Modern Europe

Sources and Perspectives from History

John C. Swanson
Utica College of Syracuse University

Michael S. Melancon
Auburn University

New York San Francisco Boston
London Toronto Sydney Tokyo Singapore Madrid
Mexico City Munich Paris Cape Town Hong Kong Montreal

Vice President/Publisher: Priscilla McGeehon
Aquisitions Editor: Erika Gutierrez
Executive Marketing Manager: Sue Westmoreland
Production Manager: Charles Annis
Project Coordination and Electronic Page Makeup: Shepherd, Inc.
Cover Design Manager: Wendy Fredericks
Cover Designer: David G. Bartow
Cover Photos: *Background:* Segovia, Spain © Emma Lee/Getty Images PhotoDisc Inc.; *Night Cafe,* 1888, Vincent van Gogh © Planet Art; Winston Churchill, Franklin Delano Roosevelt, and Joseph Stalin, seated from left to right, in the grounds of the Livadia Palace, Yalta, the U.S. headquarters in Russia, where they met for the Big Three, or Three Powers Conference, © Getty Images Hulton Archive Photos; worker in a factory in Brasov, Romania, 1990, © B. Bisson/Corbis Sygma; Napoleon © Fototeca Storica Nazioinale, 2000; Declaration of the Rights of Man of 1789, French, © Giraudon/Art Resource, Inc.
Manufacturing Buyer: Al Dorsey
Printer and Binder: Hamilton Printing
Cover Printer: Phoenix Color Corp.

Library of Congress Cataloging-in-Publication Data

Modern Europe : sources and perspectives from history / [collected by] John C. Swanson, Michael S. Melancon.
p. cm.
ISBN 0-321-08648-1
1. Europe—History—1789–1900—Sources. 2. Europe—History—20th century—Sources. 3. Europe—History—1989—Sources. I. Swanson, John C., 1965 II. Melancon, Michael S., 1940–
D299 .M56 2002
940.2—dc21

2002016086

Please visit our website at http://www.ablongman.com

ISBN 0-321-08648-1

10 9 8 7 6 5 4 3 2 1

HT—05 04 03 02

Contents

Preface

This reader provides students with direct images of European history from 1789 to the present. Certain themes that reflect significant developments in Europe stand out quite sharply. These themes are of various type and importance. Some are overtly political, others bear on society, culture, or individual life. All of them helped shape European nations, the experiences of people living in them, and, indirectly, the ways of life of much of the global population.

Individual–State Relations

Perhaps the single most important underlying theme in these selections is the relationship between the individual and the state. From the late eighteenth to the early twenty-first century, this relationship has remained in dynamic flux. One cannot help but note phases, some of them overlapping, in the working out of this problem. We suggest the following:

Phase One: In earlier eras, the individual occupied a quite passive position in state and society, with the exception, of course, of great leaders. During the late eighteenth, nineteenth, and early twentieth centuries, a series of developments—broader political participation, the rise of the nation-state, the expansion of mass education, the empowerment of women and other disenfranchised or previously unrecognized groups, a shift from rural to urban life, and technological transformations—sharply altered the relationship between individuals and the societies and states they inhabit. As democratic constitutional government with legally protected rights gradually became the norm, individuals asserted themselves more clearly, while at the same time state and society, which in some ways gained in power and uniformity, yielded somewhat in their direct control over people's lives.

Phase Two: Despite advances, the twentieth century has hardly witnessed unhindered progress for the individual in Europe. Although autocracy gave way to representative government that promoted individual rights, twentieth-century authoritarianism and totalitarianism, based in great measure upon mass political mobilization through the manipulation of modern communications, soon made their mark on the European scene. What graver threat to individual rights and indeed existence could be imagined than military dictatorship, Fascism, Nazism, and Stalinist Communism?

Phase Three: Even with the passing away of those severe challenges, problems remain in the ever-changing relationship between the individual and society. Modern technologies of all kinds exert potentially negative influences on individual privacy and freedom. As the impact of contemporary electronic communications makes itself felt, Europeans, like citizens of all modern societies, are still asking many of the same questions about the individual's place in society that they had raised during the eighteenth and nineteenth centuries. What is the proper role of the state and society in human life? The selections from the reader remind us of a range of humane, as well as inhumane, possibilities. Presumably, there is no final answer.

Politics: Modernization, Liberalism, and Nationalism

Modernization, liberalism, and nationalism are a second set of themes in these selections. If the individual's relationship to the state and society is an "underlying" theme of Europe's history during the last two centuries, modernization, liberalism, and nationalism are the "overlying" themes, that is, the ones that have dominated people's concerns and actions in an overt fashion.

Modernization signifies the more or less unceasing industrialization, urbanization, education, and technological transformation that have occurred throughout Europe during the last two centuries. The end result is a different way of life in a different environment for hundreds of millions of Europe's inhabitants.

The reader's principal political theme is an uneven, often interrupted but definite progress of constitutional democracy. The political movement that underlies constitutional democracy and its corollary, representative government, is known as *classical liberalism.* Liberal government, punctuated for briefer periods by monarchical autocracy, socialism, communism, fascism, and personal or military dictatorship, has gradually become the norm in Europe.

At the same time, *nationalism* provides a subtext for much of Europe's recent political history. Unfortunately, as various selections reveal, the early gentle vision of national equality and self-determination gave way by the end of the nineteenth century to a rampant chauvinism that led directly to two all-European wars and that still stalks the European scene in former Yugoslavia and elsewhere.

Taken together modernization, liberalism, and nationalism have constituted the primary spheres of political action and ideology during the last two centuries. In fact, they continue to be so today.

Society and Culture: Gender, Class, Culture, and Cohesion

Along with the principal historical themes mentioned above, several sub-themes of great significance thread their way through the various sections. Among these are the women's question, class conflict, cultural uncertainty, and, more recently, social integration.

The question of *women's status* arises in the first chapter with Olympe de Gouges' complaint about the French Revolution's lack of recognition of women's rights and reappears in various guises throughout much of the reader. Women eventually won the right to have property, to vote, and to work under roughly equal conditions as men. Progress indisputably has occurred for women and yet the final frontiers of women's rights remain to be conquered.

The advance of industrialization and urbanization gave rise to the development of middle and working classes as the dominant forces in European societies, as indicated in numerous selections. Throughout much of the two centuries covered, the political interests and aspirations of the two classes, the bourgeoisie and the proletariat, remained to one degree or another in opposition, a phenomenon known as *class conflict.* Although the middle classes provided broad support for liberalism and the workers for socialism, toward the end of the nineteenth century leaders of both sides began to move toward compromise.

The vast political, demographic, and technological changes of the nineteenth century eventually found their reflection in a merciless re-examination of European ideological, cultural, and religious beliefs. This scrutiny did not so much lead to new values as to a questioning of the old ones. Many of the problems of the twentieth century reflected *cultural uncertainty* and even despair.

After the radical experiments of Hitlerism and Stalinism during the second quarter of the twentieth century and the horrors of World War II, the two classes and the movements that represent their political views continued the process of compromise first noticeable during the last decade of the nineteenth century. The relatively stable post-war Western European politics, as well as the considerable prosperity, represent the results of this compromise, which now extends its sway in much of Eastern Europe as well. *Social integration* rather than class conflict now predominates in European thinking, whereas potentially destabilizing conflict about ethnicity, immigration, and religion cuts across class lines.

Europe: the Continent and the World

Another significant sub-theme that requires separate discussion concerns relations among European nations and European relations with the outside world. Both themes resonate quite differently in the two main centuries covered by this reader, the nineteenth and twentieth. As regards European interrelations, the French Revolution introduced a quarter century of wars and strife among European nations, after which European leaders and populations, exhausted by seemingly endless wars, strove to create the conditions for a lasting peace. Several phases characterized the nineteenth and twentieth centuries.

Phase one: From the time of the 1814–1815 Vienna Congress, European leaders sought and found mechanisms to prevent conflicts. The consequence was a century (roughly from 1815 to 1914) during which no major or lengthy wars threatened overall peace on the continent.

Phase two: By the onset of the twentieth century, the relative success of the Vienna arrangements floundered on the shoals of extreme nationalism, the arms race, and the race for global empires. The breakdown of peace arrangements led to two horrendous European hot wars, succeeded by the cold war's balance of fear.

Phase three: Only with Gorbachev's rise to power in the Soviet Union (1985) and the eventual collapse of the Communist regimes in Eastern Europe (1989–1991) did the conditions for general European peace prevail. Unfortunately, the last decade has witnessed a renewal of small brutal conflicts in the Balkans and the Caucasus.

The relations of European nations with the rest of the world have also witnessed sharp twists and turns. Global European commercial networks and technological advances signified a kind of European international hegemony that, especially after 1880, culminated in the division of much of the world into European empires. The European wars of the first half of the twentieth century weakened Europe's influence and relative strength in the rest of the world. One aspect of this phenomenon was decolonialization. By the 1950s and 1960s, European nations had neither the strength nor the will to maintain their global empires.

The State of Europe Today

Only now, with Europe's gradual withdrawal from its former status as a global imperial power and the rather sudden collapse of Communism, with its reduction of the Soviet Union from superpower to major power status, does the region find both its internal and external foreign relations more or less normalized. The end of the Cold War has even offered the promise of European-wide cooperation, economic integration, and a measure of political coordination. Still, the stability promised by social, economic, and even political integration finds challenges from outbursts of extreme nationalism and racism, ecological problems, and uncertainties associated with electronic and computer technologies, all matters raised in the readings. Within the realm of culture, Europeans have adjusted to living with uncertainty, just as they have become accustomed to the undeniable fact that cultural, economic, and technological predominance has shifted to other parts of the globe. Still, we might note that indirectly and by proxy, European accomplishments in economic, intellectual, cultural, and political realms play a greater role in the globe than ever before.

The Reader's Approach to Historical Understanding

The reader utilizes four types of selections: the writings of influential historical actors and theorists (Napoleon, de Staël, Marx, Freud, Hitler, Woolf, de Beauvoir), important historical documents (declarations, constitutions, and treaties), memoirs of persons who witnessed great historical events (among others Orwell, Juenger, Bloch, Ginzburg, Levi) and excerpts from fiction (novels or poetry of Eliot, Hardy, Balzac, Kafka, Pasternak, Sassoon, Akhmatova) selected to illustrate these same events. Through these prisms, each revealing in a special way, students both comprehend and experience the past.

The value of the first three—writings of great historical figures, important documents, and memoirs—are clear enough. They are what practicing historians call the *primary sources* of history. They testify directly to what happened, although, students should be aware, primary sources reflect subjectivity and are open to interpretation. Regardless, they form a major part of the historical record, subject to collection, analysis, and evaluation, used by historians to characterize the historical past. They represent a *first* kind of historical memory.

The value of *fiction*—the final of our four types of selections—for understanding real past events is of a different and less obvious nature. The fiction carefully chosen here is itself a form of memoir. The fictional excerpts come from works of authors who themselves witnessed the things they wrote about (Hugo's vivid portrayal of the French Revolution is the exception that proves the rule). These pieces add a new perspective to regular memoirs in that they reflect the efforts of talented writers who not only knew firsthand the eras they described, but who, by nature of their special literary talents captured intuitively how historical events influence the lives of living, albeit fictional, human beings. The authors of fiction employ made-up characters and situations to illustrate real life experience at the human level. In these cases, they do so against the backdrop of vast historical events such as wars, revolutions, or profound social, economic, and technological transformations. One might characterize these fictional writings as a *second* kind of historical memory.

The reader's compilers believe that all these selections will deeply enhance students' awareness of the historical events recounted and analyzed in course lectures and textbooks.

The lectures and texts are the foundations of the course. The readings illustrate thoughts, motivations, memory, and emotions or, put another way, the structures erected upon the foundations.

Taken all together, these various sources of historical knowledge and understanding create for students an historical recollection as rich in emotional and intellectual content as in facts and structure. The student will take away from the course a permanent, usable sense of the past, a *third* kind of historical memory. The readings, chosen for their centrality or insightfulness rather than for ease, will provide special rewards for the engaged and interested student.

Most of the persons whose writings comprise this reader are very well known. Students should turn to their history texts for further data about them. The chapter introductions contain brief biographical data for each of these authors. These will aid students about the less famous writers; in some cases lecturers may wish to offer supplemental biographical information. At appropriate places in the reader, the editors have provided orientation sketches for fiction pieces and bibliographical data and original publication dates for each selection utilized.

Acknowledgements

We would like to thank several individuals for useful suggestions about readings. We are grateful to Professor Louise Katainen of Auburn University for bringing to our attention Grazia Deledda's *Reeds in the Wind,* to Professor Stephan Gerson of New York University for suggesting Victor Hugo's *The Ladies Paradise,* and to Boris Gorshkov of Auburn University for making us aware of Olga Berggolts' *Second Letter to the Kama.* A great debt is also owed to our students, who shared with us their opinions about the reader and its selections, as did, most generously and effectively, the editors at Addison-Wesley Longman and the numerous readers consulted from the European history field.

Grateful acknowledgment is made to the following scholars who gave generously of their time and knowledge to provide thoughtful evaluations and helpful suggestions: Caitlin Corning, George Fox University; Guillaume de Syon, Albright University; George Esenwein, University of Florida; Oliver Hayward, University of Wisconsin-Parkside; David T. Murphy, Anderson University; H. Glenn Penny, University of Missouri-Kansas City; Jennifer Popiel, University of Wisconsin-Green Bay; Michael T. Saler, University of California-Davis; Frederick Schneid, High Point University; Douglas R. Skopp, SUNY Plattsburgh; Victoria Thompson, Arizona State University; Edward J. Woell, Marist College; Thomas G. Velek, Mississippi University for Women.

✧ PART ONE ✧

The French Revolution

During the French Revolution, the guillotine, hailed as a humane method of execution, became the instrument of choice for dispatching the revolution's victims. In this image, the head of King Louis XVI is held up for all to see.

THE FRENCH REVOLUTION

A watershed in European history, the French Revolution (1789–1815) demarcated the old regime from the modern period. For the first time Enlightenment ideals underlay a European society. Polities, economics, and even culture came to reflect the desires of the people, no longer subjects of the monarch but citizens of the state. Yet, when hostile powers attacked France in 1792, the revolution spun out of control and, under the Jacobins, became a reign of terror. In 1794 moderates imposed order by arresting and guillotining the Jacobins and creating the Directory, a dull dictatorship. In 1799 the military hero Napoleon Bonaparte overthrew the Directory. After initially taking the title First Consul, he named himself Emperor of France in 1804, although he still described himself as the "son" of the revolution. Napoleon's limitless ambition destroyed the last vestiges of the revolution, and his wars of conquest helped give rise to modern nationalism when other peoples responded to the French threat.

As one of its first acts in August 1789, the new Assembly of France promulgated the Declaration of the Rights of Man and Citizen. The document's Enlightenment language ringingly proclaimed equal rights for all men. Although the Declaration later served as the foundation of many liberationist movements, the authors had excluded women. Seeking to right this omission, Olympe de Gouges, a woman of humble birth, wrote the Declaration of the Rights of Woman in 1791 and addressed it to the queen.

Domestic turmoil plagued France throughout the revolutionary era. In his novel *Ninety-Three* (1881), Victor Hugo (1802–1885), born after the revolution, brought to life the revolutionary conflict between aristocrats and Republican forces. As the revolution deepened, Louis XVI joined a chorus of conservative voices to warn in his 1791 Declaration that it could bring no benefit to the nation or, by inference, to the world. Others had different views. In his letters, collected in *The Mind of Napoleon,* Bonaparte (1768–1821) argued that he was true heir to the revolution. His actions, he insisted, had carried to the rest of Europe the ideals of "liberty, equality, and fraternity."

✦ Reading 1 ✦

Declaration of the Rights of Man and Citizen

The representatives of the French people, organized in National Assembly, considering that ignorance, forgetfulness, or contempt of the rights of man are the sole causes of public misfortunes and of the corruption of governments, have resolved to set forth in a solemn declaration the natural, inalienable, and sacred rights of man, in order that such declaration, continually before all members of the social body, may be a perpetual reminder of their rights and duties; in order that the acts of the legislative power and those of the executive power may constantly be compared with the aim of every political institution and may accordingly be more respected; in order that the demands of the citizens, founded henceforth upon simple and incontestable principles, may always be directed towards the maintenance of the Constitution and the welfare of all.

Accordingly, the National Assembly recognizes and proclaims, in the presence and under the auspices of the Supreme Being, the following rights of man and citizen.

1. Men are born and remain free and equal in rights; social distinctions may be based only upon general usefulness.

2. The aim of every political association is the preservation of the natural and inalienable rights of man; these rights are liberty, property, security, and resistance to oppression.

3. The source of all sovereignty resides essentially in the nation; no group, no individual may exercise authority not emanating expressly therefrom.

4. Liberty consists of the power to do whatever is not injurious to others; thus the enjoyment of the natural rights of every man has for its limits only those that assure other members of society the enjoyment of those same rights; such limits may be determined only by law.

5. The law has the right to forbid only actions which are injurious to society. Whatever is not forbidden by law may not be prevented, and no one may be constrained to do what it does not prescribe.

6. Law is the expression of the general will; all citizens have the right to concur personally, or through their representatives, in its formation; it must be the same for all, whether it protects or punishes. All citizens, being equal before it, are equally admissible to all public offices, positions, and employments, according to their capacity, and without other distinction than that of virtues and talents.

7. No man may be accused, arrested, or detained except in the cases determined by law, and according to the forms prescribed thereby. Whoever solicit, expedite, or execute arbitrary orders, or have them executed, must be punished; but every citizen summoned or apprehended in pursuance of the law must obey immediately; he renders himself culpable by resistance.

8. The law is to establish only penalties that are absolutely and obviously necessary; and no one may be punished except by virtue of a law established and promulgated prior to the offence and legally applied.

9. Since every man is presumed innocent until declared guilty, if arrest be deemed indispensable, all unnecessary severity for securing the person of the accused must be severely repressed by law.

10. No one is to be disquieted because of his opinions, even religious, provided their manifestation does not disturb the public order established by law.

11. Free communication of ideas and opinions is one of the most precious of the rights of man. Consequently, every citizen may speak, write, and print freely, subject to responsibility for the abuse of such liberty in the cases determined by law.

12. The guarantee of the rights of man and citizen necessitates a public force; such a force, therefore, is

---

From: *A Documentary Survey of the French Revolution,* ed. John Hall Stewart (New York: Macmillan Company, 1951), pp. 113–115.

instituted for the advantage of all and not for the particular benefit of those to whom it is entrusted.

13. For the maintenance of the public force and for the expenses of administration a common tax is indispensable; it must be assessed equally on all citizens in proportion to their means.

14. Citizens have the right to ascertain, by themselves or through their representatives, the necessity of the public tax, to consent to it freely, to supervise its use, and to determine its quota, assessment, payment, and duration.

15. Society has the right to require of every public agent an accounting of his administration.

16. Every society in which the guarantee of rights is not assured or the separation of powers not determined has no constitution at all.

17. Since property is a sacred and inviolable right, no one may be deprived thereof unless a legally established public necessity obviously requires it, and upon condition of a just and previous indemnity.

✦ Reading 2 ✦

Declaration of the Rights of Woman

Olympe de Gouges

To be decreed by the National Assembly in its last sessions or by the next legislature.

Preamble

Mothers, daughters, sisters, female representatives of the nation ask to be constituted as a national assembly. Considering that ignorance, neglect, or contempt for the rights of woman are the sole causes of public misfortunes and governmental corruption, they have resolved to set forth in a solemn declaration the natural, inalienable, and sacred rights of woman: so that by being constantly present to all the members of the social body this declaration may always remind them of their rights and duties; so that by being liable at every moment to comparison with the aim of any and all political institutions the acts of womens's and men's powers may be the more fully respected; and so that by being founded henceforward on simple and incontestable principles the demands of the citizenesses may always tend toward maintaining the constitution, good morals, and the general welfare.

In consequence, the sex that is superior in beauty as in courage, needed in maternal sufferings, recognizes and declares, in the presence and under the auspices of the Supreme Being, the following rights of woman and the citizeness.

1. Woman is born free and remains equal to man in rights. Social distinctions may be based only on common utility.

2. The purpose of all political association is the preservation of the natural and imprescriptible rights of woman and man. These rights are liberty, property, security, and especially resistance to oppression.

3. The principle of all sovereignty rests essentially in the nation, which is but the reuniting of woman and man. No body and no individual may exercise authority which does not emanate expressly from the nation.

4. Liberty and justice consist in restoring all that belongs to another; hence the exercise of the natural rights of woman has no other limits than those that the perpetual tyranny of man opposes to them; these limits must be reformed according to the laws or nature and reason.

5. The laws of nature and reason prohibit all actions which are injurious to society. No hindrance should be put in the way of anything not prohibited by these wise and divine laws, nor may anyone be forced to do what they do not require.

6. The law should be the expression of the general will. All citizenesses and citizens should take part, in person or by their representatives, in its formation. It must be the same for everyone. All citizenesses and citizens, being equal in its eyes, should be equally admissible to all public dignities, offices, and employments, according to their ability, and with no other distinction than that of their virtues and talents.

7. No woman is exempted; she is indicted, arrested, and detained in the cases determined by the law. Women like men obey this rigorous law.

8. Only strictly and obviously necessary punishments should be established by the law, and no one may be punished except by virtue of a law established and promulgated before the time of the offense, and legally applied to women.

9. Any woman being declared guilty, all rigor is exercised by the law.

10. No one should be disturbed for his fundamental opinions; woman has the right to mount the scaffold, so she should have the right equally to mount the tribune, provided that these manifestations do not trouble public order as established by law.

From: *The French Revolution and Human Rights: A Brief Documentary History,* ed. Lynn Hunt (New York: Bedford Books, 1996), pp. 124–129.

11. The free communication of thoughts and opinions is one of the most precious of the rights of woman, since this liberty assures the recognition of children by their fathers. Every citizeness may therefore say freely, I am the mother of your child; a barbarous prejudice [against unmarried women having children] should not force her to hide the truth, so long as responsibility is accepted for any abuse of this liberty in cases determined by the law [women are not allowed to lie about the paternity of their children].

12. The safeguard of the rights of woman and citizeness requires public powers. These powers are instituted for the advantage of all and not for the private benefit of those to whom they are entrusted.

13. For maintenance of public authority and for expenses of administration, taxation of women and men is equal; she takes part in all forced labor service, in all painful tasks; she must therefore have the same proportion in the distribution of places, employments, offices, dignities, and in industry.

14. The citizenesses and citizens have the right, by themselves or through their representatives, to have demonstrated to them the necessity of public taxes. The citizenesses can only agree to them upon admission of an equal division, not only in wealth, but also in the public administration, and to determine the means of apportionment, assessment, and collection, and the duration of the taxes.

15. The mass of women, joining with men in paying taxes, have the right to hold accountable every public agent of the administration.

16. Any society in which the guarantee of rights is not assured or the separation of powers not settled has no constitution. The constitution is null and void if the majority of individuals composing the nation has not cooperated in its drafting.

17. Property belongs to both sexes whether united or separated; it is for each of them an inviolable and sacred right, and no one may be deprived of it as a true patrimony of nature, except when public necessity, certified by law, obviously requires it, and then on condition of a just compensation in advance.

Postscript

Women, wake up; the tocsin of reason sounds throughout the universe; recognize your rights. The powerful empire of nature is no longer surrounded by prejudice, fanaticism, superstition, and lies. The torch of truth has dispersed all the clouds of folly and usurpation. Enslaved man has multiplied his force and needs yours to break his chains. Having become free, he has become unjust toward his companion. Oh women! Women, when will you cease to be blind? What advantages have you gathered in the revolution? A scorn more marked, a disdain more conspicuous. During the centuries of corruption you only reigned over the weakness of men. Your empire is destroyed; what is left to you then? Firm belief in the injustices of men. The reclaiming of your patrimony founded on the wise decrees of nature; why should you fear such a beautiful enterprise? . . . Whatever the barriers set up against you, it is in your power to overcome them; you only have to want it. Let us pass now to the appalling account of what you have been in society; and since national education is an issue at this moment, let us see if our wise legislators will think sanely about the education of women.

Women have done more harm than good. Constraint and dissimulation have been their lot. What force has taken from them, ruse returned to them; they have had recourse to all the resources of their charms, and the most irreproachable man has not resisted them. Poison, the sword, women controlled everything; they ordered up crimes as much as virtues. For centuries, the French government, especially, depended on the nocturnal administration of women; officials kept no secrets from their indiscretion; ambassadorial posts, military commands, the ministry, the presidency [of a court], the papacy, the college of cardinals, in short everything that characterizes the folly of men, profane and sacred, has been submitted to the cupidity and ambition of this sex formerly considered despicable and respected, and since the revolution, respectable and despised. . . .

Under the former regime, everyone was vicious, everyone guilty. . . . A woman only had to be beautiful and amiable; when she possessed these two advantages, she saw a hundred fortunes at her feet. . . . The most indecent woman could make herself respectable with gold; the commerce in women was a kind of industry amongst the highest classes, which henceforth will enjoy no more credit. If it still did, the revolution would be lost, and in the new situation we would still be corrupted. Can reason hide the fact that every other road to fortune is closed to a woman bought by a man, bought like a slave from the coasts of Africa? The difference between them is great; this is known. The slave [that is, the woman] commands her master, but if the master gives her her freedom without compensation and at an age when the slave has lost all her charms, what does this unfortunate woman become? The plaything of disdain; even the doors of charity are closed to her; she is poor and old, they say: why did she not know how to make her fortune?

Other examples even more touching can be provided to reason. A young woman without experience, seduced by the man she loves, abandons her parents to follow him; the ingrate leaves her after a few years and the older she will have grown with him, the more his inconstancy will be inhuman. If she has children, he will still abandon her. If he is rich, he will believe himself excused from sharing his fortune with his noble victims. If some engagement ties him to his duties, he will violate it while counting on support from the law. If he is married, every other obligation loses its force. What laws then remain to be passed that would eradicate vice down to its roots? That of equally dividing [family] fortunes between men and women and of public administration of their goods. It is easy to imagine that a woman born of a rich family would gain much from the equal division of property [between children]. But what about the woman born in a poor family with merit and virtues; what is her lot? Poverty and opprobrium. If she does not excel in music or painting, she cannot be admitted to any public function, even if she is fully qualified. . . .

Marriage is the tomb of confidence and love. A married woman can give bastards to her husband with impunity, and even the family fortune which does not belong to them. An unmarried woman has only a feeble right: ancient and inhuman laws refuse her the right to the name and goods of her children's father; no new laws have been made in this matter. If giving my sex an honorable and just consistency is considered to be at this time paradoxical on my part and an attempt at the impossible, I leave to future men the glory of dealing with this matter; but while waiting, we can prepare the way with national education, with the restoration of morals and with conjugal agreements.

Form for a Social Contract between Man and Woman

We, _____ and _____, moved by our own will, unite for the length of our lives and for the duration of our mutual inclinations under the following conditions: We intend and wish to make our wealth communal property, while reserving the right to divide it in favor of our children and of those for whom we might have a special inclination, mutually recognizing that our goods belong directly to our children, from whatever bed they come [ligitimate or not], and that all of them without distinction have the right to bear the name of the fathers and mothers who have acknowledged them, and we impose on ourselves the obligation of subscribing to the law that punishes any rejection of one's own blood [refusing to acknowledge an illegitimate child]. We likewise obligate ourselves, in the case of a separation, to divide our fortune equally and to set aside the portion the law designates for our children. In the case of a perfect union, the one who dies first will give up half his property in favor of the children; and if there are no children, the survivor or will inherit by right, unless the dying person has disposed of his half of the common property in favor of someone he judges appropriate. [She then goes on to defend her contract against the inevitable objections of "hypocrites, prudes, the clergy, and all the hellish gang."]

✦ Reading 3 ✦

The King's Declaration (20 June, 1791)

Louis XVI

As long as the King could hope to see order and the welfare of the kingdom regenerated by the means employed by the National Assembly, and by his residence near that assembly in the capital of the kingdom, no sacrifice mattered to him; . . . but today, when his sole recompense for so many sacrifices consists of seeing the monarchy destroyed, all powers disregarded, property violated, personal security everywhere endangered, crimes unpunished, and total anarchy taking the place of law, while the semblance of authority provided by the new Constitution is insufficient to repair a single one of the ills afflicting the kingdom, the King, having solemnly protested against all the acts issued during his captivity, deems it his duty to place before Frenchmen and the entire universe the picture of his conduct and that of the government which has established itself in the kingdom. . . .

But the more sacrifices the King made for the welfare of his people, the more the rebels labored to disparage the value thereof, and to present the monarchy under the most false and odious colors.

The convocation of the Estates General, the doubling of the deputies of the third estate, the King's efforts to eliminate all difficulties which might delay the meeting of the Estates General and those which arose after its opening, all the retrenchments which the King made in his personal expenses, all the sacrifices which he made for his people in the session of 23 June, finally, the union of the orders, effected by the King's wish, a measure which His Majesty then deemed indispensable for the functioning of the Estates General, all his anxiety, all his efforts, all his generosity, all his devotion to his people—all have been misjudged, all have been misrepresented.

From: *A Documentary Survey of the French Revolution,* ed. John Hall Stewart (New York: Macmillan Company, 1951), pp. 205–210.

The time when the Estate General, assuming the name of National Assembly, began to occupy itself with the constitution of the kingdom, calls to mind the memoirs which the rebels were cunning enough to have sent from several provinces, and the movements of Paris to have the deputies disregard one of the principal clauses contained in their *cahiers,* namely that providing that *the making of the laws should be done in concert with the King.* In defiance of that clause, the assembly placed the King entirely outside the constitution by refusing him the right to grant or to withhold his sanction to articles which it regarded as constitutional, reserving to itself the right to include in that category those which it deemed suitable; and for those regarded as purely legislative, reducing the royal prerogative to a right of suspension until the third legislature, a purely illusory right as so many examples prove only too well.

What remains to the King other than a vain semblance of monarchy? . . .

Let us, then, examine the several branches of the government.

Justice. The King has no share in making the laws; he has only the right to obstruct, until the third legislature, matters which are not regarded as constitutional, and to request the National Assembly to apply itself to such and such matters, without possessing the right to make a formal proposal thereon. Justice is rendered in the name of the King . . . ; but it is only a matter of form . . . One of the most recent decrees of the Assembly deprived the King of one of the finest prerogatives everywhere associated with monarchy, that of pardoning and commuting penalties. . . . Morever, this provision lessens royal majesty in the eyes of the people, so long accustomed to having recourse to the King in their needs and difficulties, and to seeing in him the common father who can relieve their afflictions!

Internal Administration. There is entirely too much authority in the hands of the departments, districts, and municipalities, which impede the working of the machine, and may often thwart one another. All these bodies are elected by the people, and are not under the jurisdiction of the government, according to law, except for the execution of decrees or for those special orders which are the consequence thereof. . . . Moreover, these bodies have acquired little influence and esteem. The Societies of the Friends of the Constitution . . . are often more powerful, and, consequently, the action of the government is of no effect. . . .

According to decrees, the disposition of military forces is in the hands of the King. He has been declared the supreme head of the army and navy; but all the work of constituting these two forces has been done by committees of the assembly without the participation of the King; everything, even the slightest regulation of discipline, has been effected by them; . . . What becomes of an army when it no longer has leaders or discipline? Instead of being the power and safeguard of a state, it becomes the terror and scourge thereof. . . .

Foreign Affairs. Appointment to ministerial posts at foreign courts and the conduct of negotiations have been reserved to the King; but the King's liberty in such appointments is as void as for those of officers in the army; . . . The revision and confirmation of treaties, which is reserved to the National Assembly, and the nomination of a diplomatic committee absolutely nullify the second provision. . . .

Finances. The King declared, even before the convocation of the Estates General, that he recognized the right of the assemblies of the nation to grant subsidies, and that he no longer wished to tax the people without their consent. All the *cahiers* of the deputies to the Estates General were agreed in placing the re-establishment of the finances foremost among matters to be dealt with by that assembly; some imposed restrictions in favor of articles to be given priority. The King eliminated the difficulties which such restrictions might have occasioned, by taking the matter in his own hands and granting, in the session of 23 June, everything that was desired. On 4 February, 1790, the King urged the assembly to take effective action on such an important matter; it has done so only recently . . . There is still no exact statement of receipts and expenditures . . . The ordinary taxes are at present greatly in arrears, and the extraordinary expedient of the first one billion, two hundred millions in *assignats* is almost exhausted. . . . The regulation of funds, the collection of taxes, the assessment among the departments, the rewards for services rendered, all have been removed from the King's supervision. . . .

Finally, decrees have pronounced the King supreme head of administration of the kingdom; other subsequent enactments have regulated the organization of the ministry so that the King . . . may change nothing therein without new decisions of the assembly. . . .

This form of government, so vicious in itself, is becoming still more so for several reasons. 1st, The assembly, through its committees, constantly exceeds the limits it has prescribed for itself; it devotes itself to matters dealing only with the internal administration of the kingdom and with that of justice, and thus it acquires all authority; through its Committee on Investigations it even exercises a veritable despotism, more barbarous and insufferable than any ever known to history. 2nd, There exist in almost all the cities, and even in some towns and villages, of the kingdom associations known under the name of Friends of the Constitution. Contrary to the tenor of the law, they do not tolerate any others not affiliated with them; they constitute an immense corporation, more dangerous than any that formerly existed. Without being authorized thereto, and even in defiance of all decrees, they deliberate upon all questions of government, correspond among themselves upon all matters, make and receive declarations, post decrees, and have acquired such a preponderance that all the administrative and judicial bodies, not even excepting the National Assembly itself, usually obey their orders.

The King does not think it possible to govern a kingdom of such great extent and importance as France through the means established by the National Assembly, as they exist at present. His Majesty, in granting to all decrees, without distinction, a sanction which he well knew could not be refused, was influenced by a desire to avoid all discussion, which experience has shown to be useless to say the least; he feared, moreover, that he would be suspected of wishing to retard or to bring about the failure of the efforts of the National Assembly, in the success of which the nation took so great an interest; he placed his confidence in the wise men of that assembly . . .

But the closer the Assembly draws to the end of its labors, the more we see the wise men losing their influence, the more we see measures which only render difficult or even impossible the carrying on of government, and daily engender increasing mistrust and disfavor toward it. Other regulations, instead of applying healing balm to the wounds which still bleed in several provinces, only aggravate the discontent and embitter the malcontents. The spirit of the clubs dominates and pervades everything; thousands of calumniating and incendiary newspapers and pamphlets, distributed daily, are simply their echoes, and prepare men to think as they wish them to. The National Assembly has never dared remedy that licence, so fax removed from true liberty; it has lost its influence and even the force which it would need to retrace its steps and to change whatever it would seem desirable to correct. We judge from the spirit which prevails in the clubs, and from the manner in which they make themselves masters of the new primary assemblies, what is to be expected from them; and if they show any inclination to revise anything, it is in order to destroy the remainder of the monarchy and to establish a metaphysical and philosophical government which would be impossible to operate.

Frenchmen, is that why you sent your representatives to the National Assembly? Would you want the anarchy and despotism of the clubs to supplant the monarchical government under which the nation has prospered for fourteen hundred years? Would you want to see your King overwhelmed with insults and deprived of his liberty, while he devotes himself entirely to the establishment of yours?

Love for their kings is one of the virtues of Frenchmen, and His Majesty has personally received too many touching proofs thereof ever to be able to forget them. The rebels are well aware that, so long as this love abides, their work can never succeed; they know, likewise, that in order to enfeeble it, it is necessary, if possible, to destroy the respect which has always accompanied it; and that is the source of the outrages which the King has experienced during the past two years, and of all the ills which he has suffered. His Majesty would not here delineate the distressing picture of these if he did not wish to make known to his faithful subjects the spirit of these rebels who would rend the bosom of their *Patrie,* while feigning to desire its regeneration. . . .

In view of all these facts and the King's present inability to effect the good and prevent the evil that is perpetrated, is it astonishing that the King has sought to recover his liberty and to place himself and his family in safety?

Frenchmen, and especially you Parisians, you inhabitants of a city which the ancestors of His Majesty were pleased to call the good city of Paris, distrust the suggestions and lies of your false friends. Return to your king; he will always be your father, your best friend. What pleasure will he not take in forgetting all his personal injuries, and in beholding himself again in your midst, when a constitution, freely accepted by him, shall cause our holy religion to be respected, the government to be established upon a firm foundation and made useful by its functioning, the property and position of every person no longer to be disturbed, the laws no longer to be violated with impunity, and, finally, liberty to be established on firm and immovable foundations.

Signed, Louis

The King forbids his Ministers to sign any order in his name until they have received further instructions; he enjoins the Keeper of the Seal of State to send the Seal to him when required so to do.

Signed, Louis

Paris, 20 June, 1791.

✦ Reading 4 ✦

Ninety-Three

Victor Hugo

The protagonist in this novel is revolutionary France. The various characters, some based on historical figures, are not as important as the country that they aided or injured. Throughout the novel, Hugo repeats the question: can a good action be a bad action?

The Convention

We approach the grand summit.

Behold the Convention!

The gaze grows steady in presence of this height.

Never has a more lofty spectacle appeared on the horizon of mankind.

There is one Himalaya, and there is one Convention.

The Convention is perhaps the culminating point of History.

During its lifetime—for it lived—men did not quite understand what it was. It was precisely the grandeur which escaped its contemporaries; they were too much scared to be dazzled. Everything grand possesses a sacred horror. It is easy to admire mediocrities and hills; but whatever is too lofty, whether it be a genius or a mountain,—an assembly as well as a masterpiece,—alarms when seen too near. An immense height appears an exaggeration. It is fatiguing to climb. One loses breath upon acclivities, one slips down declivities; one is hurt by sharp, rugged heights which are in themselves beautiful; torrents in their foaming reveal the precipices; clouds hide the mountain-tops; a sudden ascent terrifies as much as a fall. Hence there is a greater sensation of fright than admiration. What one feels is fantastic enough,—an aversion to the grand. One sees the abyss and loses sight of the sublimity; one sees the monster and does not perceive the marvel. Thus the Convention was at first judged. It was measured by the purblind,—it, which needed to be looked at by eagles.

To-day we see it in perspective, and it throws across the deep and distant heavens, against a background at once serene and tragic, the immense profile of the French Revolution.

* * *

The 14th of July delivered.

The 10th of August blasted.

The 21st of September founded.

The 21st of September was the Equinox; was Equilibrium,—*Libra,* the balance. It was, according to the remark of Romme, under this sign of Equality and Justice that the Republic was proclaimed. A constellation heralded it.

The Convention is the first avatar of the peoples. It was by the Convention that the grand new page opened and the future of to-day commenced.

Every idea must have a visible enfolding; a habitation is necessary to any principle; a church is God between four walls; every dogma must have a temple. When the Convention became a fact, the first problem to be solved was how to lodge the Convention.

At first the Riding-school, then the Tuileries, was taken. A platform was raised, scenery arranged,—a great grey painting by David imitating bas-reliefs; benches were placed in order; there was a square tribune, parallel pilasters with plinths like blocks and long rectilinear stems; square enclosures, into which the spectators crowded, and which were called the public tribunes; a Roman velarium, Grecian draperies; and in these right-angles and these straight lines the Convention was installed,—the tempest confined within this geometrical plan. On

From: Victor Hugo, *Ninety-Three,* in *Works of Victor Hugo,* Volume VII (New York: Chesterfield Society), pp. 142–144, 162–163, 166–167, 226–232.

the tribune the Red Cap was painted in grey. The royalists began by laughing at this grey red cap, this theatrical hall, this monument of pasteboard, this sanctuary of papier-maché, this Pantheon of mud and spittle. How quickly it would disappear! The columns were made of the staves from hogsheads, the arches were of deal boards, the bas-reliefs of mastic, the entablatures were of pine, the statues of plaster; the marbles were paint, the walls canvas; and of this provisional shelter France has made an eternal dwelling.

When the Convention began to hold its sessions in the Riding-school, the walls were covered with the placards which sprouted over Paris at the period of the return from Varennes.

On one might be read: "The king returns. Any person who cheers him shall be beaten; any person who insults him shall be hanged." On another: "Peace! Hats on! He is about to pass before his judges." On another: "The king has aimed at the nation. He has hung fire; it is now the nation's turn." On another: "The Law! The Law!" It was within those walls that the Convention sat in judgment on Louis XVI.

At the Tuileries, where the Convention began to sit on the 10th of May, 1793, and which was called the Palais-National, the assembly-hall occupied the whole space between the Pavillon de l'Horloge, called the Pavilion of Unity, and the Pavilion Marsan, then named Pavilion of Liberty. The Pavilion of Flora was called Pavillon Egalité. The hall was reached by the grand staircase of Jean Bullant. The whole ground-floor of the palace, beneath the story occupied by the Assembly, was a kind of long guard-room, littered with bundles and camp-beds of the troops of all arms, who kept watch about the Convention. The Assembly had a guard of honour styled "the Grenadiers of the Convention."

A tricoloured ribbon separated the palace where the Assembly sat from the garden in which the people came and went.

* * *

At the same time that it threw off revolution, this Assembly produced civilization. Furnace, but forge too.

In this caldron, where terror bubbled, progress fermented. Out of this chaos of shadow, this tumultuous flight of clouds, spread immense rays of light parallel to the eternal laws,—rays that have remained on the horizon, visible forever in the heaven of the peoples, and which are, one, Justice; another, Tolerance; another, Goodness; another, Right; another, Truth; another, Love.

The Convention promulgated this grand axiom: "The liberty of each citizen ends where the liberty of another citizen commences,"—which comprises in two lines all human social law. It declared indigence sacred; it declared infirmity sacred in the blind and the deaf and dumb, who became wards of the State; maternity sacred in the girl-mother, whom it consoled and lifted up; infancy sacred in the orphan, whom it caused to be adopted by the country; innocence sacred in the accused who was acquitted, whom it indemnified. It branded the slave-trade; it abolished slavery. It proclaimed civic joint responsiblity. It decreed gratuitous instruction. It organized national education by the normal school of Paris; central schools in the chief towns; primary schools in the communes. It created the academies of music and the museums. It decreed the unity of the Code, the unity of weights and measures, and the unity of calculation by the decimal system. It established the finances of France, and caused public credit to succeed to the long monarchical bankruptcy. It put the telegraph in operation. To old age it gave endowed almshouses; to sickness, purified hospitals; to instruction, the Polytechnic School; to science, the Bureau of Longitudes; to human intellect, the Institute. At the same time that it was national it was cosmopolitan. Of the eleven thousand two hundred and ten decrees which emanated from the Convention, a third had a political aim; two thirds, a human aim. It declared universal morality the basis of society, and universal conscience the basis of law. And all that servitude abolished, fraternity proclaimed, humanity protected, human conscience rectified, the law of work transformed into right, and from onerous made honourable,—national riches consolidated, childhood instructed and raised up, letters and sciences propagated, light illuminating all heights, aid to all sufferings, promulgation of all principle,—the Convention accomplished, having in its bowels that hydra, the Vendée; and upon its sholders that heap of tigers, the kings.

* * *

Spirits which were a prey of the wind. But this was a miracle-working wind. To be a member of the Convention was to be a wave of the ocean. This was true even of the greatest there. The force of impulsion came from on high. There was a Will in the Convention which was that of all, and yet not that of any one person. This Will was an Idea,—an idea indomitable and immeasurable, which swept from the summit of heaven into the darkness below. We call this Revolution. When that Idea passed, it beat down one and raised up another; it scattered this man into foam and dashed that one upon the reefs. This Idea knew whither it was going, and drove the whirlpool before it. To ascribe the Revolution to men is to ascribe the tide to the waves.

The Revolution is a work of the Unknown. Call it good or bad, according as you yearn toward the future or the past, but leave it to the power which caused it. It seems the joint work of grand events and grand individualities mingled, but it is in reality the result of events. Events dispense, men suffer; events dictate, men sigh. The 14th of July is signed Camille Desmoulins; the 10th of August is signed Danton; the 2d of September is signed Marat; the 21st of September is signed Grégoire; the 21st of January is signed Robespierre; but Desmoulins, Danton, Marat, Grégoire, and Robespierre are mere scribes. The great and mysterious writer of these grand pages has a name,—God; and a mask, Destiny. Robespierre believed in God: yea, verily!

The Revolution is a form of the eternal phenomenon which presses upon us from every quarter, and which we call Necessity. Before this mysterious complication of benefits and sufferings arises the Wherefore of history. *Because:* this answer of him who knows nothing is equally the response of him who knows all.

In presence of these climacteric catastrophes which devastate and revivify civilization, one hesitates to judge their details. To blame or praise men on account of the result is almost like praising or blaming ciphers on account of the total. That which ought to happen happens; the blast which ought to blow blows. The Eternal Serenity does not suffer from these north winds. Above revolutions Truth and Justice remain as the starry sky lies above and beyond tempests.

* * *

The Two Poles of the Truth

At the end of a few weeks, which had been filled with the vicissitudes of civil war, the district of Fougères could talk of nothing but the two men who were opposed to each other, and yet were occupied in the same work; that is, fighting side by side the great revolutionary combat.

The savage Vendean duel continued, but the Vendée was losing ground. In Ille-et-Vilaine in particular, thanks to the young commander who had at Dol so opportunely replied to the audacity of six thousand royalists by the audacity of fifteen hundred patriots, the insurrection, if not quelled, was at least greatly weakened and circumscribed. Several lucky hits had followed that one, and out of these successes had grown a new position of affairs. Matters had changed their face, but a singular complication had arisen.

In all this portion of the Vendée the Republic had the upper hand,—that was beyond a doubt. But which republic? In the triumph which was opening out, two forms of republic made themselves felt,—the republic of terror, and the republic of clemency; the one desirous to conquer by rigour, and the other by mildness. Which would prevail? These two forms—the conciliating and the implacable—were represented by two men, each of whom possessed his special influence and authority: the one a military commander, the other a civil delegate. Which of them would prevail?

One of the two, the delegate, had a formidable basis of support; he had arrived bearing the threatening watchword of the Paris Commune to the battalions of Santerre: "No mercy; no quarter!" He had, in order to put everything under his control, the decree of the Convention, ordaining "death to whomsoever should set at liberty and help a captive rebel chief to escape." He had full powers, emanating from the Committee of Public Safety, and an injunction commanding obedience to him as delegate, signed ROBESPIERRE, DANTON, MARAT. The other, the soldier, had on his side only, this strength,—pity. He had only his own arm, which chastised the enemy; and his heart, which pardoned them. A conqueror, he believed that he had the right to spare the conquered.

Hence arose a conflict, hidden but deep, between these two men. The two stood in different atmospheres; both combating the rebellion, and each having his own thunderbolt,—that of the one, victory; that of the other, terror.

Throughout all the Bocage nothing was talked of but them; and what added to the anxiety of those who watched them from every quarter was the fact that these two men so diametrically opposed were at the same time closely united. These two antagonists were friends. Never sympathy loftier and more profound joined two hearts; the stern had saved the life of the clement, and bore on his face the wound received in the effort. These two men were the incarnation,—the one of life, the other of death; the one was the principle of destruction, the other of peace, and they loved each other. Strange problem! Imagine Orestes merciful and Pylades pitiless. Picture Arimanes the brother of Ormus!

Let us add that the one of the pair who was called "the ferocious" was, at the same time, the most brotherly of men. He dressed the wounded, cared for the sick, passed his days and nights in the ambulance and hospitals, was touched by the sight of barefooted children, had nothing for himself, gave all to the poor. He was present at all the battles; he marched at the head of the columns and in the thickest of the fight, armed,—for he had in his belt a sabre and two pistols,—yet disarmed, because no one had ever seen him draw his sabre or touch his pistols. He faced blows, and did not return them. It was said that he had been a priest.

One of these men was Gauvain; the other was Cimourdain. There was friendship between the two men, but hatred between the two principles; this hidden war could not fail to burst forth. One morning the battle began.

Cimourdain said to Gauvain: "What have we accomplished?"

Gauvain replied: "You know as well as I. I have dispersed Lantenac's bands. He has only a few men left. Then he is driven back to the forest of Fougères. In eight days he will be surrounded."

"And in fifteen days?"

"He will be taken."

"And then?"

"You have read my notice?"

"Yes. Well?"

"He will be shot."

"More clemency! He must be guillotined."

"As for me," said Gauvain, "I am for a military death."

"And I," replied Cimourdain, "for a revolutionary death." He looked Gauvain in the face, and added: "Why did you set at liberty those nuns of the convent of Saint Marc-le-Blanc?"

"I do not make war on women," answered Gauvain.

"Those women hate the people; and where hate is concerned, one woman outweighs ten men. Why did you refuse to send to the revolutionary tribunal all that herd of old fanatical priests who were taken at Louvigné?"

"I do not make war on old men."

"An old priest is worse than a young one. Rebellion is more dangerous preached by white hairs. Men have faith in wrinkles. No false pity, Gauvain! The regicides are liberators. Keep your eye fixed on the tower of the Temple."

"The Temple tower! I would bring the Dauphin out of it. I do not make war on children."

Cimourdain's eyes grew stern. "Gauvain, learn that it is necessary to make war on a woman when she calls herself Marie Antoinette, on an old man when he is named Pius VI. and Pope, and upon a child when he is named Louis Capet."

"My master, I am not a politician."

"Try not to be a dangerous man. Why, at the attack on the post of Cossé, when the rebel Jean Treton, driven back and lost, flung himself alone, sabre in hand, against the whole column, didst thou cry, 'Open the ranks! Let him pass?' "

"Because one does not set fifteen hundred to kill a single man."

"Why, at the Cailleterie d'Astillé, when you saw your soldiers about to kill the Vendean Joseph Bézier, who was wounded and dragging himself along, did you exclaim, 'Go on before! This is my affair!' and then fire your pistol in the air?"

"Because one does not kill a man on the ground."

"And you were wrong. Both are to-day chiefs of bands. Joseph Bézier is Mustache, and Jean Treton is Jambe d'Argent. In saving those two men you gave two enemies to the Republic."

"Certainly I could wish to give her friends, and not enemies."

"Why, after the victory of Landéan, did you not shoot your three hundred peasant prisoners?"

"Because Bonchamp had shown mercy to the republican prisoners, and I wanted it said that the Republic showed mercy to the royalist prisoners."

"But, then, if you take Lantenac you will pardon him?"

"No."

"Why? Since you showed mercy to the three hundred peasants?"

"The peasants are ignorant men; Lantenac knows what he does."

"But Lantenac is your kinsman."

"France is the nearest."

"Lantenac is an old man."

"Lantenac is a stranger. Lantenac has no age. Lantenac summons the English. Lantenac is invasion. Lantenac is the enemy of the country. The duel between him and me can only finish by his death or mine."

"Gauvain, remember this vow."

"It is sworn."

There was silence, and the two looked at each other.

Then Gauvain resumed: "It will be a bloody date, this year '93 in which we live."

"Take care!" cried Cimourdain. "Terrible duties exist. Do not accuse that which is not accusable. Since when is it that the illness is the fault of the physician? Yes, the characteristic of this tremendous year is its pitilessness. Why? Because it is the grand revolutionary year. This year in which we live is the incarnation of the Revolution. The Revolution has an enemy,—the old world,—and it is without pity for it; just as the surgeon has an enemy,—gangrene,—and is without pity for it. The Revolution extirpates royalty in the king, aristocracy in the noble, despotism in the soldier, superstition in the priest, barbarism in the judge; in a word, everything which is tyranny, in all which is the tyrant. The operation is fearful; the Revolution performs it with a sure hand. As to the amount of sound flesh which it sacrifices, demand of Boerhaave what he thinks in regard to that. What tumour does not cause a loss of blood in its cutting away? Does not the extinguishing of a conflagration demand an energy as fierce as that of the fire itself? These formidable necessities are the very condition of success. A surgeon resembles a butcher; a healer may have the appearance of an executioner. The Revolution devotes itself to its fatal work. It mutilates, but it saves. What! you demand pity for the virus? You wish it to be merciful to that which is poisonous? It will not listen. It holds the post,—it will exterminate it. It makes a deep wound in civilization, from whence will spring health to the human race. You suffer? Without doubt. How long will it last? The time necessary for the operation. After that you will live. The Revolution amputates the world. Hence this hemorrhage,—'93."

"The surgeon is calm," said Gauvain, "and the men that I see are violent."

"The Revolution," replied Cimourdain, "needs savage workmen to aid it! It pushes aside every hand that trembles. It has only faith in the inexorables. Danton is the terrible, Robespierre is the inflexible; Saint-Just is the immovable, Marat is the implacable. Take care, Gauvain! these names are necessary. They are worth as much as armies to us; they will terrify Europe."

"And perhaps the future also," said Gauvain. He checked himself, and resumed: "For that matter, my master, you err. I accuse no one. According to me, the true point of view of the Revolution is its irresponsibility. Nobody is innocent, nobody is guilty. Louis XVI. is a sheep thrown among lions: he wishes to escape, he tries to flee, he seeks to defend himself; he would bite if he could. But one is not a lion at will; his craze to be one passes for crime. This enraged sheep shows his teeth: 'The traitor!' cry the lions; and they eat him. That done, they fight among themselves."

"The sheep is a brute."

"And the lions, what are they?"

This retort set Cimourdain thinking. He raised his head, and answered: "These lions are consciences. These lions are ideas. These lions are principles."

"They produce the reign of Terror."

"One day, the Revolution will be the justification of this Terror."

"Beware lest the Terror become the calumny of the Revolution." Gauvain continued: "Liberty, Equality, Fraternity,—these are the dogmas of peace and harmony. Why give them an alarming aspect? What is it we want? To bring the peoples to a universal republic. Well, do not let us make them afraid. What can intimidation serve? The people can no more be attracted by a scarecrow than birds can. One must not do evil to bring about good; one does not overturn the throne in order to leave the gibbet standing. Death to kings, and life to nations! Strike off the crowns; spare the heads! The Revolution is concord, not fright. Clement ideas are ill served by cruel men. Amnesty is to me the most beautiful word in human language. I will only shed blood in risking my own. Besides, I simply know how to fight; I am nothing but a soldier. But if I may not pardon, victory is not worth the trouble it costs. During battle let us be the enemies of our enemies, and after the victory their brothers."

"Take care!" repeated Cimourdain, for the third time. "Gauvain, you are more to me than a son; take care!" Then he added thoughtfully: "In a period like ours, pity may become one of the forms of treason."

Any one listening to the talk of these two men might have fancied he heard a dialogue between the sword and the axe. . . .

✦ Reading 5 ✦

Letters

Napoleon Bonaparte

The Revolution Consolidated

[Proclamation, December 15, 1799] Citizens, the Revolution has been made fast to the principles that started it. The Revolution is ended.

[Stenographic transcript, Conseil d'Etat, 1805; subject under discussion: a proposal to maintain feudal rights in the annexed provinces of Piedmont] I say: we have had a jubilee. The social order has been overthrown; the king, who was the apex of all legislation, has been guillotined. . . . Everything has been uprooted. . . .

You cannot undo the past. The annexed territories must be just like France, and if you went on annexing everything as far as Gibraltar and Kamchatka the laws of France would have to spread there, too. I am pleading the cause of the humble folk; the others never lack good dinners and brilliant drawing rooms that will plead for them.

[Conversation, 1816] In this gigantic struggle between the present and the past, I am the natural arbiter and mediator. I tried to be its supreme judge. My whole internal administration, my whole foreign policy were determined by that great aim.

Liberty, Equality, Vanity

[Conversation, 1803] I have come to realize that men are not born to be free.

[Conversation, 1804] Liberty means a good civil code. The only thing modern nations care for is property.

[Conversation, 1800s] Liberty is a need felt by a small class of people whom nature has endowed with nobler minds than the mass of men. Consequently, it may be repressed with impunity. Equality, on the other hand, pleases the masses.

[Conversation, 1800s] In Paris—and Paris means France—people are unable to take an interest in things unless they also take an interest in persons. The old monarchic way of life has accustomed us to personify everything. This would be a bad state of affairs for a people that seriously desires liberty. But the French are unable to desire anything seriously except, perhaps, equality. Even so, they would gladly renounce it if everyone could entertain the hope of rising to the top. Equality in the sense that everyone will be master—there you have the secret of all your vanities. What must be done, then, is to give everybody the hope of being able to rise.

[Conversation, 1815] My motto has always been: A career open to all talents, without distinctions of birth.

[Conversation, 1816] Democracy, if it is reasonable, limits itself to giving everyone an equal opportunity to compete and to obtain.

[Conversation, 1816, related by Las Cases] Concerning the Legion of Honor, the Emperor said, among other things, that the variety and the specialization of the old orders of chivalry tended to strengthen caste divisions, whereas the single decoration of the Legion of Honor and the universality of its application was the symbol of equality. The old orders kept the classes divided, while the new decoration ought to bring about the cohesion of the citizen body. Its influence, its effects within the national family might become incalculable: it was the common center, the universal incentive of all the diverse ambitions.

[Conversation, early 1800s] It is very easy to govern the French through vanity.

[Conversation, 1800] When a Frenchman is torn between fear of a policeman and fear of the devil, he

---

From: *The Mind of Napoleon: A Selection from His Written and Spoken Words,* ed. and trans. J. Christopher Herold (New York: Columbia University Press, 1955), pp. 72–75, 84–85, 245, 251–256.

will side with the devil. But when he is caught between the devil and fashion, he will obey fashion.

[Letter to his brother Jérôme, then king of Westphalia, 1807] What the peoples of Germany desire most impatiently is that talented commoners should have the same right to your esteem and to public employments as the nobles, that any trace of serfdom and of an intermediate hierarchy between the sovereign and the lowest class of the people should be completely abolished. The benefits of the Code Napoléon, the publicity of judicial procedure, the creation of juries must be so many distinguishing marks of your monarchy. And, if I may give you my whole opinion, I count more firmly on their effects for the enlargement and consolidation of your kingdom than on the results of even the greatest military victories. Your people must enjoy a degree of freedom, equality, and prosperity unknown to the people of the Germanies, and this liberal regime must produce, in one way or another, the most salutary changes affecting the politics of the Confederation of the Rhine and the power of your monarchy. This manner of governing will give you a more powerful shield against Prussia than the Elbe, fortifications, and French protection. What nation would wish to return under the arbitrary Prussian government once it had tasted the benefits of a wise and liberal administration? The peoples of Germany, the peoples of France, of Italy, of Spain all desire equality and liberal ideas. I have guided the affairs of Europe for many years now, and I have had occasion to convince myself that the buzzing of the privileged classes is contrary to the general opinion. Be a constitutional king.

* * *

"A Single Party and a Single Will"

[Newspaper editorial, 1801, on the "ideologist" opposition in the Tribunate] They are a dozen or fifteen men and think they are a party. Their endless ravings they call oratory. . . . Infernal machines have been set against the First Consul, knives have been sharpened, impotent plots have been fomented. Add to this, if you will, the sarcasms and the insane notions of twelve or fifteen befogged metaphysicians. Against this handful of enemies he will pit the people of France.

[Conseil d'Etat, 1802] The opposition in England is completely harmless. Its members are not partisans. They do not long for either feudalism or Jacobinism. Their influence is legitimately owed to their talents, and they merely try to sell themselves to the Crown. With us, it is quite different. Here the opposition consists of the Jacobins and of the ex-privileged classes. Those people do not merely compete for positions or money: the former want their clubs back, the latter the old regime. There is a great difference between free discussion in a country whose institutions are long established and the opposition in a country that is still unsettled.

[Conversation, 1803] *The First Consul* (in his bathtub): An opposition, as in England, is that it? I haven't been able to understand yet what good there is in an opposition. Whatever it may be, its only result is to diminish the prestige of authority in the eyes of the people.

Joseph Bonaparte: It's easy to see that you don't like it; you have taken good care of it.

The First Consul: Let another govern in my place, and if he doesn't, like me, make an effort to silence the talkers, he'll see what will happen to him. As for me, let me tell you that in order to govern well one needs absolute unity of power. I won't shout this from the roof tops, since I mustn't frighten a lot of people who would raise loud cries of despotism, if they were allowed to talk, and who would write about it, if they were allowed to write. But I have begun to put good order into all this.

[Proclamation, 19 Brumaire, Year VIII/November 10, 1799] I have refused to be the man of any party.

[Repeated saying, 1799] I have opened up a vast road. He who marches straight ahead shall be safe. He who strays to the right or to the left shall be punished.

[Instructions to an ambassador, 1803] In France there is but a single party and a single will.

[Conversation, 1816] Who ever heard me ask, throughout the years I was in power, to what party anyone belonged, or ever had belonged to, or what he had said, done, or written? Let them imitate me! I always was known to have but one question, one aim: "Do you want to be Frenchmen with me?" And if they said yes, I pushed everyone into a defile of granite rock, closed off to the right and to the left, where he was forced to march on to the other end—

and there I stood, pointing to the honor, glory, and splendor of the fatherland.

* * *

France as the Master Nation

[Conseil d'Etat, 1800s] I want the title of French citizen to become the finest and most desirable on earth. I want every Frenchman traveling anywhere in Europe to be able to believe himself at home.

[Letter to Joseph, 1806] I believe I have already told you that I intend to place the kingdom of Naples in my family. Together with Italy, Switzerland, Holland, and the three kingdoms of Germany, it will constitute my federated states, or the true French Empire.

[Conversation, c.1810] The French Empire shall become the metropolis of all other sovereignties. I want to force every king in Europe to build a large Palace for his use in Paris. When an Emperor of the French is crowned, these kings shall come to Paris, and they shall adorn that imposing ceremony with their presence and salute it with their homages.

[Conversation, 1816] It was a part of my ceaseless dreams to make Paris the true capital of Europe. At times, for instance, I wanted it to become a city of two, three, or four million inhabitants—in a word, something fabulous, something colossal and unprecedented, with public establishments commensurate with its population.

* * *

A Political Testament

[Deathbed statement, recorded by Montholon on April 17, 1821] The Emperor spent a quiet night, although he perspired abundantly. About three o'clock, he had me called. When I arrived, he was sitting up, and the brilliance of his eyes made me fear that this fever had increased. Noticing my concern, he said to me in a kindly voice:

"I am not worse, but I have become preoccupied, while talking with Bertrand, about what the executors of my will are to say to my son when they see him. Bertrand doesn't understand me. He and Lafayette are still exactly as they were in 1791, with their utopias, their English notions, their bills of grievances and States-General. All they see in the Revolution of 1789 is a mere reform of abuses, and they refuse to admit that it constituted, all in itself, a complete social rebirth.

* * *

"There is nothing worse than decent people in a political crisis when their consciences are under the spell of false ideas. You will understand me: all you need do is remember the things I have dictated to you on the aims of my reign. But all this may be scattered here and there in your memory when the time comes for you to speak of it. I had better sum up in a few words the advice I leave to my son, so that you can explain my thought to him in detail. Write:

" 'My son must have no thought of avenging my death: he must take advantage of it. Let him never forget my accomplishments; let him forever remain, as I have been, French to the finger tips. All his efforts must tend to a reign of peace. If, merely to imitate me and without an absolute necessity, he wants to resume my wars, he would be a mere ape. To do my labors over again would mean that I have accomplished nothing. To complete my work, on the other hand, would be to demonstrate the firmness of its foundations and to make intelligible the ground plan of the edifice that I had merely sketched. One cannot do the same thing twice in a century. I have been obliged to subdue Europe by force; today, Europe must be persuaded. I have saved the Revolution, which was on the point of death; I have washed off its crimes, I have held it up to the eyes of Europe resplendent with glory. I have implanted new ideas in the soil of France and Europe: their march cannot be reversed. Let my son reap the fruit of my seed. Let him develop all the elements of prosperity contained in the soil of France—at that price, he may yet become a great ruler.

" 'The Bourbons will not last. When I am dead, there will be a universal reaction in my Favor, even in England. That is a fine inheritance for my son. It is possible that, in order to wipe out the memory of their persecutions, the English will favor the return of my son to France. But in order to live on good terms with England, it is necessary at all costs to favor her commercial interests. This necessity entails two consequences: either fight England or share the world with her. The second alternative is the only possible one in our day.

* * *

" 'France is the one country in which the leaders exercise the least influence; to lean on them is to build on quicksand. Nothing great can be accomplished in France except by leaning on the masses. Besides, a government must look for support where it can find it. There are moral laws that are as inflexible and imperious as physical laws. The Bourbons cannot find support except in the nobles and the priests, no matter what constitution they may be forced to adopt, just as water must find its level despite the pump that has temporarily lifted it. As for me, I always leaned on everybody without exception; I gave the first example of a government favoring the interests of all. I did not govern for or through the nobles, the priests, the bourgeoisie, or the workers. I have governed for the entire community, for the whole great French family. To keep a nation's interests divided is a disservice to all classes and gives rise to civil war. What nature has made one cannot be divided but only mutilated.

* * *

" 'In my youth, I had illusions. I got rid of them fast. The great orators who dominate political assemblies by the glitter of their words are generally the most mediocre statesmen. You must not fight them with words—they usually command a still more sonorous vocabulary than your own—you must counter their fluency with closely reasoned logic. Their strength consists in vagueness; you must lead them back to the reality of facts. Practice kills them. In the Conseil d'Etat there were men far more eloquent than I, but I regularly defeated them with this simple argument: Two and two is four.

" 'France is swarming with highly capable and practical-minded men. The difficulty lies merely in finding them and giving them a chance to pursue their careers. There are men behind ploughs who should be in the Conseil d'Etat, and there are ministers who ought to be behind a plough.

* * *

" 'My son should never be surprised at seeing the most reasonable-looking men suggest the most absurd plans, from agrarian reform to Oriental despotism. All systems have their apologists in France. Let him listen to everything, but also let him evaluate everything according to its true merit, and let him surround himself with all the true talents produced by the nation. The French people has two equally powerful passions which seem opposed to each other but which in fact derive from the same sentiment—love of equality and love of distinctions. A government cannot satisfy those two needs except by being exceedingly just. In its laws and its actions, the government must be the same for all; honors and rewards must be given to those men who, in the eyes of the government, are most worthy of them.

* * *

" 'My son will have to reign with a free press. In our day, this is a necessity. In order to govern, the question is not to follow out a more or less valid theory but to build with whatever materials are at hand. The inevitable must be accepted and turned to advantage.

" 'In the hands of the government, a free press may become a powerful ally by carrying sound principles and doctrines to the remotest corners of the Empire. To leave it to its own devices is to sleep next to a powder keg.

* * *

" '. . . Our enemies are the enemies of mankind. They want to put chains around the people, whom they regard as a herd. They want to oppress France and to make the river flow back to its source: let them beware lest it overflow! Under my son the conflicting interests can coexist in peace, and the new ideas can spread and grow in strength without hurt and without victims. Humanity would be spared incalculable misfortunes. But if the blind hatred of the kings pursues my blood after my death, I shall be avenged nonetheless—but cruelly avenged.

" 'Civilization will be the loser in any case. If the people break their chains, Europe will be flooded with blood; civilization will disappear amid civil and foreign wars. It will take more than three hundred years to destroy, in Europe, that royal authority which only yesterday still represented the common interest but which required several centuries to emerge from the grip of the Middle Ages. If, on the other hand, the North [i.e., Russia] should march against civilization, the struggle will be less long but the blows will be more fatal. The welfare of the people, all the achievements of so many years, will be lost, and no one can foresee what may be the disastrous consequences.

" 'The restoration of my son is in the interest of the people as well as of the kings. Outside the ideas and principles for which we have fought and which I made triumph I see nothing but slavery or confusion for France and Europe alike.

* * *

" 'Europe is marching toward an inevitable change. To retard her march is to waste strength in a futile struggle. To favor it is to strengthen the hopes and aspirations of all.

" 'There are national aspirations that must be satisfied sooner or later, and toward this aim we must march. . . . The serious questions will no longer be resolved in the North but in the Mediterranean: there is enough on its shores to satisfy the ambitions of all the powers, and with the shreds of uncivilized countries the happiness of the civilized nations can be bought. If only the kings would see the light, there would no longer be in Europe any cause for hatred among nations.

* * *

" 'In order to know whether his administration is good or bad, whether his laws are in harmony with custom, my son should ask for a yearly report on the number of sentences passed by the tribunals, together with their motivations. If crimes and misdemeanors increase, this is proof that misery is on the rise and that society is badly governed. Their decrease is proof of the contrary.

" 'Religious ideas have a more powerful influence than is thought by certain shortsighted philosophers; they can render great service to humanity. By being on good terms with the pope, it is possible even today to dominate the consciences of a hundred million men.

* * *

" 'My son should read much history and meditate upon it: it is the only true philosophy. Let him read and meditate upon the wars of the great captains: it is the only way to learn the art of war.

" 'Yet no matter what you say to him, no matter what he learns, he will profit little from it if in his innermost heart he lacks that sacred flame, that love of the good which alone inspires great deeds.' "

✧ PART TWO ✧

Restoration, Liberalism, and the Individual, 1815–1848

Eugene Delacroix's painting Liberty Leading the People *(1831) portrays the turbulence of the post-Vienna Congress era, during which the new ideologies of economic, social, and personal freedom promised to create a new and better world.*

Restoration, Liberalism, and the Individual, 1815–1848

After the tumult of the revolutionary and Napoleonic eras, European leaders restored the old dynasties and tried to head off any future social and political change. Regardless, the French and American revolutions had provided glimpses of a freer world. Tensions immediately arose between two competing world views—one aimed at retaining a hierarchical society dominated by hereditary elites and autocrats and the other at creating a fluid society guided by constitutions that favored those whose prosperity and education were of recent origin. The latter view more closely approximated the realities of post-1815 Europe: a vulgar, energetic middle class, motivated by the attainment of personal wealth and prestige, refused to be bypassed. The titles historians simultaneously use for the 1815–1848 era capture this dramatic conflict: the Age of Metternich (symbol of conservatism) and the Age of Revolutions.

The conservative Austrian minister, Prince Clemens von Metternich (1773–1859), stamped his personality on the attempted restoration of the *ancien régime*. His Confession (1820) expressed certitude in established values, yearning for an old way of life, and foreboding for the future. To the contrary, John Stuart Mill (1806–1873) welcomed the new world and its freer society and politics in *On Liberty* (1859). He and other progressive writers wished to enlist everyone's talents.

George Eliot (1819–1880) used her novel *Middlemarch* (1871–1872) to portray these acutely conflicting views of society by detailing the personal, working, and political lives of all classes in a small English town. Raucous politics, she implied, were the price of empowering the people. In *The Sorrows of Young Werther* (1774), the German writer Johann Wolfgang von Goethe (1749–1832) helped create the era's new romantic sensibility, which rejected the earlier reliance on reason in favor of an emphasis on emotion and individual expression. Despairing of attaining his high personal goals, the romantic Werther commits suicide, an act that inspired many real-life imitators among European youth unused to individual freedom and unbridled sentiment.

✦ Reading 6 ✦

Confession of Faith

Prince Metternich

Confession of Faith Metternich's Secret Memorandum to the Emperor Alexander

'*L'Europe,*' a celebrated writer has recently said, '*fait aujourd'hui pitié à l'homme d'esprit et horreur à l'homme vertueux.*'

It would be difficult to comprise in a few words a more exact picture of the situation at the time we are writing these lines!

Kings have to calculate the chances of their very existence in the immediate future; passions are let loose, and league together to overthrow everything which society respects as the basis of its existence; religion, public morality, laws, customs, rights, and duties, all are attacked, confounded, overthrown, or called in question. The great mass of the people are tranquil spectators of these attacks and revolutions, and of the absolute want of all means of defence. A few are carried off by the torrent, but the wishes of the immense majority are to maintain a repose which exists no longer, and of which even the first elements seem to be lost.

What is the cause of all these evils? By what methods has this evil established itself, and how is it that it penetrates into every vein of the social body?

Do remedies still exist to arrest the progress of this evil, and what are they?

These are doubtless questions worthy of the solicitude of every good man who is a true friend to order and public peace—two elements inseparable in principle, and which are at once the first needs and the first blessings of humanity.

Has there never been offered to the world an institution really worthy of the name? Has truth been always confounded with error ever since society has believed itself able to distinguish one from the other? Have the experiences bought at the price of so many sacrifices, and repeated at intervals, and in so many different places, been all in error? Will a flood of light be shed upon society at one stroke? Will knowledge come by inspiration? If one could believe in such phenomena it would not be the less necessary, first of all, to assure oneself of their reality. Of all things, nothing is so fatal as error; and it is neither our wish nor our intention ever to give ourselves up to it. Let us examine the matter!

The Source of the Evil

Man's nature is immutable. The first needs of society are and remain the same, and the differences which they seem to offer find their explanation in the diversity of influences, acting on the different races by natural causes, such as the diversity of climate, barrenness or richness of soil, insular or continental position, &c. &c. These local differences no doubt produce effects which extend far beyond purely physical necessities; they create and deferrable particular needs in a more elevated sphere; finally, they determine the laws, and exercise an influence even on religions.

It is, on the other hand, with institutions as with everything else. Vague in their origin, they pass through periods of development and perfection, to arrive in time at their decadence; and, conforming to the laws of man's nature, they have, like him, their infancy, their youth, their age of strength and reason, and their age of decay.

Two elements alone remain in all their strength, and never cease to exercise their indestructible influence with equal power. These are the precepts of morality, religions as well as social, and the necessities created by locality. From the time that men attempt to swerve from these bases, to become rebels

From: *Memoirs of Prince Metternich, 1815–1829,* ed. Prince Richard Metternich, trans. Mrs. Alexander Napier (London: Richard Bentley & Son, 1881), vol. 3, pp. 454–476.

against these sovereign arbiters of their destinies, society suffers from a *malaise* which sooner or later will lead to a state of convulsion. The history of every country, in relating the consequences of such errors, contains many pages stained with blood; but we dare to say, without fear of contradiction, one seeks in vain for an epoch when an evil of this nature has extended its ravages over such a vast area as it has done at the present time. The causes are natural.

History embraces but a very limited space of time. It did not begin to deserve the name of history until long after the fall of great empires. There, where it seems to conduct us to the cradle of civilisation, it really conducts us to ruins. We see republics arise and prosper, struggle, and then submit to the rule of one fortunate soldier. We see one of these republics pass through all the phases common to society, and end in an almost universal monarchy—that is to say, subjugating the scattered portions of the then civilised world. We see this monarchy suffer the fate of all political bodies: we see its first springs become enfeebled, and finally decay.

Centuries of darkness followed the irruption of the barbarians. The world, however, could not return to barbarism. The Christian religion had appeared; imperishable in its essence, its very existence was sufficient to disperse the darkness and establish civilisation on new foundations, applicable to all times and all places, satisfying all needs, and establishing the most important of all on the basis of a pure and eternal law! To the formation of new Christian States succeeded the Crusades, a curious mixture of good and evil.

A decisive influence was shortly exercised on the progress of civilisation by three discoveries—the invention of printing, that of gunpowder, and the discovery of the New World. Still later came the Reformation—another event which had incalculable effects, on account of its influence on the moral world. From that time the face of the world was changed.

The facilitation of the communication of thoughts by printing; the total change in the means of attack and defence brought about by the invention of gunpowder; the difference suddenly produced in the value of property by the quantity of metals which the discovery of America put in circulation; the spirit of adventure provoked by the chances of fortune opened in a new hemisphere; the modifications in the relations of society caused by so many and such important changes, all became more developed, and were in some sort crowned by the revolution which the Reformation worked in the moral world.

The progress of the human mind has been extremely rapid in the course of the last three centuries. This progress having been accelerated more rapidly than the growth of wisdom (the only counterpoise to passions and to error); a revolution prepared by the false systems, the fatal errors into which many of the most illustrious sovereigns of the last half of the eighteenth century fell, has at last broken out in a country advanced in knowledge, and enervated by pleasure, in a country inhabited by a people whom one can only regard as frivolous, from the facility with which they comprehend and the difficulty they experience in judging calmly.

Having now thrown a rapid glance over the first causes of the present state of society, it is necessary to point out in a more particular manner the evil which threatens to deprive it, at one blow, of the real blessings, the fruits of genuine civilisation, and to disturb it in the midst of its enjoyments. This evil may be described in one word—presumption; the natural effect of the rapid progression of the human mind towards the perfecting of so many things. This it is which at the present day leads so many individuals astray, for it has become an almost universal sentiment.

Religion, morality, legislation, economy, politics, administration, all have become common and accessible to everyone. Knowledge seems to come by inspiration; experience has no value for the presumptuous man; faith is nothing to him; he substitutes for it a pretended individual conviction, and to arrive at this conviction dispenses with all inquiry and with all study; for these means appear too trivial to a mind which believes itself strong enough to embrace at one glance all questions and all facts. Laws have no value for him, because he has not contributed to make them, and it would be beneath a man of his parts to recognise the limits traced by rude and ignorant generations. Power resides in himself; why should he submit himself to that which was only useful for the man deprived of light and knowledge? That which, according to him, was required in an age of weakness cannot be suitable in an age of reason and vigour, amounting to universal perfection, which the German innovators designate by the idea, absurd in itself, of the Emancipation of the People! Morality itself he does not attack openly, for without it he could not be sure for a single instant of his own existence; but he interprets its essence after his own fashion, and allows every other person to do so likewise, provided that other person neither kills nor robs him.

In thus tracing the character of the presumptuous man, we believe we have traced that of the society of the day, composed of like elements, if the denomination of society is applicable to an order of things which only tends in principle towards individualising all the elements of which society is composed. Presumption makes every man the guide of his own belief, the arbiter of laws according to which he is pleased to govern himself, or to allow some one else to govern him and his neighbours; it makes him, in short, the sole judge of his own faith, his own actions, and the principles according to which he guides them.

Is it necessary to give a proof of this last fact? We think we have furnished it in remarking that one of the sentiments most natural to man, that of nationality, is erased from the Liberal catechism, and that where the word is still employed, it is used by the heads of the party as a pretext to enchain Governments, or as a lever to bring about destruction. The real aim of the idealists of the party is religious and political fusion, and this being analysed is nothing else but creating in favour of each individual an existence entirely independent of all authority, or of any other will than his own, an idea absurd and contrary to the nature of man, and incompatible with the needs of human society.

The Course Which the Evil Has Followed and Still Follows

The causes of the deplorable intensity with which this evil weighs on society appear to us to be of two kinds. The first are so connected with the nature of things that no human foresight could have prevented them. The second should be subdivided into two classes, however similar they may appear in their effects.

Of these causes, the first are negative, the others positive. We will place among the first the feebleness and the inertia of Governments.

It is sufficient to cast a glance on the course which the Governments followed during the eighteenth century, to be convinced that not one among them was ignorant of the evil or of the crisis towards which the social body was tending. There were, however, some men, unhappily endowed with great talents, who felt their own strength, and were not slow to appraise the progressive course of their influence, taking into account the weakness or the inertia of their adversaries; and who had the art to prepare and conduct men's minds to the triumph of their detestable enterprise—an enterprise all the more odious as it was pursued without regard to results, simply abandoning themselves to the one feeling of hatred of God and of His immutable moral laws.

France had the misfortune to produce the greatest number of these men. It is in her midst that religion and all that she holds sacred, that morality and authority, and all connected with them, have been attacked with a steady and systematic animosity, and it is there that the weapon of ridicule has been used with the most ease and success.

Drag through the mud the name of God and the powers instituted by His divine decrees, and the revolution will be prepared! Speak of a social contract, and the revolution is accomplished! The revolution was already completed in the palaces of Kings, in the drawing-rooms and boudoirs of certain cities, while among the great mass of the people it was still only in a state of preparation.

It would be difficult not to pause here to consider the influence which the example of England had for a long time exercised on France. England is herself placed in such a peculiar situation that we believe we may safely say that not one of the forms possible to that State, not one of its customs or institutions, would suit any Continental State, and that where we might wish to take them for models, we should only obtain inconvenience and danger, without securing a single one of the advantages which accompany them.

According to the bent of minds in France, at the time of the convocation of the *notables*, and in consequence of the direction which public opinion had received for more than fifty years—a direction which, latterly, had been strengthened and in some sort adapted to France by the imprudent help which her Government had given to the American revolution—all reform in France touching the very foundations of the monarchy was soon transformed into a revolution. What might have been foreseen, and what had been foretold by everybody, the Government alone excepted, was realised but too soon. The French Revolution broke out, and has gone through a complete revolutionary cycle in a very short period, which could only have appeared long to its victims and to its contemporaries.

The scenes of horror which accompanied the first phases of the French Revolution prevented the rapid propagation of its subversive principles beyond the frontiers of France, and the wars of conquest which succeeded them gave to the public mind a direction little favourable to revolutionary principles. Thus the Jacobin propaganda failed entirely to realise criminal hopes.

Nevertheless the revolutionary seed had penetrated into every country and spread more or less. It was greatly developed under the *régime* of the military despotism of Bonaparte. His conquests displaced a number of laws, institutions, and customs; broke through bonds sacred among all nations, strong enough to resist time itself; which is more than can be said of certain benefits conferred by these innovators. From these perturbations it followed that the revolutionary spirit could in Germany, Italy, and later on in Spain, easily hide itself under the veil of patriotism.

Prussia committed a grave fault in calling to her aid such dangerous weapons as secret associations always will be: a fault which could not be justified even by the deplorable situation in which that Power then found itself. This it was that first gave a strong impulse to the revolutionary spirit in her States, and this spirit made rapid progress, supported as it was in the rest of Germany by the system of foreign despotism which since 1806 has been there developed. Many Princes of the Rhenish Confederation were secretly auxiliaries and accomplices of this system, to which they sacrificed the institutions which in their country from time immemorial had served as a protection against despotism and democracy.

The war of the Allies, by putting bounds to the predominance of France, was vigorously supported in Germany by the same men whose hatred of France was in reality nothing but hatred of the military despotism of Bonaparte, and also of the legitimate power of their own masters. With wisdom in the Governments and firmness in principles, the end of the war in 1814 might nevertheless have insured to the world the most peaceful and happy future. Great experiences had been gained and great lessons, which might have been usefully applied. But fate had decided otherwise.

The return of the usurper to France, and the completely false steps taken by the French Government from 1815 to 1820, accumulated a mass of new dangers and great calamities for the whole civilised world. It is to the first of these misfortunes that is partly due the critical state in which France and the whole social body is placed. Bonaparte destroyed in a hundred days the work of the fourteen years during which he had exercised his authority. He set free the revolution which he came to France to subdue; he brought back men's minds, not to the epoch of the 18th Brumaire, but to the principles which the National Assembly had adopted in its deplorable blindness.

What Bonaparte had thus done to the detriment of France and Europe, the grave errors which the French Government have since committed, and to which other Governments have yielded—all these unhappy influences weigh heavily on the world of to-day; they threaten with total ruin the work of restoration, the fruit of so many glorious efforts, and of a harmony between the greatest monarchs unparalleled in the records of history, and they give rise to fears of indescribable calamities to society.

In this memoir we have not yet touched on one of the most active and at the same time most dangerous instruments used by the revolutionists of all countries, with a success which is no longer doubtful. I refer to the secret societies, a real power, all the more dangerous as it works in the dark, undermining all parts of the social body, and depositing everywhere the seeds of a moral gangrene which is not slow to develop and increase. This plague is one of the worst which those Governments who are lovers of peace and of their people have to watch and fight against.

Do Remedies for This Evil Exist, and What Are They?

We look upon it as a fundamental truth, that for every disease there is a remedy, and that the knowledge of the real nature of the one should lead to the discovery of the other. Few men, however, stop thoroughly to examine a disease which they intend to combat. There are hardly any who are not subject to the influence of passion, or held under the yoke of prejudice; there are a great many who err in a way more perilous still, on account of its flattering and often brilliant appearance: we speak of *l'esprit de système;* that spirit always false, but indefatigable, audacious and irrepressible, is satisfactory to men imbued with it (for they live in and govern a world created by themselves), but it is so much the more dangerous for the inhabitants of the real world, so different from that created by *l'esprit de système.*

There is another class of men who, judging of a disease by its outward appearance, confound the accessory manifestations with the root of the disease, and, instead of directing their efforts to the source of the evil, content themselves with subduing some passing symptoms.

It is our duty to try and avoid both of these dangers.

The evil exists and it is enormous. We do not think we can better define it and its cause at all times and in all places than we have already done by the word 'presumption,' that inseparable companion of the half-educated, that spring of an unmeasured ambition, and yet easy to satisfy in times of trouble and confusion.

It is principally the middle classes of society which this moral gangrene has affected, and it is only among them that the real heads of the party are found.

For the great mass of the people it has no attraction and can have none. The labours to which this class—the real people—are obliged to devote themselves, are too continuous and too positive to allow them to throw themselves into vague abstractions and ambitions. The people know what is the happiest thing for them: namely, to be able to count on the morrow, for it is the morrow which will repay them for the cares and sorrows of to-day. The laws which afford a just protection to individuals, to families, and to property, are quite simple in their essence. The people dread any movement which injures industry and brings new burdens in its train.

Men in the higher classes of society who join the revolution are either falsely ambitious men or, in the widest acceptation of the word, lost spirits. Their career, moreover, is generally short! They are the first victims of political reforms, and the part played by the small number among them who survive is mostly that of courtiers despised by upstarts, their inferiors, promoted to the first dignities of the State; and of this France, Germany, Italy, and Spain furnish a number of living examples.

We do not believe that fresh disorders with a directly revolutionary end—not even revolutions in the palace and the highest places in the Government—are to be feared at present in France, because of the decided aversion of the people to anything which might disturb the peace they are now enjoying after so many troubles and disasters.

In Germany, as in Spain and Italy, the people ask only for peace and quiet.

In all four countries the agitated classes are principally composed of wealthy men—real cosmopolitans, securing their personal advantage at the expense of any order of things whatever—paid State officials, men of letters, lawyers, and the individuals charged with the public education.

To these classes may be added that of the falsely ambitious, whose number is never considerable among the lower orders, but is larger in the higher ranks of society.

There is besides scarcely any epoch which does not offer a rallying cry to some particular faction. This cry, since 1815, has been *Constitution.* But do not let us deceive ourselves: this word, susceptible of great latitude of interpretation, would be but imperfectly understood if we supposed that the factions attached quite the same meaning to it under the different *régimes.* Such is certainly not the case. In pure monarchies it is qualified by the name of 'national representation.' In countries which have lately been brought under the representative *régime* it is called 'development,' and promises charters and fundamental laws. In the only State which possesses an ancient national representation it takes 'reform' as its object. Everywhere it means change and trouble.

In pure monarchies it may be paraphrased thus:—'The level of equality shall pass over your heads; your fortunes shall pass into other hands; your ambitions, which have been satisfied for centuries, shall now give place to our ambitions, which have been hitherto repressed.'

In the States under a new *régime* they say:—'The ambitions satisfied yesterday must give place to those of the morrow, and this is the morrow for us.'

Lastly, in England, the only place in the third class, the rallying cry—that of Reform—combines the two meanings.

Europe thus presents itself to the impartial observer under an aspect at the same time deplorable and peculiar. We find everywhere the people praying for the maintenance of peace and tranquillity, faithful to God and their Princes, remaining proof against the efforts and seductions of the factious who call themselves friends of the people and wish to lead them to an agitation which the people themselves do not desire!

The Governments, having lost their balance, are frightened, intimidated, and thrown into confusion by the cries of the intermediary class of society, which, placed between the Kings and their subjects, breaks the sceptre of the monarch, and usurps the cry of the people—that class so often disowned by the people, and nevertheless too much listened to, caressed and feared by those who could with one word reduce it again to nothingness.

We see this intermediary class abandon itself with a blind fury and animosity which proves much more its own fears than any confidence in the success of its enterprises, to all the means which seem proper to assuage its thirst for power, applying itself to the task of persuading Kings that their rights are confined to sitting upon a throne, while those of the people are to govern, and to attack all that centuries have bequeathed as holy and worthy of man's respect—denying, in fact, the value of the past, and declaring themselves the masters of the future. We see this class take all sorts of disguises, uniting and subdividing as occasion offers, helping each other in the hour of danger, and the next day depriving each other of all their conquests. It takes possession of the press, and employs it to promote impiety, disobedience to the laws of religion and the State, and goes so far as to preach murder as a duty for those who desire what is good.

One of its leaders in Germany defined public opinion as 'the will of the strong man in the spirit of the party'—a maxim too often put in practice, and too seldom understood by those whose right and duty it is to save society from its own errors, its own weaknesses, and the crimes which the factious commit while pretending to act in its interests.

The evil is plain; the means used by the faction which causes these disorders are so blameable in principle, so criminal in their application, and expose the faction itself to so many dangers, that what men of narrow views (whose head and heart are broken by circumstances stronger than their calculations or their courage) regard as the end of society may become the first step towards a better order of things. These weak men would be right unless men stronger than they are come forward to close their ranks and determine the victory.

We are convinced that society can no longer be saved without strong and vigorous resolutions on the part of the Goverments still free in their opinions and actions.

We are also convinced that this may yet be, if the Governments face the truth, if they free themselves from all illusion, if they join their ranks and take their stand on a line of correct, unambiguous, and frankly announced principles.

By this course the monarchs will fulfil the duties imposed upon them by Him who, by entrusting them with power, has charged them to watch over the maintenance of justice, and the rights of all, to avoid the paths of error, and tread firmly in the way of truth. Placed beyond the passions which agitate society, it is in days of trial chiefly that they are called upon to despoil realities of their false appearances, and to show themselves as they are, fathers invested with the authority belonging by right to the heads of families, to prove that, in days of mourning, they know how to be just, wise, and therefore strong, and that they will not abandon the people whom they ought to govern to be the sport of factions, to error and its consequences, which must involve the loss of society. The moment in which we are putting our thoughts on paper is one of these critical moments. The crisis is great; it win be decisive according to the part we take or do not take.

There is a rule of conduct common to individuals and to States, established by the experience of centuries as by that of everyday life. This rule declares 'that one must not dream of reformation while agitated by passion; wisdom directs that at such moments we should limit ourselves to maintaining.'

Let the monarchs vigorously adopt this principle; let all their resolutions bear the impression of it. Let their actions, their measures, and even their words announce and prove to the world this determination —they will find allies everywhere. The Governments, in establishing the principle of *stability,* will in no wise exclude the development of what is good, for stability is not immobility. But it is for those who are burdened with the heavy task of government to augment the well-being of their people! It is for Governments to regulate it according to necessity and to suit the times. It is not by concessions, which the factious strive to force from legitimate power, and which they have neither the right to claim nor the faculty of keeping within just bounds, that wise reforms can be carried out. That all the good possible should be done is our most ardent wish; but that which is not good must never be confounded with that which is, and even real good should be done only by those who unite to the right of authority the means of enforcing it. Such should be also the sincere wish of the people, who know by sad experience the value of certain phrases and the nature of certain caresses.

Respect for all that is; liberty for every Government to watch over the well-being of its own people; a league between all Governments against factions in all States; contempt for the meaningless words which have become the rallying cry of the factious; respect for the progressive development of institutions in lawful ways; refusal on the part of every monarch to aid or succour partisans under any mask whatever—such are happily the ideas of the great monarchs: the world will be saved if they bring them into action—it is lost if they do not.

Union between the monarchs is the basis of the policy which must now be followed to save society from total ruin.

What is the particular object towards which this policy should be directed? The more important this question is, the more necessary it is to solve it. A principle is something, but it acquires real value only in its application.

The first sources of the evil which is crushing the world have been indicated by us in a paper which has no pretension to be anything more than a mere sketch. Its further causes have also there been pointed out: if, with respect to individuals, it may be defined by the word *presumption,* in applying it to society, taken as a whole, we believe we can best describe the existing evil as the *confusion of ideas,* to which too much generalisation constantly leads. This is what now troubles society. Everything which up to this time has been considered as fixed in principle is attacked and overthrown.

In religious matters criticism and inquiry are to take the place of faith, Christian morality is to replace the Law of Christ as it is interpreted by Christian authorities.

In the Catholic Church, the Janseuists and a number of isolated sectarians, who wish for a religion without a Church, have devoted themselves to this enterprise with ardent zeal: among the Protestant sects, the Methodists, sub-divided into almost as many sects as there are individuals; then the enlightened promoters of the Bible Societies and the Unitarians—the promoters of the fusion of Lutherans and Calvinists in one Evangelical community—all pursue the same end.

The object which these men have in common, to whatever religion they may ostensibly belong, is simply to overthrow all authority. Put on moral grounds, they wish *to enfranchise souls* in the same way as some of the political revolutionists who were not actuated by motives of personal ambition wished to *enfranchise the people.*

If the same elements of destruction which are now throwing society into convulsion have existed in all ages—for every age has seen immoral and ambitious men, hypocrites, men of heated imaginations, wrong motives, and wild projects—yet ours, by the single fact of the liberty of the press, possesses more than any preceding age the means of contact, seduction, and attraction Whereby to act on these different classes of men.

We are certainly not alone in questioning if society can exist with the liberty of the press, a scourge unknown to the world before the latter half of the seventeenth century, and restrained until the end of the eighteenth, with scarcely any exceptions but England—a part of Europe separated from the continent by the sea, as well as by her language and by her peculiar manners.

The first principle to be followed by the monarchs, united as they are by the coincidence of their desires and opinions, should be that of maintaining the stability of political institutions against the disorganised excitement which has taken possession of men's minds; the immutability of principles against the madness of their interpretation; and respect for laws actually in force against a desire for their destruction.

The hostile faction is divided into two very distinct parties. One is that of the Levellers; the other, that of the Doctrinaires. United in times of confusion, these men are divided in times of inaction. It is for the Governments to understand and estimate them at their just value.

In the class of Levellers there are found men of strong will and determination. The Doctrinaires can count none such among their ranks. If the first are more to be feared in action, the second are more dangerous in that time of deceitful calm which precedes it; as with physical storms, so with those of social order. Given up to abstract ideas inapplicable to real wants, and generally in contradiction to those very wants, men of this class unceasingly agitate the people by their imaginary or simulated fears, and disturb Governments in order to make them deviate from the right path. The world desires to be governed by facts and according to justice, not by phrases and theories; the first need of society is to be maintained by strong authority (no authority without real strength deserves the name) and not to govern itself. In comparing the number of contests between parties in mixed Governments, and that of just complaints caused by aberrations of power in a Christian State, the comparison would not be in favour of the new doctrines. The first and greatest concern for the immense majority of every nation is the stability of the laws, and their uninterrupted action—never their change. Therefore let the Governments govern, let them maintain the groundwork of their institutions, both ancient and modern; for if it is at all times dangerous to touch them, it certainly would not now, in the general confusion, be wise to do so.

Let them announce this determination to their people, and demonstrate it by facts. Let them reduce the Doctrinaires to silence within their States, and show their contempt for them abroad. Let them not encourage by their attitude or actions the suspicion of being favourable or indifferent to error: let them not allow it to be believed that experience has lost all its rights to make way for experiments which at the least are dangerous. Let them be precise and clear in all their words, and not seek by concessions to gain over those parties who aim at the destruction of all power but their own, whom concessions will never gain over, but only further embolden in their pretensions to power.

Let them in these troublous times be more than usually cautious in attempting real ameliorations, not imperatively claimed by the needs of the moment, to the end that good itself may not turn against them—which is the case whenever a Government measure seems to be inspired by fear.

Let them not confound concessions made to parties with the good they ought to do for their people, in modifying, according to their recognised needs, such branches of the administration as require it.

Let them give minute attention to the financial state of their kingdoms, so that their people may enjoy, by the reduction of public burdens, the real, not imaginary, benefits of a state of peace.

Let them be just, but strong; beneficent, but strict.

Let them maintain religious principles in all their purity, and not allow the faith to be attacked and morality interpreted according to the *social contract* or the visions of foolish sectarians.

Let them suppress Secret Societies, that gangrene of society.

In short, let the great monarchs strengthen their union, and prove to the world that if it exists, it is beneficent, and ensures the political peace of Europe: that it is powerful only for the maintenance of tranquillity at a time when so many attacks are directed against it; that the principles which they profess are paternal and protective, menacing only the disturbers of public tranquillity.

The Governments of the second order will see in such a union the anchor of their salvation, and they will be anxious to connect themselves with it. The people will take confidence and courage, and the most profound and salutary peace which the history of any time can show will have been effected. This peace will first act on countries still in a good state, but will not be without a very decided influence on the fate of those threatened with destruction, and even assist the restoration of those which have already passed under the scourge of revolution.

To every great State determined to survive the storm there still remain many chances of salvation, and a strong union between the States on the principles we have announced will overcome the storm itself.

✦ Reading 7 ✦

On Liberty

John Stuart Mill

The object of this Essay is to assert one very simple principle, as entitled to govern absolutely the dealings of society with the individual in the way of compulsion and control, whether the means used be physical force in the form of legal penalties, or the moral coercion of public opinion. That principle is, that the sole end for which mankind are warranted, individually or collectively, in interfering with the liberty of action of any of their number, is self-protection. That the only purpose for which power can be rightfully exercised over any member of a civilised community, against his will, is to prevent harm to others. His own good, either physical or moral, is not a sufficient warrant. He cannot rightfully be compelled to do or forbear because it will be better for him to do so, because it will make him happier, because, in the opinions of others, to do so would be wise, or even right. These are good reasons for remonstrating with him, or reasoning with him, or persuading him, or entreating him, but not for compelling him, or visiting him with any evil in case he do otherwise. To justify that, the conduct from which it is desired to deter him must be calculated to produce evil to some one else. The only part of the conduct of any one, for which he is amenable to society, is that which concerns others. In the part which merely concerns himself, his independence is, of right, absolute. Over himself, over his own body and mind, the individual is sovereign.

It is, perhaps hardly necessary to say that this doctrine is meant to apply only to human beings in the maturity of their faculties. We are not speaking of children, or of young persons below the age which the law may fix as that of manhood or womanhood. Those who are still in a state to require being taken care of by others, must be protected against their own actions as well as against external injury. For the same reason, we may leave out of consideration those backward states of society in which the race itself may be considered as in its nonage. The early difficulties in the way of spontaneous progress are so great, that there is seldom any choice of means for overcoming them; and a ruler full of the spirit of improvement is warranted in the use of any expedients that will attain an end, perhaps otherwise unattainable. Despotism is a legitimate mode of government in dealing with barbarians, provided the end be their improvement, and the means justified by actually effecting that end. Liberty, as a principle, has no application to any state of things anterior to the time when mankind have become capable of being improved by free and equal discussion. Until then, there is nothing for them but implicit obedience to an Akbar or a Charlemagne, if they are so fortunate as to find one. But as soon as mankind have attained the capacity of being guided to their own improvement by conviction or persuasion (a period long since reached in all nations with whom we need here concern ourselves), compulsion, either in the direct form or in that of pains and penalties for noncompliance, is no longer admissible as a means to their own good, and justifiable only for the security of others.

It is proper to state that I forego any advantage which could be derived to my argument from the idea of abstract right, as a thing independent of utility. I regard utility as the ultimate appeal on all ethical questions; but it must be utility in the largest sense, grounded on the permanent interests of man as a progressive being. Those interests, I contend, authorise the subjection of individual spontaneity to external control, only in respect to those actions of each, which concern the interest of other people. If any one does an act hurtful to others, there is a *prima facie* case for punishing him, by law, or,

From: *Mill, Texts and Commentaries,* ed. Alan Ryan (New York, London: W.W. Norton & Company, 1997), pp. 48–59, 82–83.

where legal penalties are not safely applicable, by general disapprobation. There are also many positive acts for the benefit of others, which he may rightfully be compelled to perform; such as to give evidence in a court of justice: to bear his fair share in the common defence, or in any other joint work necessary to the interest of the society of which he enjoys the protection; and to perform certain acts of individual beneficence, such as saving a fellow-creature's life, or interposing to protect the defenceless against ill-usage, things which whenever it is obviously a man's duty to do, he may rightfully be made responsible to society for not doing. A person may cause evil to others not only by his actions but by his inaction, and in either case he is justly accountable to them for the injury. The latter case, it is true, requires a much more cautions exercise of compulsion than the former. To make any one answerable for doing evil to others is the rule: to make him answerable for not preventing evil is, comparatively speaking, the exception. Yet there are many cases clear enough and grave enough to justify that exception. In all things which regard the external relations of the individual, he is *de jure* amenable to those whose interests are concerned, and, if need be, to society as their protector. There are often good reasons for not holding him to the responsibility; but these reasons must arise from the special expediencies of the case: either because it is a kind of case in which he is on the whole likely to act better, when left to his own discretion, than when controlled in any way in which society have it in their power to control him: or because the attempt to exercise control would produce other evils, greater than those which it would prevent. When such reasons as these preclude the enforcement of responsibility, the conscience of the agent himself should step into the vacant judgment seal, and protect those interests of others which have no external protection; judging himself all the more rigidly, because the case does not admit of his being made accountable to the judgment of his fellow-creatures.

But there is a sphere of action in which society, as distinguished from the individual, has, if any, only an indirect interest; comprehending all that portion of a person's life and conduct which affects only himself, or if it also affects others, only with their free, voluntary, and undeceived consent and participation. When I say only himself, I mean directly, and in the first instance; for whatever affects himself, may affect others *through* himself; and the objection which may be grounded on this contingency, will receive consideration in the sequel. This, then, is the appropriate region of human liberty. It comprises, first, the inward domain of consciousness: demanding liberty of conscience in the most comprehensive sense: liberty of thought and feeling; absolute freedom of opinion and sentiment on all subjects, practical or speculative, scientific, moral or theological. The liberty of expressing and publishing opinions may seem to fall under a different principle, since it belongs to that part of the conduct of an individual which concerns other people; but, being almost of as much importance as the liberty of thought itself, and resting in great part on the same reasons, is practically inseparable from it. Secondly, the principle requires liberty of tastes and pursuits: of framing the plan of our life to suit our own character; of doing as we like, subject to such consequences as may follow: without impediment from our fellow-creatures, so long as what we do does not harm them, even though they should think our conduct foolish, perverse, or wrong. Thirdly, from this liberty of each individual, follows the liberty, within the same limits, of combination among individuals; freedom to unite, for any purpose not involving harm to others: the persons combining being supposed to be of full age, and not forced or deceived.

No society in which these liberties are not, on the whole, respected, is free, whatever may be its form of government; and none is completely free in which they do not exist absolute and unqualified. The only freedom which deserves the name, is that of pursuing our own good in our own way, so long as we do not attempt to deprive others of theirs, or impede their efforts to obtain it. Each is the proper guardian of his own health, whether bodily, or mental and spiritual. Mankind are greater gainers by suffering each other to live as seems good to themselves, than by compelling each to live as seems good to the rest.

Though this doctrine is anything but new, and, to some persons, may have the air of a truism, there is no doctrine which stands more directly opposed to the general tendency of existing opinion and practice. Society has expended fully as much effort in the attempt (according to its lights) to compel people to conform to its notions of personal as of social excellence. The ancient commonwealths thought themselves entitled to practise, and the ancient philosophers countenanced, the regulation of every part of private conduct by public authority, on the ground that the State had a deep interest in the whole bodily and mental discipline of every one of its citizens: a mode of thinking which may have been admissible in small republics surrounded by powerful enemies, in constant peril of being subverted by foreign attack or internal commotion, and to which even a short internal of relaxed energy and self-command might so easily be fatal that they could not afford to wait for the salutary permanent effects of freedom. In the modern world, the greater size of political communities, and, above all, the separation between spiritual and temporal authority (which placed the direction of men's consciences in other hands than those which controlled their worldly affairs), prevented so great an interference by law in the details of private life; but the engines of moral repression have been wielded more strenuously against divergence from the reigning opinion in self-regarding, than even in social matters; religion, the most powerful of the elements which have entered into the formation of moral feeling, having almost always been governed either by the ambition of a hierarchy, seeking control over every department of human conduct, or by the spirit of Puritanism. And some of those modern reformers who have placed themselves in strongest opposition to the religions of the past, have been noway behind either churches or sects in their assertion of the right of spiritual domination: M. Comte, in particular, whose social system, as unfolded in his *Système de Politique Positive,* aims at establishing (though by moral more than by legal appliances) a despotism of society over the individual, surpassing anything contemplated in the political ideal of the most rigid disciplinarian among the ancient philosophers.

Apart from the peculiar tenets of individual thinkers, there is also in the world at large an increasing inclination to stretch unduly the powers of society over the individual, both by the force of opinion and even by that of legislation; and as the tendency of all the changes taking place in the world is to strengthen society, and diminish the power of the individual, this encroachment is not one of the evils which tend spontaneously to disappear, but, on the contrary, to grow more and more formidable. The disposition of mankind, whether as rulers or as fellow-citizens, to impose their own opinions and inclinations as a rule of conduct on others, is so energetically supported by some of the best and by some of the worst feelings incident to human nature, that it is hardly ever kept under restraint by anything but want of power; and as the power is not declining, but growing, unless a strong barrier of moral conviction can be raised against the mischief, we must expect, in the present circumstances of the world, to see it increase.

It will be convenient for the argument, if, instead of at once entering upon the general thesis, we confine ourselves in the first instance to a single branch of it, on which the principle here stated is, if not fully, yet to a certain point, recognised by the current opinions. This one branch is the Liberty of Thought: from which it is impossible to separate the cognate liberty of speaking and of writing. Although these liberties, to some considerable amount, form part of the political morality of all countries which profess religious toleration and free institutions, the grounds, both philosophical and practical, on which they rest, are perhaps not so familiar to the general mind, nor so thoroughly appreciated by many even of the leaders of opinion, as might have been expected. Those grounds, when rightly understood, are of much wider application than to only one division of the subject, and a thorough consideration of this part of the question will be found the best introduction to the remainder. Those to whom nothing which I am about to say will be new, may therefore, I hope, excuse me, if on a subject which for now three centuries has been so often discussed, I venture on one discussion more.

Of the Liberty of Thought and Discussion

The time, it is to be hoped, is gone by, when any defence would be necessary of the "liberty of the press" as one of the securities against corrupt or tyrannical government. No argument, we may suppose, can now be needed, against permitting a legislature or an executive, not identified in interest with the people, to prescribe opinions to them, and determine what doctrines or what arguments they shall be allowed to hear. This aspect of the question, besides, has been so often and so triumphantly enforced by preceding writers, that it needs not be specially insisted on in this place. Though the law of England, on the subject of the press, is as servile to this day as it was in the time of the Tudors, there is little danger of its being actually put in force against political discussion, except during some temporary panic, when fear of insurrection drives ministers and judges from their propriety, and, speaking generally, it is not, in constitutional countries, to be apprehended, that the government, whether completely responsible to the people or not, will often attempt to control the expression of opinion, except when in doing so it makes itself the organ of the general intolerance of the public. Let us suppose, therefore, that the government is entirely at one with the people, and never thinks of exerting any power of coercion unless in agreement with what it conceives to be their voice. But I deny the right of the people to exercise such coercion, either by themselves or by their government. The power itself is illegitimate. The best government has no more title to it than the worst. It is as noxious, or more noxious, when exerted in accordance with public opinion, than when in opposition to it. If all mankind minus one were of one opinion, and only one person were of the contrary, opinion, mankind would be no more justified in silencing that one person, than he, if he had the power, would be justified in silencing mankind. Were an opinion a personal possession of no value except to the owner; if to be obstructed in the enjoyment of it were simply a private injury, it would make some difference whether the injury was inflicted only on a few persons or on many. But the peculiar evil of silencing the expression of an opinion is, that it is robbing the human race; posterity as well as the existing generation; those who dissent from the opinion, still more than those who hold it. If the opinion is right, they are deprived of the opportunity of exchanging error for truth: if wrong, they lose, what is almost as great a benefit, the clearer perception and livelier impression of truth, produced by its collision with error.

It is necessary to consider separately these two hypotheses each of which has a distinct branch of the argument corresponding to it. We can never be sure that the opinion we are endeavouring to stifle is a false opinion; and if we were sure, stifling it would be an evil still.

First: the opinion which it is attempted to suppress by authority may possibly be true. Those who desire to suppress it, of course deny its truth; but they are not infallible. They have no authority to decide the question for all mankind, and exclude every other person from the means of judging. To refuse a hearing to an opinion, because they are sure that it is false, is to assume that *their* certainty, is the same thing as *absolute* certainty. All silencing of discussion is an assumption of infallibility. Its condemnation may be allowed to rest on this common argument, not the worse for being common.

Unfortunately for the good sense of mankind, the fact of their fallibility is far from carrying the weight in their practical judgment which is always allowed to it in theory; for while every one well knows himself to be fallible, few think it necessary to take any precautions against their own fallibility, or admit the supposition that any opinion, of which they feel very certain, may be one of the examples of the error to which they acknowledge themselves to be liable. Absolute princes, or others who are accustomed to unlimited deference, usually feel this complete confidence in their own opinions on nearly all subjects. People more happily situated, who sometimes hear their opinions disputed, and are not wholly unused to be set right when they are wrong, place the same unbounded reliance only on such of their opinions as are shared by all who surround them, or to whom they habitually defer; for in proportion to a man's want of confidence in his own solitary judgment, does he usually repose, with implicit trust, on the infallibility of "the world" in general. And the world, to each individual, means the part of it with which he comes in contact; his party, his sect, his church, his class of society; the man may be called, by comparison, almost liberal and large-minded to whom it means anything so comprehensive as his own country or his own age. Nor is his faith, in this collective authority at all shaken by his being aware that other ages, countries, sects, churches, classes, and parties have thought, and even now think, the exact reverse. He devolves upon his own world the responsibility of being in the right against the dissentient worlds of other people; and it never troubles him that mere accident has decided which of these numerous worlds is the object of his reliance, and that the same causes which make him a Churchman in London, would have made him a Buddhist or a Confucian in Pekin. Yet it is as evident in itself, as any amount of argument can make it, that ages are no more infallible than individuals; every age having held many opinions which subsequent ages have deemed not only false but absurd; and it is as certain that many opinions now general will be rejected by future ages, as it is that many, once general, are rejected by the present.

The objection likely to be made to this argument would probably take some such form as the following. There is no greater assumption of infallibility in forbidding the propagation of error, than in any other thing which is done by public authority on its own judgment and responsibility. Judgment is given to men that they may use it. Because it may be used erroneously, are men to be told that they ought not to use it at all? To prohibit what they think pernicious, is not claiming exemption from error, but fulfilling the duty incumbent on them, although fallible, of acting on their conscientious conviction. If we were never to act on our opinions, because those opinions may be wrong, we should leave all our interests uncared for, and all our duties unperformed. An objection which applies to all conduct can be no valid objection to any conduct in particular. It is the duty of governments, and of individuals, to form the truest opinions they can: to form carefully, and never impose them upon others unless they are quite sure of being right. But when they are sure (such reasoners may say), it is not conscientiousness but cowardice to shrink from acting on their opinions, and allow doctrines which they honestly think dangerous to the welfare of mankind, either in this life or in another, to be scattered abroad without restraint, because other people, in less enlightened times, have persecuted opinions now believed to be true. Let us take care, it may be said, not to make the same mistake: but governments and nations have made mistakes in other things, which are not denied to be fit subjects for the exercise of authority: they have laid on bad taxes, made unjust wars. Ought we therefore to lay on no taxes, and, under whatever provocation, make no wars? Men and governments, must act to the best of their ability. There is no such thing as absolute certainty, but there is assurance sufficient for the purposes of human life. We may, and must, assume our opinion to be true for the guidance of our own conduct: and it is assuming no more when we forbid bad men to pervert society by the propagation of opinions which we regard as false and pernicious.

I answer, that it is assuming very much more. There is the greatest difference between presuming an opinion to be true, because, with every opportunity for contesting it, it has not been refuted, and assuming its truth for the purpose of not permitting its refutation. Complete liberty of contradicting and disproving our opinion is the very condition which justifies us in assuming its truth for purposes of action: and on no other terms can a being with human faculties have any rational assurance of being right.

When we consider either the history of opinion, or the ordinary conduct of human life, to what is it to be ascribed that the one and the other are no worse than they are? Not certainly to the inherent force of the human understanding: for, on any matter not self-evident, there are ninety-nine persons totally incapable of judging of it for one who is capable; and the capacity of the hundredth person is only comparative: for the majority of the eminent men of every past generation held many opinions now known to be erroneous, and did or approved numerous things which no one will now justify. Why is it, then, that there is on the whole a preponderance among mankind of rational opinions and rational conduct? If there really is this preponderance—which there must be unless human affairs are, and have always been, in an almost desperate state—it is owing to a quality of the human mind, the source of everything respectable in man either as an intellectual or as a moral being, namely, that his errors are corrigible. He is capable of rectifying his mistakes, by discussion and experience. Not by experience alone. There must be discussion, to show how experience is to be interpreted. Wrong opinions and practices gradually yield to fact and argument; but facts and arguments, to produce any effect on the mind, must be brought before it. Very few facts are able to tell their own story, without comments to bring out their meaning. The whole strength and value, then, of human judgment, depending on the one property, that it can be set right when it is wrong, reliance can be placed on it only when the means of setting it right are kept constantly at hand. In the case of any person whose judgment is really deserving of confidence, how has it become so? Because he has kept his mind open to criticism on his opinions and conduct. Because it has been his practice to listen to all that could be said against him; to profit by as much of it as was just, and expound to himself, and upon occasion to others, the fallacy of what was fallacious. Because he has felt, that the only way in which a human being can make some approach to knowing the whole of a subject, is by hearing what can be said about it by persons of every variety of opinion, and studying all modes in which it can be looked at by every character of mind. No wise man ever acquired his wisdom in any mode but this; nor is it in the nature of human intellect to become wise in any other manner. The steady habit of correcting and completing his own opinion by collating it with those of others, so far from causing doubt and hesitation in carrying it into practice, is the only stable foundation for a just reliance on it: for, being cognisant of all that can, at least obviously, be said against him, and having taken up his position against all gainsayers—knowing that he has sought for objections and difficulties, instead of avoiding them, and has shut out no light which can be thrown upon the subject from any quarter—he has a right to think his judgment better than that of any person, or any multitude, who have not gone through a similar process.

It is not too much to require that what the wisest of mankind, those who are best entitled to trust their own judgment, find necessary to warrant their relying on it, should be submitted to by that miscellaneous collection of a few wise and many foolish individuals, called the public. The most intolerant of churches, the Roman Catholic Church, even at the canonisation of a saint, admits, and listens patiently to, a "devil's advocate." The holiest of men, it appears, cannot be admitted to posthumous honours, until all that the devil could say against him is known and weighed. If even the Newtonian philosophy were not permitted to be questioned, mankind could not feel as complete assurance of its truth as they now do. The beliefs which we have most warrant for have no safeguard to rest on, but a standing invitation to the whole world to prove them unfounded. If the challenge is not accepted, or is accepted and the attempt fails, we are far enough from certainty still: but we have done the best that the existing state of human reason admits of: we have neglected nothing that could give the truth a chance of reaching us: if the lists are kept open, we may hope that if there be a better truth, it will be found when the human mind is capable of receiving it; and in the meantime we may rely on having attained such approach to truth as is possible in our own day. This is the amount of certainty attainable by a fallible being, and this the sole way of attaining it.

Strange it is, that men should admit the validity of the arguments for free discussion, but object to their being "pushed to an extreme": not seeing that unless the reasons are good for an extreme case, they are not good for any case. Strange that they should imagine that they are not assuming infallibility, when they acknowledge that there should be free discussion on all subjects which can possibly be *doubtful,* but think that some particular principle or doctrine should be forbidden to be questioned because it is so *certain,* that is, because *they are certain* that it is certain. To call any proposition certain, while there is any one who would deny its certainty if permitted, but who is not permitted, is to assume that we ourselves; and those who agree with us, are the judges of certainty, and judges without hearing the other side.

In the present age—which has been described as "destitute of faith, but terrified at scepticism"—in which people feel sure, not so much that their opinions are true, as that they should not know what to do without them—the claims of an opinion to be protected from public attack are rested not so much on its truth, as on its importance to society. There are, it is alleged, certain beliefs so useful, not to say indispensable, to well-being that it is as much the duty of governments to uphold those beliefs, as to protect any other of the interests of society. In a case of such necessity, and so directly in the line of their duty, something less than infallibility may, it is maintained, warrant, and even bind, governments to act on their own opinion, confirmed by the general opinion of mankind. It is also often argued, and still oftener thought that none but bad men would desire to weaken these salutary beliefs; and there can be nothing wrong, it is thought, in restraining bad men, and prohibiting what only such men would wish to practise. This mode of thinking makes the justification of restraints on discussion not a question of the truth of doctrines, but of their usefulness; and flatters itself by that means to escape the responsibility of claiming to be an infallible judge of opinions. But those who thus satisfy themselves, do not perceive that the assumption of infallibility is merely shifted from one point to another. The usefulness of an opinion is itself matter of opinion: as disputable, as open to discussion, and requiring discussion as much as the opinion itself. There is the same need of an infallible judge of opinions to decide an opinion to be noxious, as to decide it to be false, unless the opinion condemned has full opportunity of defending itself. And it will not do to say that the heretic may be allowed to maintain the utility or harmlessness of his opinion, though forbidden to maintain its truth. The truth of an opinion is part of its utility. If we would know whether or not it is desirable that a proposition should be believed, is it possible to exclude the consideration of whether or not it is true? In the opinion, not of bad men, but of the best men, no belief which is contrary to truth can be really useful: and can you prevent such men from urging that plea, when they are charged with culpability for denying some doctrine which they are told is useful, but which they believe to be false? Those who are on the side of received opinions never fail to take all possible advantage of this plea: you do not find *them* handling the question of utility as if it could be completely abstracted from that of truth: on the contrary, it is, above all, because their doctrine is "the truth," that the knowledge or the belief of it is held to be so indispensable. There can be no fair discussion of the question of usefulness when an argument so vital may be employed on one side, but not on the other. And in point of fact, when law or public feeling do not permit the truth of an opinion to be disputed, they are just as little tolerant of a denial of its usefulness. The utmost they allow is an extenuation of its absolute necessity, or of the positive guilt of rejecting it.

In order more fully to illustrate the mischief of denying a hearing to opinions because we, in our own judgment, have condemned them, it will be desirable to fix down the discussion to a concrete case; and I choose, by preference, the cases which are least favourable to me—in which the argument against freedom of opinion, both on the score of truth and on that of utility, is considered the strongest. Let the opinions impugned be the belief in a God and in a future state, or any of the commonly received doctrines of morality. To fight the battle on such ground gives a great advantage to an unfair antagonist; since he will be sure to say (and many who have no desire to be unfair will say it internally). Are these the doctrines which you do not deem sufficiently certain to be taken under the protection of law? Is the belief in a God one of the opinions to feel sure of which you hold to be assuming infallibility? But I must be permitted to observe, that it is not the feeling sure of a doctrine (be it what it may) which I call an assumption of infallibility. It is the undertaking to decide that question *for others,* without allowing them to hear what can be said on the contrary side. And I denounce and reprobate this pretension not the less, if put forth on the side of my most solemn convictions. However positive any one's persuasion may be, not only of the falsity but of the pernicious consequences—not only of the pernicious consequences, but (to adopt expressions which I altogether condemn) the immorality and impiety of an opinion; yet if, in pursuance of that private judgment, though backed by the public judgment of his country or his cotemporaries, he prevents the opinion from being heard in its defence, he assumes infallibility. And so far from the assumption being less objectionable or less dangerous because the opinion is called immoral or impious, this is the case of all others in which it is most fatal. These are exactly the occasions on which the men of one generation commit those dreadful mistakes which excite the astonishment and horror of posterity. It is among such that we find the instances memorable in history, when the arm of the law has been employed to root out the best men and the noblest doctrines; with deplorable success as to the men, though some of the doctrines have survived to be (as if in mockery) invoked in defence of similar conduct towards those who dissent from *them,* or from their received, interpretation.

* * *

We have now recognised the necessity to the mental well-being of mankind (on which all their other well-being depends) of freedom of opinion, and freedom of the expression of opinion, on four distinct grounds; which we will now briefly recapitulate.

First, if any opinion is compelled to silence, that opinion may, for aught we can certainly know, be true. To deny this is to assume our own infallibility.

Secondly, though the silenced opinion be an error, it may, and very commonly does, contain a portion of truth; and since the general or prevailing opinion on any subject is rarely or never the whole truth, it is only by the collision of adverse opinions that the remainder of the truth has any chance of being supplied.

Thirdly, even if the received opinion be not only true, but the whole truth: unless it is suffered to be, and actually is, vigorously and earnestly contested, it will, by most of those who receive it, be held in the manner of a prejudice, with little comprehension or feeling of its rational grounds. And not only this, but, fourthly, the meaning of the doctrine itself will be in danger of being lost, or enfeebled, and deprived of its vital effect on the character and conduct; the dogma becoming a mere formal profession, inefficacious for good, but cumbering the ground, and preventing the growth of any real and heartfelt conviction, from reason or personal experience.

Before quitting the subject of freedom of opinion, it is fit to take some notice of those who say that the free expression of all opinions should be permitted, on condition that the manner be temperate, and do not pass the bounds of fair discussion. Much might be said on the impossibility of fixing where these supposed bounds are to be placed; for if the test be offence to those whose opinions are attacked, I think experience testifies that this offence is given when ever the attack is telling and powerful, and that every opponent who pushes them hard, and whom they find it difficult to answer, appears to them, if he shows any strong feeling on the subject, an intemperate opponent. But this, though an important consideration in a practical point of view, merges in a more fundamental objection. Undoubtedly the manner of asserting an opinion, even though it be a true one, may be very objectionable, and may justly incur severe censure. But the principal offences of the kind are such as it is mostly impossible, unless by accidental self-betrayal, to bring home to conviction. The gravest of them is, to argue sophistically, to suppress facts or arguments, to misstate the elements of the case, or misrepresent the opposite opinion. But all this, even to the most aggravated degree, is so continually done in perfect good faith, by persons who are not considered, and in many other respects may not deserve to be considered, ignorant or incompetent, that it is rarely possible, on adequate grounds, conscientiously to stamp the misrepresentation as morally culpable; and still less could law presume to interfere with this kind of controversial misconduct. With regard to what is commonly meant by intemperate discussion, namely invective, sarcasm, personality, and the like, the denunciation of these weapons would deserve more sympathy if it were ever proposed to interdict them equally to both sides; but it is only desired to restrain the employment of them against the prevailing opinion: against the unprevailing they may not only be used without general disapproval, but will be likely to obtain for him who uses them the praise of honest zeal and righteous indignation. Yet whatever mischief arises from their use is greatest when they are employed against the comparatively defenceless: and whatever unfair advantage can be derived by any opinion from this mode of asserting it, accrues almost exclusively to received opinions. The worst offence of this kind which can be committed by a polemic is to stigmatise those who hold the contrary opinion as bad and immoral men. To calumny of this sort, those who hold any unpopular opinion are peculiarly exposed, because they are in general few and uninfluential, and nobody but themselves feels much interested in seeing justice done them; but this weapon is, from the nature of the case, denied to those who attack a prevailing opinion: they can neither use it with safety to themselves, nor, if they could, would it do anything but recoil on their own cause. In general, opinions contrary to those commonly received can only obtain a hearing by studied moderation of language, and the most cautious avoidance of unnecessary offence, from which they hardly ever deviate even in a slight degree without losing ground: while unmeasured vituperation employed on the side of the prevailing opinion really does deter people from professing contrary opinions, and from listening to those who profess them. For the interest, therefore, of truth and justice, it is far more important to restrain this employment of vituperative language than the other; and, for example, if it were neccessary to choose, there would be much more need to discourage offensive attacks on infidelity than on religion. It is, however, obvious that law and authority have no business with restraining either, while opinion ought, in every instance, to determine its verdict by the circumstances of the individual case; condemning every one, on whichever side of the argument he places himself, in whose mode of advocacy either want of candour, or malignity, bigotry, or intolerance of feeling manifest themselves; but not inferring these vices from the side which a person takes, though it be the contrary side of the question to our own; and giving merited honour to every one, whatever opinion he may hold, who has calmness to see and honesty to state what his opponents and their opinions really are, exaggerating nothing to their discredit, keeping nothing back which tells, or can be supposed to tell, in their favour. This is the real morality of public discussion: and if often violated, I am happy to think that there are many controversialists who to a great extent observe it, and a still greater number who conscientiously strive towards it.

✦ Reading 8 ✦
Middlemarch
George Eliot

Ladislaw, a talented and eligible but penniless young man of Polish-English descent, makes his career as a journalist and political advisor. A mutual attraction develops between himself and a young married woman of wealth and status. Later her husband, an older, unsympathetic character, dies, opening the way for future happiness. The personal stories of these and other characters work their way out against the backdrop of a local political campaign during the years prior to the 1832 reforms.

The Dead Hand

Party is Nature too, and you shall see
By force of Logic how they both agree:
The Many in the One, the One in Many;
All is not Some, nor Some the same as
Any:
Genus holds species, both are great or
small;
One genus highest, one not high at all;
Each species has its differentia too,
This is not That, and He was never You,
Though this and that are AYES, and you
and he
Are like as one to one, or three to three.

No gossip about Mr Casaubon's will had yet reached Ladislaw: the air seemed to be filled with the dissolution of Parliament and the coming election, as the old wakes and fairs were filled with the rival clatter of itinerant shows; and more private noises were taken little notice of. The famous "dry election" was at hand, in which the depths of public feeling might be measured by the low flood-mark of drink. Will Ladislaw was one of the busiest at this time; and though Dorothea's widowhood was continually in his thought, he was so far from wishing to be spoken to on the subject, that when Lydgate sought him out to tell him what had passed about the Lowick living, he answered rather waspishly—

"Why should you bring me into the matter? I never see Mrs Casaubon, and am not likely to see her, since she is at Freshitt. I never go there. It is Tory ground, where I and the 'Pioneer' are no more welcome than a poacher and his gun."

The fact was that Will had been made the more susceptible by observing that Mr Brooke, instead of wishing him, as before, to come to the Grange oftener than was quite agreeable to himself, seemed now to contrive that he should go there as little as possible. This was a shuffling concession of Mr Brooke's to Sir James Chettam's indignant remonstrance; and Will, awake to the slightest hint in this direction, concluded that he was to be kept away from the Grange on Dorothea's account. Her friends, then, regarded him with some suspicion? Their fears were quite superfluous: they were very much mistaken if they imagined that he would put himself forward as a needy adventurer trying to win the favour of a rich woman.

Until now Will had never fully seen the chasm between himself and Dorothea—until now that he was come to the brink of it, and saw her on the other side. He began, not without some inward rage, to think of going away from the neighbourhood: it would be impossible for him to show any further interest in Dorothea without subjecting himself to disagreeable imputations—perhaps even in her mind, which others might try to poison.

"We are for ever divided," said Will. "I might as well be at Rome; she would be no farther from me." But what we call our despair is often only the painful

From: George Eliot, *Middlemarch* (Oxford, England: Clarendon Press, 1986), pp. 487–499.

eagerness of unfed hope. There were plenty of reasons why he should not go—public reasons why he should not quit his post at this crisis, leaving Mr Brooke in the lurch when he needed "coaching" for the election, and when there was so much canvassing, direct and indirect, to be carried on. Will could not like to leave his own chessmen in the heat of a game; and any candidate on the right side, even if his brain and marrow had been as soft as was consistent with a gentlemanly bearing, might help to turn a majority. To coach Mr Brooke and keep him steadily to the idea that he must pledge himself to vote for the actual Reform Bill, instead of insisting on his independence and power of pulling up in time, was not an easy task. Mr Farebrother's prophecy of a fourth candidate "in the bag" had not yet been fulfilled, neither the Parliamentary Candidate Society nor any other power on the watch to secure a reforming majority seeing a worthy nodus for interference while there was a second reforming candidate like Mr Brooke, who might be returned at his own expense; and the fight lay entirely between Pinkerton the old Tory member, Bagster the new Whig member returned at the last election, and Brooke the future independent member, who was to fetter himself for this occasion only. Mr Hawley and his party would bend all their forces to the return of Pinkerton, and Mr Brooke's success must depend either on plumpers which would leave Bagster in the rear, or on the new minting of Tory votes into reforming votes. The latter means, of course, would be preferable.

This prospect of converting votes was a dangerous distraction to Mr Brooke: his impression that waverers were likely to be allured by wavering statements, and also the liability of his mind to stick afresh at opposing arguments as they turned up in his memory, gave Will Ladislaw much trouble.

"You know there are tactics in these things," said Mr Brooke; "meeting people half-way—tempering your ideas—saying, 'Well now, there's something in that,' and so on. I agree with you that this is a peculiar occasion—the country with a will of its own—political unions—that sort of thing—but we sometimes cut with rather too sharp a knife, Ladislaw. These ten-pound householders, now: why ten? Draw the line somewhere—yes: but why just at ten? That's a difficult question, now, if you go into it."

"Of course it is," said Will, impatiently. "But if you are to wait till we get a logical Bill, you must put yourself forward as a revolutionist, and then Middlemarch would not elect you, I fancy. As for trimming, this is not a time for trimming."

Mr Brooke always ended by agreeing with Ladislaw, who still appeared to him a sort of Burke with a leaven of Shelley; but after an interval the wisdom of his own methods reasserted itself, and he was again drawn into using them with much hopefulness. At this stage of affairs he was in excellent spirits, which even supported him under large advances of money; for his powers of convincing and persuading had not yet been tested by anything more difficult than a chairman's speech introducing other orators, or a dialogue with a Middlemarch voter, from which he came away with a sense that he was a tactician by nature, and that it was a pity he had not gone earlier into this kind of thing. He was a little conscious of defeat, however, with Mr Mawmsey, a chief representative in Middlemarch of that great social power, the retail trader, and naturally one of the most doubtful voters in the borough—willing for his own part to supply an equal quality of teas and sugars to reformer and anti-reformer, as well as to agree impartially with both, and feeling like the burgesses of old that this necessity of electing members was a great burthen to a town; for even if there were no danger in holding out hopes to all parties beforehand, there would be the painful necessity at last of disappointing respectable people whose names were on his books. He was accustomed to receive large orders from Mr Brooke of Tipton; but then, there were many of Pinkerton's committee whose opinions had a great weight of grocery on their side. Mr Mawmsey thinking that Mr Brooke, as not too "clever in his intellects," was the more likely to forgive a grocer who gave a hostile vote under pressure, had become confidential in his back parlour.

"As to Reform, sir, put it in a family light," he said, rattling the small silver in his pocket, and smiling affably. "Will it support Mrs Mawmsey, and enable her to bring up six children when I am no more? I put the question *fictiously,* knowing what must be the answer. Very well, sir. I ask you what, as a husband and a father, I am to do when gentlemen come to me and say, 'Do as you like, Mawmsey; but if you vote against us, I shall get my groceries elsewhere: when I sugar my liquor I like to feel that I am benefiting the country by maintaining tradesmen of the right colour.' Those very words have been spoken to me, sir, in the very chair where you are now sitting. I don't mean by your honourable self, Mr Brooke."

"No, no, no—that's narrow, you know. Until my butler complains to me of your goods, Mr Mawmsey," said Mr Brooke, soothingly, "until I hear that you send bad sugars, spices—that sort of thing—I shall never order him to go elsewhere."

"Sir, I am your humble servant, and greatly obliged," said Mr Mawmsey, feeling that politics were clearing up a little. "There would be some pleasure in voting for a gentleman who speaks in that honourable manner."

"Well, you know, Mr Mawmsey, you would find it the right thing to put yourself on our side. This Reform will touch everybody by-and-by—a thoroughly popular measure—a sort of A, B, C, you know, that must come first before the rest can follow. I quite agree with you that you've got to look at the thing in a family light: but public spirit, now. We're all one family, you know—it's all one cupboard. Such a thing as a vote, now: why, it may help to make men's fortunes at the Cape—there's no knowing what may be the effect of a vote," Mr Brooke ended, with a sense of being a little out at sea, though finding it still enjoyable. But Mr Mawmsey answered in a tone of decisive check.

"I beg your pardon, sir, but I can't afford that. When I give a vote I must know what I'm doing; I must look to what will be the effects on my till and ledger, speaking respectfully. Prices, I'll admit, are what nobody can know the merits of—the sudden falls after you've bought in currants, which are a goods that will not keep—I've never myself seen into the ins and outs there; which is a rebuke to human pride. But as to one family, there's debtor and creditor, I hope; they're not going to reform that away; else I should vote for things staying as they are. Few men have less need to cry for change than I have, personally speaking—that is, for self and family. I am not one of those who have nothing to lose: I mean as to respectability both in parish and private business, and noways in respect of your honourable self and custom, which you was good enough to say you would not withdraw from me, vote or no vote, while the article sent in was satisfactory."

After this conversation Mr Mawmsey went up and boasted to his wife that he had been rather too many for Brooke of Tipton, and that he didn't mind so much now about going to the poll.

Mr Brooke on this occasion abstained from boasting of his tactics to Ladislaw, who for his part was glad enough to persuade himself that he had no concern with any canvassing except the purely argumentative sort, and that he worked no meaner engine than knowledge. Mr Brooke, necessarily, had his agents, who understood the nature of the Middlemarch voter and the means of enlisting his ignorance on the side of the Bill—which were remarkably similar to the means of enlisting it on the side against the Bill. Will stopped his ear occasionally; Parliament, like the rest of our lives, even to our eating and apparel, could hardly go on if our imaginations were too active about processes. There were plenty of dirty-handed men in the world to do dirty business; and Will protested to himself that his share in bringing Mr Brooke through would be quite innocent.

But whether he should succeed in that mode of contributing to the majority on the right side was very doubtful to him. He had written out various speeches and memoranda for speeches, but he had begun to perceive that Mr Brooke's mind, if it had the burthen of remembering any train of thought, would let it drop, run away in search of it, and not easily come back again. To collect documents is one mode of serving your country, and to remember the contents of a document is another. No! the only way in which Mr Brooke could be coerced into thinking of the right arguments at the right time was to be well plied with them till they took up all the room in his brain. But here there was the difficulty of finding room, so many things having been taken in beforehand. Mr Brooke himself observed that his ideas stood rather in his way when he was speaking.

However, Ladislaw's coaching was forthwith to be put to the test, for before the day of nomination Mr Brooke was to explain himself to the worthy electors at Middlemarch from the balcony of the White Hart, which looked out advantageously at an angle of the market-place, commanding a large area in front and two converging streets. It was a fine May morning, and everything seemed hopeful: there was some prospect of an understanding between Bagster's committee and Brooke's, to which Mr Bulstrode, Mr Standish as a Liberal lawyer, and such manufacturers as Mr Plymdale and Mr Vincy, gave a solidity which almost counterbalanced Mr Hawley and his associates who sat for Pinkerton at the Green Dragon. Mr Brooke, conscious of having weakened the blasts of the 'Trumpet' against him, by his reforms as a landlord in the last half-year, and hearing himself cheered a little as he drove into the town, felt his heart tolerably light under his buff-coloured waistcoat. But with regard to critical occasions, it often happens that all moments seem comfortably remote until the last.

"This looks well, eh?" said Mr Brooke as the crowd gathered. "I shall have a good audience, at any rate. I like this, now—this kind of public made up of one's own neighbours, you know."

The weavers and tanners of Middlemarch, unlike Mr Mawmsey, had never thought of Mr Brooke as a neighbour, and were not more attached to him than if he had been sent in a box from London. But they listened without much disturbance to the speakers who introduced the candidate, though one of them—a political personage from Brassing, who came to tell Middlemarch its duty—spoke so fully, that it was alarming to think what the candidate could find to say after him. Meanwhile the crowd became denser, and as the political personage neared the end of his speech, Mr Brooke felt a remarkable change in his sensations while he still handled his eye-glass, trifled with documents before him, and exchanged remarks with his committee, as a man to whom the moment of summons was indifferent.

"I'll take another glass of sherry, Ladislaw," he said, with an easy air, to Will, who was close behind him, and presently handed him the supposed fortifier. It was ill-chosen; for Mr Brooke was an abstemious man, and to drink a second glass of sherry quickly at no great interval from the first was a surprise to his system which tended to scatter his energies instead of collecting them. Pray pity him: so many English gentlemen make themselves miserable by speechifying on entirely private grounds! whereas Mr Brooke wished to serve his country by standing for Parliament—which, indeed, may also be done on private grounds, but being once undertaken does absolutely demand some speechifying.

It was not about the beginning of his speech that Mr Brooke was at all anxious: this, he felt sure, would be all right; he should have it quite pat, cut out as nearly as a set of couplets from Pope. Embarking would be easy, but the vision of open sea that might come after was alarming. "And questions, now," hinted the demon just waking up in his stomach, "somebody may put questions about the schedules.—Ladislaw," he continued, aloud, "just hand me the memorandum of the schedules."

When Mr Brooke presented himself on the balcony, the cheers were quite loud enough to counterbalance the yells, groans, brayings, and other expressions of adverse theory, which were so moderate that Mr Standish (decidedly an old bird) observed in the ear next to him, "This looks dangerous, by God! Hawley has got some deeper plan than this." Still, the cheers were exhilarating, and no candidate could look more amiable than Mr Brooke, with the memorandum in his breast-pocket, his left hand on the rail of the balcony, and his right trifling with his eye-glass. The striking points in his appearance were his buff waistcoat, short-clipped blond hair, and neutral physiognomy. He began with some confidence.

"Gentlemen—Electors of Middlemarch!"

This was so much the right thing that a little pause after it seemed natural.

"I'm uncommonly glad to be here—I was never so proud and happy in my life—never so happy, you know."

This was a bold figure of speech, but not exactly the right thing; for, unhappily, the pat opening had slipped away—even couplets from Pope may be but "failings from us, vanishings," when fear clutches us, and a glass of sherry is hurrying like smoke among our ideas. Ladislaw, who stood at the window behind the speaker, thought, "It's all up now. The only chance is that, since the best thing won't always do, floundering may answer for once." Mr Brooke, meanwhile, having lost other clues, fell back on himself and his qualifications—always an appropriate graceful subject for a candidate.

"I am a close neighbour of yours, my good friends—you've known me on the bench a good while—I've always gone a good deal into public questions—machinery, now, and machine-breaking—you're many of you concerned with machinery, and

I've been going into that lately. It won't do, you know, breaking machines: everything must go on—trade, manufactures, commerce, interchange of staples—that kind of thing—since Adam Smith, that must go on. We must look all over the globe:—'Observation with extensive view,' must look everywhere, 'from China to Peru,' as somebody says—Johnson, I think, 'The Rambler,' you know. That is what I have done up to a certain point—not as far as Peru; but I've not always stayed at home—I saw it wouldn't do. I've been in the Levant, where some of your Middlemarch goods go—and then, again, in the Baltic. The Baltic, now."

Plying among his recollections in this way, Mr Brooke might have got along easily to himself, and would have come back from the remotest seas without trouble; but a diabolical procedure had been set up by the enemy. At one and the same moment there had risen above the shoulders of the crowd, nearly opposite Mr Brooke, and within ten yards of him, the effigy of himself; buff-coloured waistcoat, eyeglass, and neutral physiognomy, painted on rag; and there had arisen, apparently in the air, like the note of the cuckoo, a parrot-like, Punch-voiced echo of his words. Everybody looked up at the open windows in the houses at the opposite angles of the converging streets; but they were either blank, or filled by laughing listeners. The most innocent echo has an impish mockery in it when it follows a gravely persistent speaker, and this echo was not at all innocent; if it did not follow with the precision of a natural echo, it had a wicked choice of the words it overtook. By the time it said, "The Baltic, now," the laugh which had been running through the audience became a general shout, and but for the sobering effects of party or that great public cause which the entanglement of things had identified with "Brooke of Tipton," the laugh might have caught his committee. Mr Bulstrode asked, reprehensively, what the new police was doing; but a voice could not well be collared, and an attack on the effigy of the candidate would have been too equivocal, since Hawley probably meant it to be pelted.

Mr Brooke himself was not in a position to be quickly conscious of anything except a general slipping away of ideas within himself: he had even a little singing in the ears, and he was the only person who had not yet taken distinct account of the echo or discerned the image of himself. Few things hold the perceptions more thoroughly captive than anxiety about what we have got to say. Mr Brooke heard the laughter; but he had expected some Tory efforts at disturbance, and he was at this moment additionally excited by the tickling, stinging sense that his lost exordium was coming back to fetch him from the Baltic.

"That reminds me," he went on, thrusting a hand into his side-pocket, with an easy air, "if I wanted a precedent, you know—but we never want a precedent for the right thing—but there is Chatham, now; I can't say I should have supported Chatham, or Pitt, the younger Pitt—he was not a man of ideas, and we want ideas, you know."

"Blast your ideas! we want the Bill," said a loud rough voice from the crowd below.

Immediately the invisible Punch, who had hitherto followed Mr Brooke, repeated, "Blast your ideas! we want the Bill." The laugh was louder than ever, and for the first time Mr Brooke being himself silent, heard distinctly the mocking echo. But it seemed to ridicule his interrupter, and in that light was encouraging; so he replied with amenity—

"There is something in what you say, my good friend, and what do we meet for but to speak our minds—freedom of opinion, freedom of the press, liberty—that kind of thing? The Bill, now—you shall have the Bill"—here Mr Brooke paused a moment to fix on his eye-glass and take the paper from his breast-pocket, with a sense of being practical and coming to particulars. The invisible Punch followed:—

"You shall have the Bill, Mr Brooke, per electioneering contest, and a seat outside Parliament as delivered, five thousand pounds, seven shillings, and fourpence."

Mr Brooke, amid the roars of laughter, turned red, let his eye-glass fall, and looking about him confusedly, saw the image of himself, which had come nearer. The next moment he saw it dolorously bespattered with eggs. His spirit rose a little, and his voice too.

"Buffoonery, tricks, ridicule the test of truth—all that is very well"—here an unpleasant egg broke on Mr Brooke's shoulder, as the echo said, "All that is very well;" then came a hail of eggs, chiefly aimed at the image, but occasionally hitting the original, as if by chance. There was a stream of new men pushing among the crowd; whistles, yells, bellowings, and fifes made all the greater hubbub because there was shouting and struggling to put them down. No voice would have had wing enough to rise above the uproar, and Mr Brooke, disagreeably anointed, stood his ground no longer. The frustration would have been less exasperating if it had been less gamesome and boyish: a serious assault of which the newspaper reporter "can aver that it endangered the learned gentleman's ribs," or can respectfully bear witness to "the soles of that gentleman's boots having been visible above the railing," has perhaps more consolations attached to it.

Mr Brooke re-entered the committee-room, saying, as carelessly as he could, "This is a little too bad, you know. I should have got the ear of the people by-and-by—but they didn't give me time. I should have gone into the Bill by-and-by, you know," he added, glancing at Ladislaw. "However, things will come all right at the nomination."

But it was not resolved unanimously that things would come right; on the contrary, the committee looked rather grim, and the political personage from Brassing was writing busily, as if he were brewing new devices.

"It was Bowyer who did it," said Mr Standish, evasively. "I know it as well as if he had been advertised. He's uncommonly good at ventriloquism, and he did it uncommonly well, by God! Hawley has been having him to dinner lately: there's a fund of talent in Bowyer."

"Well, you know, you never mentioned him to me, Standish, else I would have invited him to dine," said poor Mr Brooke, who had gone through a great deal of inviting for the good of his country.

"There's not a more paltry fellow in Middlemarch than Bowyer," said Ladislaw, indignantly, "but it seems as if the paltry fellows were always to turn the scale."

Will was thoroughly out of temper with himself as well as with his "principal," and he went to shut himself in his rooms with a half-formed resolve to throw up the 'Pioneer' and Mr Brooke together. Why should he stay? If the impassable gulf between himself and Dorothea were ever to be filled up, it must rather be by his going away and getting into a thoroughly different position than by his staying here and slipping into deserved contempt as an understrapper of Brooke's. Then came the young dream of wonders that he might do—in five years, for example: political writing, political speaking, would get a higher value now public life was going to be wider and more national, and they might give him such distinction that he would not seem to be asking Dorothea to step down to him. Five years:—if he could only be sure that she cared for him more than for others; if he could only make her aware that he stood aloof until he could tell his love without lowering himself—then he could go away easily, and begin a career which at five-and-twenty seemed probable enough in the inward order of things, where talent brings fame, and fame everything else which is delightful. He could speak and he could write; he could master any subject if he chose, and he meant always to take the side of reason and justice, on which he would carry all his ardour. Why should he not one day be lifted above the shoulders of the crowd, and feel that he had won that eminence well? Without doubt he would leave Middlemarch, go to town, and make himself fit for celebrity by "eating his dinners."

But not immediately: not until some kind of sign had passed between him and Dorothea. He could not be satisfied until she knew why, even if he were the man she would choose to marry, he would not marry her. Hence he must keep his post and bear with Mr Brooke a little longer.

But he soon had reason to suspect that Mr Brooke had anticipated him in the wish to break up their connexion. Deputations without and voices within had concurred in inducing that philanthropist to take a stronger measure than usual for the good of mankind; namely, to withdraw in favour of another candidate, to whom he left the advantages of his canvassing machinery. He himself called this a strong measure, but observed that his health was less capable of sustaining excitement than he had imagined.

"I have felt uneasy about the chest—it won't do to carry that too far," he said to Ladislaw in explaining the affair. "I must pull up. Poor Casaubon was a warning, you know. I've made some heavy advances, but I've dug a channel. It's rather coarse work—this electioneering, eh, Ladislaw? I dare say you are tired of it. However, we have dug a channel with the 'Pioneer'—put things in a track, and so on. A more ordinary man than you might carry it on now—more ordinary, you know."

"Do you wish me to give it up?" said Will, the quick colour coming in his face, as he rose from the writing-table, and took a turn of three steps with his hands in his pockets. "I am ready to do so whenever you wish it."

"As to wishing, my dear Ladislaw, I have the highest opinion of your powers, you know. But about the 'Pioneer,' I have been consulting a little with some of the men on our side, and they are inclined to take it into their hands—indemnify me to a certain extent—carry it on, in fact. And under the circumstances, you might like to give up—might find a better field. These people might not take that high view of you which I have always taken, as an *alter ego*, a right hand—though I always looked forward to your doing something else. I think of having a run into France. But I'll write you any letters, you know—to Althorpe and people of that kind. I've met Althorpe."

"I am exceedingly obliged to you," said Ladislaw, proudly. "Since you are going to part with the 'Pioneer,' I need not trouble you about the steps I shall take. I may choose to continue here for the present."

After Mr Brooke had left him Will said to himself, "The rest of the family have been urging him to get rid of me, and he doesn't care now about my going. I shall stay as long as I like. I shall go of my own movement, and not because they are afraid of me."

✦ Reading 9 ✦

The Sorrows of Young Werther

Johann Wolfgang von Goethe

Werther, a young man of the educated middle class, falls in love with Lotte, the wife of a friend. To escape the situation, he takes up employment at the court of a prince, where his brashness scandalizes the aristocrats, forcing him to resign. Failed in love and career and filled with high sentiment that merely hides his egoism, he commits suicide.

August 18

Must it so be that whatever makes man happy must later become the source of his misery?

That generous and warm feeling for living Nature which flooded my heart with such bliss, so that I saw the world around me as a Paradise, has now become an unbearable torment, a sort of demon that persecutes me wherever I go. When I formerly looked from the rock far across the river and the fertile valleys to the distant hills, and saw everything on all sides sprout and spring forth—the mountains covered with tall, thick trees from base to summit, the valleys winding between pleasant shading woods, the gently flowing river gliding among the whispering reeds and reflecting light clouds which sailed across the sky under the mild evening breeze; when I listened to the birds that bring the forest to life, while millions of midges danced in the red rays of a setting sun whose last flare roused the buzzing beetle from the grass; and all the whirring and weaving around me drew my attention to the ground underfoot where the moss, which wrests its nourishment from my hard rock, and the broom plant, which grows on the slope of the arid sand hill, revealed to me the inner, glowing, sacred life of Nature—how fervently did I take all this into my warm heart, feeling like a god in that overflowing abundance, while the beautiful forms of the infinite universe stirred and inspired my soul. Huge mountains surrounded me, precipices opened before me, and torrents gushed downward; the rivers streamed below, and wood and mountains sang; and I saw them at their mutual work of creation in the depths of the earth, all these unfathomable forces. And above the earth and below the sky swarms the variety of creatures, multifarious and multiform. Everything, everything populated with a thousand shapes; and mankind, huddled together in the security of its little houses, nesting throughout and dominating the wide world in its own way. Poor fool who belittles everything because you are yourself so small! From the inaccessible mountains, across the wasteland untrod by human foot, to the end of the unexplored seas breathes the spirit of the eternal Creator who rejoices in every atom of dust that divines Him and lives.—Oh, the times when I longed to fly on the crane's wings, as it passed overhead, to the shores of the illimitable ocean, in order to drink from the foaming cup of the Infinite an elating sensation of life, and to feel, if only for a moment, in the cramped forces of my being one drop of the bliss of that Being who creates everything in and through Himself.

My friend, only the memory of those hours eases my heart. Even the effort to recall and to express again in words those inexpressible sensations lifts my soul above itself, but also intensifies the anguish of my present state.

It is as if a curtain has been drawn away from my soul, and the scene of unending life is transformed before my eyes into the pit of the forever-open grave. Can you say: "This is!" when everything passes, everything rolls past with the speed of lightning and so rarely exhausts the whole power of its existence, alas, before it is swept away by the current, drowned and smashed on the rocks? There is not one moment

---

From: Johann Wolfgang von Goethe, *The Sorrows of Young Werther* (New York: Vintage Books, 1973), pp. 64–69, 88–94, 166–167.

which does not consume you and yours, and not one moment when you yourself are not inevitably destructive; the most harmless walk costs the lives of thousands of poor, minute worms; *one* step of your foot annihilates the painstaking constructions of ants, and stamps a small world into its ignominious grave. Ha! It is not the notable catastrophes of the world, the floods that wash away our villages, the earthquakes that swallow up our town which move me; my heart is instead worn out by the consuming power latent in the whole of Nature which has formed nothing that will not destroy its neighbor and itself. So I stagger with anxiety, Heaven and Earth and their weaving powers around me! I see nothing but an eternally devouring and ruminating monster.

August 21

In vain do I stretch my arms out for her in the morning, when I try to arouse myself from troubled dreams; in vain do I seek her at night in my bed, deluded by some happy and innocent dream in which I am sitting beside her in the meadow, holding her hand and covering it with a thousand kisses. And when, still heavy with sleep, I grope for her and suddenly find myself fully awake, a torrent of tears bursts from my oppressed heart, and I weep bitterly in view of a hopeless future.

August 22

It is disastrous, Wilhelm! All my energies are tuned to another pitch, have changed to a restless inactivity; I cannot be idle and yet the same time cannot set to work at anything. My power of imagination fails me; I am insensible to Nature, and I am sick of books. If we fail ourselves, everything fails us. I swear that I should sometimes like to be a workman so that I could see, when I wake up in the morning, some prospect for the coming day, some impetus, some hope. I often envy Albert, whom I see buried up to his ears in documents; and I imagine that I should be better off were I in his place. Already more than once the thought of writing to you and to the Minister flashed through my mind, in order to apply for the post at the Legation which, you have assured me, I would not be refused. So I myself believe. The Minister has liked me for a long time, and has freqeuntly urged me to devote myself to some work; and sometimes, for an hour or so, it seems the thing to do. But when I come to consider it a little later, I remember the fable of the horse which, tired of freedom let itself be saddled and harnessed and was ridden to death. I don't *know what* to do. And, my dear fellow, isn't my longing for a change in my situation an innate, uneasy impatience that will pursue me wherever I go?

August 28

One thing is certain; if my disease could be cured, these people would cure it. Today is my birthday, and very early in the morning I received a little parcel from Albert. When I opened it I saw immediately one of the bows of pink ribbon Lotte had been wearing when I first met her and which I had often implored her to give me. The parcel also contained two books in duodecimo: the small Homer printed by Wetstein, which I had often wished to possess, so that I should not have to drag about with me on my walks the large volume edited by Ernesti.You see! that is how they anticipate my wishes, how well they select the small tokens of friendship which are a thousand times more precious than the dazzling presents which humiliate us, betraying the vanity of the giver. I kiss the ribbon over and over again and drink in with every breath the memory of the few blissful moments in those happy and irretrievable days. Wilhelm, so it is, and I do not complain—the blossoms of life are only phantoms. How many fade, leaving no trace behind; how few bear fruit, and how few of these fruits ripen! But still enough are left; but still—O my brother! should we neglect the ripe fruit, refuse to enjoy it, and let it rot?

Farewell! It is a glorious summer, and I often sit up in the trees of Lotte's orchard and take down with a long pole the pears from the highest branches. She stands below and catches them when I lower the pole.

* * *

March 15

Something has so humiliated me that I shall be forced to leave this place, and I gnash my teeth! The Devil! The harm is done, and it is *your* fault alone—*you* spurred me on, pushed and tormented me into accepting a position that was not congenial to me. Well, here I am! and you have had your way! And in order to prevent you from telling me that it was my eccentric ideas which ruined everything, I here recount, dear sir, the story, plain and clear, as a chronicler would put it down.

Count C. is very fond of me and singles me out, as is well known, and as I have written you many times. He had invited me for dinner at his house yesterday, on the very day when the whole aristocratic set, ladies and gentlemen, are accustomed to meet there late in the evening. I had completely forgotten this fact; and it also did not occur to me that subordinate officials like myself are not welcome on such occasions. Very well. I dined with the Count, and afterward we walked up and down the great hall in conversation and were joined later by Colonel B.; so the hour of the party drew near. God knows, I did not suspect anything. Then the more-than-gracious Lady S. entered with her spouse and her nobly hatched little goose of a flat-bosomed and tight-laced daughter. *En passant,* they opened their eyes wide and turned up their noses in the traditional highly aristocratic manner. As that clique is entirely repulsive to me, I had decided to leave, only waiting until the Count could free himself from trivial chatter, when Fräulein von B. entered the room. Since I become always a little more cheerful when I see her, I stayed on, took my place behind her chair, and noticed only after some time had passed that she was not talking to me with her usual frankness but with some embarrassment. This took me by surprise. "Is she really like the rest of these people?" I asked myself and was piqued. I wanted to leave, but stayed on, because I should have liked to free her from a blame I did not believe, and still hoped for a kind word from her and—whatever you wish. Meanwhile, more and more people were filling the room. Baron F. all gotten up in a complete outfit dating back to the coronation of Francis I, Hofrat R. (but here in *qualitate* called Herr von N.) with his deaf wife, not to mention the badly-reduced-in-circumstances J., who had patched up the worn places in his old-fashioned clothes with brand-new material—all these people kept arriving in swarms; and I spoke to some of those I knew who were, however, very laconic, I thought—and paid attention only to my Fräulein von B. I did not notice that the dames at the far end of the room were whispering into each other's ears or that this whispering spread to the gentlemen; that Lady S. was talking to the Count (Fräulein von B. recounted all this to me afterward), until he finally came up to me and drew me into a window recess. "You know our strange social conventions," he said, "and I notice that the company is displeased to see you here, although I should not want you, for anything in the world—" —"Your Excellency!" I interrupted, "I apologize exceedingly; I should have thought of this before, and I know you will forgive me my inconsequence. I wanted to leave some time ago, but a malicious spirit held me back," I added, smiling and bowing to him. The Count pressed my hand with a warmth that expressed everything. I turned my back on the illustrious company, slipped away and took a cabriolet to M., to see the sunset from the hill, while reading in Homer the magnificent passage which describes how Odysseus is entertained by the faithful swineherd. All this was perfect.

In the evening I returned to the inn for supper. There were only a few people in the taproom, playing at dice at the corner of a table, having turned back the tablecloth. The honest Adelin then came in, put down his hat when he saw me, and, coming up closer, said to me in a low voice: "Did something annoy you?" "Annoy me?" I said.—"The Count asked you to leave his party."—"The Devil take it!" I said. "I was glad to get out into the fresh air."—"Good that you take it so lightly," he said. "The thing that worries me is that everyone is already talking." Now for the first time the whole thing began to irritate me. I imagined that everyone who came in for supper glanced at me and seemed to know about the incident. My blood was up.

And today when everyone pities me wherever I go and when I hear that my triumphant rivals are saying, "You see where arrogance leads, when proud people who boast of their little share of brains think they can ignore all conventions" (and whatever else these gossiping dogs may invent), one would like to take a knife and plunge it into one's heart; for, whatever one may say about independence, I should like to see the person who can allow rascals to slander him when they have the upper hand. When it is only empty talk, it is easy to ignore them.

March 16

Everything is against me. Today I met Fräulein von B. in the avenue. I could not keep myself from speaking to her; to tell her, as soon as we were at some distance from her companions, how much she had hurt me the other day. "O Werther," she said with deep feeling, "how could you, knowing my heart, interpret my confusion in such a way? How I suffered for you from the moment I entered the room! I foresaw everything, and a warning word was on the tip of my tongue a dozen times. I knew that Lady S. and Lady T. would leave with their husbands rather than remain while you were there; and I knew that the Count cannot risk their displeasure—and now all this scandal!"—"What do you mean?" I asked, concealing my alarm, because everything that Adelin had told me the previous day made me suddenly feel very uneasy.—"How much it has already cost me," said the sweet creature with tears in her eyes.—I was no longer master of myself, and was ready to throw myself at her feet. "Do tell me the truth," I cried. The tears ran down her cheeks, and I was almost out of my mind. She dried her tears without trying to conceal them. "You know my aunt," she began. "She was at the party and with her keen eyes kept a close watch on everything. Werther, I had to suffer for it last night, and this morning I was given a lecture on my friendship with you, and was forced to listen to the degrading, discrediting things she said about you, and could not—was not allowed to—defend you half as much as I wished."

Every word she spoke pierced my heart like a sword. She did not sense how charitable it would have been to keep all this from me; and she went on to say that more gossip would soon begin to run wild, and mentioned the sort of people who would gloat over it. How delighted they all would be about the punishment I had received for my arrogance and haughty contempt toward others, for which they had often blamed me. All this, Wilhelm, I had to hear from her, spoken in a tone of sincerest sympathy. I was completely crushed, and am still furious. I wish that someone would have the courage to blame me openly so that I could thrust my dagger through his body; if I saw blood, I should certainly feel better. Today I have taken up a knife a dozen times, intending to relieve with it my suffocating heart. I have been told that a noble breed of horses, when overheated and hunted almost to death, will by instinct bite open a vein and so recover their breath. I often feel the same. I should like to open one of my veins and gain eternal freedom for myself.

March 24

I have sent in my resignation to the Court, and I hope that it will be accepted. You will forgive me for not asking your permission first. It is absolutely necessary for me to leave; and everything you will say, to persuade me to stay, I myself know. And therefore—sugar the bitter pill for my mother. I cannot help myself, and she must put up with the fact that I cannot help her either. Of course, it is going to hurt her. To see the beginning brilliant career of her son, which might have mounted, perhaps, to the office of privy councilor and envoy, stop so suddenly, and the little horse brought back to its stable! Now think of the matter as you will and try to figure out, the possible conditions under which I might and should have stayed. Enough, I am going. But that you may know where I am going, let me tell you that Prince—, who likes my company extremely, when he heard of my intention, invited me to accompany him to his estates, and to spend the lovely springtime there. He has promised that I will be completely left alone, and as we understand one another very well, up to a certain point, I shall take my chance and go with him.

* * *

December 20, after eleven

. . . a neighbor saw the flash of the powder and heard the shot; but, as everything remained quiet, he did not pay further attention to it.

Next morning, around six o'clock, the servant entered the room with a candle. He found his master lying on the floor, the pistol beside him, and blood everywhere. He called, he touched him; no answer came, only a rattling in the throat. He ran for a doctor and for Albert. Lotte heard the bell; a tremor seized all her limbs. She woke her husband; they got up, and the servant, sobbing and stammering, told the news. Lotte fainted and fell to the ground at Albert's feet.

When the doctor arrived, he found the unfortunate young man on the floor, past help; his pulse was still beating; all his limbs were paralyzed. He had shot himself through the head above the right eye, and his brain was laid bare. They bled him needlessly; the blood flowed; he was still breathing.

From the blood on the back of the armchair they concluded that he had committed the act while sitting at his writing desk. He had then slid down and rolled around the chair in convulsions. He was lying on his back, facing the window, enfeebled, fully dressed, in his boots, his blue coat and yellow waistcoat.

The house, the neighborhood, the town, was in a tumult. Albert came in. They had laid Werther on his bed and bandaged his forehead; his face was already the face of a dead man; he did not move. His lungs still gave forth a dreadful rattling sound, now weak, now stronger; they expected the end.

He had drunk only one glass of the wine. Lessing's *Emilia Galotti* lay open on his desk.

I cannot describe Albert's consternation, Lotte's distress.

On hearing the news, the old bailiff rode up to the house at full speed; he kissed his dying friend and wept bitter tears. His older sons arrived soon afterward on foot; they knelt beside the bed with expressions of uncontrollable grief and kissed Werther's hands and mouth; the oldest, whom Werther had always loved most, clung to him to the bitter end, when they had to tear the boy away by force. Werther died at noon. The presence of the bailiff and the arrangements he made prevented a public disturbance. That night around eleven the bailiff had Werther buried at the place he himself had chosen. The old man and his sons followed the body to the grave; Albert was unable to. Lotte's life was in danger. Workmen carried the coffin. No clergyman attended.

PART THREE

INDUSTRIALIZATION AND SOCIALISM

As captured here with high drama in a painting by the French Impressionist Claude Monet, railroads perfectly symbolized the Industrial Revolution's relentless transformation of life. For Monet, this process had its beauty.

Industrialization and Socialism

Beginning before 1800, technological innovations transformed European economies. The Industrial Revolution enriched investors, owners, and managers but ruined artisanry and cottage industry, neither of which could compete with the new machines. Those who turned to industry for work faced the ruthless exploitation of an entrepreneurial middle class with its noninterventionist (*laissez-faire*) mentality. The plight of the proletariat—men, women, and children workers—dismayed a conscience-stricken educated elite. Even before the full achievement of a liberal, representative government, some thinkers offered socialism as an allegedly more humane alternative to the bourgeoisie's unlimited sway. At first depending on moral persuasion, later on violent revolution, socialists sought to attain economic equality as a necessary corollary of political and legal equality.

In his famous 1798 *Essay* on demographics, the British economist Thomas Malthus (1766–1834) defended *laissez faire* while abandoning Adam Smith's prediction that its application would benefit the poor. Malthus blamed British workers' continued poverty on their ignorance, bad morals, and prolific childbearing, arguing that excess population depressed salaries. The French socialist Flora Tristan (1803–1844) visited England and witnessed the horrors of early industrialization there. As an antidote, she promoted workers' unions to enlist social support and worker self-help. Like other pre-1848 socialists, Tristan's voluntaristic ideas, outlined in her 1843 essays "Factory Workers" and "How to Constitute a Working Class," visualized that workers would eventually organize labor and production under communal arrangements. In his *Communist Manifesto,* Karl Marx (1796–1877) accused the earlier socialists of "utopianism," abandoned nonviolence, and predicted proletarian revolution as the carrier of a new just world. This definitive formulation of socialism uneasily balanced scientific analysis and moral cause. Elizabeth Gaskell (1810–1865), wife of a minister, based *Mary Barton* (1848) on observation of the early industrial metropolis, Manchester. The novel starkly contrasts middle-class prosperity with the daily horrors faced by laborers.

✦ Reading 10 ✦

An Essay on the Principle of Population

Thomas Malthus

The professed object of Dr. Adam Smith's inquiry is the nature and causes of the wealth of nations. There is another inquiry, however, perhaps still more interesting, which he occasionally mixes with it, I mean an inquiry into the causes which affect the happiness of nations or the happiness and comfort of the lower orders of society, which is the most numerous class in every nation. I am sufficiently aware of the near connection of these two subjects, and that the causes which tend to increase the wealth of a State tend also, generally speaking, to increase the happiness of the lower classes of the people. But perhaps Dr. Adam Smith has considered these two inquiries as still more nearly connected than they really are; at least he has not stopped to take notice of those instances where the wealth of a society may increase (according to his definition of wealth) without having any tendency to increase the comforts of the labouring part of it. I do not mean to enter into a philosophical discussion of what constitutes the proper happiness of man, but shall merely consider two universally acknowledged ingredients, health, and the command of the necessaries and conveniences of life.

Little or no doubt can exist that the comforts of the labouring poor depend upon the increase of the funds destined for the maintenance of labour, and will be very exactly in proportion to the rapidity of this increase. The demand for labour which such increase would occasion, by creating a competition in the market, must necessarily raise the value of labour, and, till the additional number of hands required were reared, the increased funds would be distributed to the same number of persons as before the increase, and therefore every labourer would live comparatively at his ease. But perhaps Dr. Adam Smith errs in representing every increase of the revenue or stock of a society as an increase of these funds. Such surplus stock or revenue will, indeed, always be considered by the individual possessing it as an additional fund from which he may maintain more labour; but it will not be a real and effectual fund for the maintenance of an additional number of labourers, unless the whole, or at least a great part of this increase of the stock or revenue of the society, be convertible into a proportional quantity of provisions; and it will not be so convertible where the increase has arisen merely from the produce of labour, and not from the produce of land. A distinction will in this case occur, between the number of hands which the stock of the society could employ, and the number which its territory, can maintain.

To explain myself by an instance. Dr. Adam Smith defines the wealth of a nation to consist in the annual produce of its land and labour. This definition evidently includes manufactured produce, as well as the produce of the land. Now supposing a nation for a course of years was to add what it saved from its yearly revenue to its manufacturing capital solely, and not to its capital employed upon land, it is evident that it might grow richer according to the above definition, without a power of supporting a greater number of labourers, and therefore, without an increase in the real funds for the maintenance of labour. There would, notwithstanding, be a demand for labour from the power which each manufacturer would possess, or at least think he possessed, of extending his old stock in trade or of setting up fresh works. This demand would of course raise the price of labour, but if the yearly stock of provisions in the country was not increasing, this rise would soon turn out to be merely nominal, as the price of provisions must necessarily rise with it. The demand for manufacturing labourers might, indeed, entice many

From: Thomas Robert Malthus, *An Essay on the Principle of Population,* ed. Philip Appleman (New York: W.W. Norton & Company, 1976), pp. 103–105, 131–139.

from agriculture and thus tend to diminish the annual produce of the land, but we will suppose any effect of this kind to be compensated by improvements in the instruments of agriculture, and the quantity of provisions therefore to remain the same. Improvements in manufacturing machinery would of course take place, and this circumstance, added to the greater number of hands employed in manufactures, would cause the annual produce of the labour of the country to be upon the whole greatly increased. The wealth therefore of the country would be increasing annually, according to the definition, and might not, perhaps, be increasing very slowly.

The question is whether wealth, increasing in this way, has any tendency to better the condition of the labouring poor. It is a self-evident proposition that any general rise in the price of labour, the stock of provisions remaining the same, can only be a nominal rise, as it must very shortly be followed by a proportional rise in provisions. The increase in the price of labour therefore, which we have supposed, would have little or no effect in giving the labouring poor a greater command over the necessaries and conveniences of life. In this respect they would be nearly in the same state as before. In one other respect they would be in a worse state. A greater proportion of them would be employed in manufactures, and fewer, consequently, in agriculture. And this exchange of professions will be allowed, I think, by all, to be very unfavourable in respect of health, one essential ingredient of happiness, besides the greater uncertainty of manufacturing labour, arising from the capricious taste of man, the accidents of war, and other causes.

It may be said, perhaps, that such an instance as I have supposed could not occur, because the rise in the price of provisions would immediately turn some additional capital into the channel of agriculture. But this is an event which may take place very slowly, as it should be remarked that a rise in the price of labour had preceded the rise of provisions, and would therefore impede the good effects upon agriculture, which the increased value of the produce of the land might otherwise have occasioned.

It might also be said, that the additional capital of the nation would enable it to import provisions sufficient for the maintenance of those whom its stock could employ. A small country with a large navy, and great inland accommodations for carriage, such as Holland, may indeed import and distribute an effectual quantity of provisions; but the price of provisions must be very high to make such an importation and distribution answer in large countries less advantageously circumstanced in this respect.

An instance, accurately such as I have supposed, may not, perhaps, ever have occurred, but I have little doubt that instances nearly approximating to it may be found without any very laborious search. Indeed I am strongly inclined to think that England herself, since the revolution, affords a very striking elucidation of the argument in question.

The commerce of this country, internal as well as external, has certainly been rapidly advancing during the last century. The exchangeable value in the market of Europe of the annual produce of its land and labour has, without doubt, increased very considerably. But upon examination it will be found that the increase has been chiefly in the produce of labour and not in the produce of land, and therefore, though the wealth of the nation has been advancing with a quick pace, the effectual funds for the maintenance of labour have been increasing very slowly, and the result is such as might be expected. The increasing wealth of the nation has had little or no tendency to better the condition of the labouring poor.

* * *

Of Moral Restraint, and Our Obligation to Practise This Virtue

As it appears that, in the actual state of every society which has come within our review, the natural progress of population has been constantly and powerfully checked: and as it seems evident that no improved form of government, no plans of emigration, no benevolent institutions, and no degree or direction of national industry, can prevent the continued action of a great check to population in some form or other; it follows that we must submit to it as an inevitable law of nature; and the only inquiry that remains is, how it may take place with the least possible prejudice to the virtue and happiness of human society.

All the immediate checks to population, which have been observed to prevail in the same and different countries, seem to be resolvable into moral restraint, vice and misery; and if our choice be confined to these three, we cannot long hesitate in our decision respecting which it would be most eligible to encourage.

In the first edition of this essay I observed, that as from the laws of nature it appeared, that some check to population must exist, it was better that this check should arise from a foresight of the difficulties attending a family and the fear of dependent poverty, than from the actual presence of want and sickness. This idea will admit of being pursued farther; and I am inclined to think that, from the prevailing opinions respecting population, which undoubtedly originated in barbarous ages, and have been continued and circulated by that part of every community which may be supposed to be interested in their support, we have been prevented from attending to the clear dictates of reason and nature on this subject.

Natural and moral evil seem to be the instruments employed by the Deity in admonishing us to avoid any mode of conduct which is not suited to our being, and will consequently injure our happiness. If we are intemperate in eating and drinking, our health is disordered; if we indulge the transports of anger, we seldom fail to commit acts of which we afterwards repent; if we multiply too fast, we die miserably of poverty and contagious diseases. The laws of nature in all these cases are similar and uniform. They indicate to us that we have followed these impulses too far, so as to trench upon some other law, which equally demands attention. . . .

From the inattention of mankind hitherto to the consequences of increasing too fast, it must be presumed, that these consequences are not so immediately and powerfully connected with the conduct which leads to them, as in the other instances; but the delayed knowledge of particular effects does not alter their nature, or our obligation to regulate our conduct accordingly, as soon as we are satisfied of what this conduct ought to be. . . .

. . . It is of the very utmost importance to the happiness of mankind, that population should not increase too fast; but it does not appear, that the object to be accomplished would admit of any considerable diminution in the desire of marriage. It is clearly the duty of each individual not to marry till he has a prospect of supporting his children; but it is at the same time to be wished that he should retain undiminished his desire of marriage, in order that he may exert himself to realise this prospect, and be stimulated to make provision for the support of greater numbers.

It is evidently therefore regulation and direction which are required with regard to the principle of population, not diminution or alteration. And if moral restraint be the only virtuous mode of avoiding the incidental evils arising from this principle, our obligation to practise it will evidently rest exactly upon the same foundation as our obligation to practise any of the other virtues.

Whatever indulgence we may be disposed to allow to occasional failures in the discharge of a duty of acknowledged difficulty, yet of the strict line of duty we cannot doubt. Our obligation not to marry till we have a fair prospect of being able to support our children will appear to deserve the attention of the moralist, if it can be proved that an attention to this obligation is of most powerful effect in the prevention of misery; and that, if it were the general custom to follow the first impulse of nature, and marry at the age of puberty, the universal prevalence of every known virtue in the greatest conceivable degree, would fail of rescuing society from the most wretched and desperate state of want, and all the diseases and famines which usually accompany it.

* * *

Of the Only Effectual Mode of Improving the Condition of the Poor

. . . The object of those who really wish to better the condition of the lower classes of society must be to raise the relative proportion between the price of labour and the price of provisions, so as to enable the labourer to command a larger share of the necessaries and comforts of life. We have hitherto principally attempted to attain this end by encouraging the married poor and consequently increasing the number of labourers, and overstocking the market with a commodity which we still say that we wish to be dear. It would seem to have required no great spirit of divination to foretell the certain failure of such a plan of proceeding. There is nothing however like experience. It has been tried in many different countries, and for many hundred years, and the success has always been answerable to the nature of the scheme. It is really time now to try something else.

When it was found that oxygen, or pure vital air, would not cure consumptions as was expected, but rather aggravated their symptoms, trial was made of an air of the most opposite kind. I wish we had acted with the same philosophical spirit in our attempts to cure the disease of poverty: and having found that the pouring in of fresh supplies of labour only tended to aggravate the symptoms, had tried what would be the effect of withholding a little these supplies.

In all old and fully-peopled states it is from this method, and this alone, that we can rationally expect any essential and permanent melioration in the condition of the labouring classes of the people.

In an endeavour to raise the proportion of the quantity of provisions to the number of consumers in any country, out attention would naturally be first directed to the increasing of the absolute quantity of provisions; but finding that, as fast as we did this, the number of consumers more than kept pace with it, and that with all our exertions we were still as far as ever behind, we should be convinced that our efforts directed only in this way would never succeed. It would appear to be setting the tortoise to catch the hare. Finding, therefore, that from the laws of nature we could not proportion the food to the population, our next attempt should naturally be to proportion the population to the food. If we can persuade the hare to go to sleep the tortoise may have some chance of overtaking her.

We are not, however, to relax our efforts in increasing the quantity of provisions, but to combine another effort with it: that of keeping the population, when once it has been overtaken, at such a distance behind as to effect the relative proportion which we desire: and thus unite the two grand *desiderata,* a great actual population and a state of society in which abject poverty and dependence are comparatively but little known: two objects which are far from being incompatible.

If we be really serious in what appears to be the object of such general research, the mode of essentially and permanently bettering the condition of the poor, we must explain to them the true nature of their situation, and show them that the withholding of the supplies of labour is the only possible way of really raising its price, and that they themselves, being the possessors of this commodity, have alone the power to do this.

* * *

Plan of the Gradual Abolition of the Poor Laws Proposed

If the principles in the preceding chapters should stand the test of examination, and we should ever feel the obligation of endeavouring to act upon them, the next inquiry would be in what way we ought practically to proceed. The first grand obstacle which presents itself in this country is the system of the poor-laws, which has been justly stated to be an evil in comparison of which the national debt, with all its magnitude of terror, is of little moment. The rapidity with which the poor's rates have increased of late years presents us indeed with the prospect of such an extraordinary proportion of paupers in the society as would seem to be incredible in a nation flourishing in arts, agriculture, and commerce, and with a government which has generally been allowed to be the best that has hitherto stood the test of experience.

* * *

I have reflected much on the subject of the poor-laws, and hope therefore that I shall be excused in venturing to suggest a mode of their gradual abolition to which I confess that at present I can see no material objection. Of this indeed I feel nearly convinced that, should we ever become so fully sensible of the widespreading tyranny, dependence, indolence, and unhappiness which they create as seriously to make an effort to abolish them, we shall be compelled by a sense of justice to adopt the principle, if not the plan, which I shall mention. It seems impossible to get rid of so extensive a system of support, consistently with humanity, without applying ourselves directly to its vital principle, and endeavouring to counteract that deeply-seated cause which occasions the rapid growth of all such establishments and invariably renders them inadequate to their object.

As a previous step even to any considerable alteration in the present system, which would contract or stop the increase of the relief to be given, it appears to me that we are bound in justice and honour formally to disclaim the *right* of the poor to support.

To this end, I should propose a regulation to be made, declaring that no child born from any marriage, taking place after the expiration of a year from the date of the law, and no illegitimate child born two years from the same date, should ever be entitled to parish assistance. And to give a more general knowledge of this law, and to enforce it more strongly on the minds of the lower classes of people, the clergyman of each parish should, after the publication of banns, read a short address stating the strong obligation on every man to support his own children; the impropriety, and even immorality, of marrying without a prospect of being able to do this; the evils which had resulted to the poor themselves from the attempt which had been made to assist by public institutions in a duty which ought to be exclusively appropriated to parents; and the absolute necessity which had at length appeared of abandoning all such institutions, on account of their producing effects totally opposite to those which were intended.

This would operate as a fair, distinct, and precise notice, which no man could well mistake; and, without pressing hard on any particular individuals, would at once throw off the rising generation from that miserable and helpless dependence upon the government and the rich, the moral as well as physical consequences of which are almost incalculable.

After the public notice which I have proposed had been given, and the system of poor-laws had ceased with regard to the rising generation, if any man chose to marry, without a prospect of being able to support a family, he should have the most perfect liberty so to do. Though to marry, in this case, is, in my opinion, clearly an immoral act, yet it is not one which society can justly take upon itself to prevent or punish; because the punishment provided for it by the laws of nature falls directly and most severely upon the individual who commits the act, and through him, only more remotely and feebly, on the society. When nature will govern and punish for us, it is a very miserable ambition to wish to snatch the rod from her hand and draw upon ourselves the odium of executioner. To the punishment therefore of nature he should be left, the punishment of want. He has erred in the face of a most clear and precise warning, and can have no just reason to complain of any person but himself when he feels the consequences of his error. All parish assistance should be denied him; and he should be left to the uncertain support of private charity. He should be taught to know that the laws of nature, which are the laws of God, had doomed him and his family to suffer for disobeying their repeated admonitions; that he had no claim of *right* on society for the smallest portion of food, beyond that which his labour would fairly purchase; and that if he and his family were saved from feeling the natural consequences of his imprudence he would owe it to the pity of some kind benefactor, to whom, therefore, he ought to be bound by the strongest ties of gratitude.

If this system were pursued, we need be under no apprehensions that the number of persons in extreme want would be beyond the power and the will of the benevolent to supply. The sphere for the exercise of private charity would, probably, not be greater than it is at present; and the principal difficulty would be to restrain the hand of benevolence from assisting those in distress in so indiscriminate a manner as to encourage indolence and want of foresight in others.

With regard to illegitimate children, after the proper notice had been given, they should not be allowed to have any claim to parish assistance, but be left entirely to the support of private charity. If the parents desert their child, they ought to be made answerable for the crime. The infant is, comparatively speaking, of little value to the society, as others will immediately supply its place. . . .

Of the Modes of Correcting the Prevailing Opinions on Population

It is not enough to abolish all the positive institutions which encourage population; but we must endeavour, at the same time, to correct the prevailing opinions which have the same, or perhaps even a more powerful effect. This must necessarily be a work of time; and can only be done by circulating juster notions on these subjects in writing and conversation; and by endeavouring to impress as strongly as possible on the public mind that it is not the duty of man simply to propagate his species, but to propagate virtue and happiness; and that, if he has not a tolerably fair prospect of doing this, he is by no means called upon to leave descendants.

. . . The fairest chance of accomplishing this end would probably be by the establishment of a system of parochial education upon a plan similar to that proposed by Adam Smith. In addition to the usual subjects of instruction, and those which he has mentioned, I should be disposed to lay considerable stress on the frequent explanation of the real state of the lower classes of society as affected by the principle of population, and their consequent dependence on themselves for the chief part of their happiness or misery. . . .

The principal argument which I have heard advanced against a system of national education in England is, that the common people would be put in a capacity to read such works as those of Paine, and that the consequences would probably be fatal to government. But on this subject I agree most cordially with Adam Smith in thinking that an instructed and well-informed people would be much less likely to be led away by inflammatory writings, and much better able to detect the false declamation of interested and ambitious demagogues, than an ignorant people. . . .

In most countries, among the lower classes of people, there appears to be something like a standard of wretchedness, a point below which they will not continue to marry and propagate their species. This standard is different in different countries, and is formed by various concurring circumstances of soil, climate, government, degree of knowledge, and civilisation, etc. The principal circumstances which contribute to raise it are liberty, security of property, the diffusion of knowledge, and a taste for the conveniences and the comforts of life. Those which contribute principally to lower it are despotism and ignorance.

In an attempt to better the condition of the labouring classes of society our object should be to raise this standard as high as possible, by cultivating a spirit of independence, a decent pride, and a taste for cleanliness and comfort. The effect of a good government in increasing the prudential habits and personal respectability of the lower classes of society has already been insisted on; but certainly this effect will always be incomplete without a good system of education; and, indeed, it may be said that no government can approach to perfection that does not provide for the instruction of the people. The benefits derived from education are among those which may be enjoyed without restriction of numbers; and, as it is in the power of governments to confer these benefits, it is undoubtedly their duty to do it.

Of Our Rational Expectations Respecting the Future Improvement of Society

* * *

It is less the object of the present work to propose new plans of improving society than to inculcate the necessity of resting contented with that mode of improvement which already has in part been acted upon as dictated by the course of nature, and of not obstructing the advances which would otherwise be made in this way.

It would be undoubtedly highly advantageous that all our positive institutions, and the whole tenour of our conduct to the poor, should be such as actively to co-operate with that lesson of prudence inculcated by the common course of human events; and if we take upon ourselves sometimes to mitigate the natural punishents of imprudence, that we could balance it by increasing the rewards of an opposite conduct. But much would be done if merely the institutions which directly tend to encourage marriage were gradually changed, and we ceased to circulate opinions and inculcate doctrines which positively counteract the lessons of nature.

The limited good which it is sometimes in our power to effect, is often lost by attempting too much, and by making the adoption of some particular plan essentially necessary even to a partial degree of success. In the practical application of the reasonings of this work, I hope that I have avoided this error. I wish to press on the recollection of the reader that, though I may have given some new views of old facts, and may have indulged in the contemplation of a considerable degree of *possible* improvement, that I might not shut out that prime cheerer hope; yet in my expectations of probable improvement and in suggesting the means of accomplishing it, I have been very cautious. . . .

From a review of the state of society in former periods compared with the present, I should certainly say that the evils resulting from the principle of population have rather diminished than increased, even under the disadvantage of an almost total ignorance of the real cause. And if we can indulge the hope that this ignorance will be gradually dissipated, it does not seem unreasonable to expect that they will be still further diminished. The increase of absolute population, which will of course take place, will evidently tend but little to weaken this expectation, as everything depends upon the relative proportion between population and food, and not on the absolute number of people. In the former part of this work it appeared that the countries which possessed the fewest people often suffered the most from the effects of the principle of population; and it can scarcely be doubled that, taking Europe throughout, fewer famines and fewer diseases arising from want have prevailed in the last century than in those which preceded it.

On the whole, therefore, though our future prospects respecting the mitigation of the evils arising from the principle of population may not be so bright as we could wish, yet they are far from being entirely disheartening, and by no means preclude that gradual and progressive improvement in human society which, before the late wild speculations on this subject, was the object of rational expectation. To the laws of property and marriage, and to the apparent narrow principle of self-interest which prompts each individual to exert himself in bettering his condition, we are indebted for all the noblest exertions of human genius, for everything that distinguishes the civilised from the savage state. A strict inquiry into the principle of population obliges us to conclude that we shall never be able to throw down the ladder by which we have risen to this eminence; but it by no means proves that we may not rise higher by the same means. The structure of society, in its great features, will probably always remain unchanged. We have every reason to believe that it will always consist of a class of proprietors and a class of labourers; but the condition of each, and the proportion which they bear to each other, may be so altered as greatly to improve the harmony and beauty of the whole. It would indeed be a melancholy reflection that, while the views of physical science are daily enlarging, so as scarcely to be bounded by the most distant horizon, the science of moral and political philosophy should be confined within such narrow limits, or at best be so feeble in its influence, as to be unable to counteract the obstacles to human happiness arising from a single cause. But however formidable these obstacles may have appeared in some parts of this work, it is hoped that the general result of the inquiry is such as not to make us give up the improvement of human society in despair. The partial good which seems to be attainable is worthy of all our exertions; is sufficient to direct our efforts, and animate our prospects. And although we cannot expect that the virtue and happiness of mankind will keep pace with the brilliant career of physical discovery; yet, if we are not wanting to ourselves, we may confidently indulge the hope that, to no unimportant extent, they will be influenced by its progress and will partake in its success.

✦ Reading 11 ✦

Two Essays: Factory Workers and How to Constitute a Working Class

Flora Tristan

Factory Workers

Slavery shows itself at the dawn of every society. The evils it produces make it essentially transitory, and its duration is inversely proportional to its severity. If our ancestors had had no more humanity for their serfs than the English manufacturers have for their workers, serfdom would not have lasted through the Middle Ages. The English proletariat, in whatever occupation, has such an atrocious existence that the negroes who have left the sugar plantations of Guadaloupe and Martinique in order to partake of English liberty on Dominique and Saint-Lucia return to their former masters whenever they can. Far be it from me to have the sacrilegious thought of defending any kind of slavery! I only want to prove by this example that English law is harder on the proletariat than the *arbitrary will* of the French master toward his negro. The English wage slave has an infinitely worse time earning his daily bread and paying the taxes that are imposed on him.

The negro is exposed only to the caprices of his master, while the existence of the English proletarian, his wife, and his children is at the mercy of the producer. Should calico or some such article be lowered in price, those immediately affected by the drop, whether spinners, cutters, potters, etc., of one accord reduce wages, with no consideration at all for the subsistence of the workers; they also increase the number of work hours. Where pieceworkers are concerned, the producers demand more highly finished work while paying less, and when all the conditions are not exactly fulfilled the work is not paid for. Cruelly exploited by his employer, the worker is further pressured by the tax collector and starved by the landowners. He almost always dies at an early age. His life is shortened by the excess and nature of his work. His wife and children do not long survive him; tied to the factory, they succumb for the same reasons. If they have no work in the winter, they die of hunger in the street.

The division of labor pushed to its extreme limit, which has been the cause of such progress in manufacturing, has destroyed intelligence and reduced man to being only a gear of the machine. If the worker could still do different parts of one or several manufacturing processes, he would derive satisfaction from being more independent; the cupidity of the master would have fewer means of torturing him; his body would be able to resist the deleterious effects of an occupation that lasted only a few hours. Tool-grinders in English factories do not live past thirty-five years of age; the use of the grindstone does not harm our Châtellerault workers because the grinding is only a part of their work and of their time, whereas in the English workshops, the grinders do nothing else. If the worker could be employed in several parts of the manufacturing process instead of repeating the same thing all day long, he would not be overwhelmed by his own unimportance and by the perpetual inactivity of his mind. He would no longer need strong brandies to rouse him from the torpor into which the monotony of his work plunges him, and drunkenness would not be the last degree of his misfortune.

To get a good idea of the physical sufferings and moral debasement of this class of the population, one must visit the manufacturing cities and see the worker in Birmingham, Manchester, Glasgow, Sheffield, and in Staffordshire, etc. It is impossible to

From: Flora Tristan, *Utopian Feminist: Her Travel Diaries and Personal Crusade,* selected by Doris and Paul Beik (Bloomington: Indiana University Press, 1993), pp. 61–67, 107–111.

We entered the great heating room. The two rows of furnaces on each side were lighted. That fiery furnace calls to mind rather well the descriptions that the ancient poets have left us of Vulcan's forges, except that divine activity and intelligence animated the Cyclops, whereas the black servants of the English furnaces are morose, silent, and exhausted. There were about twenty men working there, accurately, but slowly. Those not occupied stood motionless, their eyes on the ground. They did not even have enough energy to dry the perspiration that poured off them. Three or four looked at me with eyes that immediately shifted from mine. The others did not turn their heads. The foreman told me that the stokers where chosen from the strongest men but that, even so, all became consumptive at the end of seven or eight years of the work and died of tuberculosis. That explained the sadness and apathy on the faces and in the movements of these unfortunates.

A kind of work is required of them that the human physique cannot bear. They are naked except for a small loincloth. When they leave, they throw a jacket over their shoulders.

Although the space between the two rows of furnaces seemed to me to be fifty or sixty feet, the floor was so hot that the heat immediately penetrated my shoes to much that I had to lift my feet as if I were stepping on burning coals. I had to step up onto a large stone and even though it was off the ground, it was *hot*. I could not stay in this hell; my lungs were full, the smell of gas went to my head, and the heat suffocated me. The foreman took me to the back of the furnace room, to a balcony from which I could see everything without being so uncomfortable.

We made the tour of the establishment. I had great admiration for all these machines, this perfection and order with which the work is done. However, the precautions taken do not prevent all accidents, and frequently there are great disasters, injuring the men and sometimes killing them. My God! Progress, then, can only take place at the expense of the lives of a certain number of individuals!

The gas from this factory goes in pipes to light the district from Oxford Street to Regent Street.

The air that one breathes in this factory is really poisonous! Every minute noxious fumes assail you. I left the shed, hoping to breathe purer air in the courtyard; but everywhere I was pursued by the infectious exhalations of gas and the odors of oil, tar, etc.

I must say also that the site is very dirty. The courtyard full of stagnant water and pieces of garbage shows extreme negligence in everything concerning the property. In truth, the nature of the materials from which one obtains gas is such as to require a very active cleaning service but two men would be enough for the job, and with only a slight increase in expense the establishment would be made healthful.

I was asphyxiated and I was hurrying to get out of this stench when the foreman said to me: "Stay a minute more—you will see something interesting. The firemen are going to take the coke from the ovens."

I again perched on the balcony. From there I saw one of the most frightening sights I had ever witnessed.

The heating room is on the second floor; below is the chamber to receive the coke. The stokers, armed with long iron rakes, opened the ovens and drew out the coke, which, all fiery, fell in torrents into the chamber. Nothing could be more terrible or majestic than those mouths vomiting forth flames! Nothing could be more magical than the chamber suddenly illuminated by burning coals plunging like the waters of a cataract from a high rock and, like them, being swallowed in the abyss! Nothing could be more frightening than the sight of the stokers dripping as if they were emerging from water, lighted on all sides by those horrible coals whose fiery tongues seem to advance as if to devour them. No, one could not see anything more frightening!

When the furnaces were half empty, men on top of the vats at the four corners of the chamber threw down water to extinguish the fires; then the scene in the heating room changed: a whirlwind of black, thick, glowing smoke rose majestically from the hole and went out through the roof, which had been expressly opened for it. I could no longer see the mouths of the ovens except through this cloud that made the flames redder and the tongues of flame more frightening. The white bodies of the firemen became black and those unfortunates, whom one would have thought to be devils, became lost in this infernal chaos. Surprised by the smoke from the coke, I just had time to get down in a hurry.

I waited for the end of the operation, curious to know what was going to become of the poor stokers. I was amazed to see no woman arrive. My God, I thought, these workers, then, have no mothers, sisters, wives, or daughters waiting at the door when they leave this fiery furnace, to bathe them in warm water, wrap them in flannel shirts, make them drink a nourishing, strengthening beverage, and then give them such words of friendship and love as may console, encourage, and help man to bear the cruelest miseries. I was concerned; not a woman appeared. I asked the foreman if these men, drenched in sweat, were going to get some rest.

"They are going to throw themselves on a bed in this shed," he answered me coldly, "and at the end of a couple of hours they will fire up again."

This shed, open to every wind, only keeps out the rain; it was icy cold in there. A kind of mattress, hardly distinguishable from the coal around it, was in one of the corners. I saw the stokers stretch out on this hard-as-a-stone mattress. They were covered with very dirty overcoats, impregnated with so much sweat and coal dust that one couldn't even guess the color of them. "There," the foreman said to me, "that is how the men become consumptive—by going from hot to cold without precautions."

The foreman's last observation had such an effect on me that I left the factory in a complete state of exasperation.

That is how men's lives are bought for money; and when the exacted task causes deaths, the industrialist suffers no inconvenience except having to raise wages! Why, that is even worse than the negro *slave trade!* I see nothing surpassing this enormous monstrosity except cannibalism! The owners of factories and manufacturing plants can, with no legal impediment, have at their disposal the youth and the vigor of hundreds of men, purchase their lives and sacrifice them, in order to gain money! All at wages of seven to eight shillings a day, eight francs, seventy-five centimes to ten francs!

I do not know that any heads of factories such as those of whom I have just been speaking have had the humanity to make available a room moderately heated, with baths of warm water, mattresses, and wool covers, where the stokers could go, on leaving their furnaces, to wash and rest, well wrapped up, in an atmosphere not unlike the one they had left. It is really a shame and a national disgrace for such things as I have just described to occur.

In England when the horses arrive at the post stations, someone hurries to throw a blanket over them, dry their sweat and wash their feet; then they are put in a closed stable well lined with very dry straw.

A few years ago relay stations were placed closer together after it was realized that too great distances between them shortened the lives of the horses; yes, but a horse costs the industralist forty to fifty pounds sterling, whereas the country furnishes him men *for nothing!*

How to Constitute the Working Class

It is very important that the workers understand clearly the difference between the WORKERS' UNION as I have conceived of it and what exists today under various names such as *association, compagnonnage, union, mutual aid,* etc.

The common aim of all these distinct and differing associations is simply for *members of the same society* to provide each other with aid and assistance, mutually and individually. And so these societies were established in preparation for cases of *sickness, accidents,* and *long periods of unemployment.*

Given the present state of isolation, abandonment, and poverty characteristic of the working class, these societies are very useful, for their aim is to help, in small ways, the most needy, and thereby to lessen personal suffering that often exceeds the strength and courage of its victims. I therefore heartily approve of these societies, and I encourage workers to increase their number while at the same time purifying them of the abuses to which they can be subject. But to *relieve distress* is not to *destroy it;* to lessen an evil is not to *remove* it. If at last one decides to attack the evil at its root, clearly something more is needed than *private organizations* whose only purpose is to *minister to the sufferings of individuals. . . .*

Workers, you must therefore abandon as quickly as possible your habits of division and isolation and march courageously and fraternally in the only direction that is suitable for you—toward *unity.* The project of union as I have conceived of it rests on a broad base, and its spirit is capable of fully satisfying the moral and material requirements of a great people.

What is the objective and what will be the result of the *universal union of workingmen and workingwomen?*

It has as objectives: (1) To CONSTITUTE the compact, indissoluble UNITY of the WORKING CLASS; (2) to make the WORKERS' UNION the possessor of an enormous capital, by means of a voluntary contribution from each worker; (3) to acquire, by means of this capital, some real power, that of money; (4) by means of this power, to prevent poverty and to eradicate the evil at its root, in giving children of the working class a solid, rational education, capable of making them into trained, reasonable, intelligent men and women who art also skillful in their professions; (5) to compensate all sorts of labor amply and worthily.

This is too beautiful! someone will cry. It is too beautiful: *it is impossible.*

Readers, before paralyzing the impulses of your heart and imagination by this glacial phrase, *it is impossible,* always keep in mind that France contains seven to eight million workers; that at two francs apiece there will accumulate at the end of a year fourteen million; at four francs, twenty-eight million; at eight francs, fifty-six million. This result is in no way chimerical. Among the workers some are well-to-do, and very many are generous; some will give two francs, others four, eight, ten, or twenty francs, and think of your number, seven million! . . .* I have said by means of this capital the WORKERS' UNION could gain real power, that which money gives. Let us see how.

For example, the Irish people by means of their union have been able to establish and maintain what is called THE ASSOCIATION . . . ; moreover, they have been able to set up, by voluntary contributions, . . . a colossal fortune, at the disposition of a man of heart and talent, O'Connell. . . .

What is the social position of the working class in France today, and what rights remain for it to claim?

*The WORKERS' UNION, in my view, would have for its aim, at first, "to constitute the working class, properly speaking," and eventually to "*rally*" to the same cause the twenty-five million French working people of all kinds who are "not proprietors," in order that they might defend their interests and demand their rights. The working class is not the only one to suffer from the privileges of property. . . .

In principle the organic law that has regulated French society since the Declaration of the Rights of Man of 1791 is the highest expression of justice and equity, for this law is the solemn recognition that legitimates the sanctity of the principle of absolute equality, and not only the equality before God demanded by Jesus but also that *living equality* practiced in the name of both the spirit and the flesh in the presence of humanity. . . .

. . . But let us hasten to say that to enjoy equality and liberty *in principle* is to live *in spirit,* and if he who brought to the world *the law of the spirit* spoke wisely in saying that "man does not live by bread alone," I believe that it is also wise to say that "man does not live by spirit alone."

In reading the Charter of 1830 one is struck by a serious omission. Our constitutional legislators forgot that prior to the rights of man and of the citizen there exists an imperious, imprescriptible fight that precedes and governs all the others, the *right to live.* Now, for the poor worker who possesses neither land nor houses, nor capital, nor absolutely anything except *his arms,* the rights of man and citizen are of no value (and in this case they even become for him a bitter mockery), if first one does not recognize *his right to live,* and, for the worker, the right to live is *the right to work,* the *only one* that can give him the possibility of *eating,* and consequently of living.

The first of the rights belonging to everyone from birth is precisely that which was *overlooked* in the writing of the charter. It is therefore *this first right* that is still to be proclaimed.*

Today the working class must concentrate on a single demand because this demand is based on the strictest equity and because this claim cannot be refused without violating the *right to life.* What, in fact, does the working class demand?

THE RIGHT TO WORK.

*The National Convention had "almost" recognized "the right to work" or at least "to public assistance." Art. XXI: "Public assistance is a sacred obligation. Society owes subsistence to unfortunate citizens, whether by finding work for them, or by guaranteeing the means of existence to those who are unable to work." *Declaration of the Rights of Man and of the Citizen,* June 27, 1793.

Its own property, the only one that it can ever possess, is *its arms.* Yes, its arms! They are its patrimony, its unique wealth! Its arms are the *only instruments of labor* in its possession. They therefore constitute *its property,* and the *legitimacy,* and above all the *utility,* of this property cannot, I think, be contested, for if the earth produces, it is thanks to *the work people's arms.*

To deny that *arms are property* is to refuse to understand the *spirit* of article 8 of the charter. Nevertheless, arms as a form of property cannot be contested, and when the day comes that this matter can be discussed, there can be on this subject only one conclusion. But for the working class to be *secure* and *guaranteed* in the enjoyment of its property (as article 8 stipulates), the *free use* and guarantee of that property must be recognized in *principle* (and also in reality). Now the actual free use of this property would consist, for the working class, in being able to *make use of its arms,* whenever and however it wished, and to make this possible it must possess the *right to work.* And as for the guarantee of this property, it consists of a wise and equitable ORGANIZATION OF LABOR.

The working class has therefore two important claims to make: (1) THE RIGHT TO WORK; (2) THE ORGANIZATION OF LABOR.

But, someone is going to say again, what you demand for the working class is *impossible.* The right to work! They won't get it. This claim, however just and legal, will be considered an attack on property properly so called (land, houses, capital), and the organization of labor will be considered an attack on the rights of free competition. Now since those who manage the governmental machine are the owners of land and capital, it is evident that they will never consent to grant such rights to the working class.

Let us understand each other. If in their present condition of division and isolation the workers decide to demand the *right to work* and *the organization of labor,* the proprietors will not even do them the honor of considering their demand as an attack: they will simply not listen. A worker of merit (Adolphe Boyer) wrote a little book in which he made both demands: no one read his book. The unfortunate man, from chagrin and poverty, and possibly with the thought that his tragic end would move people to read his proposals, killed himself. Briefly the press took notice, for four days, perhaps eight; then the suicide and Adolphe Boyer's little book were completely forgotten. . . . Boyer was a poor worker who wrote all alone in his corner; he defended the cause of his unfortunate brothers, that is true, but he was not linked to them by shared thoughts or even by shared emotions or interests; and so be killed himself because he lacked 200 francs to pay the expenses of his small book. Can you believe that this would have happened if Boyer had been part of a vast union? Without doubt, no. . . .

Workers, you see the situation. If you want to save yourselves, you have only one means: you must UNITE.

If I preach UNION to you, it is because I understand the strength and capacity you will find in it. Open your eyes, look around you, and see the advantages enjoyed by all those who have formed a UNION in order to serve the same cause and the same interests.

Notice the procedure adopted by all men of intelligence, for example the founders of religions. Their first preoccupation was with the founding of a UNION. Moses unites his people, and by attachments so strong that time itself cannot break them. . . . What does Jesus do before his death? He gathers his twelve apostles and UNITES them. . . . The master dies. No matter! THE UNION IS CONSTITUTED. . . . Jesus Christ *lives in his apostles* with an *eternal life,* for after John comes Peter, and after Peter comes Paul, and so on, to the end of time.

Twelve men UNITED established the *Catholic Church,* a vast union that became so powerful that for 2,000 years this union has governed most of the earth.

Examine on a smaller scale the same principle of strength in operation: Luther, Calvin, and all of the Catholic dissidents. From the moment of their joining together in a UNION they become powerful.

And now, another order of events: the revolution of '89 breaks out. Like a torrent that sweeps everything before it, it overthrows, it exiles, it kills. But the ROYALIST UNION is *constituted.* Although overwhelmingly outnumbered, it is so strong that it survives the destructions of '93, and twenty years later it returns to France, *its king as its head!* And in the face of such accomplishments you would persist in remaining in your isolation! No, no! Short of madness, you can persist no longer.

In '89 the bourgeois class won its independence. Its own charter dates from the taking of the Bastille. Workers, for 200 years and more the bourgeois fought with courage and persistence against the privileges of the nobility and for the triumph of their *rights.* But with victory achieved, although they recognized equality of rights for everyone, *in fact they seized for themselves alone* all the gains and advantages of this conquest.

Since '89 the bourgeois class HAS BEEN CONSTITUTED. Notice what force a body united by the same interests can have. Once this class IS CONSTITUTED it becomes so strong that it can appropriate ever power in the land. Finally, in 1830, its strength reaches its peak, and without regard for consequences it pronounces the *dismissal the last king of France;* it chooses its *own* king, arranges for his selection without consulting the rest of the nation, and finally, being in fact *sovereign,* takes charge of affairs and governs the country according to its own tastes.

This bourgeois-proprietor class *represents itself* in the Chamber and before the nation, not in order to *defend its interests* there, for no one threatens them, but in order to *impose* its conditions on the twenty-five million proletarians, its subordinates. In a word, it makes itself *judge* and *party,* absolutely as the feudal lords behaved whom it has overthrown. As proprietor of the soil, it makes laws relating to the *products it markets,* and thus, regulates *as it pleases* the prices of the wine, the meat, and even the *bread* consumed by the people.

You see, the *noble class* has been succeeded by the *bourgeois class,* already much *more numerous* and *more useful;* it now remains to CONSTITUTE THE WORKING CLASS. It is necessary, therefore, for the workers, the enduring part of the nation, in their turn to form a vast UNION and CONSTITUTE THEMSELVES IN UNITY. Oh, then the working class will be strong, then it will be able to demand of messieurs the bourgeois both its RIGHT TO WORK and the ORGANIZATION OF LABOR; and insist on being heard.

The advantage enjoyed by all of the great *constituted* bodies is to be able to count for something in the state and thereby to *enjoy representation.* Today the ROYALIST UNION has its representative in the Chamber, its delegate before the nation to defend its interests; and that defender is the most eloquent man in France, M. Berryer. THE COLONIAL UNION has its representatives in the Chamber, its delegates before the mother country to defend its interests. Well, why then should not the working class, once it is CONSTITUTED AS A BODY, the class that by its number, and especially its importance, is certainly the equal of the royalists and the colonial proprietors, have, too, its representative in the Chamber and its delegate before the nation *to defend its interests there?*

Workers, consider this well: the first thing you must do is to have yourselves *represented before the nation.*

I said above that the WORKERS' UNION would enjoy real power, that of money. It will in fact be easy for it, out of twenty to thirty million francs, to devote 500,000 a year to the ample rapport of a defender worthy of serving its cause!

We need not doubt that there will easily be found in our beautiful France. so generous, so chivalrous, men with the devotion and talents of an O'Connel.

If, then, the WORKERS' UNION really understands its position and its true interests, its first act must be a solemn APPEAL to those men possessed of sufficient love, strength, courage, and talent to dare assume the defense of the holiest of causes, that of the workers.

Oh, who knows what France still possesses in the way of generous hearts and capable men! Who could foresee the effect of an appeal in the name of seven million workers demanding the RIGHT TO WORK?

Poor workers! Isolated, you count for nothing in the nation; but once the WORKERS' UNION IS CONSTITUTED the working class will become a powerful and respectable body; and men of the highest merit will solicit the honor of being chosen as defenders of the WORKERS' UNION. . . .

✦ Reading 12 ✦

The Communist Manifesto

Karl Marx

A spectre is haunting Europe—the spectre of Communism. All the powers of old Europe have entered into a holy alliance to exorcise this spectre: Pope and Tsar, Metternich and Guizot, French Radicals and German police-spies.

Where is the party in opposition that has not been decried as communistic by its opponents in power? Where is the Opposition that has not hurled back the branding reproach of Communism, against the more advanced opposition parties, as well as against its reactionary adversaries?

Two things result from this fact:

I. Communism is already acknowledged by all European powers to be itself a power.

II. It is high time that Communists should openly, in the face of the whole world, publish their views, their aims, their tendencies, and meet this nursery tale of the spectre of Communism with a manifesto of the party itself.

To this end, Communists of various nationalities have assembled in London, and sketched the following manifesto, to be published in the English, French, German, Italian, Flemish and Danish languages:

I: Bourgeois and Proletarians[*]

The history of all hitherto existing society[†] is the history of class struggles.

From: Karl Marx, *The Communist Manifesto,* commentary and notes by Emile Burns (New York: Avenel Books, 1982), pp. 22–59. NOTE: The footnotes were written by Engels for the English edition of 1888.

*By bourgeoisie is meant the class of modern capitalists, owners of the means of social production and employers of wage-labour. By proletariat, the class of modern wage-labourers who, having no means of production of their own, are reduced to selling their labour power in order to live.

Freeman and slave, patrician and plebeian, lord and serf, guild-master[‡] and journeyman, in a word, oppressor and oppressed, stood in constant opposition to one another, carried on an uninterrupted, now hidden, now open fight, a fight that each time ended, either in a revolutionary reconstitution of society at large, or in the common ruin of the contending classes.

In the earlier epochs of history, we find almost everywhere a complicated arrangement of society into various orders, a manifold gradation of social rank. In ancient Rome we have patricians, knights, plebeians, slaves; in the Middle Ages, feudal lords, vassals, guild-masters, journeymen, apprentices,

†That is, all *written* history. In 1847, the pre-history of society, the social organisation existing previous to recorded history, was all but unknown. Since then Haxthausen [August von, 1792–1866] discovered common ownership of land in Russia, Maurer [Georg Ludwig von] proved it to be the social foundation from which all Teutonic races started in history, and, by and by, village communities were found to be, or to have been, the primitive form of society everywhere from India to Ireland. The inner organization of this primitive communistic society was laid bare, in its typical form, by Morgan's [Henry, 1818–1881] crowning discovery of the true nature of the *gens* and its relation to the *tribe.* With the dissolution of these primæval communities, society begins to be differentiated into separate and finally antagonistic classes. I have attempted to retrace this process of dissolution in *Der Ursprung der Familie, des Privaleigenthums und des Staats,* 2nd edition, Stuttgart, 1886. (*The Origin of the Family, Private Property and the State.*)

‡Guild-master, that is a full member of a guild, a master within, not a head of a guild.

serfs; in almost all of these classes, again, subordinate gradations.

The modern bourgeois society that has sprouted from the ruins of feudal society has not done away with class antagonisms. It has but established new classes, new conditions of oppression, new forms of struggle in place of the old ones.

Our epoch, the epoch of the bourgeoisie, possesses, however, this distinctive feature: it has simplified the class antagonisms. Society as a whole is more and more splitting up into two great hostile camps, into two great classes directly facing each other—bourgeoisie and proletariat.

From the serfs of the Middle Ages sprang the chartered burghers of the earliest towns. From these burgesses the first elements of the bourgeoisie were developed.

The discovery of America, the rounding of the Cape, opened up fresh ground for the rising bourgeoisie. The East-Indian and Chinese markets, the colonisation of America, trade with the colonies, the increase in the means of exchange and in commodities generally, gave to commerce, to navigation, to industry, an impulse never before known, and thereby, to the revolutionary element in the tottering feudal society, a rapid development.

The feudal system of industry, in which industrial production was monopolised by closed guilds, now no longer sufficed for the growing wants of the new markets. The manufacturing system took its place. The guild-masters were pushed aside by the manufacturing middle class; division of labour between the different corporate guilds vanished in the face of division of labour in each single workshop.

Meantime the markets kept ever growing, the demand ever rising. Even manufacture no longer sufficed. Thereupon, steam and machinery revolutionised industrial production. The place of manufacture was taken by the giant, modern industry, the place of the industrial middle class, by industrial millionaires, the leaders of whole industrial armies, the modern bourgeois.

Modern industry has established the world market, for which the discovery of America paved the way. This market has given an immense development to commerce, to navigation, to communication by land. This development has, in its turn, reacted on the extension of industry; and in proportion as industry, commerce, navigation, railways extended, in the same proportion the bourgeoisie developed, increased its capital, and pushed into the background every class handed down from the Middle Ages.

We see, therefore, how the modern bourgeoisie is itself the product of a long course of development, of a series of revolutions in the modes of production and of exchange.

Each step in the development of the bourgeoisie was accompanied by a corresponding political advance of that class. An oppressed class under the sway of the feudal nobility, an armed and self-governing association in the mediæval commune;* here independent urban republic (as in Italy and Germany), there taxable "third estate" of the monarchy (as in France); afterwards, in the period of manufacture proper, serving either the semi-feudal or the absolute monarchy as a counterpoise against the nobility, and, in fact, corner-stone of the great monarchies in general, the bourgeoisie has at last, since the establishment of Modern Industry and of the world market, conquered for itself, in the modern representative State, exclusive political sway. The executive of the modern State is but a committee for managing the common affairs of the whole bourgeoisie.

The bourgeoisie, historically, has played a most revolutionary part.

The bourgeoisie, wherever it has got the upper hand, has put an end to all feudal, patriarchal, idyllic relations. It has pitilessly torn asunder the motley feudal ties that bound man to his "natural superiors," and has left no other nexus between man and man than naked self-interest, than callous "cash payment." It has drowned the most heavenly ecstasies of religious fervour, of chivalrous enthusiasm, of philistine sentimentalism, in the icy water of egotistical calculation. It has resolved personal worth into exchange value, and in place of the

*"Commune" was the name taken, in France, by the nascent town even before they had conquered from their feudal lords and masters, local self-government and political rights as "the Third Estate." Generally speaking, for the economical development of the bourgeoisie, England is here taken as the typical country, for its political development France.

numberless indefeasible chartered freedoms, has set up that single, unconscionable freedom—Free Trade. In one word, for exploitation, veiled by religious and political illusions, it has substituted naked, shameless, direct, brutal exploitation.

The bourgeoisie has stripped of its halo every occupation hitherto honoured and looked up to with reverent awe. It has converted the physician, the lawyer, the priest, the poet, the man of science, into its paid wage-labourers.

The bourgeoisie has torn away from the family its sentimental veil, and has reduced the family relation to a mere money relation.

The bourgeoisie has disclosed how it came to pass that the brutal display of vigour in the Middle Ages, which reactionaries so much admire, found its fitting complement in the most slothful indolence. It has been the first to show what man's activity can bring about. It has accomplished wonders far surpassing Egyptian pyramids, Roman aqueducts, and Gothic cathedrals; it has conducted expeditions that put in the shade all former Exoduses of nations and crusades.

The bourgeoisie cannot exist without constantly revolutionising the instruments of production, and thereby the relations of production, and with them the whole relations of society. Conservation of the old modes of production in unaltered form, was, on the contrary, the first condition of existence for all earlier industrial classes. Constant revolutionising of production, uninterrupted disturbance of all social conditions, everlasting uncertainty and agitation distinguish the bourgeois epoch from all earlier ones. All fixed, fast-frozen relations, with their train of ancient and venerable prejudices and opinions, are swept away, all new-formed ones become antiquated before they can ossify. All that is solid melts into air, all that is holy is profaned, and man is at last compelled to face with sober senses his real conditions of life and his relations with his kind.

The need of a constantly expanding market for its products chases the bourgeoisie over the whole surface of the globe. It must nestle everywhere, settle everywhere, establish connections everywhere.

The bourgeoisie has through its exploitation of the world market given a cosmopolitan character to production and consumption in every country. To the great chagrin of reactionaries, it has drawn from under the feet of industry the national ground on which it stood. All old-established national industries have been destroyed or are daily being destroyed. They are dislodged by new industries, whose introduction becomes a life and death question for all civilised nations, by industries that no longer work up indigenous raw material, but raw material drawn from the remotest zones; industries whose products are consumed, not only at home, but in every quarter of the globe. In place of the old wants, satisfied by the production of the country, we find new wants, requiring for their satisfaction the products of distant lands and climes. In place of the old local and national seclusion and self-sufficiency, we have intercourse in every direction, universal inter-dependence of nations. And as in material, so also in intellectual production. The intellectual creations of individual nations become common property. National one-sidedness and narrow-mindedness become more and more impossible, and from the numerous national and local literatures there arises a world literature.

The bourgeoisie, by the rapid improvement of all instruments of production, by the immensely facilitated means of communication, draws all, even the most barbarian, nations into civilisation. The cheap prices of its commodities are the heavy artillery with which it batters down all Chinese walls, with which it forces the barbarians' intensely obstinate hatred of foreigners to capitulate. It compels all nations, on pain of extinction, to adopt the bourgeois mode of production; it compels them to introduce what it calls civilisation into their midst, i.e., to become bourgeois themselves. In one word, it creates a world after its own image.

The bourgeoisie has subjected the country to the rule of the towns. It has created enormous cities, has greatly increased the urban population as compared with the rural, and has thus rescued a considerable part of the population from the idiocy of rural life. Just as it has made the country dependent on the towns, so it has made barbarian and semi-barbarian countries dependent on the civilised ones, nations of peasants on nations of bourgeois, the East on the West.

The bourgeoisie keeps more and more doing away with the scattered state of the population, of the means of production, and of property. It has agglomerated population, centralised means of production, and has concentrated property in a few hands. The necessary consequence of this was political centralisation. Independent, or but loosely connected provinces, with separate interests, laws, governments and systems of taxation, became lumped together into one nation, with one government, one code of laws, one national class interest, one frontier and one customs tariff.

The bourgeoisie, during its rule of scarce one hundred years, has created more massive and more colossal productive forces than have all preceding generations together. Subjection of nature's forces to man, machinery, application of chemistry to industry and agriculture, steam-navigation, railways, electric telegraphs, clearing of whole continents for cultivation, canalisation of rivers, whole populations conjured out of the ground—what earlier century had even a presentiment that such productive forces slumbered in the lap of social labour?

We see then; the means of production and of exchange, on whose foundation the bourgeoisie built itself up, were generated in feudal society. At a certain stage in the development of these means of production and of exchange, the conditions under which feudal society produced and exchanged, the feudal organisation of agriculture and manufacturing industry, in one word, the feudal relations of property became no longer compatible with the already developed productive forces; they became so many fetters. They had to be burst asunder; they were burst asunder.

Into their place stepped free competition, accompanied by a social and political constitution adapted to it, and by the economical and political sway of the bourgeois class.

A similar movement is going on before our own eyes. Modern bourgeois society with its relations of production, of exchange and of property, a society that has conjured up such gigantic means of production and of exchange, is like the sorcerer who is no longer able to control the powers of the nether world whom he has called up by his spells. For many a decade past the history of industry and commerce is but the history of the revolt of modern productive forces against modern conditions of production, against the property relations that are the conditions for the existence of the bourgeoisie and of its rule. It is enough to mention the commercial crises that by their periodical return put the existence of the entire bourgeois society on its trial, each time more threateningly. In these crises a great part not only of the existing products, but also of the previously created productive forces, are periodically destroyed. In these crises there breaks out an epidemic that, in all earlier epochs, would have seemed an absurdity—the epidemic of overproduction. Society suddenly finds itself put back into a state of momentary barbarism; it appears as if a famine, a universal war of devastation had cut off the supply of every means of subsistence; industry and commerce seem to be destroyed. And why? Because there is too much civilisation, too much means of subsistence, too much industry, too much commerce. The productive forces at the disposal of society no longer tend to further the development of the conditions of bourgeois property; on the contrary, they have become too powerful for these conditions, by which they are fettered, and so soon as they overcome these fetters, they bring disorder into the whole of bourgeois society, endanger the existence of bourgeois property. The conditions of bourgeois society are too narrow to comprise the wealth created by them. And how does the bourgeoisie get over these crises? On the one hand by enforced destruction of a mass of productive forces; on the other, by the conquest of new markets, and by the more thorough exploitation of the old ones. That is to say, by paving the way for more extensive and more destructive crises, and by diminishing the means whereby crises are prevented.

The weapons with which the bourgeoisie felled feudalism to the ground are now turned against the bourgeoisie itself.

But not only has the bourgeoisie forged the weapons that bring death to itself; it has also called into existence the men who are to wield those weapons—the modern working class—the proletarians.

In proportion as the bourgeoisie, i.e., capital, is developed, in the same proportion is the proletariat, the modern working class, developed—a class of labourers, who live only so long as they find work, and who find work only so long as their labour increases capital. These labourers, who must sell themselves piecemeal, are a commodity, like every other article of commerce, and are consequently exposed to all the vicissitudes of competition, to all the fluctuations of the market.

Owing to the extensive use of machinery and to division of labour, the work of the proletarians has lost all individual character, and, consequently, all charm for the workman. He becomes an appendage of the machine, and it is only the most simple, most monotonous, and most easily acquired knack, that is required of him. Hence, the cost of production of a workman is restricted, almost entirely, to the means of subsistence that he requires for his maintenance, and for the propagation of his race. But the price of a commodity, and therefore, also of labour, is equal to its cost of production. In proportion, therefore, as the repulsiveness of the work increases, the wage decreases. Nay, more, in proportion as the use of machinery and division of labour increases, in the same proportion the burden of toil also increases, whether by prolongation of the working hours, by increase of the work exacted in a given time, or by increased speed of the machinery, etc.

Modern industry has converted the little workshop of the patriarchal master into the great factory of the industrial capitalist. Masses of labourers, crowded into the factory are organised like soldiers. As privates of the industrial army they are placed under the command of a perfect hierarchy of officers and sergeants. Not only are they slaves of the bourgeois class, and of the bourgeois state; they are daily and hourly enslaved by the machine, by the over looker, and, above all, by the individual bourgeois manufacturer himself. The more openly this despotism proclaim gain to be its end and aim, the more petty, the more hateful and the more embittering it is.

The less the skill and exertion of strength implied in manual labour, in other words, the more modern industry becomes developed, the more is the labour of men superseded by that of women. Differences of age and sex have no longer any distinctive social validity for the working class. All are instruments of labour, more or less expensive to use, according to their age and sex.

No sooner is the exploitation of the labourer by the manufacturer so far at an end that he receives his wages in cash than he is set upon by the other portions of the bourgeoisie, the landlord, the shopkeeper, the pawnbroker, etc.

The lower strata of the middle class—the small tradespeople, shopkeepers, and retired tradesmen generally, the handicraftsmen and peasants—all these sink gradually into the proletariat, partly because their diminutive capital does not suffice for the scale on which modern industry is carried on, and is swamped in the competition with the large capitalists, partly because their specialised skill is rendered worthless by new methods of production. Thus the proletariat is recruited from all classes of the population.

The proletariat goes through various stages of development. With its birth begins its struggle with the bourgeoisie. At first the contest is carried on by individual labourers, then by the work people of a factory, then by the operatives of one trade, in one locality, against the individual bourgeois who directly exploits them. They direct their attacks not against the bourgeois conditions of production, but against the instruments of production themselves; they destroy imported wares that compete with their labour, they smash to pieces machinery, they set factories ablaze, they seek to restore by force the vanished status of the workman of the Middle Ages.

At this stage the labourers still form an incoherent mass scattered over the whole country, and broken up by their mutual competition. If anywhere they unite to form more compact bodies, this is not yet the consequence of their own active union, but of the union of the bourgeoisie, which class, in order to attain its own political ends, is compelled to set the whole proletariat in motion, and is moreover yet, for a time, able to do so. At this stage, therefore, the proletarians do not fight their enemies, but the enemies of their enemies, the remnants of absolute monarchy, the landowners, the non-industrial bourgeois, the petty bourgeoisie. Thus the whole historical movement is concentrated in the hands of the bourgeoisie; every victory so obtained is a victory for the bourgeoisie.

But with the development of industry the proletariat not only increases in number; it becomes concentrated in greater masses, its strength grows, and it feels that strength more. The various interests and conditions of life within the ranks of the proletariat are more and more equalised, in proportion as machinery obliterates all distinctions of labour, and nearly everywhere reduces wages to the same low level. The growing competition among the bourgeois, and the resulting commercial crises, make the wages of the workers ever more fluctuating. The unceasing improvement of machinery, ever more rapidly developing, makes their livelihood more and more precarious; the collisions between individual workmen and individual bourgeois take more and more the character of collisions between two classes. Thereupon the workers begin to form combinations (trades' unions) against the bourgeois; they club together in order to keep up the rate of wages; they found permanent associations in order to make provision beforehand for these occasional revolts. Here and there the contest breaks out into riots.

Now and then the workers are victorious, but only for a time. The real fruit of their battles lies, not in the immediate result, but in the ever expanding union of the workers. This union is helped on by the improved means of communication that are created by modern industry, and that place the workers of different localities in contact with one another. It was just this contact that was needed to centralise the numerous local struggles, all of the same character, into one national struggle between classes. But every class struggle is a political struggle. And that union, to attain which the burghers of the Middle Ages, with their miserable highways, required centuries, the modern proletarians, thanks to railways, achieve in a few years.

This organisation of the proletarians into a class, and consequently into a political party, is continually being upset again by the competition between the workers themselves. But it ever rises up again, stronger, firmer, mightier. It compels legislative recognition of particular interests of the workers, by taking advantage of the divisions among the bourgeoisie itself. Thus the ten-hours' bill in England was carried.

Altogether, collisions between the classes of the old society further in many ways the course of development of the proletariat. The bourgeoisie finds itself involved in a constant battle. At first with the aristocracy; later on, with those portions of the bourgeoisie itself, whose interests have become antagonistic to the progress of industry; at all times with the bourgeoisie of foreign countries. In all these battles it sees itself compelled to appeal to the proletariat, to ask for its help, and thus to drag it into the political arena. The bourgeoisie itself, therefore, supplies the proletariat with its own elements of political and general education, in other words, it furnishes the proletariat with weapons for fighting the bourgeoisie.

Further, as we have already seen, entire sections of the ruling classes are, by the advance of industry, precipitated into the proletariat, or are at least threatened in their conditions of existence. These also supply the proletariat with fresh elements of enlightenment and progress.

Finally, in times when the class struggle nears the decisive hour, the process of dissolution going on within the ruling class, in fact within the whole range of old society, assumes such a violent, glaring character that a small section of the ruling class cuts itself adrift and joins the revolutionary class, the class that holds the future in its hands. Just as, therefore, at an earlier period, a section of the nobility went over to the bourgeoisie, so now a portion of the bourgeoisie goes over to the proletariat, and, in particular, a portion of the bourgeois ideologists, who have raised themselves to the level of comprehending theoretically the historical movement as a whole.

Of all the classes that stand face to face with the bourgeoisie to-day, the proletariat alone is a really revolutionary class. The other classes decay and finally disappear in the face of modern industry; the proletariat is its special and essential product.

The lower middle class, the small manufacturer, the shopkeeper, the artisan, the peasant, all these fight against the bourgeoisie, to save from extinction their existence as fractions of the middle class. They are therefore not revolutionary, but conservative. Nay, more, they are reactionary, for they try to roll back the wheel of history. If by chance they are revolutionary, they are so only in view of their impending transfer into the proletariat; they thus defend not their present, but their future interests; they desert their own standpoint to place themselves at that of the proletariat.

The "dangerous class," the social scum, that passively rotting mass thrown off by the lowest layers of old society, may, here and there, be swept into the movement by a proletarian revolution; its conditions of life, however, prepare it far more for the part of a bribed tool of reactionary intrigue.

In the conditions of the proletariat, those of old society at large are already virtually swamped. The proletarian is without property; his relation to his wife and children has no longer anything in common with the bourgeois family relations; modern industrial labour, modern subjection to capital, the same in England as in France, in America as in Germany, has stripped him of every trace of national character. Law, morality, religion, are to him so many bourgeois prejudices, behind which lurk in ambush just as many bourgeois interests.

All the preceding classes that got the upper hand, sought to fortify their already acquired status by subjecting society at large to their conditions of appropriation. The proletarians cannot become masters of the productive forces of society, except by abolishing their own previous mode of appropriation, and thereby also every other previous mode of appropriation. They have nothing of their own to secure and to fortify; their mission is to destroy all previous securities for, and insurances of, individual property.

All previous historical movements were movements of minorities, or in the interest of minorities. The proletarian movement is the self-conscious, independent movement of the immense majority, in the interest of the immense majority. The proletariat, the lowest stratum of our present society, cannot stir, cannot raise itself up, without the whole superincumbent strata of official society being sprung into the air.

Though not in substance, yet in form, the struggle of the proletariat with the bourgeoisie is at first a national struggle. The proletariat of each country must, of course, first of all settle matters with its own bourgeoisie.

In depicting the most general phases of the development of the proletariat, we traced the more or less veiled civil war, raging within existing society, up to the point where that war breaks out into open revolution, and where the violent overthrow of the bourgeoisie lays the foundation for the sway of the proletariat.

Hitherto, every form of society has been based, as we have already seen, on the antagonism of oppressing and oppressed classes. But in order to oppress a class, certain conditions must be assured to it under which it can, at least, continue its slavish existence. The serf, in the period of serfdom, raised himself to membership in the commune, just as the petty bourgeois, under the yoke of feudal absolutism, managed to develop into a bourgeois. The modern labourer, on the contrary, instead of rising with the progress of industry, sinks deeper and deeper below the conditions of existence of his own class. He becomes a pauper, and pauperism develops more rapidly than population and wealth. And here it becomes evident that the bourgeoisie is unfit any longer to be the ruling class in society and to impose its conditions of existence upon society as an over-riding law. It is unfit to rule because it is incompetent to assure an existence to its slave within his slavery, because it cannot help letting him sink into such a state, that it has to feed him, instead of being fed by him. Society can no longer live under this bourgeoisie; in other words, its existence is no longer compatible with society.

The essential condition for the existence and for the sway of the bourgeois class is the formation and augmentation of capital; the condition for capital is wage-labour. Wage-labour rests exclusively on competition between the labourers. The advance of industry, whose involuntary promoter is the bourgeoisie, replaces the isolation of the labourers, due to competition, by their revolutionary combination, due to association. The development of modern industry, therefore, cuts from under its feet the very foundation on which the bourgeoisie produces and appropriates products. What the bourgeoisie therefore produces, above all, are its own grave-diggers. Its fall and the victory of the proletariat are equally inevitable.

II: Proletarians and Communists

In what relation do the Communists stand to the proletarians as a whole?

The Communists do not form a separate party opposed to other working class parties.

They have no interests separate and apart from those of the proletariat as a whole.

They do not set up any sectarian principles of their own, by which to shape and mould the proletarian movement.

The Communists are distinguished from the other working class parties by this only: 1. In the national struggles of the proletarians of the different countries, they point out and bring to the front the common interests of the entire proletariat, independently of all nationality. 2. In the various stages of development which the struggle of the working class against the bourgeoisie has to pass through, they always and everywhere represent the interests of the movement as a whole.

The Communists, therefore, are on the one hand, practically, the most advanced and resolute section of the working class parties of every country, that section which pushes forward all others; on the other hand, theoretically, they have over the great mass of the proletariat the advantage of clearly understanding the line of march, the conditions, and the ultimate general results of the proletarian movement.

The immediate aim of the Communists is the same as that of all the other proletarian parties: formation of the proletariat into a class, overthrow of the bourgeois supremacy, conquest of political power by the proletariat.

The theoretical conclusions of the Communists are in no way based on ideas or principles that have been invented, or discovered, by this or that would-be universal reformer.

They merely express, in general terms, actual relations springing from an existing class struggle, from a historical movement going on under our very eyes. The abolition of existing property relations is not at all a distinctive feature of Communism.

All property relations in the past have continually been subject to historical change consequent upon the change in historical conditions.

The French revolution, for example, abolished feudal property in favour of bourgeois property.

The distinguishing feature of Communism is not the abolition of property generally but the abolition of bourgeois property. But modern bourgeois private property is the final and most complete expression of the system of producing and appropriating products that is based on class antagonisms, on the exploitation of the many by the few.

In this sense, the theory of the Communists may be summed up in the single sentence: Abolition of private property.

We Communists have been reproached with the desire of abolishing the right of personally acquiring property as the fruit of a man's own labour, which property is alleged to be the groundwork of all personal freedom, activity and independence.

Hard-won, self-acquired, self-earned property! Do you mean the property of the petty artisan and of the small peasant, a form of property that preceded the bourgeois form? There is no need to abolish that; the development of industry has to a great extent already destroyed it, and is still destroying it daily.

Or do you mean modern bourgeois private property?

But does wage-labour create any property for the labourer? Not a bit. It creates capital, i.e., that kind of property which exploits wage-labour and which cannot increase except upon condition of begetting a new supply of wage-labour for fresh exploitation. Property, in its present form, is based on the antagonism of capital and wage-labour. Let us examine both sides of this antagonism.

To be a capitalist is to have not only a purely personal, but a social, *status* in production. Capital is a collective product, and only by the united action of many members, nay, in the last resort, only by the united action of all members of society, can it be set in motion.

Capital is therefore not a personal, it is a social power.

When, therefore, capital is converted into common property, into the property of all members of society, personal property is not thereby transformed into social property. It is only the social character of the property that is changed. It loses its class character.

Let us now take wage-labour.

The average price of wage-labour is the minimum wage, i.e., that quantum of the means of subsistence which is absolutely requisite to keep the labourer in bare existence as a labourer. What, therefore, the wage-labourer appropriates by means of his labour merely suffices to prolong and reproduce a bare existence. We by no means intend to abolish this personal appropriation of the products of labour, an appropriation that is made for the maintenance and reproduction of human life, and that leaves no surplus wherewith to command the labour of others. All that we want to do away with is the miserable character of this appropriation, under which the labourer lives merely to increase capital, and is allowed to live only in so far as the interest of the ruling class requires it.

In bourgeois society, living labour is but a means to increase accumulated labour. In Communist society, accumulated labour is but a means to widen, to enrich, to promote the existence of the labourer.

In bourgeois society, therefore, the past dominates the present; in Communist society, the present dominates the past. In bourgeois society capital is independent and has individuality, while the living person is dependent and has no individuality.

And the abolition of this state of things is called by the bourgeois abolition of individuality and freedom! And rightly so. The abolition of bourgeois individuality, bourgeois independence, and bourgeois freedom is undoubtedly aimed at.

By freedom is meant, under the present bourgeois conditions of production, free trade, free selling and buying.

But if selling and buying disappears, free selling and buying disappears also. This talk about free selling and buying, and all the other "brave words" of our bourgeoisie about freedom in general, have a meaning, if any, only in contrast with restricted selling and buying, with the fettered traders of the Middle Ages, but have no meaning when opposed to the Communist abolition of buying and selling, of the bourgeois conditions of production, and of the bourgeoisie itself.

You are horrified at our intending to do away with private property. But in your existing society, private property is already done away with for nine-tenths of the population; its existence for the few is solely due to its non-existence in the hands of those nine-tenths. You reproach us, therefore, with intending to do away with a form of property, the necessary condition for whose existence is the non-existence of any property for the immense majority of society.

In one word, you reproach us with intending to do away with your property. Precisely so; that is just what we intend.

From the moment when labour can no longer be converted into capital, money, or rent, into a social power capable of being monopolised, i.e., from the moment when individual property can no longer be transformed into bourgeois property, into capital, from that moment, you say, individuality vanishes.

You must, therefore, confess that by "individual" you mean no other person than the bourgeois, than the middle class owner of property. This person must, indeed, be swept out of the way, and made impossible.

Communism deprives no man of the power to appropriate the products of society; all that it does is to deprive him of the power to subjugate the labour of others by means of such appropriation.

It has been objected that upon the abolition of private property all work will cease, and universal laziness will overtake us.

According to this, bourgeois society ought long ago to have gone to the dogs through sheer idleness; for those of its members who work acquire nothing, and those who acquire anything do not work. The whole of this objection is but another expression of the tautology: There can no longer be any wage-labour when there is no longer any capital.

All objections urged against the Communistic mode of producing and appropriating material products have, in the same way, been urged against the Communistic modes of producing and appropriating intellectual products. Just as to the bourgeois the disappearance of class property is the disappearance of production itself so the disappearance of class culture is to him identical with the disappearance of all culture.

That culture, the loss of which he laments, is, for the enormous majority, a mere training to act as a machine.

But don't wrangle with us so long as you apply, to our intended abolition of bourgeois property, the standard of your bourgeois notions of freedom, culture, law, etc. Your very ideas are but the outgrowth of the conditions of your bourgeois production and bourgeois property, just as your jurisprudence is but the will of your class made into a law for all, a will whose essential character and direction are determined by the economical conditions of existence of your class.

The selfish misconception that induces you to transform into eternal laws of nature and of reason, the social forms springing from your present mode of production and form of property—historical relations that rise and disappear in the progress of production—this misconception you share with every ruling class that has preceded you. What you see clearly in the case of ancient property, what you admit in the case of feudal property, you are of course forbidden to admit in the case of your own bourgeois form of property.

Abolition of the family! Even the most radical flare up at this infamous proposal of the Communists.

On what foundation is the present family, the bourgeois family, based? On capital, on private gain. In its completely developed form this family exists only among the bourgeoisie. But this state of things finds its complement in the practical absence of the family among the proletarians, and in public prostitution.

The bourgeois family will vanish as a matter of course when its complement vanishes, and both will vanish with the vanishing of capital.

Do you charge us with wanting to stop the exploitation of children by their parents? To this crime we plead guilty.

But, you will say, we destroy the most hallowed of relations, when we replace home education by social.

And your education! Is not that also social, and determined by the social conditions under which you educate, by the intervention, direct or indirect, of society, by means of schools, etc.? The Communists have not invented the intervention of society in education; they do but seek to alter the character of that intervention, and to rescue education from the influence of the ruling class.

The bourgeois claptrap about the family and education, about the hallowed correlation of parent and child, becomes all the more disgusting the more, by the action of modern industry, all family ties among the proletarians are torn asunder, and their children transformed into simple articles of commerce and instruments of labour.

But you Communists would introduce community of women, screams the whole bourgeoisie in chorus.

The bourgeois sees in his wife a mere instrument of production. He hears that the instruments of production are to be exploited in common, and, naturally, can come to no other conclusion than that the lot of being common to all will likewise fall to the women.

He has not even a suspicion that the real point aimed at is to do away with the status of women as mere instruments of production.

For the rest, nothing is more ridiculous than the virtuous indignation of our bourgeois at the community of women which, they pretend, is to be openly and officially established by the Communists. The Communists have no need to introduce community of women; it has existed almost from time immemorial.

Our bourgeois, not content with having the wives and daughters of their proletarians at their disposal, not to speak of common prostitutes, take the greatest pleasure in seducing each other's wives.

Bourgeois marriage is in reality a system of wives in common and thus, at the most, what the Communists might possibly be reproached with is that they desire to introduce, in substitution for a hypocritically concealed, an openly legalised community of women. For the rest, it is self-evident that the abolition of the present system of production must bring with it the abolition of the community of women springing from that system, i.e., of prostitution both public and private.

The Communists are further reproached with desiring to abolish countries and nationality.

The working men have no country. We cannot take from them what they have not got. Since the proletariat must first of all acquire political supremacy, must rise to be the leading class of the nation, must constitute itself *the* nation, it is, so far, itself national, though not in the bourgeois sense of the word.

National differences and antagonisms between peoples are daily more and more vanishing, owing to the development of the bourgeoisie, to freedom of commerce, to the world market, to uniformity in mode of production and in the conditions of life corresponding thereto.

The supremacy of the proletariat will cause them to vanish still faster. United action of the leading civilised countries at least is one of the first conditions for the emancipation of the proletariat.

In proportion as the exploitation of one individual by another is put an end to, the exploitation of one nation by another will also be put an end to. In proportion as the antagonism between classes within the nation vanishes, the hostility of one nation to another will come to an end.

The charges against Communism made from a religious, a philosophical and, generally, from an ideological standpoint are not deserving of serious examination.

Does it require deep intuition to comprehend that man's ideas, views, and conceptions, in one word, man's consciousness, changes with every change in the conditions of his material existence, in his social relations and in his social life?

What else does the history of ideas prove than that intellectual production changes its character in proportion as material production is changed? The ruling ideas of each age have ever been the ideas of its ruling class.

When people speak of ideas that revolutionise society, they do but express the fact that within the old society the elements of a new one have been created, and that the dissolution of the old ideas keeps even pace with the dissolution of the old conditions of existence.

When the ancient world was in its last throes, the ancient religions were overcome by Christianity. When Christian ideas succumbed in the eighteenth century to rationalist ideas, feudal society fought its death-battle with the then revolutionary bourgeoisie. The ideas of religious liberty and freedom of conscience merely gave expression to the sway of free competition within the domain of knowledge.

"Undoubtedly," it will be said, "religious, moral, philosophical and juridical ideas have been modified in the course of historical development. But religion, morality, philosophy, political science, and law constantly survived this change."

"There are, besides, eternal truths, such as Freedom, Justice, etc., that are common to all states of society. But Communism abolishes eternal truths, it abolishes all religion, and all morality, instead of constituting them on a new basis; it therefore acts in contradiction to all past historical experience."

What does this accusation reduce itself to? The history of all past society has consisted in the development of class antagonisms, antagonisms that assumed different forms at different epochs.

But whatever form they may have taken, one fact is common to all past ages, viz., the exploitation of one part of society by the other. No wonder, then, that the social consciousness of past ages, despite all the multiplicity and variety it displays, moves within certain common forms, or general ideas, which cannot completely vanish except with the total disappearance of class antagonisms.

The Communist revolution is the most radical rupture with traditional property relations; no wonder that its development involves the most radical rupture with traditional ideas.

But let us have done with the bourgeois objections to Communism.

We have seen above that the first step in the revolution by the working class is to raise the proletariat to the position of ruling class, to win the battle of democracy.

The proletariat will use its political supremacy to wrest, by degrees, all capital from the bourgeoisie, to centralise all instruments of production in the hands of the State, i.e., of the proletariat organised as the ruling class; and to increase the total of productive forces as rapidly as possible.

Of course, in the beginning, this cannot be effected except by means of despotic inroads on the rights of property, and on the conditions of bourgeois production; by means of measures, therefore, which appear economically insufficient and untenable, but which, in the course of the movement, outstrip themselves, necessitate further inroads upon the old social order, and are unavoidable as a means of entirely revolutionising the mode of production.

These measures will, of course, be different in different countries.

Nevertheless in the most advanced countries, the following will be pretty generally applicable:

1. Abolition of property in land and application of all rents of land to public purposes.
2. A heavy progressive or graduated income tax.
3. Abolition of all right of inheritance.
4. Confiscation of the property of all emigrants and rebels.
5. Centralisation of credit in the hands of the State, by means of a national bank with State capital and an exclusive monopoly.
6. Centralisation of the means of communication and transport in the hands of the State.
7. Extension of factories and instruments of production owned by the State; the bringing into cultivation of waste lands, and the improvement of the soil generally in accordance with a common plan.
8. Equal obligation of all to work. Establishment of industrial armies, especially for agriculture.
9. Combination of agriculture with manufacturing industries; gradual abolition of the distinction between town and country, by a more equable distribution of the population over the country.
10. Free education for all children in public schools. Abolition of children's factory labour in its

present form. Combination of education with industrial production, etc.

When, in the course of development, class distinctions have disappeared, and all production has been concentrated in the hands of a vast association of the whole nation, the public power will lose its political character. Political power, properly so called, is merely the organised power of one class for oppressing another. If the proletariat during its contest with the bourgeoisie is compelled, by the force of circumstances, to organise itself as a class; if, by means of a revolution, it makes itself the ruling class, and, as such, swoops away by force the old conditions of production, then it will, along with these conditions, have swept away the conditions for the existence of class antagonisms and or classes generally, and will thereby have abolished its own supremacy as a class.

In place of the old bourgeois society, with its classes and class antagonisms, we shall have an association in which the free development of each is the condition for the free development of all.

III: Socialist and Communist Literature

1. Reactionary Socialism

a. Feudal Socialism

Owing to their historical position, it became the vocation of the aristocracies of France and England to write pamphlets against modern bourgeois society. In the French revolution of July 1830, and in the English reform agitation, these aristocracies again succumbed to the hateful upstart. Thenceforth, a serious political struggle was altogether out of the question. A literary battle alone remained possible. But even in the domain of literature the old cries of the restoration period* had become impossible.

In order to arouse sympathy, the aristocracy was obliged to lose sight, apparently, of its own interests, and to formulate its indictment against the bourgeoisie in the interest of the exploited working class alone. Thus the aristocracy took their revenge by singing lampoons on their new master, and whispering in his ears sinister prophecies of coming catastrophe.

In this way arose feudal socialism: half lamentation, half lampoon; half echo of the past, half menace of the future; at times, by its bitter, witty and incisive criticism, striking the bourgeoisie to the very heart's core, but always ludicrous in its effect, through total incapacity to comprehend the march of modern history.

The aristocracy, in order to rally the people to them, waved the proletarian alms-bag in front for a banner. But the people so often as it joined them saw on their hindquarters the old feudal coats of arms and deserted with loud and irreverent laughter.

One section of the French Legitimists and "Young England," exhibited this spectacle.

In pointing out that their mode of exploitation was different to that of the bourgeoisie, the feudalists forget that they exploited under circumstances and conditions that were quite different, and that are now antiquated. In showing that, under their rule, the modern proletariat never existed, they forget that the modern bourgeoisie is the necessary offspring of their own form of society.

For the rest, so little do they conceal the reactionary character of their criticism that their chief accusation against the bourgeoisie amounts to this, that under the bourgeois regime a class is being developed which is destined to cut up root and branch the old order of society.

What they upbraid the bourgeoisie with is not so much that it creates a proletariat as that it creates a *revolutionary* proletariat.

In political practice, therefore, they join in all coercive measures against the working class; and in ordinary life, despite their high-faluting phrases, they stoop to pick up the golden apples dropped from the tree of industry, and to barter truth, love, and honour for traffic in wool, beetroot-sugar, and potato spirits.*

*Not the English Restoration, 1660 to 1689, but the French Restoration, 1814 to 1830.

*This applies chiefly to Germany where the landed aristocracy and squirearchy have large portions of their estates cultivated for their own account by stewards, and are, moreover, extensive beetroot-sugar manufacturers and distillers of potato spirits. The wealthier British aristocracy are, as yet, rather above that; but they, too, know how to make up for declining rents by lending their names to floaters of more or less shady joint-stock companies.

As the parson has ever gone hand in hand with the land lord, so has Clerical Socialism with Feudal Socialism.

Nothing is easier than to give Christian asceticism a Socialist tinge. Has not Christianity declaimed against private property, against marriage, against the State? Has it not preached in the place of these, charity and poverty, celibacy and mortification of the flesh, monastic life and Mother Church? Christian Socialism is but the holy water with which the priest consecrates the heart-burnings of the aristocrat.

b. Petty Bourgeois Socialism

The feudal aristocracy was not the only class that was ruined by the bourgeoisie, not the only class whose conditions of existence pined and perished in the atmosphere of modern bourgeois society. The mediæval burgesses and the small peasant proprietors were the precursors of the modern bourgeoisie. In those countries which are but little developed, industrially and commercially, these two classes still vegetate side by side with the rising bourgeoisie.

In countries where modern civilisation has become fully developed, a new class of petty bourgeois has been formed fluctuating between proletariat and bourgeoisie, and ever renewing itself as a supplementary part of bourgeois society. The individual members of this class, however, are being constantly hurled down into the proletariat by the action of competition, and, as modern industry develops, they even see the moment approaching when they will completely disappear as an independent section of modern society, to be replaced, in manufactures, agriculture and commerce, by overlookers, bailiffs and shopmen.

In countries like France, where the peasants constitute far more than half of the population, it was natural that writers who sided with the proletariat against the bourgeoisie should use, in their criticism of the bourgeois régime the standard of the peasant and petty bourgeois, and from the standpoint of these intermediate classes should take up the cudgels for the working class. Thus arose petty bourgeois Socialism. Sismondi was the head of this school, not only in France but also in England.

This school of Socialism dissected with great acuteness the contradictions in the conditions of modern production. It laid bare the hypocritical apologies of economists. It proved, incontrovertibly, the disastrous effects of machinery and division of labour; the concentration of capital and land in a few hands; overproduction and crises; it pointed out the inevitable ruin of the petty bourgeois and peasant, the misery of the proletariat, the anarchy in production, the crying inequalities in the distribution of wealth, the industrial war of extermination between nations, the dissolution of old moral bonds, of the old family relations, of the old nationalities.

In its positive aims, however, this form of Socialism aspires either to restoring the old means of production and of exchange, and with them the old property relations, and the old society, or to cramping the modern means of production and of exchange within the framework of the old property relations that have been, and were bound to be exploded by those means. In either case, it is both reactionary and Utopian.

Its last words are: Corporate guilds for manufacture; patriarchal relations in agriculture.

Ultimately, when stubborn historical facts had dispersed all intoxicating effects of self-deception, this form of Socialism ended in a miserable fit of the blues.

c. German or "True" Socialism

The Socialist and Communist literature of France, a literature that originated under the pressure of a bourgeoisie in power, and that was the expression of the struggle against this power, was introduced into Germany at a time when the bourgeoisie in that country had just begun its contest with feudal absolutism.

German philosophers, would-be philosophers, and men of letters eagerly seized on this literature, only forgetting that when these writings immigrated from France into Germany, French social conditions had not immigrated along with them. In contact with German social conditions, this French literature lost all its immediate practical significance, and assumed a purely literary aspect. Thus, to the German philosophers of the eighteenth century, the demands of the "Practical Reason" in general—and the utterance of the will of the first French Revolution were nothing more than the demands of revolutionary French bourgeoisie—signified in their eyes the laws of pure will, of will as it was bound to be, of true human will generally.

The work of the German *literati* consisted solely in bringing the new French ideas into harmony with their ancient philosophical conscience, or, rather, in annexing the French ideas without deserting their own philosophic point of view.

This annexation took place in the same way in which a foreign language is appropriated, namely, by translation.

It is well known how the monks wrote silly lives of Catholic saints *over* the manuscripts on which the classical works of ancient heathendom had been written. The German *literati* reversed this process with the profane French literature. They wrote their philosophical nonsense beneath the French original. For instance, beneath the French criticism of the economic functions of money, they wrote "alienation of humanity," and beneath the French criticism of the bourgeois State they wrote, "dethronement of the category of the general," and so forth.

The introduction of these philosophical phrases at the back of the French historical criticisms they dubbed "Philosophy of Action," "True Socialism," "German Science of Socialism," "Philosophical Foundation of Socialism," and so on.

The French Socialist and Communist literature was thus completely emasculated. And, since it ceased in the hands of the German to express the struggle of one class with the other, he felt conscious of having overcome "French onesidedness" and of representing, not true requirements, but the requirements of truth; not the interests of the proletariat, but the interests of human nature, of man in general, who belongs to no class, has no reality, who exists only in the misty realm of philosophical phantasy.

This German Socialism, which took its schoolboy task so seriously and solemnly, and extolled its poor stock-in-trade in such mountebank fashion, meanwhile gradually lost its pedantic innocence.

The fight of the German and especially of the Prussian bourgeoisie against feudal aristocracy and absolute monarchy, in other words, the liberal movement, became more earnest.

By this, the long-wished-for opportunity was offered to "True" Socialism of confronting the political movement with the Socialist demands, of hurling the traditional anathemas against liberalism, against representative government, against bourgeois competition, bourgeois freedom of the press, bourgeois legislation, bourgeois liberty and equality, and of preaching to the masses that they had nothing to gain, and everything to lose, by this bourgeois movement. German Socialism forgot, in the nick of time, that the French criticism, whose silly echo it was, presupposed the existence of modern bourgeois society, with its corresponding economic conditions of existence, and the political constitution adapted thereto, the very things whose attainment was the object of the pending struggle in Germany.

To the absolute governments, with their following of parsons, professors, country squires and officials, it served as a welcome scarecrow against the threatening bourgeoisie.

It was a sweet finish after the bitter pills of floggings and bullets with which these same governments, just at that time, dosed the German working class risings.

While this "True" Socialism thus served the governments as a weapon for fighting the German bourgeoisie, it, at the same time, directly represented a reactionary interest, the interest of the German Philistines. In Germany the petty bourgeois class, a relic of the sixteenth century, and since then constantly cropping up again under various forms, is the real social basis of the existing state of things.

To preserve this class is to preserve the existing state of things in Germany. The industrial and political supremacy of the bourgeoisie threatens it with certain destruction— on the one hand, from the concentration of capital; on the other, from the rise of a revolutionary proletariat. "True" Socialism appeared to kill these two birds with one stone. It spread like an epidemic.

The robe of speculative cobwebs, embroidered with flowers of rhetoric, steeped in the dew of sickly sentiment, this transcendental robe in which the German Socialists wrapped their sorry "eternal truths," all skin and bone, served to wonderfully increase the sale of their goods amongst such a public.

And on its part, German Socialism recognised, more and more, its own calling as the bombastic representative of the petty bourgeois Philistine.

It proclaimed the German nation to be the model nation, and the German petty Philistine to be the typical man. To every villainous meanness of this model man it gave a hidden, higher, socialistic interpretation, the exact contrary of its real character. It went to the extreme length of directly opposing the "brutally destructive" tendency of Communism, and of proclaiming its supreme and impartial contempt of all class struggles. With very few exceptions, all the so-called Socialist and Communist publications that now (1847) circulate in Germany belong to the domain of this foul and enervating literature.

2. Conservative or Bourgeois Socialism

A part of the bourgeoisie is desirous of redressing social grievances, in order to secure the continued existence of bourgeois society.

To this section belong economists, philanthropists, humanitarians, improvers of the condition of the working class, organisers of charity, members of societies for the prevention of cruelty to animals, temperance fanatics, hole-and-corner reformers of every imaginable kind. This form of Socialism has, moreover, been worked out into complete systems.

We may cite Proudhon's *Philosophie de la Misère* (Philosophy of Poverty) as an example of this form.

The socialistic bourgeois want all the advantages of modern social conditions without the struggles and dangers necessarily resulting therefrom. They desire the existing state of society minus its revolutionary and disintegrating elements. They wish for a bourgeoisie without a proletariat. The bourgeoisie naturally conceives the world in which it is supreme to be the best; and bourgeois Socialism develops this comfortable conception into various more or less complete systems. In requiring the proletariat to carry out such a system, and thereby to march straightway into the social New Jerusalem, it but requires in reality that the proletariat should remain within the bounds of existing society, but should cast away all its hateful ideas concerning the bourgeoisie.

A second and more practical, but less systematic, form of this Socialism sought to depreciate every revolutionary movement in the eyes of the working class, by showing that no mere political reform, but only a change in the material conditions of existence, in economical relations, could be of any advantage to them. By changes in the material conditions of existence, this form of Socialism, however, by no means understands abolition of the bourgeois relations of production, an abolition that can be effected only by a revolution, but administrative reforms, based on the continued existence of these relations; reforms, therefore, that in no respect affect the relations between capital and labour, but, at the best, lessen the cost, and simplify the administrative work of bourgeois government.

Bourgeois Socialism attains adequate expression, when, and only when, it becomes a mere figure of speech.

Free trade: for the benefit of the working class. Protective duties: for the benefit of the working class. Prison reform: for the benefit of the working class. This is the last word and the only seriously meant word of bourgeois Socialism.

It is summed up in the phrase: the bourgeois is a bourgeois—for the benefit of the working class.

3. Critical-Utopian Socialism and Communism

We do not here refer to that literature which, in every great modern revolution, has always given voice to the demands of the proletariat, such as the writings of Babeuf and others.

The first direct attempts of the proletariat to attain its own ends, made in times of universal excitement, when feudal society was being overthrown—these attempts necessarily failed, owing to the then undeveloped state of the proletariat, as well as to the absence of the economic conditions for its emancipation, conditions that had yet to be produced, and could be produced by the impending bourgeois epoch alone. The revolutionary literature that accompanied these first movements of the proletariat had necessarily a reactionary character. It inculcated universal asceticism and social levelling in its crudest form.

The Socialist and Communist systems properly so called, those of St. Simon, Fourier, Owen and others, spring into existence in the early undeveloped period, described above, of the struggle between proletariat and bourgeoisie (see Section I. Bourgeois and Proletarians).

The founders of these systems see, indeed, the class antagonisms, as well as the action of the decomposing elements in the prevailing form of society. But the proletariat, as yet in its infancy, offers to them the spectacle of a class without any historical initiative or any independent political movement.

Since the development of class antagonism keeps even pace with the development of industry, the economic situation, as they find it, does not as yet offer to them the material conditions for the emancipation of the proletariat. They therefore search after a new social science, after new social laws, that are to create these conditions.

Historical action is to yield to their personal inventive action; historically created conditions of emancipation to phantastic ones; and the gradual, spontaneous class organisation of the proletariat to an organisation of society specially contrived by these inventors. Future history resolves itself, in their eyes, into the propaganda and the practical carrying out of their social plans.

In the formation of their plans they are conscious of caring chiefly for the interests of the working class, as being the most suffering class. Only from the point of view of being the most suffering class does the proletariat exist for them.

The undeveloped state of the class struggle, as well as their own surroundings, causes Socialists of this kind to consider themselves far superior to all class antagonisms. They want to improve the condition of every member of society, even that of the most favoured. Hence, they habitually appeal to society at large, without distinction of class; nay, by preference, to the ruling class. For how can people, when once they understand their system, fail to see in it the best possible plan of the best possible state of society?

Hence, they reject all political, and especially all revolutionary action; they wish to attain their ends by peaceful means, and endeavour, by small experiments, necessarily doomed to failure, and by the force of example, to pave the way for the new social gospel.

Such phantastic pictures of future society, painted at a time when the proletariat is still in a very undeveloped state and has but a phantastic conception of its own position, correspond with the first instinctive yearnings of that class for a general reconstruction of society.

But these Socialist and Communist publications contain also a critical element. They attack every principle of existing society. Hence they are full of the most valuable materials for the enlightenment of the working class. The practical measures proposed in them—such as the abolition of the distinction between town and country, of the family, of the carrying on of industries for the account of private individuals, and of the wage-system, the proclamation of social harmony, the conversion of the functions of the State into a mere superintendence of production—all these proposals point solely to the disappearance of class antagonisms which were, at that time, only just cropping up, and which, in these publications, are recognised in their earliest, indistinct and undefined forms only. These proposals, therefore, are of a purely Utopian character.

The significance of Critical-Utopian Socialism and Communism bears an inverse relation to historical development. In proportion as the modern class struggle develops and takes definite shape, this phantastic standing apart from the contest, these phantastic attacks on it, lose all practical value and all theoretical justification. Therefore, although the originators of these systems were, in many respects, revolutionary, their disciples have, in every case, formed mere reactionary sects. They hold fast by the original views of their masters, in opposition to the progressive historical development of the proletariat. They, therefore, endeavour, and that consistently, to deaden the class struggle and to reconcile the class antagonisms. They still dream of experimental realization of their social Utopias, of founding isolated *phalansteres,* of establishing "Home Colonies," or setting up a "Little Icaria"*—pocket editions of the New Jerusalem—and to realise all these castles in the air, they are compelled to appeal to the feelings and purses of the bourgeois. By degrees they sink into the category of the reactionary conservative Socialists depicted above, differing from these only by more systematic pedantry, and by their fanatical and superstitious belief in the miraculous effects of their social science.

They, therefore, violently oppose all political action on the part of the working class; such action, according to them, can only result from blind unbelief in the new gospel.

The Owenites in England, and the Fourierists in France, respectively, oppose the Chartists and the *Reformistes.*

**Phalansteres* were socialist colonies on the plan of Charles Fourier; Icaria was the name given by Cabet to his Utopia and, later on, to his American Communist colony.

IV: Position of the Communists in Relation to the Various Existing Opposition Parties

Section II has made clear the relations of the Communists to the existing working class parties, such as the Chartists in England and the Agrarian Reformers in America.

The Communists fight for the attainment of the immediate aims, for the enforcement of the momentary interests of the working class; but in the movement of the present, they also represent and take care of the future of that movement. In France the Communists ally themselves with the Social-Democrats,* against the conservative and radical bourgeoisie, reserving, however, the right to take up a critical position in regard to phrases and illusions traditionally handed down from the great Revolution.

In Switzerland they support the Radicals, without losing sight of the fact that this party consists of antagonistic elements, partly of Democratic Socialists, in the French sense, partly of radical bourgeois.

In Poland they support the party that insists on an agrarian revolution as the prime condition for national emancipation, that party which fomented the insurrection of Cracow in 1846.

In Germany they fight with the bourgeoisie whenever it acts in a revolutionary way, against the absolute monarchy, the feudal squirearchy, and the petty bourgeoisie.

But they never cease, for a single instant, to instil into the working class the clearest possible recognition of the hostile antagonism between bourgeoisie and proletariat, in order that the German workers may straightway use, as so many weapons against the bourgeoisie, the social and political conditions that the bourgeoisie must necessarily introduce along with its supremacy, and in order that, after the fall of the reactionary classes in Germany, the fight against the bourgeoisie itself may immediately begin.

The Communists turn their attention chiefly to Germany, because that country is on the eve of a bourgeois revolution that is bound to be carried out under more advanced conditions of European civilisation and with a much more developed proletariat than that of England was in the seventeenth, and of France in the eighteenth century, and because the bourgeois revolution in Germany will be but the prelude to an immediately following proletarian revolution.

In short, the Communists everywhere support every revolutionary movement against the existing social and political order of things.

In all these movements they bring to the front, as the leading question in each, the property question, no matter what its degree of development at the time.

Finally, they labour everywhere for the union and agreement of the democratic parties of all countries.

The Communists disdain to conceal their views and aims. They openly declare that their ends can be attained only by the forcible overthrow of all existing social conditions. Let the ruling classes tremble at a Communist revolution. The proletarians have nothing to lose but their chains. They have a world to win.

Working men of all countries, unite!

*The party then represented in Parliament by Ledru-Rollin, in literature by Louis Blanc [1811–1882], in the daily press by the *Reform*. The name of Social-Democracy signifies, with these its inventors, a section of the Democratic or Republican Party more or less tinged with Socialism.

✦ Reading 13 ✦

Mary Barton: A Tale of Manchester Life

Elizabeth Gaskell

The Barton family are textile workers in Manchester mills. Tom Barton, whose wife has died, is determined that their daughter Mary will never toil in the mills. Meanwhile, the mill owner's son plots to seduce the innocent Mary. These characters' interactions disclose the startling differences in their lives.

'How little can the rich man know
Of what the poor man feels,
When Want, like some dark demon foe,
Nearer and nearer steals!
He never tramp'd the weary round,
A stroke of work to gain,
And sicken'd at the dreaded sound
Telling him 'twas in vain.
Foot-sore, heart-sore, he never came
Back through the winter's wind,
To a dark cellar, there no flame,
No light, no food, to find.
He never saw his darlings lie
Shivering, the grass their bed;
He never heard that maddening cry,
"Daddy, a bid of bread!"'

Manchester Song

John Barton was not far wrong in his idea that the Messrs Carson would not be over much grieved for the consequences of the fire in their mill. They were well insured; the machinery lacked the improvements of late years, and worked but poorly in comparison with that which might now be procured. Above all, trade was very slack; cottons could find no market, and goods lay packed and piled in many a warehouse. The mills were merely worked to keep the machinery, human and metal, in some kind of order and readiness for better times. So this was an excellent time, Messrs Carson thought, for refitting their factory with first-rate improvements, for which the insurance money would amply pay. They were in no hurry about the business, however. The weekly drain of wages given for labour, useless in the present state of the market, was stopped. The partners had more leisure than they had known for years; and promised wives and daughters all manner of pleasant excursions, as soon as the weather should become more genial. It was a pleasant thing to be able to lounge over breakfast with a review or newspaper in hand; to have time for becoming acquainted with agreeable and accomplished daughters, on whose education no money had been spared, but whose fathers, shut up during a long day with calicoes and accounts, had so seldom had leisure to enjoy their daughters' talents. There were happy family evenings, now that the men of business had time for domestic enjoyments. There is another side to the picture. There were homes over which Carsons' fire threw a deep, terrible gloom; the homes of those who would fain work, and no man gave unto them—the homes of those to whom leisure was a curse. There, the family music was hungry wails, when week after week passed by, and there was no work to be had, and consequently no wages to pay for the bread the children cried aloud for in their young impatience of suffering. There was no breakfast to lounge over; their lounge was taken in bed, to try and keep warmth in them that bitter March weather, and, by being quiet, to deaden the gnawing wolf within. Many a penny that would have gone little way enough in oatmeal or potatoes, bought

From: Elizabeth Gaskell, *Mary Barton: A Tale of Manchester Life* (London: Penguin, 1970), pp. 95–113.

opium to still the hungry little ones, and make them forget their uneasiness in heavy troubled sleep. It was mothers mercy. The evil and the good of our nature came out strongly then. There were desperate fathers; there were bitter-tongued mothers (O God! what wonder!); there were reckless children; the very closest bonds of nature were snapt in that time of trial and distress. There was Faith such as the rich can never imagine on earth; there was 'Love strong as death'; and self-denial, among rude, coarse men, akin to that of Sir Philip Sidney's most glorious deed. The vices of the poor sometimes astound us *here;* but when the secrets of all hearts shall be made known, their virtues will astound us in far greater degree. Of this I am certain.

As the cold bleak spring came on (spring, in name alone), and consequently as trade continued dead, other mills shortened hours, turned off hands, and finally stopped work altogether.

Barton worked short hours; Wilson, of course, being a hand in Carsons' factory, had no work at all. But his son, working at an engineer's, and a steady man, obtained wages enough to maintain all the family in a careful way. Still it preyed on Wilson's mind to be so long indebted to his son. He was out of spirits and depressed. Barton was morose, and soured towards mankind as a body, and the rich in particular. One evening, when the clear light at six o'clock contrasted strangely with the Christmas cold, and when the bitter wind piped down every entry, and through every cranny, Barton sat brooding over his stinted fire, and listening for Mary's step, in unacknowledged trust that her presence would cheer him. The door was opened, and Wilson came breathless in.

'You've not got a bit o' money by you, Barton?' asked he.

'Not I; who has now, I'd like to know. Whatten you want it for?'

'I donnot want it for mysel, tho' we've none to spare. But don ye know Ben Davenport as worked at Carsons'? He's down wi' the fever, and ne'er a stick o' fire, nor a cowd potato in the house.'

'I han got no money, I tell ye,' said Barton. Wilson looked disappointed. Barton tried not to be interested, but he could not help it in spite of his gruffness. He rose, and went to the cupboard (his wife's pride long ago). There lay the remains of his dinner, hastily put there ready for supper. Brad, and a slice of cold fat boiled bacon. He wrapped them in his handkerchief, put them in the crown of his hat, and said—'Come, let's be going.'

'Going—art thou going to work this time o' day?'

'No, stupid, to be sure not. Going to see the fellow thou spoke on.' So they put on their hats and set out. On the way Wilson said Davenport was a good fellow, though too much of the Methodee; that his children were too young to work, but not too young to be cold and hungry; that they had sunk lower and lower, and pawned thing after thing, and that now they lived in a cellar in Berry Street, off Store Street. Barton growled inarticulate words of no benevolent import to a large class of mankind, and so they went along till they arrived in Berry Street. It was unpaved; and down the middle a gutter forced its way, every now and then forming pools in the holes with which the street abounded. Never was the Old Edinburgh cry of 'Gardez l'eau,' more necessary than in this street. As they passed, women from their doors tossed household slops of *every* description into the gutter; they ran into the next pool, which overflowed and stagnated. Heaps of ashes were the stepping-stones, on which the passer-by, who cared in the least for cleanliness, took care not to put his foot. Our friends were not dainty, but even they picked their way till they got to some steps leading down into a small area, where a person standing would have his head about one foot below the level of the street, and might at the same time, without the least motion of his body, touch the window of the cellar and the damp muddy wall right opposite. You went down one step even from the foul area into the cellar in which a family of human beings lived. It was very dark inside. The window-panes were many of them broken and stuffed with rags, which was reason enough for the dusky light that pervaded the place even at mid-day. After the account I have given of the state of the street, no one can be surprised that on going into the cellar inhabited by Davenport, the smell was so foetid as almost to knock the two men down. Quickly recovering themselves, as those inured to such things do, they began to penetrate the thick darkness of the place, and to see three or four little children rolling on the damp, nay wet, brick floor, through which the stagnant, filthy moisture of the street oozed up; the fire-place was empty and black; the wife sat on her husband's chair, and cried in the dank loneliness.

'See, missis, I'm back again.—Hold your noise, children, and don't mither your mammy for bread, here's a chap as has got some for you.'

In that dim light, which was darkness to strangers, they clustered round Barton, and tore from him the food he had brought with him. It was a large hunch of bread, but it had vanished in an instant.

'We mun do summut for 'em,' said he to Wilson. 'Yo stop here, and I'll be back in half-an-hour.'

So he strode, and ran, and hurried home. He emptied into the ever-useful pocket-handkerchief the little meal remaining in the mug. Mary would have her tea at Miss Simmonds'; her food for the day was safe. Then he went up-stairs for his better coat, and his one, gay, red-and-yellow silk pocket-handkerchief—his jewels, his plate, his valuables, these were. He went to the pawn-shop; he pawned them for five shillings; he stopped not, nor stayed, till he was once more in London Road, within five minutes' walk of Berry Street—then he loitered in his gait, in order to discover the shops he wanted. He bought meat, and a loaf of bread, candles, chips, and from a little retail yard he purchased a couple of hundredweights of coals. Some money, yet remained—all destined for them, but he did not yet know how best to spend it. Food, light, and warmth, he had instantly seen were necessary; for luxuries he would wait. Wilson's eyes filled with tears when he saw Barton enter with his purchases. He understood it all, and longed to be once more in work, that he might help in some of these material ways, without feeling that he was using his son's money. But though 'silver and gold he had none,' he gave heart-service, and love-works of far more value. Nor was John Barton behind in these. 'The fever' was (as it usually is in Manchester), of a low, putrid, typhoid kind; brought on by miserable living, filthy neighbourhood, and great depression of mind and body. It is virulent, malignant, and highly infectious. But the poor are fatalists with regard to infection; and well for them it is so, for in their crowded dwellings no invalid can be isolated. Wilson asked Barton if he thought he should catch it, and was laughed at for his idea.

The two men, rough, tender nurses as they were, lighted the fire, which smoked and puffed into the room as if it did not know the way up the damp, unused chimney. The very smoke seemed purifying and healthy in the thick clammy air. The children clamoured again for bread; but this time Barton took a piece first to the poor, helpless, hopeless woman, who still sat by the side of her husband, listening to his anxious miserable mutterings. She took the bread, when it was put into her hand, and broke a bit, but could not eat. She was past hunger. She fell down on the floor with a heavy unresisting bang. The men looked puzzled. 'She's well-nigh clemmed,' said Barton. 'Folk do say one mustn't give clemmed people much to eat; but, bless us, she'll eat naught.'

'I'll tell you what I'll do,' said Wilson. I'll take these two big lads, as does nought but fight, home to my missis's for to-night, and I will get a jug o' tea. Them women always does best with tea and such like slop.'

So Barton was now left alone with a little child, crying (when it had done eating) for mammy; with a fainting, dead-like woman; and with the sick man, whose mutterings were rising up to screams and shrieks of agonized anxiety. He carried the woman to the fire, and chafed her hands. He looked around for something to raise her head. There was literally nothing but some loose bricks. However, those he got; and taking off his coat he covered them with it as well as he could. He pulled her feet to the fire, which now began to emit some faint heat. He looked round for water, but the poor woman had been too weak to drag herself out to the distant pump, and water there was none. He snatched the child, and ran up the area-steps to the room above, and borrowed their only saucepan with some water in it. Then he began, with the useful skill of a working-man, to make some gruel; and when it was hastily made he seized a battered iron table-spoon (kept when many other little things had been sold in a lot), in order to feed baby, and with it he forced one or two drops between her clenched teeth. The mouth opened mechanically to receive more, and gradually she revived. She sat up and looked round; and recollecting all, fell down again in weak and passive despair. Her little child crawled to her, and wiped with its fingers the thick-coming tears which she now had strength to weep. It was now high time to attend to the man. He lay on straw, so damp and mouldy no dog would have chosen it in preference to flags; over it was a piece of sacking, coming next to his worn skeleton of a body; above him was mustered every article of clothing that could be spared by mother or children this bitter weather; and in addition to his own, these might have given as much warmth as one blanket, could they have been kept on him; but as he restlessly tossed to and fro, they fell off and left him shivering in spite of the burning heat of his skin. Every now and then he started up in his naked madness, looking like the prophet of woe in the fearful plague-picture; But he soon fell again in exhaustion, and Barton found he must be closely watched, lest in these falls he should injure himself against the hard brick floor. He was thankful when Wilson reappeared, carrying in both hands a jug of steaming tea, intended for the poor wife; but when the delirious husband saw drink, he snatched at it with animal instinct, with a selfishness he had never shown in health.

Then the two men consulted together. It seemed decided without a word being spoken on the subject, that both should spend the night with the forlorn couple; that was settled. But could no doctor be had? In all probability no; the next day an infirmary order might be begged, but meanwhile the only medical advice they could have must be from a druggist's. So Barton (being the moneyed man) set out to find a shop in London Road.

It is a pretty sight to walk through a street with lighted shops; the gas is so brilliant, the display of goods so much more vividly shown than by day, and of all shops a druggist's looks the most like the tales of our childhood, from Aladdin's garden of enchanted fruits to the charming Rosamond with her purple jar. No such associations had Barton; yet he felt the contrast between the well-filled, well-lighted shops and the dim gloomy cellar, and it made him moody that such contrasts should exist. They are the mysterious problem of life to more than him. He wondered if any in all the hurrying crowd, had come from such a house of mourning. He thought they all looked joyous, and he was angry with them. But he could not, you cannot, read the lot of those who daily pass you by in the street. How do you know the wild romances of their lives; the trials, the temptations they are even now enduring, resisting, sinking under? You may be elbowed one instant by the girl desperate in her abandonment, laughing in mad merriment with her outward gesture, while her soul is longing for the rest of the dead, and bringing itself to think of the cold-flowing river as the only mercy of God remaining to her here. You may pass the criminal, meditating crimes at which you will to-morrow shudder with honor as you read them. You may push against one, humble and unnoticed, the last upon earth, who in Heaven will for ever be in the immediate light of God's countenance. Errands of mercy—errands of sin—did you ever think where all the thousands of people you daily meet are bound? Barton's was an errand of mercy; but the thoughts of his heart were touched by sin, by bitter hatred of the happy, whom he, for the time, confounded with the selfish.

He reached a druggist's shop, and entered. The druggist (whose smooth manners seemed to have been salved over with his own spermaceti) listened attentively to Barton's description of Davenport's illness; concluded it was typhus fever, very prevalent in that neighbourhood; and proceeded to make up a bottle of medicine, sweet spirits of nitre, or some such innocent potion, very good for slight colds, but utterly powerless to stop, for an instant, the raging fever of the poor man it was intended to relieve. He recommended the same course they had previously determined to adopt, applying the next morning for an infirmary order; and Barton left the shop with comfortable faith in the physic given him; for men of his class, if they believe in physic at all, believe that every description is equally efficacious.

Meanwhile, Wilson had done what he could at Davenport's home. He had soothed, and covered the man many a time; he had fed and hushed the little child, and spoken tenderly to the woman, who lay still in her weakness and her weariness. He had opened a door but only for an instant; it led into a back cellar, with a grating instead of a window, down which dropped the moisture from pigstyes, and worse abominations. It was not paved; the floor was one mass of bad smelling mud. It had never been used, for there was not an article of furniture in it; nor could a human being, much less a pig, have lived there many days. Yet the 'back apartment' made a difference in the rent. The Davenports paid threepence more for having two rooms. When he turned round again, he saw the woman suckling the child from her dry, withered breast.

'Surely the lad is weaned!' exclaimed he, in surprise. 'Why, how old is he?'

'Going on two year,' she faintly answered. 'But, Oh! it keeps him quiet when I've nought else to gi' him, and he'll get a bit of sleep lying there, if he's getten nought beside. We han done our best to gi' the childer food, howe'er we pinched ourselves.'

'Han ye had no money fra th' town?'

'No, my master is Buckinghamshire born; and he's feared the town would send him back to his parish, if he went to th' board; so we've just borne on in hope o' better times. But I think they'll never come in my day'; and the poor woman began her weak high-pitched cry again.

'Here, sup this drop o' gruel, and then try and get a bit o' sleep. John and I'll watch by your master to-night.'

'God's blessing be on you.'

She finished the gruel, and fell into a dead sleep. Wilson covered her with his coat as well as he could, and tried to move lightly for fear of disturbing her; but there need have been no such dread, for her sleep was profound and heavy with exhaustion. Once only she roused to pull the coat round her little child.

And now all Wilson's care, and Barton's to boot, was wanted to restrain the wild mad agony of the fevered man. He started up, he yelled, he seemed infuriated by overwhelming anxiety. He cursed and swore, which surprised Wilson, who knew his piety in health, and who did not know the unbridled tongue of delirium. At length he seemed exhausted, and fell asleep; and Barton and Wilson drew near the fire, and talked together in whispers. They sat on the floor, for chairs there were none; the sole table was an old tub turned upside-down. They put out the candle and conversed by the flickering fire-light.

'Han yo known this chap long?' asked Barton.

'Better nor three year. He's worked wi' Carsons that long, and were alway a steady, civil-spoken fellow, though, as I said afore, somewhat of a Methodee. I wish I'd gotten a letter he sent his missis, a week or two agone, when he were on tramp for work. It did my heart good to read it; for, yo see, I were a bit grumbling mysel; it seemed hard to be spunging on Jem, and taking a' his flesh-meat money to buy bread for me and them as I ought to be keeping. But, yo know, though I can earn nought, I mun eat summut. Well, as I telled ye, I were grumbling, when she (indicating the sleeping woman by a nod) brought me Ben's letter, for she could na read hersel. It were as good as Bible-words; ne'er a word o' repining; a' about God being our father, and that we mun bear patiently whate'er he sends.'

'Don ye think he's th' masters' father, too? I'd be loath to have 'em for brothers.'

'Eh, John I donna talk so; sure there's many and many a master as good or better nor us.'

'If you think so, tell me this. How comes it they're rich, and we're poor? I'd like to know that. Han they done as they'd be done by for us?'

But Wilson was no arguer. No speechifier as he would have called it. So Barton, seeing he was likely to have it his own way, went on.

'You'll say (at least many a one does), they'n getten capital an' we'n getten none. I say, our labour's our capital and we ought to draw interest on that. They get interest on their capital somehow a' this time, while ourn is lying idle, else how could they all live as they do? Besides, there's many on 'em as had nought to begin wi'; there's Carsons, and Duncombes, and Mengles, and many another, as comed into Manchester with clothes to their back, and that were all, and now they're worth their tens of thousands, a' getten out of our labour; why the very land as fetched but sixty pound twenty year agone is now worth six hundred, and that, too, is owing to our labour: but look at yo, and see me, and poor Davenport yonder; whatten better are we? They'n screwed us down to th' lowest peg, in order to make their great big fortunes, and build their great big houses, and we, why we're just clemming, many and many of us. Can you say there's nought wrong in this?'

'Well, Barton, I'll not gainsay ye. But Mr Carson spoke to me after th' fire, and says he, "I shall ha' to retrench, and be very careful in my expenditure during these bad times, I assure ye"; so yo see th' masters suffer too.'

'Han they ever seen a child o' their'n die for want o' food?' asked Barton, in a low, deep voice.

'I donnot mean,' continued he, 'to say as I'm so badly off. I'd scorn to speak for mysel; but when I see such men as Davenport there dying away, for very clemming, I cannot stand it. I've but gotten Mary, and she keeps hersel pretty much. I think we'll ha' to give up house-keeping; but that I donnot mind.'

And in this kind of talk the night the long heavy night of watching, wore away. As far as they could judge, Davenport continued in the same state, although the symptoms varied occasionally. The wife slept on, only roused by a cry of her child now and then, which seemed to have power over her, when far louder noises failed to disturb her. The watchers agreed, that as soon as it was likely Mr Carson would be up and visible, Wilson should go to his house, and beg for an Infirmary order. At length the grey dawn penetrated even into the dark cellar; Davenport slept, and Barton was to remain there until Wilson's return; so stepping out into the fresh air, brisk and reviving, even in that street of abominations, Wilson took his way to Mr Carson's.

Wilson had about two miles to walk before he reached Mr Carson's house, which was almost in the country. The streets were not yet bustling and busy. The shop-men were lazily taking down the shutters, although it was near eight o'clock; for the day was long enough for the purchases people made in that quarter of the town, while trade was so flat. One or two miserable-looking women were setting off on their day's begging expedition. But there were few people abroad. Mr Carson's was a good house, and furnished with disregard to expense. But in addition to lavish expenditure, there was much taste shown, and many articles chosen for their beauty and elegance adorned his rooms. As Wilson passed a window which a housemaid had thrown open, he saw pictures and gilding, at which he was tempted to stop and look; but then he thought it would not be respectful. So he hastened on to the kitchen door. The servants seemed very busy with preparations for breakfast; but good-naturedly, though hastily, told him to step in, and they could soon let Mr Carson know he was there. So he was ushered into a kitchen hung round with glittering tins, where a roaring fire burnt merrily, and where numbers of utensils hung round, at whose nature and use Wilson amused himself by guessing. Meanwhile, the servants bustled to and fro; an out-door man-servant came in for orders, and sat down near Wilson; the cook broiled steaks, and the kitchen-maid toasted bread, and boiled eggs.

The coffee steamed upon the fire, and altogether the odours were so mixed and appetizing, that Wilson began to yearn for food to break his fast, which had lasted since dinner the day before. If the servants had known this, they would have willingly given him meat and bread in abundance; but they were like the rest of us, and not feeling hunger themselves, forgot it was possible another might. So Wilson's craving turned to sickness, while they chattered on, making the kitchen's free and keen remarks upon the parlour.

'How late you were last night, Thomas!'

'Yes, I was right weary of waiting; they told me to be at the rooms by twelve; and there I was. But it was two o'clock before they called me.'

'And did you wait all that time in the street?' asked the housemaid who had done her work for the present, and come into the kitchen for a bit of gossip.

'My eye as like! you don't think I'm such a fool as to catch my' death of cold, and let the horses catch their death too, as we should ha' done if we'd stopped there. No! I put th' horses up in th' stables at th' Spread Eagle, and went mysel', and got a glass or two by th' fire. They're driving a good custom, them, wi' coachmen. There were five on us, and we'd many a quart o' ale, and gin wi' it, to keep out cold.'

'Mercy on us, Thomas; you'll get a drunkard at last!'

'If I do, I know whose blame it will be. It will be missis's, and not mine. Flesh and blood can't sit to be starved to death on a coach-box, waiting for folks as don't know their own mind.'

A servant, semi-upper-housemaid, semi-lady's-maid, now came down with orders from her mistress.

'Thomas, you must ride to the fishmonger's, and say missis can't give above half-a-crown a pound for salmon for Tuesday; she's grumbling because trade's so bad. And she'll want the carriage at three to go to the lecture, Thomas; at the Royal Execution, you know.'

'Ay, ay, I know.'

'And you'd better all of you mind your P's and Q's, for she's very black this morning. She's got a bad headache.'

'It's a pity Miss Jenkins is not here to match her. Lord! how she and missis did quarrel which had got the worst headaches, it was that Miss Jenkins left for; she would not give up having bad headaches, and missis could not abide any one to have 'em but herself.'

'Missis will have her breakfast up-stairs, cook, and the cold partridge as was left yesterday, and put plenty of cream in her coffee, and she thinks there's a roll left, and she would like it well buttered.'

So saying, the maid left the kitchen to be ready to attend to the young ladies' bell when they chose to ring, after their late assembly the night before.

In the luxurious library, at the well-spread breakfast-table, sat the two Mr Carsons, father and son. Both were reading; the father a newspaper, the son a review, while they lazily enjoyed their nicely prepared food. The father was a prepossessing-looking old man; perhaps self-indulgent you might guess. The son was strikingly handsome, and knew it. His dress was neat and well appointed, and his manners far more gentlemanly than his father's. He was the only son, and his sisters were proud of him; his father and mother were proud of him: he could not set up his judgement against theirs; he was proud of himself.

The door opened and in bounded Amy, the sweet youngest daughter of the house, a lovely girl of sixteen, fresh and glowing, and bright as a rosebud. She was too young to go to assemblies, at which her father rejoiced, for he had little Amy with her pretty jokes, and her bird-like songs, and her playful caresses all the evening to amuse him in his loneliness; and she was not too much tired, like Sophy and Helen, to give him her sweet company at breakfast the next morning.

He submitted willingly while she blinded him with her hands, and kissed his rough red face all over. She took his newspaper away after a little pretended resistance and would not allow her brother Harry to go on with his review.

'I'm the only lady this morning, papa, so you know you must make a great deal of me.'

'My darling, I think you have your own way always, whether you're the only lady or not.'

'Yes, papa, you're pretty good and obedient, I must say that; but I'm sorry to say Harry is very naughty, and does not do what I tell him; do you, Harry?'

'I'm sure I don't know what you mean to accuse me of, Amy; I expected praise and not blame; for did not I get you that eau de Portugal from town, that you could not meet with at Hughes', you little ungrateful puss?'

'Did you! Oh sweet Harry; you're as sweet as eau de Portugal yourself; you're almost as good as papa; but still you know you did go and forget to ask Bigland for that rose, that new rose they say he has got.'

'No, Amy, I did not forget. I asked him, and he has got the Rose, *sans reproche;* but do you know, little Miss Extravagance, a very small one is half a guinea?'

'Oh, I don't mind. Papa will give it me, won't you, dear father? He knows his little daughter can't live without flowers and scents?'

Mr Carson tried to refuse his darling, but she coaxed him into acquiescence, saying she must have it, it was one of her necessaries. Life was not worth having without flowers.

'Then, Amy,' said her brother, 'try and be content with peonies and dandelions.'

'Oh you wretch! I don't call them flowers. Besides, you're every bit as extravagant. Who gave half-a-crown for a bunch of lilies of the valley at Yates', a month ago, and then would not let his poor little sister have them, though she went on her knees to beg them? Answer me that, Master Hal.'

'Not on compulsion,' replied her brother, smiling with his mouth, while his eyes had an irritated expression, and he went first red, then pale, with vexed embarrassment.

'If you please, sir,' said a servant, entering the room, 'here's one of the mill people wanting to see you; his name is Wilson, he says.'

'I'll come to him directly; stay, tell him to come in here.'

Amy danced off into the conservatory which opened out of the room, before the gaunt, pale, unwashed, unshaven weaver was ushered in. There he stood at the door, sleeking his hair with old country habit, and every now and then stealing a glance round at the splendour of the apartment.

'Well, Wilson, and what do you want today, man?'

'Please, sir, Davenport's ill of the fever, and I'm come to know if you've got an Infirmary order for him?'

'Davenport—Davenport; who is the fellow? I don't know the name.'

'He's worked in your factory better nor three year, sir.'

'Very likely, I don't pretend to know the names of the men I employ; that I leave to the overlooker. So he's ill, eh?'

'Ay, sir, he's very bad; we want to get him in at the fever wards.'

'I doubt if I have an in-patients order to spare; they're always wanted for accidents, you know. But I'll give you an out-patient's, and welcome.'

So saying, he rose up, unlocked a drawer, pondered a minute, and then gave Wilson an out-patient's order to be presented the following Monday. Monday! How many days there were before Monday!

Meanwhile, the younger Mr Carson had ended his review, and began to listen to what was going on. He finished his breakfast, got up, and pulled five shillings out of his pocket, which he gave to Wilson as he passed him, for the 'poor fellow'. He went past quickly, and calling for his horse, mounted gaily, and rode away. He was anxious to be in time to have a look and a smile from lovely Mary Barton, as she went to Miss Simmonds'. But today he was to be disappointed. Wilson left the house, not knowing whether to be pleased or grieved. It was long to Monday, but they had all spoken kindly to him, and who could tell if they might not remember this, and do something before Monday. Besides, the cook, who, when she had had time to think, after breakfast was sent in, had noticed his paleness, had had meat and bread ready to put in his hand when he came out of the parlour; and a full stomach makes every one of us more hopeful.

When he reached Berry Street, he had persuaded himself he bore good news, and felt almost elated in his heart. But it fell when he opened the cellar-door, and saw Barton and the wife both bending over the sick man's couch with awe-struck, saddened look.

'Come here,' said Barton. 'There's a change comed over him sin' yo left, is there not?'

Wilson looked. The flesh was sunk, the features prominent, bony, and rigid. The fearful clay-colour of death was over all. But the eyes were open and sensible, though the films of the grave were settling upon them.

'He wakened fra his sleep, as yo left him in, and began to mutter and moan; but he soon went off again, and we never knew he were awake till he called his wife, but now she's here he's gotten nought to say to her.'

Most probably, as they all felt, he could not speak, for his strength was fast ebbing. They stood round him still and silent; even the wife checked her sobs, though her heart was like to break. She held her child to her breast, to try and keep him quiet. Their eyes were all fixed on the yet living one, whose moments of life were passing so rapidly away. At length he brought, (with jerking, convulsive effort) his two hands into the attitude of prayer. They saw his lips move, and bent to catch the words, which came in gasps, and not in tones.

'Oh Lord God! I thank thee, that the hard struggle of living is over.'

'Oh, Ben! Ben!' wailed forth his wife, 'have you no thought for me? Oh, Ben! Ben! do say one word to help me through life.'

He could not speak again. The trump of the archangel would set his tongue free; but not a word more would it utter till then. Yet he heard, he understood, and though sight failed, he moved his hand gropingly over the covering. They knew what he meant, and guided it to her head, bowed and hidden in her hands, when she had sunk in her woe. It rested there, with a feeble pressure of endearment. The face grew beautiful, as the soul neared God. A peace beyond understanding came over it. The hand was a heavy, stiff weight on the wife's head. No more grief or sorrow for him. They reverently laid out the corpse—Wilson fetching his only spare shirt to array it in. The wife still lay hidden in the clothes, in a stupor of agony.

There was a knock at the door, and Barton went to open it. It was Mary, who had received a message from her father, through a neighbour, telling her where he was; and she had set out early to come and have a word with him before her day's work; but some errands she had to do for Miss Simmonds had detained her until now.

'Come in, wench!' said her father. 'Try if thou canst comfort yon poor, poor woman, kneeling down there. God help her.' Mary did not know what to say, or how to comfort; but she knelt down by her, and put her arm round her neck, and in a little while fell to crying herself so bitterly, that the source of tears was opened by sympathy in the widow, and her full heart was, for a time, relieved.

And Mary forgot all purposed meeting with her gay lover, Harry Carson; forgot Miss Simmonds' errands, and her anger, in the anxious desire to comfort the poor lone woman. Never had her sweet face looked more angelic, never had her gentle voice seemed so musical as when she murmured her broken sentences of comfort.

'Oh, don't cry so, dear Mrs Davenport, pray don't take on so. Sure he's gone where he'll never know care again. Yes, I know how lonesome you must feel; but think of your children. Oh! we'll all help to earn food for 'em. Think how sorry *he'd* be, if he sees you fretting so. Don't cry so, please don't.'

And she ended by crying herself, as passionately as the poor widow.

It was agreed that the town must bury him; he had paid to a burial club as long as he could; but by a few weeks' omission, he had forfeited his claim to a sum of money now. Would Mrs Davenport and the little child go home with Mary? The latter brightened up as she urged this plan; but no! where the poor, fondly loved remains were, there would the mourner be; and all that they could do was to make her as comfortable as their funds would allow, and to beg a neighbour to look in and say a word at times. So she was left alone with her dead, and they went to work that had work, and he who had none, took upon him the arrangements for the funeral.

Mary had many a scolding from Miss Simmonds that day for her absence of mind. To be sure Miss Simmonds was much put out by Mary's non-appearance in the morning with certain bits of muslin, and shades of silk which were wanted to complete a dress to be worn that night; but it was true enough that Mary did not mind what she was about; she was too busy planning how her old black gown (her best when her mother died) might be spunged, and turned, and lengthened into something like decent mourning for the widow. And when she went home at night (though it was very late, as a sort of retribution for her morning's negligence), she set to work at once, and was so busy, and so glad over her task, that she had, every now and then, to check herself in singing merry ditties, that she felt little accorded with the sewing on which she was engaged.

So when the funeral day came, Mrs Davenport was neatly arrayed in black, a satisfaction to her poor heart in the midst of her sorrow. Barton and Wilson both accompanied her, as she led her two elder boys, and followed the coffin. It was a simple walking funeral, with nothing to grate on the feelings of any; far more in accordance with its purpose, to my mind, than the gorgeous hearses, and nodding plumes, which form the grotesque funeral pomp of respectable people. There was no 'rattling the bones over the stones', of the pauper's funeral. Decently and patiently was he followed to the grave by one determined to endure her woe meekly for his sake. The only mark of pauperism attendant on the burial concerned the living and joyous, far more than the dead, or the sorrowful. When they arrived in the churchyard, they halted before a raised and handsome tombstone; in reality a wooden mockery of stone respectabilities which adorned the burial-ground. It was easily raised in a very few minutes, and below was the grave in which pauper bodies were piled until within a foot or two of the surface; when the soil was shovelled over, and stamped down, and the wooden cover went to do temporary duty over another hole.* But little they recked of this who now gave up their dead.

*The case, to my certain knowledge, in one churchyard in Manchester. There may be more.

✧ PART FOUR ✧

Rural and Small Town Landscapes

John Constable's painting The Cornfields *evokes the almost mystically idyllic preindustrial Europe of romantic memory.*

Rural and Small Town Landscapes

Throughout the nineteenth and early twentieth centuries, millions of rural and small town dwellers moved to cities, where they adopted new ways. The rhythms and traditions of small town and agricultural life soon faded among an urban population and, by the mid-twentieth century, seemed poised to pass away forever. In his *Years of Childhood* (1856), Sergei Aksakov (1791–1859) recalled life on the estates of his serf-owning Russian noble family. His memoir evoked a way of life that endured in parts of Europe well into the nineteenth century. Domesticated life had only just overtaken the wilds of nature in the distant Ural province on Europe's uttermost eastern peripheries, where Aksakov's grandfather had deliberately settled to escape the pettiness of social customs. The fictional writings of Honoré de Balzac (1799–1850) and Thomas Hardy (1840–1928), such as *Lost Illusions* (1837), *Tess of the d'Urbevilles* (1891), and *Mayor of Casterbridge* (1886), trace their characters' life trajectories from agriculture through artisanry and petty commerce toward prosperity and a more genteel, urban way of life. A fall from grace into tragedy always threatens. Kaleidoscopic rural and town scenes form the backdrop for their lives, as for those of Eliot's *Middlemarch.*

In *Reeds in the Wind* (1913), Nobel prize-winning author Grazia Deledda (1871–1936) depicts the timeless mores of Italian Sardinia. Both religiously devout and abjectly superstitious, the peasants confront incomprehensible social and economic change. Joseph Roth (1894–1939) decribes remote late nineteenth century garrisons of Austria-Hungary in his novel *The Radetzky March* (1932). Through the eyes of a rather insecure army officer-baron, Roth portrays a turn-of-the-century world denuded of certainties. Europe's landscapes were filled with such scenes throughout the nineteenth century and beyond, as the changes in people's lives paralleled transfigurations of the physical world—from golden fields, wooded expanses, and picturesque dwellings to drab, crowded cities whose "satanic" mills and furnaces poisoned air and water. Regardless, villagers entered the middle class in droves and led lives their grandparents might have envied. In the end, not much remained of the pristine country that had been early nineteenth century Europe.

✦ Reading 14 ✦

Years of Childhood

Sergei Aksakov

In these scenes, Aksakov describes life on his family estate in the Ural Mountains.

Parashino

From level upper country the road suddenly ran downhill, and at last there before us, lying in a hollow, lay revealed the prosperous village of Parashino, with its stone church and a small mere where the spring waters had cut their channel. The manor farmyard with its rows of stacks of corn was just like a little town, and there were quite a number of stacks of last year's corn to be seen even in the peasants' own yards.

My father was delighted to see such quantities of corn. "There's peasants indeed!" he cried. "Those are the peasants for you! A delight to the heart!" I shared his pleasure, though it again struck me that my mother was quite indifferent to what he had just said.

At last we entered the village. At that very moment the priest was just setting out from the church to bless the waters of Jordan. He was in full canonicals, bearing the cross on his head, while in front of him processed the deacon with his censer and the icons and banners. A huge crowd of people followed. We at once reined in our carriage and got out to join the congregation. Mother held my hand, and Nurse carried my little sister, who stared at this sight, something she had never seen before, with unusual interest, and although I for my part had had the opportunity of seeing the like in Ufa, I nonetheless also watched most excitedly.

When the blessing of the waters was over, we all in turn kissed the cross and were aspersed with holy water; the priest then congratulated us on our safe arrival at journey's end, and we at last entered Parashino manor courtyard, which was only just across the road from the church. The folk crowded close around us, all of them as happy and pleased to see us as the peasants in the harvest fields had been. A group of senior men pressed their way forward, bowing and greeting us most cordially. The leader among them was a short-statured, broad-shouldered, elderly peasant with grizzled hair and eyes so unusual that I felt quite frightened when he looked hard at me. The concourse of peasants now conducted us to the porch of the manor guest house, when they dispersed, while this peasant with the unusual eyes ran up the steps, unlocked the door, and invited us to step inside, constantly assuring my parents how cordially welcome they were and addressing them as "little Father" and "little Mother" Alexey Stepanych and Sofia Nikolavna.

We stepped indoors. Everything seemed to have been got ready specially for our coming. But later I learned that my great-aunt's principal steward and manager regularly put up there whenever he happened to come to Parashino. My parents spoke rather familiarly of him as "Mikhailushka," but everybody else always referred to him with great respect as "Mikhail Maksimych"—anyway, he proved to be the real reason why the guest apartments at Parashino were always ready.

From something my father said I now guessed that the short-statured peasant with the terrible eyes was none other than the man they called Mironych about whom I had made inquiries while we were still in our carriage. Father was now inquiring of him about all aspects of the farm management. At last, dismissing him, Father said he would send for him when he needed him, and told Mironych to send to him a number of the older men, whom he indicated by name. Small though I was, it struck me then that Father's instructions were not much to Mironych's

---

From: Sergei Aksakov, *Years of Childhood* (New York: Vintage Books, 1960), pp. 39–52.

liking. He said "Very well, sir" in such a way that I can hear him to this very moment, and the words really meant: "That's not at all the thing to do."

When Mironych had gone, I heard a conversation between my parents which absolutely flabbergasted me. Mother said that this man Mironych must be a rogue, and Father just grinned and said it did look rather like it: he had heard a lot of bad things about the man previously, but Mironych was a kinsman and pet of Mikhailushka's, and Aunt Praskovia trusted Mikhailushka implicitly. Father explained that he had given orders for elder men of the Bagrovo peasants to be sent to him—men who would tell him the full truth, knowing that he would not betray their trust—and that this had not suited Mironych's book at all. Father added that after dinner he thought he would drive around and have a look at all the field work. He asked Mother if she would go with him, but she said flatly she would not, she could not bear the sight of it all, but if he liked, he could take the boy. I was overjoyed, and asked if I might go, and my Father readily consented. "Yes," he said, "and what's more, when we've had a cup of tea, Sergey and I'll walk around and have a look at the stables. From there we can go round by the springs and the mill."

I need not say how welcome this additional suggestion was to me, and what was still better was that my mother agreed. We drank our tea; then we set out for the stable yard, which was at the far end of the grass-grown Parashino courtyard. At the stable doors we were met by the chief horseman, Grigori Kovliaga, waiting for us, together with the other stable men. At first glance I liked Kovliaga very much; he was very nice to me, too. But before we had had time even to go inside the stables, there was that loathsome Mironych, and from then on he did not leave my father all day.

Through the big doorway we entered a funny, long building. There were passages down each side of it, and off these, to left and right, between partitions, were huge, grown-up, fat horses. And in some of these partitions there were also young horses, still nice and slender. At this point I learned that the partitioned-off spaces were called "boxes." On the wall, facing the entrance, there was an icon, and Kovliaga told me this was "Nicholas the Miracle-performer."

When he had inspected both sides of the stables and praised their cleanliness, my father went out into the yard again and had some of the horses led out. It was Kovliaga who did this, with the help of another stable man. Well foddered and well rested, the proud creatures reared on their bind legs and whinnied, lifting the two stable men up into the air, so they just hung from their necks, their right hands holding fast to the bridle. I was scared and pressed close to my father, but when they made some of those glorious horses run and jump at the end of a long rope that, digging their heels into the ground and scarcely able to manage, the stable man held, I loved watching them.

Mironych put his spoke in everywhere, and I was very annoyed when familiarly and without any respect instead of "Grigori Kovliaga" he called him "Grishka Kovlazhenok," whereas Father called him quite properly: Grigori. "And where do you turn the horses out to pasture?" Father asked Grigori, but it was Mironych who answered and said one herd went out to "Koshelga" [*the "Punnet"*] and the other to "Kamenni Vrag" ["Stony Hollow"], and added: "But, perhaps, *Batiushka* Alexey Stepanych, you would like me to send 'em out to the fallow land—we mean to have the dedication service tomorrow and start sowing—that won't be so far, then we can have a look at the manor rye and spring-wheat crops." Father said: "Very well."

From the stable yard we went to the springs. My father was very fond of any sort of waters, but especially natural spring waters, while I could not even see water running in the gutters in the street without excitement, so the magnificent Parashino springs, of which there were more than twenty, enraptured me. Some of the springs were very powerful indeed, breaking out of the hillside halfway up, others came bubbling out at the foot of the hill, and those which were up the slope were fenced in with piles and roofed over, with troughs of limewood set in these huts, and the troughs were full of water so clear that they looked quite empty, the troughs were brimful, with the water streaming over and down the sides like glass curtains.

I saw the peasant women bringing their buckets, saw how they tapped out the wooden plug at the end of the trough and put their buckets under the stream of water, which shot out in a big curve, because the end of the trough was high above the ground, as it stood on big stone blocks (the sides of the ravine consisted of nothing but natural blocks of stone). A bucket was full in a minute; then the other was filled. The water from all the springs flowed down into the mill pool. There were a lot of springs which were not built over, but they too all flowed to the mere in little brooks, over a shingly bed, and in these, Father and I found ever so many lovely stones, just as if polished. They were quite round and rather long, so they were like sugar leaves. They were called "devil's fingers." This was the first time I had ever seen any. I found them wonderful things and stuffed my pockets full, only Father could not give me any explanation of the name, and I plagued him with questions for a long time as to what sort of an animal a devil was to have such strong fingers.

Still full of new and pleasant impressions, now I suddenly passed on to new ones that, though not quite so pleasing, were nonetheless very interesting ones; my father took me to the mill, a thing about which I had no notion whatsoever. A mill pond was fed by the springs, and it was rather deep. The perpendicular-walled channel that the waters had cut was fenced across by a broad wall, which could be moved, and dammed it. In the center of it was a little wooden house, and in this mill there was the milling machinery, which only ground well at high water, though this, as my father explained to me, was not because there was not much water in the mere, but because the dam was all leaks.

This wretched little mill seemed to me to be a miracle of human artifice. The first thing I looked at was the stream of water which poured out of the sluice funnel on to the water wheel, which had become quite green from wetness and turned rather slowly with a lot of splashing and foaming, while with the noise of the water mingled some other humming and hissing. Then my father pointed out the wooden hopper, which was the box, broad at the top and narrower at the bottom (as I saw later), into which the wheat was poured. Then we went downstairs, and I could see the mill stone turning and above it the hopper shaking away, out of which the grains of wheat poured under the stone. This had a wooden rim all around it, and it kept on turning and grinding the grains and turning them into flour, which poured out underneath onto a sort of wooden shovel. When I peeped in sideways, I could see another wheel, which was called the "dry wheel." This turned a lot faster than the bobbin wheel and kept catching at the trundle head with a sort of hands, so that it turned the stone that was fastened to it.

The mill house was full of flour dust and all a-quiver and sometimes it simply hopped up into the air. For a long time I was absolutely astounded, gazing at these wonderful things and remembering having seen something like it in children's toys. We spent a very long time in the mill, where there was an old man who was very feeble and bent, whom they called the "tipper-in"; he was all gray and tottering, and he was milling all the tailings for feeding the master's horses, he said. He was absolutely white from flour dust. I would have asked him all sorts of questions, but when I saw how often he coughed till he could not get his breath back, I felt very sorry for him, and I put all the rest of my questions to my father, but here, too, the loathsome Mironych would keep putting his word in, although I would rather not have heard a thing he said.

When we came out of the mill, I saw that we, too, were white with flour dust, though not as white as the tipper-in. I at once turned to ask my father to have the old man put to bed and given hot tea to drink. My father smiled, then, turning to Mironych, said: "Old Vassily Terentiev, the tipper-in, is frightfully old and ailing, isn't he? That cough has quite got him down, and the tail-wheat dust is no good for him. He ought to be retired from old man's work and not made to keep on being tipper-in." "It shall be as you wish, sir," was Mironych's response. "Only won't other old men be envious? If we retire him, then we ought to retire the others, too. There are a lot of men who don't earn their keep and idlers, you know. Who'll take on the old-man jobs?" My father's reply was that not all the old men were as tottery—besides, ailing people should be looked after and given peace; they had already done enough work in their lifetimes. "Don't you forget that you yourself will soon be getting on in years," my father said, "you too will not earn your keep, and when that time comes, you will want to have rest." Mironych's reply was: "Very well, sir, your orders shall be carried out, though this Vassily Terentiev of yours does not deserve kindly treatment. His grandson is a young rebel: only the other day he threatened to slit my throat." To this my father replied with a vigor and a tone of voice which I had never once heard from him before: "So you'd punish the old man for his grandson's faults, eh? Well, now you just tackle the man who's to blame, will you!" Mironych was quick to agree. "Don't you fear,

Batiushka Alexey Stepanych, it shall all be exactly as you say."

Why, I do not know, but I began to feel shivery inside. Seeing that we had paused, Vassily Terentiev, who had meant to follow us, so now heard what was said, stood rooted to the spot, trembling all over and never stopping bowing. Even when we had got to the top of the hill and I looked back, the old man was still standing there, bowing to the ground.

As soon as we reached our apartments, I forgot all about the springs and the mill, but lost no time in telling my mother about the old man. Mother was very moved by my story, and if she had had her way, she would have sent for Mironych at once and dressed him down and suspended him from his duties, while she hurried to write and tell Aunt Praskovia all about it. . . . Indeed, my father had no easy task restraining her from such hasty action.

There followed a lengthy discussion—indeed, a dispute. There was a lot I did not understand and much that I have forgotten; all indeed that I recall clearly is my father saying: "My dear, don't meddle in what does not concern you, you'll spoil it all, you will be the ruin of the whole family. Now, Mironych will never touch them, he will be bound to be afraid lest I write to Auntie, though if it came to a plain demand for his dismissal, Mikhailushka would never let the man go, and then I would not be able to show my face at Parashino, and nothing at all would have been achieved, except, indeed, annoying Aunt Praskovia." My mother argued back a while, but in the end gave way.

Heavens! What a mish-mash of notions there was now in my mind! What was it that this poor, dear, ailing old man was made to suffer for? And what exactly was this nasty Mironych? What sorts of powers were Mikhailushka and Father's Aunt Praskovia? Why exactly would Father not let Mother dismiss Mironych at once? For did this not mean that my father could have done so? Then why did he not do so? For Father was kind, was he not?—he was never angry. These were the questions that seethed in my mind then. The solution I found for myself was that Mikhailushka and Grandmother Praskovia Kurolessov were bad people, and my father was afraid of them.

The "devil's fingers" I gave away to my darling sister, she had missed me so much. We added our new treasure to the precious things we already possessed—our "billets" and those stones that came from the river Bielaia, which I always called "ores" (I had adopted this word from old Anichkov). With enthusiasm I told my dear sister about all I had seen. I always kept her informed about everything that happened to me without her. But it began to dawn on me that my little sister did not always understand, so I now began to adopt the language Nurse used and talk in a tongue that a little child could really understand.

After dinner Father and I set off for the fields in a long, low farm wagon. The loathsome Mironych also came with us. This was the first time in my life I had ridden on *rospuski,* as they called the cart, and I liked it very much indeed. Sitting on a felt rug folded in four, I swayed about just as if I were in a cradle slung on the whippy branch of a tree. In the ruts of the road over the steppe this wagon went down so low that the tall-growing grass and flowers whipped at my legs and my arms, and I found that very great fun. I even managed to pick some wild flowers. But it struck me that grown-ups found sitting like that uncomfortable because they could not let their feet down, but had to keep pulling them in and holding them in the air, so they did not touch the ground, whereas I could go on sitting with my legs almost full length, yet the grass only reached to my shoes.

When we drove between the wheat fields up the broad headlands overgrown with sour cherry trees with their reddish fruit and dwarf almonds with fruits that were still green, I begged Father to stop a moment, and with my own hands gathered a whole handful of those wild morellos. They were tiny and hard, like large peas. Father would not let me eat them. He said they were sour because they were not ripe; as for the fruit of the wild peach, which the peasants call *bobovnik,* I gathered a whole pocketful of these. I was also going to stuff my other pocket, to take my darling mother some, but Father said: "Your mother won't care about that rubbish," they would squash in my pocket, and I had better throw them away. I was sorry to part from them so quickly, and held them in my hand a long time, but at last I was obliged to throw them away, though I remember neither how nor when.

Wherever the rye had not drooped—was not laid, as one says—it was so tall that we and our wagon and the horses were quite hidden from view, and this new sight also delighted me very much. We drove for a long time along headlands, then a strange faraway sound, mixed with men's voices, began to be audible. The nearer we came to it, the more audible it became, till at last through the unreaped rye we began to get glimpses of the glint of sickles and of handfuls of bunched ears of the cut-off rye swept up into the air by unseen hands. Soon the shoulders and backs of peasant men and women bending double could be seen.

The moment we drove out on to the *desiatina* [2.7 *acre strip*] on which about ten men were working, their talk at once ceased and the rasp of the sickle blades through the straw also increased and filled the whole field with those sounds that were unusual and that I had never heard before. We drew up and got down out of the wagon and walked across toward the reapers, men and women, and in a kindly sort of voice my father cried: "God aid ye all!"

At once they all left their work, turned to face us, and bowed very low, while some of the men, those who were older, greeted my father and me. Real delight was to be read on their sun-tanned faces. Some of them were breathing hard, others had their bare feet and their fingers bandaged with dirty rags, but they were all cheerful. My father asked how many men worked on a *desiatina,* if they found the work hard, and for answer got the statement: " 'Tis a bit hard-like, but how can you help it? 'Tis powerful rye, but we'll manage by nightfall." Father said: "Then carry on, and God be wi' ye!" In a moment the sickles all flashed, handfuls of rye flashed over the workers' heads, and the sound of cutting through the tough straw was louder and spread more vigorously over the whole field. I stood lost in wonder.

All at once the whimpering of a baby attracted my attention, and then I saw that in various places cradles were dangling from three sticks planted in the ground and tied together at the top. A young woman now stuck her sickle in the sheaf she had just tied, unhurriedly went to her baby, who was crying, took him in her arms, sat down under a stook, and, kissing and fondling him, gave the babe her breast. The babe was soon soothed and fell asleep, when his mother put him in the cradle, took up her sickle, and set to work reaping with extra vigor, so as to catch up with the other women and not be left behind them.

Father had been talking to Mironych, and I had had time to take a good look at everything all about me. My heart was seized with an inexpressible sense of sympathy for these people working at such strain under the scorching sun, and many a time after that, when I found myself in the harvest field, I would recall that first impression.

From this *desiatina* we drove on to another, then yet another, and still another. At first we would get out of the wagon and go over to the reapers, but afterward we would merely drive up close to them and halt a while. Father would say: "God aid ye!" It was the same performance everywhere, the same bows, the same kindly, delighted faces, and the same simple words of thanks to their "dear master Alexey Stepanych." It was impossible to make a stop everywhere. There would not have been enough time. We drove through all the spring wheat fields that were also beginning to ripen, about which my father and Mironych talked with alarm, as they did not know where to find the labor or how they were to get the corn in. "There you have the trouble, and a real trouble it is, Master," said the chief foreman. "The rye ripened late and now, as you see, here's the spring wheat's coming on, even the late oats are coming into the picture, and it's already time to start sowings. Yesterday Providence granted a shower big enough to break the crust, now the soil's nice and moist, so tomorrow I'm going to get 'em all on to sowing. So you can just see for yourself, can't you—we're not going to get a lot harvested with only the womenfolk, yet there's half the rye still unreaped. I wondered if you wouldn't think of ordering them all to turn out on a free day?"

My father replied that Mironych ought to know well enough that the folk needed to get in their own corn, too, and it was not at all right to take a day of their own time in the height of August heat—far better to have a round robin for labor and call on the neighboring estates to help out. The foreman was beginning to spread word about how any neighbors they had were a long distance away and not very used to the idea of helping out, but at this point we had reached the pea fields and the poppy fields, and these took our attention.

Father told Mironych to break off a few poppy heads, which were still quite green, and pluck out a handful of peas, root and all, with their young stalks and fresh green, still unplimped pods. All this he gave into my care, and even let me eat one pod, and the flat little peas seemed very sweet and tasty to me. At any other time this would have occupied my attention more strongly, but just now it was the rye fields with all the reapers, men and women, which occupied my imagination, and I just held those dozen poppy heads with their slender stems and the handful of green peas in my hand and did not take much interest in them.

On the way back we went around by the fallow lands. They were overgrown with green sow-thistle and goat's beard, about which my father remarked to Mironych, but he made the excuse that these fields were so far out that there was no possibility of pasturing either the manor or the peasants' herds on them, and he made out that the peasants' plows would cut under all those weeds and they wouldn't "belch" any more—that is, would not spring up again. In spite of all this talk, my father was not particularly pleased with the fallows. He said the feed was very poor in places and the furrows were far apart and that was why there was such a lot of weed growth.

The sun was sinking now, and we hardly had time at all to inspect the two herds of the manor horses, which had been specially turned out close to the fallow lands. One consisted of a great number of fillies and mares of all ages and of mares with foals, and these to some extent took my mind off the harvest fields and cheered me up with their prancing and nuzzling their mothers. The other herd, to which we were told we should be very cautions about going near, only my father looked at, walking across to it with the herdsmen. In it were a number of unbroken, bad-tempered horses, which were liable to attack strangers. It was getting quite dark when we got back, and Mother was beginning to get alarmed and regret having let me go. It was quite true; I was far too tired, and fell asleep without even waiting for tea.

I got up rather late because nobody awakened me, and then saw that there was a great deal of excitement going on all around, a lot of fuss and packing. A great many peasants had come to see Father, with all sorts of requests, things Mironych could not take it on himself to do—so he said—or, most likely, things he did not want to do. All this I found out afterward, from the discussions between Father and Mother. However, my father would not assume any authority at all, and his answer to them all was that his aunt had told him only to inspect the estate and report to her about everything, but she had not told him to interfere in any arrangements made by the steward.

All the same, when he had Mironych alone, I did hear Father say that Mironych might do so-and-so for such-and-such a peasant, and something else for another. To any such observation the steward's usual reply was: "Yes, sir, it shall be done," although my father would repeat several times: "My dear man, I am not giving any orders, I am only asking you if you don't think yourself that that is what should be done. But I shall make a point of it to my aunt that I have given no instructions, so don't you refer her back to me about anything."

Still more peasant women came to see my mother than peasants came to see Father. Some of them had requests about poll tax that was due, others about all sorts of ailments. Mother would not even listen to the healthy women's tales, but she did give the ailing ones her advice and even some medicines out of her traveling medicine chest. The evening before, while I was asleep, my father had had a meeting with the older men whom he had had sent to him, and clearly they had not had anything particularly bad to say about Mironych, because Father was nicer to him than he had been yesterday and even praised him for his good work.

The priest and his wife also came to bid us farewell and they, too, spoke well of Mironych. One of the things that the priest said was that the steward was a yes-man, he did whatever he was told to do, and, with a smile, the priest added that it was only God who was faultless; the only thing he himself regretted was that Mironych had so many kinsfolk in the village and favored them. I did not understand at all what that could mean—indeed, it seemed to me that the more kinsfolk Mironych had and the more he favored them, the better.

Why our packing took so long I do not know, but we did not start out till about midday. Mironych and some of the older men, with a crowd of peasant boys and girls, accompanied us to the boundary. We now had forty-five versts to go, to spend a night on the river "Ik," which, so my father said, was at least as good as the Djoma and full of fish, so pleasant thoughts stirred again in my head.

✦ Reading 15 ✦

Lost Illusions

Honoré de Balzac

David, the educated son of an illiterate worker in the print trade, and his school friend Lucien, a would-be poet, start their careers attempting to manage the provincial printing business now owned by David's father. Unimagined complications await them.

A Provincial Printing-Office

At the time when this story begins, the Stanhope press and inking-rollers were not yet in use in small provincial printing-offices. Angoulême, although its paper-making industry kept it in contact with Parisian printing, was still using those wooden presses from which the now obsolete metaphor 'making the presses groan' originated. Printing there was so much behind the times that the pressmen still used leather balls spread with ink to dab on the characters. The bed of the press holding the letter-failed 'forme' to which the paper is applied was still made of stone and so justified its name 'marble'. The ravenous machines of our times have so completely superseded this mechanism—to which, despite its imperfections, we owe the fine books produced by the Elzevirs, the Plantins, the Aldi and the Didots—that it is necessary to mention this antiquated equipment which Jérôme-Nicolas Séchard held in superstitious affection; it has its part to play in this great and trivial story.

Séchard had been one of those journeymen pressmen who, in the typographical jargon used by the workmen occupied in putting type together, are known as 'bears'. No doubt this nickname is due to the to-and-fro motion, resembling that of a caged bear, which carried the pressmen backwards and forwards between the ink-block and the press. In retaliation, the 'bears' call compositors 'monkeys' because of the antics these persons continuously perform in snatching up the letters from the hundred and fifty-two boxes which contain them. In the calamitous period of 1793, Séchard was about fifty, and a married man. His age and marital status saved him from the great call-up which bore off almost all working-men to the armed forces. The old pressman was the only hand left in the printing-office whose owner, known as 'the gaffer', had just died, leaving a childless widow. It looked as if the business was doomed to immediate extinction: the solitary 'bear' could not change into a 'monkey', because, being a mere pressman, he could neither read nor write. Taking no account of his incompetence, a 'Representative of the People', in a hurry to promulgate the eloquent decrees issued by the National Convention, invested the pressman with a licence as master printer and requisitioned the printing-press. After accepting this dangerous licence, Citizen Séchard indemnified his master's widow by paying over his own wife's savings, with which he bought the whole plant at half its value. So far so good, but the Republican decrees had to be accurately and punctually printed. Faced with this difficult problem, Jérôme-Nicolas Séchard was lucky enough to come upon a nobleman from Marseilles who did not relish the idea of losing his estates by emigrating or of risking his head by showing himself in public, and could only earn his daily bread by taking on some sort of employment. And so Monsieur le Comte de Maucombe donned the humble overalls of a foreman in a provincial printing-office. He set up, read and himself corrected the decrees which imposed the death penalty on citizens who gave concealment to noblemen; the 'bear', who had now become the 'gaffer', struck them off and posted them up; and both of them came through safe and sound. By 1795 the

---

From: Honoré de Balzac, *Lost Illusions* (London: Penguin, 1971), pp. 3–24.

squall of the Terror was over, and Nicolas Séchard had to find another factotum as compositor, proofreader and foreman. An Abbé, who was destined to become a bishop under the Restoration for having, refused to conform to the Civil Constitutions, replaced the Comte de Maucombe until the day when the First Consul re-established the Catholic religion. Later the Count and the bishop were to find themselves both sitting on the same bench in the House of Peers. Although in 1802 Jérôme-Nicolas Séchard was no better at reading and writing than in 1793, his 'makings' were enough for him to be able to engage a foreman. The journeyman once so unconcerned about his future had become quite a martinet to his 'monkeys' and 'bears'. Avarice begins where poverty ends. No sooner had the printer espied the possibility of making a fortune than self-interest developed in him a material understanding of his craft, but he became greedy, wary and sharp-sighted. With him practice made a long nose at theory. In the end he was able to appraise at a glance the cost of a page or folio according to the kind of character required. He proved to his ignorant customers that heavy type cost more to set than light; and when it came to the smaller type he averred that this was more difficult to handle. Composing being that part of printing of which he understood nothing, he was afraid of undercharging that he never made anything but excessive estimates. If his compositors worked on a time-contract he never took his eyes off them. If he knew that a paper-manufacturer was in difficulties, he bought his stock for next to nothing and put it in store. And so by now he was already owner of the building which had housed the printing-office from time immemorial. He had every sort of good luck: he lost his wife, and had only one son, whom he sent to the town *lycée,* not so much in order to have him educated as to prepare the way for a successor: he treated him harshly in order to prolong the duration of his paternal authority; thus, during holidays, he made him work at the type-case, telling him that he must earn his living so that one day he might repay his poor father who was bleeding himself white in order to educate him. When the Abbé departed, Séchard chose a new foreman from among his four compositors, one whom the future bishop had singled out as being as honest as he was intelligent. He was thus in a position to look forward to the time when his son would be able to run the business so that it might expand in young and able hands. David Séchard was a brilliant pupil at the *lycée* of Angoulême. Although the elder Séchard was only a 'bear' who had made good without knowledge or education and had a healthy contempt for learning, he sent his son to Paris to study more advanced typography; but he so vehemently recommended him to amass a fair sum of money in the capital, which he called the 'working-man's paradise', and so often warned him not to count on dipping into his father's purse, that it was obvious that he looked on his son's sojourn in that 'home of sapience' as a means for gaining his own ends. While learning his trade in Paris, David completed his education: the foreman of the Didot works became a scholar. Towards the end of 1819 he left Paris without having cost his father a penny. The latter was now recalling him in order to hand over the management to him. At that time the Séchard press owned the only journal for legal notices that existed in the *département.* It also did all the printing for the prefectoral and episcopal administrations: these three clients were enough to give great prosperity to an energetic young man.

At that period precisely, a firm of paper-manufacturers, the brothers Cointet, purchased the second printer's licence in the Angoulême district. Up to then Séchard senior had managed to keep it completely inoperative by taking advantage of the military crisis which, during the Empire, damped down all industrial enterprise. For this reason he had not bothered to buy it himself and his parsimony was destined to bring ruin in the end to his ancient printing-press. When he learnt of this acquisition, old Séchard thanked his stars that the conflict likely to ensue between his own establishment and that of the Cointets would be sustained by his son, and not himself. 'I should have had the worst of it', he told himself. 'But a young man trained by the Didots will come out all right.' The septuagenarian was sighing for the moment when he could take his ease. His knowledge of high-class typography was scanty, but, to compensate for this, he was known us a past master in an art which workmen printers have jestingly dubbed *tipsiography*: an art held in great esteem by the divine author of *Pan-*

tagruel, but one whose cultivation, persecuted as it is by so-called Temperance Societies, has fallen more and more into disrepute. Jérôme-Nicolas Séchard, true to the destiny which his patronymic marked out for him, was endowed with an unquenchable thirst. This passion for the crushed grape—a taste so natural with 'bears' that Monsieur de Chateaubriand has discovered its effects in the genuine bears of North America—had for long been kept within just bounds by his wife; but philosophers have observed that habits contracted in early life attack old age with renewed vigour. Séchard's case confirmed this moral law: the older he grew, the more he loved imbibing. This passion left such marks on his ursine countenance as to make it truly unique: his nose had assumed the shape and contours of a capital A of triple canon size, while both of his veinous cheeks resembled the kind of vine-leaf which is swollen with violet, purple and often multi-coloured gibbosities: it made one think of a monstrous truffle wrapped round with autumn shoots. Lurking behind tufty eyebrows which were like two snow-laden bushes, his small grey eyes, sparkling with the cunning of avarice that was killing all other emotions, even fatherly affection, in him, showed that he kept his wits about him even when he was drunk. His cranium, completely bald on top, though it was still fringed with greying curls, called to mind the Franciscan friars in La Fontaine's *Tales.* He was short and pot-bellied like many of those old-fashioned lampions which consume more oil than wick—for excesses of every sort urge the body along its appointed path. Drunkenness, like addiction to study, makes a fat man fatter and a thin man thinner. For thirty years Jérôme-Nicolas Séchard had been wearing the famous three-cornered municipal hat still to be seen on the heads of town-criers in certain provinces. His waistcoat and trousers were of greenish velvet. Finally, he wore an old brown frock-coat, stockings of patterned cotton and shoes with silver buckles. This costume, thanks to which the artisan was still manifest behind the bourgeois, was so suited to his vices and habits, so expressive of his way of life, that he looked as if he had come into the world fully clad: you could no more have imagined him without his clothes than you could imagine an onion without its peel.

If this aged printer had not long since shown how far his blind cupidity could go, his plan for retirement would suffice to depict his character. In spite of the expert knowledge that his son must have acquired while training in the great Didot firm, he was proposing to strike a profitable deal with him—one which he had long been meditating. If the father was to make a good bargain, it had to be a bad one for the son. For this sorry individual recognized no father-and-son relationship in business. If in the beginning he had thought of David as being an only child, he later had only looked on him as an obvious purchaser whose interests were opposed to his own: he wanted to sell dear, whereas David would want to buy cheap; therefore his son was an enemy to be vanquished. This transformation of feeling into self-interest, which in educated people is usually a slow, tortuous and hypocritical process, was rapid and undeviating in the old 'bear', who thus showed how easily guileful *tipsiography* could triumph over expertise in typography. When his son arrived home, the old man displayed the commercial-minded tenderness which wily people show to their intended dupes: he fussed over him as a lover might have fussed over a mistress; he took him by the arm and told him where to step in order not to get mud on his shoes; he had had his bed warmed, a fire lit, a supper prepared. Next day, after trying to get his son intoxicated in the course of a copious dinner, Jérôme-Nicolas Séchard, by now well-seasoned, said to him: 'Let's talk business': a proposal so strangely sandwiched between two hiccoughs that David begged him to put it off until the following morning. But the old 'bear' was too expert at drawing advantage from his own tipsiness to delay so long-prepared a battle. Moreover, he said, having had his nose so close to the grindstone for fifty years, he did not intend to keep it there one single hour more. Tomorrow his son would be the 'gaffer'.

Here perhaps a word about Séchard's establishment is needed. The printing-office stood at the spot where the rue de Beaulieu runs into the Place du Mûrier, and had been set up in the building towards the end of the reign of Louis XV. And so a long time had elapsed since these premises had been adapted to the needs of this industry. The ground-floor consisted of one enormous room to which light came from the street through an old glazed window, and from an inner court through a large sash-frame. There was also an alley, leading to the master-printer's office. But in provincial towns the processes of printing always arouse such lively curiosity that customers preferred to come in by the front entrance, even though this meant walking down a few steps, since the workshop floor was below street level. Gaping visitors never minded the inconvenience of threading their devious way through the workshop. If they paid heed to the sheets of paper hanging like cradles from cords attached to the ceiling, they stumbled against rows of cases, or had their hats knocked off by the iron bars which supported the presses. If they watched the agile movements of a compositor plucking his letters out of the hundred-and-fifty-two compartments of type, reading his copy, re-reading the line in his composing-stick and slipping in a lead, they bumped into a ream of damp paper lying under its weights, or caught their hips against the corner of a bench: all to the great amusement of 'monkeys' and 'bears'. No one had ever arrived without mishap at the two large cages at the farther end of this cavern which formed two dismal annexes giving on to the court-yard and in which, on one side, the foreman sat in state and, on the other side, the master-printer. The courtyard walls were pleasantly decorated with vine-trellises which, given the owner's reputation, lent an appetizing touch of local colour. At the farther end a tumbledown lean-to, in which the paper was damped and cut, backed on to a jet-black party wall. There too was the sink in which, before and after the printing-off, the 'formes' were washed. From this sink seeped away a decoction of ink mingled with the household slops, and that gave the peasants passing by on market-days the idea that the Devil was taking his ablutions inside the house. On one side of the lean-to was the kitchen, on the other a wood-pile. The first floor of the house, which had only two attic bedrooms above it, contained three rooms. The first, which ran the whole length of the alley except for the well of the old wooden staircase and received its light from the street through a little wooden casement, and from a court-yard through a bull's-eye window, served both as antechamber and dining-room. Having no other decoration than white-wash, it exemplified the cynical simplicity of commercial greed; the dirty flags had never been washed; it was furnished with three rickety chairs, a round table and a sideboard standing between two doors which gave access, one to a bedroom, the other to the living-room; the windows and doors were brown with grime; as a rule it was cluttered with blank or printed paper, the bales of which were often covered with the remains of Jérôme-Nicolas Séchard's dinner: dessert, dishes and bottles. The bedroom, whose leaded window-panes drew their light from the courtyard, was hung with some of those old tapestries which in provincial towns are displayed along the house-fronts on Corpus Christi day. The bed was a curtained four-poster with a coarse linen counterpane and a red serge coverlet over the foot; there were worm-eaten armchairs, two upholstered walnut chairs, an old writing-desk and a wall-dock hanging over the chimney-piece. This room owed its atmosphere of patriarchal simplicity and its abundance of brown tints to the worthy Rouzeau, Séchard's predecessor and former employer. The living-room had been modernized by the late Madame Séchard and shocked the eye with its appalling wainscots painted in wig-maker's blue; the panels were decorated with wall-paper depicting Oriental scenes in sepia on a white ground; the furniture consisted of six chairs with blue roan seats and backs in the shape of lyres. The two crudely-arched windows looking out on to the Place du Mûrier had no curtains; the chimney-piece was devoid of candelabra, clock and mirror. Madame Séchard had died when she was only half-way through with her plans for embellishment, and the 'bear', seeing no purpose in unproductive improvements, had abandoned them. It was into this room that Jérôme-Nicholas Séchard, *pede titubante,* ush ered his son and pointed to a round table, on which was a statement of his printing-house stock drawn up by the foreman at his direction.

'Read that, my boy', said Jérôme-Nicolas as his besotted eyes rolled from the document to his son and from his son to the document. 'You'll see what a champion printing-office I'm giving you.'

'Three wooden presses supported by iron bars, with imposing-stone of cast iron. . . '

'One of my improvements,' said the old man, interrupting his son's reading.

'With all their appurtenances: ink-troughs, balls and benches, etc. Sixteen hundred francs! . . . Why, father,' said David, letting the inventory fail, 'your presses are just old lumber, not worth three hundred francs. All they're fit for is firewood.'

'Old lumber, are they? . . .' Séchard senior exclaimed, 'Old lumber! Take the inventory and come downstairs! You'll see whether the new-fangled ironmongery they make nowadays works like these good, well-tried tools. And then you'll be ashamed to cry down honest presses which roll along like the mail-coaches and will go on running the rest of your life without needing the slightest repair. Old lumber! Yes, but good enough to keep your pot boiling! Old lumber which your father has been handling for twenty years and which helped him to make you just what you are!'

The old man clattered down the rugged, worn, rickety staircase without tumbling over himself, opened the alley door leading to the workshop, rushed to the first of his presses which he had been crafty enough to have oiled and cleaned, and pointed to the strong oaken side-pieces which his apprentices had polished.

'Isn't that a jewel of a press?' he asked. There was a wedding-invitation on it. The old 'bear' lowered the frisket on to the tympan and the tympan on to the carriage and rolled it under the press; he pulled the bar, unrolled the cord to draw back the carriage, and raised tympan and frisket with all the agility a young 'bear' might have shown. Thus handled, the press gave a pretty little squeak like that of a bird fluttering away after striking against a window-pane.

'Is there a single English press that can do such quick work?' said the father to his astonished son.

The old man ran to the second and third presses in succession and performed the same operation on each of them with equal adroitness. The last one revealed to his wine-blurred gaze a spot which his apprentice had overlooked: with a resounding oath the drunkard gave it a rub with his coat-tail, like a horse-coper smoothing the hide of a horse he wants to sell.

'With these presses, and without a foreman, you can earn yourself nine thousand francs a year, David. As your future partner, I am against your replacing them by those accursed iron presses which wear out the type. You went into raptures in Paris over the invention of that damned Englishman, an enemy of France, trying to make a fortune for the type-founders. Oh yes! You wanted Stanhope presses! To hell with your Stanhope presses. They cost two thousand five hundred francs apiece, almost twice is much as my three beauties put together, and wear down the type because there's no give in them. I'm not educated like you, but bear this in mind: Stanhope presses may last longer, but they spell ruin for the type. My three presses will give you good service, the work will be pulled clean, and that's all the people in Angoulême will ask for. Print with iron or wood, gold or silver, they won't pay you a farthing more.'

'*Item,*' said David. 'Five thousand pounds of type from the Vaflard foundry . . .' The pupil of the Didots could not repress a smile on reading this name.

'All right, laugh away! After a dozen years, the characters are as good as new. There's a type-founder for you! Monsieur Vaflard is an honest man who turns out hard-wearing material; and in my opinion the best founder is the one you go to least often.'

'Valued at ten thousand francs,' David continued. 'Ten thousand francs, father! But that works out at forty sous a pound, and Messrs Didot only charge thirty-six sous a pound for their new pica. Your old batter is only worth the metal it's cast in—ten sous a pound.'

'So you call it better, do you? Bastard, italic and round type made by Monsieur Gillé, formerly printer to the Emperor: type worth six francs a pound, masterpieces of punch-cutting which I bought five years ago. And look, some of them still have the white of the casting on them!' Séchard senior caught up a handful of still unused 'sorts' and showed them to his son. 'I'm no scholar and can't read or write, but I know enough about it to guess that the English script types used by your precious Didots were cribbed from those of the Gillé foundry. Here's a *ronde,*' he added, pointing to a case and taking an M from it: 'a *ronde* in pica size which is still brand-new.'

David perceived that there could be no arguing with his father. He had to take it or leave it, accept or refuse the lot: The old 'bear' had included everything in the inventory, even the ropes in the drying zoom. The smallest job-chase, the wetting-boards, the basins, the stone and brushes for cleaning, everything was priced with miserly precision. The total amounted to thirty thousand francs, including the master-printer's licence and the good-will. David was mentally computing whether the transaction was feasible or not. Seeing his son musing in silence over the figure, Séchard senior grew anxious, for he preferred heated bargaining to mute acceptance. In this sort of dealing, bargaining denotes a business man capable of defending his interests. 'The man who never haggles never pays,' old Séchard used to say. As he watched his son closely to guess his thoughts, he ran through the list of his sorry utensils, all of them needed, he argued, for running a provincial printing-office. He took David round to a glazing-press and a trimmer for jobbing-work, and boasted of their usefulness and soundness.

'Old tools are always best,' he said. 'In the printing business they ought to fetch a better price than the new ones, as they do in the gold-beaters' trade.'

Hideous vignettes representing Hymens and Cupids, dead people pushing up the lids of their sepulchres and representing a V or an M, and enormous play-bill borders complete with mummers' masks were transformed, by virtue of Jérôme-Nicolas's wine-sodden eloquence, into articles of tremendous value. He told his son that provincial people were strongly rooted in their habits, and that any attempt to provide them with better products would be wasted. He, Jérôme-Nicolas Séchard, had tried to sell them better almanacs than the *Double Liégois,* which was printed on sugar-bag paper. Well, they had preferred the original *Double Liégois* to the most splendid almanacs. David would soon recognize the importance of such old-fashioned stuff, which would sell better than the most costly novelties.

'Ha! Ha! my boy! The provinces are one thing, Paris is another. If a man from L'Houmeau comes and orders wedding cards, and if you print them without a Cupid and garlands, he won't think he's properly married: he'll bring them back to you if he only sees an M on them, as with your Messrs Didot. They are the glory of the printing-trade, but their new-fangled ideas won't take on in the provinces for a hundred years. And that's the truth.'

Generous souls make poor business men. David was one of those shy and sensitive people who shrink from argument and give way as soon as their opponent's foil pricks too near to their heart. His lofty sentiments and the deference he still paid to the old drunkard made him even less fit to hold his own in discussion with his father, particularly since he credited him with the best intentions—for at first he put down the pressman's voracious selfishness to affection for his tools. Nonetheless, since Jérôme-Nicolas Séchard had bought the entire concern from Rouzeau's widow for ten thousand francs in *assignats,* and since at present values thirty thousand francs was an exorbitant price, young David exclaimed:

'But father, you are bleeding me white!'

'I who brought you into the world . . .' said the old sot, with his arms raised towards the drying-poles. 'How much then do you reckon, David, for the printer's licence? Do you know what the *Advertising Journal* is worth at ten sous a line? It's a monopoly, and it brought in five hundred francs last month. My lad, take a look at the ledgers and see what comes in from the prefecture posters and registers and the work we do for the Mayor and the Bishop. You're a lazy-bones with no thought of getting on. You're boggling about the price of a horse which will carry you to some fine piece of property like the Marsac one.'

To the inventory was appended a deed of partnership between father and son. The benevolent father was letting his house to the firm for twelve hundred francs a year, although he had bought it for less than six thousand francs; and he was reserving one of the two attic rooms for his own use. Until such time as David Séchard had paid off the thirty thousand francs, profits were to be equally divided; once he had repaid this sum to his father, he would become the one and only owner of the printing-office. David computed the value of the licence, the goodwill and the journal without taking the plant into account; he decided he would be able to make good and accepted the terms. His father, accustomed to the niggling cautiousness of the peasant class, and knowing nothing of the wider scope of Parisian calculations, was astonished at so prompt a conclusion.

'Can my son have made money?' he wondered. 'Or is he even now thinking of not paying up?' With this thought in mind, he questioned him in order to find out if he had money with him, so as to take it from him as a first instalment. The father's curiosity awakened the son's suspicions, and the latter remained as tight as a clam. The next day, Séchard senior ordered his apprentice to remove to the second-floor bedroom all the furniture which he planned to have transported to his country cottage in carts which would be returning there empty. He stripped the three first-floor rooms bare and handed them over to his son; he also put him in possession of the printing-works without giving him a farthing for the workmen's wages. When David asked his father, as a partner, to contribute to the outlay needed for their joint enterprise, the old pressman affected not to understand. He was not obliged, he said, to hand over money as well as the printing-office; his capital was already sunk in it. His son's logic became more pressing, and he replied that, when he had bought the printing-works from Rouzeau's widow, he had managed without a penny in his pocket. If he, a poor and completely ignorant workman, had succeeded, a pupil of the Didots would do better still. Moreover, David had been earning money thanks to the education his old father had paid for by the sweat of his brow, and now he could very well put it to use.

'What have you done with your earnings?' he asked, returning to the attack in order to clear up the problem which his son's silence had left unsolved the previous day.

'Well, I had to live, and I had to buy books,' David answered indignantly.

'Oh, you bought books! You won't do well in business. People who buy books can't be much good at printing them,' the 'bear' replied.

David experienced the most horrible of humiliations: a father's degradation. He had to endure the spate of mean, tearful, shifty, mercenary arguments which the old miser used to express his refusal. Realizing that he had to stand alone, without support, finding that he was dealing with a speculator instead of a father, he thrust back his grief and tried, out of philosophical curiosity, to get to the bottom of his character. He drew his attention to the fact that he had never asked him to render an account of his mother's fortune. Even if this fortune could not be set off against the price asked for the printing-works, it should at least go towards the running of the new partnership.

'Why', old Séchard replied, 'all your mother owned was her brains and beauty.'

At this reply, David saw through his father completely, and realized that, in order to extract such a reckoning from him, he would have to take legal proceedings, and that these would be interminable, costly and discreditable. The noble-hearted young man decided to shoulder the burden—a heavy one, for he knew what an effort it would be to discharge the obligations he was contracting towards his father.

'I will work hard,' he told himself. 'After all, if I find it heavy going, so did the old fellow. Besides, shall I not be working for myself?'

Séchard senior was worried by his son's silence. 'I'm leaving you a treasure,' he said.

David asked what this treasure was.

'Marion,' he replied.

Marion was a sturdy country girl, indispensable for the running of the printing-works. She wetted the paper and trimmed it, ran errands, did the cooking, washed the clothes, unloaded the paper from the vans, went round collecting debts and cleaned the ink-balls. Had she had been able to read, old Séchard would have made a compositor of her.

He set off on foot for the country. Although well pleased with his sale, which he was passing off as a venture in partnership, he was anxious about the way payment would be made. After the agony of making a sale, there always comes the agony of turning it into cash. All passions are essentially jesuitical. This man, who regarded education as useless, strove hard to believe in the effect it produces. His thirty thousand francs were so to speak lent out on mortgage, and the security for them was the sense of honour which education must have developed in his son. As a properly brought-up young man, David would sweat blood in order to meet his engagements; his knowledge of the trade would suggest ways and means; he had shown plenty of fine sentiments; he would certainly pay! Many fathers who act thus believe they have really been paternal, and old Séchard had managed to persuade himself of this by the time he reached his vineyard at Marsac, a little village some ten miles away from Angoulême. This domain, on which the previous owner had built a pleasant habitation, had grown in size from year to year since 1809, when the old 'bear' had acquired it. It was there that he exchanged the care of the printing-press for that of the winepress and, as he used to say, he had had too much to do with wine not to know all about the vine.

For the first year of his retirement to the country, old Séchard showed a troubled countenance as he leaned over his vine-poles, for he spent all his time in his vineyard, just as formerly he had remained inside his workship. The unhoped-for thirty thousand francs went to his head even more than his cloudy September vintage: in his mind's eye he could already see himself fingering them lovingly. The less he deserved this money, the more he desired to lay hands on it. And so anxiety often brought him back from Marsac to Angoulême. He toiled up the slopes of the rock on whose pinnacle the town is perched and entered the workshop to see how his son was getting on. The presses were in their usual place. The one and only apprentice, with a paper cap on his head, would be cleaning the ink-balls. The old 'bear' could hear the press creaking over an invitation card, recognize his old type and see his son and the foreman, each in his cage, reading what he supposed to be the proofs of a book. After dining with David, he returned to his Marsac property, brooding over his fears. Avarice, like love, is endowed with second sight as regards future contingencies; it sniffs them out and worries them. At a distance from the workshop where the sight of his apparatus fascinated him and carried him back to the days when he was prospering, the vine-grower could detect disquieting symptoms of inactivity in his son's demeanour. He took fright at the very name of *Cointet Brothers*, and could see it eclipsing that of *Séchard and Son*. In short the old man could scent misfortune in the wind, for misfortune was indeed hovering over the Séchard firm. But there is a divinity that looks after misers and, through a combination of unforeseen circumstances, this divinity was about to pour the proceeds of his usurious sale into the drunkard's lap.

The reason for the Séchard printing-office being on the decline in spite of factors making for prosperity was David's indifference to the religious reaction which set in under the Restoration government, equalled by his unconcern about the Liberal movement. He maintained in political and religious matters a neutrality which was most injurious to his interests. He was living in a period when provincial tradespeople had to line up with a party in order to get customers: in fact they had to choose between the patronage either of the Liberals or the Royalists. David had fallen in love; this, together with his scientific preoccupations and his inherent good nature, prevented his having that avidity for gain which goes to the making of a genuine business man and which might have induced him to study the differences existing between provincial and Parisian industry. Shades of opinion, which stand out so clearly in the *départements*, are obliterated in the great swirl of Parisian activity. The brothers Cointet adopted the views of the monarchist party, made an open show of keeping fast-days, haunted the Cathedral, cultivated the society of priests and brought out reprints of books of devotion as soon as they came into demand. Thus they took the lead in a lucrative sideline, and slandered David by accusing him of liberalism and atheism. How, they asked, could one give work to a man whose father had sided with the Terrorists, who was a drunkard, a Bonapartist, an old miser who sooner or later would surely leave piles of gold to his heir? They themselves were poor men with large families, whereas David was a bachelor and would be rolling in wealth; that was why he was taking things easy. And so forth. Influenced by the accusations thus launched against David, the prefectoral and episcopal officials at length transferred their custom to the Cointets. Soon these greedy opponents, emboldened by their rival's indifference, founded a second advertising journal. All that the older press had left was jobbing-work from the townspeople; the profits from its advertising journal were reduced by half. Soon the Cointet firm, considerably enriched by the sale of prayer-books and works of piety, offered to buy the Séchard journal in order to monopolize the printing of departmental notices and judicial announcements. The moment David passed on the news to his father, the old vine-grower, appalled by the progress the Cointet firm was making, swooped down from Marsac to the Place du Mûrier with the swiftness of a crow scenting corpses on the battle-field.

'Leave me to deal with the Cointets,' he said to his son. 'You keep out of this.'

The old man was quick to see through the Cointet's intentions, and they were alarmed by his shrewd appraisal of the situation. His son, he said, was making a blunder, and he was going to prevent it. Where would their custom come from if the journal were handed over? Every solicitor, notary and tradesman in L'Houmeau was a Liberal. Well, the Cointets had tried to ruin the Séchards by making out they were Liberals. But this was as good as throwing out a lifeline, for it meant that *Séchard and Son* would keep all the Liberal advertisements. Sell the journal? Just as well sell out completely, stock and printer's licence!

Thereupon he demanded sixty thousand francs of the Cointets for the printing-works, to save his son from ruin. He loved his son; he was protecting his son. The vine-grower made use of his son as peasants make use of their wives: his son wanted this, or he didn't want that, according to the propositions he extorted one by one from the Cointets. By this means he persuaded them, not without great effort, to pay twenty-two thousand francs for the *Charente Advertiser*. But David was to undertake never to print any periodical whatsoever, under a penalty of thirty thousand francs' damages. This sale spelled suicide for the Séchard press, but the vine-grower cared little for that. Theft always leads to murder. The old reprobate counted on applying this sum to the recovery of his capital, and to lay his fingers on that he would have handed David over into the bargain, the more readily because this nuisance of a son had a right to one half of the unexpected windfall. By way of compensation, the generous father made over the printing-works to him—but he still kept the rent for the house at the prodigious figure of twelve hundred francs a year.

After this sale of the *Charente Advertiser* to the Cointets, the old man rarely came to town, alleging his great age; but the real reason was his lack of interest in a printing-office which no longer belonged to him. Nevertheless he was unable entirely to repudiate the long-standing affection he felt for his apparatus. When his concerns brought him to Angoulême, it would have been very difficult to decide what most attracted him to the house—his wooden presses or his son, whom he visited in order to make *pro forma* requests for his rent. His erstwhile foreman, who had now gone over to the Cointets, well knew what to make of this paternal generosity: the wily old fox, he said, was thus reserving to himself the right of intervening in his son's affairs, since the accumulation of unpaid rents made him a preferential creditor.

David Séchard's negligence was due to causes which will throw light on the young man's character. A few days after settling in at his father's printing-office, he had met one of his school friends, Lucien Chardon, a young man of about twenty-one, who at that time was living in the utmost poverty. He was the son of a former medical officer in the Republican armies who had been invalided out as a result of a wound. Nature had made a chemist of Monsieur Chardon senior, and chance had set him up as a pharmacist in Angoulême. Death overtook him just as he was working his way to a lucrative discovery after spending several years at scientific research. He was trying to find a cure for all kinds of gout. Gout is a rich man's disease, and rich men will pay any price to recover their health once lost. And so, among all the problems which had given him subject for meditation, he had singled out this one for resolution. Divided between science and his practice as a pharmacist, the late Chardon had realized that science alone could bring him prosperity: he had accordingly studied the causes of the disease and based his remedy on a certain diet suited to every constitution. He died during a stay in Paris while soliciting the approval of the Academy of Science, and thus lost the fruit of his labours. Anticipating prosperous times, the pharmacist had spared no expense for the education of his son and daughter, so that budgeting for the family constantly ate away the income from his chemist's shop. Consequently, he not only left his children in poverty but also, unfortunately for them, he had brought them up in the expectation of a brilliant future, which his death extinguished. The illustrious doctor Desplein tended him in his last moments and watched him die in convulsions of rage. The prime motive for his ambition had been the ardent love he bore his wife, the last representative of the Rubempré family, whom he had miraculously saved from the scaffold in 1793. Without getting the girl's consent for the fiction, he had gained time by alleging she was pregnant. After having to some extent established the right to marry her, he did in fact marry her in spite of their mutual poverty. His children, like all love-children, inherited their mother's beauty and nothing more: a present which so often proves fatal when it goes with poverty. Madame Chardon's keen participation in her husband's hopes, labours and disappointments had made deep inroads into her beauty, just as her standard of living had suffered from the gradual deterioration which indigence inflicts; but her courage, and that of her children, proved equal to this adversity. The poverty-stricken widow sold the chemist's shop situated in the High Street of L'Houmeau, Angoulême's principal suburb. The proceeds allowed her to purchase an income of three hundred francs a year, a sum insufficient to provide even for her own needs; but she and her daughter accepted their situation without shame and went out to work to earn a living. The mother became a nurse for women in labour, and her gentle manners gained her the preference over all others in the rich households, in which she lived without costing her children anything and in fact earned twenty sous a day. To spare her son the humiliation of seeing his mother reduced to such humble employment, she had assumed the name of 'Madame Charlotte'. People in need of her services applied to Monsieur Postel, Chardon's successor. Lucien's sister worked in a laundry which handled fine linen and belonged to a neighbour, a very decent woman much esteemed in L'Houmeau, a Madame Prieur, and there she was earning about fifteen sous a day. She was in charge of the laundry-women and so enjoyed a sort of superiority which raised her somewhat above the class of working-girls. The meagre proceeds of their toil, added to Madame Chardon's income of three hundred francs, amounted to about eight hundred francs a year, which had to provide these three people with food, clothes and lodging. Even strict economy made this seem scarcely adequate, for it was almost entirely absorbed by Lucien's requirements. Madame Chardon and her daughter Eve believed in Lucien as fervently as Mahomet's wife believed in her husband: there were no bounds to the sacrifices they made for his future. This hard-up family lived in L'Houmeau in a dwelling rented for a very modest sum from Monsieur Chardon's successor; it lay at the further end of an inner court, over the dispensary. Lucien occupied a shabby room in the attic. Spurred on by his father who, with his passion for the natural sciences, had at first urged his son in the same direction, Lucien was one of the most brilliant pupils in the College of Angoulême; he had reached a senior class at the time Séchard was finishing his studies there.

When chance brought these two school friends together again Lucien, tired of drinking from the rudely-fashioned cup of poverty, was on the verge of making one of those drastic decisions which young men of twenty are apt to make. David offered to teach Lucien the art of proof-reading, although he had absolutely no need of a foreman, and paid him a wage of forty francs a month, which saved him from despair. The ties of a friendship dating from schooldays, thus renewed, were strengthened both by the similarity of their predicament and the differences in their characters. Both of them, full of varied ideas for making their fortune, were possessed of that soaring intelligence which makes a man capable of the highest achievements. Yet there they were, at the very bottom of the social ladder. The injustice of their lot forged a powerful bond between them. Moreover, each of them was a poet, although they had climbed different slopes on their way to Parnassus. Although he had been destined for the highest speculation of natural science, Lucien had an ardent thirst for literary glory, while David, whose meditative genius predisposed him to poetry, felt drawn towards the exact sciences. This interchange of roles engendered a kind of spiritual affinity between them. Lucien was not slow in communicating to David the lofty views transmitted to him by his father on the application of science to industry; and David opened Lucien's eyes to new paths in literature along which he might venture in order to make his name and fortune. In a few days the friendship between these two young people developed into the kind of passion that occurs only as one emerges from adolescence. David soon caught a glimpse of the beautiful Eve and fell in love with all the fervour natural to a melancholic and meditative spirit. The liturgical *Et nunc et semper et in secula seculorum* is the guiding maxim for those sublime, unknown poets whose only works are the magnificent epics which two hearts conceive but never consign to paper. When Eve's admirer fathomed the secret hopes which Lucien's mother and sister were setting on his handsome, poetic brow, when he became aware of their blind devotion, he found it sweet to draw closer to his beloved by sharing her hopes and self-denial. And so Lucien became a chosen brother to David. Like the 'Ultras' who were then trying to be more royalist than the King himself, David carried to excess the faith which mother and sister placed in Lucien's genius, and indulged him as a mother does her child. During one of the frequent conversations in which, under the stress of frustrating penury, they were ruminating as all young people do over means of prompt enrichment—shaking the branches of all the trees which earlier marauders had already denuded of their fruit—Lucien remembered two ideas put forward by his father. Monsieur Chardon had talked of halving the price of sugar by the use of a new chemical reagent, and of a similar reduction in the cost of paper to be achieved by importing from America certain inexpensive vegetable substances analogous to those used by the Chinese. David recognized the importance of this problem over which the Didots had already cogitated, and he seized on the idea, seeing a promise of enrichment in it; and so he looked on Lucien as a benefactor whom he would never be able to repay.

Anyone will divine the incompetence of these two friends to manage a printing-press, obsessed as they were by their schemes and their cult of the inner life. Far from bringing in between fifteen and twenty thousand a year, as did the printing-office of the Cointet brothers, printers and publishers to the diocese, proprietors of the *Charente Advertiser,* which was now the only periodical in the *département,* the press belonging to young Séchard scarcely produced three hundred francs a month; and from this had to be deducted the proof-reader's salary, Marion's wages, taxes and rent; and that only left David with about one hundred francs a month. In enterprising and industrious hands the type would have been renewed, steel presses bought and a contract made with Paris publishers for cheap reprints of their books. But master-printer and foreman were so absorbed in their intellectual pursuits that they were content to carry out the orders placed by their sole remaining customers. The Cointet brothers were now so fully aware of David's character and manner of life that they slandered him no more; on the contrary, a wiser policy was to let his press rub along in honest mediocrity so that it should not fall into the hands of some rival to be feared; they themselves passed the so-called town custom on to it. Thus, without knowing it, David owed his commercial survival to the cunning calculation of his competitors. Pleased with what they called his mania, the Cointets made a show of rectitude and loyalty in their dealings with him; but in reality they were behaving like the Public Transport Service when it stages bogus competition in order to ward off a genuine one.

✦ Reading 16 ✦

Tess of the D'Urbevilles

Thomas Hardy

Tess is the daughter of a poor farming family with high, if distant, connections. The father, having become aware of their old family name, wants Tess to improve her lot, a daunting task as her tribulations will reveal. This scene portrays a first meeting between Tess and a young man of wealth. Their later acquaintanceship will prove disastrous for both of them.

The village of Marlott lay amid the north-eastern undulations of the beautiful Vale of Blakemore, or Blackmoor, aforesaid, an engirdled and secluded region, for the most part untrodden as yet by tourist or landscape-painter, though within a four hours' journey from London.

It is a vale whose acquaintance is best made by viewing it from the summits of the hills that surround it—except perhaps during the droughts of summer. An unguided ramble into its recesses in bad weather is apt to engender dissatisfaction with its narrow, tortuous, and miry ways.

This fertile and sheltered tract of country, in which the fields are never brown and the springs never dry, is bounded on the south by the bold chalk ridge that embraces the prominences of Hambledon Hill, Bulbarrow, Nettlecombe-Tout, Dogbury, High Stoy, and Bubb Down. The traveller from the coast, who, after plodding northward for a score of miles over calcareous downs and cornlands, suddenly reaches the verge of one of these escarpments is surprised and delighted to behold, extended like a map beneath him, a country differing absolutely from that which he has passed through. Behind him the hills are open, the sun blazes down upon fields so large as to give an unenclosed character to the landscape, the lanes are white, the hedges low and plashed, the atmosphere colourless. Here, in the valley, the world seems to be constructed upon a smaller and more delicate scale; the fields are mere paddocks, so reduced that from this height their hedgerows appear a network of dark green threads overspreading the paler green of the grass. The atmosphere beneath is languorous, and is so tinged with azure that what artists call the middle distance partakes also of that hue, while the horizon beyond is of the deepest ultramarine. Arable lands are few and limited; with but slight exceptions the prospect is a broad, rich mass of grass and trees, mantling minor hills and dales within the major. Such is the Vale of Blackmoor.

The district is of historic, no less than of topographical, interest. The vale was known in former times as the Forest of White Hart, from a curious legend of King Henry III's reign, in which the killing by a certain Thomas de la Lynd of a beautiful white hart which the King had run down and spared was made the occasion of a heavy fine. In those days, and till comparatively recent times, the country was densely wooded. Even now, traces of its earlier condition are to be found in the old oak copses and irregular belts of timber that yet survive upon its slopes and the hollow-trunked trees that shade so many of its pastures.

The forests have departed, but some old customs of their shades remain. Many, however, linger only in a metamorphosed or disguised form. The May Day dance, for instance, was to be discerned on the afternoon under notice in the guise of the chub-revel, or "club-walking," as it was there called.

It was an interesting event to the younger inhabitants of Marlott, though its real interest was not observed by the participators in the ceremony. Its singularity lay less in the retention of a custom of walking in procession and dancing on each anniversary than in the members being solely women. In

From: Thomas Hardy, *Tess of the D'Urbevilles: A Pure Woman* (New York: Signet, 1999), pp. 6–13.

men's clubs such celebrations were, though expiring, less uncommon; but either the natural shyness of the softer sex or a sarcastic attitude on the part of male relatives had denuded such women's clubs as remained (if any other did) of this their glory and consummation. The club of Marlott alone lived to uphold the local Cerealia. It had walked for hundreds of years, if not as benefit-club, as votive sisterhood of some sort; and it walked still.

The banded ones were all dressed in white gowns—a gay survival from Old Style days, when cheerfulness and May-time were synonyms—days before the habit of taking long views had reduced emotions to a monotonous average. Their first exhibition of themselves was in a processional march of two and two round the parish. Ideal and real clashed slightly as the sun lit up their figures against the green hedges and creeper-laced house-fronts, for, though the whole troop wore white garments, no two whites were alike among them. Some approached pure blanching; some had a bluish pallor; some worn by the older characters (which had possibly lain by folded for many a year) inclined to a cadaverous tint and to a Georgian style.

In addition to the distinction of a white frock, every woman and girl carried in her right hand a peeled willow wand and in her left a bunch of white flowers. The peeling of the former and the selection of the latter had been an operation of personal care.

There were a few middle-aged and even elderly women in the train, their silver-wiry hair and wrinkled faces, scourged by time and trouble, having almost a grotesque, certainly a pathetic, appearance in such a jaunty situation. In a true view, perhaps, there was more to be gathered and told of each anxious and experienced one, to whom the years were drawing nigh when she should say, "I have no pleasure in them," than of her juvenile comrades. But let the elder be passed over here for those under whose bodices the life throbbed quick and warm.

The young girls formed, indeed, the majority of the band, and their heads of luxuriant hair reflected in the sunshine every tone of gold and black and brown. Some had beautiful eyes, others a beautiful nose, others a beautiful mouth and figure: few, if any, had all. A difficulty of arranging their lips in this crude exposure to public scrutiny, an inability to balance their heads and to dissociate self-consciousness from their features, was apparent in them and showed that they were genuine country-girls, unaccustomed to many eyes.

And as each and all of them were warmed without by the sun, so each had a private little sun for her soul to bask in; some dream, some affection, some hobby, at least some remote and distant hope which, though perhaps starving to nothing, still lived on, as hopes will. Thus they were all cheerful, and many of them merry.

They came round by The Pure Drop Inn, and were turning out of the high road to pass through a wicket-gate into the meadows when one of the women said, "The Lord-a-Lord! Why, Tess Durbeyfield, if there isn't thy father riding home in a carriage!"

A young member of the band turned her head at the exclamation. She was a fine and handsome girl—not handsomer than some others, possibly—but her mobile peony mouth and large innocent eyes added eloquence to colour and shape. She wore a red ribbon in her hair and was the only one of the white company who could boast of such a pronounced adornment. As she looked round Durbeyfield was seen moving along the road in a chaise belonging to The Pure Drop, driven by a frizzle-headed brawny damsel with her gown-sleeves rolled above her elbows. This was the cheerful servant of that establishment, who, in her part of factotum, turned groom and ostler at times. Durbeyfield, leaning back, and with his eyes closed luxuriously, was waving his hand above his head and singing in a slow recitative:
"I've-got-a-gr't-family-vault-at-Kingsbere—and knighted-fore-fathers-in-lead-coffins-there!"

The clubbists tittered, except the girl called Tess—in whom a slow heat seemed to rise at the sense that her father was making himself foolish in their eyes.

"He's tired, that's all," she said hastily, "and he has got a lift home because our own horse has to rest today."

"Bless thy simplicity, Tess," said her companions. "He's got his market-nitch, Haw-haw!"

"Look here; I won't walk another inch with you if you say any jokes about him!" Tess cried, and the colour upon her cheeks spread over her face and neck. In a moment her eyes grew moist and her glance drooped to the ground. Perceiving that they had really pained her, they said no more, and order again prevailed. Tess's pride would not allow her to turn her head again, to learn what her father's meaning was, if he had any; and thus she moved on with the whole body to the enclosure where there was to be dancing on the green. By the time the spot was reached, she had recovered her equanimity and tapped her neighbour with her wand and talked as usual.

Tess Durbeyfield at this time of her life was a mere vessel of emotion untinctured by experience. The dialect was on her tongue to some extent, despite the village school: the characteristic intonation of that dialect for this district being the voicing approximately rendered by the syllable UR, probably as rich an utterance as any to be found in human speech. The pouted-up, deep red mouth to which this syllable was native had hardly as yet settled into its definite shape, and her lower lip had a way of thrusting the middle of her top one upward when they closed together after a word.

Phases of her childhood lurked in her aspect still. As she walked along to-day, for all her bouncing, handsome womanliness, you could sometimes see her twelfth year in her cheeks or her ninth sparkling from her eyes; and even her fifth would flit over the curves of her mouth now and then.

Yet few knew, and still fewer considered this. A small minority, mainly strangers, would look long at her in casually passing by, and grow momentarily fascinated by her freshness, and wonder if they would ever see her again; but to almost everybody she was a fine and picturesque country-girl, and no more.

Nothing was seen or heard further of Durbeyfield in his triumphal chariot under the conduct of the ostleress, and the club having entered the allotted spaced, dancing began. As there were no men in the company, the girls danced at first with each other, but when the hour for the close of labour drew on, the masculine inhabitants of the village, together with other idlers and pedestrians, gathered round the spot and appeared inclined to negotiate for a partner.

Among these on-lookers were three young men of a superior class, carrying small knapsacks strapped to their shoulders and stout sticks in their hands. Their general likeness to each other and their consecutive ages would almost have suggested that they might be what in fact they were, brothers. The elder wore the white tie, high waistcoat, and thin-brimmed hat of the regulation curate; the second was the normal undergraduate; the appearance of the third and youngest would hardly have been sufficient to characterize him; there was an uncribbed, uncabined aspect in his eyes and attire, implying that he had hardly as yet found the entrance to his professional groove. That he was a desultory, tentative student of something and everything might only have been predicted of him.

These three brethren told casual acquaintance that they were spending their Whitsun holidays in a walking tour through the Vale of Blackmoor, their course being south-westerly from the town of Shaston on the northeast.

They leant over the gate by the highway and inquired as to the meaning of the dance and the white-frocked maids. The two elder of the brothers were plainly not intending to linger more than a moment, but the spectacle of a bevy of girls dancing without male partners seemed to amuse the third and make him in no hurry to move on. He unstrapped his knapsack, put it, with his stick, on the hedge-bank, and opened the gate.

"What are you going to do, Angel?" asked the eldest.

"I am inclined to go and have a fling with them. Why not all of us—just for a minute or two—it will not detain us long?"

"No—no; nonsense!" said the first. "Dancing in public with a troop of country hoydens—suppose we should be seen! Come along, or it will be dark before we get to Stourcastle, and there's no place we can sleep at nearer than that; besides, we must get through another chapter of *A Counterblast to Agnosticism* before we turn in, now I have taken the trouble to bring the book."

"All right—I'll overtake you and Cuthbert in five minutes; don't stop; I give my word that I will, Felix."

The two elder reluctantly left him and walked on, taking their brother's knapsack to relieve him in following, and the youngest entered the field.

"This is a thousand pities," he said gallantly to two or three of the girls nearest him as soon as there was a pause in the dance. "Where are your partners, my dears?"

"They've not left off work yet," answered one of the boldest. "They'll be here by and by. Till then, will you be one, sir?"

"Certainly. But what's one among so many!"

"Better than none. 'Tis melancholy work facing and footing it to one of your own sort, and no clipsing and colling at all. Now, pick and choose."

" 'Ssh—don't be so for'ard!" said a shyer girl.

The young man, thus invited, glanced them over and attempted some discrimination; but, as the group were all so new to him, he could not very well exercise it. He took almost the first that came to hand, which was not the speaker, as she had expected; nor did it happen to be Tess Durbeyfield. Pedigree, ancestral skeletons, monumental record, the d'Urberville lineaments, did not help Tess in her life's battle as yet even to the extent of attracting to her a dancing-partner over the heads of the commonest peasantry. So much for Normal blood unaided by Victorian lucre.

The name of the eclipsing girl, whatever it was, has not been handed down; but she was envied by all as the first who enjoyed the luxury of a masculine partner that evening. Yet such was the force of example that the village young men, who had not hastened to enter the gate while no intruder was in the way, now dropped in quickly, and soon the couples became leavened with rustic youth to a marked extent, till at length the plainest woman in the club was no longer compelled to foot it on the masculine side of the figure.

The church clock struck, when suddenly the student said that he must leave—he had been forgetting himself—he had to join his companions. As he fell out of the dance his eyes lighted on Tess Durbeyfield, whose own large orbs wore, to tell the truth, the faintest aspect of reproach that he had not chosen her. He, too, was sorry then that, owing to her backwardness, he had not observed her; and with that in his mind he left the pasture.

On account of his long delay he started in a flying-run down the lane westward, and had soon passed the hollow and mounted the next rise. He had not yet overtaken his brothers, but he paused to get breath, and looked back. He could see the white figures of the girls in the green enclosure whirling about as they had whirled when he was among them. They seemed to have quite forgotten him already.

All of them, except, perhaps, one. This white shape stood apart by the hedge alone. From her position he knew it to be the pretty maiden with whom he had not danced. Trifling as the matter was, he yet instinctively felt that she was hurt by his oversight. He wished that he had asked her; he wished that he had inquired her name. She was so modest, so expressive, she had looked so soft in her thin white gown that he felt he had acted stupidly.

However, it could not be helped, and, turning and bending himself to a rapid walk, he dismissed the subject from his mind.

✦ Reading 17 ✦

The Mayor of Casterbridge

Thomas Hardy

Susan Henchard and her daughter return to the Casterbridge area after many years abroad. Elizabeth-Ann believes her father died in her infancy, whereas in reality, in a fit of drunkenness, he had literally sold wife and infant daughter to the highest bidder at a fair. To Susan's surprise, her husband, a completely reformed character and prosperous businessman in the wheat trade, is mayor of Casterbridge.

Henchard's wife acted for the best, but she had involved herself in difficulties. A hundred times she had been upon the point of telling her daughter Elizabeth-Jane the true story of her life, the tragical crisis of which had been the transaction at Weydon Fair, when she was not much older than the girl now beside her. But she had refrained. An innocent maiden had thus grown up in the belief that the relations between the genial sailor and her mother were the ordinary ones that they had always appeared to be. The risk of endangering a child's strong affection by disturbing ideas which had grown with her growth was to Mrs. Henchard too fearful a thing to contemplate. It had seemed, indeed, folly to think of making Elizabeth-Jane wise.

But Susan Henchard's fear of losing her dearly loved daughter's heart by a revelation had little to do with any sense of wrong-doing on her own part. Her simplicity—the original ground of Henchard's contempt for her—had allowed her to live on in the conviction that Newson had acquired a morally real and justifiable right to her by his purchase—though the exact bearings and legal limits of that right were vague. It may seem strange to sophisticated minds that a sane young matron could believe in the seriousness of such a transfer, and were there not numerous other instances of the same belief the thing might scarcely be credited. But she was by no means the first or last peasant woman who had religiously adhered to her purchaser, as too many rural records show.

From: Thomas Hardy, *The Mayor of Casterbridge* (New York: Signet, 1984), pp. 32–38.

The history of Susan Henchard's adventures in the interim can be told in two or three sentences. Absolutely helpless she had been taken off to Canada, where they had lived several years without any great worldly success, though she worked as hard as any woman could to keep their cottage cheerful and well-provided. When Elizabeth-Jane was about twelve years old the three returned to England and settled at Falmouth, where Newson made a living for a few years as boatman and general handy shoreman.

He then engaged in the Newfoundland trade, and it was during this period that Susan had an awakening. A friend to whom she confided her history ridiculed her grave acceptance of her position; and all was over with her peace of mind. When Newson came home at the end of one winter he saw that the delusion he had so carefully sustained had vanished for ever.

There was then a time of sadness, in which she told him her doubts if she could live with him longer. Newson left home again on the Newfoundland trade when the season came round. The vague news of his loss at sea a little later on solved a problem which had become torture to her meek conscience. She saw him no more.

Of Henchard they heard nothing. To the liege subjects of Labour, the England of those days was a continent, and a mile a geographical degree.

Elizabeth-Jane developed early into womanliness. One day, a month or so after receiving intelligence of Newson's death off the Bank of Newfoundland, when the girl was about eighteen, she was sitting on a willow chair in the cottage they still occupied, working twine nets for the fishermen. Her mother was in a back corner of the same room, engaged in the same labour; and dropping the heavy wood needle she was filling she surveyed her daughter thoughtfully. The sun shone in at the door upon the young woman's head and hair, which was worn loose, so that the rays streamed into its depths as into a hazel copse. Her face, though somewhat wan and incomplete, possessed the raw materials of beauty in a promising degree. There was an underhandsomeness in it, struggling to reveal itself through the provisional curves of immaturity, and the casual disfigurements that resulted from the straitened circumstances of their lives. She was handsome in the bone, hardly as yet handsome in the flesh. She possibly might never be fully handsome, unless the carking accidents of her daily existence could be evaded before the mobile parts of her countenance had settled to their final mould.

The sight of the girl made her mother sad—not vaguely, but by logical inference. They both were still in that strait-waistcoat of poverty from which she had tried so many times to be delivered for the girl's sake. The woman had long perceived how zealously and constantly the young mind of her companion was struggling for enlargement; and yet now, in her eighteenth year, it still remained but little unfolded. The desire—sober and repressed—of Elizabeth-Jane's heart was indeed to see, to hear, and to understand. How could she become a woman of wider knowledge, higher repute—"better," as she termed it—this was her constant inquiry of her mother. She sought further into things than other girls in her position ever did, and her mother groaned as she felt she could not aid in the search.

The sailor, drowned or no, was probably now lost to them; and Susan's staunch, religious adherence to him as her husband in principle, till her views had been disturbed by enlightenment, was demanded no more. She asked herself whether the present moment, now that she was a free woman again, were not as opportune a one as she would find in a world where anything had been so inopportune, for making a desperate effort to advance Elizabeth. To pocket her pride and search for the first husband seemed, wisely or not, the best initiatory step. He had possibly drunk himself into his tomb. But he might, on the other hand, have had too much sense to do so; for in her time with him he had been given to bouts only, and was not a habitual drunkard.

At any rate, the propriety of returning to him, if he lived, was unquestionable. The awkwardness of searching for him lay in enlightening Elizabeth, a proceeding which her mother could not endure to contemplate. She finally resolved to undertake the search without confiding to the girl her former relations with Henchard, leaving it to him if they found him to take what steps he might choose to that end. This will account for their conversation at the fair and the half-informed state in which Elizabeth was led onward.

In this attitude they proceeded on their journey, trusting solely to the dim light afforded of Henchard's whereabouts by the furmity woman. The strictest economy was indispensable. Sometimes they might have been seen on foot, sometimes on farmers' waggons, sometimes in carriers' vans; and thus they drew near to Casterbridge. Elizabeth-Jane discovered to her alarm that her mother's health was not what it once had been, and there was ever and anon in her talk that renunciatory tone which showed that, but for the girl, she would not be very sorry to quit a life she was growing thoroughly weary of.

It was on a Friday evening, near the middle of September, and just before dusk, that they reached the summit of a hill within a mile of the place they sought. There were high-banked hedges to the coach-road here, and they mounted upon the green turf within, and sat down. The spot commanded a full view of the town and its environs.

"What an old-fashioned place it seems to be!" said Elizabeth-Jane, while her silent mother mused on other things than topography. "It is huddled all together; and it is shut in by a square wall of trees, like a plot of garden ground by a box-edging."

Its squareness was, indeed, the characteristic which most struck the eye in this antiquated borough, the borough of Casterbridge—at that time, recent as it was, untouched by the faintest sprinkle of modernism. It was compact as a box of dominoes. It had no suburbs—in the ordinary sense. Country and town met at a mathematical line.

To birds of the more soaring kind Casterbridge must have appeared on this fine evening as a mosaic-work of subdued reds, browns, greys, and crystals, held together by a rectangular frame of deep green. To the level eye of humanity it stood as an indistinct mass behind a dense stockade of limes and chestnuts, set in the midst of miles of rotund down and concave field. The mass became gradually dissected by the vision into towers, gables, chimneys, and casements, the highest glazings shining bleared and bloodshot with the coppery fire they caught from the belt of sunlit cloud in the west.

From the centre of each side of this tree-bound square ran avenues east, west, and south into the wide expanse of corn-land and coomb to the distance of a mile or so. It was by one of these avenues that the pedestrians were about to enter. Before they had risen to proceed two men passed outside the hedge, engaged in argumentative conversation.

"Why, surely," said Elizabeth, as they receded, "those men mentioned the name of Henchard in their talk—the name of our relative?"

"I thought so too," said Mrs. Newson.

"That seems a hint to us that he is still here."

"Yes."

"Shall I run after them, and ask them about him—"

"No, no, no! Not for the world just yet. He may be in the workhouse, or in the stocks, for all we know."

"Dear me—why should you think that, Mother?"

" 'Twas just something to say—that's all! But we must make private inquiries."

Having sufficiently rested they proceeded on their way at evenfall. The dense trees of the avenue rendered the road dark as a tunnel, though the open land on each side was still under a faint daylight; in other words, they passed down a midnight between two gloamings. The features of the town had a keen interest for Elizabeth's mother, now that the human side came to the fore. As soon as they had wandered about they could see that the stockade of gnarled trees which framed in Casterbridge was itself an avenue, standing on a low green bank or escarpment, with a ditch yet visible without. Within the avenue and bank was a wall more or less discontinuous, and within the wall were packed the abodes of the burghers.

Though the two women did not know it these external features were but the ancient defences of the town, planted as a promenade.

The lamplights now glimmered through the engirdling trees, conveying a sense of great snugness and comfort inside, and rendering at the same time the unlighted country without strangely solitary and vacant in aspect, considering its nearness to life. The difference between burgh and champaign was increased, too, by sounds which now reached them above others—the notes of a brass band. The travellers returned into the High Street, where there were timber houses with overhanging stories, whose small-paned lattices were screened by dimity curtains on a drawing-string, and under whose barge-boards old cobwebs waved in the breeze. There were houses of brick-nogging, which derived their chief support from those adjoining. There were slate roofs patched with tiles, and tile roofs patched with slate, with occasionally a roof of thatch.

The agricultural and pastoral character of the people upon whom the town depended for its existence was shown by the class of objects displayed in the shop windows. Scythes, reap-hooks, sheep-shears, bill-hooks, spades, mattocks, and hoes at the ironmonger's; beehives, butter-firkins, churns, milking stools and pails, hay-rakes, field-flagons, and seed-lips at the cooper's; cart-ropes and plough-harness at the saddler's; carts, wheelbarrows, and mill-gear at the wheelwright's and machinist's; horse-embrocations at the chemists's; at the glover's and leather-cutter's, hedging-gloves, thatchers' knee-caps, ploughmen's leggings, villagers' patterns and clogs.

They came to a grizzled church, whose massive square tower rose unbroken into the darkening sky, the lower parts being illuminated by the nearest lamps sufficiently to show how completely the mortar from the joints of the stonework had been nibbled out by time and weather, which had planted in the crevices thus made little tufts of stonecrop and grass almost as far up as the very battlements. From this tower the clock struck eight, and thereupon a bell began to toll with a peremptory clang. The curfew was still rung in Casterbridge, and it was utilized by the inhabitants as a signal for shutting their shops. No sooner did the deep notes of the bell throb between the housefronts than a clatter of shutters arose through the whole length of the High Street. In a few minutes business at Casterbridge was ended for the day.

Other clocks struck eight from time to time—one gloomily from the gaol, another from the gable of an almshouse, with a preparative creak of machinery, more audible than the note of the bell; a row of tall, varnished case-clocks from the interior of a clockmaker's shop joined in one after another just as the shutters were enclosing them, like a row of actors delivering their final speeches before the fall of the curtain; then chimes were heard stammering out the Sicilian Mariners' Hymn; so that chronologists of the advanced school were appreciably on their way to the next hour before the whole business of the old one was satisfactorily wound up.

In an open space before the church walked a woman with her gown-sleeves rolled up so high that the edge of her underlinen was visible and her skirt tucked up through her pocket hole. She carried a loaf under her arm from which she was pulling pieces of bread, and handing them to some other women who walked with her; which pieces they nibbled critically. The sight reminded Mrs. Henchard-Newson and her daughter that they had an appetite; and they inquired of the woman for the nearest baker's.

"Ye may as well look for manna-food as good bread in Casterbridge just now," she said, after directing them. "They can blare their trumpets and thump their drums, and have their roaring dinners"—waving her hand towards a point further along the street, where the brass band could be seen standing in front of an illuminated building—"but we must needs be put-to for want of a wholesome crust. There's less good bread than good beer in Casterbridge now."

"And less good beer than swipes," said a man with his hands in his pockets.

"How does it happen there's no good bread?" asked Mrs. Henchard.

"Oh, 'tis the corn-factor—he's the man that our millers and bakers all deal wi', and he has sold 'em growed wheat, which they didn't know was growed, so they *say,* till the dough ran all over the ovens like quicksilver, so that the loaves be as flat as toads, and like suet pudden inside. I've been a wife, and I've been a mother, and I never see such unprincipled bread in Casterbridge as this before.—But you must be a real stranger here not to know what's made all the poor volks' insides plim like blowed bladders this week?"

"I am," said Elizabeth's mother shyly.

Not wishing to be observed further till she knew more of her future in this place, she withdrew with her daughter from the speaker's side. Getting a couple of biscuits at the shop indicated as a temporary substitute for a meal, they next bent their steps instinctively to where the music was playing.

✦ Reading 18 ✦

Reeds in the Wind

Grazia Deledda

Tied to the past, the servant Efix, of local peasant stock, tends to the needs of his mistresses, impoverished sisters of noble birth. They live out their lives in a decaying grand house on a tiny farm, all that remains of vast estates.

Efix, the Pintor sisters' servant, had worked all day to shore up the primitive river embankment that he had slowly and laboriously built over the years. At nightfall he was contemplating his work from where he was sitting in front of his hut halfway up white Doves' Hill. A blue-green fringe of reeds rustled behind him.

Silently stretching out before him down to the river sparkling in the twilight was the little farm that Efix considers more his than the owners': thirty years of possession and work had certainly made it his, and the two hedgerows of prickly pear that enclose it like two gray walls meandering from terrace to terrace, from the hill to the river, are like the boundaries of the world to him.

In his survey the servant ignored the land on either side of the farm because it had once been Pintor property. Why dredge up the past? Useless regret. Better to think about the future and hope in God's help.

And God promised a good year, or at least He had covered all the almond and peach trees in the valley with blossoms; and this valley, between two rows of white hills covered with spring vegetation, water, scrub, flowers, together with the distant blue mountains to the west and the blue sea to the east, gave the impression of a cradle billowing with green veils and blue ribbons, with the river murmuring monotonously like a sleepy child.

But the days were already too hot and Efix was also thinking about the torrential rains that swell the bankless river and make it leap like an all-destroying monster. One could hope, but had to be watchful, like the reeds along the riverbank beating their leaves together with every breath of wind as though warning of danger.

That was why he had worked all day and now, waiting for night, he wove a reed mat so as not to waste time and prayed that God make his work worthwhile. What good is a little embankment if God's will doesn't make it as formidable as a mountain?

Seven reeds across a willow twig, and seven prayers to the Lord and to Our Lady of Rimedio, bless her. In the intense twilight blue her little church and the quiet circle of cabins around it down below lay like a centuries-old abandoned prehistoric village. At this hour, as the moon bloomed like a big rose in the bushes on the hill and euphorbia spread its perfume along the river, Efix's mistresses were also praying. Donna Ester, the oldest, bless her, was certainly remembering him, the sinner. This was enough to make him feel happy, compensated for his efforts.

Footsteps in the distance made him look up. They sounded familiar. It was the light, swift stride of a boy, the stride of an angel hurrying with some happy or sad announcement. God's will be done. It's He who sends good and bad news; but Efix's heart began to pound, and his black cracked fingers trembled on the silvery reeds shining in the moonlight like threads of water.

The footsteps were no longer heard. Nevertheless, Efix remained motionless, waiting.

The moon rose before him, and evening voices told him the day had ended: a cuckoo's rhythmical cry, the early crickets' chirping, a bird calling; the reeds sighing and the ever more distinct voice of the river; but most of all a breathing, a mysterious panting that seemed to come from the earth itself. Yes, man's working day was done, but the fantastic life

From: Grazia Deledda, *Reeds in the Wind* (New York: Ithaca Press, 1999), 1–10.

of elves, fairies, wandering spirits was beginning. Ghosts of the ancient Barons came down from the Castle ruins above Galte on Efix's left and ran along the river hunting wild boar and fox. Their guns gleamed in the short alder trees along the riverbed, and the faint sound of barking dogs in the distance was a sign of their passing.

Efix could hear the sound that the *panas*—women who died in childbirth—made while washing their clothes down by the river, beating them with a dead man's shin bone, and he believed he saw the *ammattadore* (the elf with seven caps where he hid his treasure) jumping about under the almond woods, followed by vampires with steel tails.

It was the elf that caused the branches and rocks to glitter under the moon. And along with the evil spirits were spirits of unbaptized babies—white spirits that flew through the air changing themselves into little silvery clouds behind the moon. And dwarfs and *janas*—the little fairies who stay in their small rock houses during the day weaving gold cloth on their golden looms—were dancing in the large phillyrea bushes, while giants looked out from the rocks on the moonstruck mountains, holding the bridles of enormous horses that only they can mount, squinting to see if down there within the expanse of evil euphorbia a dragon was lurking. Or if the legendary *cananèa,* living from the time of Christ, was slithering around on the sandy marshland.

During moonlit nights especially this entire mysterious population animates the hills and valleys. Man has no right to disturb it with his presence, just as the spirits have respected him during the sun's course; therefore it's time to retire and close one's eyes under the protection of guardian angels.

Efix made the sign of the cross and stood up, but he was still waiting for someone. Nevertheless he shoved the plank that served as a door across the entry way and leaned a big reed cross against it to keep spirits and temptation from entering his hut.

Through the cracks the moonlight illuminated the corners of the low, narrow room—but a room large enough for someone like him who was as small and scrawny as a young boy. From the conical cane and reed roof over the dry stone walls, with a hole in the middle for the smoke to escape, hung bunches of onions and dry herbs, palm crosses and blessed olive branches, a painted candle, a scythe for keeping vampires away, and a little sack of barley for protection against the *panas.* With every breath of air everything quivered and spider webs shone in the moonlight. On the floor a two-handled pitcher lay on its side, and a pan rested upside down next to it.

Efix unrolled his mat but didn't lie down. He thought he kept hearing the sound of a boy's footsteps. Someone was certainly coming, and in fact dogs on nearby farms suddenly began to bark, and the whole countryside, which a few moments earlier seemed to sleep amid prayers murmured by nocturnal voices, was full of echoes and rustling almost as though it had suddenly jerked awake.

Efix pushed the plank aside. A black figure was coming over the rise where the low bean plants grew silvery under the moonlight, and he, to whom even human shapes seemed mysterious at night, made the sign of the cross again. But a voice he recognized called out to him. It was the clear but slightly breathless voice of the boy who lived next door to the Pintor sisters.

"Zio Efisè, Zio Efisè!"

"What's happened, Zuannantò? Are the women all right?"

"They seem all right to me. They sent me to tell you to go to town early tomorrow, because they need to talk to you. Maybe it's because of the yellow letter I saw in Donna Noemi's hand."

"A letter? Do you know who it's from?"

"I don't know. I don't know how to read. But grandmother says maybe it's from their nephew, Giacinto."

Yes, Efix felt it had to be. Nevertheless, head down, he thoughtfully rubbed his cheek, and hoped and feared he was wrong.

The tired boy sat down on a rock in front of the hut and unlaced his boots, asking if there was something to eat.

"I ran like a deer. I was afraid of the spirits. . . ."

Efix raised his olive-colored face, hard as a bronze mask, and gazed at the boy with his little bluish eyes, deep set and surrounded by wrinkles. Those lively, shining eyes were full of childish anxiety.

"They said for me to go to town tomorrow or tonight?"

"Tomorrow, I told you! I'll stay here to guard the farm while you're in town."

The servant was accustomed to obeying the women without asking questions. He pulled an onion from the bunch, a piece of bread from his bag, and while the boy ate, laughing and crying from the sharp onion, they began to talk. The town's most important people entered their conversation. First came the Rector, then the Rector's sister, then Milese who had married a daughter of the Rector and had gone from hawking oranges and amphoras to being the richest merchant in the village. The mayor, Don Predu, came next, the Pintor sisters' cousin. Don Predu was also rich, but not like Milese. Then came Kallina the usurer, she also rich, but in a mysterious way.

"Thieves tried to break down her wall. Impossible. It's bewitched. And she was laughing this morning in her courtyard, saying: even if they get in they'll only find ashes and nails, poor as Christ. But my grandmother says that Zia Kallina has a little sack of gold hidden in the wall."

These stories were really of little interest to Efix. Lying on his mat, with one hand tucked under his arm and the other on his cheek, he felt his heart beating, and the reeds rustling on the riverbank sounded like an evil spirit sighing.

A yellow letter! An ugly color, yellow. Who knows what had happened to those women. For twenty years whenever some event broke the monotonous life at the Pintor house it was inevitably a disaster.

The boy also lay down, but he didn't feel like sleeping.

"Zio Efix, just today my grandmother said that the Pintors were once as rich as Don Predu. Is that true?"

"It's true," the servant said with a sigh. "But now's not the time to be thinking about these things. Go to sleep."

The boy yawned. "But my grandmother said that after saintly old Donna Maria Cristina died she walked around her house like an excommunicated soul. Is that true or not?"

"Go to sleep, I say. Now's not the time. . . ."

"Let me talk! Why did Donna Lia run away? My grandmother says you knew about it and you helped her, you went to the bridge with Donna Lia where she hid until a cart came by that would take her to the sea to get on a boat. And that her father Don Zame looked for her till he died. He died there, by the bridge. Who killed him? My grandmother says you know. . . ."

"Your grandmother is a witch! She and you, both of you, should leave the dead in peace!" shouted Efix; but his voice was hoarse and the boy laughed insolently.

"Don't get mad 'cause it's not good for you, Zio Efix! My grandmother says a goblin killed Don Zame. It that true or not?"

Efix didn't answer. He closed his eyes and put his hand over his ear, but the boy's voice buzzed in the dark and it sounded to him the voice of spirits from the past.

Little by little they all gathered around him, entering through the cracks like moonbeams: Donna Maria Cristina, beautiful and calm as a saint; Don Zame, red and violent as the devil; their four daughters whose pale faces have the serenity of their mother and their father's flame in the depths of their eyes; maidservants and menservants, relatives, friends—everyone who invades the rich house of the Barons' descendants. But once the wind of misfortune blows, people disperse like little clouds around the moon when the wind blows off the mountains.

Donna Cristina dies; her daughters' pale faces lose some of their serenity, and the deep flame in their eyes grows. It grows to such a degree that after his wife's death, Don Zame becomes as domineering as his Baron ancestors, and like them keeps his four daughters shut up in the house like slaves while they wait for husbands worthy of them. And like slaves they had to work, make bread, weave, sew, cook, know how to take care of their things. But above all they couldn't raise their eyes to men, or even allow themselves to think about anyone not destined to become a husband. But the years went by and the husbands didn't come along. And the older his daughters became the more Don Zame expected them to adhere to a strict manner of comportment. If he saw them at the windows overlooking the lane behind the house or if they went out without his permission, he would slap them and shout insults, while threatening death to the young men who passed by on the lane more than twice in succession.

Don Zame spent his days roaming around town or sitting on the stone bench in front of the shop belonging to the Rector's sister. When people saw him they would slink away, afraid as they were of his tongue. He quarreled with everyone, and was so envious of others that when he passed by a nice farm he would say, "may lawsuits devour you." But lawsuits ended up devouring his land, and an unspeakable catastrophe struck him suddenly like punishment from God for his pride and his prejudices. His third daughter, Donna Lia, disappeared one night from the paternal house and nothing more was known about her for a long time. A deathly shadow fell over the house. Never had the town known such a scandal; never had such a noble and well-brought up young woman like Lia run away like that. Don Zame seemed to go mad; he ran around here and there searching for Lia all over the Baronia district and along the Coast; but no one could give him any information. At last she wrote her sisters saying she was safe and happy to have broken her chains. However, her sisters didn't forgive her or answer her. Don Zame became even more tyrannical. He sold what was left of his inheritance, mistreated the servant, annoyed half the world with lawsuits, kept traveling in the hopes of tracking down his daughter and bringing her back home. The shadow of dishonor over him and his entire family because of Lia's flight weighed on him like a cloak of the damned. One morning they found him dead on the bridge outside town. A stroke must have killed him, because there was not a sign of violence—only a small green mark on the back of his neck.

People said that maybe Don Zame had quarreled with someone who had struck him with a walking stick. But in time this rumor faded and the certainty prevailed that he had died of a broken heart over his daughter's leaving.

While her sisters, dishonored by her escape, were unable to find husbands, Lia wrote announcing her marriage. Her husband was a cattle dealer that she had met by chance. They lived at Civitavecchia, were comfortably well off, and would soon have a child.

Her sisters did not forgive her this new wrong: marriage with a common man met in such a sorry manner. They did not reply.

Some time later Lia wrote announcing Giacinto's birth. They sent a present to their little nephew, but didn't write his mother.

The years went by. Giacinto grew up, and every year he wrote his aunts at Easter time and Christmas, and his aunts sent him a present. Once he wrote that he was studying, another time that he wanted to join the navy, and still another time that he had found a job; then he wrote about his father's death, then his mother's, and finally he expressed the desire to visit them and settle down if he could find work in town. He didn't like his job with the Customs Office: it was menial and tiresome, a waste of his youth. Of course he loved to work, but out in the open. Everyone advised him to go to his mother's island and try his luck with an honest job.

His aunts began to talk it over, and the more they talked the less they agreed.

"Work?" said Ruth, the calmest sister. "If the little town can't provide work even for those who were born here?"

Ester, on the other hand, was sympathetic with their nephew's plans; while the youngest, Noemi, smiled coldly and scornfully.

"Perhaps he thinks to come here to play the gentleman. Come right ahead! He can go fishing in the river. . . ."

"He says he wants to work, Noemi! Then he'll work: he might be a trader like his father."

"He needs experience first. Our family has never dealt with cattle."

"In the past, dear Noemi! Nowadays gentlemen are merchants. See Milese? He says he's the Baron of Galte now."

Noemi laughed with an evil look deep in her eyes, and her laugh was more discouraging to Ester than all her other sister's arguments.

Everyday it was the same story: Giacinto's name resounded throughout the house, and even when the three sisters were silent he was in their midst, as he had always been anyway from the day he was born, his unknown shape filling the decaying house with life.

Efix didn't remember ever taking part directly in their discussions. He didn't dare. First of all because they didn't consult him, and then not to have qualms of conscience. But he wanted the boy to come.

He loved him. He had always loved him like a member of the family.

After Don Zame's death, Efix had remained with the three women to help them settle their tangled affairs. Their relatives didn't care about them, they even held them in contempt and spurned them. The sisters were only capable of domestic tasks and knew nothing about the little farm, their last remaining inheritance.

"I'll stay another year in their service," Efix had said, moved to pity by their helplessness. And he had stayed twenty years.

The three women lived on the income from the farm he cultivated. In lean years, Donna Ester would say to Efix when the moment came to pay him (thirty scudi a year and a pair of boots): "Be patient, for the love of God. You'll get what's coming to you."

He was patient, and their debt to him grew year after year, so much that Donna Ester, half joking, half serious, promised to leave him the farm and house, although he was older than they. Old now, and weak, but he was still a man, and his shadow was still enough to protect the three women.

Now it was he who dreamed about good fortune for them. At least that Noemi might find a husband! What if the yellow letter brought good news, after all? What if it was about an inheritance? What if it was a marriage request for Noemi? The Pintor sisters still had rich relatives living in Sassari and Nuoro. Why couldn't one of them marry Noemi? Don Predu himself could have written the yellow letter. . . .

And there in the servant's tired imagination things have suddenly changed as from night to day; everything is light, sweetness. His noble mistresses have become young again, they rise on wings like eagles taking flight; their house rises up from ruin and all around everything blooms again like the valley in spring.

And for him, the poor servant, there's nothing left to do but retire to the little farm for the remainder of his life, to spread out his mat and rest with God, while in the silence of the night the reeds whisper the prayer of the sleeping earth.

✦ Reading 19 ✦

The Radetzky March

Joseph Roth

When Lieutenant-Baron von Trotta's only friend, the regimental doctor Demant, is killed in a senseless duel, he seeks reassignment to an area near the home village of his Slovene peasant grandfather, who was awarded a title for saving the emperor's life at the Battle of Solferino. Instead he is sent to the far eastern frontiers of the empire.

In those days before the Great War when the events narrated in this book took place, it had not yet become a matter of indifference whether a man lived or died. When one of the living had been extinguished another did not at once take his place in order to obliterate him: there was a gap where he had been, and both close and distant witnesses of his demise fell silent whenever they became aware of this gap. When fire had eaten away a house from the row of others in a street, the burnt-out space remained long empty. Masons worked slowly and cautiously. Close neighbors and casual passers-by alike, when they saw the empty space, remembered the aspect and walls of the vanished house. That was how things were then. Everything that grew took its time in growing and everything that was destroyed took a long time to be forgotten. And everything that had once existed left its traces so that in those days people lived on memories, just as now they live by the capacity to forget quickly and completely.

The deaths of Count Tattenbach and the regimental surgeon moved and troubled the minds of the officers and men of this regiment of Uhlans—and indeed, of the civilian population—for a long time. The dead were buried in accordance with the usual religious and military rites. Although (except among themselves) none of the soldiers had uttered a word as to the manner in which the two had died, nevertheless there was a rumor among the townspeople of the little garrison that both men had fallen victim to their rigid code of honor. So that, from that day on, it was as if each surviving officer bore upon his forehead the mark of close, violent death. To the shopkeepers and artisans of the little town these strange gentlemen became stranger still. The officers moved among them like incomprehensible worshippers of some remote, unappeasable god, whose gaily decked-out, gaudy victims they were. People shook their heads as they saw them pass, they even pitied them. They have all kinds of privileges, the people said to themselves, they can swagger about with their swords and attract women; the Emperor himself takes a personal interest in them and cares for them as if they were his sons. And yet, at any moment, if one insults the other, it has to be avenged in red blood.

Indeed, those of whom such things were being said were not to be envied. Even Captain Taittinger, who was rumored to have taken part in a few other fatal duels in other regiments, began to change his habits. Whereas the noisy and light-hearted became quiet and subdued, a strange restlessness took possession of the sweet-toothed, quiet, lean Captain. He could no longer sit for hours behind the glass doors of his little pastry shop devouring pastries, or play silent games of chess and dominoes with himself or his colonel. He was afraid of solitude. He literally clung to others. If no brother officer was about, he would go into a shop and buy something he didn't want. He would hang around for a long time and chatter foolishly to the shopkeeper, unable to make up his mind to leave the shop, unless, by chance, he saw a casual acquaintance passing in the street, in which case he would immediately run out. So changed was the world. The club was empty. The officers desisted from the companionable jaunts to

From: Joseph Roth, *The Radetzky March* (Woodstock, NY: The Overlook Press, 1983), pp. 107–30.

Frau Resi's. The orderlies were less busy. Anyone who ordered a cognac thought, as he looked at his glass, that it might be the very one out of which Tattenbach had drunk a few days ago. They continued to tell the old anecdotes but these no longer evoked loud guffaws—smiles at most. Lieutenant Trotta was never about except on duty.

A deft magic hand had wiped every trace of youth off Carl Joseph's face. In the whole Royal and Imperial Army not another lieutenant like him could have been found. He felt the need for some extraordinary achievement, but near or far, he found nothing extraordinary to achieve. It went without saying that now he would leave the regiment and enter another. But he searched for some difficult task to perform. In fact, he was looking for a self-imposed penance. He could never have managed to say it, but we may, after all, say it of him: it oppressed him unspeakably to feel himself the instrument of misfortune. In this state of mind he wrote to his father, announcing the outcome of the duel, with news of his inevitable transfer to another regiment. He withheld the fact that at this point a short leave was due to him, since he feared to look his father in the face. But it turned out that he underestimated the old man. For the District Commissioner, that model of civil servants, was well up in military usage. And oddly enough, he seemed just as conversant with the griefs and perplexities of his son, as could clearly be read between the lines of his reply. It was as follows:

My dear son,

I thank you for your precise account and for your confidence. The fate which has overtaken your brother officers moves me deeply. They died like men of honor.

Duels were even more frequent in my time, and honor seemed far more precious to us than life. It also seems to me that in my time officers were made of tougher stuff. You, my son, are an officer, and the grandson of the hero of Solferino. You will know how to bear your innocent and involuntary connection with this tragic affair. No doubt you will be sorry to leave the regiment, but remember that wherever you may be serving, in whatever regiment of our entire army, you will be serving our Emperor.

Your Father
FRANZ VON TROTTA

P.S. The fortnight's leave to which your transfer entitles you you may spend either at home with me, or, better still, in your new garrison, which will give you time to become acquainted with your new surroundings.

F. v. T.

Lieutenant Trotta could not read this letter without a feeling of shame. His father had guessed everything. In the Lieutenant's eyes, the image of the District Commissioner swelled to fearsome dimensions: he assumed almost the stature of his grandfather. And if Carl Joseph had felt anxiety before at the thought of confronting the old man, now it was out of the question to spend his leave at home. Later, later when I get my regular leave, the Lieutenant thought. He was cast in a different mold altogether from the Lieutenants of the District Commissioner's youth. "No doubt you will be sorry to leave the regiment," his father wrote. Had he written it because he could sense the contrary? What was there that Carl Joseph did *not* want to leave? Perhaps this window with its view of the men's quarters? The men themselves, perched on their cots, the melancholy sound of their mouth organs and their singing, the remote songs which sounded like uncomprehended echoes of similar songs sung by the peasants of Sipolje? Perhaps I ought to go to Sipolje, thought the Lieutenant. He went over to look at the ordnance map, the one piece of decoration in his room. He could have found Sipolje in his sleep. The pleasant, quiet village lay in the extreme south of the monarchy. Traced on a lightly cross-hatched bronze-coloured background were the hair-thin, minute letters, faint as the breath of which the name Sipolje was composed. Near it were a draw well, a water mill, the little station of a light railway running its single track through a wood, a mosque, a church, a young plantation, narrow forest paths, solitary huts. It is evening in Sipolje. The women stand in the sunset by the fountains, the colored kerchiefs on their heads stained gold by the vanishing sun. Moslems pray in their mosques on faded carpets. The miniature engine of the railway puffs clanging into the dark-green gloom of pines. The water mill clatters; the stream murmurs. It was the familiar game he had played as a cadet. The familiar images rose at once. Above them all shone his grandfather's mysterious gaze. There was probably not a cavalry garrison near Sipolje. He would have to transfer to the infantry. Cavalry officers cannot regard their foot-slogging brothers without a certain element of pity. Not without a certain element of pity would they regard the transferred Trotta. His grandfather had been only a plain infantry captain. To march on foot across one's own native earth would almost be like a return to his peasant forebears. Their heavy feet had trodden the hard soil, they had dug their plowshares into the fertile soil of the fields and had scattered fruitful seed with gestures that were a blessing. No, the Lieutenant was not in the least sorry to leave the regiment and perhaps the cavalry. His father would have to give his consent. He would have to go through an undoubtedly rather tedious course of infantry training.

He had to make his farewells. An evening at the club. A round of drinks. A short speech by the Colonel. A bottle of wine. A firm handshake from his brother officers, who were already gossiping behind his back. A bottle of champagne. Who could say, perhaps it might even end up in a general turn out all together to Frau Resi's. Another round of cognac. Oh, if only the leave-taking were over and done with. He would take his batman Onufrij with him. He did not want to go through the trouble of getting used to another name. He would avoid visiting his father. Altogether, he would try to avoid as much as possible the unpleasantness usually connected with a change of regiment. There remained only the difficult visit to the widow of the late Dr Demant.

What a visit! Carl Joseph tried to tell himself that Frau Eva Demant had gone back to Vienna to her father after her husband's funeral. He would therefore stand on the doorstep of the house, ring the bell for a long time and receive no answer, get her Vienna address, write her a letter as brief and sympathetic as possible. It was very convenient that he only had to write to her. I am not in the least plucky, the Lieutenant thought at the same time. Wasn't he constantly aware of the dark mysterious gaze of his grandfather, who knew how miserably he might have to lurch through this hard life. He grew brave only when he thought of the hero of Solferino. He had to keep going back to his grandfather for a little fortitude. So slowly, the Lieutenant set out on the difficult visit. It was three o'clock in the afternoon. Little shopkeepers looked miserable, freezing in front of their shops as they waited for their sparse customers. Creative, familiar sounds rang from the artisans' workshops. There was the sound of jovial hammering from the blacksmith, the plumber clanked forth his hollow, tinny thunderings, quick taps sounded from the cobblers' cellars, and the saws sang in the joiner's workshop. The Lieutenant knew all the sounds and faces of these workshops. Every day from the saddle he had seen them over the tops of the faded blue signs. Every day he had caught morning glimpses of first-floor rooms, the unmade beds, the coffeepots, and men in shirtsleeves, women with their hair still down; the flowerpots along the window sills; dried fruit and pickled gherkins behind ornamental ironwork.

Now he was on the doorstep of Dr Demant's house. The front door creaked. He went inside. The servant let him in. The Lieutenant waited. Frau Demant arrived. He trembled a little. He remembered the condolence visit he had paid Sergeant-Major Slama. He could feel the man's heavy, moist, cold, loose handshake. He could see the dark hall, the reddish parlor. He had in his mouth the stale aftertaste of the raspberry cordial. So she's not in Vienna, the Lieutenant thought—but only until the actual moment he saw the widow. Her black dress came as a surprise. It was as if he had only just been informed that Frau Demant was the widow of a regimental surgeon. The room, too, which he now entered was not the same as the one he had been in when his friend was still alive. On the opposite wall, festooned in black, hung a large likeness of the deceased. It receded further and further, like the Emperor's portrait in the club: it was as though it were not within sight and touching distance, as though it were immeasurably far beyond the wall—out of reach, as though he were seeing it through glass.

"Thank you for coming," said Frau Demant.

"I wanted to say good-by," answered Trotta.

Frau Demant raised her pale face. The Lieutenant saw the gray, clear beauty of her wide, shining eyes. They were turned straight on his face, two rounds of light, of glittering ice. In the winter-afternoon dusk of the room only the woman's eyes shone out. Quickly the Lieutenant glanced above them at her narrow white forehead, then at the wall, at the distant portrait of her dead husband. These preliminaries were taking far too long, it was high time she asked him to sit down, but she said nothing. Meanwhile, he could feel the gathering darkness of approaching evening close in on him through the windows, and he was childishly afraid that they might never turn the lights on in this house. No appropriate words occurred to him. He heard the woman's quiet breathing. She said at last, "But what are we standing like this for? Let's sit down." They sat down facing each other across a table. As before, at Sergeant-Major Slama's, he had the door behind him. As on that occasion, he felt the threat of the door. It seemed for no reason at all to open slowly from time to time and then noiselessly shut again. The dusk thickened. Frau Demant's black dress merged into the dusk, which now enveloped her. Her white face hovered naked, bared on the dark surface of the evening. The dead man's portrait had vanished from the wall opposite. "My husband," Frau Demant's voice was saying out of the darkness. The Lieutenant saw the gleam of her teeth—they were whiter than her face. Gradually, too he began to distinguish again the bright gleam of her eyes. "You were his only friend, he often said so. How often he spoke of you! If you only knew—I can't believe he's dead. And," she whispered, "that it is my fault."

"It is *my* fault," said the Lieutenant. His voice was very loud and hard and sounded strange to his own ears. There was no consolation for Demant's widow. "My fault," he repeated. "I ought to have taken you home more circumspectly. I ought never to have brought you along by the club."

The woman began to sob. Her white face bent lower and lower over the table, sinking slowly like a large white oval flower. Suddenly, to the right and left of it, white hands came up out of the darkness, receiving the sinking face, cushioning it. And now, for a while, for a whole minute, and then another, nothing could be heard except the woman's sobs. An eternity for the Lieutenant. I'd better get up and leave her to cry and go away, he thought. In fact, he got up.

Her hands fell back at once upon the table. In a calm voice which seemed to come from another throat, not the one with which she had just been sobbing, she said to him, "Where are you going?"

"To turn on the light," said Trotta.

She got up, went past him around the table, brushing him. His nostrils caught the faint whiff of her scent; she was past him, the scent dispersed. The light was hard. He forced himself to stare straight at the lamp. Frau Demant kept one hand in front of her eyes.

"Turn on that little lamp above the bracket," she told him. The Lieutenant obeyed. She waited by the door, shading her eyes. When the little lamp under its pale-gold shade was lit, she switched off the ceiling light. She took her hand from her eyes as if removing a visor. She looked very bold in her black dress with her pale face, which she turned full on Trotta. She was angry and brave. Her cheeks showed faint streaks of drying tears. Her eyes were shining, just as before.

"Sit down," ordered Frau Demant. "Over there, on the sofa." And Carl Joseph sat down. Soft, comfortable cushions seemed to be gliding against him, off the sofa back, out of the corners, sly and insinuating, from all sides. He felt that it was dangerous to sit here and moved decisively to the edge of the sofa. He put his hands on the hilt of his upright sword and watched Frau Demant advance upon him. She looked like the dangerous commandant of all these cushions. On the wall, to the right of the sofa, hung his dead friend's portrait. Frau Eva sat down. A smooth little cushion lay between them. Trotta did not stir. He was doing what he always did when he could see no way out of one of the numerous awkward situations he always seemed to be slipping into; namely, he told himself that he could go.

"So they're going to transfer you?" asked Frau Demant.

"I've applied to be transferred," he told her, his eyes on the carpet, his chin on his hands, and his hands on his sword hilt.

"Must you?"

"Yes, I must."

"I'm sorry, very sorry."

Frau Demant sat like him, her knees supporting her elbows her chin on her hands, her eyes on the carpet. She was probably expecting a word of comfort and charity. He was silent. He enjoyed the luxurious sensation of cruelly avenging his friend's death by a callous silence. Stories of dangerous, murderous, pretty little women, an ever-recurring theme of his brother officers, came back to him. She most probably belonged to the dangerous sisterhood of weak murderesses. He must take good care to keep clear of her. He began to get ready to leave. At that instant, Frau Demant changed her position. She removed her hands from under her chin, cautiously, and softly her left hand felt its way along the silk braid of the sofa's edge. Her fingers, along the narrow, glossy path, slowly advanced, then steadily retreated, and again advanced on Lieutenant Trotta. They slid into his field of vision. He longed for blinkers. The white fingers were involving him in a voiceless but quite inevitable conversation. A cigarette—splendid inspiration. He pulled out his cigarette case and matches. "Will you give me one?" asked Frau Demant.

He was forced to look into her face as he held the match. He disapproved of her smoking, as if the enjoyment of nicotine were unseemly for someone in mourning: And the way she inhaled her first puff—her lips set in a small coral round which sent out a soft bluish cloud—was vicious and arrogant!

"Haven't you any idea where they'll transfer you?"

"No," the Lieutenant said, "but I shall do my best to get sent as far away as possible."

"Far away? But where, for instance?"

"Perhaps to Bosnia."

"Do you think you'll be happy there?"

"I don't think I shall ever be happy anywhere."

"Oh, I hope you will." Glib, far too glib, it seemed to Trotta. She stood up, came back with an ashtray, and put it between them on the floor.

She said "So I suppose we're never likely to meet again."

Never. That word, the dread and shoreless ocean of soundless eternity. He could never see Katherina again, nor Dr Demant, nor this woman. Carl Joseph said, "No, I suppose not, unfortunately." He would have liked to add, "And I won't see Max Demant again." Widows should be burnt. Trotta remembered one of Taittinger's daring phrases as he spoke.

The front doorbell rang; there were sounds in the passage. "That's my father," said Frau Demant. Herr Knopfmacher was already in the room.

"Oh, it's you, it's you," he said, bringing a sharp tang of snow with him. He unfolded a large snow-white pocket handkerchief and blew his nose resoundingly. He stowed the handkerchief carefully in his breast pocket like a precious object, thrust out a hand toward the door and switched on the ceiling light. He came up to Trotta, who had risen at Knopfmacher's arrival. In his handshake, Herr Knopfmacher indicated all the grief that needed to be expressed at the death of the doctor. Already he was saying to his daughter, pointing to the ceiling lamp, "I'm sorry, I can't stand these artistic glooms." It was as if he had flung a stone at the crape-enveloped portrait of the dead man.

"Well, you aren't looking too grand," Knopfmacher said the next instant in an exultant voice. "It's taken a lot out of you, I suppose, this terrible affair, yes?"

"He was my only friend."

"You know," Knopfmacher said and sat down at the table—"Oh, please stay where you are"—and he went on when the Lieutenant had settled on the sofa again, "that was just exactly what he said about you when he was alive. What a business!" He shook his head a few times and his full, rosy cheeks quivered a little.

Frau Demant drew a wisp of lace from her sleeve, dabbed her eyes, got up, and hurried from the room.

"Who knows how she'll get over it," said Knopfmacher. "Well, I talked to her long enough beforehand. But, of course, she wouldn't take any notice of me. You see, my dear Lieutenant, every profession has its dangers. But an officer! An officer—forgive me—really ought never to marry. Between you and me, though of course he's certain to have told you, he'd thought of sending in his papers and devoting all his time to science. I can't tell you how pleased I was to hear it. He'd certainly have become a famous doctor. Dear, kind Max." Herr Knopfmacher raised his eyes to the portrait, allowed them to linger on it, and ended his obituary. "An authority."

Frau Demant brought her father's favorite *slivovitz*.

"You'll have a drink?" Knopfmacher asked, filling some glasses. With cautious hand, he carried the brimming glass across to the sofa.

The Lieutenant rose, the stale taste of raspberry cordial still in his mouth, as on the previous occasion. He finished the alcohol in a gulp.

"When did you see him last?" inquired Knopfmacher.

"One day before."

"He asked Eva to go to Vienna without giving her any hint. She went in complete ignorance. Then we got his farewell letter. I saw at once there was nothing to be done."

"No, there was nothing to be done."

"I hope you won't mind my saying that this code of honor seems out of date. After all, we're in the twentieth century. Why, we've got the gramophone, you can telephone hundreds of miles away, and people like Blériot go flying about in the air. I don't know if you're much of a newspaper reader, are you at all interested in politics? But everyone seems to be saying that the whole constitution is going to be radically changed. Here and abroad, all sorts of things have been happening, since universal secret suffrage was brought in. Our Emperor, God bless him and keep him, isn't nearly as old-fashioned as some people think. Of course, these conservatives may not be altogether wrong, things have to be done slowly, cautiously, step by step. No use rushing things."

"I don't know anything about politics," said Trotta.

Knopfmacher was beginning to feel irritated. He was angry with the whole stupid army and its idiotic institutions. His child was a widow, his son-in-law dead. He'd have to find a new one, a civilian this time, and he'd probably have to wait for his councilorship. It was high time to stop such nonsense. These young, frivolous lieutenants must not be allowed to get out of hand, not in the twentieth century. The nations were insisting on their rights, and so were the citizens. Down with aristocratic privileges. Social democracy might be a bit risky, but it was a good counterweight. There was a lot of talk about war, but no doubt there wouldn't be one. They'd show them. The times were enlightened. In England, for instance, the king had no powers at all.

"Naturally," he said, "there's no use for politics in the army. But he. . . ." Knopfmacher indicated the portrait. "Well, anyway, he knew something about it."

"He was very wise," said Trotta very quietly.

"There was nothing to be done," Knopfmacher repeated.

"Perhaps," said the Lieutenant, and was himself aware that he was speaking with borrowed wisdom, wisdom hidden in those vast tomes of the silver-bearded king of publicans, "perhaps he was very wise and quite alone." He turned pale. He could feel Frau Demant's barefaced glances. He would have to leave. It grew very quiet. There was nothing more to be said. "Father, we won't see Baron Trotta again, they're going to transfer him," said Frau Demant.

"You'll keep in touch," asked Knopfmacher.

"You will write to me?" said Frau Demant.

Carl Joseph rose.

"Good luck," said Knopfmacher. His hand was large and soft, it felt like warm velvet.

Frau Demant went on ahead. The servant came to hold his coat. Frau Demant stood next to him. She said very rapidly, "You will write? I will want to know what becomes of you." It was a swift, warm breath, dispersed immediately. The servant was opening the door, he was out on the steps. The gate appeared in front of him, just as it had when he had left Sergeant-Major Slama.

He hurried back to the town, stopped at the first café he passed, stood at the bar and drank a brandy, then another. "We only drink Hennessy," he could hear the District Commissioner saying. He hurried on, to the barracks.

Outside the door of his room, Onufrij was waiting, a dark-blue streak against bare whitewash. The office orderly had brought him a package, by colonel's orders. It stood in the corner, a long, narrow brown-paper object. On the table lay a letter. The Lieutenant read it:

"My dear Friend, I leave you my sword and my watch. Max Demant."

Trotta unpacked the sword. From its hilt dangled Demant's smooth silver watch. It was not going. The hands stood at ten to twelve. The Lieutenant wound it and held it to his ear. Its quick quiet voice ticked consolingly. He opened the case with his pocketknife, inquisitive and playful, like a boy. On the inside were the initials M.D. He drew the sword from its sheath. With his penknife, Dr Demant had scratched a clumsy line of sprawling letters on the steel. LIVE IN HAPPINESS AND FREEDOM the inscription read. The Lieutenant hung the sword in his cupboard. He held up the sword hanger. Its wired silk glided through his fingers like cool gold rain. Trotta shut the cupboard. He was closing a coffin.

He switched off the light and lay down fully dressed on his bed. The yellow glow from the men's quarters opposite spilled on the white lacquer of his door, its reflections caught by the glittering handle. From across the way came the hoarse sighing music of mouth organs accompanying the men's deep-throated roar. They were singing the Ukrainian song which tells of the Emperor and his Empress. The

Empress had long been dead, but Ruthenian peasants thought she was still alive.

* * *

Eastward to the frontiers of the Tsar, the Habsburg sun shot forth its rays. It was the same sun which had fostered the growth of the Trottas to nobility and esteem. Francis Joseph had a long memory for gratitude and his favor had a wide reach. If one of his favorite children was about to commit some folly, the servants and ministers of the Emperor intervened in good time to force the erring child into prudence and reason. It would scarcely have been fitting to permit the sole heir of this recently created baronetcy of Trotta von Sipolje to serve in the native province of the hero of Solferino, the grandson of illiterate Slovenian peasants, the son of a gendarmery sergeant-major. This young nobleman might, of course, if he chose, exchange his service in the Uhlans for a modest commission in an infantry regiment; it merely proved him faithful to the memory of his grandfather, who had saved his Emperor's life as a plain lieutenant in the line. But the prudence of the Imperial and Royal Ministry of War avoided sending the bearer of such a title, a title identical with the actual Slovenian village in which the first baron had been born, to serve in the neighborhood of the village. The District Commissioner, son of the hero of Solferino, agreed with the authorities. Though with a heavy heart he allowed his son to transfer to the infantry, he was not at all pleased with Carl Joseph's request to serve in the Slovenian province. He himself, the District Commissioner, had never felt any desire to see the home of his fathers. He was an Austrian, civil servant of the Habsburgs, his home the Imperial Hofburg in Vienna. Had he entertained political notions of any useful reshaping of the great and multifarious monarchy it would have seemed fitting to him that all the crownlands should simply form large and colorful outer courts of the Imperial Hofburg; and to see in all the nations of the monarchy subjects of the Habsburgs. He was a District Commissioner; within his district he represented the Apostolic Majesty. He wore the gold collar, cocked hat, and sword. He had no wish at all to drive a furrow into the blessed Slovenian earth. His final decisive letter to his son contained the following sentence: "Fate has raised our stock from peasant frontiersmen to Austrians. Let us remain such."

So it came about that Carl Joseph, Baron Trotta von Sipolje, found the southern frontiers inaccessible. He had only the choice between serving in the interior of Austria or on its eastern border. He chose a battalion of Jaeger stationed not more than two miles from the Russian frontier. Near it was the village of Burdlaki, Onufrij's home. This district was akin to the home of Ukrainian peasants, their melancholy concertinas and their unforgettable songs; it was the northern sister of Slovenia.

For seventeen hours Carl Joseph sat in the train. In the eighteenth there came into sight the last eastern railway station of the monarchy. Here he got out. His batman came with him. The Jaeger barracks stood at the center of the small town. Onufrij crossed himself three times before they entered the barrack square. It was morning. Spring, which had long since reached the inner provinces of the Empire, had only recently arrived here. The laburnum glowed on the arches of the railway viaduct. Violets flowered in the moist woods. Frogs croaked in the endless marshes. Storks circled above the low-thatched roofs of the village huts in search of old wheels to use as foundations for their summer nests.

At that time the borderland between Austria and Russia in the north-eastern corner was one of the most remarkable areas of the monarchy. Carl Joseph's Jaeger battalion garrisoned a town of ten thousand inhabitants. It lay around a wide circular market-place at whose center two main roads intersected, east to west, north to south. One led from the cemetery to the railway station, the other from the castle ruins to the steam mill. About a third of the town's ten thousand inhabitants were craftsmen of various kinds; another third lived in poverty off meager small holdings. The rest engaged in trade of a sort.

We call it "trade of a sort" since neither the goods nor the business methods corresponded in any way to the notions which the so-called civilized world has formed of trade. In these parts the tradesmen made their living far more by hazard than by design, more by the unpredictable grace of God than by any commercial reckonings in advance. Every trader was ready at any moment to seize on whatever floating merchandise heaven might throw in his way, or even to invent his goods if God had provided him with none. The livelihood of these traders was indeed a mystery. They displayed no shopfronts, they had no names. They had no credit. But they possessed a keen, miraculous sharp instinct for any remote and hidden sources of profit. Though they lived on other people's work, they created work for strangers. They were frugal. They lived as meanly as if they survived by the toil of their hands. And yet the toil was never theirs. Forever shifting, ever on the road, with glib tongues and clear, quick brains, they might have had possession of half the world if they had had any notion of the world. But they had none. They lived remote from it, wedged between East and West, cramped between day and night, themselves a species of living ghosts spawned by the night and haunting the day.

Cramped? The character of their native soil left them unconscious of it. Nature had forged endless horizons for these dwellers on the frontier, drawing around them a mighty circle of green forests and blue hills. When they walked in the twilight of pinewoods, they might even have felt themselves privileged by God, had their daily cares for the sustenance of wives and children left them time to perceive His goodness. But they entered their forests only to gather wood to trade with native shopkeepers as soon as winter drew near. For they also dealt in wood. They dealt in coral for the peasant girls of nearby villages and for those other peasants over the border, on Russian soil. They dealt in feathers for featherbeds, in tobacco, in horsehair, in bar silver, in jewelry, in Chinese tea, in fruit from the south, in cattle and horses, poultry and eggs, fish and vegetables, jute and wool, butter and cheese, woodlands and fields, Italian marble, human hair from China for making wigs, raw-silk and finished-silk merchandise, Manchester cotton and Brussels lace, galoshes from Moscow, Viennese linen, lead from Bohemia. No cheap bit of goods or splendid merchandise thrown up by the earth in profusion was unknown to the tradesmen of this district. What the law forbade them to come by and to sell, they would get one way or another in defiance of it—slick and secretive, adroitly prudent and bold. Some traded in live human flesh. They shipped off deserters from the Russian army to America and peasant girls to Brazil and Argentina. They had shipping agents and business connections with foreign brothels. Yet, with it all, their gains were meager, and they had no inkling of the vast superfluity in which a man may live. Their senses, so acutely edged for the sniffing out of petty gain, their hands which could strike gold from gravel like sparks from a flint, were not capable of bringing pleasure to their hearts or health to their bodies. The people in this district were swamp-begotten. For evil swamps lay far and wide to either side of the highroad and over the whole face of the land. Swamps that spawned frogs and fever, deceptive grass, dreadful enticements to a dreadful death for the unsuspecting stranger. Many had perished in the swamps with no one hearing their cries for help. But all who had been born here were familiar with the malignity of the marshland, and they themselves were tinged with this same malignity. In spring and summer, the air was thick with the deep and endless croaking of the frogs. Under the sky, equally jubilant larks rejoiced. It was an untiring dialogue between sky and marshland.

Many of these traders were Jews. A *lusus naturae,* perhaps a mysterious law obeyed by some secret branch of the legendary tribe of Khazars, determined that many among these frontier Jews were red-headed. The hair flamed from their heads. Their beards were like torches. On the backs of their nimble hands wiry hairs bristled like minute spears. And delicate reddish wool burgeoned out of their ears, like fumes of the red fires which might be glowing in their heads.

A stranger who settled here was bound to degenerate in time. No one was as strong as the swamp. No one could hold out against the borderland. At this time gentlemen in high places in Vienna and St Petersburg were already beginning preparations for the Great War. The people at the frontier were conscious of its approach sooner than others, not only because they sensed the future out of habit, but because from day to day they observed omens of disaster. They turned these preparations to profit. Many lived by espionage and counterespionage, drew Austrian gulden from the Austrian police and Russian rubles from the Russian. The isolation and swampy boredom of the garrison sometimes drove an officer to despair, to gambling, to debt, and into the company of sinister men. The cemeteries of the frontier garrisons concealed many young corpses of weak men.

But here, as in every garrison in the monarchy, privates drilled. Every day the Jaeger battalion, bespattered with shiny mud, their boots gray with slime, turned back to barracks. Major Zoglauer rode at their head. Lieutenant Trotta was in charge of the first platoon of the second company. A long sober blast from the bugler set the pace for the marching Jaeger—not the proud fanfare which had pierced the clattering hoofs of the Uhlan horses, and had checked and surrounded them. Carl Joseph tramped along, persuading himself that he preferred it. Around him crunched the hobnail boots of the Jaeger, over sharp-edged gravel freshly strewn week after week in spring, by request of the military authorities, only to be sucked down by the swampy highroad. All the stones, millions of them, disappeared into the insatiable ground. And everywhere triumphant silver-gray shiny mud oozed up out of the depths, devouring mortar and gravel, slapping up around the stamping boots of the men.

The barracks stood behind the municipal park. Next to it on the left was the District Court, and facing it the official enclosure of the District Commissioner's office buildings. Behind those ornate but crumbling walls stood two churches, one Roman Catholic, the other Greek Orthodox. To the right of the barracks stood the grammar school. The town was so small you could cross it in twenty minutes. The major buildings clustered together in irksome proximity. Like convicts in their prison yard, the townspeople exercised every evening round and round the unbroken ring of their park. It was a good half hour's walk to the station. The mess of the Jaeger officers was situated in two small rooms of a private house. Most preferred to eat in the station restaurant, including Carl Joseph. He was glad to tramp through the oozing slime if only to see a station. This was the last of all stations in the monarchy, but even so, it displayed two pairs of glittering lines stretching away without break into the heart of the monarchy. Like all the others, this station had shining signals of brightly colored glass, ringing with gentle messages from home; and there was a Morse keyboard ticking away incessantly on which the confused, delightful voices of a lost and distant world were hammered out, stitched as on some busy sewing machine.

This station, like all others, had its porter and this porter swung a clanging bell and the bell signified "All aboard, all aboard!" Once a day, at lunchtime, he went swinging his bell alongside a train on its way to Cracow, Oderberg, Vienna. A cozy, nice train. It stood there, almost the whole of lunch-time, just in front of the first-class refreshment-room windows, behind which the officers sat. Not until the coffee arrived did the engine whistle. Gray steam rolled against the windows. By the time it had begun to collect in drops and run down in streaks, the train had departed. They finished their coffee and went back in a slow, disconsolate group, through the silver slime. Even generals on tours of inspection took care not to come here. They did not come, nobody came. Only twice a year the one hotel in the town where most of the Jaeger officers were billeted was visited by rich hop merchants from Nuremberg and Prague and Saaz. When they had completed their incomprehensible deals, they hired a band and played cards in the only café, which belonged to the hotel.

Carl Joseph could see the whole town from his room on the second floor of the Hotel Brodnitzer. He could see the gable roofs of the District Court, the little white tower of the District Commissioner's offices, the black-and-yellow flag over the barracks, the double cross of the Greek church, the weathercock on the municipal building and all the slate-gray shingled roofs of the little, one-storied houses. The Hotel Brodnitzer was the tallest building in the area. It was as much a landmark as the church or the municipal and government buildings. The streets had no names and the little houses no numbers, so that anyone in search of a specific place had to find his way by vague description. So-and-so lived behind the church, so-and-so just opposite the jail. So-and-so somewhere to the right of the District Court. They lived like villagers. The secrets of the people in these low houses leaked out through chinks and rafters into the slimy streets and even into the ever-inaccessible barrack yard. So-and-so's wife had betrayed him, so-and-so had sold his daughter to a Russian cavalry captain; in this house they dealt in rotten eggs, the whole family over the way lived by contraband; so-and-so had been in jail, but the other had got off scot free. So-and-So lent officers money, and his neighbor collected a third of the pay. The officers, mainly middle class, of German parentage, had been stationed in this garrison for years. They were used to it and accepted the inevitable. Cut off from their homes and the German language, which here became merely an official language, exposed to the endless desolation of the swamps, they took up gambling and drank the fiery local brandy manufactured locally and sold under the label NINETY PERCENT. From the harmless mediocrity to which cadet schools and drill had educated them, they sank into the corruption of the area—already overcast by the vast breath of the hostile empire of the Tsars. They were scarcely fourteen kilometers out of Russia. Not infrequently Russian officers from the frontier garrison came across in their long pale-lemon and dove-gray army coats, with heavy gold and silver epaulettes on their broad shoulders, and shiny galoshes drawn over their shimmering top-boots in all weathers. Indeed, there was a certain amount of friendly exchange between the garrisons. Sometimes they would go in little canvas-roofed baggage carts across the frontier to watch the Cossacks display their horsemanship and drink the Russian brandy. Over there, in the Russian garrison, spirit casks stood on the edge of the wooden pavements, guarded by Russian privates with grounded rifles and long, triple-edged fixed bayonets. At dusk, these little casks rolled and bumped along uneven streets, kicked by Cossack boots to the Russian club, a soft slap and gurgle from inside betraying their contents to the townspeople. The officers of the Tsar showed the officers of His Apostolic Majesty what Russian hospitality really meant. And none of the Tsar's officers and none of His Apostolic Majesty's officers knew at that time how, above the goblets from which they drank, death was already crossing his haggard invisible hands.

In the open space between the two frontier woods, the sotnias of Cossacks galloped and wheeled like winds in military formation, uniformed winds on the swift little ponies of their native steppes, flourishing their lances above their tall fur caps like streaks of lightning on long wooden stems, coquettish blades with graceful pennons. On the soft swampy ground the clatter of hoofs was almost inaudible. The wet earth gave no more than a low sigh under the flying thud of their hoofs. The dark-green meadow grass scarcely bent beneath them. It was as though these Cossacks hovered above the plain. And when they crossed the dusty, coppery highway, there rose up a tall, bright-yellow, fine-grained sandstorm, glittering with sunlight, drifting wide, sinking to earth in myriad tiny clouds. The guests sat watching them from rough wooden stands. These riders' movements were almost quicker than the eyes of the watchers. The Cossacks ducked from their saddles to snatch blue and scarlet handkerchiefs off the ground in their strong tawny horse teeth, suddenly falling right under the bellies of their mounts in full gallop, their legs still pressing the flanks in glistening riding boots. Others flung their lances high in the air, and, far beyond them, the shafts glittered and twirled, to fall obediently back in the riders' hands, returning, as falcons might, to their masters. Others again, crouching down flat across their horses' backs, their mouths pressing the beasts' soft muzzles fraternally, jumped through iron hoops, astonishingly narrow, each just wide enough to girt a small beer keg. The horses stretched all four feet out from their bodies, their manes soared like wings, their tails acting as rudders, their narrow heads like the slim bows of canoes skidding along. Another could jump his beast over twenty beer barrels set edge to edge. The horse whinnied before taking them. The rider came galloping from a distance; a gray speck, he grew in scorching speed to a streak. The body, the rider, became a huge, legendary bird, half-horse, half-man, a winged centaur, until at last, after the jump, he stood stock-still a hundred paces beyond the casks: a monument, a lifeless image. Others again fired at flying targets as they sped like arrows, themselves looking like arrows, targets which were held up to them on big white rounds by riders galloping away. The marksmen galloped, fired, and hit. Many tumbled to the earth. The men, coming from behind, sped gently across their bodies, no hoof touched them. There were riders with horses galloping beside them who could leap in full gallop from saddle to saddle, return to the first, suddenly tumble back into the second, until at last, with one band set on each horse, their legs dangling down between the galloping bodies, they pulled both up with a jerk at the given stopping place, reining them in to stand there motionless, like steeds in bronze.

Such displays of horsemanship were not the sole diversion provided by the outpost between the monarchy and Russia. A regiment of Dragoons was also stationed in the garrison. Between Jaeger officers, Dragoons and the gentlemen of the Russian regiment, Count Chojnicki established intimate relations. He was one of the wealthiest Polish landowners in the district.

Count Wojciech Chojnicki, a connection of the Ledochowskis and Potockis, a cousin of the Sternbergs, a friend of the Thuns, was a man of the world. Forty years old (though he might have been any age), a cavalry captain in the Reserve, a bachelor, he was frivolous and at the same time melancholy, a lover of horses, alcohol, society, both flippant and serious. He spent his winters in cities and in the gambling casinos of the Riviera. But he returned like a migrating bird to the home of his ancestors when the laburnum began to bloom on the railway bridges. He brought with him a faintly scented whiff of society and tales of gallantry and adventure. He was the kind of man who can have no enemies but no friends either; he had only associates, boon companions, or casual acquaintances. Chojnicki, with his pale, intelligent, rather prominent eyes, his shining baldness smooth as a pebble, his wisp of a yellow mustache, and his narrow shoulders, his thin, disproportionately long legs, could attract whomever he chose or whomever chance had set in his way.

He lived alternately in two houses, known to the townspeople and respected by them, as the old and the new Schloss. The so-called old Schloss was a huge dilapidated hunting lodge which, for mysterious reasons, the Count refused to put into repair. The new Schloss was a spacious, two-storey country house, the upper storey often filled with strange and sometimes rather shady-looking visitors. These were the Count's poor relations. The closest possible study of family history would never have enabled Count Chojnicki to trace the exact degrees of kinship of his guests. Gradually they had made it a habit to arrive and stay the summer at the new Schloss, as family pensioners and connections. Having rested and fed, sometimes clothed in new suits provided by the Count's local tailor, these guests departed when starlings twittered in the night and the time of cuckoo weed was approaching—back into the unknown regions from which they had come. The master of the house noticed neither their arrival, nor their presence, nor their departure. His Jewish steward had standing orders to examine their family credentials, regulate their habits, and get rid of them at the approach of winter. The house had two entrances. While the Count and any guest who was not a kinsman used the front door, the relations had to go the long way around, across the fruit garden and in by the little side door in its wall. Apart from this, these uninvited guests were free to do anything they pleased.

Twice a week, on Mondays and Thursdays, Count Chojnicki held his little evenings, and once a month he gave a party. On little evenings only six rooms were lit up, for the parties twelve. On little evenings the footmen wore drab yellow livery and no gloves. Parties meant white-gloved footmen in dark-brown coats with silver buttons and velvet facings. All occasions began with vermouth and dry Spanish wines from which the guests passed on to Burgundy and Bordeaux. Then it was time for the champagne, which was followed by cognac. An evening ended with a fitting tribute to local patriotism—namely the local product, Ninety Percent.

The officers of the ultrafeudal Dragoons and the chiefly middle-class Jaeger swore lifelong friendship with great emotion at Count Chojnicki's parties. Through the wide curved windows of the Schloss, summer dawns would witness a colorful confusion of infantry and cavalry uniforms. Toward five a.m. a swarm of despairing batmen came running to the Schloss to wake their masters; for regimental parades began at six. The host, in whom alcohol engendered no fatigue, had long since gone to his little hunting lodge. There he would fiddle about with weird test tubes, chemical apparatus, and minute flames. Local gossip had it that Chojnicki was trying to make gold. Indeed, it certainly looked as though he were occupied with some foolish experiment in alchemy. However, even if he failed to produce gold, he was certainly making money at roulette. Sometimes he would drop hints about infallible systems passed on to him by a deceased gambler.

For years he had been a deputy to the Reichsrat, always re-elected by his district, quelling any local opposition by money, influence, or sudden attack. He was the spoilt darling of every government and despised the parliament he served in. He had never made a speech nor asked a question. Unbelieving and contemptuous, fearless and without scruple, Chojnicki was in the habit of saying that the Emperor was a thoughtless old man, the government officials a set of fools, the Reichsrat a well-meaning assemblage of pathetic idiots, the Civil Service venal, cowardly, and indolent. German-Austrians were waltzing apes, Hungarians stank, Czechs were born lick-spittles, Ruthenians treacherous Russians in disguise, Croats and Slovenes, whom he always called Crovots and Schlaviners, were tinkers, peddlars, and sots. His own nation, the Poles, were snobs, hairdressers, and fashion-plate photographers.

After every return from Vienna, or any other part of that society in which he kicked his heels up so familiarly, the Count would give an ominous lecture, somewhat as follows:

"The monarchy is bound to end. The minute the Emperor is dead, we shall splinter into a hundred fragments. The Balkans will be more powerful than we are. Each nation will set up its own dirty little government, even the Jews will proclaim a king in Palestine. Vienna's begun to stink of the sweat of democrats—I can't stand the Ringstrasse any more. The workers all wave red flags and don't want to work any more. The mayor of Vienna is a pious shopkeeper. Even the parsons are going red, they've started preaching in Czech in the churches. At the Burgtheater all the performances are filthy Jewish plays. And every week another Hungarian water-closet manufacturer is made a baron. I tell you, gentlemen, if we don't start shooting pretty soon, it'll be the end. You just wait and see what's coming to us."

His listeners laughed and had another drink. They couldn't see what the fuss was all about. Now and again, of course, you did some shooting, at election times, for instance, to secure the safe return of Count Chojnicki, which proved that things were not being allowed to go to the dogs just like that. The Emperor was still alive. He would be followed by his successor. The army continued to drill, resplendent in every regulation hue. The people loved their dynasty and acclaimed it, in many different kinds of peasant costume. Chojnicki was a joker.

But Trotta was more sensitive than his comrades, sadder than they, his mind forever full of echoes, darkness, and the rustling wings of death he had already twice encountered. Lieutenant Trotta could sometimes feel the dismal force of these prophecies.

✧ PART FIVE ✧

1848 AND NATIONALISM

This image of revolutionary conflict in Frankfurt during 1848 could serve as a template for most of the capitals of continental Europe that year as movements for national and political liberation confronted the forces of conservatism.

1848 and Nationalism

The year 1848 abruptly closed the curtain on the era of Metternich and revolutions. From the English Channel to the Russian frontier, uprisings swept away monarchies in favor of liberal political goals and national self-determination. Angry middle classes found allies among workers with socialist slogans and, sometimes, peasants attacking serfdom's last vestiges. Frightened by anarchy, millions soon welcomed back recently overturned regimes. One commentator described 1848 as the "turning point in history when history failed to turn." Even so, the 1848 tumult forewarned elites about widespread, irresistible popular aspirations. Of special note was nationalism, the idea that a people sharing the same history, language, and culture should constitute a nation-state. Beginning in 1820 and accelerating after 1848, national aspirations in many parts of Europe achieved recognition.

Now commonplace, the idea of national self-rule played little role in pre-1800 thinking about states and peoples. Earlier writers focused on all Europe as "Christendom" and the Enlightenment stressed common rational capacities. Monarchies ruled over whatever territories and peoples they inherited or obtained. Inspired by German romantic writers, Madame (Anne-Louise-Germaine) de Staël (1766–1817), daughter of a famous pre-revolutionary statesman, first popularized the idea of national character. Published between 1810 and 1818, her evenhanded descriptions of the German, English, and Russian peoples highlighted individual national histories and cultures. By the middle of the century, Joseph Mazzini (1805–1872) preached the full-fledged nationalist cause. His writings, such as *The Duties of Man* (1844), spurred the 1848 Italian uprisings and inspired Italian national unification a decade and a half later. He and other writers about nationalism created the intellectual basis for the nation-state. Early Russian socialist, Alexander Herzen (1812–1870), fled persecution and arrived in Western Europe just in time to participate in the 1848 uprisings and witness their brutal repression by resurgent governments. His disenchanted recollections written in 1855 reflect the revolutions' failure.

✦ Reading 20 ✦

Germany, England, and Russia

Madame de Staël

Germany

The Customs and the Character of the Germans

Only a few basic characteristics are held in common by the entire German nation, for the diversities of this country are such that one is at a loss to combine from one viewpoint religions, governments, climates, and even peoples so different. The Germany of the South is, in many respects, entirely distinct from the North; the commercial cities are unlike the cities famous for their universities; the small states differ considerably from the two great monarchies of Prussia and Austria. Germany was an aristocratic federation. This domain had no common center of enlightenment and public spirit; it was not a solid nation, for the separate elements were not tied together. This division of Germany, fatal to her political influence, was nevertheless very favorable to all efforts of talent and the imagination. In respect to literary and metaphysical ideas, there was a sort of mild and peaceful anarchy that permitted each person to develop fully his own way of looking at things.

Since there is no capital where the elite of Germany gathers, the spirit of society exercises little power there: the sway of taste and the weapon of ridicule have no influence. Most writers and thinkers work in solitude or surrounded only by a little circle that they dominate.

In literature, as in politics, the Germans have too much consideration for foreigners and not enough national predilections. This self-abnegation and esteem of others is a virtue in individuals, but the patriotism of nations ought to be self-centered.

From: Madame de Staël-Holstein, *On Politics, Literature, and National Character,* ed. Monroe Berger (Garden City, NJ: Doubleday, 1964), pp. 277–285, 342–348, 362–369.

I shall examine separately the Germany of the South and of the North but I shall confine myself now to some reflections applicable to the whole nation. The Germans are in general sincere and faithful; they rarely break their word, and deceit is foreign to them.

The power of work and reflection is another distinctive trait of the German nation. They are naturally literary and philosophical; but the separation of the classes, which is more pronounced in Germany than anywhere else because society does not subdue its distinctions, is in some respects harmful to the understanding properly so called. The nobility have too few ideas and the men of letters too little practical experience. It is imagination, rather than understanding, that characterizes the Germans.

In leaving France, it is very difficult to get used to the slowness and dullness of the German people. They never hurry, and they find obstacles to everything. You hear "it is impossible" a hundred times in Germany for one time in France. When it comes to action, the Germans do not know how to wrestle with difficulties. Their respect for power arises more from its resemblance to destiny than from self-interest. The lower classes have rather coarse manners, especially when they are rubbed the wrong way. They naturally feel, more than the nobility, that holy antipathy for foreign manners, customs, and languages that strengthens the national bond in every country. The offer of money does not disturb their usual ways, nor does fear; in short, they are very capable of that steadiness in all things that is an excellent basis for morality; for the man who is always moved by fear, and even more by hope, passes easily from one opinion to another whenever his interest requires it.

Once we rise a little above the lowest class of people in Germany, we can easily observe the inner life, the poetry of the soul, that characterizes the Germans. Almost all the inhabitants of town and country, the soldiers and the peasants, know music. I had the experience of entering poor homes blackened by tobacco-smoke and of suddenly hearing not only the mistress but also the master of the house improvising on the harpsichord, as the Italians improvise in verse.

We must also be grateful to the Germans for the good will they display in the respectful bows and in politeness filled with formalities that foreigners have so often held up to ridicule. They might easily have substituted cold and indifferent manners for the grace and elegance they are accused of being unable to reach. Indifference always silences mockery, for mockery applies itself especially to useless efforts. But benevolent people would rather expose themselves to mockery than preserve themselves from it by the haughty and reserved air so easy for anyone to assume.

One is constantly struck, in Germany, by the contrast between sentiments and habits, between talents and tastes: civilization and nature do not yet seem to be well blended. Sometimes the most truthful men are affected in their expressions and appearance, as if they had something to hide. Sometimes, on the other hand, gentleness of soul does not prevent rudeness in manners: often this contradiction goes still further, and weakness of character reveals itself through the rough language and conduct. Enthusiasm for the arts and poetry is joined to rather common behavior in social life. There is no country where the men of letters or the young people studying in the universities are better acquainted with ancient languages and antiquity, but also there is none where superannuated practices more generally still persist. The memories of Greece and the taste for the fine arts seem to have reached them indirectly, but feudal institutions and the old customs of the Germans are still held in honor there, although, unhappily for the military power of the country, they no longer have the same strength.

There is no more bizarre combination than the military appearance of all Germany—the soldiers one meets at every step, and the kind of domesticated life people lead there. They are afraid of hardship and bad weather, as though the nation were entirely made up of merchants and men of letters; yet all their institutions tend—and necessarily so—to give the nation military habits.

Stoves, beer, and tobacco-smoke surround the lower classes of Germany with a heavy and hot atmosphere from which they do not like to emerge. This atmosphere is harmful to alertness, which is no less important than courage in war. Determination is sluggish and discouragement is easy because such a generally melancholy life does not afford much confidence in fortune.

The demarcation of classes, much more positive in Germany than it was in France, necessarily destroyed the military spirit in the middle class. This demarcation is not offensive, for, I repeat, amiability suffuses everything in Germany, even aristocratic pride. Differences in rank are reduced to a few court privileges, to a few gatherings that do not afford enough pleasure to warrant much regret. Nothing is bitter, no matter how regarded, when society—and through it, ridicule—has little influence. Men can wound their own souls only by duplicity or mockery; in a serious and truthful country there is always justice and happiness. But the barrier in Germany that separated the nobles from the citizens necessarily made the entire nation less warlike.

Imagination, which is the dominant feature of artistic and literary Germany, inspires the fear of danger if this natural emotion is not combated by the influence of judgment and the exaltation of honor. It is important to know whether domestic affections, the habit of reflection, and the very gentleness of soul do not lead to the fear of death; and if all the power of a state consists in its military spirit, it is essential to examine the causes that have weakened this spirit in the German nation.

Three chief motives usually lead men to battle: love of country and of freedom, love of glory, and religious fanaticism.

There cannot be much love of country in a realm divided for several centuries, where Germans fought Germans almost always through foreign instigation. Love of glory has little vitality where there is no center, no capital, no society. The type of impartiality, a luxury of justice, that characterizes the Germans makes them susceptible to being more inflamed by abstract ideas than by the concerns of life. The general who loses a battle is more certain of indulgence than the general who wins one is of applause. In such a nation there is not enough difference between success and failure to excite much ambition.

Religion in Germany is deep-seated, but it has a character of meditation and self-containment that does not inspire the vigor necessary to exclusive feelings. That same separateness in opinion, individuals, and states, so harmful to the power of the German Empire, is found in religion too: a large number of different sects divide Germany. Even Catholicism, which by its nature exerts a uniform and strict discipline, is interpreted by each one in his own way. A political and social bond among peoples, one government, one religion, one law, common interests, a classical literature, a prevailing point of view—none of these things is found among the Germans.

The love of liberty is not developed among the Germans; they have not learned its value through possession or deprivation of it. There are several examples of federated governments that lend as much vigor to public spirit as does unity in government, but they are associations of equal states and of free citizens. The German federation was composed of strong and weak states, citizens and serfs, rivals and even enemies—these were old elements joined by circumstances and respected by men.

The very independence enjoyed in Germany, in almost all respects, made the Germans indifferent to liberty. Independence is a possession, and liberty is a right. And precisely because no one in Germany was injured in respect to his rights or possessions, no need was felt for any means to preserve this happy condition.

The Germans, with a few exceptions, are hardly able to succeed in anything that calls for tact and facility. Everything makes them anxious, everything hinders them, and they feel the need of a method in doing things just as much as they feel the need of independence in ideas. The French, on the contrary, approach action with the freedom of art, and ideas with the bondage of custom. The Germans, who cannot endure the yoke of rules in literature, prefer everything to be laid out for them in advance when it comes to behavior. They do not know how to deal with people; and the less occasion they have in this respect to decide for themselves, the more satisfied they are.

Only political institutions can shape the character of a nation. The nature of the government of Germany was antithetical to the philosophical enlightenment of the Germans. That is why they combine boldness of thought with the most obedient character. The pre-eminence of the military regime and the distinctions of rank have accustomed them to the strictest submission in the relations of social life. Among them obedience is a matter of regularity, not servility; they are scrupulous in the execution of the orders they receive, as though every order were a duty.

The enlightened men of Germany heatedly argue among themselves in the domain of theory, where they will brook no interference. But they rather willingly abandon to the powerful of this earth all the realities of life. These realities, which they so despise, nonetheless find purchasers, who then disturb and repress the realm of the imagination. The mind and character of the Germans appear not to be in touch with each other: the one cannot bear any restriction, the other submits to every yoke. The one is very venturesome, the other very timid. In short, the enlightenment of the one rarely lends strength to the other, and that is easily explained. The spread of knowledge in modern times only weakens character when the latter is not fortified by the practice of business and the exercise of the will. To see and understand everything is a great cause of uncertainty; and vigor of action develops only in those free and powerful countries where patriotic sentiments are to the soul like blood to the veins and grow cold only as life ends.

The Women

Nature and society have given women a great capacity for endurance, and it seems to me that it cannot be denied that in our day they are in general more meritorious than men.

German women have a charm all their own—a touching voice, fair hair, a dazzling complexion. They are modest, but less timid than English women; it seems that they less often meet men who are superior to them and that, moreover, they have less to fear from harsh judgments of the public. They seek to please by their sensibility and to interest by their imagination. They are familiar with the language of poetry and the fine arts. They flirt wholeheartedly, whereas French women do so wittily and jokingly. The perfect loyalty that is peculiar to the character of the Germans makes love less dangerous for the happiness of women, and they possibly approach this sentiment with more confidence because it is clothed in more romantic colors, and disdain and infidelity are less to be feared there than elsewhere.

Love is a religion in Germany, but a poetic religion that too readily tolerates whatever sensibility excuses. It cannot be denied that the ease of divorce in Protestant areas strikes at the sacredness of marriage. Husbands and wives are changed there as calmly as if it were a matter of arranging the incidents of a play. Owing to the good nature of men and women, no bitterness enters into these easy separations; and since the Germans have more imagination than genuine passion, the most bizarre events occur with extraordinary tranquillity. But it is in this way that manners and character lose all solidity. The spirit of paradox shakes the most sacred institutions, and there are no fixed rules on any subject.

One may justifiably laugh at the absurdities of some German women who become enthusiastic to the point of affectation, and whose saccharine expressions obliterate everything pointed and striking in mind and character. They are not frank, yet neither are they false. It is merely that they see and judge nothing accurately, and real events pass before their eyes like a phantasmagoria. Even when it occurs to them to be gay, they still maintain a tinge of that sentimentality that is so honored in their country.

Despite these absurdities, there are many German women with genuine feelings and simple manners. Their careful upbringing and natural purity of soul make them a gentle and steady influence. But we seldom find among them the quick wit that animates conversation and stimulates ideas; this kind of delight is hardly to be found except in the smartest and wittiest Paris society.

* * *

England

The Prosperity of England and the Causes That Have Hitherto Increased It

Reaching England, I was thinking of no particular person: I knew hardly anyone there, but I went with confidence. I was persecuted by an enemy of liberty, so I believed myself certain of honorable sympathy in a country whose every institution was in harmony with my political sentiments. I counted much, also, on the memory of my father to protect me, and I was not deceived. The waves of the North Sea, which I crossed in coming from Sweden, still filled me with terror as I made out from afar the green island that alone had resisted the enslavement of Europe. Those who will not acknowledge the influence of liberty in the power of England constantly repeat that the English would have been conquered by Bonaparte, like all the Continental nations, had they not been protected by the sea. This opinion cannot be refuted by experience. I have no doubt that if, by a stroke of Leviathan, Great Britain had been joined to the European continent, it would certainly have suffered more and its wealth would have diminished. But the public spirit of a free nation is such that it would never have yielded to the yoke of foreigners.

From Harwich to London one travels a highway about seventy miles long bordered almost entirely by country houses to the right and left: a succession of dwellings with gardens, interrupted by towns. Almost everyone is well-clothed, hardly a cottage is in decay; even the animals seem peaceful and thriving, as if there were rights for them, too, in this great structure of social order. The price of everything is necessarily very high, but most of these prices are fixed; there is in this country such an aversion for anything arbitrary that, besides the law itself, a rule and then a custom are established to ensure, as far as possible, in the smallest details, some degree of exactness and stability. The high cost of living resulting from extremely high taxes is of course a disadvantage. But assuming the war was absolutely necessary, what other nation—that is, what other form of government—could be equal to it?

The amount accomplished in England through private contributions is enormous: hospitals, educational establishments, missions, Christian societies were not only maintained but increased during the war; and foreigners who underwent disasters from it—the Swiss, Germans, Dutch—constantly received private aid from England, the result of voluntary gifts.

But to what are these miracles of liberal prosperity to be attributed? To liberty—that is, to the nation's trust in a government that makes publicity the first principle of finances, in a government enlightened by discussion and by freedom of the press. The nation, which cannot be deceived under such an arrangement, knows the use of the taxes it pays, and public credit supports the unbelievable weight of the

English debt. If something proportionately similar were tried in any non-representative state on the European continent, it would not be able to go far in such an undertaking. Five hundred thousand owners of government bonds constitute a strong guarantee of payment of the debt in a country where each man's opinion and interest is influential.

The government never meddles in anything that private individuals can do just as well. Respect for individual freedom extends to the exercise of everyone's abilities, and the people are so anxious to manage their own affairs, when it is possible, that in many respects London lacks the police necessary for the convenience of the city because the ministers may not encroach upon the local authorities.

Political security, without which there can be neither credit nor capital accumulation, is still not enough to develop all the resources of a nation: emulation must stimulate men to labor, while the law assures them of its fruit. Commerce and industry must be honored, not by rewards to this or that individual—this presupposes two classes in a country, one of which thinks it has the right to reward the other—but by an order of things that allows each man to rise to the highest level if he deserves it. In fact, the absurd prejudice that forbade the nobility of France to go into business did more harm to the growth of French fortunes than any other abuse of the Old Regime. In England peerages have been recently granted to leading businessmen. Once peers, they do not remain in commerce, because they are expected to serve the country in another way; but it is their function as government officials, and not the prejudices of caste, that divorces them from business, into which the younger sons of the highest nobility enter without hesitation when circumstances call them to it. The same family often has peers on one side and on the other the most ordinary merchants of some provincial town. This political order enhances all the faculties of every individual, because there are no limits to the advantages that wealth and talent can bring, and because the lowest English citizen, if he is worthy of being the highest, is barred from no marriage, employment, society, or title.

All classes of well-bred men in England meet often in various committees engaged in some venture or charity supported by private contributions. Publicity in all matters is a principle so widely accepted that, though the English are by nature the most reserved of men and the most reluctant to speak before others, there are almost always, in the rooms where the committees meet, seats for spectators and a platform from which the speakers address the assembly.

I attended one of these discussions, in which the reasons calculated to stimulate the listeners' generosity were forcefully presented. It concerned the sending of help to the people of Leipzig after the battle fought beneath its walls. The first speaker was the Duke of York, second son of the king. After the Duke of York, the Duke of Sussex, the fifth son of the king, who expresses himself with much elegance and ease, also spoke in his turn; and the most beloved and respected man in all of England, Mr. Wilberforce, could hardly make himself heard above the applause. Humble men, and with no other status in society than their wealth or devotion to humanity, followed these illustrious names. The listeners contributed as they left, and considerable sums were the result of this meeting. Thus are formed the ties that strengthen the unity of the nation and thus the social order bases itself upon reason and humanity.

The object of these worthy assemblies is not merely to encourage works of charity; some of them serve especially to strengthen the union of the nobility and the businessmen, the nation and the government.

Liberty and Public Spirit among the English

The greatest support of liberty is individual security, and nothing is finer than English legislation in this respect. A criminal trial is a horrible spectacle anywhere. In England the excellence of the procedure, the humanity of the judges, the precautions of every kind taken to protect the lives of the innocent, and the means of defense of the guilty inject a feeling of admiration into the anguish of such a trial. The admirable institution of the jury, which goes back in England to remote antiquity, introduces equity into justice.

English civil law is much less worthy of praise; the trials are too costly and too long. It will certainly be improved with time, as it already has been in several respects, for what distinguishes English government above all is the possibility of orderly improvement.

"Very well," exclaim the enemies of all public virtue, "even if praise of England were fully warranted, it would only mean that it is a skillfully and wisely governed country, just as any other country might be. But it is not free in the way that the *philosophes* understand freedom, for the ministers are the masters of everything, there as elsewhere. They buy the votes of Parliament in such a way as always to assure themselves a majority, and the whole English constitution of which people speak with admiration is nothing but the art of putting political venality to work."

Can anyone honestly convince himself that the English ministers give money to the members of the House of Commons or of the higher chamber to vote with the government? How could the English ministers, who account for public funds so exactly, find sums large enough to corrupt men of such great wealth, to say nothing of their character?

Fidelity to party is one of the virtues based upon public spirit, from which comes the greatest advantage for English liberty. If tomorrow the ministers with whom one voted go out of office, those to whom they have given posts leave with them. A man would be disgraced in England if he parted from his political allies for his private interest. One never hears the same mouth uttering two opposite opinions; but in the present state of things in England differences are a matter of shades rather than colors. The Tories, it has been said, approve liberty and love the monarchy, while the Whigs approve the monarchy and love liberty. But between these two parties there is no question as to a republic or a monarchy, the old or the new dynasty, liberty or servitude.

For nearly fifty years the members of the Opposition have held ministerial office only three or four years, yet their fidelity to party has not been shaken.

The existence of a Government party and an Opposition party, though it cannot be prescribed by law, is an essential support of liberty based on the nature of things. In every country where you see an assembly of men always in agreement, be certain that there is a despotism, or that despotism will be the result of unanimity if it is not the cause of it. Now, since power and the favors it disposes have attraction for men, liberty could exist only with this fidelity to party which imposes, so to speak, a discipline of honor in the ranks of the deputies enrolled under various banners.

But if opinions are settled in advance, how can truth and eloquence influence the assembly? How can the majority change when circumstances require it to do so, and of what use is debate if no one can vote according to his conviction? That is not the situation. What is called fidelity to party means that one must not separate one's personal interests from the interests of one's political allies, nor deal separately with the men in power. But it often happens that circumstances or arguments influence the bulk of the assembly and that the considerable number of neutrals, that is, those who do not play an active role in politics, are able to change the majority. It is in the nature of English government that the ministers cannot stay in office without this majority in their favor. Yet Mr. Pitt, though he temporarily lost it at the time of the King's first illness, could remain in office because public opinion, which was favorable to him, enabled him to dissolve Parliament and to resort to a new election. In short, opinion rules in England; it is this that establishes the liberty of a state.

Enlightenment and the strength of public spirit are a more than adequate answer to the arguments of those who maintain that, if England were a Continental power, the army would encroach upon its liberty. It is undoubtedly an advantage to the English that their strength lies in the navy rather than in ground forces. It requires greater knowledge to be a captain of a ship than a colonel, and the habits acquired at sea do not lead to the desire to interfere in the internal affairs of one's country. But if nature, turned lavish, created ten Lord Wellingtons and if the world saw ten more Battles of Waterloo, it would not occur to those who so readily give their lives for their country to turn their power against it; if they did, they would face an insuperable obstacle in men just as brave as themselves and more enlightened, who detest the military spirit though they admire and practice warlike qualities.

The kind of prejudice that convinced the French nobility that they could serve their country only in a military career does not exist at all in England. A great many sons of peers are lawyers; the bar shares the respect felt for the law, and in all walks of life civil occupations are respected. In such a country people need not yet fear the inroads of military power; only unenlightened nations have a blind admiration for the sword.

* * *

Russia

The Road from Kiev to Moscow

I have seen nothing barbaric in these people. On the contrary, their manners have something elegant and gentle that is not found elsewhere. I am quite aware that one may reasonably raise, in objection to my view, the great atrocities found in Russian history. But, first, I should place the blame for them upon the Boyars, depraved by the despotism they practiced or suffered, rather than upon the nation itself. Moreover, political dissension, in all places and times, perverts the national character. Nothing in history is more deplorable than a succession of masters elevated and overturned by crime. But such is the inevitable condition of absolute power upon this earth.

If tyranny had on its side only its fully convinced advocates, it could never maintain itself. The astonishing thing, which more than anything else reveals human wretchedness, is that most ordinary men are at the service of success. They do not have the power to think beyond a bare fact, and when an oppressor has triumphed and a victim is destroyed, they hasten to justify not the tyrant, precisely, but the fate of which he is the instrument. Weakness of mind and character is no doubt the cause of this servility, but there is also in man a certain need to justify fate, whatever it may be, as if that were a way to live in peace with it.

Everywhere in Europe one sees the contrast between wealth and poverty, but in Russia neither the one nor the other, so to speak, is conspicuous. The populace are not poor; the upper class can, when necessary, lead the same life as the populace. What characterizes this country is the mixture of the severest hardships and the most exquisite pleasures. Those very noblemen whose houses combine the most striking luxuries from various parts of the world live, while traveling, on much worse food than do our French peasants and can endure a very disagreeable physical existence not only in war but in many circumstances of life. The severity of the climate, the marshlands, forests, and deserts, which make up a large part of the country, put man in a struggle against nature. What the English call *comfort,* and what we call *l'aisance,* is hardly to be found in Russia. You will find nothing of any kind perfect enough to satisfy the fancy of the Russian nobles. But when this poetry of abundance falls short, they drink hydromel, sleep on a plank, and travel day and night in an open carriage without missing the luxury to which one would think them accustomed. They love wealth for its magnificence rather than for the pleasures it affords; in this too they are like Orientals, who practice hospitality toward strangers, overwhelm them with presents, and often neglect their own ordinary comfort. This is one of the reasons that explain the great courage with which they have borne the ruin inflicted upon them by the burning of Moscow. More accustomed to external pomp than to solicitude for themselves, they are not debilitated by luxury; to give away money satisfies their pride as much as or more than lavish spending. A gigantic quality in all things characterizes this nation; ordinary dimensions do not at all apply to it. I do not mean by this that neither true greatness nor stability are to be found in it. But the boldness, the imagination, of the Russians knows no bounds. Among them everything is colossal rather than proportional, audacious rather than thoughtful, and if the target is not hit it is because it is overshot.

Appearance of the Country. Character of the Russian People

On the eve of my arrival in Moscow, I stopped, the night of a very warm day, in a pleasant enough meadow. Some peasant women, dressed picturesquely in accordance with the habit of the locality, were returning from their labors singing Ukrainian tunes whose words praise love and liberty with a kind of melancholy akin to regret. I asked them to dance and they consented to do so. I was struck by the gentle gaiety of these peasant women, as I had been by that of most of the common people I met in Russia. I can well believe that they are terrible when their passions are aroused; and as they have no education, they do not know how to curb their violence. As a result of this ignorance, they have few moral principles, and theft is very frequent in Russia, but so is hospitality. They give to you as they take from you, according to whether trickery or generosity strikes their fancy; both arouse the admiration of this nation. There is a little resemblance to uncivilized people in this way of living, but it seems to me that at present the only vigorous European nations are

those that are called either barbarous—that is to say, unenlightened—or free.

One thing worth noting is the degree to which public spirit is marked in Russia. The reputation for invincibility which a great many successes have given this nation, the pride natural to the nobility, the self-sacrifice ingrained in the character of the nation, the profound influence of religion, the hatred of foreigners which Peter I tried to destroy in order to enlighten and civilize his country but which remains nonetheless in the blood of the Russians and is occasionally aroused—all these causes combine to make this nation a very energetic one. Some wretched anecdotes about earlier reigns, some Russians who ran up debts in Paris, and some *bon mots* of Diderot put it into the heads of Frenchmen that Russia consisted only of a corrupt Court, officers and chamberlains, and a population of slaves. This is a great error.

The welcome the Russians extend is so kind that from the first day one thinks he is intimate with them, but very likely one would not really know them even after ten years. Russian silence is absolutely extraordinary; it is induced only by what arouses their deep interest. Of everything else, they talk as much as one would like, but their conversation reveals only their politeness: it betrays neither their feelings nor their opinions. Moreover, as they are in general not highly educated, they find little pleasure in serious conversation and do not take pride in scintillating by the wit that may be displayed in it. Poetry, eloquence, and literature are not found in Russia. Luxury, power, and courage are the main goals of pride and ambition; all other ways of distinguishing oneself still seem effeminate and hollow to this nation.

But, it will be said, the people are slaves. What kind of character can they be credited with? I certainly do not have to point out that all enlightened people hope that the Russian nation will emerge from this condition, and the one who probably desires it most is Emperor Alexander. But this Russian slavery does not resemble the kind we are familiar with in the West. It is not, as under the feudal *régime,* a matter of conquerors who imposed their harsh laws upon the conquered. The relationship between the nobles and the populace is more like what was called the family of slaves among the ancients than the status of serfs among the moderns. There is no third estate in Russia. This is a great hindrance to the progress of literature and the fine arts, for it is usually in this middle class that learning is developed. But the result of this absence of an intermediary between the nobility and the populace is that they have greater affection for each other. The distance between the two classes seems the greater because there is nothing between these two extremes, but in actual fact they are the closer to one another for not being separated by a middle class. This is a social organization entirely unfavorable to the enlightenment of the upper classes but not to the happiness of the lower. Moreover, where there is no representative government, that is, in countries where the monarch still decrees the laws he is to execute, men are often more degraded by the loss of their reason and their character than in this vast domain where a few simple religious and patriotic ideas govern a large mass guided by a few leaders. The immense extent of the Russian realm also prevents the despotism of the nobles from bearing heavily upon the people in everyday affairs. Finally, above all, the religious and military spirit is so predominant in the nation that many faults may be forgiven in consideration of these two great sources of noble deeds.

Moscow

Gilded cupolas announced Moscow from afar; yet, as the surrounding country is only a plain like all of Russia, one can reach that large city without being impressed by its extent. Someone has said with reason that Moscow is rather a province than a city. Indeed, one sees there huts, houses, palaces, a bazaar as in the Orient, churches, public buildings, bodies of water, woods, and parks. The diversity of manners and of nations that make up Russia is revealed in this vast region. I was asked: Would you like to buy some Kashmir shawls in the Tartar district? Have you seen Chinatown? Asia and Europe are combined in this immense city. People in it enjoy more liberty than in Petersburg, where the Court necessarily exercises great influence. The nobles settled in Moscow do not strive for high places; but they show their patriotism by large gifts to the state, whether for public purposes in time of peace or for relief in time of war. The colossal fortunes of the Russian nobles are used for building up collections of all kinds, for commercial enterprises, and for entertainments modeled after the *Thousand and One Nights,* and these fortunes are also very often lost through the unrestrained passions of their owners.

When I arrived in Moscow, there was talk of nothing but the sacrifices made for the war.

No sooner does a Russian become a soldier than his beard is cut, and from this moment he is free. People wished that everyone who served in the militia would also be regarded as free, but then the whole nation would have been free, for it rose up almost in its entirety. Let us hope that this liberation, so much desired, will be brought about peacefully. But, in the meantime, one wishes the beards would be preserved, so much strength and dignity do they lend the face.

The Kremlin, that citadel where the emperors of Russia defended themselves against the Tartars, is surrounded by a high wall crenelated and flanked with turrets whose unusual shapes recall a Turkish minaret rather than a fortress like most of those in the West. But though the external character of the city's buildings is Oriental, the imprint of Christianity is found in the multitude of churches, so revered, which attract one's notice at every step.

The Russians played no role in the Age of Chivalry; they were not involved in the Crusades. Constantly at war with the Tartars, Poles, and Turks, the military spirit took shape among them in the midst of atrocities of all kinds brought about by the barbarity of the Asian nations and of the tyrants who governed Russia. In social relations, which are so new to them, the Russians do not distinguish themselves by the spirit of chivalry as the peoples of the West conceive it; rather, they have always shown themselves to be unmerciful toward their enemies. So many massacres took place in the interior of Russia down to and after the reign of Peter the Great that the morality of the nation, and especially that of the nobility, necessarily suffered much from them. These despotic governments, whose only limit is the assassination of the despot, overthrow the principles of honor and duty in the minds of men. But patriotism and attachment to religious beliefs have maintained themselves in all their strength through the wreckage of this bloody history, and the nation that preserves such virtues may yet astonish the world.

In Moscow I saw the most enlightened men in the field of the sciences and literature. But there, as at Petersburg, almost all the professorial posts are filled by Germans. There is a great scarcity of educated men in every field in Russia. The young people, for the most part, do not go to the university except to enter the military profession sooner. Civil offices in Russia confer a rank corresponding to a grade in the army; the spirit of the nation is entirely directed toward the war. In everything else, in administration, political economy, public education, etc., the other nations have until now surpassed the Russians. They are, however, making attempts in literature. The softness and vividness of the sounds of their language are obvious even to those who do not understand it; it should be well suited to music and poetry. But the Russians, like so many other nations on the Continent, make the mistake of imitating French literature which, by its very beauty, is appropriate only to the French. It seems to me that the Russians should find their literary heritage in the Greeks rather than in the Latins. The letters of Russian script, which are so much like those of the Greeks, the former connections between the Russians and the Byzantine empire, their future destinies, which may lead them toward the illustrious monuments of Athens and Sparta—all this should induce the Russians to study Greek. But above all their writers must draw their poetry from the deepest source in their own souls. Their works, until now, have been composed, so to speak, only from their lips, but so vigorous a nation can never be stirred by such weak notes.

✦ Reading 21 ✦

The Duties of Man

Joseph Mazzini

To the Italian Working-Men

I want to speak to you of your duties. I want to speak to you, as my heart dictates to me, of the most sacred things which we know—of God, of Humanity, of the Fatherland, of the Family. Listen to me with love, even as I shall speak to you with love. My words are words of conviction matured by long years of sorrow and of observation and of study. The duties which I am going to point out to you I strive and shall strive as long as I live to fulfil, to the utmost of my power. I may make mistakes, but my heart is true. I may deceive myself, but I will not deceive you. Hear me therefore as a brother; judge freely among yourselves, whether it seems to you that I speak the truth; abandon me if you think that I preach what is false; but follow me and do according to my teaching if you find me an apostle of truth. To be mistaken is a misfortune to be pitied; but to know the truth and not to conform one's actions to it is a crime which Heaven and Earth condemn.

Why do I speak to you of your *duties* before speaking to you of your *rights?* Why in a society in which all, voluntarily or involuntarily, oppress you, in which the exercise of all the rights which belong to man is constantly denied you, in which misery is your lot, and what is called happiness is for other classes of men, why do I speak to you of self-sacrifice and not of conquest; of virtue, moral improvement, education, and not of material *well-being?* This is a question which I must answer before going further, because here precisely lies the difference between our school and many others which are being preached to-day in Europe; because, moreover, it is a question which rises readily in the indignant mind of the suffering working-man.

We are poor, enslaved, unhappy; speak to us of better material conditions, of liberty, of happiness. Tell us if we are doomed to suffer for ever, or if we too may enjoy in our turn. Preach Duty to our masters, to the classes above us which treat us like machines, and monopolise the blessings which belong to all. To us speak of rights; speak of the means of vindicating them; speak of our strength. Wait till we have a recognized existence; then you shall speak to us of duties and of sacrifice. This is what many of our working-men say, and follow teachers and associations which respond to their desires. They forget one thing only, and that is, that the doctrine which they invoke has been preached for the last fifty years without producing the slightest material improvement in the condition of the working-people.

For the last fifty years whatever has been done for the cause of progress and of good against absolute governments and hereditary aristocracies has been done in the name of the Rights of Man; in the name of liberty as the means, and of *well-being* as the object of existence. All the acts of the French Revolution and of the revolutions which followed and imitated it were consequences of a Declaration of the Rights of Man. All the works of the philosophers who prepared it were based upon a theory of liberty, and upon the need of making known to every individual his own rights. All the revolutionary schools preached that man is born for happiness, that he has the right to seek it by all the means in his power, that no one has the right to impede him in this search, and that he has the right of overthrowing all the obstacles which he may encounter on his path. And the obstacles were overthrown; liberty was conquered. It endured for years in many countries; in some it still endures. Has the condition of the people improved? Have the millions who live by the daily

From: Joseph Mazzini, *The Duties of Man and Other Essays* (New York: Dutton, 1966), pp. 7–20, 51–59.

labour of their hands gained the least fraction of the well-being hoped for and promised to them?

No; the condition of the people has not improved; rather it has grown and grows worse in nearly every country, and especially here where I write the price of the necessaries of life has gone on continually rising, the wages of the working-man in many branches of industry falling, and the population multiplying. In nearly every country the lot of workers has become more uncertain, more precarious, and the labour crises which condemn thousands of working-men to idleness for a time have become more frequent. The yearly increase of emigration from one country to another, and from Europe to other parts of the world, and the ever-growing number of beneficent institutions, the increase of poor rates and provisions for the destitute, are enough to prove this. The latter prove also that public attention is waking more and more to the ills of the people; but their inability to lessen those ills to any visible extent points to a no less continual increase of poverty among the classes which they endeavour to help.

And nevertheless, in these last fifty years, the sources of social wealth and the sum of material blessings have steadily increased. Production has doubled. Commerce, amid continual crises, inevitable in the utter absence of organisation, has acquired a greater force of activity and a wider sphere for its operations. Communication has almost everywhere been made secure and rapid, and the price of commodities has fallen in consequence of the diminished cost of transport. And, on the other hand, the idea of rights inherent in human nature is to-day generally accepted; accepted in word and, hypocritically, even by those who seek to evade it in deed. Why, then, has the condition of the people not improved? Why is the consumption of products, instead of being divided equally among all the members of the social body in Europe, concentrated in the hands of a small number of men forming a new aristocracy? Why has the new impulse given to industry and commerce produced, not the well-being of the many, but the luxury of the few?

The answer is clear to those who will look a little closely into things. Men are creatures of education, and act only according to the principle of education given to them. The men who have promoted revolutions hitherto have based them upon the idea of the rights belonging to the individual; the revolutions conquered liberty—individual liberty, liberty of teaching, liberty of belief, liberty of trade, liberty in everything and for everybody. But of what use was the recognition of their rights to those who had no means of exercising them? What did liberty of teaching mean to those who had neither time nor means to profit by it, or liberty of trade to those who had nothing to trade with, neither capital nor credit? In all the countries where these principles were proclaimed society was composed of a small number of individuals who possessed the land, the credit, the capital, and of vast multitudes of men who had nothing but their own hands and were forced to give the labour of them to the former class, on any terms, in order to live, and forced to spend the whole day in material and monotonous toil. For these, constrained to battle with hunger, what was liberty but an illusion and a bitter irony? To make it anything else it would have been necessary for the men of the well-to-do classes to consent to reduce the hours of labour, to increase the remuneration, to institute free and uniform education for the masses, to make the instruments of labour accessible to all, and to provide a bonus fund for the working-man endowed with capacity and good intentions. But why should they do it? Was not *well-being* the supreme object in life? Were not material blessings desirable before all other things? Why should they lessen their own enjoyment for the advantage of others? Let those who could, help themselves. When society has secured to everybody who can use them the free exercise of the rights belonging to human nature, it does all that is required of it. If there be any one who is unable from the fatality of his own circumstances to exercise any of these rights, he must resign himself and not blame others.

It was natural that they should say thus, and thus, in fact, they did say. And this attitude of mind towards the poor in the classes privileged by fortune soon became the attitude of every individual towards every other. Each man looked after his own rights and the improvement of his own condition without seeking to provide for others; and when his rights clashed with those of others, there was war; not a war of blood, but of gold and of cunning; a war less manly than the other, but equally destructive; cruel war, in which those who had the means and were strong relentlessly crushed the weak or the unskilled. In this continual warfare, men were educated in egoism and in greed for material welfare exclusively. Liberty of belief destroyed all community of faith. Liberty of education produced moral anarchy. Men without a common tie, without unity of religious belief and of aim, and whose sole vocation was enjoyment, sought every one his own road, not heeding if in pursuing it they were trampling upon the heads of their brothers—brothers in name and enemies in fact. To this we are come to-day, thanks to the theory of *rights*.

Certainly rights exist; but where the rights of an individual come into conflict with those of another, how can we hope to reconcile and harmonise them, without appealing to something superior to all rights? And where the rights of an individual, or of many individuals, clash with the rights of the Country, to what tribunal are we to appeal? If the right to *well-being*, to the greatest possible well-being, belongs to every living person, who will solve the difficulty between the workingman and the manufacturer? If the right to existence is the first and inviolable right of every man, who shall demand the sacrifice of that existence for the benefit of other men? Will you demand it in the name of Country, of Society, of the multitude of your brothers? What is Country, in the opinion of those of whom I speak, but the place in which our individual rights are most secure? What is Society but a collection of men who have agreed to bring the strength of the many in support of the rights of each? And after having taught the individual for fifty years that Society is established for the purpose of *assuring to him the exercise of his rights*, would you ask him to sacrifice them all to Society, to submit himself, if need be, to continuous toil, to prison, to exile, for the sake of improving it? After having preached to him everywhere that the object of life is *well-being*, would you all at once bid him give up well-being and life itself to free his country from the foreigner, or to procure better conditions for a class which is not his own? After having talked to him for years of *material* interests, how can you maintain that, finding wealth and power in his reach, he ought not to stretch out his hand to grasp them, even to the injury of his brothers?

Italian Working-men, this is not a chance thought of my mind, without a foundation in fact. It is history, the history of our own times, a history the pages of which drip with blood, the blood of the people. Ask all the men who transformed the revolution of 1830 into a mere substitution of one set of persons for another, and, for example, made the bodies of your French comrades, who were killed fighting in the Three Days, into stepping-stones to raise themselves to power; all their doctrines, before 1830, were founded on the old theory of the *rights* of man, not upon a belief in his *duties*. You call them to-day traitors and apostates, and yet they were only consistent with their own doctrine. They fought with sincerity against the Government of Charles X, because that Government was directly hostile to the classes from which they sprang, and violated and endeavoured to suppress their rights. They fought in the name of the well-being which they did not possess as much of as they thought they ought to have. Some were persecuted for freedom of thought; others, men of powerful mind, saw themselves neglected, shut out from offices occupied by men of capacity inferior to their own. Then the wrongs of the people angered them also. Then they wrote boldly and in good faith about the rights which belong to every man. Afterwards, when their own political and intellectual rights had been secured, when the path to office was opened to them, when they had conquered the *well-being* which they sought, they forgot the people, forgot that the millions, inferior to them in education and in aspirations, were seeking the exercise of other rights and the achievement of *well-being* of another sort, and they set their minds at rest and troubled no longer about anybody but themselves. Why call them traitors? Why not rather call their doctrine treacherous?

There lived and wrote at that time in France a man whom you ought never to forget, more powerful in mind than all of them put together. He was our opponent then; but he believed in Duty; in the duty of sacrificing the whole existence to the common good, to the pursuit and triumph of Truth. He studied the men and the circumstances of the time deeply, and did not allow himself to be led astray by applause, or to be discouraged by disappointment. When he had tried one way and failed, he tried yet another for the amelioration of the masses. And when the course of events had shown him that there was one power alone capable of achieving it, when the people had proved themselves in the field of action more virtuous and more believing than all those who had pretended to deal with their cause, he, Lamennais, author of the *Words of a Believer,* which you have all read, became the best apostle of the cause in which we are brothers. There you see in him, and in the men of whom I have been speaking, the difference between the men of *rights* and those of *duty.* To the first the acquisition of their individual rights, by withdrawing stimulus, proves a sufficient check to further effort; the work of the second only ceases here on earth with life.

And among the peoples who are completely enslaved, where the conflict has very different dangers, where every step made towards a better state of things is signed with the blood of a martyr, where the operations against injustice in high places are necessarily secret and lack the consolation of publicity and of praise, what obligation, what stimulus to constancy can maintain upon the path of progress men who degrade the holy social war which we carry on to a mere battle for their *rights?* I speak, be it understood, of the generality and not of the exceptions to be met with in all schools of thought. When the hot blood and the impulse of reaction against tyranny which naturally draw youth into the conflict have calmed down, what can prevent these men, after a few years of effort, after the disappointments inevitable in any such enterprise, from growing weary? Why should they not prefer any sort of repose to an unquiet existence, agitated by continual struggles and danger, and liable to end any day in imprisonment, or the scaffold, or exile? It is the too common story of most of the Italians of to-day, imbued as they are with the old French ideas; a very sad story, but how can it be altered except by changing the principle with which they start as their guide? How and in whose name are they to be convinced that danger and disappointment ought to make them stronger, that they have got to fight not for a few years, but for their whole lives? Who shall say to a man, *Go on struggling for your rights,* when to struggle for them costs him dearer than to abandon them?

And even in a society constituted on a juster basis than our own, who shall convince a believer in the theory of *rights* solely that he has to work for the common purpose and devote himself to the development of the social *idea ?* Suppose he should rebel; suppose he should feel himself strong and should say to you: *I break the social compact; my inclinations, my faculties, call me elsewhere; I have a sacred and inviolable right to develop them, and I choose to be at war with everybody:* what answer can you give him while he keeps to his theory of rights? What right have you, because you are a majority, to compel his obedience to laws which do not accord with his desires and with his individual aspirations? What right have you to punish him if he violates them? Rights belong equally to every individual; the fact of living together in a community does not create a single one. Society has greater strength, not more rights, than the individual. How, then, are you going to prove to the individual that he must merge his will in the will of those who are his brothers, whether in the Country or in the wider fellowship of Humanity? By means of the executioner, of the prison? Societies existing up till now have used such means. But that is war, and we want peace; that is tyrannical repression, and we want education.

Education, we have said; and this is the great word which sums up our whole doctrine. The vital question agitating our century is a question of education. What we have to do is not to establish a new order of things by violence. An order of things so established is always tyrannical even when it is better than the old. *We have to overthrow by force the brute force which opposes itself to-day to every attempt at improvement,* and then propose for the approval of the nation, free to express its will, what we believe to be the best order of things and by every possible means educate men to develop it and act in conformity with it. The theory of *rights* enables us to rise and overthrow obstacles, but not to found a strong and lasting accord between all the elements which compose the nation. With the theory of happiness, of *well-being,* as the primary aim of existence we shall only form egoistic men, worshippers of the material, who will carry the old passions into the new order of things and corrupt it in a few months. We have therefore to find a principle of education superior to any such theory, which shall guide men to better things, teach them constancy in self-sacrifice and link them with their fellow men without making them dependent on the ideas of a single man or on the strength of all. And this principle is

Duty. We must convince men that they, sons of one only God, must obey one only law, here on earth; that each one of them must live, not for himself, but for others; that the object of their life is not to be more or less happy, but to make themselves and others better; that to fight against injustice and error for the benefit of their brothers is not only a *right,* but a *duty;* a duty not to be neglected without sin,—the duty of their whole life.

Italian Working-men, my Brothers! understand me fully. When I say that the knowledge of their *rights* is not enough to enable men to effect any appreciable or lasting improvement, I do not ask you to renounce these rights; I only say that they cannot exist except as a consequence of duties fulfilled, and that one must begin with the latter in order to arrive at the former. And when I say that by proposing *happiness, well-being,* or *material* interest as the aim of existence, we run the risk of producing egoists, I do not mean that you should never strive after these things. I say that material interests pursued alone, and not as a means, but as an end, lead always to this most disastrous result. When under the Emperors, the old Romans asked for nothing but *bread* and *amusements,* they became the most abject race conceivable, and after submitting to the stupid and ferocious tyranny of the Emperors they basely fell into slavery to the invading Barbarians. In France and elsewhere the enemies of all social progress have sown corruption and tried to divert men's minds from ideas of change by furthering the development of *material* activity. And shall we help the enemy with our own hands? Material improvement is essential, and we shall strive to win it for ourselves; but not because the one thing necessary for man is to be well fed and housed, but rather because you cannot have a sense of your own dignity or any moral development while you are engaged, as at the present day, in a continual duel with want. You work ten or twelve hours a day: how can you find *time* to educate yourselves? Most of you earn hardly enough to keep yourselves and your families: how can you then find *means* to educate yourselves? The uncertainty of your employment and the frequent interruptions in it cause you to alternate between too much work and periods of idleness: how are you to acquire habits of order, regularity, and assiduity? The scantiness of your earnings does away with any hope of saving enough to be useful some day to your children, or to your own old age: how are you to educate yourselves into habits of economy? Many of you are compelled by poverty to separate your children, we will not say from the careful bringing-up—what sort of bringing-up can the poor wives of working-men give their children?—but from the love and the watchful eye of their mothers, and to send them out, for the sake of a few halfpence, to unwholesome labour in factories: how, in such conditions, can family affection unfold itself and be ennobled? You have not the rights of citizens, nor any participation, by election or by vote, in the laws which regulate your actions and your life: how should you feel the pride of citizenship or have any zeal for the State, or sincere affection for the laws? Justice is not dealt out to you with the same equal hand as to the other classes: whence, then, are you to learn respect and love for justice? Society treats you without a shadow of sympathy: whence are you to learn sympathy with society? You need, then, a change in your material conditions to enable you to develop morally; you need to work less so as to have some hours of your day to devote to the improvement of your minds; you need a sufficient remuneration of your labour to put you in a position to accumulate savings, and so set your minds at rest about the future, and to purify yourselves above all of every sentiment of *retaliation,* every impulse of revenge, every thought of injustice towards those who have been unjust to you. You must strive, then, for this change, and you will obtain it, but you must strive for it as a *means,* not as an *end;* strive for it from a sense of *duty,* not only as a *right;* strive for it in order to make yourselves better, not only to make yourselves *materially* happy. If not, what difference would there be between you and your tyrants? They are tyrants precisely because they do not think of anything but *well-being,* pleasure and power.

To make yourselves better; this must be the aim of your life. You cannot make yourselves permanently less unhappy except by improving yourselves. Tyrants will arise by the thousand among you, if you fight only in the name of material interests, or of a particular organisation. A change of social organisation makes little difference if you and the other classes keep the passions and the egoism of to-day; organisations are like certain plants which yield poison or remedies according to the way in which they are administered. Good men make bad organisations good, and bad men make good organisations bad. You have got to improve the classes which, voluntarily or involuntarily, oppress you to-day, and convince them of their duties; but you will never succeed in this unless you begin by making yourselves better as far as possible.

When therefore you hear men who preach the necessity of a social transformation telling you that they can accomplish it by invoking your *rights* only, be grateful to them for their good intentions, but distrustful of the outcome. The ills of the poor man are known, in part at least, to the well-to-do classes; *known* but not *felt*. In the general indifference born of the absence of a common faith; in the egoism, inevitably resulting from the continual preaching through so many years of the doctrine of material *well-being,* those who do not suffer have grown accustomed little by little to consider these ills as a sad necessity of the social order and to leave the trouble of remedying them to the generations to come. The difficulty is not to convince them, but to shake them out of inertia and to induce them, when they are convinced, to *act,* to associate themselves, to unite with you in brotherly fellowship for the purpose of creating such a social organisation as shall put an end, as far as the conditions of humanity allow, to your ills and to their own fears. Now, this is a work of faith, of faith in the mission which God has given to the human creature here upon earth; of faith in the responsibility weighing upon all those who do not fulfil that mission, and in the duty which bids every one work continually, and with self-sacrifice, for the cause of Truth. All possible theories of rights and of material *well-being* can only lead you to attempts which, so long as they remain isolated and dependent on your strength only, will not succeed, but can only bring about the worst of social crimes, a civil war between class and class.

Italian Working-men, my Brothers! When Christ came and changed the face of the world, He did not speak of rights to the rich, who had no need to conquer them; nor to the poor, who would perhaps have abused them, in imitation of the rich. He did not speak of utility or of self-interest to a people whom utility and self-interest had corrupted. He spoke of Duty, He spoke of Love, of Sacrifice, of Faith: He said that *they only should be first among all who had done good to all by their work.* And these thoughts, breathed into the ear of a society which had no longer any spark of life, reanimated it, conquered the millions, conquered the world, and caused the education of the human race to progress a degree. Italian Working-men ! we live in an epoch like Christ's. We live in the midst of a society rotten as that of the Roman Empire, and feel in our souls the need of reviving and transforming it, of associating all its members and its workers in one single faith, under one single law, and for one purpose; the free and progressive development of all the faculties which God has planted in His creatures. We seek the reign of God upon earth as in heaven, or better, that the earth shall be a preparation for heaven, and society an endeavour towards a progressive approach to the Divine Idea.

But every act of Christ's represented the faith which He preached, and round Him there were apostles who embodied in their acts the faith which they had accepted. Be such as they, and you will conquer. Preach Duty to the men of the classes above you, and fulfil, as far as possible, your own duties; preach virtue, sacrifice, love; and be yourselves virtuous and prompt to self-sacrifice and love. Declare with courage your needs and your ideas; but without wrath, without vindictiveness, without threats. The most powerful threat, if there are any who need threats, is firm, not angry, speech. While you propagate among your companions the conception of their future destinies, the conception of a nation which will give them a name, education, work, and fair wages, together with the self-respect and vocation of men, while you kindle their spirit for the inevitable struggle for which they must prepare themselves, so that they may conquer all this in spite of all the forces of our evil government and of the foreigner, strive to instruct yourselves, to grow better, and to educate yourselves to the full knowledge and to the practice of your duties. This is an impossible task for the masses in a great part of Italy; no plan of popular education could be realised among us without a change in the material condition of the people, and without a political revolution; they who deceive themselves into hoping for it, and preach it as an indispensable preparation for any attempt at emancipation, preach a gospel of inertia, nothing else. But the few among you whose circumstances are somewhat better, and to whom a sojourn in foreign lands has afforded more liberal means of education, can do it, and therefore ought to do it. And these few, once imbued with the true principles upon which the education of a people depends, will be enough to spread them among the thousands as a guide for their path and a protection from the fallacies and the false doctrines which will come to waylay them.

* * *

Duties to Country

Your first Duties—first, at least, in importance—are, as I have told you, to Humanity. You are *men* before you are *citizens* or *fathers*. If you do not embrace the whole human family in your love, if you do not confess your faith in its unity—consequent on the unity of God—and in the brotherhood of the Peoples who are appointed to reduce that unity to fact—if wherever one of your fellowmen groans, wherever the dignity of human nature is violated by falsehood or tyranny, you are not prompt, being able, to succour that wretched one, or do not feel yourself called, being able, to fight for the purpose of relieving the deceived or oppressed—you disobey your law of life, or do not comprehend the religion which will bless the future.

But what can *each* of you, with his isolated powers, *do* for the moral improvement, for the progress of Humanity? You can, from time to time, give sterile expression to your belief; you may, on some rare occasion, perform an act of *charity* to a brother not belonging to your own land, no more. Now, *charity* is not the watchword of the future faith. The watchword of the future faith is *association,* fraternal cooperation towards a common aim, and this is as much superior to *charity* as the work of many uniting to raise with one accord a building for the habitation of all together would be superior to that which you would accomplish by raising a separate hut each for himself, and only helping one another by exchanging stones and bricks and mortar. But divided as you are in language tendencies, habits, and capacities, you cannot attempt this common work. The *individual* is too weak, and Humanity too vast. *My God,* prays the Breton mariner as he puts out to sea, *protect me, my ship is so little, and Thy ocean so great!* And this prayer sums up the condition of each of you, if no means is found of multiplying your forces and your powers of action indefinitely. But God gave you this means when he gave you a Country, when, like a wise overseer of labour, who distributes the different parts of the work according to the capacity of the workmen, he divided Humanity into distinct groups upon the face of our globe, and thus planted the seeds of nations. Bad governments have disfigured the design of God, which you may see clearly marked out, as far, at least, as regards Europe, by the courses of the great rivers, by the lines of the lofty mountains, and by other geographical conditions; they have disfigured it by conquest, by greed, by jealousy of the just sovereignty of others; disfigured it so much that to-day there is perhaps no nation except England and France whose confines correspond to this design. They did not, and they do not, recognise any country except their own families and dynasties, the egoism of caste. But the divine design will infallibly be fulfilled. Natural divisions, the innate spontaneous tendencies of the peoples will replace the arbitrary divisions sanctioned by bad governments. The map of Europe will be remade. The Countries of the People will rise, defined by the voice of the free, upon the ruins of the Countries of Kings and privileged castes. Between these Countries there will be harmony and brotherhood. And then the work of Humanity for the general amelioration, for the discovery and application of the real law of life, carried on in association and distributed according to local capacities, will be accomplished by peaceful and progressive development; then each of you, strong in the affections and in the aid of many millions of men speaking the same language, endowed with the same tendencies, and educated by the same historic tradition, may hope by your personal effort to benefit the whole of Humanity.

To you, who have been born in Italy, God has allotted, as if favouring you specially, the best-defined country in Europe. In other lands, marked by more uncertain or more interrupted limits, questions may arise which the pacific vote of all will one day solve, but which have cost, and will yet perhaps cost, tears and blood; in yours, no. God has stretched round you sublime and indisputable boundaries; on one side the highest mountains of Europe, the Alps; on the other the sea, the immeasurable sea. Take a map of Europe and place one point of a pair of compasses in the north of Italy on Parma; point the other to the mouth of the Var, and describe a semicircle with it in the direction of the Alps; this point, which will fall, when the semicircle is completed, upon the mouth of the Isonzo, will have marked the frontier which God has given you. As far as this frontier your language is spoken and understood; beyond this you have no rights. Sicily, Sardinia, Corsica, and the smaller islands between them and the mainland of Italy belong undeniably to you. Brute force may for a little while contest these frontiers with you, but they have been recognised from of old by the tacit general consent of the peoples; and the day when, rising with one accord for the final trial, you plant your tricoloured flag upon that frontier, the whole of Europe will acclaim re-risen Italy, and receive her into the community of the nations. To this final trial all your efforts must be directed.

Without Country you have neither name, token, voice, nor rights, no admission as brothers into the fellowship of the Peoples. You are the bastards of Humanity. Soldiers without a banner, Israelites among the nations, you will find neither faith nor protection; none will be sureties for you. Do not beguile yourselves with the hope of emancipation from unjust social conditions if you do not first conquer a Country for yourselves; where there is no Country there is no common agreement to which you can appeal; the egoism of self-interest rules alone, and he who has the upper hand keeps it, since there is no common safeguard for the interests of all. Do not be led away by the idea of improving your material conditions without first solving the national question. You cannot do it. Your industrial associations and mutual help societies are useful as a means of educating and disciplining yourselves; as an economic fact they will remain barren until you have an Italy. The economic problem demands, first and foremost, an increase of capital and production; and while your Country is dismembered into separate fragments—while shut off by the barrier of customs and artificial difficulties of every sort, you have only restricted markets open to you—you cannot hope for this increase. To-day—do not delude yourselves—you are not the working-class of Italy; you are only fractions of that class; powerless, unequal to the great task which you propose to yourselves. Your emancipation can have no practical beginning until a National Government, understanding the signs of the times, shall, seated in Rome, formulate a Declaration of Principles to be the guide for Italian progress, and shall insert into it these words, *Labour is sacred, and is the source of the wealth of Italy.*

Do not be led astray, then, by hopes of material progress which in your present conditions can only be illusions. Your Country alone, the vast and rich Italian Country, which stretches from the Alps to the farthest limit of Sicily, can fulfil these hopes. You cannot obtain your *rights* except by obeying the commands of *Duty*. Be worthy of them, and you will have them. O my Brothers! love your Country. Our Country is our home, the home which God has given us, placing therein a numerous family which we love and are loved by, and with which we have a more intimate and quicker communion of feeling and thought than with others; a family which by its concentration upon a given spot, and by the homogeneous nature of its elements, is destined for a special kind of activity. Our Country is our field of labour; the products of our activity must go forth from it for the benefit of the whole earth; but the instruments of labour which we can use best and most effectively exist in it, and we may not reject them without being unfaithful to God's purpose and diminishing our own strength. In labouring according to true principles for our Country we are labouring for Humanity; our Country is the fulcrum of the lever which we have to wield for the common good. If we give up this fulcrum we run the risk of becoming useless to our Country and to Humanity. Before *associating* ourselves with the Nations which compose Humanity we must exist as a Nation. There can be no association except among equals; and you have no recognised collective existence.

Humanity is a great army moving to the conquest of unknown lands, against powerful and wary enemies. The Peoples are the different corps and divisions of that army. Each has a post entrusted to it; each a special operation to perform; and the common victory depends on the exactness with which the different operations are carried out. Do not disturb the order of the battle. Do not abandon the banner which God has given you. Wherever you may be, into the midst of whatever people circumstances may have driven you, fight for the liberty of that people if the moment calls for it; but fight as Italians, so that the blood which you shed may win honour and love, not for you only, but for your Country. And may the constant thought of your soul be for Italy, may all the acts of your life be worthy of her, and may the standard beneath which you range yourselves to work for Humanity be Italy's. Do not say *I;* say *we.* Be every one of you an incarnation of your Country, and feel himself and make himself responsible for his fellow-countrymen; let each one of you learn to act in such a way that in him men shall respect and love his Country.

Your Country is one and indivisible. As the members of a family cannot rejoice at the common table if one of their number is far away, snatched from the affection of his brothers, so you should have no joy or repose as long as a portion of the territory upon which your language is spoken is separated from the Nation.

Your Country is the token of the mission which God has given you to fulfil in Humanity. The faculties, the strength of *all* its sons should be united for the accomplishment of this mission. A certain number of common duties and rights belong to every man who answers to the *Who are you?* of the other peoples, *I am an Italian.* Those duties and those rights cannot be represented except by one *single* authority resulting from your votes. A Country must have, then, a single government. The politicians who call themselves federalists, and who would make Italy into a brotherhood of different states, would dismember the Country, not understanding the idea of Unity. The States into which Italy is divided today are not the creation of our own people; they are the result of the ambitions and calculations of princes or of foreign conquerors, and serve no purpose but to flatter the vanity of local aristocracies for which a narrower sphere than a great Country is necessary. What you, the people, have created, beautified, and consecrated with your affections, with your joys, with your sorrows, and with your blood, is the City and the Commune, not the Province or the State. In the City, in the Commune, where your fathers sleep and where your children will live, where you exercise your faculties and your personal rights, you live out your lives as *individuals.* It is of your City that each of you can say what the Venetians say of theirs: *Venezia la xe nostra : l'avemo fatta nu.** In your City you have need of *liberty* as in your Country you have need of *association.* The Liberty of the Commune and the Unity of the Country—let that, then, be your faith. Do not say Rome and Tuscany, Rome and Lombardy, Rome and Sicily; say Rome and Florence, Rome and Siena, Rome and Leghorn, and so through all the Communes of Italy. Rome for all that represents Italian life; your Commune for whatever represents the *individual* life. All the other divisions are artificial, and are not confirmed by your national tradition.

A Country is a fellowship of free and equal men bound together in a brotherly concord of labour towards a single end. You must make it and maintain it such. A Country is not an aggregation, it is an *association.* There is no true Country without a uniform right. There is no true Country where the uniformity of that right is violated by the existence of caste, privilege, and inequality—where the powers and faculties of a large number of individuals are suppressed or dormant—where there is no common principle accepted, recognised, and developed by all. In such a state of things there can be no Nation, no People, but only a multitude, a fortuitous agglomeration of men whom circumstances have brought together and different circumstances will separate. In the name of your love for your Country you must combat without truce the existence of every privilege, every inequality, upon the soil which has given you birth. One privilege only is lawful—the privilege of Genius when Genius reveals itself in brotherhood with Virtue; but it is a privilege conceded by God and not by men, and when you acknowledge it and follow its inspirations, you acknowledge it freely by the exercise of your own reason and your own choice. Whatever privilege claims your submission in virtue of force or heredity, or any right which is not a common right, is a usurpation and a tyranny, and you ought to combat it and annihilate it. Your Country should be your Temple. God at the summit, a People of equals at the base. Do not accept any other formula, any other moral law, if you do not want to dishonour your Country and yourselves. Let the secondary laws for the gradual regulation of your existence be the progressive application of this supreme law.

And in order that they should be so, it is necessary that *all* should contribute to the making of them. The laws made by one fraction of the citizens only can never by the nature of things and men do otherwise than reflect the thoughts and aspirations and desires of that fraction; they represent, not the whole country, but a third, a fourth part, a class, a zone of the country. The law must express the general aspiration, promote the good of all, respond to a beat of the nation's heart. The whole nation therefore should be, directly or indirectly, the legislator. By yielding this mission to a few men, you put the egoism of one class in the place of the Country, which is the union of *all* the classes.

A Country is not a mere territory; the particular territory is only its foundation. The Country is the idea which rises upon that foundation; it is the sentiment of love, the sense of fellowship which binds together all the sons of that territory. So long as a single one of your brothers is not represented by his own vote in the development of the national life—so long as a single one vegetates uneducated among the educated—so long as a single one able and willing to work languishes in poverty for want of work—you have not got a Country such as it ought to be, the Country of all and for all. *Votes, education, work* are the three main pillars of the nation; do not rest until your hands have solidly erected them.

And when they have been erected—when you have secured for every one of you food for both body and soul—when freely united, entwining your right hands like brothers round a beloved mother, you advance in beautiful and holy concord towards the development of your faculties and the fulfilment of the Italian mission—remember that that mission is the moral unity of Europe; remember the immense duties which it imposes upon you. Italy is the only land that has twice uttered the great word of unification to the disjoined nations. Twice Rome has been the metropolis, the temple, of the European world; the first time when our conquering eagles traversed the known world from end to end and prepared it for union by introducing civilised institutions; the second time when, after the Northern conquerors had themselves been subdued by the potency of Nature, of great memories and of religious inspiration, the genius of Italy incarnated itself in the Papacy and undertook the solemn mission—abandoned four centuries ago—of preaching the union of souls to the peoples of the Christian world. To-day a third mission is dawning for our Italy; as much vaster than those of old as the Italian People, the free and united Country which you are going to found, will be greater and more powerful than Caesars or Popes. The presentiment of this mission agitates Europe and keeps the eye and the thought of the nations chained to Italy.

Your duties to your Country are proportioned to the loftiness of this mission. You have to keep it pure from egoism, uncontaminated by falsehood and by the arts of that political Jesuitism which they call diplomacy.

The government of the country will be based through your labours upon the worship of principles, not upon the idolatrous worship of interests and of opportunity. There are countries in Europe where Liberty is sacred within, but is systematically violated without; peoples who say, *Truth is one thing, utility another: theory is one thing, practice another.* Those countries will have inevitably to expiate their guilt in long isolation, oppression, and anarchy. But you know the mission of our Country, and will pursue another path. Through you Italy will have, with one only God in the heavens, one only truth, one only faith, one only rule of political life upon earth. Upon the edifice, sublimer than Capitol or Vatican, which the people of Italy will raise, you will plant the banner of Liberty and of Association, so that it shines in the sight of all the nations, nor will you lower it ever for terror of despots or lust for the gains of a day. You will have boldness as you have faith. You will speak out aloud to the world, and to those who call themselves the lords of the world, the thought which thrills in the heart of Italy. You will never deny the sister nations. The life of the Country shall grow through you in beauty and in strength, free from servile fears and the hesitations of doubt, keeping as its *foundation* the people, as its *rule* the consequences of its principles logically deduced and energetically applied, as its *strength* the strength of all, as its *outcome* the amelioration of all, as its *end* the fulfilment of the mission which God has given it. And because you will be ready to die for Humanity, the life of your Country will be immortal.

✦ Reading 22 ✦

My Past and Thoughts

Alexander Herzen

The Revolution of 1848 in France

. . . The spectacle of the Café Lamblin was still new to me; at that time I was not familiar with the back premises of the revolution. It is true that I had been about in Rome and in the Cage delle Belle Arti and in the square; I had been in the Circolo Romano and in the Circolo Popolare; but the movement in Rome had not then that character of political garishness which particularly developed after the failures of 1848. Ciceruacchio and his friends had a naïveté of their own, their southern gesticulations which strike one as commonplace and their Italian phrases which seem to us to be rant; but they were in a period of youthful enthusiasm, they had not yet come to themselves after three centuries of sleep. *Il popolano* Ciceruacchio was not in the least a political agitator by trade; he would have liked nothing better than to retire once more in peace to his little house in Strada Ripetta and to carry on his trade in wood and timber within his family-circle like a *paterfamilias* and free *civis romanus*.

The men surrounding him were free from that brand of vulgar, babbling pseudo-revolutionism, of that *taré* character which is so dismally common in France.

I need hardly say that in speaking of the café agitators and revolutionary *lazzaroni* I was not thinking of those mighty workers for the emancipation of humanity, those martyrs for the love of their fellow-creatures and fiery evangelists of independence whose words could not be suppressed by prison, exile, proscription or Poverty—of the drivers, the motive powers of events, by whose blood, tears and words a new historical order is established. I was talking about the incrusted border covered with barren weeds, for which agitation itself is goal and reward, who like the process of national revolution for its own sake, as Chichikov's Petrushka liked the process of reading, or as Nicholas liked military drill.

There is nothing for reaction to rejoice at in this, for it is overgrown with worse burdocks and toadstools, not only on the borders but everywhere. In its ranks are whole multitudes of officials who tremble before their superiors, prying spies, volunteer assassins ready to fight on either side, officers of every repulsive species from the Prussian *junker* to the predatory French Algerian, from the guardsman to the *page de chambre*—and here we still have touched only on the secular side of the reaction, and have said nothing of the mendicant fraternity, the intriguing Jesuits, the priestly police, or the other members of the ranks of angels and archangels.

If there are among reactionaries any who resemble our dilettante revolutionaries, they are the courtiers employed for ceremonies, the men of exits and entrances, the people who are conspicuous at *levées*, christenings, royal weddings, coronations, and funerals, the people who exist for the uniform, for gold lace, who represent the rays and fragrance of power.

In the Café Lamblin, where the desperate *citoyens* were sitting over their *petits verres* and big glasses, I learned that they had no plan, that the movement had no real centre of momentum and no programme. Inspiration was to descend upon them as the Holy Ghost once descended upon the heads of the apostles. There was only one Point on which all were agreed—to *come to the meeting-place unarmed*. After two hours of empty chatter we went off to the office of the *True Republic*, agreeing to meet at eight o'clock next morning at the Boulevard Bonne Nouvelle, facing the Château d'Eau.

The editor was not at home: he had gone to the 'Montagnards' for instructions. About twenty people, for the most part Poles and Germans, were in the big,

---

From: *My Past and Thoughts: The Memoirs of Alexander Herzen,* abridged by Dwight Macdonald (Berkeley: University of California, 1982), pp. 351–357.

grimy, poorly lit and still more poorly furnished room which served the editorial board as an assembly hall and a committee room. Sazonov took a sheet of paper and began writing something; when he had written it he read it out to us: it was a protest in the name of the *émigrés* of all nationalities against the occupation of Rome, and a declaration of their readiness to take part in the movement. Those who wished to immortalise their names by associating them with the glorious morrow he invited to sign it. Almost all wished to immortalise their names, and signed. The editor came in, tired and dejected, trying to suggest to everyone that he knew a great deal but was bound to keep silent; I was convinced that he knew nothing at all.

'Citoyens,' said Thorez, *'la Montagne est en permanence.'*

Well, who could doubt its success—*en permanence!* Sazonov gave the editor the protest of the democracy of Europe. The editor read it through and said:

'That's splendid, splendid! France thanks you, *citoyens;* but why the signatures? There are so few that if we are unsuccessful our enemies will vent all their anger upon you.'

Sazonov insisted that the signatures should remain; many agreed with him.

'I won't take the responsibility for it,' the editor objected; 'excuse me, I know better than you the people we have to deal with.'

With that he tore off the signatures and delivered the names of a dozen candidates for immortality to a holocaust in the candle, and the text he sent to the printer.

It was daybreak when we left the office; groups of ragged boys and wretched, poorly dressed women were standing, sitting, and lying on the pavement near the various newspaper offices, waiting for the piles of newspapers—some to fold them, and others to run with them all over Paris. We walked out on to the boulevard: there was absolute stillness; now and then one came upon a patrol of National Guards, and police-sergeants strolled about looking slyly at us.

'How free from care the city sleeps,' said my comrade, 'with no foreboding of the storm that will wake it up to-morrow!'

'Here are those who keep vigil for us all,' I said to him, pointing upwards—that is, to a lighted window of the *Maison d'Or.*

'And very appropriately, too. Let us go in and have some absinthe; my stomach is a bit upset.'

'And I feel empty; it wouldn't be amiss to have some supper too. How they eat in the Capitole I don't know, but in the Conciergerie the food is abominable.'

From the bones left after our meal of cold turkey no one could have guessed either that cholera was raging in Paris, or that in two hours' time we were going to change the destinies of Europe. We ate at the *Maison d'Or* as Napoleon slept before Austerlitz.

Between eight and nine o'clock, when we reached the Boulevard Bonne Nouvelle, numerous groups of people were already standing there, evidently impatient to know what they were to do; their faces showed perplexity, but at the same time something in the peculiar look of the groups manifested great exasperation. Had those people found real leaders the day would not have ended in a farce.

There was a minute when it seemed to me that something was really going to happen. A gentleman rode on horseback rather slowly down the boulevard. He was recognised as one of the ministers (Lacroix), who probably was having a ride so early not for the sake of fresh air alone. He was surrounded by a shouting crowd, who pulled him off his horse, tore his coat and then let him go—that is, another group rescued him and escorted him away. The crowd grew; by ten o'clock there may have been twenty-five thousand people. No one we spoke to, no one we questioned, knew anything. Chersosi, a *carbonaro* of old days assured us that the *banlieue* was coming to the Arc de Triomphe with a shout of *'Vive la République!'*

'Above all,' the elders of the democracy repeated again, 'be unarmed, or you will spoil the character of the affair—the sovereign people must show the National Assembly its will peacefully and solemnly in order to give the enemy no occasion for calumny.'

At last columns were formed; we foreigners made up an honorary phalanx immediately behind the leaders, among whom were E. Arago in the uniform of a colonel, Bastide, a former minister, and other celebrities of 1848. We moved down the boulevard, voicing various cries and singing the Marseillaise One who has not heard the Marseillaise, sung by thousands of voices in that state of nervous excitement and irresolution which is inevitable before certain conflict, can hardly realise the overwhelming effect of the revolutionary hymn.

At that minute there was really something grand about the demonstration. As we slowly moved down the boulevards all the windows were thrown open; ladies and children crowded to them and came out on to the balconies; the gloomy, alarmed faces of their husbands, the fathers and proprietors, looked out from behind them, not observing that in the fourth storeys and attics other heads, those of poor seamstresses and working girls were thrust out—they waved handkerchiefs, nodded and greeted us. From time to time, as we passed by the houses of well known people, various shouts were uttered.

In this way we reached the point where the Rue de la Pays joins the boulevards; it was closed by a squad of the Vincennes Chasseurs, and when our column came up to it the chasseurs suddenly moved apart like the scenery in a theatre, and Changarnier, mounted upon a small horse, galloped up at the head of a squadron of dragoons. With no summons to the crowd to disperse, with no beat of drum or other formalities prescribed by law, he threw the foremost ranks into confusion, cut them off from the others and, deploying the dragoons in two directions ordered them to clear the street in quick time. The dragoons in a frenzy fell to riding down people, striking them with the flat of their swords and using the edge at the slightest resistance. I hardly had time to take in what was happening when I found myself nose to nose with a horse which was almost snorting in my face, and a dragoon swearing likewise in my face and threatening to give me one with the flat if I did not move aside. I retreated to the right, and in an instant was carried away by the crowd and squeezed against the railings of the Rue Basse des Remparts. Of our rank the only one left beside me was Müller Strübing. Meanwhile the dragoons were pressing back the foremost ranks with their horses, and people who had no room to get away were thrust back upon us. Arago leaped down into the Rue Basse des Remparts, slipped and dislocated his leg; Strübing and I jumped down after him. We looked at each other in a frenzy of indignation; Strübing turned round and shouted loudly: *'Aux armes! Aux armes!'* A man in a workman's blouse caught him by the collar, shoved him out of the way and said:

'Have you gone mad? Look there!'

Thickly bristling bayonets were moving down the street—the Chaussée d'Antin it must have been.

'Get away before they hear you and cut off all escape. All is lost, all!' he added, clenching his fist; he hummed a tune as though there was nothing the matter, and walked rapidly away. We made our way to the Place de la Concorde. In the Champs-Elysées there was not a single squad from the *banlieue;* why, Chersosi must have known that there was not. It had been a diplomatic lie to save the situation, and it would perhaps have been the destruction of anyone who had believed it.

The shamelessness of attacking unarmed people aroused great resentment. If anything really had been prepared, had there been leaders, nothing would have been easier than for fighting to have begun in earnest. Instead of showing itself in its full strength the *Montagne,* on hearing how ludicrously the sovereign people had been dispersed by horses, hid itself behind a cloud. Ledru-Rollin carried on negotiations with Guinard. Guinard, the artillery commander of the National Guard, wanted to join the movement, wanted to give men, agreed to give cannon, but would not on any consideration give ammunition—he seems to have wished to act by the moral influence of the guns; Forestier was doing the same with his legion. Whether this helped them much we saw by the Versailles trial. Everyone wanted to do something, but no one dared; the most foresight was shown by some young men who hoped for a new order—they bespoke themselves prefects' uniforms, which they declined to take after the failure of the movement, and the tailor was obliged to hang them up for sale.

When the hurriedly rigged-up government was installed at the *Arts et Métiers* the workmen, after walking about the streets with inquiring faces and finding neither advice nor leadership, went home, convinced once more of the bankruptcy of the *Montagnard* fathers of the country: perhaps they gulped down their tears like the man who said to us, 'All is lost!'—or perhaps laughed in their sleeves at the way the *Montagne* had been tousled.

But the dilatoriness of Ledru-Rollin, the pedantry of Guinard—these were the external causes of the failure, and were just as *à propos* as are decisive characters and fortunate circumstances when they are needed. The internal cause was the poverty of the republican idea in which the movement originated. Ideas that have outlived their day may hobble about the world for years—may even, like Christ, appear after death once or twice to their devotees; but it is hard for them ever again to lead and dominate life. Such ideas never gain complete possession of a man, or gain possession only of incomplete people. If the *Montagne* had been victorious on the 13th of June, what would it have done? There was nothing new they could call their own. It would have been a photograph in black and white of the grim, glowing Rembrandt or Salvator Rosa picture of 1793 without the Jacobins, without the war, without even the naïve guillotine. . . .

After the 13th of June [1849] and the attempted rising at Lyons, arrests began. The mayor came to us with the police at Ville d'Avray to look for Karl Blind and Arnold Ruge; some of our acquaintances were seized. The Conciergerie was full to overflowing. In one small room there were as many as sixty men; in the middle stood a large slop-bucket, which was emptied once in the twenty-four hours—and all this in civilised Paris, with the cholera raging. Having not the least desire to spend some two months among those comforts, fed on rotten beans and putrid meat, I got a passport from a Moldo-Wallachian and went to Geneva.*

*How well founded my apprehensions were was shown by a police search of my mother's house at Ville d'Avray two days after my departure. They seized all the papers, even the correspondence of her maid with my cook. I thought it inopportune to publish my account of the 13th of June at the time.

PART SIX

Women in the Domestic, Work, and Public Spheres

The arrest and bodily removal of Emmeline Pankhurst, the subject of this photograph, remind us of the obstacles faced by women in the struggle for equal rights.

Women in the Domestic, Work, and Public Spheres

A few exceptional women, mostly writers, made their mark in a nineteenth century Europe that offered scant opportunities for women. Farming women toiled arduously, and hundreds of thousands entered the industrial workforce only to face stark exploitation. Middle- and upper-class women contended with male control. Society accepted women's endeavors in running the household, raising children, and pleasing husbands, with charitable work as the sole nondomestic exception. Only the truly economically independent could hope to overstep these boundaries. Regardless, the growing political liberation movements eventually addressed the plight of women, especially of the laboring classes. Later in the century, with the advent of universal male suffrage in Europe, a powerful movement arose for female voting rights that, after World War I, finally attained its goal. Still, full equal rights for women came neither easily nor quickly.

During the first half of the nineteenth century, social commentator Flora Tristan (1803–1844) portrayed the plight of laboring women, as did Elizabeth Gaskell's *Mary Barton* and other fiction and non-fiction works. In her 1850 essay "Why I Mention Women," Tristan noted the historically debased status of women, often viewed as virtually bestial in mental and spiritual capacities. In her view, only equal rights and education would eliminate poor women's frequent resort to prostitution and criminality. Later in the century, women of an educated English family, Emmeline, Sylvia, and Christabel Pankhurst, broadened their critical analysis to include questions of suffrage for all women, an example of which is "Why We Are Militant" by Emmeline Pankhurst (1858–1928). The Pankhursts supplemented analysis with persistent militant activism. Throughout the century, novelists such as Balzac, Hardy, Eliot, and many others portrayed women's experiences. In *The Ladies' Paradise* (1883), Emile Zola (1840–1902) describes the phenomenon of shopping, itself a form of self-expression for middle- and upper-class women. The rise of department stores with their extravagant displays of merchandise reflected in part the economic growth and pretensions of Napoleon III's Second Empire. The heroine is, however, not a shopper but an employee. Department stores and the production of the goods in them provided prosperous women with preoccupation and working- and lower-middle class women with occupation.

✦ Reading 23 ✦

Why I Mention Women

Flora Tristan

Workers, you my brothers, for whom I work with love, because you represent the most vital, numerous, and useful part of humanity, and because from that point of view I find my own satisfaction in serving your cause, I beg you earnestly to read this with the greatest attention. For, you must be persuaded, it concerns your material interests to understand why when I mention women I always designate them as *female workers* or *all the women.*

The intelligent person enlightened by rays of divine love and love for humanity, can easily grasp the logical chain of relationships that exist between causes and effects. For him, all of philosophy and religion can be summed up by two questions: First, how can and must one love God and serve Him for the universal well-being of all men and women? Second, how can and must one love and treat woman, for the sake of all men and women? Asked in this manner, these two questions, with respect to natural order, underlie everything produced in the moral and physical worlds (one results or flows from the other).

I don't believe this is the place to answer these two questions. Later, if the workers wish it, I shall gladly treat metaphysically and philosophically questions of the highest order. But, for the time being, one need only pose the questions, as the formal declaration of an absolute principle. Without going directly back to causes, let us limit our analysis to the effects.

Up to now, woman has counted for nothing in human society. What has been the result of this? That the priest, the lawmaker, and the philosopher have treated her as a true *pariah*. Woman (one half of humanity) has been cast out of the Church, out of the law, out of society. For her, there are no functions in the Church, no representation before the law, no functions in the State. The priest told her, "Woman, you are temptation, sin, and evil; you represent flesh, that is, corruption and rottenness. Weep for your condition, throw ashes on your head, seek refuge in a cloister, and mortify your heart, which is made for love, and your female organs, which are made for motherhood. And when thus you have mutilated your heart and body, offer them all bloody and dried up to your God for remission from the original sin committed by your mother Eve." Then the lawmaker tells her, "Woman, by yourself you are nothing; you have no active role in human affairs; you cannot expect to find a seat at the social banquet. If you want to live, you must serve as an appendage to your lord and master, man. So, young girl, you will obey your father; when married you shall obey your husband; widowed and old, you will be left alone." Then, the learned philosopher tells her, "Woman, it has been scientifically observed that, according to your constitution, you are inferior to man. Now, you have no intelligence, no comprehension for lofty questions, no logic in ideas, no ability for the so-called exact sciences, no aptitude for serious endeavors. Finally, you are a feeble-minded and weak-bodied being, cowardly, superstitious; in a word, you are nothing but a capricious child, spontaneous, frivolous, for ten or fifteen years of your life you are a nice little doll, but full of faults and vices. That is why, woman, man must be your master and have complete authority over you."

So that is how for the six thousand years the world has existed, the wisest among the wise have judged the female race.

Such a terrible condemnation, repeated for six thousand years, is likely to impress the masses, for

From: Flora Tristan, *The Workers' Union,* translated by Beverly Livingston (Urbana: University of Illinois Press, 1983), pp. 75–88.

the sanction of time has great authority over them. However, what must make us hope that this sentence can be repealed is that the wisest of the wise have also for six thousand years pronounced a no less horrible verdict upon another race of humanity—the proletariat. Before 1789, what was the proletarian in French society? A serf, a peasant, who was made into a taxable, drudging beast of burden. Then came the Revolution of 1789, and all of a sudden the wisest of the wise proclaimed that the lower orders are to be called the *people,* that the serfs and peasants are to be called *citizens.* Finally, they proclaimed the *rights of man* in full national assembly.

The proletarian, considered until then a brute, was quite surprised to learn that it had been the neglect and scorn for his rights that had caused all the world's misfortunes. He was quite surprised to learn that he would enjoy civil, political, and social rights, and finally would become the *equal* of his former lord and master. His surprise grew when he was told that he possessed a brain of the same quality as the royal prince's. What a change! However, it did not take long to realize that this second judgment on the proletariat was truer than the first. Hardly had they proclaimed that proletarians were capable of all kinds of civil, military, and social functions, than out of their ranks came generals the likes of which Charlemagne, Henri IV, and Louis XIV could not recruit from the ranks of their proud and brilliant nobility. Then, as if by magic, from the ranks of the proletariat surged learned men, artists, poets, writers, statesmen, and financiers who gave France a luster she had never had. Then military glory came upon her like a halo; scientific discoveries enriched her; the arts embellished her; her commerce made immense strides, and in less than thirty years the wealth of the country trebled. These facts cannot be disputed: everyone agrees today that men are born indistinct, with essentially equal faculties, and that the sole thing we should be concerned about is how to develop an individual's total faculties for the sake of the general well-being.

What happened to the proletariat, it must be agreed, is a good omen for women when their "1789" rings out. According to a very simple calculation, it is obvious that wealth will increase immeasurably on the day women are called upon to participate with their intelligence, strength, and ability in the social process. This is as easy to understand as two is the double of one. But, alas! We are not yet there. Meanwhile, let us take a look at what is happening in 1843.

The Church having said that woman was sin; the lawmaker that by herself she was nothing, that she was to enjoy no rights; the learned philosopher that by her constitution she had no intellect, it was concluded that she is a poor being disinherited by God; so men and society treated her as such.

Once woman's inferiority was proclaimed and postulated, notice what disastrous consequences resulted for the universal well-being of all men and women.

Those who believed that woman by nature lacked the strength, intelligence, and capacity to do serious and useful work, very logically deduced that it would be a waste of time to give her a rational, solid, and strict education, the kind that would make her a useful member of society. So she has been raised to be a nice doll and a slave destined for amusing and serving her master. In truth, from time to time some intelligent, sensitive men, showing empathy with their mothers, wives, and daughters, have cried out against the barbarity and absurdity of such an order of things, energetically protesting against such an iniquitous condemnation. On several occasions, society has been moved for a moment; but when pushed by logic, has replied, "Well then! Let us suppose that women are not what the wise men have believed, that they have great moral strength and intelligence. Well, in that case, what good would it be to develop their faculties, since they would not be able to employ them usefully in this society which rejects them? What an awful torture, to feel one has force and power to act, and to see oneself condemned to inaction!"

This reasoning was irrefutably true. So everyone repeated, "It's true, women would suffer too much if their God-given talents were developed, if from childhood on they were raised to understand their dignity and to be conscious of their value as members of society. Then never would they be able to bear the degradation imposed upon them by the Church, the law, and prejudice. It is better to treat them like children and leave them in the dark about themselves: they will suffer less."

Follow closely, and you will see what horrible consequences result from accepting a false premise.

In order not to stray too far from my subject, even though it is a good opportunity to speak from a general standpoint, I am returning to the question of the working class.

In the life of the workers, woman is everything. She is their sole providence. If she is gone, they lack everything. So they say, "It is woman who makes or unmakes the home," and this is the clear truth: that is why it has become a proverb. However, what education, instruction, direction, moral or physical development does the working-class woman receive? None. As a child, she is left to the mercy of a mother and grandmother who also have received no education. One of them might have a brutal and wicked disposition and beat and mistreat her for no reason; the other might be weak and uncaring, and let her do anything. (As with everything I am suggesting, I am speaking in general terms; of course, there are numerous exceptions.) The poor child will be raised among the most shocking contradictions—hurt by unfair blows and treatment one day, then pampered and spoiled no less perniciously the next.

Instead of being sent to school, she is kept at home in deference to her brothers and so that she can share in the housework, rock the baby, run errands, or watch the soup, etc. At the age of twelve she is made an apprentice. There she continues to be exploited by her mistress and often continues to be as mistreated as she was at home.

Nothing embitters the character, hardens the heart, or makes the spirit so mean as the continuous suffering a child endures from unfair and brutal treatment. First, the injustice hurts, afflicts, and causes despair; then when it persists, it irritates and exasperates us and finally, dreaming only of revenge, we end up by becoming hardened, unjust, and wicked. Such will be the normal condition for a poor girl of twenty. Then she will marry, without love, simply because one must marry in order to get out from under parental tyranny. What will happen? I suppose she will have children, and she, in turn, will be unable to raise them suitably. She will be just as brutal to them as her mother and grandmother were to her.

Working class women, take note, I beg you, that by mentioning your ignorance and incapacity to raise your children, I have no intention in the least of accusing *you* or *your nature*. No, I am accusing society for leaving you uneducated—you, women and mothers, who actually need so much to be instructed and formed in order to be able to instruct and develop the men and children entrusted to your care.

Generally women of the masses are brutal, mean, and sometimes hard. This being true, where does this situation come from, so different from the sweet, good, sensitive, and generous nature of woman?

Poor working women! They have so many reasons to be irritated! First, their husbands. (It must be agreed that there are few working-class couples who are happily married,) Having received more instruction, being the head by law and also by the money he brings home, the husband thinks he is (and he is, in fact) very superior to his wife, who only brings home her small daily wage and is merely a very humble servant in her home.

Consequently, the husband treats his wife with nothing less than great disdain. Humiliated by his every word or glance, the poor woman either openly or silently revolts, depending upon her personality. This creates violent, painful scenes that end up producing an atmosphere of constant irritation between the master and the slave (one can indeed say *slave*, because the woman is, so to speak, her husband's property). This state becomes so painful that, instead of staying home to talk with his wife, the husband hurries out; and as if he had no other place to go, he goes to the tavern to drink blue wine in the hope of getting drunk, with the other husbands who are just as unhappy as he.

This type of distraction makes things worse. The wife, waiting for payday (Sunday) to buy weekly provisions for the family, is in despair seeing her husband spend most of the money at the tavern. Then she reaches a peak of irritation, and her brutality and wickedness redouble. You have to have personally seen these working-class households (especially the bad ones) to have an idea of the husband's misfortune and the wife's suffering. It passes from reproaches and insults to blows, then tears; from discouragement to despair.

And following the acute chagrins caused by the husband come the pregnancies, illnesses, unemployment, and poverty, planted by the door like Medusa's head. Add to all that the endless tension provoked by four or five loud, turbulent, and bothersome children clamoring about their mother, in a small worker's room too small to turn around in. My! One would have to be an angel from heaven not to be irritated, not to become brutal and mean in such a situation. However, in this domestic setting, what becomes of the children? They see their father only in the evening or on Sunday. Always either upset or drunk, their father speaks to them only angrily and gives them only insults and blows. Hearing their mother continuously complain, they begin to feel hatred and scorn for her. They fear and obey her, but they do not love her, for a person is made that way—he cannot love someone who mistreats him. And isn't it a great misfortune for a child not to be able to love his mother! If he is unhappy, to whose breast will he go to cry? If he thoughtlessly makes a bad mistake or is led astray, in whom can he confide? Having no desire to stay close to his mother, the child will seek any pretext to leave the parental home. Bad associations are easy to make, for girls as for boys. Strolling becomes vagrancy, and vagrancy often becomes thievery.

Among the poor girls in houses of prostitution and the poor men moaning in jails, how many can say, "If we had had a *mother able to raise us,* then we would not be here."

I repeat, woman is everything in the life of a worker. As mother, she can influence him during his childhood. She and only she is the one from whom he gets his first notions of that science which is so important to acquire—the science of life, which teaches us how to live well for ourselves and for others, according to the milieu in which fate has placed us. As lover, she can influence him during his youth, and what a powerful influence could be exerted by a young, beautiful, and beloved girl! As wife, she can have an effect on him for three-quarters of his life. Finally, as daughter, she can act upon him in his old age. Note that the worker's position is very different from an idle person's. If the rich child has a mother unable to raise him, he is placed in a boarding school or given a governess. If the young rich fellow has no mistress, he can busy his heart and imagination with studying the arts and sciences. If the rich man has no spouse, he does not fail to find distractions in society. If the old rich man has no daughter, he finds some old friends or young nephews who willingly come and play cards with him; whereas the worker, for whom all these pleasures are denied, has only the company of the women in his family, his companions in misfortune, for all his joy and solace. The result of this situation is that it would be most important, from the point of view of intellectually, morally, and materially improving the working class, that the women receive from childhood a rational and solid education, apt to develop all their potential so that they can become skilled in their trades, good mothers capable of raising and guiding their children and to be for them, as *La Presse* says, free and natural schoolteachers, and also so that they can serve as moralizing agents for the men whom they influence from birth to death.

Are you beginning to understand, you men, who cry scandal before being willing to examine the issue, why I demand rights for women? Why I would like women placed in society on a footing of *absolute equality* with men to enjoy the legal birthright all beings have? I call for woman's rights because I am convinced that *all* the misfortunes in the world come from this neglect and scorn shown until now for the natural and inalienable rights of woman. I call for woman's rights because it is the only way to have her educated, and woman's education depends upon man's in general, and particularly the working-class man's. I call for woman's rights because it is the only way to obtain her rehabilitation before the church, the law, and society, and this rehabilitation is necessary before working men themselves can be rehabilitated. All working-class ills can be summed up in two words: poverty and ignorance. Now in order to get out of this maze, I see only one way: begin by educating women, because the women are in charge of instructing boys and girls.

Workers, in the current state of things, you know what goes on in your households. You, the master with rights over your wife, do you live with her with a contented heart? Say, are you happy? No, it is easy to see, in spite of your rights, you are neither contented nor happy. Between master and slave there can only be the weariness of the chain's weight tying them together. Where the lack of freedom is felt, happiness cannot exist.

Men always complain about the bad moods and the devious and silently wicked characters women show in all their relationships. Oh, would I have a very bad opinion of women, if in the state of abjection where the law and customs place them, they were to submit without a murmur to the yoke weighing on them! Thanks be to God, that it is not so! Their protest, since the beginning of time, has always been relentless. But since the declaration of the rights of man, a solemn act proclaiming the neglect and scorn the new men gave to women, their protest has taken on new energy and violence which proves that the slave's exasperation has peaked.

Workers, you who have good sense and with whom one can reason, because, as Fourier says, you do not have minds stuffed with systems, suppose for a moment that by right woman is the equal of man? What would come of that? (1) That as soon as one would no longer have to fear the dangerous consequences necessarily caused by the moral and physical development of woman's faculties because of her current enslavement, she would be carefully educated so as to bring out the best possible in her intelligence and work; (2) that you, men of the people, you would have clever workers for mothers, earning a good wage, instructed, well-raised and very able to teach and raise you, workers, as it is appropriate for free men; (3) that your sisters, lovers, wives, and friends would be educated, well-raised women whose daily companionship would be most pleasant for you, for nothing is sweeter or gentler to a man's heart than a woman's conversation when she is well educated, good, and speaks with logic and benevolence.

We have quickly glanced over what is currently going on in the workers' households. Let us now examine what would occur in these same households if woman were man's equal.

Knowing that his wife has rights equal to his, the husband would not treat her anymore with the disdain and scorn shown to inferiors. On the contrary, he would treat her with the respect and deference one grants to equals. Then the woman will no longer have cause for irritation; and once that is destroyed, she will no longer appear brutal, devious, grouchy, angry, exasperated, or mean. No longer considered the husband's servant at home, but his associate, friend, and companion, she will naturally take an interest in the association and do all she can to make the little household flourish. With theoretical and practical knowledge, she will employ all her intelligence to keep her house neat, economical, and pleasant. Educated and aware of the utility of an education, she will put all her ambition into raising her children well. She will lovingly teach them herself, watch over their schoolwork, and place them in good apprenticeships; and finally, she will always guide them with care, tenderness, and discernment. Then what a contented heart, peace of mind, and happy soul the man, the husband, the worker will have who possesses such a woman! Finding his wife has intelligence, common sense and educated opinions, he will be able to talk with her about serious subjects, tell her about his plans, and work with her to further improve their position. Flattered by his confidence in her, she will help him with good advice or collaboration in his endeavors and business. The worker, also educated and well brought up, will find it delightful to teach and develop his young children. Workers in general are kindhearted and love children very much. How diligently a man will work all week knowing that he is to spend Sunday in his wife's company, that he will enjoy his two little mischievous, affectionate girls and his two already educated boys who are able to talk with their father about serious things! How hard this father will work to earn a few extra cents to buy pretty bonnets for his little girls, a book for his sons, an engraving or something else which he knows will please them? With what joyful ecstasy these little gifts will be received, and what happiness for the mother to see the reciprocal love between father and children! It is clear that this, hypothetically, would be the most desirable domestic life for the worker. Comfortable at home, happy and satisfied in the company of his kind, old mother and young wife and children, it would never occur to him to leave the house to seek a good time at the tavern, that place of perdition which wastes the worker's time, money and health, and dulls his intellect. With half of what a drunkard spends in the tavern, a worker's whole family living together could go for meals in the country in summer. So little is necessary for people who know how to live soberly. Out in the open air, the children would all be happy to run with their father and mother, who would be like children to amuse them; and in the evening, with contented hearts and limbs slightly weary from the week's work, the family would return home very satisfied with their day. In winter, the family would go to a show. These amusements offer a dual advantage: they instruct children while entertaining them. How many objects of study an intelligent mother can find to teach her children in a day spent in the country or an evening at the theater!

Under the circumstances I have just outlined, the home would create well-being rather than ruin for the worker. Who doesn't know how love and contentment of the heart treble or quadruple a man's strength? We have seen it in a few rare cases. It has happened that a worker, adoring his family and getting the idea of teaching his children, did the work that three unmarried men would not have been able to do in order to attain this noble goal. Then there is the question of deprivations. Single men spend generously; they don't deny themselves anything. What does it matter, they say, after all, we can gaily live and drink since we have no one to feed. But the married man who loves his family finds satisfaction in depriving himself and lives with exemplary frugality.

Workers, this vaguely sketched picture of the situation the proletariat would enjoy if woman were recognized as man's equal must lead to thought about the evil existing and the goodness which might exist. That ought to make you become very determined.

Workers, you probably have no power to abrogate the old laws or to make new ones. But you have the power to protest against the inequity and absurdity of laws that impede humanity's progress and make you in particular suffer. You can and must then energetically use thought, speaking, and writing to protest the laws oppressing you for it is your sacred duty. So now, try to understand: the law which enslaves woman and deprives her of education oppresses you, proletarian men.

To be raised, educated, and taught the science of the world, the son of the wealthy has governesses and knowledgeable teachers, able advisers and finally, beautiful *marquises,* elegant, witty women whose functions in high society consist in taking over the son's education after he leaves school. It's a very useful role for the well-being of those gentlemen of high nobility. These ladies teach them to have proper manners, tact, finesse, wit; in a word, they make them into men who *know how to live,* the right kind of men. No matter how capable a young man is, if he is fortunate enough to be the protégé of one of these amiable ladies, his fortune is made. At thirty-five he is certain of becoming an ambassador or a minister. While you, poor workers, to rear and teach you, you have only your mother; to make you into civilized men, you only have women of your class, your companions in ignorance and misery.

Thus it is not in the name of woman's superiority (as I will unfailingly be accused) that I tell you to demand rights for women; not really. First of all, before discussing her superiority, one must recognize her social individuality. My support has a more solid basis. In the name of your own interest and improvement, men; and finally in the name of the universal well-being of all men and women, I invite you to appeal for women's rights, and meanwhile at least to recognize them in principle.

Thus, workers, it is up to you, who are the victims of real inequality and injustice, to establish the rule of justice and absolute equality between man and woman on this earth. Give a great example to the world, an example that will prove to your oppressors that you want to triumph through your right and not by brute force. You seven, ten, fifteen million proletarians, could avail yourselves of that brute force! In calling for justice, prove that you are just and equitable. You, the strong men, the men with bare arms, proclaim your recognition that woman is your equal, and as such, you recognize her equal right to the benefits of the *universal union of working men and women.*

Workers, perhaps in three or four years you will have your first palace, ready to admit six hundred old persons and six hundred children. Well! Proclaim through your statutes, which will become your charter, the rights of women for equality. Let it be written in your charter that an equal number of girls and boys will be admitted to the Workers' Union palace to receive intellectual and vocational training.

Workers, in 1791, your fathers proclaimed the immortal declaration of the *rights of man,* and it is to that solemn declaration that today you owe your being free and equal men before the law. May your fathers be honored for this great work! But, proletarians, there remains for you men of 1843 a no less great work to finish. In your turn, emancipate the last slaves still remaining in French society; proclaim the *rights of woman,* in the same terms your fathers proclaimed yours:

"We, French proletarians, after fifty-three years of experience, recognize that we are duly enlightened and convinced that the neglect and scorn perpetrated upon the natural rights of woman are the only cause of unhappiness in the world, and we have resolved to expose her sacred and inalienable rights in a solemn declaration inscribed in our charter. We wish women to be informed of our declaration, so that they will not let themselves be oppressed and degraded any more by man's injustice and tyranny, and so that men will respect the freedom and equality they enjoy in their wives and mothers.

1. The goal of society necessarily being the common happiness of men and women, the Workers' Union guarantees them the enjoyment of their rights as working men and women.

2. Their rights include equal admission to the Workers' Union palaces, whether they be children, or disabled or elderly.

3. Woman being man's equal, we understand that girls will receive as rational, solid, and extensive (though different) an education in moral and professional matters as the boys.

4. As for the disabled and the elderly, in every way, the treatment will be the same for women as for men.

Workers, rest assured, if you have enough equity and justice to inscribe in your Charter the few lines I have just traced, this declaration of the rights of woman will soon become custom, then law, and within twenty-five years you will see absolute equality of man and woman inscribed at the head of the book of law.

Then, my brothers, and only then, will human unity be established.

Sons of '89, that is the work your fathers bequeathed to you!

✦ Reading 24 ✦

Why We Are Militant

Emmeline Pankhurst

A Speech Delivered in New York October 21st, 1913

I know that in your minds there are questions like these; you are saying, 'Woman Suffrage is sure to come; the emancipation of humanity is an evolutionary process, and how is it that some women, instead of trusting to that evolution, instead of educating the masses of people of their country, instead of educating their own sex to prepare them for citizenship, how is it that these militant women are using violence and upsetting the business arrangements of the country in their undue impatience to attain their end?'

Let me try to explain to you the situation.

Although we have a so-called democracy, and so-called representative government there, England is the most conservative country on earth. Why, your forefathers found that out a great many years ago! If you had passed your life in England as I have, you would know that there are certain words which certainly, during the last two generations, certainly till about ten years ago, aroused a feeling of horror and fear in the minds of the mass of the people. The word revolution, for instance, was identified in England with all kind of horrible ideas. The idea of change, the idea of unsettling the established order of things was repugnant.

Now, in America it is the proud boast of some of the most conservative men and women that I have met, that they are descended from the heroes of the Revolution. You have an organisation, I believe, called the Daughters of the Revolution, whose members put an interpretation upon the word revolution which is quite different from the interpretation given to it in Great Britain. Perhaps that will help you to realise how extremely difficult it is in Great Britain to get anything done. All my life I have heard people talking in advocacy of reforms which it was self-evident would be for the good of the people, and yet it has all ended in talk; they are still talking about these reforms, and unless something happens of a volcanic nature they will go on talking about them until the end of time. Nothing ever has been got out of the British Parliament without something very nearly approaching a revolution. You need something dynamic in order to force legislation through the House of Commons; in fact, the whole machinery of government in England may almost be said to be an elaborate arrangement for not doing anything.

The extensions of the franchise to the men of my country have been preceded by very great violence, by something like a revolution, by something like civil war. In 1832, you know we were on the edge of a civil war and on the edge of revolution, and it was at the point of the sword—no, not at the point of the sword—it was after the practice of arson on so large a scale that half the city of Bristol was burned down in a single night, it was because more and greater violence and arson were feared that the Reform Bill of 1832 was allowed to pass into law. In 1867, John Bright urged the people of London to crowd the approaches to the Houses of Parliament in order to show their determination, and he said that if they did that no Parliament, however obdurate, could resist their just demands. Rioting went on all over the country, and as the result of that rioting, as the result of that unrest, which resulted in the pulling down of the Hyde Park railings, as a result of the fear of more rioting and violence the Reform Act of 1867 was put upon the statute books.

In 1884 came the turn of the agricultural labourer. Joseph Chamberlain, who afterwards be-

From: *Suffrage and the Pankhursts,* ed. Jane Marcus (London: Routledge & Kegan Paul, 1984), pp. 153–162.

came a very conservative person, threatened that, unless the vote was given to the agricultural labourer, he would march 100,000 men from Birmingham to know the reason why. Rioting was threatened and feared, and so the agricultural labourers got the vote.

Meanwhile, during the '80's, women, like men, were asking for the franchise. Appeals, larger and more numerous than for any other reform, were presented in support of Woman's Suffrage. Meetings of the great corporations, great town councils, and city councils, passed resolutions asking that women should have the vote. More meetings were held, and larger, for Woman Suffrage than were held for votes for men, and yet the women did not get it. Men got the vote because they were and would be violent. The women did not get it because they were constitutional and law-abiding. Why, is it not evident to everyone that people who are patient where misgovernment is concerned may go on being patient! Why should anyone trouble to help them? I take to myself some shame that through all those years, at any rate from the early '80's, when I first came into the Suffrage movement, I did not learn my political lessons.

I believed, as many women still in England believe, that women could get their way in some mysterious manner, by purely peaceful methods. We have been so accustomed, we women, to accept one standard for men and another standard for women, that we have even applied that variation of standard to the injury of our political welfare.

Having had better opportunities of education, and having had some training in politics, having in political life come so near to the 'superior' being as to see that he was not altogether such a fount of wisdom as they had supposed, that he had his human weaknesses as we had, the twentieth century women began to say to themselves. 'Is it not time, since our methods have failed and the men's have succeeded, that we should take a leaf out of their political book?'

We were led to that conclusion, we older women, by the advice of the young—you know there is a French proverb which says, 'If youth knew; if age could,' but I think that when you can bring together youth and age, as we have done, and get them to adopt the same methods and take the same point of view, then you are on the high road to success.

Well, we in Great Britain, on the eve of the General Election of 1905, a mere handful of us—why, you could almost count us on the fingers of both hands—set out on the wonderful adventure of forcing the strongest Government of modern times to give the women the vote. Only a few in number; we were not strong in influence, and we had hardly any money, and yet we quite gaily made our little banners with the words 'Votes for Women' upon them, and we set out to win the enfranchisement of the women of our country.

The Suffrage movement was almost dead. The women had lost heart. You could not get a Suffrage meeting that was attended by members of the general public. We used to have about 24 adherents in the front row. We carried our resolutions and heard no more about them.

Two women changed that in a twinkling of an eye at a great Liberal demonstration in Manchester, where a Liberal leader, Sir Edward Grey, was explaining the programme to be carried out during the Liberals' next turn of office. The two women put the fateful question, 'When are you going to give votes to women?' and refused to sit down until they had been answered. These two women were sent to gaol, and from that day to this the women's movement, both militant and constitutional, has never looked back. We had little more than one moribund society for Woman Suffrage in those days. Now we have nearly 50 societies for Woman Suffrage, and they are large in membership, they are rich in money, and their ranks are swelling every day that passes. That is how militancy has put back the clock of Woman Suffrage in Great Britain.

Now, some of you have said how wicked it is (the immigration commissioners told me that on Saturday afternoon), how wicked it is to attack the property of private individuals who have done us no harm. Well, you know there is a proverb which says that you cannot make omelettes without breaking eggs. I wish we could.

I want to say here and now that the only justification for violence, the only justification for damage to property, the only justification for risk to the comfort of other human beings is the fact that you have tried all other available means and have failed to secure justice, and as a law-abiding person—and I am by nature a law-abiding person, as one hating violence, hating disorder—I want to say that from the moment we began our militant agitation to this day I have felt absolutely guiltless in this matter.

I tell you that in Great Britain there is no other way. We can show intolerable grievances. The Chancellor of the Exchequer, Mr Lloyd George, who is no friend of the woman's movement, although a professed one, said a very true thing when speaking of the grievances of his own country, of Wales. He said that there comes a time in the life of human beings suffering from intolerable grievances when the only way to maintain their self respect is to revolt against that injustice.

Well, I say the time is long past when it became necessary for women to revolt in order to maintain their self respect in Great Britain. The women who are waging this war are women who would fight, if it were only for the idea of liberty—if it were only that they might be free citizens of a free country—I myself would fight for that idea alone. But we have, in addition to this love of freedom, intolerable grievances to redress.

We do not feel the weight of those grievances in our own persons. I think it is very true that people who are crushed by personal wrongs are not the right people to fight for reform. The people who can fight best are the people who have happy lives themselves, the fortunate ones. At any rate, in our revolution it is the happy women, the fortunate women, the women who have drawn prizes in the lucky bag of life, in the shape of good fathers, good husbands and good brothers, they are the women who are fighting this battle. They are fighting it for the sake of others more helpless than themselves, and it is of the grievances of those helpless ones that I want to say a few words to-night to make you understand the meaning of our militant campaign.

Those grievances are so pressing that, so far from it being a duty to be patient and to wait for evolution, in thinking of those grievances the idea of patience is intolerable. We feel that patience is something akin to crime when our patience involves continued suffering on the part of the oppressed.

We are fighting to get the power to alter bad laws; but some people say to us, 'Go to the representatives in the House of Commons, point out to them that these laws are bad, and you will find them quite ready to alter them.'

Ladies and gentlemen, there are women in my country who have spent long and useful lives trying to get reforms, and because of their voteless condition, they are unable even to get the ear of Members of Parliament, much less are they able to secure those reforms.

Our marriage and divorce laws are a disgrace to civilisation. I sometimes wonder, looking back from the serenity of past middle age, at the courage of women. I wonder that women have the courage to take upon themselves the responsibilities of marriage and motherhood when I see how little protection the law of my country affords them. I wonder that a woman will face the ordeal of childbirth with the knowledge that after she has risked her life to bring a child into the world she has absolutely no parental rights over the future of that child. Think what trust women have in men when a woman will marry a man, knowing, if she has knowledge of the law, that if that man is not all she in her love for him thinks him, he may even bring a strange woman into the house, bring his mistress into the house to live with her, and she cannot get legal relief from such a marriage as that.

How often is women's trust misplaced, and yet how whole-hearted and how touching that trust must be when a woman, in order to get love and companionship, will run such terrible risks in entering into marriage! Yet women have done it, and as we get to know more of life we militant Suffragists have nerved ourselves and forced ourselves to learn something of how other people live. As we get that knowledge we realise how political power, how political influence, which would enable us to get better laws, would make it possible for thousands upon thousands of unhappy women to live happier lives.

Well, you may say, the laws may be inadequate, the laws may be bad, but human nature, after all, is not much influenced by laws, and upon the whole, people are fairly happy. Now, for those who are fortunate it is very comfortable to have that idea, but if you will really look at life as we see it in our centralised civilisation in Europe, you will find that after all the law is a great educator, and if men are brought up to think the law allows them to behave badly to those who should be nearest and dearest to them, the worst kind of man is very apt to take full advantage of all the laxity of the law.

What have we been hearing of so much during the last few years! It is a very remarkable thing, ladies, and gentlemen, that along with this woman's movement, along with this woman's revolt, you are having a great uncovering of social sores. We are having light let into dark places, whether it is in the United States or whether it is in the old countries of Europe, you find the social ills from which humanity suffers, are very much the same. Every civilised country has been discussing how to deal with that most awful slavery, the white slave traffic.

When I was a very tiny child the great American people were divided into hostile sections on the question of whether it was right that one set of human beings of one colour should buy and sell human beings of another colour, and you had a bloody war to settle that question. I tell you that throughout the civilised world to-day there is a slavery more awful than negro slavery in its worst form ever was. It is called prostitution, but in that awful slavery there are slaves of every shade and colour, and they are all of one sex.

Well, in my country we have been having legislation to deal with it. We have now a White Slave Act, and in that Act of Parliament they have put a flogging clause. Certain men are to be flogged if they are convicted and found guilty under that Act of Parliament, and the British House of Commons, composed of men of varying moral standard, waxed highly eloquent on the need of flogging these tigers of the human race, men engaged in the white slave traffic.

Well, we women looked on and we read their speeches, but in our hearts we said, 'Why don't they decide to go to the people for whom the white slave traffic exists? What is the use of dealing with the emissaries, with the slave hunters, with the purveyors? Why don't they go to the very foundation of the evil; why don't they attack the customers? If there was no demand there would be no traffic, because business does not exist if there is no demand for it?' And so we women said, 'It's no use, gentlemen, trying to put us off with sentimental legislation on the white slave traffic. We don't trust you to settle it; we want to have a hand in settling it ourselves, because we think we know how.' And we have a right to distrust that legislation. They passed the Act very, very quickly; they put it on the Statute Book, and we have seen it in operation, and we know that the time of Parliament and the time of the nation was wasted on a piece of legislation which I fear was never intended to be taken very seriously; something to keep the women quiet, something to lull us into a sense of security, something to make us believe that now, at least, the Government were really grappling with the situation.

And so we attacked this great evil. We said, 'How can we expect real legislation to deal with the white slave traffic on a small scale when the Government of the country is the biggest white slave trading firm that we have got?'

And it is true; because you know, although we have suppressed such regulation of vice in England, we have got it in full swing in the great dependencies that we own all over the world, and we have only to turn to India and look to other places where our Army is stationed to find the Government, which is in no way responsible to women, actually taking part in that awful trade, in absolute cold bloodedness where native women are concerned, all, forsooth, in the name of the health of the men of our forces.

Well, we have been speaking out, ladies and gentlemen; we have been saying to our nation and the rulers of our nation, 'We will not have the health of one-half of the community, their pretended health, maintained at the expense of the degradation and sorrow and misery of the other half.'

I want to ask you whether, in all the revolutions of the past, in your own revolt against British rule, you had deeper or greater reasons for revolt than women have to-day?

Take the industrial side of the question: have men's wages for a hard day's work ever been so low and inadequate as are women's wages to-day? Have men ever had to suffer from the laws, more injustice than women suffer? Is there a single reason which men have had for demanding liberty that does not also apply to women?

Why, if you were talking to the *men* of any other nation you would not hesitate to reply in the affirmative. There is not a man in this meeting who has not felt sympathy with the uprising of the men of other lands when suffering from intolerable tyranny, when deprived of all representative rights. You are full of sympathy with men in Russia. You are full of sympathy with nations that rise against the domination of the Turk. You are full of sympathy with all struggling people striving for independence. How is it, then, that some of you have nothing but ridicule and contempt and reprobation for women who are fighting for exactly the same thing?

All my life I have tried to understand why it is that men who value their citizenship as their dearest possession seem to think citizenship ridiculous when it is to be applied to the women of their race. And I find an explanation, and it is the only one I can think of. It came to me when I was in a prison cell, remembering how I had seen men laugh at the idea of women going to prison. Why they would confess they could not bear a cell door to be shut upon themselves for a single hour without asking to be let out. A thought came to me in my prison cell, and it was this: that to men women are not human beings like themselves. Some men think we are superhuman; they put us on pedestals; they revere us; they think we are too fine and too delicate to come down into the hurly-burly of life. Other men think us sub-human; they think we are a strange species unfortunately having to exist for the perpetuation of the race. They think that we are fit for drudgery, but that in some strange way our minds are not like theirs, our love for great things is not like theirs, and so we are a sort of sub-human species.

We are neither superhuman nor are we sub-human. We are just human beings like yourselves.

Our hearts burn within us when we read the great mottoes which celebrate the liberty of your country; when we go to France and we read the words, liberty, fraternity and equality, don't you think that we appreciate the meaning of those words? And then when we wake to the knowledge that these things are not for us, they are only for our brothers, then there comes a sense of bitterness into the hearts of some women, and they say to themselves, 'Will men never understand?' But so far as we in England are concerned, we have come to the conclusion that we are not going to leave men any illusions upon the question.

When we were patient, when we believed in argument and persuasion, they said, 'You don't really want it because, if you did, you would do something unmistakable to show you were determined to have it.' And then when we did something unmistakable they said, 'You are behaving so badly that you show you are not fit for it.'

Now, gentlemen, in your heart of hearts you do not believe that. You know perfectly well that there never was a thing worth having that was not worth fighting for. You know perfectly well that if the situation were reversed, if you had no constitutional rights and we had all of them, if you had the duty of paying and obeying and trying to look as pleasant, and we were the proud citizens who could decide our fate and yours, because we knew what was good for you better than you knew yourselves, you know perfectly well that you wouldn't stand it for a single day, and you would be perfectly justified in rebelling against such intolerable conditions.

Well, in Great Britain, we have tried persuasion, we have tried the plan of showing (by going upon public bodies, where they allowed us to do work they hadn't much time to do themselves) that we are capable people. We did it in the hope that we should convince them and persuade them to do the right and proper thing. But we had all our labour for our pains, and now we are fighting for our rights, and we are growing stronger and better women in the process. We are getting more fit to use our rights because we have such difficulty in getting them.

And now may I say a word about the reason for my coming to America.

Always when human beings have been struggling for freedom they have looked to happier parts of the world for support and sympathy. In your hour of trouble you went to other peoples and asked them for help. It seems to me, looking into the past, into my recollections of history, that a great man named Benjamin Franklin went to France to ask the French people to help in the struggle for American independence. You didn't apologise for sending him, and I am sure he didn't apologise for going. There may have been people in France who said, 'Why does this pestilent, rebellious fellow come over trying to stir up people here in our peaceful country?' But, in the main, the people of France welcomed him. Their hearts thrilled at the idea of a brave and courageous struggle, and they sent money and they sent men to help to fight and win the independence of the American people.

Those who have been struggling for freedom in other lands have come to you, and I can't help remembering that right through the struggle of the Irish people they sent law-breakers to plead with you for help for law-breakers in Ireland.

Yes, and like all political law breaking done by men, the form their violence has taken has not been merely to break some shop windows or to set on fire the house of some rich plutocrat, but it has found its expression in the taking of human life, in the injury even of poor, dumb animals who could have no part in the matter. And yet you looked at that agitation in a large way. You said, 'In times of revolution and revolt you cannot curb the human spirit, you cannot bind men and women down to narrow rules of conduct which are proper and right in times of peace,' and you sent help and cheer to the Irish people in their struggle for greater freedom.

Why, then, should not I come to ask for help for British women? Whatever helps them is going to help women all over the world. It will be the hastening of your victory. It has not as yet been necessary in the United States for women to be militant in the sense that we are, and perhaps one of the reasons why it is not necessary and why it may never be necessary is that we are doing the militant work for you. And we are glad to do that work. We are proud to do that work. If there are any men who are fighters in this hall, any men who have taken part in warfare, I tell you, gentlemen, that amongst the other good things that you, consciously or unconsciously, have kept from women, you have kept the joy of battle.

We know the joy of battle. When we have come out of the gates of Holloway at the point of death, battered, starved, forcibly fed as some of our women have been—their mouths forced open by iron gags—their bodies bruised, they have felt when the prison bars were broken and the doors have opened, even at the point of death, they have felt the joy of battle and the exultation of victory.

People have said that women could never vote, never share in the government, because government rests upon force. We have proved that is not true. Government rests not upon force; government rests upon the consent of the governed; and the weakest woman, the very poorest woman, if she withholds her consent cannot be governed.

They sent me to prison, to penal servitude for three years. I came out of prison at the end of nine days. I broke my prison bars. Four times they took me back again; four times I burst the prison door open again. And I left England openly to come and visit America, with only three or four weeks of the three years' sentence of penal servitude served. Have we not proved, then, that they cannot govern human beings who withhold their consent?

And so we are glad we have had the fighting experience, and we are glad to do all the fighting for all the women all over the world. All that we ask of you is to back us up. We ask you to show that although, perhaps, you may not mean to fight as we do, yet you understand the meaning of our fight; that you realise we are women fighting for a great idea; that we wish the betterment of the human race, and that we believe this betterment is coming through the emancipation and uplifting of women.

✦ Reading 25 ✦

The Ladies' Paradise

Emile Zola

After the death of her parents, Denise arrives from the provinces with her young brothers to live in Paris with her uncle, who has commercial connections. Mesmerized by the extravagant Paris department stores, she arranges for a position in one of them, The Ladies' Paradise.

The following Monday, the 10th of October, a clear, victorious sun pierced the grey clouds which had darkened Paris during the previous week. It had drizzled all the previous night, a sort of watery mist, the humidity of which dirtied the streets; but in the early morning, thanks to the sharp wind which was driving the clouds away, the pavement had become drier, and the blue sky had a limpid, spring-like gaiety.

Thus The Ladies' Paradise, after eight o'clock, blazed forth beneath the clear rays of the sun, in all the glory of its great sale of winter novelties. Flags were flying at the door, and pieces of woollens were flapping about in the fresh morning air, animating the Place Gaillon with the bustle of a country fair; whilst in both streets the windows developed symphonies of displays, the clearness of the glass showing up still further the brilliant tones. It was like a debauch of colour, a street pleasure which burst forth there, a wealth of goods publicly displayed, where everybody could go and feast their eyes.

But at this hour very few people entered, only a few rare customers, housewives of the neighbourhood, women desirous of avoiding the afternoon crush. Behind the stuffs which decorated it, one could feel the shop to be empty, under arms and waiting for customers, with its waxed floors and counters overflowing with goods.

The busy morning crowd barely glanced at the windows, without lingering a moment. In the Rue Neuve-Saint-Augustin and in the Place Gaillon, where the carriages were to take their stand, there were only two cabs at nine o'clock. The inhabitants of the district, especially the small traders, stirred up by such a show of streamers and decorations, formed little groups in the doorways, at the corners of the streets, gazing at the shop, making bitter remarks. What most filled them with indignation was the sight of one of the four delivery vans just introduced by Mouret, which was standing in the Rue de la Michodière, in front of the delivery office. They were green, picked out with yellow and red, their brilliantly varnished panels sparkling in the sun with the brightness of purple and gold. This van, with its brand-new medley of colours, the name of the house painted on each side, and surmounted with an advertisement of the day's sale, finished by going off at a trot, drawn by a splendid horse, after being filled up with the previous night's parcels; and Baudu, who was standing on the threshold of The Old Elbeuf, watched it as far as the boulevard, where it disappeared, to spread all over Paris in a starry radiance the hated name of The Ladies' Paradise.

However, a few cabs were arriving and forming a line. Every time a customer entered, there was a movement amongst the shop messengers, who were drawn up under the lofty doorway, dressed in livery consisting of a light green coat and trousers, and striped red and yellow waistcoat. Jouve, the inspector and retired captain, was also there, in a frock-coat and white tie, wearing his decoration like a sign of respectability and probity, receiving the ladies with a gravely polite air, bending over them to point out the

From: Emile Zola, *The Ladies' Paradise* (Berkeley: University of California Press, 1992), pp. 77–82.

departments. Then they disappeared in the vestibule, which was transformed into an oriental saloon.

From the very threshold it was a marvel, a surprise, which enchanted all of them. It was Mouret who had been struck with this idea. He was the first to buy, in the Levant, at very advantageous rates, a collection of old and new carpets, articles which up to the present had only been sold at curiosity shops, at high prices; and he intended to flood the market with these goods, selling them at a little over cost price, simply drawing from them a splendid decoration destined to attract the best class of art customers to his establishment. From the centre of the Place Gaillon could be seen this oriental saloon, composed solely of carpets and door curtains which had been hung under his orders. The ceiling was covered with a quantity of Smyrna carpets, the complicated designs of which stood out boldly on a red ground. Then from each side there hung Syrian and Karamanian door-curtains, speckled with green, yellow, and vermilion; Diarbekir door-curtains of a commoner type, rough to the touch, like shepherds' cloaks; besides these there were carpets which could be used as door-curtains and hangings—long Ispahan, Teheran, and Kermancha rugs, the larger Schoumaka and Madras carpets, a strange florescence of peonies and palms, the fancy let loose in a garden of dreams. On the floor were more carpets, a heap of greasy fleeces: in the centre was an Agra carpet, an extraordinary article with a white ground and a broad delicate blue border, through which ran violet-coloured ornaments of exquisite design. Everywhere there was an immense display of marvellous fabrics; Mecca carpets with a velvety reflection, prayer carpets from Daghestan with a symbolic point, Kurdistan carpets covered with blossoming flowers; and finally, piled up in a corner, a heap of Gherdes, Koula, and Kirchur rugs from fifteen francs a piece.

This sumptuous pacha's tent was furnished with divans and arm-chairs, made with camel sacks, some ornamented with many-coloured lozenges, others with primitive roses. Turkey, Arabia, and the Indies were all there. They had emptied the palaces, plundered the mosques and bazaars. A barbarous gold tone prevailed in the weft of the old carpets, the faded tints of which still preserved a sombre warmth, as of an extinguished furnace, a beautiful burnt hue suggestive of the old masters. Visions of the East floated beneath the luxury of this barbarous art, amid the strong odour which the old wools had retained of the country of vermin and of the rising sun.

In the morning at eight o'clock, when Denise, who was to commence on that very Monday, had crossed the oriental saloon, she stood there, lost in astonishment, unable to recognise the shop entrance, entirely overcome by this harem-like decoration planted at the door. A messenger having shown her to the top of the house, and handed her over to Madame Cabin, who cleaned and looked after the rooms, this person installed her in No. 7, where her box had already been put. It was a narrow cell, opening on the roof by a skylight, furnished with a small bed, a walnut-wood wardrobe, a toilet-table, and two chairs. Twenty similar rooms ran along the convent-like corridor, painted yellow; and, out of the thirty-five young ladies in the house, the twenty who had no friends in Paris slept there, whilst the remaining fifteen lodged outside, a few with borrowed aunts and cousins. Denise at once took off her shabby woollen dress, worn thin by brushing and mended at the sleeves, the only one she had brought from Valognes; she then put on the uniform of her department, a black silk dress which had been altered for her and which she found ready on the bed. This dress was still too large, too wide across the shoulders; but she was so hurried in her emotion that she paid no heed to these details of coquetry. She had never worn silk before. When she went downstairs again, dressed up, uncomfortable, she looked at the shining skirt, feeling ashamed of the noisy rustling of the silk.

Down below, as she was entering her department, a quarrel burst out. She heard Clara say, in a shrill voice:

"Madame, I came in before her."

"It isn't true," replied Marguerite. "She pushed past me at the door, but I had already one foot in the room."

It was for the inscription on the list of turns, which regulated the sales. The saleswomen wrote their names on a slate in the order of their arrival, and whenever one of them had served a customer, she re-wrote her name beneath the others. Madame Aurélie finished by deciding in Marguerite's favour.

"Always some injustice here!" muttered Clara, furiously.

But Denise's entry reconciled these young ladies. They looked at her, then smiled to each other. How could a person truss herself up in that way! The young girl went and awkwardly wrote her name on the list, where she found herself last. Meanwhile, Madame Aurélie was examining her with an anxious face. She could not help saying:

"My dear, two like you could get into your dress; you must have it taken in. Besides, you don't know how to dress yourself. Come here and let me arrange you a bit."

And she placed herself before one of the tall glasses alternating with the doors of the cupboards containing the dresses. The vast apartment, surrounded by these glasses and the wood-work in carved oak, the floor covered with red Wilton carpet of a large pattern, resembled the commonplace drawing-room of an hotel, traversed by a continual stream of travellers. The young ladies completed the resemblance, dressed in the regulation silk, promenading their commercial charms about, without ever sitting down on the dozen chairs reserved for the customers. All wore between two buttonholes of the body of their dresses, as if stuck in their bosoms, a long pencil, with its point in the air; and half out of their pockets, could be seen the white cover of the book of debit-notes. Several risked wearing jewellery—rings, brooches, chains; but their great coquetry, the luxury they all struggled for in the forced uniformity of their dress, was their bare hair, quantities of it, augmented by plaits and chignons when their own did not suffice, combed, curled, and decked out in every way.

"Pull the waist down in front," said Madame Aurélie. "There, you have now no hump on your back. And your hair, how can you massacre it like that? It would be superb, if you only took a little trouble."

This was, in fact, Denise's only beauty. Of a beautiful flaxen hue, it fell down to her ankles; and when she did it up, it was so troublesome that she simply rolled it in a knot, keeping it together under the strong teeth of a bone comb. Clara, greatly annoyed by this head of hair, affected to laugh at it, so strange did it look, twisted up anyhow in its savage grace. She made a sign to a saleswoman in the under-linen department, a girl with a large face and agreeable manner. The two departments, which were close together, were in continual hostility; but the young ladies sometimes joined together in laughing at other people.

"Mademoiselle Cugnot, just look at that mane," said Clara, whom Marguerite was nudging, feigning also to be on the point of bursting out laughing.

But Mademoiselle Cugnot was not in the humour for joking. She had been looking at Denise for a moment, and she remembered what she had suffered herself during the first few months of her arrival in the establishment.

"Well, what?" said she. "Everybody hasn't got a mane like that!"

And she returned to her place, leaving the two others very crestfallen. Denise, who had heard all, followed her with a look of thanks, while Madame Aurélie gave our heroine a book of debit-notes with her name on it, saying: "To-morrow you'll get yourself up better; and, now, try and pick up the ways of the house, wait your turn for selling. To-day's work will be very hard; we shall be able to judge of your capabilities."

However, the department still remained deserted; very few customers came up at this early hour. The young ladies reserved themselves, prudently preparing for the fatigues of the afternoon. Denise, intimidated by the thought that they were watching her, sharpened her pencil, for the sake of something to do; then, imitating the others, she stuck it into her bosom, between two buttonholes, and summoned up all her courage, determined to conquer a position. The previous evening they had told her she entered as a probationer, that is to say without any fixed salary; she would simply have the commission and a certain allowance on everything she sold. But she fully hoped to earn twelve hundred francs a year in this way, knowing that the good saleswomen earned as much as two thousand, when they liked to take the trouble. Her expenses were regulated; a hundred francs a month would enable her to pay Pépé's board and lodging, assist Jean, who did not earn a sou, and procure some clothes and linen for herself. But, in order to attain this large sum, she would have to show herself industrious and pushing, taking no notice of the ill-will displayed by those around her, fighting for her share, even snatching it from her comrades if necessary. As she was thus working herself up for the struggle, a tall young man, passing the department, smiled at her; and when she saw it was Deloche, who had been engaged in the lace department the previous day, she returned his smile, happy at the friendship which thus presented itself, accepting this smile as a good omen.

At half-past nine a bell rang for the first luncheon. Then a fresh peal announced the second; and still no customers appeared. The second-hand Madame Frédéric, who, in her disagreeable widow's harshness, delighted in prophesying disasters, declared in short sentences that the day was lost, that they would not see a soul, that they might close the cupboards and go away; predictions which darkened Marguerite's flat face, she being a girl who looked sharp after her profits, whilst Clara, with her runaway-horse appearance, was already dreaming of an excursion to the Verrières woods, if the house failed. As for Madame Aurélie, she was there, silent and serious, promenading her Caesar-like mask about the empty department, like a general who has a certain responsibility in victory and in defeat. About eleven o'clock a few ladies appeared. Denise's turn for serving had arrived. Just at that moment a customer came up.

"The fat old girl from the country," murmured Marguerite.

It was a woman of forty-five, who occasionally journeyed to Paris from the depths of some out-of-the-way place. There she saved up for months; then, hardly out of the train, she made straight for The Ladies' Paradise, and spent all her savings. She very rarely ordered anything by letter, she liked to see and handle the goods, and laid in a stock of everything, even down to needles, which she said were excessively dear in her small town. The whole staff knew her, that her name was Boutarel, and that she lived at Albi, but troubled no further about her, neither about her position nor her mode of life.

"How do you do, madame?" graciously asked Madame Aurélie, who had come forward. "And what can we show you? You shall be attended to at once." Then, turning round: "Now, young ladies!"

Denise approached; but Clara had sprung forward. As a rule, she was very careless and idle, not caring about the money she earned in the shop, as she could get plenty outside, without trouble. But the idea of doing the new-comer out of a good customer spurred her on. . . .

European Civilization, 1850–1914

This brooding image of the German Philosopher Friedrich Nietzche, who challenged Christian morality and conventional values, suggests European culture's loss of certainty at the turn of the 20th century.

EUROPEAN CIVILIZATION, 1850–1914

European civilization changed dramatically in the decades before World War I. Rapid industrial developments and the rise of mass politics transformed economic, social, and political life. Despite severe economic fluctuations, the introduction of the internal combustion engine, the telephone, and the gramophone constituted a virtual second industrial revolution toward century's end. Europe's population increased and more people moved to cities. The late nineteenth century also witnessed the growing influence of political parties. European lives and views altered irrevocably. After World War I, some reminisced about the good old days, "la belle époche," while others recalled, more darkly, the "fin de siècle," an end of the century cultural crisis.

In 1859 Charles Darwin (1809–1882) published *The Origin of Species,* which offered a scientific account for the differentiation of species. Minute differences adapted individuals within existing species to specific environments and, claimed Darwin, promoted survival. Widespread varied cumulative adaptations eventually resulted in species proliferation. Change in the natural world resembled a sort of competition, an approach that reflected industrial Europe's capitalist, laissez-faire economics. Darwin did not apply his theories to human societies but others quickly did. By the late nineteenth century, evolutionary theory heavily influenced people's views of one another. This and other factors associated with the demise of traditional values led to a cultural crisis across Europe, accompanied by an increase in nervous disorders, alcoholism, and drug use. Sigmund Freud (1856–1939), a Viennese doctor, used his *Lectures on Psychoanalysis* (1915–1917) to explore the human unconscious as a basis for society's problems, a strategy that implied the inadequacy of the Enlightenment's rationalism. Friedrich Nietzsche (1844–1900) exceeded Freud's antirationalism by arguing in *Beyond Good and Evil* (1886) that humankind progressed only under the often brutal leadership of outstanding individuals. He denounced concepts of "equal and inalienable rights to life, liberty, and the pursuit of happiness" and urged instead an aristocracy of "supermen" willing to act decisively and mercilessly for humankind's betterment.

✦ Reading 26 ✦

The Origin of Species

Charles Darwin

Recapitulation and Conclusion

As this whole volume is one long argument, it may be convenient to the reader to have the leading facts and inferences briefly recapitulated.

That many and serious objections may be advanced against the theory of descent with modification through variation and natural selection, I do not deny. I have endeavoured to give to them their full force. Nothing at first can appear more difficult to believe than that the more complex organs and instincts have been perfected, not by means superior to, though analogous with, human reason, but by the accumulation of innumerable slight variations, each good for the individual possessor. Nevertheless, this difficulty, though appearing to our imagination insuperably great, cannot be considered real if we admit the following propositions, namely, that all parts of the organisation and instincts offer, at least, individual differences—that there is a struggle for existence leading to the preservation of profitable deviations of structure or instinct—and, lastly, that gradations in the state of perfection of each organ may have existed, each good of its kind. The truth of these propositions cannot, I think, be disputed.

It is, no doubt, extremely difficult even to conjecture by what gradations many structures have been perfected, more especially amongst broken and failing groups of organic beings, which have suffered much extinction, but we see so many strange gradations in nature, that we ought to be extremely cautious in saying that any organ or instinct, or any whole structure, could not have arrived at its present state by many graduated steps. There are, it must be admitted, cases of special difficulty opposed to the theory of natural selection; and one of the most curious of these is the existence in the same community of two or three defined castes of workers or sterile female ants; but I have attempted to show how these difficulties can be mastered.

* * *

Turning to geographical distribution, the difficulties encountered on the theory of descent with modification are serious enough. All the individuals of the same species, and all the species of the same genus, or even higher group, are descended from common parents; and therefore, in however distant and isolated parts of the world they may now be found, they must in the course of successive generations have travelled from some one point to all the others. We are often wholly unable even to conjecture how this could have been effected. Yet, as we have reason to believe that some species have retained the same specific form for very long periods of time, immensely long as measured by years, too much stress ought not to be laid on the occasional wide diffusion of the same species; for during very long periods there will always have been a good chance for wide migration by many means. A broken or interrupted range may often be accounted for by the extinction of the species in the intermediate regions. It cannot be denied that we are as yet very ignorant as to the full extent of the various climatal and geographical changes which have affected the earth during modern periods; and such changes will often have facilitated migration. As an example, I have attempted to show how potent has been the influence of the Glacial period on the distribution of the same and of allied species throughout the world. We are as yet profoundly ignorant of the many occasional means of transport. With respect to distinct species of the same genus inhabiting distant and isolated regions, as the

---

From: Charles Darwin, *The Origin of Species by Means of Natural Selection; or, The Preservation of Favored Races in the Struggle for Life* (New York: The Modern Library), p. 353, pp. 355–374.

process of modification has necessarily been slow, all the means of migration will have been possible during a very long period; and consequently the difficulty of the wide diffusion of the species of the same genus is in some degree lessened.

As according to the theory of natural selection an interminable number of intermediate forms must have existed, linking together all the species in each group by gradations as fine as are our existing varieties, it may be asked: Why do we not see these linking forms all around us? Why are not all organic beings blended together in an inextricable chaos? With respect to existing forms, we should remember that we have no right to expect (excepting in rare cases) to discover *directly* connecting links between them, but only between each and some extinct and supplanted form. Even on a wide area, which has during a long period remained continuous, and of which the climatic and other conditions of life change insensibly in proceeding from a district occupied by one species into another district occupied by a closely allied species, we have no just right to expect often to find intermediate varieties in the intermediate zones. For we have reason to believe that only a few species of a genus ever undergo change; the other species becoming utterly extinct and leaving no modified progeny. Of the species which do change, only a few within the same country change at the same time; and all modifications are slowly effected. I have also shown that the intermediate varieties which probably at first existed in the intermediate zones, would be liable to be supplanted by the allied forms on either hand; for the latter, from existing in greater numbers, would generally be modified and improved at a quicker rate than the intermediate varieties, which existed in lesser numbers; so that the intermediate varieties would, in the long run, be supplanted and exterminated.

On this doctrine of the extermination of an infinitude of connecting links, between the living and extinct inhabitants of the world, and at each successive period between the extinct and still older species, why is not every geological formation charged with such links? Why does not every collection of fossil remains afford plain evidence of the gradation and mutation of the forms of life? Although geological research has undoubtedly revealed the former existence of many links, bringing numerous forms of life much closer together, it does not yield the infinitely many fine gradations between past and present species required on the theory; and this is the most obvious of the many objections which may be urged against it. Why, again, do whole groups of allied species appear, though this appearance is often false, to have come in suddenly on the successive geological stages? Although we now know that organic beings appeared on this globe, at a period incalculably remote, long before the lowest bed of the Cambrian system was deposited, why do we not find beneath this system great piles of strata stored with the remains of the progenitors of the Cambrian fossils? For on the theory, such strata must somewhere have been deposited at these ancient and utterly unknown epochs of the world's history.

I can answer these questions and objections only on the supposition that the geological record is far more imperfect than most geologists believe. The number of specimens in all our museums is absolutely as nothing compared with the countless generations of countless species which have certainly existed. The parent-form of any two or more species would not be in all its characters directly intermediate between its modified offspring, any more than the rock-pigeon is directly intermediate in crop and tail between its descendants, the pouter and fantail pigeons. We should not be able to recognise a species as the parent of another and modified species, if we were to examine the two ever so closely, unless we possessed most of the intermediate links; and owing to the imperfection of the geological record, we have no just right to expect to find so many links. If two or three, or even more linking forms were discovered, they would simply be ranked by many naturalists as so many new species, more especially if found in different geological sub-stages, let their differences be ever so slight. Numerous existing doubtful forms could be named which are probably varieties; but who will pretend that in future ages so many fossil links will be discovered, that naturalists will be able to decide whether or not these doubtful forms ought to be called varieties? Only a small portion of the world has been geologically explored. Only organic beings of certain classes can be preserved in a fossil condition, at least in any great number. Many species when once formed never undergo any further change but become extinct without leaving modified descendants; and the periods, during which species have undergone modification, though long as measured by years, have probably been short in comparison with the periods during which they retain the same form. It is the dominant and widely ranging species which vary most frequently and vary most, and varieties are often at first local—both causes rendering the discovery of intermediate links in any one formation less likely. Local varieties will not spread into other and distant regions until they are considerably modified and improved; and when they have spread, and are discovered in a geological formation, they appear as if suddenly created there, and will be simply classed as new species. Most formations have been intermittent in their accumulation; and their duration has probably been shorter than the average duration of specific forms. Successive formations are in most cases separated from each other by blank intervals of time of great length; for fossiliferous formations thick enough to resist future degradations can as a general rule be accumulated only where much sediment is deposited on the subsiding bed of the sea. During the alternate periods of elevation and of stationary level the record will generally be blank. During these latter periods there will probably be more variability in the forms of life; during periods of subsidence, more extinction.

With respect to the absence of strata rich in fossils beneath the Cambrian formation, I can recur only to the hypothesis given in the tenth chapter; namely, that though our continents and oceans have endured for an enormous period in nearly their present relative positions, we have no reason to assume that this has always been the case; consequently formations much older than any now known may lie buried beneath the great oceans. With respect to the lapse of time not having been sufficient since our planet was consolidated for the assumed amount of organic change, and this objection, as urged by Sir William Thompson, is probably one of the gravest as yet advanced, I can only say, firstly, that we do not know at what rate species change as measured by years, and secondly, that many philosophers are not as yet willing to admit that we know enough of the constitution of the universe and of the interior of our globe to speculate with safety on its past duration.

That the geological record is imperfect all will admit; but that it is imperfect to the degree required by our theory, few will be inclined to admit. If we look to long enough intervals of time, geology plainly declares that species have all changed; and they have changed in the manner required by the theory, for they have changed slowly and in a graduated manner. We clearly see this in the fossil remains from consecutive formations invariably being much more closely related to each other, than are the fossils from widely separated formations.

Such is the sum of the several chief objections and difficulties which may be justly urged against the theory; and I have now briefly recapitulated the answers and explanations which, as far as I can see, may be given. I have felt these difficulties far too heavily during many years to doubt their weight. But it deserves especial notice that the more important objections relate to questions on which we are confessedly ignorant; nor do we know how ignorant we are. We do not know all the possible transitional gradations between the simplest and the most perfect organs; It cannot be pretended that we know all the varied means of Distribution during the long lapse of years, or that we know how imperfect is the Geological Record. Serious as these several objections are, in my judgment they are by no means sufficient to overthrow the theory of descent with subsequent modification.

Now let us turn to the other side of the argument. Under domestication we see much variability, caused, or at least excited, by changed conditions of life; but often in so obscure a manner, that we are tempted to consider the variations as spontaneous. Variability is governed by many complex laws,—by correlated growth, compensation, the increased use and disuse of parts, and the definite action of the surrounding conditions. There is much difficulty in ascertaining how largely our domestic productions have been modified; but we may safely infer that the amount has been large, and that modifications can be inherited for long periods. As long as the conditions of life remain the same, we have reason to believe that a modification, which has already been inherited for many generations, may continue to be inherited for an almost infinite number of generations. On the other hand, we have evidence that variability when it has once come into play, does not cease under domestication for a very long period; nor do we know that it ever ceases, for new varieties are still occasionally produced by our oldest domesticated productions.

Variability is not actually caused by man; he only unintentionally exposes organic beings to new conditions of life, and then nature acts on the organisation and causes it to vary. But man can and does select the variations given to him by nature, and thus accumulates them in any desired manner. He thus adapts animals and plants for his own benefit or pleasure. He may do this methodically, or he may do it unconsciously by preserving the individuals most useful or pleasing to him without any intention of altering the breed. It is certain that he can largely influence the character of a breed by selecting, in each successive generation, individual differences so slight as to be inappreciable except by an educated eye. This unconscious process of selection has been the great agency in the formation of the most distinct and useful domestic breeds. That many breeds produced by man have to a large extent the character of natural species, is shown by the inextricable doubts whether many of them are varieties or aboriginally distinct species.

There is no reason why the principles which have acted so efficiently under domestication should not have acted under nature. In the survival of favoured individuals and races, during the constantly-recurrent Struggle for Existence, we see a powerful and ever-acting form of Selection. The struggle for existence inevitably follows from the high geometrical ratio of increase which is common to all organic beings. This high rate of increase is proved by calculation,—by the rapid increase of many animals and plants during a succession of peculiar seasons, and when naturalised in new countries. More individuals are born than can possibly survive. A grain in the balance may determine which individuals shall live and which shall die,—which variety or species shall increase in number, and which shall decrease, or finally become extinct. As the individuals of the same species come in all respects into the closest competition with each other, the struggle will generally be most severe between them; it will be almost equally severe between the varieties of the same species, and next in severity between the species of the same genus. On the other hand the struggle will often be severe between beings remote in the scale of nature. The slightest advantage in certain individuals, at any age or during any season, over those with which they come into competition, or better adaptation in however slight a degree to the surrounding physical conditions, will, in the long run, turn the balance.

With animals having separated sexes, there will be in most cases a struggle between the males for the possession of the females. The most vigorous males, or those which have most successfully struggled with their conditions of life, will generally leave most progeny. But success will often depend on the males having special weapons, or means of defence, or charms; and a slight advantage will lead to victory.

As geology plainly proclaims that each land has undergone great physical changes, we might have expected to find that organic beings have varied under nature, in the same way as they have varied under domestication. And if there has been any variability under nature, it would be an unaccountable fact if natural selection had not come into play. It has often been asserted, but the assertion is incapable of proof, that the amount of variation under nature is a strictly limited quantity. Man, though acting on external characters alone and often capriciously, can produce within a short period a great result by adding up mere individual differences in his domestic productions; and every one admits that species present individual differences. But, besides such differences, all naturalists admit that natural varieties exist, which are considered sufficiently distinct to be worthy of record in systematic works. No one has drawn any clear distinction between individual differences and slight varieties; or between more plainly marked varieties and sub-species, and species. On separate continents, and on different parts of the same continent when divided by barriers of any kind, and on outlying islands, what a multitude of forms exist, which some experienced naturalists rank as varieties, others as geographical races or sub-species, and others as distinct, though closely allied species!

If then, animals and plants do vary, let it be ever so slightly or slowly, why should not variations or individual differences, which are in any way beneficial, be preserved and accumulated through natural selection, or the survival of the fittest? If man can by patience select variations useful to him, why, under changing and complex conditions of life, should not variations useful to nature's living products often arise, and be preserved or selected? What limit can be put to this power, acting during long ages and rigidly scrutinising the whole constitution, structure, and habits of each creature,—favouring the good and rejecting the bad? I can see no limit to this power, in slowly and beautifully adapting each form to the most complex relations of life. The theory of natural selection, even if we look no farther than this, seems to be in the highest degree probable. I have already recapitulated, as fairly as I could, the opposed difficulties and objections: now let us turn to the special facts and arguments in favour of the theory.

On the view that species are only strongly marked and permanent varieties, and that each species first existed as a variety, we can see why it is that no line of demarcation can be drawn between species, commonly supposed to have been produced by special acts of creation, and varieties which are acknowledged to have been produced by secondary laws. On this same view we can understand how it is that in a region where many species of a genus have been produced, and where they now flourish, these same species should present many varieties; for where the manufactory of species has been active, we might expect, as a general rule, to find it still in action; and this is the case if varieties be incipient species. Moreover, the species of the larger genera, which afford the greater number of varieties or incipient species, retain to a certain degree the character of varieties; for they differ from each other by a less amount of difference than do the species of smaller genera. The closely allied species also of the larger genera apparently have restricted ranges, and in their affinities they are clustered in little groups round other species—in both respects resembling varieties. These are strange relations on the view that each species was independently created, but are intelligible if each existed first as a variety.

As each species tends by its geometrical rate of reproduction to increase inordinately in number; and as the modified descendants of each species will be enabled to increase by as much as they become more diversified in habits and structure, so as to be able to seize on many and widely different places in the economy of nature, there will be a constant tendency in natural selection to preserve the most divergent offspring of any one species. Hence, during a long-continued course of modification, the slight differences characteristic of varieties of the same species, tend to be augmented into the greater differences characteristic of the species of the same genus. New and improved varieties will inevitably supplant and exterminate the older, less improved, and intermediate varieties; and thus species are rendered to a large extent defined and distinct objects. Dominant species belonging to the larger groups within each class tend to give birth to new and dominant forms; so that each large group tends to become still larger, and at the same time more divergent in character. But as all groups cannot thus go on increasing in size, for the world would not hold them, the more dominant groups beat the less dominant. This tendency in the large groups to go on increasing in size and diverging in character, together with the inevitable contingency of much extinction, explains the arrangement of all the forms of life in groups subordinate to groups, all within a few great classes, which has prevailed throughout all time. This grand fact of the grouping of all organic beings under what is called the Natural System, is utterly inexplicable on the theory of creation.

As natural selection acts solely by accumulating slight, successive, favourable variations, it can produce no great or sudden modifications; it can act only by short and slow steps. Hence, the canon of "Natura non facit saltum," which every fresh addition to our knowledge tends to confirm, is on this theory intelligible. We can see why throughout nature the same general end is gained by an almost infinite diversity of means, for every peculiarity when once acquired is long inherited, and structures already modified in many different ways have to be adapted for the same general purpose. We can, in short, see why nature is prodigal in variety, though niggard in innovation. But why this should be a law of nature if each species has been independently created no man can explain.

Many other facts are, as it seems to me, explicable on this theory. How strange it is that a bird, under the form of a woodpecker, should prey on insects on the ground; that upland geese which rarely or never swim should possess webbed feet; that a thrush-like bird should dive and feed on sub-aquatic insects; and that a petrel should have the habits and structure fitting it for the life of an awk! and so in endless other cases. But on the view of each species constantly trying to increase in number, with natural selection always ready to adapt the slowly varying descendants of each to any unoccupied or ill-occupied place in nature, these facts cease to be strange, or might even have been anticipated.

We can to a certain extent understand how it is that there is so much beauty throughout nature; for this may be largely attributed to the agency of selection. That beauty, according to our sense of it, is not universal, must be admitted by every one who will look at some venomous snakes, at some fishes, and at certain hideous bats with a distorted resemblance to the human face. Sexual selection has given the most brilliant colours, elegant patterns, and other ornaments to the males, and sometimes to both sexes of many birds, butterflies, and other animals. With birds it has often rendered the voice of the male musical to the female, as well as to our ears. Flowers and fruit have been rendered conspicuous by brilliant colours in contrast with the green foliage, in order that the flowers may be readily seen, visited and fertilised by insects, and the seeds disseminated by birds. How it comes that certain colours, sounds, and forms should give pleasure to man and the lower animals,—that is, how the sense of beauty in its simplest form was first acquired,—we do not know any more than how certain odours and flavours were first rendered agreeable.

As natural selection acts by competition, it adapts and improves the inhabitants of each country only in relation to their co-inhabitants; so that we need feel no surprise at the species of any one country, although on the ordinary view supposed to have been created and specially adapted for that country, being beaten and supplanted by the naturalised productions from another land. Nor ought we to marvel if all the contrivances in nature be not, as far as we can judge, absolutely perfect, as in the case even of the human eye; or if some of them be abhorrent to our ideas of fitness. We need not marvel at the sting of the bee, when used against an enemy, causing the bee's own death; at drones being produced in such great numbers for one single act, and being then slaughtered by their sterile sisters; at the astonishing waste of pollen by our fir-trees; at the instinctive hatred of the queen-bee for her own fertile daughters; at the ichneumonidæ feeding within the living bodies of caterpillars; or at other such cases. The wonder indeed is, on the theory of natural selection, that more cases of the want of absolute perfection have not been detected.

The complex and little known laws governing the production of varieties are the same, as far as we can judge, with the laws which have governed the production of distinct species. In both cases physical conditions seem to have produced some direct and definite effect, but how much we cannot say. Thus, when varieties enter any new station, they occasionally assume some of the characters proper to the species of that station. With both varieties and species, use and disuse seem to have produced a considerable effect; for it is impossible to resist this conclusion when we look, for instance, at the logger-headed duck, which has wings incapable of flight, in nearly the same condition as in the domestic duck; or when we look at the burrowing tucu-tucu, which is occasionally blind, and then at certain moles, which are habitually blind and have their eyes covered with skin; or when we look at the blind animals inhabiting the dark caves of America and Europe. With varieties and species, correlated variation seems to have played an important part, so that when one part has been modified other parts have been necessarily modified. With both varieties and species, reversions to long-lost characters occasionally occur. How inexplicable on the theory of creation is the occasional appearance of stripes on the shoulders and legs of the several species of the horse-genus and of their hybrids! How simply is this fact explained if we believe that these species are all descended from a striped progenitor, in the same manner as the several domestic breeds of the pigeon are descended from the blue and barred rock-pigeon!

On the ordinary view of each species having been independently created, why should specific characters, or those by which the species of the same genus differ from each other, be more variable than generic characters in which they all agree? Why, for instance, should the colour of a flower be more likely to vary in any one species of a genus, if the other species possess differently coloured flowers, than if all possessed the same coloured flowers? If species are only well-marked varieties, of which the characters have become in a high degree permanent, we can understand this fact; for they have already varied since they branched off from a common progenitor in certain characters, by which they have come to be specifically distinct from each other; therefore these same characters would be more likely again to vary than the generic characters which have been inherited without change for an immense period. It is inexplicable on the theory of creation why a part developed in a very unusual manner in one species alone of a genus, and therefore, as we may naturally infer, of great importance to that species, should be eminently liable to variation; but, on our view, this part has undergone, since the several species branched off from a common progenitor, an unusual amount of variability and modification, and therefore we might expect the part generally to be still variable. But a part may be developed in the most unusual manner, like the wing of a bat, and yet not be more variable than any other structure, if the part be common to many subordinate forms, that is, if it has been inherited for a very long period; for in this case, it will have been rendered constant by long-continued natural selection.

Glancing at instincts, marvellous as some are, they offer no greater difficulty than do corporeal structures on the theory of the natural selection of successive slight, but profitable modifications. We can thus understand why nature moves by graduated steps in endowing different animals of the same class with their several instincts. I have attempted to show how much light the principle of gradation throws on the admirable architectural powers of the hive-bee. Habit no doubt often comes into play in modifying instincts; but it certainly is not indispensable, as we see in the case of neuter insects, which leave no progeny to inherit the effects of long-continued habit. On the view of all the species of the same genus having descended from a common parent, and having inherited much in common, we can understand how it is that allied species, when placed under widely different conditions of life, yet follow nearly the same instincts; why the thrushes of tropical and temperate South America, for instance, line their nests with mud like our British species. On the view of instincts having been slowly acquired through natural selection, we need not marvel at some instincts being not perfect and liable to mistakes, and at many instincts causing other animals to suffer.

If species be only well-marked and permanent varieties, we can at once see why their crossed offspring should follow the same complex laws in their degrees and kinds of resemblance to their parents,—in being absorbed into each other by successive crosses, and in other such points,—as do the crossed offspring of acknowledged varieties. This similarity would be a strange fact, if species had been independently created and varieties had been produced through secondary laws.

If we admit that the geological record is imperfect to an extreme degree, then the facts, which the record does give, strongly support the theory of descent with modification. New species have come on the stage slowly and at successive intervals; and the amount of change, after equal intervals of time, is widely different in different groups. The extinction of species and of whole groups of species which has played so conspicuous a part in the history of the organic world, almost inevitably follows from the principle of natural selection; for old forms are supplanted by new and improved forms. Neither single species nor groups of species reappear when the chain of ordinary generation is once broken. The gradual diffusion of dominant forms, with the slow modification of their descendants, causes the forms of life, after long intervals of time, to appear as if they had changed simultaneously throughout the world. The fact of the fossil remains of each formation being in some degree intermediate in character between the fossils in the formations above and below, is simply explained by their intermediate position in the chain of descent. The grand fact that all extinct beings can be classed with all recent beings, naturally follows from the living and the extinct being the offspring of common parents. As species have generally diverged in character during their long course of descent and modification, we can understand why it is that the more ancient forms, or early progenitors of each group, so often occupy a position in some degree intermediate between existing groups. Recent forms are generally looked upon as being, on the whole, higher in the scale of organisation than ancient forms; and they must be higher, in so far as the later and more improved forms have conquered the older and less improved forms in the struggle for life; they have also generally had their organs more specialised for different functions. This fact is perfectly compatible with numerous beings still retaining simple and but little improved structures, fitted for simple conditions of life; it is likewise compatible with some forms having retrograded in organisation, by having become at each stage of descent better fitted for new and degraded habits of life. Lastly, the wonderful law of the long endurance of allied forms on the same continent,—of marsupials in Australia, of edentata in America, and other such cases,—is intelligible, for within the same country the existing and the extinct will be closely allied by descent.

Looking to geographical distribution, if we admit that there has been during the long course of ages much migration from one part of the world to another, owing to former climatal and geographical changes and to the many occasional and unknown means of dispersal, then we can understand, on the theory of descent with modification, most of the great leading facts in Distribution. We can see why there should be so striking a parallelism in the distribution of organic beings throughout space, and in their geological succession throughout time; for in both cases the beings have been connected by the bond of ordinary generation, and the means of modification have been the same. We see the full meaning of the wonderful fact, which has struck every traveller, namely, that on the same continent, under the most diverse conditions, under heat and cold, on mountain and lowland, on deserts and marshes, most of the inhabitants within each great class are plainly related; for they are the descendants of the same progenitors and early colonists. On this same principle of former migration, combined in most cases with modification, we can understand, by the aid of the Glacial period, the identity of some few plants, and the close alliance of many others, on the most distant mountains, and in the northern and southern temperate zones; and likewise the close alliance of some of the inhabitants of the sea in the northern and southern temperate latitudes, though separated by the whole intertropical ocean. Although two countries may present physical conditions as closely similar as the same species ever require, we need feel no surprise at their inhabitants being widely different, if they have been for a long period completely sundered from each other; for as the relation of organism to organism is the most important of all relations, and as the two countries will have received colonists at various periods and in different proportions, from some other country or from each other, the course of modification in the two areas will inevitably have been different.

On this view of migration, with subsequent modification, we see why oceanic islands are inhabited by only few species, but of these, why many are peculiar or endemic forms. We clearly see why species belonging to those groups of animals which cannot cross wide spaces of the ocean, as frogs and terrestrial mammals, do not inhabit oceanic islands; and why, on the other hand, new and peculiar species of bats, animals which can traverse the ocean, are found on islands far distant from any continent. Such cases as the presence of peculiar species of bats on oceanic islands and the absence of all other terrestrial mammals, are facts utterly inexplicable on the theory of independent acts of creation.

The existence of closely allied or representative species in any two areas, implies, on the theory of descent with modification, that the same parent-forms formerly inhabited both areas; and we almost invariably find that wherever many closely allied species inhabit two areas, some identical species are still common to both. Wherever many closely allied yet distinct species occur, doubtful forms and varieties belonging to the same groups likewise occur. It is a rule of high generality that the inhabitants of each area are related to the inhabitants of the nearest source whence immigrants might have been derived. We see this in the striking relation of nearly all plants and animals of the Galapagos archipelago, of Juan Fernandez, and of the other American islands, to the plants and animals of the neighbouring American mainland; and of those of the Cape de Verde archipelago, and of the other African islands to the African mainland. It must be admitted that these facts receive no explanation on the theory of creation.

The fact, as we have seen, that all past and present organic beings can be arranged within a few great classes, in groups subordinate to groups, and with the extinct groups often falling in between the recent groups, is intelligible on the theory of natural selection with its contingencies of extinction and divergence of character. On these same principles we see how it is, that the mutual affinities of the forms within each class are so complex and circuitous. We see why certain characters are far more serviceable than others for classification;—why adaptive characters, though of paramount importance to the beings, are of hardly any importance in classification; why characters derived from rudimentary parts, though of no service to the beings, are often of high classificatory value; and why embryological characters are often the most valuable of all. The real affinities of all organic beings, in contradistinction to their adaptive resemblances, are due to inheritance or community of descent. The Natural System is a genealogical arrangement, with the acquired grades of difference, marked by the terms, varieties, species, genera, families, &c.; and we have to discover the lines of descent by the most permanent characters whatever they may be and of however slight vital importance.

The similar framework of bones in the hand of a man, wing of a bat, fin of the porpoise, and leg of the horse,—the same number of vertebræ forming the neck of the giraffe and of the elephant,—and innumerable other such facts, at once explain themselves on the theory of descent with slow and slight successive modifications. The similarity of pattern in the wing and in the leg of a bat, though used for such different purpose,—in the jaws and legs of a crab,—in the petals, stamens, and pistils of a flower, is likewise, to a large extent, intelligible on the view of the gradual modification of parts or organs, which were aboriginally alike in an early progenitor in each of these classes. On the principle of successive variations not always supervening at an early age, and being inherited at a corresponding not early period of life, we clearly see why the embryos of mammals, birds, reptiles, and fishes should be so closely similar, and so unlike the adult forms. We may cease marvelling at the embryo of an air-breathing mammal or bird having branchial slits and arteries running in loops, like those of a fish which has to breathe the air dissolved in water by the aid of well-developed branchiæ.

Disuse, aided sometimes by natural selection, will often have reduced organs when rendered useless under changed habits or conditions of life; and we can understand on this view the meaning of rudimentary organs. But disuse and selection will generally act on each creature, when it has come to maturity and has to play its full part in the struggle for existence, and will thus have little power on an organ during early life; hence the organ will not be reduced or rendered rudimentary at this early age. The calf, for instance, has inherited teeth, which never cut through the gums of the upper jaw, from an early progenitor having well-developed teeth; and we may believe, that the teeth in the mature animal were formerly reduced by disuse, owing to the tongue and palate, or lips. having become excellently fitted through natural selection to browse without their aid; whereas in the calf, the teeth have been left unaffected, and on the principle of inheritance at corresponding ages have been inherited from a remote period to the present day. On the view of each organism with all its separate parts having been specially created, how utterly inexplicable is it that organs bearing the plain stamp of inutility, such as the teeth in the embryonic calf or the shrivelled wings under the soldered wing-covers of many beetles, should so frequently occur. Nature may be said to have taken pains to reveal her scheme of modification, by means of rudimentary organs, of embryological and homologous structures, but we are too blind to understand her meaning.

I have now recapitulated the facts and considerations which have thoroughly convinced me that species have been modified, during a long course of descent. This has been effected chiefly through the natural selection of numerous successive, slight, favourable variations; aided in an important manner by the inherited effects of the use and disuse of parts; and in an unimportant manner, that is in relation to adaptive structures, whether past or present, by the direct action of external conditions, and by variations which seem to us in our ignorance to arise spontaneously. It appears that I formerly underrated the frequency and value of these latter forms of variation, as leading to permanent modifications of structure independently of natural selection. But as my conclusions have lately been much misrepresented, and it has been stated that I attribute the modification of species exclusively to natural selection, I may be permitted to remark that in the first edition of this work, and subsequently, I placed in a most conspicuous position—namely, at the close of the Introduction—the following words: "I am convinced that natural selection has been the main but not the exclusive means of modification." This has been of no avail. Great is the power of steady misrepresentation; but the history of science shows that fortunately this power does not long endure.

It can hardly be supposed that a false theory would explain, in so satisfactory a manner as does the theory of natural selection, the several large classes of facts above specified. It has recently been objected that this is an unsafe method of arguing; but it is a method used in judging of the common events of life, and has often been used by the greatest natural philosophers. The undulatory theory of light has thus been arrived at; and the belief in the revolution of the earth on its own axis was until lately supported by hardly any direct evidence. It is no valid objection that science as yet throws no light on the far higher problem of the essence or origin of life. Who can explain what is the essence of the attraction of gravity? No one now objects to following out the results consequent on this unknown element of attraction; notwithstanding that Leibnitz formerly accused Newton of introducing "occult qualities and miracles into philosophy."

I see no good reason why the views given in this volume should shock the religious feelings of any one. It is satisfactory, as showing how transient such impressions are, to remember that the greatest discovery ever made by man, namely, the law of the attraction of gravity, was also attacked by Leibnitz, "as subversive of natural, and inferentially of revealed, religion." A celebrated author and divine has written to me that "he has gradually learnt to see that it is just as noble a conception of the Deity to believe that He created a few original forms capable of self-development into other and needful forms, as to believe that He required a fresh act of creation to supply the voids caused by the action of His laws."

Why, it may be asked, until recently did nearly all the most eminent living naturalists and geologists disbelieve in the mutability of species? It cannot be asserted that organic beings in a state of nature are subject to no variation; it cannot be proved that the amount of variation in the course of long ages is a limited quality; no clear distinction has been, or can be, drawn between species and well-marked varieties. It cannot be maintained that species when intercrossed are invariably sterile, and varieties invariably fertile; or that sterility is a special endowment and sign of creation. The belief that species were immutable productions was almost unavoidable as long as the history of the world was thought to be of short duration; and now that we have acquired some idea of the lapse of time, we are too apt to assume, without proof, that the geological record is so perfect that it would have afforded us plain evidence of the mutation of species, if they had undergone mutation.

But the chief cause of our natural unwillingness to admit that one species has given birth to clear and distinct species, is that we are always slow in admitting great changes of which we do not see the steps. The difficulty is the same as that felt by so many geologists, when Lyell first insisted that long lines of inland cliffs had been formed, and great valleys excavated, by the agencies which we see still at work. The mind cannot possibly grasp the full meaning of the term of even a million years; it cannot add up and perceive the full effects of many slight variations, accumulated during an almost infinite number of generations.

Although I am fully convinced of the truth of the views given in this volume under the form of an abstract, I by no means expect to convince experienced naturalists whose minds are stocked with a multitude of facts all viewed, during a long course of years, from a point of view directly opposite to mine. It is so easy to hide our ignorance under such expressions as the "plan of creation," "unity of design," &c., and to think that we give an explanation when we only re-state a fact. Any one whose disposition leads him to attach more weight to unexplained difficulties than to the explanation of a certain number of facts will certainly reject the theory. A few naturalists, endowed with much flexibility of mind, and who have already begun to doubt the immutability of species, may be influenced by this volume; but I look with confidence to the future,—to young and rising naturalists, who will be able to view both sides of the question with impartiality. Whoever is led to believe that species are mutable will do good service by conscientiously expressing his conviction; for thus only can the load of prejudice by which this subject is overwhelmed be removed.

Several eminent naturalists have of late published their belief that a multitude of reputed species in each genus are not real species; but that other species are real, that is, have been independently created. This seems to me a strange conclusion to arrive at. They admit that a multitude of forms, which till lately they themselves thought were special creations, and which are still thus looked at by the majority of naturalists, and which consequently have all the external characteristic features of true species,—they admit that these have been produced by variation, but they refuse to extend the same view to other and slightly different forms. Nevertheless they do not pretend that they can define, or even conjecture, which are the created forms of life, and which are those produced by secondary laws. They admit variation as a *vera causa* in one case, they arbitrarily reject it in another, without assigning any distinction in the two cases. The day will come when this will be given as a curious illustration of the blindness of preconceived opinion. These authors seem no more startled at a miraculous act of creation than at an ordinary birth. But do they really believe that at innumerable periods in the earth's history certain elemental atoms have been commanded suddenly to flash into living tissues? Do they believe that at each supposed act of creation one individual or many were produced? Were all the infinitely numerous kinds of animals and plants created as eggs or seed, or as full grown? and in the case of mammals, were they created bearing the false marks of nourishment from the mother's womb? Undoubtedly some of these same questions cannot be answered by those who believe in the appearance or creation of only a few forms of life, or of some one form alone. It has been maintained by several authors that it is as easy to believe in the creation of a million beings as of one; but Maupertuis' philosophical axiom "of least action" leads the mind more willingly to admit the smaller number; and certainly we ought not to believe that innumerable beings within each great class have been created with plain, but deceptive, marks of descent from a single parent.

As a record of a former state of things, I have retained in the foregoing paragraphs, and elsewhere, several sentences which imply that naturalists believe in the separate creation of each species; and I have been much censured for having thus expressed myself. But undoubtedly this was the general belief when the first edition of the present work appeared. I formerly spoke to very many naturalists on the subject of evolution, and never once met with any sympathetic agreement. It is probable that some did then believe in evolution, but they were either silent, or expressed themselves so ambiguously that it was not easy to understand their meaning. Now things are wholly changed, and almost every naturalist admits the great principle of evolution. There are, however, some who still think that species have suddenly given birth, through quite unexplained means, to new and totally different forms: but, as I have attempted to show, weighty evidence can be opposed to the admission of great and abrupt modifications. Under a scientific point of view, and as leading to further investigation, but little advantage is gained by believing that new forms are suddenly developed in an inexplicable manner from old and widely different forms, over the old belief in the creation of species from the dust of the earth.

It may be asked how far I extend the doctrine of the modification of species. The question is difficult to answer, because the more distinct the forms are which we consider, by so much the arguments in favour of community of descent become fewer in number and less in force. But some arguments of the greatest weight extend very far. All the members of whole classes are connected together by a chain of affinities, and all can be classed on the same principle, in groups subordinate to groups. Fossil remains sometimes tend to fill up very wide intervals between existing orders.

Organs in a rudimentary condition plainly show that an early progenitor had the organ in a fully developed condition; and this in some cases implies an enormous amount of modification in the descendants. Throughout whole classes various structures are formed on the same pattern, and at a very early age the embryos closely resemble each other. Therefore I cannot doubt that the theory of descent with modification embraces all the members of the same great class or kingdom. I believe that animals are descended from at most only four or five progenitors, and plants from an equal or lesser number.

Analogy would lead me one step farther, namely, to the belief that all animals and plants are descended from some one prototype. But analogy may be a deceitful guide. Nevertheless all living things have much in common, in their chemical composition, their cellular structure, their laws of growth, and their liability to injurious influences. We see this even in so trifling a fact as that the same poison often similarly affects plants and animals; or that the poison secreted by the gall-fly produces monstrous growths on the wild rose or oak-tree. With all organic beings excepting perhaps some of the very lowest, sexual production seems to be essentially similar. With all, as far as is at present known the germinal vesicle is the same; so that all organisms start from a common origin. If we look even to the two main divisions—namely, to the animal and vegetable kingdoms—certain low forms are so far intermediate in character that naturalists have disputed to which kingdom they should be referred. As Professor Asa Gray has remarked, "the spores and other reproductive bodies of many of the lower algæ may claim to have first a characteristically animal, and then an unequivocally vegetable existence." Therefore, on the principle of natural selection with divergence of character, it does not seem incredible that, from such low and intermediate form, both animals and plants may have been developed; and, if we admit this, we must likewise admit that all the organic beings which have ever lived on this earth may be descended from some one primordial form. But this inference is chiefly grounded on analogy and it is immaterial whether or not it be accepted. No doubt it is possible, as Mr. G. H. Lewes has urged, that at the first commencement of life many different forms were evolved; but if so we may conclude that only a very few have left modified descendants. For, as I have recently remarked in regard to the members of each great kingdom, such as the Vertebrata Articulata &c., we have distinct evidence in their embryological homologous and rudimentary structures that within each kingdom all the members are descended from a single progenitor.

When the views advanced by me in this volume, and by Mr. Wallace, or when analogous views on the origin of species are generally admitted, we can dimly foresee that there will be a considerable revolution in natural history. Systematists will be able to pursue their labours as at present; but they will not be incessantly haunted by the shadowy doubt whether this or that form be a true species. This, I feel sure and I speak after experience, will be no slight relief. The endless disputes whether or not some fifty species of British brambles are good species will cease. Systematists will have only to decide (not that this will be easy) whether any form be sufficiently constant and distinct from other forms, to be capable of definition; and if definable, whether the differences be sufficiently important to deserve a specific name. This latter point will become a far more essential consideration than it is at present; for differences, however slight, between any two forms if not blended by intermediate gradations, are looked at by most naturalists as sufficient to raise both forms to the rank of species.

Hereafter we shall be compelled to acknowledge that the only distinction between species and well-marked varieties is, that the latter are known, or believed, to be connected at the present day by intermediate gradations, whereas species were formerly thus connected. Hence, without rejecting the consideration of the present existence of intermediate gradations between any two forms we shall be led to weigh more carefully and to value higher the actual amount of difference between them. It is quite possible that forms now generally acknowledged to be merely varieties may hereafter be thought worthy of specific names; and in this case scientific and common language will come into accordance. In short, we shall have to treat species in the same manner as those naturalists treat genera, who admit that genera are merely artificial combinations made for convenience. This may not be a cheering prospect; but we shall at least be free from the vain search for the undiscovered and undiscoverable essence of the term species.

The other and more general departments of natural history will rise greatly in interest. The terms used by naturalists, of affinity, relationship, community of type, paternity, morphology, adaptive characters, rudimentary and aborted organs, &c., will cease to be metaphorical, and will have a plain signification. When we no longer look at an organic being as a savage looks at a ship, as something wholly beyond his comprehension; when we regard every production of nature as one which has had a long history; when we contemplate every complex structure and instinct as the summing up of many contrivances, each useful to the possessor, in the same way as any great mechanical invention is the summing up of the labour, the experience, the reason, and even the blunders of numerous workmen;

when we thus view each organic being, how far more interesting—I speak from experience—does the study of natural history become!

A grand and almost untrodden field of inquiry will be opened, on the causes and laws of variation, on correlation, on the effects of use and disuse, on the direct action of external conditions, and so forth. The study of domestic productions will rise immensely in value. A new variety raised by man will be a more important and interesting subject for study than one more species added to the infinitude of already recorded species. Our classifications will come to be, as far as they can be so made, genealogies; and will then truly give what may be called the plan of creation. The rules for classifying will no doubt become simpler when we have a definite object in view. We possess no pedigrees or armorial bearings; and we have to discover and trace the many diverging lines of descent in our natural genealogies, by characters of any kind which have long been inherited. Rudimentary organs will speak infallibly with respect to the nature of long-lost structures. Species and groups of species which are called aberrant, and which may fancifully be called living fossils, will aid us in forming a picture of the ancient forms of life. Embryology will often reveal to us the structure, in some degree obscured, of the prototype of each great class.

When we feel assured that all the individuals of the same species, and all the closely allied species of most genera, have within a not very remote period descended from one parent, and have migrated from some one birth-place; and when we better know the many means of migration, then, by the light which geology now throws, and will continue to throw, on former changes of climate and of the level of the land, we shall surely be enabled to trace in an admirable manner the former migrations of the inhabitants of the whole world. Even at present, by comparing the differences between the inhabitants of the sea on the opposite sides of a continent, and the nature of the various inhabitants on that continent, in relation to their apparent means of immigration, some light can be thrown on ancient geography.

The noble science of Geology loses glory from the extreme imperfection of the record. The crust of the earth with its imbedded remains must not be looked at as a well-filled museum, but as a poor collection made at hazard and at rare intervals. The accumulation of each great fossiliferous formation will be recognised as having depended on an unusual concurrence of favourable circumstances, and the blank intervals between the successive stages as having been of vast duration. But we shall be able to gauge with some security the duration of these intervals by a comparison of the preceding and succeeding organic forms. We must be cautious in attempting to correlate as strictly contemporaneous two formations, which do not include many identical species, by the general succession of the forms of life. As species are produced and exterminated by slowly acting and still existing causes, and not by miraculous acts of creation; and as the most important of all causes of organic change is one which is almost independent of altered and perhaps suddenly altered physical conditions, namely, the mutual relation of organism to organism,—the improvement of one organism entailing the improvement or the extermination of others; it follows, that the amount of organic change in the fossils of consecutive formations probably serves as a fair measure of the relative though not actual lapse of time. A number of species, however, keeping in a body might remain for a long period unchanged, whilst within the same period several of these species by migrating into new countries and coming into competition with foreign associates, might become modified; so that we must not overrate the accuracy of organic change as a measure of time.

In the future I see open fields for far more important researches. Psychology will be securely based on the foundation already well laid by Mr. Herbert Spencer, that of the necessary acquirement of each mental power and capacity by gradation. Much light will be thrown on the origin of man and his history.

Authors of the highest eminence seem to be fully satisfied with the view that each species has been independently created. To my mind it accords better with what we know of the laws impressed on matter by the Creator, that the production and extinction of the past and present inhabitants of the world should have been due to secondary causes, like those determining the birth and death of the individual. When I view all beings not as special creations, but as the lineal descendants of some few beings which lived long before the first bed of the Cambrian system was deposited, they seem to me to become ennobled. Judging from the past, we may safely infer that not one living species will transmit its unaltered likeness to a distant futurity. And of the species now living very few will transmit progeny of any kind to a far distant futurity; for the manner in which all organic beings are grouped, shows that the greater number of species in each genus, and all the species in many genera, have left no descendants, but have become utterly extinct. We can so far take a prophetic glance into futurity as to foretell that it will be the common and widely-spread species, belonging to the larger and dominant groups within each class, which will ultimately prevail and procreate new and dominant species. As all the living forms of life are the lineal descendants of those which lived long before the Cambrian epoch, we may feel certain that the ordinary succession by generation has never once been broken, and that no cataclysm has desolated the whole world. Hence we may look with some confidence to a secure future of great length. And as natural selection works solely by and for the good of each being, all corporeal and mental endowments will tend to progress towards perfection.

It is interesting to contemplate a tangled bank, clothed with many plants of many kinds, with birds singing on the bushes, with various insects flitting about, and with worms crawling through the damp earth, and to reflect that these elaborately constructed forms, so different from each other, and dependent upon each other in so complex a manner, have all been produced by laws acting around us. These laws, taken in the largest sense, being Growth with Reproduction; Inheritance which is almost implied by reproduction; Variability from the indirect and direct action of the conditions of life, and from use and disuse: a Ratio of Increase so high as to lead to a Struggle for Life, and as a consequence to Natural Selection, entailing Divergence of Character and the Extinction of less-improved forms. Thus, from the war of nature, from famine and death, the most exalted object which we are capable of conceiving, namely, the production of the higher animals, directly follows. There is grandeur in this view of life, with its several powers, having been originally breathed by the Creator into a few forms or into one; and that, whilst this planet has gone cycling on according to the fixed law of gravity, from so simple a beginning endless forms most beautiful and most wonderful have been, and are being evolved.

✦ Reading 27 ✦

A General Introduction to Psychoanalysis

Sigmund Freud

First Lecture

Introduction

I do not know what knowledge any of you may already have of psycho-analysis, either from reading or from hearsay. But having regard to the title of my lectures—Introductory Lectures on Psycho-Analysis—I am bound to proceed as though you knew nothing of the subject and needed instruction, even in its first elements.

One thing, at least, I may pre-suppose that you know—namely, that psycho-analysis is a method of medical treatment for those suffering from nervous disorders; and I can give you at once an illustration of the way in which psycho-analytic procedure differs from, and often even reverses, what is customary in other branches of medicine. Usually, when we introduce a patient to a new form of treatment we minimize its difficulties and give him confident assurances of its success. This is, in my opinion, perfectly justifiable, for we thereby increase the probability of success. But when we undertake to treat a neurotic psychoanalytically we proceed otherwise. We explain to him the difficulties of the method, its long duration, the trials and sacrifices which will be required of him; and, as to the result, we tell him that we can make no definite promises, that success depends upon his endeavours, upon his understanding, his adaptability and his perseverance. We have, of course, good reasons, into which you will perhaps gain some insight later on, for adopting this apparently perverse attitude.

Now forgive me if I begin by treating you in the same way as I do my neurotic patients, for I shall positively advise you against coming to hear me a second time. And with this intention I shall explain to you how of necessity you can obtain from me only an incomplete knowledge of psycho-analysis and also what difficulties stand in the way of your forming an independent judgment on the subject. For I shall show you how the whole trend of your training and your accustomed modes of thought must inevitably have made you hostile to psycho-analysis, and also how much you would have to overcome in your own minds in order to master this instinctive opposition. I naturally cannot foretell what degree of understanding of psycho-analysis you may gain from my lectures, but I can at least assure you that by attending them you will not have learnt how to conduct a psycho-analytic investigation, nor how to carry out a psycho-analytic treatment. And further, if any one of you should feel dissatisfied with a merely cursory acquaintance with psycho-analysis and should wish to form a permanent connection with it, I shall not merely discourage him, but I shall actually warn him against it. For as things are at the present time, not only would the choice of such a career put an end to all chances of academic success, but, upon taking up work as a practitioner, such a man would find himself in a community which misunderstood his aims and intentions, regarded him with suspicion and hostility, and let loose upon him all the latent evil impulses harboured within it. Perhaps you can infer from the accompaniments of the war now raging in Europe what a countless host that is to reckon with.

However, there are always some people to whom the possibility of a new addition to knowledge will prove an attraction strong enough to survive all such inconveniences. If there are any such among you who will appear at my second lecture in spite of my words of warning they will be welcome. But all of you have

From: Sigmund Freud, *A General Introduction to Psychoanalysis: A Course of Twenty-Eight Lectures Delivered at the University of Vienna,* trans. Joan Riviere (New York: Liveright Publishing Corporation, 1920), pp. 17–24, 75–89.

a right to know what these inherent difficulties of psycho-analysis are to which I have alluded.

First of all, there is the problem of the teaching and exposition of the subject. In your medical studies you have been accustomed to use your eyes. You see the anatomical specimen, the precipitate of the chemical reaction, the contraction of the muscle as the result of the stimulation of its nerves. Later you come into contact with the patients; you learn the symptoms of disease by the evidence of your senses; the results of pathological processes can be demonstrated to you, and in many cases even the exciting cause of them in an isolated form. On the surgical side you are witnesses of the measures by which the patient is helped, and are permitted to attempt them yourselves. Even in psychiatry, demonstration of patients, of their altered expression, speech and behaviour, yields a series of observations which leave a deep impression on your minds. Thus a teacher of medicine acts for the most part as an exponent and guide, leading you as it were through a museum, while you gain in this way a direct relationship to what is displayed to you and believe yourselves to have been convinced by your own experience of the existence of the new facts.

But in psycho-analysis, unfortunately, all this is different. In psycho-analytic treatment nothing happens but an exchange of words between the patient and the physician. The patient talks, tells of his past experiences and present impressions, complains, and expresses his wishes and his emotions. The physician listens, attempts to direct the patient's thought-processes, reminds him, forces his attention in certain directions, gives him explanations and observes the reactions of understanding or denial thus evoked. The patient's unenlightened relatives—people of a kind to be impressed only by something visible and tangible, preferably by the sort of 'action' that may be seen at a cinema—never omit to express their doubts of how "mere talk can possibly cure anybody." Their reasoning is of course as illogical as it is inconsistent. For they are the same people who are always convinced that the sufferings of neurotics are purely "in their own imagination." Words and magic were in the beginning one and the same thing, and even to-day words retain much of their magical power. By words one of us can give to another the greatest happiness or bring about utter despair; by words the teacher imparts his knowledge to the student; by words the orator sweeps his audience with him and determines its judgements and decisions. Words call forth emotions and are universally the means by which we influence our fellow-creatures. Therefore let us not despise the use of words in psycho-therapy and let us be content if we may overhear the words which pass between the analyst and the patient.

But even that is impossible. The dialogue which constitutes the analysis will admit of no audience; the process cannot be demonstrated. One could, of course, exhibit a neurasthenic or hysterical patient to students at a psychiatric lecture. He would relate his case and his symptoms, but nothing more. He will make the communications necessary to the analysis only under the conditions of a special affective relationship to the physician; in the presence of a single person to whom he was indifferent he would become mute. For these communications relate to all his most private thoughts and feelings, all that which as a socially independent person he must hide from others, all that which, being foreign to his own conception of himself, he tries to conceal even from himself.

It is impossible, therefore, for you to be actually present during a psycho-analytic treatment; you can only be told about it, and can learn psycho-analysis, in the strictest sense of the word, only by hearsay. This tuition at second hand, so to say, puts you in a very unusual and difficult position as regards forming your own judgement on the subject, which will therefore largely depend on the reliance you can place on your informant.

Now imagine for a moment that you were present at a lecture in history instead of in psychiatry, and that the lecturer was dealing with the life and conquests of Alexander the Great. What reason would you have to believe what he told you? The situation would appear at first sight even more unsatisfactory than in the case of psycho-analysis, for the professor of history had no more part in Alexander's campaigns than you yourselves; the psycho-analyst at least informs you of matters in which he himself has played a part. But then we come to the question of what evidence there is to support the historian. He can refer you to the accounts of early writers who were either contemporaries or who lived not long after the events in question, such as Diodorus, Plutarch, Arrian, and others; he can lay before you reproductions of the preserved coins and statues of the king, and pass round a photograph of the mosaic at Pompeii representing the battle at Issus. Yet, strictly speaking, all these documents only prove that the existence of Alexander and the reality of his deeds were already believed in by former generations of men, and your criticism might begin anew at this point. And then you would find that not everything reported of Alexander is worthy of belief or sufficiently authenticated in detail, but I can hardly suppose that you would leave the lecture-room in doubt altogether as to the reality of Alexander the Great. Your conclusions would be principally determined by two considerations: first, that the lecturer could have no conceivable motive for attempting to persuade you of something which he did not himself believe to be true, and secondly, that all the available authorities agree more or less in their accounts of the facts. In questioning the accuracy of the early writers you would apply these tests again, the possible motives of the authors and the agreement to be found between them. The result of such tests would certainly be convincing in the case of Alexander, probably less so in regard to figures like Moses and Nimrod. Later on you will perceive clearly enough what doubts can be raised against the credibility of an exponent of psycho-analysis.

Now you will have a right to ask the question: If no objective evidence for psycho-analysis exists and no possibility of demonstrating the process, how is it possible to study it at all or to convince oneself of its truth? The study of it is indeed not an easy matter, nor are there many people who have thoroughly learned it; still, there is, of course, some way of learning it. Psycho-analysis is learnt first of all on oneself, through the study of one's own personality. This is not exactly what is meant by introspection, but it may be so described for want of a better word. There is a whole series of very common and well-known mental phenomena which can be taken as material for self-analysis when one has acquired some knowledge of the method. In this way one may obtain the required conviction of the reality of the processes which psycho-analysis describes, and of the truth of its conceptions, although progress on these lines is not without its limitations. One gets much further by submitting oneself to analysis by a skilled analyst, undergoing the working of the analysis in one's own person and using the opportunity to observe the finer details of the technique which the analyst employs. This, eminently the best way, is of course only practicable for individuals and cannot be used in a class of students.

The second difficulty you will find in connection with psycho-analysis is not, on the other hand, inherent in it, but is one for which I must hold you yourselves responsible, at least in so far as your medical studies have influenced you. Your training will have induced in you an attitude of mind very far removed from the psycho-analytical one. You have been trained to establish the functions and disturbances of the organism on an anatomical basis, to explain them in terms of chemistry and physics, and to regard them from a biological point of view; but no part of your interest has ever been directed to the mental aspects of life, in which, after all, the development of the marvellously complicated organism culminates. For this reason a psychological attitude of mind is still foreign to you, and you are accustomed to regard it with suspicion, to deny it a scientific status, and to leave it to the general public, poets, mystics, and philosophers. Now this limitation in you is undoubtedly detrimental to your medical efficiency; for on meeting a patient it is the mental aspects with which one first comes into contact, as in most human relationships, and I am afraid you will pay the penalty of having to yield a part of the curative influence at which you aim to the quacks, mystics, and faith-healers whom you despise.

I quite acknowledge that there is an excuse for this defect in your previous training. There is no auxiliary philosophical science that might be of service to you in your profession. Neither speculative philosophy nor descriptive psychology, nor even the so-called experimental psychology which is studied in connection with the physiology of the sense-organs, as they are taught in the schools, can tell you anything useful of the relations existing between mind and body, or can give you a key to comprehension of a possible disorder of the mental functions. It is true that the psychiatric branch of medicine occupies itself with describing the different forms of recognizable mental disturbances and grouping them in clinical pictures, but in their best moments psychiatrists themselves are doubtful whether their purely descriptive formulations deserve to be called science. The origin, mechanism, and interrelation of the symptoms which make up these clinical pictures are undiscovered: either they cannot be correlated with any demonstrable changes in the brain, or only with such changes as in no way explain them. These mental disturbances are open to therapeutic influence only when they can be identified as secondary effects of some organic disease.

This is the lacuna which psycho-analysis is striving to fill. It hopes to provide psychiatry with the missing psychological foundation, to discover the common ground on which a correlation of bodily and mental disorder becomes comprehensible. To this end it must dissociate itself from every foreign preconception, whether anatomical, chemical, or physiological, and must work throughout with conceptions of a purely psychological order, and for this very reason I fear that it will appear strange to you at first.

For the next difficulty I shall not hold you, your training or your mental attitude, responsible. There are two tenets of psycho-analysis which offend the whole world and excite its resentment; the one conflicts with intellectual, the other with moral and æsthetic prejudices. Let us not underestimate these prejudices; they are powerful things, residues of valuable, even necessary, stages in human evolution. They are maintained by emotional forces, and the fight against them is a hard one.

The first of these displeasing propositions of psycho-analysis is this: that mental processes are essentially unconscious, and that those which are conscious are merely isolated acts and parts of the whole psychic entity. Now I must ask you to remember that, on the contrary, we are accustomed to identify the mental with the conscious. Consciousness appears to us as positively the characteristic that defines mental life, and we regard psychology as the study of the content of consciousness. This even appears so evident that any contradiction of it seems obvious nonsense to us, and yet it is impossible for psycho-analysis to avoid this contradiction, or to accept the identity between the conscious and the psychic. The psycho-analytical definition of the mind is that it comprises processes of the nature of feeling, thinking, and wishing, and it maintains that there are such things as unconscious thinking and unconscious wishing. But in doing so psycho-analysis has forfeited at the outset the sympathy of the sober and scientifically minded, and incurred the suspicion of being a fantastic cult occupied with dark and unfathomable mysteries. You yourselves must find it difficult to understand why I should stigmatize an abstract proposition, such as "The psychic is the conscious," as a prejudice; nor can you guess yet what evolutionary process could have led to the denial of the unconscious, if it does indeed exist, nor what advantage could have been achieved by this denial. It seems like an empty wrangle over words to argue whether mental life is to be regarded as coextensive with consciousness or whether it may be said to stretch beyond this limit, and yet I can assure you that the acceptance of unconscious mental processes represents a decisive step towards a new orientation in the world and in science.

As little can you suspect how close is the connection between this first bold step on the part of psycho-analysis and the second to which I am now coming. For this next proposition, which we put forward as one of the discoveries of psycho-analysis, consists in the assertion that impulses, which can only be described as sexual in both the narrower and the wider sense, play a peculiarly large part, never before sufficiently appreciated, in the causation of nervous and mental disorders. Nay, more, that these sexual impulses have contributed invaluably to the highest cultural, artistic, and social achievements of the human mind.

In my opinion, it is the aversion from this conclusion of psycho-analytic investigation that is the most significant source of the opposition it has encountered. Are you curious to know how we ourselves account for this? We believe that civilization has been built up, under the pressure at the struggle for existence, by sacrifices in gratification of the primitive impulses, and that it is to a great extent for ever being re-created, as each individual, successively joining the community, repeats the sacrifice of his instinctive pleasures for the common good. The sexual are amongst the most important of the instinctive forces thus utilized: they are in this way sublimated, that is to say, their energy is turned aside from its sexual goal and diverted towards other ends, no longer sexual and socially more valuable. But the structure thus built up is insecure, for the sexual impulses are with difficulty controlled; in each individual who takes up his part in the work of civilization there is a danger that a rebellion of the sexual impulses may occur, against this diversion of their energy. Society can conceive of no more powerful menace to its culture than would arise from the liberation of the sexual impulses and a return of them to their original goal. Therefore society dislikes this sensitive place in its development being touched upon; that the power of the sexual instinct should be recognized, and the significance of the individual's sexual life revealed, is very far from its interests; with a view to discipline it has rather taken the course of diverting attention away from this whole field. For this reason, the revelations of psycho-analysis are not tolerated by it, and it would greatly prefer to brand them as æsthetically offensive, morally reprehensible, or dangerous. But since such objections are not valid arguments against conclusions which claim to represent the objective results of scientific investigation, the opposition must be translated into intellectual terms before it can be expressed. It is a characteristic of human nature to be inclined to regard anything which is disagreeable as untrue, and then without much difficulty to find arguments against it. So society pronounces the unacceptable to be untrue, disputes the results of psycho-analysis with logical and concrete arguments, arising, however, in affective sources, and clings to them with all the strength of prejudice against every attempt at refutation.

But we, on the other hand, claim to have yielded to no tendency in propounding this objectionable theory. Our intention has been solely to give recognition to the facts as we found them in the course of painstaking researches. And we now claim the right to reject unconditionally any such introduction of practical considerations into the field of scientific investigation, even before we have determined whether the apprehension which attempts to force these considerations upon us is justified or not.

These, now, are some of the difficulties which confront you at the outset when you begin to take an interest in psycho-analysis. It is probably more than enough for a beginning. If you can overcome their discouraging effect, we will proceed further.

* * *

Fifth Lecture

Difficulties and Preliminary Approach to the Subject

One day the discovery was made that the symptoms of disease in certain nervous patients have meaning. It was upon this discovery that the psycho-analytic method of treatment was based. In this treatment it happened that patients in speaking of their symptoms also mentioned their dreams, whereupon the suspicion arose that these dreams too had meaning.

However, we will not pursue this historical path, but will strike off in the opposite direction. Our aim is to demonstrate the meaning of dreams, in preparation for the study of the neuroses. There are good grounds for this reversal of procedure, since the study of dreams is not merely the best preparation for that of the neuroses, but a dream is itself a neurotic symptom and, moreover, one which possesses for us the incalculable advantage of occurring in all healthy people. Indeed, if all human beings were healthy and would only dream, we could gather almost all the knowledge from their dreams which we have gained from studying the neuroses.

So dreams become the object of psycho-analytic research—another of these ordinary, under-rated occurrences, apparently of no practical value, like "errors," and sharing with them the characteristic of occurring in healthy persons. But in other respects the conditions of work are rather less favourable. Errors had only been neglected by science, people had not troubled their heads much about them, but at least it was no disgrace to occupy oneself with them. True, people said, there are things more important but still something may possibly come of it. To occupy oneself with dreams, however, is not merely unpractical and superfluous, but positively scandalous: it carries with it the taint of the unscientific and arouses the suspicion of personal leanings towards mysticism. The idea of a medical student troubling himself about dreams when there is so much in neuropathology and psychiatry itself that is more serious— tumours as large as apples compressing the organ of the mind, hæmorrhages, chronic inflammatory conditions in which the alterations in the tissues can be demonstrated under the microscope! No, dreams are far too unworthy and trivial to be objects of scientific research.

There is yet another factor involved which, in itself, sets at defiance all the requirements of exact investigation. In investigating dreams even the object of research, the dream itself, is indefinite. A delusion, for example, presents clear and definite outlines. "I am the Emperor of China," says your patient plainly. But a dream? For the most part it cannot be related at all. When a man tells a dream, has he any guarantee that he has told it correctly, and not perhaps altered it in the telling or been forced to invent part of it on account of the vagueness of his recollection? Most dreams cannot be remembered at all and are forgotten except for some tiny fragments. And is a scientific psychology or a method of treatment for the sick to be founded upon material such as this?

A certain element of exaggeration in a criticism may arouse our suspicions. The arguments brought against the dream as an object of scientific research are clearly extreme. We have met with the objection of triviality already in "errors," and have told ourselves that great things may be revealed even by small indications. As to the indistinctness of dreams, that is a characteristic like any other—we cannot dictate to things their characteristics; besides, there are also dreams which are clear and well-defined. Further, there are other objects of psychiatric investigation which suffer in the same way from the quality of indefiniteness, e.g. the obsessive ideas of many cases, with which nevertheless many psychiatrists of repute and standing have occupied themselves. I will recall the last case of the kind which came before me in medical practice. The patient, a woman, presented her case in these words: "I have a certain feeling, as if I had injured, or had meant to injure, some living creature—perhaps a child—no, no, a dog rather, as if perhaps I had pushed it off a bridge—or done something else." Any disadvantage resulting from the uncertain recollection of dreams may be remedied by deciding that exactly what the dreamer tells is to count as the dream, and by ignoring all that he may have forgotten or altered in the process of recollection. Finally, one cannot maintain in so sweeping a fashion that dreams are unimportant things. We know from our own experience that the mood in which we awake from a dream may last throughout the day, and cases have been observed by medical men in which mental disorder began with a dream, the delusion which had its source in this dream persisting; further, it is told of historical persons that impulses to momentous deeds sprang from their dreams. We may therefore ask: what is the real cause of the disdain in which dreams are held in scientific circles? In my opinion it is the reaction from the over-estimation of them in earlier times. It is well known that it is no easy matter to reconstruct the past, but we may assume with certainty (you will forgive my jest) that as early as three thousand years ago and more our ancestors dreamt in the same way as we do. So far as we know, all ancient peoples attached great significance to dreams and regarded them as of practical value; they obtained from them auguries of the future and looked for portents in them. For the Greeks and other Orientals, it was at times as unthinkable to undertake a campaign without a dream-interpreter as it would be to-day without air-scouts for intelligence. When Alexander the Great set out on his campaign of conquest the most famous interpreters of dreams were in his following. The city of Tyre, still at that time on an island, offered so stout a resistance to the king that he entertained the idea of abandoning the siege; then one night he dreamed of a satyr dancing in triumph, and when he related this dream to his interpreters they informed him that it foretold his victory over the city; he gave the order to attack and took Tyre by storm. Among the Etruscans and Romans other methods of foretelling the future were employed, but during the whole of the Græco-Roman period the interpretation of dreams was practised and held in high esteem. Of the literature on this subject the principal work at any rate has come down to us, namely, the book of Artemidorus of Daldis, who is said to have lived at the time of the Emperor Hadrian. How it happened that the art of dream-interpretation declined later and dreams fell into disrepute, I cannot tell you. The progress of learning cannot have had very much to do with it, for in the darkness of the middle ages things far more absurd than the ancient practice of the interpretation of dreams were faithfully retained. The fact remains that the interest in dreams gradually sank to the level of superstition and could hold its own only amongst the uneducated. In our day, there survive, as a final degradation of the art of dream-interpretation, the attempts to find out from dreams numbers destined to draw prizes in games of chance. On the other hand, exact science of the present day has repeatedly concerned itself with the dream, but always with the sole object of illustrating *physiological* theories. By medical men, naturally, a dream was never regarded as a mental process but as the mental expression of physical stimuli. Binz in 1876 pronounced the dream to be "a physical process, always useless and in many cases actually morbid, a process above which the conception of the world-soul and of immortality stands as high as does the blue sky above the most low-lying, weed-grown stretch of sand." Maury compares dreams with the spasmodic jerkings of St. Vitus' dance, contrasted with the co-ordinated movements of the normal human being; in an old comparison a parallel is drawn between the content of a dream and the sounds which would be produced if "someone ignorant of music let his ten fingers wander over the keys of an instrument."

"Interpretation" means discovering a hidden meaning, but there can be no question of attempting this while such an attitude is maintained towards the dream-performance. Look up the description of dreams given in the writings of Wundt, Jodl and other recent philosophers: they are content with the bare enumeration of the divergences of the dream-life from waking thought with a view to depreciating the dreams: they emphasize the lack of connection in the associations, the suspended exercise of the critical faculty, the elimination of all knowledge, and other indications of diminished functioning. The single valuable contribution to our knowledge about dreams for which we are indebted to exact science relates to the influence upon the dream-content of physical stimuli operating during sleep. We have the work of a Norwegian author who died recently—J. Mourly Vold—two large volumes on experimental investigation of dreams (translated into German in 1910 and 1912), which are concerned almost entirely with the results obtained by change in the position of the limbs. These investigations have been held up to us as models of exact research in the subject of dreams. Now can you imagine what would be the comment of exact science on learning that we intend to try to find out the *meaning* of dreams? The comment that has perhaps been made already! However, we will not allow ourselves to be appalled at the thought. If it was possible for errors to have an underlying meaning, it is possible that dreams have one too; and errors have, in very many cases, a meaning which has eluded the researches of exact science. Let us adopt the assumption of the ancients and of simple folk, and follow in the footsteps of the dream-interpreters of old.

First of all, we must take our bearings in this enterprise, and make a survey of the field of dreams. What exactly is a dream? It is difficult to define it in a single phrase. Yet we need not seek after a definition, when all we need is to refer to something familiar to everyone. Still we ought to pick out the essential features in dreams. How are we to discover these features? The boundaries of the region we are entering comprise such vast differences, differences whichever way we turn. That which we can show to be common to all dreams is probably what is essential.

Well then—the first common characteristic of all dreams would be that we are asleep at the time. Obviously, the dream is the life of the mind during sleep, a life bearing certain resemblances to our waking life and, at the same time, differing from it widely. That, indeed, was Aristotle's definition. Perhaps dream and sleep stand in yet closer relationship to each other. We can be waked by a dream; we often have a dream when we wake spontaneously or when we are forcibly roused from sleep. Dreams seem thus to be an intermediate condition between sleeping and waking. Hence, our attention is directed to sleep itself: what then is sleep?

That is a physiological or biological problem concerning which much is still in dispute. We can come to no decisive answer, but I think we may attempt to define one psychological characteristic of sleep. Sleep is a condition in which I refuse to have anything to do with the outer world and have withdrawn my interest from it. I go to sleep by retreating from the outside world and warding off the stimuli proceeding from it. Again, when I am tired by that world I go to sleep. I say to it as I fall asleep: "Leave me in peace, for I want to sleep." The child says just the opposite: "I won't go to sleep yet; I'm not tired, I want more things to happen to me!" Thus the biological object of sleep seems to be recuperation, its psychological characteristic the suspension of interest in the outer world. Our relationship with the world which we entered so unwillingly seems to be endurable only with intermission; hence we withdraw again periodically into the condition prior to our entrance into the world: that is to say, into intrauterine existence. At any rate, we try to bring about quite similar conditions—warmth, darkness and absence of stimulus—characteristic of that state. Some of us still roll ourselves tightly up into a ball resembling the intra-uterine position. It looks as if we grown-ups do not belong wholly to the world, but only by two-thirds; one-third of us has never yet been born at all. Every time we wake in the morning it is as if we were newly born. We do, in fact, speak of the condition of waking from sleep in these very words: we feel "as if we were newly born,"—and in this we are probably quite mistaken in our idea of the general sensations of the new-born infant; it may be assumed on the contrary that it feels extremely uncomfortable. Again, in speaking of birth we speak of "seeing the light of day."

If this is the nature of sleep, then dreams do not come into its scheme at all, but seem rather to be an unwelcome supplement to it; and we do indeed believe that dreamless sleep is the best, the only proper sleep. There should be no mental activity during sleep; if any such activity bestirs itself, then in so far have we failed to reach the true pre-natal condition of peace; we have not been able to avoid altogether some remnants of mental activity, and the act of dreaming would represent these remnants. In that event it really does seem that dreams do not need to have meaning. With errors it was different, for they were at least activities manifested in waking life; but if I sleep and have altogether suspended mental activity, with the exception of certain remnants which I have not been able to suppress, there is no necessity whatever that they should have any meaning. In fact, I cannot even make use of any such meaning, seeing that the rest of my mind is asleep. It can really then be a matter of spasmodic reactions only, of such mental phenomena only as have their origin in physical stimulation. Hence, dreams must be remnants of the mental activity of waking life disturbing sleep, and we might as well make up our minds forthwith to abandon a theme so unsuited to the purposes of psycho-analysis.

Superfluous as dreams may be, however, they do exist nevertheless, and we can try to account for their existence to ourselves. Why does not mental life go off to sleep? Probably because there is something that will not leave the mind in peace; stimuli are acting upon it and to these it is bound to react. Dreams therefore are the mode of reaction of the mind to stimuli acting upon it during sleep. We note here a possibility of access to comprehension of dreams. We can now endeavour to find out, in various dreams, what are the stimuli seeking to disturb sleep, the reaction to which takes the form of dreams. By doing this we should have worked out the first characteristic common to all dreams.

Is there any other common characteristic? Yes, there is another, unmistakable, and yet much harder to lay hold of and describe. The character of mental processes during sleep is quite different from that of waking processes. In dreams we go through many experiences, which we fully believe in, whereas in reality we are perhaps only experiencing the single disturbing stimulus. For the most part our experiences take the form of visual images; there may be feeling as well, thoughts, too, mixed up with them, and the other senses may be drawn in; but for the most part dreams consist of visual images. Part of the difficulty of reciting a dream comes from the fact that we have to translate these images into words. "I could draw it," the dreamer often says to us, "but I do not know how to put it into words." Now this is not exactly a diminution in the mental capacity, as seen in a contrast between a feeble-minded person and a man of genius. The difference is rather a qualitative one, but it is difficult to say precisely wherein it lies. G. T. Fechner once suggested that the stage whereon the drama of the dream (within the mind) is played out is other than that of the life of waking ideas. That is a saying which we really do not understand, nor do we know what it is meant to convey to us, but it does actually reproduce the impression of strangeness which most dreams make upon us. Again, the comparison of the act of dreaming with the performances of an unskilled hand in music breaks down here, for the piano will certainly respond with the same notes, though not with melodies, to a chance touch on its keys. We will keep this second common characteristic of dreams carefully in view, even though we may not understand it.

Are there any other qualities common to all dreams? I can think of none, but can see differences only, whichever way I look, differences too in every respect—in apparent duration, definiteness, the part played by affects, persistence in the mind, and so forth. This is really not what we should naturally expect in the case of a compulsive attempt, at once meagre and spasmodic, to ward off a stimulus. As regards the length of dreams, some are very short, containing only one image, or very few, or a single thought, possibly even a single word; others are peculiarly rich in content, enact entire romances and seem to last a very long time. There are dreams as distinct as actual experiences, so distinct that for some time after waking we do not realize that they were dreams at all; others, which are ineffably faint, shadowy and blurred; in one and the same dream, even, there may be some parts of extraordinary vividness alternating with others so indistinct as to be almost wholly elusive. Again, dreams may be quite consistent or at any rate coherent, or even witty or fantastically beautiful; others again are confused, apparently imbecile, absurd or often absolutely mad. There are dreams which leave us quite cold, others in which every affect makes itself felt—pain to the point of tears, terror so intense as to wake us, amazement, delight, and so on. Most dreams are forgotten soon after waking; or they persist throughout the day, the recollection becoming fainter and more imperfect as the day goes on; others remain so vivid (as, for example, the dreams of childhood) that thirty years later we remember them as clearly as though they were part of a recent experience. Dreams, like people, may make their appearance once and never come back; or the same person may dream the same thing repeatedly, either in the same form or with slight alterations. In short, these scraps of mental activity at night-time have at command an immense repertory, can in fact create everything that by day the mind is capable of—only, it is never the same.

One might attempt to account for these diversities in dream by assuming that they correspond to different intermediate states between sleeping and waking, different levels of imperfect sleep. Very well; but then in proportion as the mind approached the waking state there should be not merely an increase in the value, content, and distinctness of the dream-performance, but also a growing perception that it *is* a dream; and it ought not to happen that side by side with a clear and sensible element in the dream there is one which is nonsensical or indistinct, followed again by a good piece of work. It is certain that the mind could not vary its depth of sleep so rapidly as that. This explanation therefore does not help; there is in fact no short cut to an answer.

For the present we will leave the "meaning" of the dream out of question, and try instead, by starting from the common element in dreams, to clear a path to a better understanding of their nature. From the relationship of dreams to sleep we have drawn the conclusion that dreams are the reaction to a stimulus disturbing sleep. As we have heard, this is also the single point at which exact experimental psychology can come to our aid; it affords proof of the fact that stimuli brought to bear during sleep make their appearance in dreams. Many investigations have been made on these lines, culminating in those of Mourly Vold whom I mentioned earlier; we have all, too, been in a position to confirm their results by occasional observations of our own. I will choose some of the earlier experiments to tell you. Maury had tests of this kind carried out upon himself. Whilst dreaming, he was made to smell some eau de Cologne, whereupon he dreamt he was in Cairo, in the shop of Johann Maria Farina, and this was followed by some crazy adventures. Again, someone gave his neck a gentle pinch, and he dreamt of the application of a blister and of a doctor who had treated him when he was a child. Again, they let a drop of water fall on his forehead and he was immediately in Italy, perspiring freely and drinking the white wine of Orvieto.

The striking feature about these dreams produced under experimental conditions will perhaps become still clearer to us in another series of "stimulus"-dreams. These are three dreams of which we have an account by a clever observer, Hildebrandt, and all three are reactions to the sound of an alarum-clock:

"I am going for a walk on a spring morning, and I saunter through fields just beginning to grow green, till I come to a neighbouring village, where I see the inhabitants in holiday attire making their way in large numbers to the church, their hymn-books in their hands. Of course! it is Sunday and the morning service is just about to begin. I decide to take part in it, but first as I am rather overheated I think I will cool down in the churchyard which surrounds the church. Whilst reading some of the epitaphs there I hear the bell-ringer go up into the tower, where I now notice, high up, the little village bell which will give the signal for the beginning of the service. For some time yet it remains motionless, then it begins to swing, and suddenly the strokes ring out, clear and piercing—so clear and piercing that they put an end to my sleep. But the sound of the bell comes from the alarum-clock."

Here is another combination of images. "It is a bright winter day, and the roads are deep in snow. I have promised to take part in a sleighing expedition, but I have to wait a long time before I am told that the sleigh is at the door. Now follow the preparations for getting in, the fur rug is spread out and the foot-muff fetched and finally I am in my place. But there is still a delay while the horses wait for the signal to start. Then the reins are jerked and the little bells, shaken violently, begin their familiar janizary music, so loudly that in a moment the web of the dream is rent. Again it is nothing but the shrill sound of the alarum-clock."

Now for the third example! "I see a kitchen-maid with dozens of piled-up plates going along the passage to the dining-room. It seems to me that the pyramid of china in her arms is in danger of overbalancing. I call out a warning: 'Take care, your whole load will fall to the ground.' Of course I receive the usual answer: that they are accustomed to carrying china in that way, and so on; meanwhile I follow her as she goes with anxious looks. I thought so—the next thing is a stumble on the threshold, the crockery falls, crashing and clattering in a hundred pieces on the ground. But—I soon become aware that that interminably prolonged sound is no real crash, but a regular ringing—and this ringing is due merely to the alarum-clock, as I realize at last on awakening."

These dreams are very pretty, perfectly sensible, and by no means so incoherent as dreams usually are. We have no quarrel with them on those grounds. The thing common to them all is that in each case the situation arises from a noise, which the dreamer on waking recognizes as that of the alarum-clock. Hence we see here how a dream is produced, but we find out something more. In the dream there is no recognition of the clock, which does not even appear in it, but for the noise of the clock another noise is substituted; the stimulus which disturbs sleep is interpreted, but interpreted differently in each instance. Now why is this? There is no answer; it appears to be mere caprice. But to understand the dream we should be able to account for its choice of just this noise and no other to interpret the stimulus given by the alarum-clock. In analogous fashion we must object to Maury's experiments that, although it is clear that the stimulus brought to bear on the sleeper does appear in the dream, yet his experiments don't explain why it appears exactly in that form, which is one that does not seem explicable by the nature of the stimulus disturbing sleep. And further, in Maury's experiments there was mostly a mass of other dream-material attached to the direct result of the stimulus, for example, the crazy adventures in the eau de Cologne dream, for which we are at a loss to account.

Now will you reflect that the class of dreams which wake one up affords the best opportunity for establishing the influence of external disturbing stimuli. In most other cases it will be more difficult. We do not wake up out of all dreams, and if in the morning we remember a dream of the night before, how are we to assign it to a disturbing stimulus operating perhaps during the night? I once succeeded in subsequently establishing the occurrence of a sound-stimulus of this sort, but only, of course, because of peculiar circumstances. I woke up one morning at a place in the Tyrolese mountains knowing that I had dreamt that the Pope was dead. I could not explain the dream to myself, but later my wife asked me: "Did you hear quite early this morning the dreadful noise of bells breaking out in all the churches and chapels?" No, I had heard nothing, my sleep is too sound, but thanks to her telling me this I understood my dream. How often may such causes of stimulus as this induce dreams in the sleeper without his ever hearing of them afterwards? Possibly very often: and possibly not. If we can get no information of any stimulus we cannot be convinced on the point. And apart from this we have given up trying to arrive at an estimation of the sleep-disturbing external stimuli, since we know that they only explain a fragment of the dream and not the whole dream-reaction.

We need not on that account give up this theory altogether; there is still another possible way of following it out. Obviously it is a matter of indifference what disturbs sleep and causes the mind to dream. If it cannot always be something external acting as a stimulus to one of the senses, it is possible that, instead, a stimulus operates from the internal organs—a so-called somatic stimulus. This supposition lies very close, and moreover it corresponds to the view popularly held with regard to the origin of dreams, for it is a common saying that they come from the stomach. Unfortunately, here again we must suppose that in very many cases information respecting a somatic stimulus operating during the night would no longer be forthcoming after waking, so that it would be incapable of proof. But we will not overlook the fact that many trustworthy experiences support the idea that dreams may be derived from somatic stimuli; on the whole it is indubitable that the condition of the internal organs can influence dreams. The relation of the content of many dreams to distention of the bladder or to a condition of excitation of the sex-organs is so plain that it cannot be mistaken. From these obvious cases we pass to others, in which, to judge by the content of the dream, we are at least justified in suspecting that some such somatic stimuli have been at work, since there is something in this content which can be regarded as elaboration, representation, or interpretation of these stimuli. Scherner, the investigator of dreams (1861), emphatically supported the view which traces the origin of dreams to organic stimuli, and contributed some excellent examples towards it. For instance, he sees in a dream "two rows of beautiful boys, with fair hair and delicate complexions, confronting each other pugnaciously, joining in combat, seizing hold of one another, and again letting go their hold, only to take up the former position and go through the whole process again"; his interpretation of the two rows of boys as the teeth is in itself plausible and seems to receive full confirmation when after this scene the dreamer "pulls a long tooth from his jaw." Again, the interpretation of "long, narrow, winding passages" as being suggested by a stimulus originating in the intestine seems sound and corroborates Scherner's assertion that dreams primarily endeavour to represent, by like objects, the organ from which the stimulus proceeds.

We must therefore be prepared to admit that internal stimuli can play the same rôle in dreams as external ones. Unfortunately, evaluation of this factor is open to the same objections. In a great number of instances the attribution of dreams to somatic stimuli must remain uncertain or incapable of proof; not all dreams, but only a certain number of them, rouse the suspicion that stimuli from internal organs have something to do with their origin; and lastly, the internal somatic stimulus will suffice no more than the external sensory stimulus to explain any other part of the dream than the direct reaction to it. The origin of all the rest of the dream remains obscure.

Now, however, let us direct our attention to a certain peculiarity of the dream-life which appears when we study the operation of these stimuli. The dream does not merely reproduce the stimulus, but elaborates it, plays upon it, fits it into a context, or replaces it by something else. This is a side of the dream-work which is bound to be of interest to us because possibly it may lead us nearer to the true nature of dreams. The scope of a man's production is not necessarily limited to the circumstance which immediately gives rise to it. For instance, Shakespeare's *Macbeth* was written as an occasional drama on the accession of the king who first united in his person the crowns of the three kingdoms. But does this historical occasion cover the whole content of the drama, or explain its grandeur and its mystery? Perhaps in the same way the external and internal stimuli operating upon the sleeper are merely the occasion of the dream and afford us no insight into its true nature.

The other element common to all dreams, their peculiarity in mental life, is on the one hand very difficult to grasp and on the other seems to afford no clue for further inquiry. Our experiences in dreams for the most part take the form of visual images. Can these be explained by the stimuli? Is it really the stimulus that we experience? If so, why is the experience visual, when it can only be in the very rarest instance that any stimulus has operated upon our eyesight? Or, can it be shown that when we dream of speech any conversation or sounds resembling conversation reached our ears during sleep? I venture to discard such a possibility without any hesitation whatever.

If we cannot get any further with the common characteristics of dreams as a starting-point, let us try beginning with their differences. Dreams are often meaningless, confused, and absurd, yet there are some which are sensible, sober, and reasonable.

Let us see whether these latter sensible dreams can help to elucidate those which are meaningless. I will tell you the latest reasonable dream which was told to me, the dream of a young man: "I went for a walk in the Kärntnerstrasse and there I met Mr. X.; after accompanying him for a short time I went into a restaurant. Two ladies and a gentleman came and sat down at my table. At first I was annoyed and refused to look at them, but presently I glanced across at them and found that they were quite nice." The dreamer's comment on this was that the evening before he had actually been walking in the Kärntnerstrasse, which is the way he usually goes, and that he had met Mr. X. there. The other part of the dream was not a direct reminiscence, but only bore a certain resemblance to an occurrence of some time previously. Or here we have another prosaic dream, that of a lady. Her husband says to her: "Don't you think we ought to have the piano tuned?" and she replies: "It is not worth it, for the hammers need fresh leather anyhow." This dream repeats a conversation which took place in almost the same words between herself and her husband the day before the dream. What then do we learn from these two prosaic dreams? Merely that there occur in them recollections of daily life or of matters connected with it. Even that would be something if it could be asserted of all dreams without exception. But that is out of the question; this characteristic too belongs only to a minority of dreams. In most dreams we find no connection with the day before, and no light is thrown from this quarter upon meaningless and absurd dreams. All we know is that we have met with a new problem. Not only do we want to know what a dream is saying, but if as in our examples that is quite plain, we want to know further from what cause and to what end we repeat in dreams this which is known to us and has recently happened to us.

I think you would be as tired as I of continuing the kind of attempts we have made up to this point. It only shows that all the interest in the world will not help us with a problem unless we have also an idea of some path to adopt in order to arrive at a solution. Till now we have not found this path. Experimental psychology has contributed nothing but some (certainly very valuable) information about the significance of stimuli in the production of dreams. Of philosophy we have nothing to expect, unless it be a lofty repetition of the reproach that our object is intellectually contemptible; while from the occult sciences we surely do not choose to borrow. History and the verdict of the people tell us that dreams are full of meaning and importance, and of prophetic significance; but that is hard to accept and certainly does not lend itself to proof. So then our first endeavours are completely baffled.

But unexpectedly there comes a hint from a direction in which we have not hitherto looked. Colloquial speech, which is certainly no matter of chance but the deposit as it were, of ancient knowledge—a thing which must not indeed be made too much of—our speech, I say, recognizes the existence of something to which, strangely enough, it gives the name of "day-dreams." Day-dreams are phantasies (products of phantasy); they are very common phenomena, are observable in healthy as well as in sick persons, and they also can easily be studied by the subject himself. The most striking thing about these 'phantastic' creations is that they have received the name of "day-dreams," for they have nothing in common with the two universal characteristics of dreams. Their name contradicts any relationship to the condition of sleep and, as regards the second universal characteristic, no experience or hallucination takes place in them, we simply imagine something; we recognize that they are the work of phantasy, that we are not seeing but thinking. These day-dreams appear before puberty, often indeed in late childhood, and persist until maturity is reached when they are either given up or retained as long as life lasts. The content of these phantasies is dictated by a very transparent motivation. They are scenes and events which gratify either the egoistic cravings of ambition or thirst for power, or the erotic desires of the subject. In young men, ambitious phantasies predominate; in women, whose ambition centres on success in love, erotic phantasies; but the erotic requirement can often enough in men too be detected in the background, all their heroic deeds and successes are really only intended to win the admiration and favour of women. In other respects these day-dreams show great diversity and their fate varies. All of them are either given up after a short time and replaced by a new one, or retained, spun out into long stories, and adapted to changing circumstances in life. They march with the times; and they receive as it were "date-stamps" upon them which show the influence of new situations. They form the raw material of poetic production; for the writer by transforming, disguising, or curtailing them creates out of his day-dreams the situations which he embodies in his stories, novels, and dramas. The hero of a day-dream is, however, always the subject himself, either directly imagined in the part or transparently identified with someone else.

Perhaps day-dreams are so called on account of their similar relation to reality, as an indication that their content is no more to be accepted as real than is that of dreams. But it is possible that they share the name of dreams because of some mental characteristic of the dream which we do not yet know but after which we are seeking. On the other hand, it is possible that we are altogether wrong in regarding this similarity of name as significant. That is a question which can only be answered later.

✦ Reading 28 ✦

Beyond Good and Evil

Friedrich Nietzsche

Prejudices of Philosophers

1.

The Will to Truth, which is to tempt us to many a hazardous enterprise, the famous Truthfulness of which all philosophers have hitherto spoken with respect, what questions has this Will to Truth not laid before us! What strange, perplexing, questionable questions! It is already a long story; yet it seems as if it were hardly commenced. Is it any wonder if we at last grow distrustful, lose patience, and turn impatiently away? That this Sphinx teaches us at last to ask questions ourselves? *Who* is it really that puts questions to us here? *What* really is this "Will to Truth" in us? In fact we made a long halt at the question as to the origin of this Will—until at last we came to an absolute standstill before a yet more fundamental question. We inquired about the *value* of this Will. Granted that we want the truth: *why not rather* untruth? And uncertainty? Even ignorance? The problem of the value of truth presented itself before us—or was it we who presented ourselves before the problem? Which of us is the Œdipus here? Which the Sphinx? It would seem to be a rendezvous of questions and notes of interrogation. And could it be believed that it at last seems to us as if the problem had never been propounded before, as if we were the first to discern it, get a sight of it, and *risk raising* it. For there is risk in raising it, perhaps there is no greater risk.

2.

"*How could* anything originate out of its opposite? For example, truth out of error? or the Will to Truth out of the will to deception? or the generous deed out of selfishness? or the pure sun-bright vision of the wise man out of covetousness? Such genesis is impossible; whoever dreams of it is a fool, nay, worse than a fool; things of the highest value must have a different origin, an origin of *their own*—in this transitory, seductive, illusory, paltry world, in this turmoil of delusion and cupidity, they cannot have their source. But rather in the lap of Being, in the intransitory, in the concealed God, in the 'Thing-in-itself'—*there* must be their source, and nowhere else!"—This mode of reasoning discloses the typical prejudice by which metaphysicians of all times can be recognised, this mode of valuation is at the back of all their logical procedure; through this "belief" of theirs, they exert themselves for their "knowledge," for something that is in the end solemnly christened "the Truth." The fundamental belief of metaphysicians is *the belief in antitheses of values.* It never occurred even to the wariest of them to doubt here on the very threshold (where doubt, however, was most necessary); though they had made a solemn vow, "*de omnibus dubitandum.*" For it may be doubted, firstly, whether antitheses exist at all; and secondly, whether the popular valuations and antitheses of value upon which metaphysicians have set their seal, are not perhaps merely superficial estimates, merely provisional perspectives, besides being probably made from some corner, perhaps from below—"frog perspectives," as it were, to borrow an expression current among painters. In spite of all the value which may belong to the true, the positive, and the unselfish, it might be possible that a higher and more fundamental value for life generally should be assigned to pretence, to the will to delusion, to selfishness, and cupidity. It might even be possible that *what* constitutes the value of those good and respected things, consists precisely in their being insidiously related, knotted, and crocheted to these evil and apparently opposed things—perhaps

From: Friedrich Nietzsche, *Beyond Good and Evil: Prelude to a Philosophy of the Future,* trans. Helen Zimmern (New York: Russell & Russell, Inc., 1964), pp. 5–8, 20–22, 33–34, 223–232, 234–237, 255–256.

even in being essentially identical with them. Perhaps! But who wishes to concern himself with such dangerous "Perhapses"! For that investigation one must await the advent of a new order of philosophers, such as will have other tastes and inclinations, the reverse of those hitherto prevalent—philosophers of the dangerous "Perhaps" in every sense of the term. And to speak in all seriousness, I see such new philosophers beginning to appear.

3.

Having kept a sharp eye on philosophers, and having read between their lines long enough, I now say to myself that the greater part of conscious thinking must be counted amongst the instinctive functions, and it is so even in the case of philosophical thinking; one has here to learn anew, as one learned anew about heredity and "innateness." As little as the act of birth comes into consideration in the whole process and procedure of heredity, just as little is "being-conscious" *opposed* to the instinctive in any decisive sense; the greater part of the conscious thinking of a philosopher is secretly influenced by his instincts, and forced into definite channels. And behind all logic and its seeming sovereignty of movement, there are valuations, or to speak more plainly, physiological demands, for the maintenance of a definite mode of life. For example, that the certain is worth more than the uncertain, that illusion is less valuable than "truth": such valuations, in spite of their regulative importance for *us,* might notwithstanding be only superficial valuations, special kinds of *niaiserie,* such as may be necessary for the maintenance of beings such as ourselves. Supposing, in effect, that man is not just the "measure of things."

* * *

13.

Psychologists should bethink themselves before putting down the instinct of self-preservation as the cardinal instinct of an organic being. A living thing seeks above all to *discharge* its strength—life itself is *Will to Power;* self-preservation is only one of the indirect and most frequent *results* thereof. In short, here, as everywhere else, let us beware of *superfluous* teleological principles!—one of which is the instinct of self-preservation (we owe it to Spinoza's inconsistency). It is thus, in effect, that method ordains, which must be essentially economy of principles.

14.

It is perhaps just dawning on five or six minds that natural philosophy is only a world-exposition and world-arrangement (according to us, if I may say so!) and *not* a world-explanation; but in so far as it is based on belief in the senses, it is regarded as more, and for a long time to come must be regarded as more—namely, as an explanation. It has eyes and fingers of its own, it has ocular evidence and palpableness of its own: this operates fascinatingly, persuasively, and *convincingly* upon an age with fundamentally plebeian tastes—in fact, it follows instinctively the canon of truth of eternal popular sensualism. What is clear, what is "explained"? Only that which can be seen and felt—one must pursue every problem thus far. Obversely, however, the charm of the Platonic mode of thought, which was an *aristocratic* mode, consisted precisely in *resistance to* obvious sense-evidence—perhaps among men who enjoyed even stronger and more fastidious senses than our contemporaries, but who knew how to find a higher triumph in remaining musters of them: and this by means of pale, cold, grey conceptional networks which they threw over the motley whirl of the senses—the mob of the senses, as Plato said. In this overcoming of the world, and interpreting of the world in the manner of Plato, there was an *enjoyment* different from that which the physicists of to-day offer us—and likewise the Darwinists and antiteleologists among the physiological workers, with their principle of the "smallest possible effort," and the greatest possible blunder. "Where there is nothing more to see or to grasp, there is also nothing more for men to do"—that is certainly an imperative different from the Platonic one, but it may notwithstanding be the right imperative for a hardy, laborious race of machinists and bridge-builders of the future, who have nothing but *rough* work to perform.

* * *

23.

All psychology hitherto has run aground on moral prejudices and timidities, it has not dared to launch out into the depths. In so far as it is allowable to recognise in that which has hitherto been written, evidence of that which has hitherto been kept silent, it seems as if nobody had yet harboured the notion of psychology as the Morphology and *Development-doctrine of the Will to Power,* as I conceive of it. The power of moral prejudices has penetrated deeply into the most intellectual world, the world apparently most indifferent and unprejudiced, and has obviously operated in an injurious, obstructive, blinding, and distorting manner. A proper physio-psychology has to contend with unconscious antagonism in the heart of the investigator, it has "the heart" against it: even a doctrine of the reciprocal conditionalness of the "good" and the "bad" impulses, causes (as refined immorality) distress and aversion in a still strong and manly conscience—still more so, a doctrine of the derivation of all good impulses from bad ones. If, however, a person should regard even the emotions of hatred, envy, covetousness, and imperiousness as life-conditioning emotions, as factors which must be present, fundamentally and essentially, in the general economy of life (which must, therefore, be further developed if life is to be further developed), he will suffer from such a view of things as from sea-sickness. And yet this hypothesis is far from being the strangest and most painful in this immense and almost new domain of dangerous knowledge; and there are in fact a hundred good reasons why every one should keep away from it who *can* do so! On the other hand, if one has once drifted hither with one's bark, well! very good! now let us set our teeth firmly! let us open our eyes and keep our hand fast on the helm! We sail away right *over* morality, we crush out, we destroy perhaps the remains of our own morality by daring to make our voyage thither—but what do *we* matter! Never yet did a *profounder* world of insight reveal itself to daring travellers and adventurers, and the psychologist who thus "makes a sacrifice"—it is *not* the *sacrifizio dell' intelletto,* on the contrary!—will at least be entitled to demand in return that psychology shall once more be recognised as the queen of the sciences, for whose service and equipment the other sciences exist. For psychology is once more the path to the fundamental problems.

* * *

What is Noble?

257.

Every elevation of the type "man," has hitherto been the work of an aristocratic society—and so will it always be—a society believing in a long scale of gradations of rank and differences of worth among human beings, and requiring slavery in some form or other. Without the *pathos of distance,* such as grows out of the incarnated difference of classes, out of the constant outlooking and downlooking of the ruling caste on subordinates and instruments, and out of their equally constant practice of obeying and commanding, of keeping down and keeping at a distance—that other more mysterious pathos could never have arisen, the longing for an ever new widening of distance within the soul itself, the formation of ever higher, rarer, further, more extended, more comprehensive states, in short, just the elevation of the type "man," the continued "self-surmounting of man," to use a moral formula in a supermoral sense. To be sure, one must not resign oneself to any humanitarian illusions about the history of the origin of an aristocratic society (that is to say, of the preliminary condition for the elevation of the type "man"): the truth is hard. Let us acknowledge unprejudicedly how every higher civilisation hitherto has *originated!* Men with a still natural nature, barbarians in every terrible sense of the word, men of prey, still in possession of unbroken strength of will and desire for power, threw themselves upon weaker, more moral, more peaceful races (perhaps trading or cattle-rearing communities), or upon old mellow civilisations in which the final vital force was flickering out in brilliant fireworks of wit and depravity. At the commencement, the noble caste was always the barbarian caste: their superiority did not consist first of all in their physical, but in their psychical power—they were more *complete* men (which at every point also implies the same as "more complete beasts").

258.

Corruption—as the indication that anarchy threatens to break out among the instincts, and that the foundation of the emotions, called "life," is convulsed—is something radically different according to the organisation in which it manifests itself. When, for instance, an aristocracy like that of France at the beginning of the Revolution, flung away its privileges with sublime disgust and sacrificed itself to an excess of its moral sentiments, it was corruption:—it was really only the closing act of the corruption which had existed for centuries, by virtue of which that aristocracy had abdicated step by step its lordly prerogatives and lowered itself to a *function* of royalty (in the end even to its decoration and parade-dress). The essential thing, however, in a good and healthy aristocracy is that it should *not* regard itself as a function either of the kingship or the commonwealth, but as the *significance* and highest justification thereof—that it should therefore accept with a good conscience the sacrifice of a legion of individuals, who, *for its sake,* must be suppressed and reduced to imperfect men, to slaves and instruments. Its fundamental belief must be precisely that society is *not* allowed to exist for its own sake, but only as a foundation and scaffolding, by means of which a select class of beings may be able to elevate themselves to their higher duties, and in general to a higher *existence:* like those sun-seeking climbing plants in Java—they are called *Sipo Matador,*— which encircle an oak so long and so often with their arms, until at last, high above it, but supported by it, they can unfold their tops in the open light, and exhibit their happiness.

259.

To refrain mutually from injury, from violence, from exploitation, and put one's will on a par with that of others: this may result in a certain rough sense in good conduct among individuals when the necessary conditions are given (namely, the actual similarity of the individuals in amount of force and degree of worth, and their co-relation within one organisation). As soon, however, as one wished to take this principle more generally, and if possible even as *the fundamental principle of society,* it would immediately disclose what it really is—namely, a Will to the *denial* of life, a principle of dissolution and decay. Here one must think profoundly to the very basis and resist all sentimental weakness: life itself is *essentially* appropriation, injury, conquest of the strange and weak, suppression, severity, obtrusion of peculiar forms, incorporation, and at the least, putting it mildest, exploitation;—but why should one for ever use precisely these words on which for ages a disparaging purpose has been stamped? Even the organisation within which, as was previously supposed, the individuals treat each other as equal—it takes place in every healthy aristocracy—must itself, if it be a living and not a dying organisation, do all that towards other bodies, which the individuals within it refrain from doing to each other: it will have to be the incarnated Will to Power, it will endeavour to grow, to gain ground, attract to itself and acquire ascendency—not owing to any morality or immorality, but because it *lives,* and because life *is* precisely Will to Power. On no point, however, is the ordinary consciousness of Europeans more unwilling to be corrected than on this matter; people now rave everywhere, even under the guise of science, about coming conditions of society in which "the exploiting character" is to be absent:—that sounds to my ears as if they promised to invent a mode of life which should refrain from all organic functions. "Exploitation" does not belong to a depraved, or imperfect and primitive society: it belongs to the *nature* of the living being as a primary organic function; it is a consequence of the intrinsic Will to Power, which is precisely the Will to Life.—Granting that as a theory this is a novelty—as a reality it is the *fundamental fact* of all history: let us be so far honest towards ourselves!

260.

In a tour through the many finer and coarser moralities which have hitherto prevailed or still prevail on the earth, I found certain traits recurring regularly together and connected with one another, until finally two primary types revealed themselves to me, and a radical distinction was brought to light. There is *master-morality* and *slave-morality;*—I would at once add, however, that in all higher and mixed civilisations, there are also attempts at the reconciliation of the two moralities; but one finds still oftener the confusion and mutual misunderstanding of them, indeed, sometimes their close juxtaposition—even in the same man, within one soul. The distinctions of moral values have either originated in a ruling caste, pleasantly conscious of being different from the ruled—or among the ruled class, the slaves and dependents of all sorts. In the first case, when it is the rulers who determine the conception "good," it is the exalted, proud disposition which is regarded as the distinguishing feature, and that which determines the order of rank. The noble type of man separates from himself the beings in whom the opposite of this exalted, proud disposition displays itself: he despises them. Let it at once be noted that in this first kind of morality the antithesis "good" and "bad" means practically the same as "noble" and "despicable";—the antithesis "good" and "*evil*" is of a different origin. The cowardly, the timid, the insignificant, and those thinking merely of narrow utility are despised; moreover, also, the distrustful, with their constrained glances, the self-abasing, the dog-like kind of men who let themselves be abused, the mendicant flatterers, and above all the liars:—it is a fundamental belief of all aristocrats that the common people are untruthful. "We truthful ones"—the nobility in ancient Greece called themselves. It is obvious that everywhere the designations of moral value were at first applied to *men,* and were only derivatively and at a later period applied to *actions;* it is a gross mistake, therefore, when historians of morals start with questions like, "Why have sympathetic actions been praised?" The noble type of man regards *himself* as a determiner of values; he does not require to be approved of; he passes the judgment: "What is injurious to me is injurious in itself"; he knows that it is he himself only who confers honour on things; he is a *creator of values.* He honours whatever he recognises in himself: such morality is self-glorification. In the foreground there is the feeling of plenitude, of power, which seeks to overflow, the happiness of high tension, the consciousness of a wealth which would fain give and bestow:—the noble man also helps the unfortunate, but not—or scarcely—out of pity, but rather from an impulse generated by the superabundance of power. The noble man honours in himself the powerful one, him also who has power over himself, who knows how to speak and how to keep silence, who takes pleasure in subjecting himself to severity and hardness, and has reverence for all that is severe and hard. "Wotan placed a hard heart in my breast," says an old Scandinavian Saga: it is thus rightly expressed from the soul of a proud Viking. Such a type of man is even proud of *not* being made for sympathy; the hero of the Saga therefore adds warningly: "He who has not a hard heart when young, will never have one." The noble and brave who think thus are the furthest removed from the morality which sees precisely in sympathy, or in acting for the good of others, or in *désintéressement,* the characteristic of the moral; faith in oneself, pride in oneself, a radical enmity and irony towards "selflessness," belong as definitely to noble morality, as do a careless scorn and precaution in presence of sympathy and the "warm heart."—It is the powerful who *know* how to honour, it is their art, their domain for invention. The profound reverence for age and for tradition—all law rests on this double reverence,—the belief and prejudice in favour of ancestors and unfavourable to newcomers, is typical in the morality of the powerful; and if, reversely, men of "modern ideas" believe almost instinctively in "progress" and the "future," and are more and more lacking in respect for old age, the ignoble origin of these "ideas" has complacently betrayed itself thereby. A morality of the ruling class, however, is more especially foreign and irritating to present-day taste in the sternness of its principle that one has duties only to one's equals; that one may act towards beings of a lower rank, towards all that is foreign, just as seems good to one, or "as the heart desires," and in any case "beyond good and evil": it is here that sympathy and similar sentiments can have a place. The ability and obligation to exercise prolonged gratitude and prolonged revenge—both only within the circle of equals,—artfulness in retaliation, *raffinement* of the idea in friendship, a certain necessity to have enemies (as outlets for the emotions of envy, quarrelsomeness, arrogance—in fact, in order to be a good *friend*): all these are typical characteristics of the noble morality, which, as has been pointed out, is not the morality of "modern ideas," and is therefore at present difficult to realise, and also to unearth and disclose.—It is otherwise with the second type of morality, *slave-morality*. Supposing that the abused, the oppressed, the suffering, the unemancipated, the weary, and those uncertain of themselves, should moralise, what will be the common element in their moral estimates? Probably a pessimistic suspicion with regard to the entire situation of man will find expression, perhaps a condemnation of man, together with his situation. The slave has an unfavourable eye for the virtues of the powerful; he has a scepticism and distrust, a *refinement* of distrust of everything "good" that is there honoured—he would fain persuade himself that the very happiness there is not genuine. On the other hand, *those* qualities which serve to alleviate the existence of sufferers are brought into prominence and flooded with light; it is here that sympathy, the kind, helping hand, the warm heart, patience, diligence, humility, and friendliness attain to honour; for here these are the most useful qualities, and almost the only means of supporting the burden of existence. Slave-morality is essentially the morality of utility. Here is the seat of the origin of the famous antithesis "good" and "*evil*":—power and dangerousness are assumed to reside in the evil, a certain dreadfulness, subtlety, and strength, which do not admit of being despised. According to slave-morality, therefore, the "evil" man arouses fear; according to master-morality, it is precisely the "good" man who arouses fear and seeks to arouse it, while the bad man is regarded as the despicable being. The contrast attains its maximum when, in accordance with the logical consequences of slave-morality, a shade of depreciation—it may be slight and well-intentioned—at last attaches itself even to the "good" man of this morality; because, according to the servile mode of thought, the good man must in any case be the *safe* man: he is good-natured, easily deceived, perhaps a little stupid, *un bonhomme*. Everywhere that slave-morality gains the ascendency, language shows a tendency to approximate the significations of the words "good" and "stupid."—A last fundamental difference: the desire for *freedom*, the instinct for happiness and the refinements of the feeling of liberty belong as necessarily to slave-morals and morality, as artifice and enthusiasm in reverence and devotion are the regular symptoms of an aristocratic mode of thinking and estimating.—Hence we can understand without further detail why love *as a passion*—it is our European speciality—must absolutely be of noble origin; as is well known, its invention is due to the Provençal poet-cavaliers, those brilliant ingenious men of the "*gai saber*," to whom Europe owes so much, and almost owes itself.

* * *

262.

A *species* originates, and a type becomes established and strong in the long struggle with essentially constant *unfavourable* conditions. On the other hand, it is known by the experience of breeders that species which receive superabundant nourishment, and in general a surplus of protection and care, immediately tend in the most marked way to develop variations, and are fertile in prodigies and monstrosities (also in monstrous vices). Now look at an aristocratic commonwealth, say an ancient Greek *polis*, or Venice, as a voluntary or involuntary contrivance for the purpose of *rearing* human beings; there are there men beside one another, thrown upon their own resources, who want to make their species prevail, chiefly because they *must* prevail, or else run the terrible danger of being exterminated. The favour, the superabundance, the protection are there lacking under which variations are fostered; the species needs itself as species, as something which, precisely by virtue of its hardness, its uniformity, and simplicity of structure, can in general prevail and make itself permanent in constant struggle with its neighbours, or with rebellious or rebellion-threatening vassals. The most varied experience teaches it what are the qualities to which it principally owes the fact that it still exists, in spite of all Gods and men, and has hitherto been victorious: these qualities it calls virtues, and these virtues alone it develops to maturity. It does so with severity, indeed it desires severity; every aristocratic morality is intolerant in the education of youth, in the control of women, in the marriage customs, in the relations of old and young, in the penal laws (which have an eye only for the degenerating): it counts intolerance itself among the virtues, under the name of "justice." A type with few, but very marked features, a species of severe, warlike, wisely silent, reserved and reticent men (and as such, with the most delicate sensibility for the charm and *nuances* of society) is thus established, unaffected by the vicissitudes of generations; the constant struggle with uniform *unfavourable* conditions is, as already remarked, the cause of a type becoming stable and hard. Finally, however, a happy state of things results, the enormous tension is relaxed; there are perhaps no more enemies among the neighbouring peoples, and the means of life, even of the enjoyment of life, are present in superabundance. With one stroke the bond and constraint of the old discipline severs: it is no longer regarded as necessary, as a condition of existence—if it would continue, it can only do so as a form of *luxury,* as an archaïsing *taste.* Variations, whether they be deviations (into the higher, finer, and rarer), or deteriorations and monstrosities, appear suddenly on the scene in the greatest exuberance and splendour; the individual dares to be individual and detach himself. At this turning-point of history there manifest themselves, side by side, and often mixed and entangled together, a magnificent, manifold, virgin-forest-like up-growth and up-striving, a kind of *tropical tempo* in the rivalry of growth, and an extraordinary decay and self-destruction, owing to the savagely opposing and seemingly exploding egoisms, which strive with one another "for sun and light," and can no longer assign any limit, restraint, or forbearance for themselves by means of the hitherto existing morality. It was this morality itself which piled up the strength so enormously, which bent the bow in so threatening a manner:—it is now "out of date," it is getting "out of date." The dangerous and disquieting point has been reached when the greater, more manifold, more comprehensive life *is lived beyond* the old morality; the "individual" stands out, and is obliged to have recourse to his own law-giving, his own arts and artifices for self-preservation, self-elevation, and self-deliverance. Nothing but new "Whys," nothing but new "Hows," no common formulas any longer, misunderstanding and disregard in league with each other, decay, deterioration, and the loftiest desires frightfully entangled, the genius of the race overflowing from all the cornucopias of good and bad, a portentous simultaneousness of Spring and Autumn, full of new charms and mysteries peculiar to the fresh, still inexhausted, still unwearied corruption. Danger is again present, the mother of morality, great danger; this time shifted into the individual, into the neighbour and friend, into the street, into their own child, into their own heart, into all the most personal and secret recesses of their desires and volitions. What will the moral philosophers who appear at this time have to preach? They discover, these sharp onlookers and loafers, that the end is quickly approaching, that everything around them decays and produces decay, that nothing will endure until the day after to-morrow, except one species of man, the incurably *mediocre.* The mediocre alone have a prospect of continuing and propagating themselves—they will be the men of the future, the sole survivors; "be like them! become mediocre!" is now the only morality which has still a significance, which still obtains a hearing.—But it is difficult to preach this morality of mediocrity! it can never avow what it is and what it desires! it has to talk of moderation and dignity and duty and brotherly love—it will have difficulty *in concealing its irony!*

* * *

287.

—What is noble? What does the word "noble" still mean for us nowadays? How does the noble man betray himself, how is he recognised under this heavy overcast sky of the commencing plebeianism, by which everything is rendered opaque and leaden?—It is not his actions which establish his claim—actions are always ambiguous, always inscrutable; neither is it his "works." One finds nowadays among artists and scholars plenty of those who betray by their works that a profound longing for nobleness impels them; but this very *need of* nobleness is radically different from the needs of the noble soul itself, and is in fact the eloquent and dangerous sign of the lack thereof. It is not the works, but the *belief* which is here decisive and determines the order of rank—to employ once more an old religious formula with a new and deeper meaning,—it is some fundamental certainty which a noble soul has about itself, something which is not to be sought, is not to be found, and perhaps, also, is not to be lost.—*The noble soul has reverence for itself.*—

PART EIGHT

EUROPEAN IMPERIALISM

Here German bacteriologists examine blood samples in East Africa to seek the cause of a regional plague, sleeping sickness. The image also suggests the mixed motives of post-1880 New Imperialism by its careful juxtaposition of efficient white Europeans and dependent, ill Africans.

European Imperialism

In the 1880s the centuries-old colonial question took on new meaning. Europe (joined by Japan and the United States) entered a period of renewed imperialism, during which European and other powers carved up Africa, much of Asia, and the Pacific islands. In the decades before World War I, Europeans alone seized 10 million square miles and subjugated a half billion people. Unlike the earlier forms of colonialism, the new imperialism had behind it popular support—the power of nationalism. The scramble for Africa turned into an inter-European competition that almost led to war. In 1885 the Berlin Conference established rules for the continued dismemberment of Africa, although tensions about global empires persisted.

Charles Darwin may not have applied his theories to human society but, as noted, others did. Herbert Spencer (1820–1903), later known as a Social Darwinist, shared Darwin's interest in aspects of evolutionary theory, except that he applied the concept of evolutionary competition to human society. His *Social Growth* (1897) argues that states, like animal species, struggle to survive and only the most highly developed prevail. Spencer emphasized the phrase "survival of the fittest" as equivalent to Darwin's "natural selection." To justify building new empires, most European states drew on the newly influential Social Darwinist mentality, which assumed the "superiority" of technologically advanced nations. The French talked about their "civilizing" mission, the Germans of spreading "culture," and the British of "the white man's burden." The poem "The White Man's Burden," written by Rudyard Kipling (1865–1936) in 1899, epitomizes the British view of the new imperialism. The essay "Shooting an Elephant" (1936) by George Orwell (1903–1950) depicts the relationship between imperialists and a subject community, in this case Burma between 1922 and 1927. Prominent among various explanations offered for the renewed imperialism is that of Vladimir Lenin (1870–1924). His *Imperialism: The Highest Stage of World Capitalism* (1916) portrayed it as the last desperate attempt of over-industrialized capitalist nations to avoid collapse.

✦ Reading 29 ✦

Social Growth

Herbert Spencer

Societies, like living bodies, begin as germs—originate from masses which are extremely minute in comparison with the masses some of them eventually reach. That out of small wandering hordes have arisen the largest societies, is a conclusion not to be contested. The implements of prehistoric peoples, ruder even than existing savages use, imply absence of those arts by which alone great aggregations of men are made possible. Religious ceremonies that survived among ancient historic races pointed back to a time when the progenitors of those races had flint knives, and got fire by rubbing together pieces of wood, and must have lived in such small clusters as are alone possible before the rise of agriculture.

The implication is that by integrations, direct and indirect, there have in course of time been produced social aggregates a million times in size the aggregates which alone existed in the remote past. Here, then, is a growth reminding us, by its degree, of growth in living bodies.

Between this trait of organic evolution and the answering trait of super-organic evolution, there is a further parallelism: the growths in aggregates of different classes are extremely various in their amounts.

Glancing over the entire assemblage of animal types, we see that the members of one large class, the *Protozoa,* rarely increase beyond the microscopic size with which every higher animal begins. Among the multitudinous kinds of *Coelenterata,* the masses range from that of the small hydra to that of the large medusa. The annulose and molluscous types respectively show us immense contrasts between their superior and inferior members. And the vertebrate animals, much larger on the average than the rest, display among themselves enormous differences.

From: *The Evolution of Society: Selections from Herbert Spencer's Principles of Sociology,* ed. Robert L. Carneiro (Chicago: The University of Chicago Press, 1967), pp. 9–13, 214–217.

Kindred unlikenesses of size strike us where we contemplate the entire assemblage of human societies. Scattered over many regions there are minute hordes—still extant samples of the primordial type of society. We have Wood Veddas living sometimes in pairs, and only now and then assembling; we have Bushmen wandering about in families, and forming larger groups but occasionally; we have Fuegians clustered by the dozen or the score. Tribes of Australians, of Tasmanians, of Andamanese, are variable within the limits of perhaps twenty to fifty. And similarly, if the region is inhospitable, as with the Eskimos, or if the arts of life are undeveloped, as with the Digger Indians, or if adjacent higher races are obstacles to growth, as with Indian Hill tribes like the Juangs, this limitation to primitive size continues. Where a fruitful soil affords much food, and where a more settled life, leading to agriculture, again increases the supply of food, we meet with larger social aggregates: instance those in the Polynesian Islands and in many parts of Africa. Here a hundred or two, here several thousands, here many thousands, are held together more or less completely as one mass. And then in the highest societies, instead of partially aggregated thousands, we have completely aggregated millions.

The growths of individual and social organisms are allied in another respect. In each case size augments by two processes which go on sometimes separately, sometimes together. There is increase by simple multiplication of units, causing enlargement of the group; there is increase by union of groups, and again by union of groups of groups. The first parallelism is too simple to need illustration but the facts which show us the second must be set forth.

Organic integration . . . must be here summarized to make the comparison intelligible. . . . The smallest animal, like the smallest plant, is essentially a minute group of living molecules. There are many forms and stages showing us the clustering of such smallest animals. Sometimes, as in the compound *Vorticellae* and in the sponges, their individualities are scarcely at all masked; but as evolution of the composite aggregate advances, the individualities of the component aggregates become less distinct. In some *Coelenterata,* though they retain considerable independence, which they show by moving about like amoebae when separated, they have their individualities mainly merged in that of the aggregate formed of them: instance the common hydra. Tertiary aggregates similarly result from the massing of secondary ones. . . .

Social growth proceeds by an analogous compounding and recompounding. The primitive social group, like the primitive group of living molecules with which organic evolution begins, never attains any considerable size by simple increase. Where, as among Fuegians, the supplies of wild food yielded by an inclement habitat will not enable more than a score or so to live in the same place—where, as among Andamanese, limited to a strip of shore backed by impenetrable bush, forty is about the number of individuals who can find prey without going too far from their temporary abode . . . —where, as among Bushmen, wandering over barren tracts, small hordes are alone possible and even families "are sometimes obliged to separate, since the same spot will not afford sufficient sustenance for all" . . . we have extreme instances of the limitation of simple groups, and the formation of migrating groups when the limit is passed.

Even in tolerably productive habitats, fission of the groups is eventually necessitated in a kindred manner. Spreading as its number increases, a primitive tribe presently reaches a diffusion at which its parts become incoherent, and it then gradually separates into tribes that become distinct as fast as their continually diverging dialects pass into different languages. Often nothing further happens than repetition of this. Conflicts of tribes, dwindlings or extinctions of some, growths and spontaneous divisions of others, continue.

The formation of a larger society results only by the joining of such smaller societies, which occurs without obliterating the divisions previously caused by separations. This process may be seen now going on among uncivilized races, as it once went on among the ancestors of the civilized races. Instead of absolute independence of small hordes, such as the lowest savages show us, more advanced savages show us slight cohesions among larger hordes. In North America each of the three great tribes of Comanches consists of various bands having such feeble combination only as results from the personal character of the great chief. . . . So of the Dakotas there are, according to Burton . . . , seven principal bands, each including minor bands, numbering altogether, according to Catlin, forty-two. . . . And in like manner the five Iroquois nations had severally eight tribes.

Closer unions of these slightly coherent original groups arise under favorable conditions, but they only now and then become permanent. A common form of the process is that described by Mason as occurring among the Karens. . . . "Each village, with its scant domain, is an independent state, and every chief a prince; but now and then a little Napoleon arises, who subdues a kingdom to himself, and builds up an empire. The dynasties, however, last only with the controlling mind." The like happens in Africa. Livingstone says, "Formerly all the Maganja were united under the government of their great Chief, Undi; . . . but after Undi's death it fell to pieces. . . . This has been the inevitable fate of every African Empire from time immemorial." . . .

Only occasionally does there result a compound social aggregate that endures for a considerable period, as Dahomey or as Ashanti, which is "an assemblage of states owing a kind of feudal obedience to the sovereign". . . . The histories of Madagascar and of sundry Polynesian islands also display these transitory compound groups, out of which at length come in some cases permanent ones. During the earliest times of the extinct civilized races, like stages were passed through. In the words of Maspero, Egypt was "divided at first into a great number of tribes, which at several points simultaneously began to establish small independent states, every one of which had its laws and its worship". . . . The compound groups of Greeks first formed were those minor ones resulting from the subjugation of weaker towns by stronger neighboring towns. And in northern Europe during pagan days the numerous German tribes, each with its cantonal divisions, illustrated this second stage of aggregation.

After such compound societies are consolidated, repetition of the process on a larger scale produces doubly compound societies which, usually cohering but feebly, become in some cases quite coherent. Maspero infers that the Egyptian nomes described above as resulting from integrations of tribes, coalesced into the two great principalities, Upper Egypt and Lower Egypt, which were eventually united, the small states becoming provinces. The boasting records of Mesopotamian kings similarly show us this union of unions going on. So, too, in Greece the integration at first occurring locally, began afterwards to combine the minor societies into two confederacies. During Roman days there arose for defensive purposes federations of tribes which eventually consolidated, and subsequently these were compounded into still larger aggregates. Before and after the Christian era, the like happened throughout Northern Europe. Then after a period of vague and varying combinations, there came, in later times, as is well illustrated by French history, a massing of small feudal territories into provinces, and a subsequent massing of these into kingdoms.

So that in both organic and superorganic growths we see a process of compounding and recompounding carried to various stages. In both cases, after some consolidation of the smallest aggregates there comes the process of forming larger aggregates by union of them; in both cases repetition of this process makes secondary aggregates into tertiary ones.

Organic growth and superorganic growth have yet another analogy. As above said, increase by multiplication of individuals in a group and increase by union of groups may go on simultaneously, and it does this in both cases.

The original clusters, animal and social, are not only small, but they lack density. Creatures of low types occupy large spaces considering the small quantities of animal substance they contain, and low-type societies spread over areas that are wide relatively to the numbers of their component individuals. But as integration in animals is shown by concentration as well as by increase of bulk, so that social integration which results from the clustering of clusters is joined with augmentation of the number contained by each cluster. If we contrast the sprinklings in regions inhabited by wild tribes with the crowds filling equal regions in Europe or if we contrast the density of population in England under the Heptarchy with its present density, we see that besides the growth produced by union of groups there has gone on interstitial growth. Just as the higher animal has become not only larger than the lower but more solid, so, too, has the higher society.

Social growth, then, equally with the growth of a living body, shows us the fundamental trait of evolution under a twofold aspect. Integration is displayed both in the formation of a larger mass and in the progress of such mass towards that coherence due to closeness of parts.

It is proper to add, however, that there is a model of social growth to which organic growth affords no parallel—that caused by the migration of units from one society to another. Among many primitive groups and a few developed ones this is a considerable factor but, generally, its effect bears so small a ratio to the effects of growth by increase of population and coalescence of groups that it does not much qualify the analogy.

* * *

Summary

. . . We [have seen] . . . that societies are aggregates which grow; that in the various types of them there are great varieties in the growths reached; that types of successively larger sizes result from the aggregation and reaggregation of those of smaller sizes; and that this increase by coalescence, joined with interstitial increase, is the process through which have been formed the vast civilized nations.

Along with increase of size in societies goes increase of structure. Primitive hordes are without established distinctions of parts. With growth of them into tribes habitually come some unlikenesses, both in the powers and occupations of their members. Unions of tribes are followed by more unlikenesses, governmental and industrial—social grades running through the whole mass, and contrasts between the differently occupied parts in different localities. Such differentiations multiply as the compounding progresses. They proceed from the general to the special. First the broad division between ruling and ruled; then within the ruling part divisions into political, religious, military, and within the ruled part divisions into food-producing classes and handicraftsmen; then within each of these divisions minor ones, and so on.

Passing from the structural aspect to the functional aspect, we note that so long as all parts of a society have like natures and activities, there is hardly any mutual dependence, and the aggregate scarcely forms a vital whole. As its parts assume different functions they become dependent on one another, so that injury to one hurts others, until, in highly evolved societies, general perturbation is caused by derangement of any portion. This contrast between undeveloped and developed societies arises from the fact that with increasing specialization of functions comes increasing inability in each part to perform the functions of other parts.

The organization of every society begins with a contrast between the division which carries on relations habitually hostile with environing societies and the division which is devoted to procuring necessaries of life, and during the earlier stages of development these two divisions constitute the whole. Eventually there arises an intermediate division serving to transfer products and influences from part to part. And in all subsequent stages, evolution of the two earlier systems of structures depends on evolution of this additional system.

While the society as a whole has the character of its sustaining system determined by the character of its environment, inorganic and organic, the respective parts of this system differentiate in adaptation to local circumstances, and, after primary industries have been thus localized and specialized, secondary industries dependent on them arise in conformity with the same principle. Further, as fast as societies become compounded and recompounded and the distributing system develops, the parts devoted to each kind of industry, originally scattered, aggregate in the most favorable localities, and the localized industrial structures, unlike the governmental structures, grow regardless of the original lines of division.

Increase of size, resulting from the massing of groups, necessitates means of communication, both for achieving combined offensive and defensive actions, and for exchange of products. Faint tracks, then paths, rude roads, finished roads, successively arise, and as fast as intercourse is thus facilitated, there is a transition from direct barter to trading carried on by a separate class, out of which evolves a complex mercantile agency of wholesale and retail distributors. The movement of commodities effected by this agency, beginning as a slow flux to and reflux from certain places at long intervals, passes into rhythmical, regular, rapid currents, and materials for sustentation distributed hither and thither, from being few and crude become numerous and elaborated. Growing efficiency of transfer with greater variety of transferred products, increases the mutual dependence of parts at the same time that it enables each part to fulfil its function better.

Unlike the sustaining system, evolved by converse with the organic and inorganic environments, the regulating system is evolved by converse, offensive and defensive, with environing societies. In primitive headless groups temporary chieftainship results from temporary war; chronic hostilities generate permanent chieftainship; and gradually from the military control results the civil control. Habitual war, requiring prompt combination in the actions of parts, necessitates subordination. Societies in which there is little subordination disappear, and leave outstanding those in which subordination is great, and so there are produced societies in which the habit fostered by war and surviving in peace brings about permanent submission to a government. The centralized regulating system thus evolved, is in early stages the sole regulating system. But in large societies which have become predominantly industrial there is added a decentralized regulating system for the industrial structures, and this, at first subject in every way to the original system, acquires at length substantial independence. Finally there arises for the distributing structures also an independent controlling agency.

Societies fall firstly into the classes of simple, compound, doubly compound, trebly compound, and from the lowest the transition to the highest is through these stages. Otherwise, though less definitely, societies may be grouped as militant and industrial, of which the one type in its developed form is organized on the principle of compulsory cooperation, while the other in its developed form is organized on the principle of voluntary cooperation. The one is characterized not only by a despotic central power, but also by unlimited political control of personal conduct, while the other is characterized not only by a democratic or representative central power, but also by limitation of political control over personal conduct.

Lastly we noted the corollary that change in the predominant social activities brings metamorphosis. If, where the militant type has not elaborated into so rigid a form as to prevent change, a considerable industrial system arises, there come mitigations of the coercive restraints characterizing the militant type, and weakening of its structure. Conversely, where an industrial system largely developed has established freer social forms, resumption of offensive and defensive activities causes reversion towards the militant type. . . .

The many facts contemplated unite in proving that social evolution forms a part of evolution at large. Like evolving aggregates in general, societies show *integration,* both by simple increase of mass and by coalescence and recoalescence of masses. The change from *homogeneity* to *heterogeneity* is multitudinously exemplified, up from the simple tribe, alike in all its parts, to the civilized nation, full of structural and functional unlikenesses. With progressing integration and heterogeneity goes increasing *coherence.* We see the wandering group dispersing, dividing, held together by no bonds; the tribe with parts made more coherent by subordination to a dominant man; the cluster of tribes united into a political plexus under a chief with subchiefs; and so on up to the civilized nation, consolidated enough to hold together for a thousand years or more. Simultaneously comes increasing *definiteness.* Social organization is at first vague; advance brings settled arrangements which grow slowly more precise; customs pass into laws which, while gaining fixity, also become more specific in their applications to varieties of actions; and all institutions, at first confusedly intermingled, slowly separate, at the same time that each within itself marks off more distinctly its component structures. Thus in all respects is fulfilled the formula of evolution. There is progress towards greater size, coherence, multiformity, and definiteness.

Besides these general truths, a number of special truths have been disclosed by our survey. Comparisons of societies in their ascending grades have made manifest certain cardinal facts respecting their growths, structures, and functions—facts respecting the systems of structures, sustaining, distributing, regulating, of which they are composed; respecting the relations of these structures to the surrounding conditions and the dominant forms of social activities entailed; and respecting the metamorphoses of types caused by changes in activities. The inductions arrived at, thus constituting in rude outline an empirical sociology, show that in social phenomena there is a general order of co-existence and sequence, and that therefore social phenomena form the subject matter of a science. . . .

✦ **Reading 30** ✦

The White Man's Burden (1899)

Rudyard Kipling

(The United States and the Philippine Islands)

Take up the White Man's burden—
  Send forth the best ye breed—
Go bind your sons to exile
  To serve your captives' need;
To wait in heavy harness
  On fluttered folk and wild—
Your new-caught, sullen peoples,
  Half devil and half child.

Take up the White Man's burden—
  In patience to abide,
To veil the threat of terror
  And check the show of pride;
By open speech and simple,
  An hundred times made plain,
To seek another's profit,
  And work another's gain.

Take up the White Man's burden—
  The savage wars of peace—
Fill full the mouth of Famine
  And bid the sickness cease;
And when your goal is nearest
  The end for others sought,
Watch Sloth and heathen Folly
  Bring all your hope to nought.

Take up the White Man's burden—
  No tawdry rule of kings,
But toil of serf and sweeper—
  The tale of common things.
The ports ye shall not enter,
  The roads ye shall not tread,
Go make them with your living,
  And mark them with your dead!

Take up the White Man's burden—
  And reap his old reward:
The blame of those ye better,
  The hate of those ye guard—
The cry of hosts ye humour
  (Ah, slowly!) toward the light:—
'Why brought ye us from bondage,
  'Our loved Egyptian night?'

Take up the White Man's burden—
  Ye dare not stoop to less—
Nor call too loud on Freedom
  To cloak your weariness;
By all ye cry or whisper,
  By all ye leave or do,
The silent, sullen peoples
  Shall weigh your Gods and you.

Take up the White Man's burden—
  Have done with childish days—
The lightly proffered laurel,
  The easy, ungrudged praise.
Comes now, to search your manhood
  Through all the thankless years,
Cold-edged with dear-bought wisdom,
  The judgment of your peers!

From: T. S. Eliot, *A Choice of Kipling's Verse,* (New York: Charles Scribner's Sons, 1943), pp. 136–137.

✦ Reading 31 ✦

Shooting an Elephant

George Orwell

In Moulmein, in Lower Burma, I was hated by large numbers of people—the only time in my life that I have been important enough for this to happen to me. I was sub-divisional police officer of the town, and in an aimless, petty kind of way anti-European feeling was very bitter. No one had the guts to raise a riot, but if a European woman went through the bazaars alone somebody would probably spit betel juice over her dress. As a police officer I was an obvious target and was baited whenever it seemed safe to do so. When a nimble Burman tripped me up on the football field and the referee (another Burman) looked the other way, the crowd yelled with hideous laughter. This happened more than once. In the end the sneering yellow faces of young men that met me everywhere, the insults hooted after me when I was at a safe distance, got badly on my nerves. The young Buddhist priests were the worst of all. There were several thousands of them in the town and none of them seemed to have anything to do except stand on street corners and jeer at Europeans.

All this was perplexing and upsetting. For at that time I had already made up my mind that imperialism was an evil thing and the sooner I chucked up my job and got out of it the better. Theoretically—and secretly, of course—I was all for the Burmese and all against their oppressors, the British. As for the job I was doing, I hated it more bitterly than I can perhaps make clear. In a job like that you see the dirty work of Empire at close quarters. The wretched prisoners huddling in the stinking cages of the lock-ups, the grey, cowed faces of the long-term convicts, the scarred buttocks of the men who had been flogged with bamboos—all these oppressed me with an intolerable sense of guilt. But I could get nothing into perspective. I was young and ill-educated and I had had to think out my problems in the utter silence that is imposed on every Englishman in the East. I did not even know that the British Empire is dying, still less did I know that it is a great deal better than the younger empires that are going to supplant it. All I knew was that I was stuck between my hatred of the empire I served and my rage against the evil-spirited little beasts who tried to make my job impossible. With one part of my mind I thought of the British Raj as an unbreakable tyranny, as something clamped down, in *saecula saeculorum,* upon the will of prostrate peoples; with another part I thought that the greatest joy in the world would be to drive a bayonet into a Buddhist priest's guts. Feelings like these are the normal by-products of imperialism; ask any Anglo-Indian official, if you can catch him off duty.

One day something happened which in a roundabout way was enlightening. It was a tiny incident in itself, but it gave me a better glimpse than I had had before of the real nature of imperialism—the real motives for which despotic governments act. Early one morning the sub-inspector at a police station the other end of the town rang me up on the 'phone and said that an elephant was ravaging the bazaar. Would I please come and do something about it? I did not know what I could do, but I wanted to see what was happening and I got on to a pony and started out. I took my rifle, an old .44 Winchester and much too small to kill an elephant, but I thought the noise might be useful *in terrorem.* Various Burmans stopped me on the way and told me about the elephant's doings. It was not, of course, a wild elephant, but a tame one which had gone "must." It had been chained up, as tame elephants always are when their attack of "must" is due, but on the previous night it had broken its chain and escaped. Its mahout, the only person who could manage it when it was in that state, had set out in pursuit, but had taken the wrong direction and was now twelve hours'

From: George Orwell, *A Collection of Essays,* (New York: Doubleday Anchor Books, 1954), pp. 154–162.

journey away, and in the morning the elephant had suddenly reappeared in the town. The Burmese population had no weapons and were quite helpless against it. It had already destroyed somebody's bamboo hut, killed a cow and raided some fruit-stalls and devoured the stock; also it had met the municipal rubbish van and, when the driver jumped out and took to his heels, had turned the van over and inflicted violences upon it.

The Burmese sub-inspector and some Indian constables were waiting for me in the quarter where the elephant had been seen. It was a very poor quarter, a labyrinth of squalid bamboo huts, thatched with palm-leaf, winding all over a steep hillside. I remember that it was a cloudy, stuffy morning at the beginning of the rains. We began questioning the people as to where the elephant had gone and, as usual, failed to get any definite information. That is invariably the case in the East; a story always sounds clear enough at a distance, but the nearer you get to the scene of events the vaguer it becomes. Some of the people said that the elephant had gone in one direction, some said that he had gone in another, some professed not even to have heard of any elephant. I had almost made up my mind that the whole story was a pack of lies, when we heard yells a little distance away. There was a loud, scandalized cry of "Go away, child! Go away this instant!" and an old woman with a switch in her hand came round the corner of a hut, violently shooing away a crowd of naked children. Some more women followed, clicking their tongues and exclaiming; evidently there was something that the children ought not to have seen. I rounded the hut and saw a man's dead body sprawling in the mud. He was an Indian, a black Dravidian coolie, almost naked, and he could not have been dead many minutes. The people said that the elephant had come suddenly upon him round the corner of the hut, caught him with its trunk, put its foot on his back and ground him into the earth. This was the rainy season and the ground was soft, and his face had scored a trench a foot deep and a couple of yards long. He was lying on his belly with arms crucified and head sharply twisted to one side. His face was coated with mud, the eyes wide open, the teeth bared and grinning with an expression of unendurable agony. (Never tell me, by the way, that the dead look peaceful. Most of the corpses I have seen looked devilish.) The friction of the great beast's foot had stripped the skin from his back as neatly as one skins a rabbit. As soon as I saw the dead man I sent an orderly to a friend's house nearby to borrow an elephant rifle. I had already sent back the pony, not wanting it to go mad with fright and throw me if it smelt the elephant.

The orderly came back in a few minutes with a rifle and five cartridges, and meanwhile some Burmans had arrived and told us that the elephant was in the paddy fields below, only a few hundred yards away. As I started forward practically the whole population of the quarter flocked out of the houses and followed me. They had seen the rifle and were all shouting excitedly that I was going to shoot the elephant. They had not shown much interest in the elephant when he was merely ravaging their homes, but it was different now that he was going to be shot. It was a bit of fun to them, as it would be to an English crowd; besides they wanted the meat. It made me vaguely uneasy. I had no intention of shooting the elephant—I had merely sent for the rifle to defend myself if necessary—and it is always unnerving to have a crowd following you. I marched down the hill, looking and feeling a fool, with the rifle over my shoulder and an ever-growing army of people jostling at my heels. At the bottom, when you got away from the huts, there was a metalled road and beyond that a miry waste of paddy fields a thousand yards across, not yet ploughed but soggy from the first rains and dotted with coarse grass. The elephant was standing eight yards from the road, his left side towards us. He took not the slightest notice of the crowd's approach. He was tearing up bunches of grass, beating them against his knees to clean them and stuffing them into his mouth.

I had halted on the road. As soon as I saw the elephant I knew with perfect certainty that I ought not to shoot him. It is a serious matter to shoot a working elephant—it is comparable to destroying a huge and costly piece of machinery—and obviously one ought not to do it if it can possibly be avoided. And at that distance, peacefully eating, the elephant looked no more dangerous than a cow. I thought then and I think now that his attack of "must" was already passing off; in which case he would merely wander harmlessly about until the mahout came back and caught him. Moreover, I did not in the least want to shoot him. I decided that I would watch him for a little while to make sure that he did not turn savage again, and then go home.

But at that moment I glanced round at the crowd that had followed me. It was an immense crowd, two thousand at the least and growing every minute. It blocked the road for a long distance on either side. I looked at the sea of yellow faces above the garish clothes—faces all happy and excited over this bit of fun, all certain that the elephant was going to be shot. They were watching me as they would watch a conjurer about to perform a trick. They did not like me, but with the magical rifle in my hands I was momentarily worth watching. And suddenly I realized that I should have to shoot the elephant after all. The people expected it of me and I had got to do it; I could feel their two thousand wills pressing me forward, irresistibly. And it was at this moment, as I stood there with the rifle in my hands, that I first grasped the hollowness, the futility of the white man's dominion in the East. Here was I, the white man with his gun, standing in front of the unarmed native crowd—seemingly the leading actor of the piece; but in reality I was only an absurd puppet pushed to and fro by the will of those yellow faces behind. I perceived in this moment that when the white man turns tyrant it is his own freedom that he destroys. He becomes a sort of hollow, posing dummy, the conventionalized figure of a sahib. For it is the condition of his rule that he shall spend his life in trying to impress the "natives," and so in every crisis he has got to do what the "natives" expect of him. He wears a mask, and his face grows to fit it. I had got to shoot the elephant. I had committed myself to doing it when I sent for the rifle. A sahib has got to act like a sahib; he has got to appear resolute, to know his own mind and do definite things. To come all that way, rifle in hand, with two thousand people marching at my heels, and then to trail feebly away, having done nothing—no, that was impossible. The crowd would laugh at me. And my whole life, every white man's life in the East, was one long struggle not to be laughed at.

But I did not want to shoot the elephant. I watched him beating his bunch of grass against his knees, with that preoccupied grandmotherly air that elephants have. It seemed to me that it would be murder to shoot him. At that age I was not squeamish about killing animals, but I had never shot an elephant and never wanted to. (Somehow it always seems worse to kill a *large* animal.) Besides, there was the beast's owner to be considered. Alive, the elephant was worth at least a hundred pounds; dead, he would only be worth the value of his tusks, five pounds, possibly. But I had got to act quickly. I turned to some experienced-looking Burmans who had been there when we arrived, and asked them how the elephant had been behaving. They all said the same thing: he took no notice of you if you left him alone, but he might charge if you went too close to him.

It was perfectly clear to me what I ought to do. I ought to walk up to within, say, twenty-five yards of the elephant and test his behavior. If he charged, I could shoot; if he took no notice of me, it would be safe to leave him until the mahout came back. But also I knew that I was going to do no such thing. I was a poor shot with a rifle and the ground was soft mud into which one would sink at every step. If the elephant charged and I missed him, I should have about as much chance as a toad under a steamroller. But even then I was not thinking particularly of my own skin, only of the watchful yellow faces behind. For at that moment, with the crowd watching me, I was not afraid in the ordinary sense, as I would have been if I had been alone. A white man mustn't be frightened in front of "natives"; and so, in general, he isn't frightened. The sole thought in my mind was that if anything went wrong those two thousand Burmans would see me pursued, caught, trampled on and reduced to a grinning corpse like that Indian up the hill. And if that happened it was quite probable that some of them would laugh. That would never do. There was only one alternative. I shoved the cartridges into the magazine and lay down on the road to get a better aim.

The crowd grew very still, and a deep, low, happy sigh, as of people who see the theatre curtain go up at last, breathed from innumerable throats. They were going to have their bit of fun after all. The rifle was a beautiful German thing with cross-hair sights. I did not then know that in shooting an elephant one would shoot to cut an imaginary bar running from ear-hole to ear-hole. I ought, therefore, as the elephant was sideways on, to have aimed straight at his ear-hole; actually I aimed several inches in front of this, thinking the brain would be further forward.

When I pulled the trigger I did not hear the bang or feel the kick—one never does when a shot goes home—but I heard the devilish roar of glee that went up from the crowd. In that instant, in too short a time, one would have thought, even for the bullet to get there, a mysterious, terrible change had come over the elephant. He neither stirred nor fell, but every line of his body had altered. He looked suddenly stricken, shrunken, immensely old, as though the frightful impact of the bullet had paralysed him without knocking him down. At last, after what seemed a long time—it might have been five seconds, I dare say—he sagged flabbily to his knees. His mouth slobbered. An enormous senility seemed to have settled upon him. One could have imagined him thousands of years old. I fired again into the same spot. At the second shot he did not collapse but climbed with desperate slowness to his feet and stood weakly upright, with legs sagging and head drooping. I fired a third time. That was the shot that did for him. You could see the agony of it jolt his whole body and knock the last remnant of strength from his legs. But in falling he seemed for a moment to rise, for as his hind legs collapsed beneath him he seemed to tower upward like a huge rock toppling, his trunk reaching skywards like a tree. He trumpeted, for the first and only time. And then down he came, his belly towards me, with a crash that seemed to shake the ground even where I lay.

I got up. The Burmans were already racing past me across the mud. It was obvious that the elephant would never rise again, but he was not dead. He was breathing very rhythmically with long rattling gasps, his great mound of a side painfully rising and falling. His mouth was wide open—I could see far down into caverns of pale pink throat. I waited a long time for him to die, but his breathing did not weaken. Finally I fired my two remaining shots into the spot where I thought his heart must be. The thick blood welled out of him like red velvet, but still he did not die. His body did not even jerk when the shots hit him, the tortured breathing continued without a pause. He was dying, very slowly and in great agony, but in some world remote from me where not even a bullet could damage him further. I felt that I had got to put an end to that dreadful noise. It seemed dreadful to see the great beast lying there, powerless to move and yet powerless to die, and not even to be able to finish him. I sent back for my small rifle and poured shot after shot into his heart and down his throat. They seemed to make no impression. The tortured gasps continued as steadily as the ticking of a clock.

In the end I could not stand it any longer and went away. I heard later that it took him half an hour to die. Burmans were bringing dahs and baskets even before I left, and I was told they had stripped his body almost to the bones by the afternoon.

Afterwards, of course, there were endless discussions about the shooting of the elephant. The owner was furious, but he was only an Indian and could do nothing. Besides, legally I had done the right thing, for a mad elephant has to be killed, like a mad dog, if its owner fails to control it. Among the Europeans opinion was divided. The older men said I was right, the younger men said it was a damn shame to shoot an elephant for killing a coolie, because an elephant was worth more than any damn Coringhee coolie. And afterwards I was very glad that the coolie had been killed; it put me legally in the right and it gave me a sufficient pretext for shooting the elephant. I often wondered whether any of the others grasped that I had done it solely to avoid looking a fool.

✦ Reading 32 ✦

Imperialism: The Highest Stage of World Capitalism

V. I. Lenin

Preface to the Russian Edition

The pamphlet here presented to the reader was written in Zürich in the spring of 1916. In the conditions in which I was obliged to work there I naturally suffered somewhat from a shortage of French and English literature and from a serious dearth of Russian literature. However, I made use of the principal English work, *Imperialism,* J. A. Hobson's book, with all the care that, in my opinion, that work deserves.

This pamphlet was written with an eye to the tsarist censorship. Hence, I was not only forced to confine myself strictly to an exclusively theoretical, mainly economic analysis of facts, but to formulate the few necessary observations on politics with extreme caution, by hints, in that Æsopian language—in that cursed Æsopian language—to which tsarism compelled all revolutionaries to have recourse whenever they took up their pens to write a "legal" work.

It is very painful, in these days of liberty, to read these cramped passages of the pamphlet, crushed, as they seem, in an iron vise, distorted on account of the censor. Of how imperialism is the eve of the socialist revolution; of how social-chauvinism (socialism in words, chauvinism in deeds) is the utter betrayal of socialism, complete desertion to the side of the bourgeoisie; of how the split in the labour movement is bound up with the objective conditions of imperialism, etc., I had to speak in a "slavish" tongue. . . . In order to show, in a guise acceptable to the censors, how shamefully the capitalists and the social-chauvinist deserters (whom Kautsky opposes with so much inconsistency) lie on the question of annexations; in order to show with what cynicism they *screen* the annexations of *their* capitalists, I was forced to quote as an example—Japan! The careful reader will easily substitute Russia for Japan, and Finland, Poland, Courland, the Ukraine, Khiva, Bokhara, Estonia or other regions peopled by non-Great Russians, for Korea.

I trust that this pamphlet will help the reader to understand the fundamental economic question, *viz.,* the question of the economic essence of imperialism, for unless this is studied, it will be impossible to understand and appraise modern war and modern politics.

* * *

Imperialism, the Highest Stage of Capitalism

During the last fifteen or twenty years, especially since the Spanish-American War (1898), and the Anglo-Boer War (1899–1902), the economic and also the political literature of the two hemispheres has more and more often adopted the term "imperialism" in order to define the present era. In 1902, a book by the English economist, J. A. Hobson, *Imperialism,* was published in London and New York. This author, who adopts the point of view of bourgeois social reformism and pacifism which, in essence, is identical with the present point of view of the ex-Marxist, K. Kautsky, gives an excellent and comprehensive description of the principal economic and political characteristics of imperialism. In 1910, there appeared in Vienna the work of the Austrian Marxist, Rudolf Hilferding, *Finance Capital.* In spite of the mistake the author commits on the theory of money, and in spite of a certain inclination on his part to reconcile Marxism with opportunism, this work gives a very valuable theoretical analysis, as its sub-title tells us, of "the latest phase of capitalist development." Indeed, what has been said of imperialism during the last few years, especially in a

---

From: V. I. Lenin, *Imperialism: The Highest Stage of World Capitalism* (New York: International Publishers, 1939), pp. 7–8, 15, 123–128.

great many magazine and newspaper articles, and also in the resolutions, for example, of the Chemnitz and Basle Congresses which took place in the autumn of 1912, has scarcely gone beyond the ideas put forward, or, more exactly, summed up by the two writers mentioned above.

Later on we shall try to show briefly, and as simply as possible, the connection and relationships between the *principal* economic features of imperialism. We shall not be able to deal with non-economic aspects of the question, however much they deserve to be dealt with. . . .

* * *

The Place of Imperialism in History

We have seen that the economic quintessence of imperialism is monopoly capitalism. This very fact determines its place in history, for monopoly that grew up on the basis of free competition, and precisely out of free competition, is the transition from the capitalist system to a higher social-economic order. We must take special note of the four principal forms of monopoly, or the four principal manifestations of monopoly capitalism, which are characteristic of the epoch under review.

Firstly, monopoly arose out of the concentration of production at a very advanced stage of development. This refers to the monopolist capitalist combines, cartels, syndicates and trusts. We have seen the important part that these play in modern economic life. At the beginning of the twentieth century, monopolies acquired complete supremacy in the advanced countries. And although the first steps towards the formation of the cartels were first taken by countries enjoying the protection of high tariffs (Germany, America), Great Britain, with her system of free trade, was not far behind in revealing the same basic phenomenon, namely, the birth of monopoly out of the concentration of production.

Secondly, monopolies have accelerated the capture of the most important sources of raw materials, especially for the coal and iron industries, which are the basic and most highly cartelised industries in capitalist society. The monopoly of the most important sources of raw materials has enormously increased the power of big capital, and has sharpened the antagonism between cartelised and noncartelised industry.

Thirdly, monopoly has sprung from the banks. The banks have developed from modest intermediary enterprises into the monopolists of finance capital. Some three or five of the biggest banks in each of the foremost capitalist countries have achieved the "personal union" of industrial and bank capital, and have concentrated in their hands the disposal of thousands upon thousands of millions which form the greater part of the capital and income of entire countries. A financial oligarchy, which throws a close net of relations of dependence over all the economic and political institutions of contemporary bourgeois society without exception—such is the most striking manifestation of this monopoly.

Fourthly, monopoly has grown out of colonial policy. To the numerous "old" motives of colonial policy, finance capital has added the struggle for the sources of raw materials, for the export of capital, for "spheres of influence," *i.e.,* for spheres for profitable deals, concessions, monopolist profits and so on; in fine, for economic territory in general. When the colonies of the European powers in Africa, for instance, comprised only one-tenth of that territory (as was the case in 1876), colonial policy was able to develop by methods other than those of monopoly—by the "free grabbing" of territories, so to speak. But when nine-tenths of Africa had been seized (approximately by 1900), when the whole world had been divided up, there was inevitably ushered in a period of colonial monopoly and, consequently, a period of particularly intense struggle for the division and the redivision of the world.

The extent to which monopolist capital has intensified all the contradictions of capitalism is generally known. It is sufficient to mention the high cost of living and the oppression of the cartels. This intensification of contradictions constitutes the most powerful driving force of the transitional period of history, which began from the time of the definite victory of world finance capital.

Monopolies, oligarchy, the striving for domination instead of the striving for liberty, the exploitation of an increasing number of small or weak nations by an extremely small group of the richest or most powerful nations—all these have given birth to those distinctive characteristics of imperialism which compel us to define it as parasitic or decaying capitalism. More and more prominently there emerges, as one of the tendencies of imperialism, the creation of the "bondholding" (rentier) state, the usurer state, in which the bourgeoisie lives on the proceeds of capital exports and by "clipping coupons." It would be a mistake to believe that this tendency to decay precludes the possibility of the rapid growth of capitalism. It does not. In the epoch of imperialism, certain branches of industry, certain strata of the bourgeoisie and certain countries betray, to a more or less degree, one or other of these tendencies. On the whole, capitalism is growing far more rapidly than before. But this growth is not only becoming more and more uneven in general; its unevenness also manifests itself, in particular, in the decay of the countries which are richest in capital (such as England).

In regard to the rapidity of Germany's economic development, Riesser, the author of the book on the big German banks, states.

"The progress of the preceding period (1848–70), which had not been exactly slow, stood in about the same ratio to the rapidity with which the whole of Germany's national economy, and with it German banking, progressed during this period (1870–1905) as the mail coach of the Holy Roman Empire of the German nation stood to the speed of the present-day automobile . . . which in whizzing past, it must be said, often endangers not only innocent pedestrians in its path, but also the occupants of the car."

In its turn, this finance capital which has grown so rapidly is not unwilling (precisely because it has grown so quickly) to pass on to a more "tranquil" possession of colonies which have to be seized—and not only by peaceful methods—from richer nations. In the United States, economic development in the last decades has been even more rapid than in Germany, and *for this very reason* the parasitic character of modern American capitalism has stood out with particular prominence. On the other hand, a comparison of, say, the republican American bourgeoisie with the monarchist Japanese or German bourgeoisie shows that the most pronounced political distinctions diminish to an extreme degree in the epoch of imperialism—not because they are unimportant in general, but because in all these cases we are discussing a bourgeoisie which has definite features of parasitism.

The receipt of high monopoly profits by the capitalists in one of the numerous branches of industry, in one of numerous countries, etc., makes it economically possible for them to corrupt certain sections of the working class, and for a time a fairly considerable minority, and win them to the side of the bourgeoisie of a given industry or nation against all the others. The intensification of antagonisms between imperialist nations for the division of the world increases this striving. And so there is created that bond between imperialism and opportunism, which revealed itself first and most clearly in England, owing to the fact that certain features of imperialist development were observable there much earlier than in other countries.

Some writers, L. Martov, for example, try to evade the fact that there is a connection between imperialism and opportunism in the labour movement—which is particularly striking at the present time—by resorting to "official optimistic" arguments (*à la* Kautsky and Huysmans) like the following: the cause of the opponents of capitalism would be hopeless if it were precisely progressive capitalism that led to the increase of opportunism, or, if it were precisely the best paid workers who were inclined towards opportunism, etc. We must have no illusion regarding "optimism" of this kind. It is optimism in regard to opportunism; it is optimism which serves to conceal opportunism. As a matter of fact the extraordinary rapidity and the particularly revolting character of the development of opportunism is by no means a guarantee that its victory will be durable: the rapid growth of a malignant abscess on a healthy body only causes it to burst more quickly and thus to relieve the body of it. The most dangerous people of all in this respect are those who do not wish to understand that the fight against imperialism is a sham and humbug unless it is inseparably bound up with the fight against opportunism.

From all that has been said in this book on the economic nature of imperialism, it follows that we must define it as capitalism in transition, or, more precisely, as moribund capitalism. It is very instructive in this respect to note that the bourgeois economists, in describing modern capitalism, frequently employ terms like "interlocking," "absence of isolation," etc.; "in conformity with their functions and course of development," banks are "not purely private business enterprises; they are more and more outgrowing the sphere of purely private business regulation." And this very Riesser, who uttered the words just quoted, declares with all seriousness that the "prophecy" of the Marxists concerning "socialisation" has "not come true"!

What then does this word "interlocking" express? It merely expresses the most striking feature of the process going on before our eyes. It shows that the observer counts the separate trees, but cannot see the wood. It slavishly copies the superficial, the fortuitous, the chaotic. It reveals the observer as one who is overwhelmed by the mass of raw material and is utterly incapable of appreciating its meaning and importance. Ownership of shares and relations between owners of private property "interlock in a haphazard way." But the underlying factor of this interlocking, its very base, is the changing social relations of production. When a big enterprise assumes gigantic proportions, and, on the basis of exact computation of mass data, organises according to plan the supply of primary raw materials to the extent of two-thirds, or three-fourths of all that is necessary for tens of millions of people; when the raw materials are transported to the most suitable place of production, sometimes hundreds or thousands of miles away, in a systematic and organised manner; when a single centre directs all the successive stages of work right up to the manufacture of numerous varieties of finished articles; when these products are distributed according to a single plan among tens and hundreds of millions of consumers (as in the case of the distribution of oil in America and Germany by the American "oil trust")—then it becomes evident that we have socialisation of production, and not mere "interlocking"; that private economic relations and private property relations constitute a shell which is no longer suitable for its contents, a shell which must inevitably begin to decay if its destruction be delayed by artificial means; a shell which may continue in a state of decay for a fairly long period (particularly if the cure of the opportunist abscess is protracted), but which will inevitably be removed.

The enthusiastic admirer of German imperialism, Schulze-Gaevernitz, exclaims:

"Once the supreme management of the German banks has been entrusted to the hands of a dozen persons, their activity is even today more significant for the public good than that of the majority of the Ministers of State." (The "interlocking" of bankers, ministers, magnates of industry and rentiers is here conveniently forgotten.) . . . "If we conceive of the tendencies of development which we have noted as realised to the utmost: the money capital of the nation united in the banks; the banks themselves combined into cartels; the investment capital of the nation cast in the shape of securities, then the brilliant forecast of Saint-Simon will be fulfilled: 'The present anarchy of production caused by the fact that economic relations are developing without uniform regulation must make way for organisation in production. Production will no longer be shaped by isolated manufacturers, independent of each other and ignorant of man's economic needs, but by a social institution. A central body of management, being able to survey the large fields of social economy from a more elevated point of view, will regulate it for the benefit of the whole of society, will be able to put the means of production into suitable hands, and above all will take care that there be constant harmony between production and consumption. Institutions already exist which have assumed as part of their task a certain organisation of economic labour: the banks.' The fulfilment of the forecasts of Saint-Simon still lies in the future, but we are on the way to its fulfilment—Marxism, different from what Marx imagined, but different only in form."

A crushing "refutation" of Marx, indeed! It is a retreat from Marx's precise, scientific analysis to Saint-Simon's guesswork, the guesswork of a genius, but guesswork all the same.

PART NINE

EUROPEAN POLITICS AND SOCIETY, 1850–1930

The stormy politics of this era, which resulted in two world wars, are captured in this image. It portrays the January 1871 proclamation of the Second German Empire, with Otto von Bismarck, architect of German unification, in attendance. The site of the event, the Hall of Mirrors at the Palace of Versailles outside Paris, and the timing, after Germany's victory in the 1870–1871 Franco-Prussian War, ensured future conflict.

European Politics and Society, 1850–1930

The decades after 1848 witnessed rapid industrial expansion. Conscience and the desire to prevent further revolutions motivated governments to intervene on behalf of the workers and the poor, thus compromising *laissez-faire* and creating the underpinnings of the modern welfare state. This in turn helped to prevent the feared violent clash between workers and the bourgeoisie. By the end of the century, most European industrial states rested firmly on entire populations, workers included. World War I further unified social elements in the patriotic struggle, as governments asserted strong control over national economies to feed modern warfare's prodigious appetite for resources. These developments foreshadowed a cohesive state of politically awakened masses united by omnipotent governments and swollen armed forces. Participatory democracy hung in uneasy balance with a still obscure darker version. Representative government and national self-determination vied with colossus states without internal or external boundaries.

Because of improvements witnessed by the proletariat in the capitalist state, many European workers and their leaders had rejected Marx's stern vision of violent revolution by the 1890s. In his 1898 *Evolutionary Socialism,* the German Social Democrat Eduard Bernstein (1850–1932) outlined a revisionist socialist program of gradual reform. Worker patriotism at the outbreak of the war in 1914 burned away most remaining traces of proletarian revolutionism, except in Russia where labor conditions were still onerous. By the 1920s, the economist J. M. Keynes (1883–1946) spoke of *The End of Laissez-Faire* (1926) as he described a new corporatist state that combined free enterprise with full social benefits. This optimistic version found competition from pessimistic novels such as *We* (1924), written by Evgenii Zamiatin (1884–1937), an author who prior to and during 1917 had been close to the revolutionary movement but who had developed misgivings. This and other later dystopias (George Orwell's *1984* and Aldous Huxley's *Brave New World*) cast an alarming light on future mass society with humans as automatons of the leviathan state, which controls even thought. Indeed, by the early 1920s Italian fascism and Soviet communism already challenged the vaunted goals of individual freedom, representative government, and national self-determination. Renewed crisis could (and did) threaten the existence of post-World War I democracies.

✦ Reading 33 ✦

Evolutionary Socialism

Eduard Bernstein

Ultimate Aim and Tendency

Reference has already been made in different passages of this book to the great influence which tradition exercises, even amongst socialists, upon judgments regarding facts and ideas. I say expressly "even amongst socialists" because this power of tradition is a very widespread phenomenon from which no party, no literary or artistic line of thought, is free, and which penetrates deeply even into most of the sciences. It will probably never be quite rooted out. A certain interval of time must always pass before men so far recognise the inconsistency of tradition with what exists as to put the former on the shelf. Until this happens tradition usually forms the most powerful means of linking those together whom no strong, constant, effective interest or external pressure knits together. Hence the intuitive preference of all men of action, however revolutionary they may be in their aims, for tradition. "Never swap horses whilst crossing a stream." This motto of old Lincoln is rooted in the same thought as Lassalle's well-known anathema against the "nagging spirit of liberalism, the complaint of individual opining and wanting to know better." Whilst tradition is essentially conservative, criticism is almost always destructive. At the moment of important action, therefore, criticism, even when most justified by facts, can be an evil, and therefore be reprehensible.

To recognise this is, of course, not to call tradition sacred and to forbid criticism. Parties are not always in the midst of rapids when attention is paid to one task only.

For a party which has to keep up with a real evolution, criticism is indispensable and tradition can become an oppressive burden, a restraining fetter.

But men in very few cases willingly and fully account for the importance of the changes which take place in their traditional assumptions. Usually they prefer to take into account only such changes as are concerned with undeniable facts and to bring them into unison as far as can be with the traditional catchwords. The method is called pettifogging, and the apologies and explanations for it are called cant.

Cant—the word is English, and is said to have been first used in the sixteenth century as a description of the saintly sing-song of the Puritans. In its more general meaning it denotes an unreal manner of speech, thoughtlessly imitative, or used with the consciousness of its untruth, to attain any kind of object, whether it be in religion, politics, or be concerned with theory or actuality. In this wider meaning cant is very ancient—there were no worse "canters," for example, than the Greeks of the past classic period—and it permeates in countless forms the whole of our civilised life. Every nation, every class and every group united by theory or interest has its own cant. It has partly become such a mere matter of convention, of pure form, that no one is any longer deceived by its emptiness, and a fight against it would be shooting idly at sparrows. But this does not apply to the cant that appears in the guise of science and the cant which has become a political battle cry.

My proposition, "To me that which is generally called the ultimate aim of socialism is nothing, but the movement is everything," has often been conceived as a denial of every definite aim of the socialist movement, and Mr. George Plechanow has even discovered that I have quoted this "famous sentence" from the book *To Social Peace,* by Gerhard von Schulze-Gävernitz. There, indeed, a passage reads that it is certainly indispensable for revolutionary socialism to take as its ultimate aim the nationalisation of all the means of production, but not

From: Eduard Bernstein *Evolutionary Socialism* (New York: Schocken Books, 1970), pp. 200–224.

for practical political socialism which places near aims in front of distant ones. Because an ultimate aim is here regarded as being dispensable for practical objects, and as I also have professed but little interest for ultimate aims, I am an "indiscriminating follower" of Schulze-Gävernitz. One must confess that such demonstration bears witness to a striking wealth of thought.

When eight years ago I reviewed the Schulze-Gävernitz book in *Neue Zeit,* although my criticism was strongly influenced by assumptions which I now no longer hold, yet I put on one side as immaterial that opposition of ultimate aim and practical activity in reform, and admitted—without encountering a protest—that for England a further peaceful development, such as Schulze-Gävernitz places in prospect before her was not improbable. I expressed the conviction that with the continuance of free development, the English working classes would certainly increase their demands, but would desire nothing that could not be shown each time to be necessary and attainable beyond all doubt. That is at the bottom nothing else than what I say to-day. And if anyone wishes to bring up against me the advances in social democracy made since then in England, I answer that with this extension a development of the English social democracy has gone hand in hand from the Utopian, revolutionary sect, as Engels repeatedly represented it to be, to the party of political reform which we now know.* No socialist capable of thinking, dreams to-day in England of an imminent victory for socialism by means of a violent revolution—none dreams of a quick conquest of Parliament by a revolutionary proletariat. But they rely more and more on work in the municipalities and other self-governing bodies. The early contempt for the trade union movement has been given up; a closer sympathy has been won for it and, here and there also, for the co-operative movement.

And the ultimate aim? Well, that just remains an ultimate aim. "The working classes have no fixed and perfect Utopias to introduce by means of a vote of the nation. They know that in order to work out their own emancipation—and with it that higher form of life which the present form of society irresistibly makes for by its own economic development—they, the working classes, have to pass through long struggles, a whole series of historical processes, by means of which men and circumstances will be completely transformed. They have no ideals to realise, they have only to set at liberty the elements of the new society which have already been developed in the womb of the collapsing bourgeois society." So writes Marx in *Civil War in France.* I was thinking of this utterance, not in every point, but in its fundamental thought in writing down the sentence about the ultimate aim. For after all what does it say but that the movement, the series of processes, is everything, whilst every aim fixed beforehand in its details is immaterial to it. I have declared already that I willingly abandon the form of the sentence about the ultimate aim as far as it admits the interpretation that every general aim of the working class movement formulated as a principle should be declared valueless. But the preconceived theories about the drift of the movement which go beyond such a generally expressed aim, which try to determine the direction of the movement and its character without an ever-vigilant eye upon facts and experience, must necessarily always pass into Utopianism, and at some time or other stand in the way, and hinder the real theoretical and practical progress of the movement.

Whoever knows even but a little of the history of German social democracy also knows that the party has become important by continued action in contravention of such theories and of infringing resolutions founded on them. What Engels says in the preface to the new edition of *Civil War* with regard to the Blanquists and Proudhonists in the Paris Commune of 1871, namely that they both had been obliged in practice to act against their own theory, has often been repeated in another form. A theory or declaration of principle which does not allow attention being paid at every stage of development to the actual interests of the working classes, will always be set aside just as all foreswearing of reforming detail work and of the support of neighbouring middle class parties has again and again been forgotten; and again and again at the congresses of the party will the complaint be heard that here and there in the electoral contest the ultimate aim of socialism has not been put sufficiently in the foreground.

*I use the words "social democracy" here in the wider sense of the whole independent socialist movement. (English edition.)

In the quotation from Schulze-Gävernitz which Plechanow flings at me, it runs that by giving up the dictum that the condition of the worker in modern society is hopeless, socialism would lose its revolutionary point and would be absorbed in carrying out legislative demands. From this contrast it is clearly inferred that Schulze-Gävernitz always used the concept "revolutionary" in the sense of a struggle having revolution by violence in view. Plechanow turns the thing round, and because I have not maintained the condition of the worker to be hopeless, because I acknowledge its capability of improvement and many other facts which bourgeois economists have upheld, he carts me over to the "opponents of scientific socialism."

Unfortunately for the scientific socialism of Plechanow, the Marxist propositions on the hopelessness of the position of the worker have been upset in a book which bears the title, *Capital: A Criticism of Political Economy*. There we read of the "physical and moral regeneration" of the textile workers in Lancashire through the Factory Law of 1847, which "struck the feeblest eye." A bourgeois republic was not even necessary to bring about a certain improvement in the situation of a large section of workers! In the same book we read that the society of to-day is no firm crystal, but an organism capable of change and constantly engaged in a process of change, that also in the treatment of economic questions on the part of the official representatives of this society an "improvement was unmistakable." Further that the author had devoted so large a space in his book to the results of the English Factory Laws in order to spur the Continent to imitate them and thus to work so that the process of transforming society may be accomplished in ever more humane forms. All of which signifies not hopelessness but capability of improvement in the condition of the worker. And, as since 1866, when this was written, the legislation depicted has not grown weaker but has been improved, made more general, and has been supplemented by laws and organisations working in the same direction, there can be no more doubt to-day than formerly of the hopefulness of the position of the worker. If to state such facts means following the "immortal Bastiat," then among the first ranks of these followers is—Karl Marx.

Now, it can be asserted against me that Marx certainly recognised those improvements, but that the chapter on the historical tendency of capitalist accumulation at the end of the first volume of *Capital* shows how little these details influenced his fundamental mode of viewing things. To which I answer that as far as that is correct it speaks against that chapter and not against me.

One can interpret this chapter in very different kinds of ways. I believe I was the first to point out, and indeed repeatedly, that it was a summary characterisation of the tendency of a development which is found in capitalist accumulation, but which in practice is not carried out completely and which therefore need not be driven to the critical point of the antagonism there depicted. Engels has never expressed himself against this interpretation of mine, never, either verbally or in print, declared it to be wrong. Nor did he say a word against me when I wrote, in 1891, in an essay on a work of Schulze-Gävernitz on the questions referred to: "It is clear that where legislation, this systematic and conscious action of society, interferes in an appropriate way, the working of the tendencies of economic development is thwarted, under some circumstances can even be annihilated. Marx and Engels have not only never denied this, but, on the contrary, have always emphasised it." If one reads the chapter mentioned with this idea, one will also, in a few sentences, silently place the word "tendency" and thus be spared the need of bringing this chapter into accord with reality by distorting arts of interpretation. But then the chapter itself would become of less value the more progress is made in actual evolution. For its theoretic importance does not lie in the argument of the general tendency to capitalistic centralisation and accumulation which had been affirmed long before Marx by bourgeois economists and socialists, but in the presentation, peculiar to Marx, of circumstances and forms under which it would work at a more advanced stage of evolution, and of the results to which it would lead. But in this respect actual evolution is really always bringing forth new arrangements, forces, facts, in face of which that presentation seems insufficient and loses to a corresponding extent the capability of serving as a sketch of the coming evolution. That is how I understand it.

One can, however, understand this chapter differently. One can conceive it in this way, that all the improvements mentioned there, and some possibly ensuing, only create temporary remedies against the oppressive tendencies of capitalism, that they signify unimportant modifications which cannot in the long run effect anything substantially against the critical point of antagonisms laid down by Marx, that this will finally appear—if not literally yet substantially—in the manner depicted, and will lead to catastrophic change by violence. This interpretation can be founded on the categoric wording of the last sentences of the chapter, and receives a certain confirmation because at the end reference is again made to the *Communist Manifesto,* whilst Hegel also appeared shortly before with his negation of the negation—the restoration on a new foundation of individual property negatived by the capitalist manner of production.

According to my view, it is impossible simply to declare the one conception right and the other absolutely wrong. To me the chapter illustrates a dualism which runs through the whole monumental work of Marx, and which also finds expression in a less pregnant fashion in other passages—a dualism which consists in this, that the work aims at being a scientific inquiry and also at proving a theory laid down long before its drafting; a formula lies at the basis of it in which the result to which the exposition should lead is fixed beforehand. The return to the *Communist Manifesto* points here to a real residue of Utopianism in the Marxist system. Marx had accepted the solution of the Utopians in essentials, but had recognised their means and proofs as inadequate. He therefore undertook a revision of them, and this with the zeal, the critical acuteness, and love of truth of a scientific genius. He suppressed no important fact, he also forebore belittling artificially the importance of these facts as long as the object of the inquiry had no immediate reference to the final aim of the formula to be proved. To that point his work is free of every tendency necessarily interfering with the scientific method.

For the general sympathy with the strivings for emancipation of the working classes does not in itself stand in the way of the scientific method. But, as Marx approaches a point when that final aim enters seriously into the question, he becomes uncertain and unreliable. Such contradictions then appear as were shown in the book under consideration, for instance, in the section on the movement of incomes in modern society. It thus appears that this great scientific spirit was, in the end, a slave to a doctrine. To express it figuratively, he has raised a mighty building within the framework of a scaffolding he found existing, and in its erection he kept strictly to the laws of scientific architecture as long as they did not collide with the conditions which the construction of the scaffolding prescribed, but he neglected or evaded them when the scaffolding did not allow of their observance. Where the scaffolding put limits in the way of the building, instead of destroying the scaffolding, he changed the building itself at the cost of its right proportions and so made it all the more dependent on the scaffolding. Was it the consciousness of this irrational relation which caused him continually to pass from completing his work to amending special parts of it? However that may be, my conviction is that wherever that dualism shows itself the scaffolding must fall if the building is to grow in its right proportions. In the latter, and not in the former, is found what is worthy to live in Marx.

Nothing confirms me more in this conception than the anxiety with which some persons seek to maintain certain statements in *Capital,* which are falsified by facts. It is just some of the more deeply devoted followers of Marx who have not been able to separate themselves from the dialectical form of the work—that is the scaffolding alluded to—who do this. At least, that is only how I can explain the words of a man, otherwise so amenable to facts as Kautsky, who, when I observed in Stuttgart that the number of wealthy people for many years had increased, not decreased, answered: "If that were true then the date of our victory would not only be very long postponed, but we should never attain our goal. If it be capitalists who increase and not those with no possessions, then we are going ever further from our goal the more evolution progresses, then capitalism grows stronger, not socialism."

That the number of the wealthy increases and does not diminish is not an invention of bourgeois "harmony economists," but a fact established by the boards of assessment for taxes, often to the chagrin of those concerned, a fact which can no longer be disputed. But what is the significance of this fact as regards the victory of socialism? Why should the realisation of socialism depend on its refutation? Well, simply for this reason: because the dialectical scheme seems so to prescribe it; because a post threatens to fall out of the scaffolding if one admits that the social surplus product is appropriated by an increasing instead of a decreasing number of possessors. But it is only the speculative theory that is affected by this matter; it does not at all affect the actual movement. Neither the struggle of the workers for democracy in politics nor their struggle for democracy in industry is touched by it. The prospects of this struggle do not depend on the theory of concentration of capital in the hands of a diminishing number of magnates, nor on the whole dialectical scaffolding of which this is a plank, but on the growth of social wealth and of the social productive forces, in conjunction with general social progress, and, particularly, in conjunction with the intellectual and moral advance of the working classes themselves.

Suppose the victory of socialism depended on the constant shrinkage in the number of capitalist magnates, social democracy, if it wanted to act logically, either would have to support the heaping up of capital in ever fewer hands, or at least to give no support to anything that would stop this shrinkage. As a matter of fact it often enough does neither the one nor the other. These considerations, for instance, do not govern its votes on questions of taxation. From the standpoint of the catastrophic theory a great part of this practical activity of the working classes is an undoing of work that ought to be allowed to be done. It is not social democracy which is wrong in this respect. The fault lies in the doctrine which assumes that progress depends on the deterioration of social conditions.

In his preface to the *Agrarian Question,* Kautsky turns upon those who speak of the necessity of a triumph over Marxism. He says that he sees doubt and hesitation expressed, but that these alone indicate no development. That is so far correct in that doubt and hesitation are no positive refutation. They can, however, be the first step towards it. But is it altogether a matter of triumphing over Marxism, or is it not rather a rejection of certain remains of Utopianism which adhere to Marxism, and which are the cause of the contradictions in theory and practice which have been pointed out in Marxism by its critics? This treatise has become already more voluminous than it ought to have been, and I must therefore abstain from going into all the details of this subject. But all the more I consider it my duty to declare that I hold a whole series of objections raised by opponents against certain items in Marx's theory as unrefuted, some as irrefutable. And I can do this all the more easily as these objections are quite irrelevant to the strivings of social democracy.

We ought to be less susceptible in this respect. It has repeatedly happened that conclusions by followers of Marx, who believed that they contradicted the theories of Marx, have been disputed with great zeal, and, in the end, the supposed contradictions were proved for the most part not to exist. Amongst others I have in my mind the controversy concerning the investigations of the late Dr. Stiebling on the effect of the concentration of capital on the rate of exploitation. In his manner of expression, as well as in separate items of his calculations, Stiebling made some great blunders, which it is the merit of Kautsky to have discovered. But on the other hand the third volume of *Capital* has shown that the fundamental thought of Stiebling's works—the decrease of the rate of exploitation with the increasing concentration of capital did not stand in such opposition to Marx's doctrine as then appeared to most of us, although his proof of the phenomenon is different from that of Marx. Yet in his time Stiebling had to hear (from Kautsky) that if what he inferred was correct, the theoretical foundation of the working class movement, the theory of Marx, was false. And as a matter of fact those who spoke thus could refer to various passages from Marx. An analysis of the controversy which was entered into over the essays of Stiebling could very well serve as an illustration of some of the contradictions of the Marxist theory of value.

Similar conflicts exist with regard to the estimate of the relation of economics and force in history, and they find their counterpart in the criticism on the practical tasks and possibilities of the working class movement which has already been discussed in another place. This is, however, a point to which it is necessary to recur. But the question to be investigated is not how far originally, and in the further course of history, force determined economy and *vice versa,* but what is the creative power of force in a given society.

Now it would be absurd to go back to the prejudices of former generations with regard to the capabilities of political power, for such a thing would mean that we would have to go still further back to explain those prejudices. The prejudices which the Utopians, for example, cherished rested on good grounds; indeed, one can scarcely say that they were prejudices, for they rested on the real immaturity of the working classes of the period as a result of which, only a transitory mob rule on the one side or a return to the class oligarchy on the other was the only possible outcome of the political power of the masses. Under these circumstances a reference to politics could appear only to be a turning aside from more pressing duties. To-day these conditions have been to some extent removed, and therefore no person capable of reflecting will think of criticising political action with the arguments of that period.

Marxism first turned the thing round, as we have seen, and preached (in view of the potential capacity of the industrial proletariat) political action as the most important duty of the movement. But it was thereby involved in great contradictions. It also recognised, and separated itself thereby from the demagogic parties, that the working classes had not yet attained the required maturity for their emancipation, and also that the economic preliminary conditions for such were not present. But in spite of that it turned again and again to tactics which supposed both preliminary conditions as almost fulfilled. We come across passages in its publications where the immaturity of the workers is emphasised with an acuteness which differs very little from the doctrinairism of the early Utopian socialists, and soon afterwards we come across passages according to which we should assume that all culture, all intelligence, all virtue, is only to be found among the working classes—passages which make it incomprehensible why the most extreme social revolutionaries and physical force anarchists should not be right. Corresponding with that, political action is ever directed towards a revolutionary convulsion expected in an imminent future, in the face of which legislative work for a long time appears only as a *pis aller*—a merely temporary device. And we look in vain for any systematic investigation of the question of what can be expected from legal, and what from revolutionary action.

It is evident at the first glance that great differences exist in the latter respect. But they are usually found to be this: that law, or the path of legislative reform, is the slower way, and revolutionary force the quicker and more radical. But that only is true in a restricted sense. Whether the legislative or the revolutionary method is the more promising depends entirely on the nature of the measures and on their relation to different classes and customs of the people.

In general, one may say here that the revolutionary way (always in the sense of revolution by violence) does quicker work as far as it deals with removal of obstacles which a privileged minority places in the path of social progress: that its strength lies on its negative side.

Constitutional legislation works more slowly in this respect as a rule. Its path is usually that of compromise, not the prohibition, but the buying out of acquired rights. But it is stronger than the revolution scheme where prejudice and the limited horizon of the great mass of the people appear as hindrances to social progress, and it offers greater advantages where it is a question of the creation of permanent economic arrangements capable of lasting; in other words, it is best adapted to positive social-political work.

In legislation, intellect dominates over emotion in quiet times; during a revolution emotion dominates over intellect. But if emotion is often an imperfect leader, the intellect is a slow motive force. Where a revolution sins by over haste, the every-day legislator sins by procrastination. Legislation works as a systematic force, revolution as an elementary force.

As soon as a nation has attained a position where the rights of the propertied minority have ceased to be a serious obstacle to social progress, where the negative tasks of political action are less pressing than the positive, then the appeal to a revolution by force becomes a meaningless phrase. One can overturn a government or a privileged minority, but not a nation. When the working classes do not possess very strong economic organisations of their own, and have not attained, by means of education on self-governing bodies, a high degree of mental independence, the dictatorship of the proletariat means the dictatorship of club orators and writers. I would not wish that those who see in the oppression and tricking of the working men's organisations and in the exclusion of working men from the legislature and government the highest point of the art of political policy should experience their error in practice. Just as little would I desire it for the working class movement itself.

One has not overcome Utopianism if one assumes that there is in the present, or ascribes to the present, what is to be in the future. We have to take working men as they are. And they are neither so universally pauperised as was set out in the *Communist Manifesto,* nor so free from prejudices and weaknesses as their courtiers wish to make us believe. They have the virtues and failings of the economic and social conditions under which they live. And neither these conditions nor their effects can be put on one side from one day to another.

Have we attained the required degree of development of the productive forces for the abolition of classes? In face of the fantastic figures which were formerly set up in proof of this and which rested on generalisations based on the development of particularly favoured industries, socialist writers in modern times have endeavoured to reach by carefully detailed calculations, appropriate estimates of the possibilities of production in a socialist society, and their results are very different from those figures. Of a general reduction of hours of labour to five, four, or even three or two hours, such as was formerly accepted, there can be no hope at any time within sight, unless the general standard of life is much reduced. Even under a collective organisation of work, labour must begin very young and only cease at a rather advanced age, if it is to be reduced considerably below an eight-hours' day. Those persons ought to understand this first of all who indulge in the most extreme exaggerations regarding the ratio of the number of the non-propertied classes to that of the propertied. But he who thinks irrationally on one point does so usually on another. And, therefore, I am not surprised if the same Plechanow, who is angered to see the position of working men represented as not hopeless, has only the annihilating verdict, "Philistine," for my conclusions on the impossibility at any period within sight of abandoning the principle of the economic self-responsibility of those capable of working. It is not for nothing that one is the philosopher of irresponsibility.

But he who surveys the actual workers' movement will also find that the freedom from those qualities which appeared Philistine to a person born in the bourgeoisie, is very little valued by the workers, that they in no way support the morale of proletarianism, but, on the contrary, tend to make a "Philistine" out of a proletarian. With the roving proletarian without a family and home, no lasting, firm trade union movement would be possible. It is no bourgeois prejudice, but a conviction gained through decades of labour organisation, which has made so many of the English labour leaders—socialists and non-socialists—into zealous adherents of the temperance movement. The working class socialists know the faults of their class, and the most conscientious among them, far from glorifying these faults, seek to overcome them with all their power.

We cannot demand from a class, the great majority of whose members live under crowded conditions, are badly educated, and have an uncertain and insufficient income, the high intellectual and moral standard which the organisation and existence of a socialist community presupposes. We will, therefore, not ascribe it to them by way of fiction. Let us rejoice at the great stock of intelligence, renunciation, and energy which the modern working class movement has partly revealed, partly produced; but we must not assign, without discrimination to the masses, the millions, what holds good, say, of hundreds of thousands. I will not repeat the declarations which have been made to me on this point by working men verbally and in writing; I do not need to defend myself before reasonable persons against the suspicion of Pharisaism and the conceit of pedantry. But I confess willingly that I measure here with two kinds of measures. Just because I expect much of the working classes I censure much more everything that tends to corrupt their moral judgment than I do similar habits of the higher classes, and I see with the greatest regret that a tone of literary decadence is spreading here and there in the working class press which can only have a confusing and corrupting effect. A class which is aspiring needs a sound morale and must suffer no deterioration. Whether it sets out for itself an ideal ultimate aim is of secondary importance if it pursues with energy its proximate aims. The important point is that these aims are inspired by a definite principle which expresses a higher degree of economy and of social life, that they are an embodiment of a social conception which means in the evolution of civilisation a higher view of morals and of legal rights.

From this point of view I cannot subscribe to the proposition: "The working class has no ideas to realise." I see in it rather a self-deception, if it is not a mere play upon words on the part of its author.

And in this mind, I, at the time, resorted to the spirit of the great Königsberg philosopher, the critic of pure reason, against the cant which sought to get a hold on the working class movement and to which the Hegelian dialetic offers a comfortable refuge. I did this in the conviction that social democracy required a Kant who should judge the received opinion and examine it critically with deep acuteness, who should show where its apparent materialism is the highest—and is therefore the most easily misleading—ideology, and warn it that the contempt of the ideal, the magnifying of material factors until they become omnipotent forces of evolution, is a self-deception, which has been and will be exposed as such at every opportunity by the action of those who proclaim it. Such a thinker, who with convincing exactness could show what is worthy and destined to live in the work of our great champions, and what must and can perish, would also make it possible for us to hold a more unbiassed judgment on those works which, although not starting from premises which to-day appear to us as decisive, yet are devoted to the ends for which social democracy is fighting. No impartial thinker will deny that socialist criticism often fails in this and discloses all the dark sides of epigonism. I have myself done my share in this, and therefore cast a stone at no one. But just because I belong to the school, I believe I am justified in giving expression to the need for reform. If I did not fear that what I write should be misunderstood (I am, of course, prepared for its being misconstrued), I would translate *Back to Kant* by *Back to Lange*. For, just as the philosophers and investigators who stand by that motto are not concerned with going back to the letter of what the Königsberg philosopher wrote, but are only concerned with the fundamental principles of his criticism, so social democracy would just as little think of going back to all the social-political views of Frederick Albert Lange. What I have in mind is the distinguishing union in Lange of an upright and intrepid championship of the struggles of the working classes for emancipation with a large scientific freedom from prejudice which was always ready to acknowledge mistakes and recognise new truths. Perhaps such a great broad-mindedness as meets us in Lange's writings is only to be found in persons who are wanting in the penetrating acuteness which is the property of pioneer spirits like Marx. But it is not every epoch that produces a Marx, and even for a man of equal genius the working class movement of to-day is too great to enable him to occupy the position which Marx fills in its history. To-day it needs, in addition to the fighting spirit, the co-ordinating and constructive thinkers who are intellectually enough advanced to be able to separate the chaff from the wheat, who are great enough in their mode of thinking to recognise also the little plant that has grown on another soil than theirs, and who, perhaps, though not kings, are warm-hearted republicans in the domain of socialist thought.

✦ Reading 34 ✦

The End of Laissez-Faire

John Maynard Keynes

Finally, Individualism and *laissez-faire* could not, in spite of their deep roots in the political and moral philosophies of the late eighteenth and early nineteenth centuries, have secured their lasting hold over the conduct of public affairs, if it had not been for their conformity with the needs and wishes of the business world of the day. They gave full scope to our erstwhile heroes, the great business men. "At least one-half of the best ability in the Western world," Marshall used to say, "is engaged in business." A great part of "the higher imagination" of the age was thus employed. It was on the activities of these men that our hopes of Progress were centred. "Men of this class," Marshall wrote, "live in constantly shifting visions, fashioned in their own brains, of various routes to their desired end; of the difficulties which Nature will oppose to them on each route, and of the contrivances by which they hope to get the better of her opposition. This imagination gains little credit with the people, because it is not allowed to run riot; its strength is disciplined by a stronger will; and its highest glory is to have attained great ends by means so simple that no one will know, and none but experts will even guess, how a dozen other expedients, each suggesting as much brilliancy to the hasty observer, were set aside in favour of it. The imagination of such a man is employed, like that of the master chess-player, in forecasting the obstacles which may be opposed to the successful issue of his far-reaching projects, and constantly rejecting brilliant suggestions because he has pictured to himself the counter-strokes to them. His strong nervous force is at the opposite extreme of human nature from that nervous irresponsibility which conceives hasty Utopian schemes, and which is rather to be compared to the bold facility of a weak player, who will speedily solve the most difficult chess problem by taking on himself to move the black men as well as the white."

This is a fine picture of the great Captain of Industry, the Master-Individualist, who serves us in serving himself, just as any other artist does. Yet this one, in his turn, is becoming a tarnished idol. We grow more doubtful whether it is he who will lead us into Paradise by the hand.

These many elements have contributed to the current intellectual bias, the mental make-up, the orthodoxy of the day. The compelling force of many of the original reasons has disappeared, but, as usual, the vitality of the conclusions outlasts them. To suggest social action for the public good to the City of London is like discussing the *Origin of Species* with a Bishop sixty years ago. The first reaction is not intellectual, but moral. An orthodoxy is in question, and the more persuasive the arguments the graver the offence. Nevertheless, venturing into the den of the lethargic monster, at any rate I have traced his claims and pedigree so as to show that he has ruled over us rather by hereditary right than by personal merit.

Let us clear from the ground the metaphysical or general principles upon which, from time to time, *laissez-faire* has been founded. It is *not* true that individuals possess a prescriptive "natural liberty" in their economic activities. There is *no* "compact" conferring perpetual rights on those who Have or on those who Acquire. The world is *not* so governed from above that private and social interest always coincide. It is *not* so managed here below that in practice they coincide. It is *not* a correct deduction from the Principles of Economics that enlightened self-interest always operates in the public interest. Nor is it true that self-interest generally *is* enlightened; more often individuals acting separately to promote their

From: John Maynard Keynes, *The End of Laissez-Faire* (London, Hogarth Press, 1927), pp. 36–54.

own ends are too ignorant or too weak to attain even these. Experience does *not* show that individuals, when they make up a social unit, are always less clear-sighted than when they act separately.

We cannot therefore settle on abstract grounds, but must handle on its merits in detail what Burke termed "one of the finest problems in legislation, namely, to determine what the State ought to take upon itself to direct by the public wisdom, and what it ought to leave, with as little interference as possible, to individual exertion." We have to discriminate between what Bentham, in his forgotten but useful nomenclature, used to term *Agenda* and *Non-Agenda,* and to do this without Bentham's prior presumption that interference is, at the same time, "generally needless" and "generally pernicious." Perhaps the chief task of Economists at this hour is to distinguish afresh the *Agenda* of Government from the *Non-Agenda;* and the companion task of Politics is to devise forms of Government within a Democracy which shall be capable of accomplishing the *Agenda.* I will illustrate what I have in mind by two examples.

(1) I believe that in many cases the ideal size for the unit of control and organisation lies somewhere between the individual and the modern State. I suggest, therefore, that progress lies in the growth and the recognition of semi-autonomous bodies within the State—bodies whose criterion of action within their own field is solely the public good as they understand it, and from whose deliberations motives of private advantage are excluded, though some place it may still be necessary to leave, until the ambit of men's altruism grows wider, to the separate advantage of particular groups, classes, or faculties—bodies which in the ordinary course of affairs are mainly autonomous within their prescribed limitations, but are subject in the last resort to the sovereignty of the democracy expressed through Parliament.

I propose a return, it may be said, towards mediæval conceptions of separate autonomies. But, in England at any rate, corporations are a mode of government which has never ceased to be important and is sympathetic to our institutions. It is easy to give examples, from what already exists, of separate autonomies which have attained or are approaching the mode I designate—the Universities, the Bank of England, the Port of London Authority, even perhaps the Railway Companies. In Germany there are doubtless analogous instances.

But more interesting than these is the trend of Joint Stock Institutions, when they have reached a certain age and size, to approximate to the status of public corporations rather than that of individualistic private enterprise. One of the most interesting and unnoticed developments of recent decades has been the tendency of big enterprise to socialise itself. A point arrives in the growth of a big institution—particularly a big railway or big public utility enterprise, but also a big bank or a big insurance company—at which the owners of the capital, *i.e.* the shareholders, are almost entirely dissociated from the management, with the result that the direct personal interest of the latter in the making of great profit becomes quite secondary. When this stage is reached, the general stability and reputation of the institution are more considered by the management than the maximum of profit for the shareholders. The shareholders must be satisfied by conventionally adequate dividends; but once this is secured, the direct interest of the management often consists in avoiding criticism from the public and from the customers of the concern. This is particularly the case if their great size or semi-monopolistic position renders them conspicuous in the public eye and vulnerable to public attack. The extreme instance, perhaps, of this tendency in the case of an institution, theoretically the unrestricted property of private persons, is the Bank of England. It is almost true to say that there is no class of persons in the Kingdom of whom the Governor of the Bank of England thinks less when he decides on his policy than of his shareholders. Their rights, in excess of their conventional dividend, have already sunk to the neighbourhood of zero. But the same thing is partly true of many other big institutions. They are, as time goes on, socialising themselves.

Not that this is unmixed gain. The same causes promote conservatism and a waning of enterprise. In fact, we already have in these cases many of the faults as well as the advantages of State Socialism. Nevertheless we see here, I think, a natural line of evolution. The battle of Socialism against unlimited private profit is being won in detail hour by hour. In these particular fields—it remains acute elsewhere—this is no longer the pressing problem. There is, for instance, no so-called important political question so really unimportant, so irrelevant to the re-organisation of the economic life of Great Britain, as the Nationalisation of the Railways.

It is true that many big undertakings, particularly Public Utility enterprises and other business requiring a large fixed capital, still need to be semi-socialised. But we must keep our minds flexible regarding the forms of this semi-socialism. We must take full advantage of the natural tendencies of the day, and we must probably prefer semi-autonomous corporations to organs of the Central Government for which Ministers of State are directly responsible.

I criticise doctrinaire State Socialism, not because it seeks to engage men's altruistic impulses in the service of Society, or because it departs from *laissez-faire,* or because it takes away from man's natural liberty to make a million, or because it has courage for bold experiments. All these things I applaud. I criticise it because it misses the significance of what is actually happening; because it is, in fact, little better than a dusty survival of a plan to meet the problems of fifty years ago, based on a misunderstanding of what someone said a hundred years ago. Nineteenth-century State Socialism sprang from Bentham, free competition, etc., and is in some respects a clearer, in some respects a more muddled version of just the same philosophy as underlies nineteenth-century individualism. Both equally laid all their stress on freedom, the one negatively to avoid limitations on existing freedom, the other positively to destroy natural or acquired monopolies. They are different reactions to the same intellectual atmosphere.

(2) I come next to a criterion of *Agenda* which is particularly relevant to what it is urgent and desirable to do in the near future. We must aim at separating those services which are *technically social* from those which are *technically individual.* The most important *Agenda* of the State relate not to those activities which private individuals are already fulfilling, but to those functions which fall outside the sphere of the individual, to those decisions which are made by *no one* if the State does not make them. The important thing for Government is not to do things which individuals are doing already, and to do them a little better or a little worse; but to do those things which at present are not done at all.

It is not within the scope of my purpose on this occasion to develop practical policies. I limit myself, therefore, to naming some instances of what I mean from amongst those problems about which I happen to have thought most.

Many of the greatest economic evils of our time are the fruits of risk, uncertainty, and ignorance. It is because particular individuals, fortunate in situation or in abilities, are able to take advantage of uncertainty and ignorance, and also because for the same reason big business is often a lottery, that great inequalities of wealth come about; and these same factors are also the cause of the Unemployment of Labour, or the disappointment of reasonable business expectations, and of the impairment of efficiency and production. Yet the cure lies outside the operations of individuals; it may even be to the interest of individuals to aggravate the disease. I believe that the cure for these things is partly to be sought in the deliberate control of the currency and of credit by a central institution, and partly in the collection and dissemination on a great scale of data relating to the business situation, including the full publicity, by law if necessary, of all business facts which it is useful to know. These measures would involve Society in exercising directive intelligence through some appropriate organ of action over many of the inner intricacies of private business, yet it would leave private initiative and enterprise unhindered. Even if these measures prove insufficient, nevertheless they will furnish us with better knowledge than we have now for taking the next step.

My second example relates to Savings and Investment. I believe that some coordinated act of intelligent judgment is required as to the scale on which it is desirable that the community as a whole should save, the scale on which these savings should go abroad in the form of foreign investments, and whether the present organisation of the investment market distributes savings along the most nationally productive channels. I do not think that these matters should be left entirely to the chances of private judgment and private profits, as they are at present.

My third example concerns Population. The time has already come when each country needs a considered national policy about what size of Population, whether larger or smaller than at present or the same, is most expedient. And having settled this policy, we must take steps to carry it into operation. The time may arrive a little later when the community as a whole must pay attention to the innate quality as well as to the mere numbers of its future members.

These reflections have been directed towards possible improvements in the technique of modern Capitalism by the agency of collective action. There is nothing in them which is seriously incompatible with what seems to me to be the essential characteristic of Capitalism, namely the dependence upon an intense appeal to the money-making and money-loving instincts of individuals as the main motive force of the economic machine. Nor must I, so near to my end, stray towards other fields. Nevertheless I may do well to remind you, in conclusion, that the fiercest contests and the most deeply felt divisions of opinion are likely to be waged in the coming years not round technical questions, where the arguments on either side are mainly economic, but round those which, for want of better words, may be called psychological or, perhaps, moral.

In Europe, or at least in some parts of Europe—but not, I think, in the United States of America—there is a latent reaction, somewhat widespread, against basing Society to the extent that we do upon fostering, encouraging, and protecting the money-motives of individuals. A preference for arranging our affairs in such a way as to appeal to the money-motive as little as possible, rather than as much as possible, need not be entirely *a priori,* but may be based on the comparison of experiences. Different persons, according to their choice of profession, find the money-motive playing a large or a small part in their daily lives, and historians can tell us about other phases of social organisation in which this motive has played a much smaller part than it does now. Most religions and most philosophies deprecate, to say the least of it, a way of life mainly influenced by considerations of personal money profit. On the other hand, most men to-day reject ascetic notions and do not doubt the real advantages of wealth. Moreover, it seems obvious to them that one cannot do without the money-motive, and that, apart from certain admitted abuses, it does its job well. In the result the average man averts his attention from the problem, and has no clear idea what he really thinks and feels about the whole confounded matter.

Confusion of thought and feeling leads to confusion of speech. Many people, who are really objecting to Capitalism as a way of life, argue as though they were objecting to it on the ground of its inefficiency in attaining its own objects. Contrariwise, devotees of Capitalism are often unduly conservative, and reject reforms in its technique, which might really strengthen and preserve it, for fear that they may prove to be first steps away from Capitalism itself. Nevertheless a time may be coming when we shall get clearer than at present as to when we are talking about Capitalism as an efficient or inefficient technique, and when we are talking about it as desirable or objectionable in itself. For my part, I think that Capitalism, wisely managed, can probably be made more efficient for attaining economic ends than any alternative system yet in sight, but that in itself it is in many ways extremely objectionable. Our problem is to work out a social organisation which shall be as efficient as possible without offending our notions of a satisfactory way of life.

The next step forward must come, not from political agitation or premature experiments, but from thought. We need by an effort of the mind to elucidate our own feelings. At present our sympathy and our judgment are liable to be on different sides, which is a painful and paralysing state of mind. In the field of action reformers will not be successful until they can steadily pursue a clear and definite object with their intellects and their feelings in tune. There is no party in the world at present which appears to me to be pursuing right aims by right methods. Material Poverty provides the incentive to change precisely in situations where there is very little margin for experiments. Material Prosperity removes the incentive just when it might be safe to take a chance. Europe lacks the means, America the will, to make a move. We need a new set of convictions which spring naturally from a candid examination of our own inner feelings in relation to the outside facts.

✦ Reading 35 ✦

We

Evgenii Zamiatin

In a futuristic Europe called the United State in which people are known as "Numbers" and the ruler is called the "Well-Doer," the hero of this tale helps design an interplanetary rocket (the *Integral*). He begins to question state-imposed beliefs—that no life exists beyond the Green Wall, that Numbers' existence is perfect, and that those questioning the state are enemies of "happiness" who must be destroyed or reprogrammed. He visits beyond the wall and becomes involved with a woman opposed to the existing state, but eventually he is captured, surgically altered, and returned to unquestioning belief.

Record 1

An Announcement
The Wisest of Lines
A Poem

This is merely a copy, word for word, of what was published this morning in the State newspaper:

"In another hundred and twenty days the building of the *Integral* will be completed. The great historic hour is near, when the first *Integral* will rise into the limitless space of the universe. One thousand years ago your heroic ancestors subjected the whole earth to the power of the United State. A still more glorious task is before you: the integration of the indefinite equation of the Cosmos by the use of the glass, electric, fire-breathing *Integral*. Your mission is to subjugate to the grateful yoke of reason the unknown beings who live on other planets, and who are perhaps still in the primitive state of freedom. If they will not understand that we are bringing them a mathematically faultless happiness, our duty will be to force them to be happy. But before we take up arms, we shall try the power of words.

"In the name of the Well-Doer, the following is announced herewith to all Numbers of the United State:

"Whoever feels capable must consider it his duty to write treatises, poems, manifestoes, odes, and other compositions on the greatness and the beauty of the United State.

"This will be the first cargo which the *Integral* will carry.

"Long live the United State! Long live the Numbers!! Long live the Well-Doer!!!"

I feel my cheeks burn as I write this. To integrate the colossal, universal equation! To unbend the wild curve, to straighten it out to a tangent—to a straight line! For the United State is a straight line, a great, divine, precise, wise line, the wisest of lines!

I, D-503, the builder of the *Integral,* I am only one of the many mathematicians of the United State. My pen, which is accustomed to figures, is unable to express the march and rhythm of consonance; therefore I shall try to record only the things I see, the things I think, or, to be more exact, the things *we* think. Yes, "we"; that is exactly what I mean, and *We,* therefore, shall be the title of my records. But this will only be a derivative of our life, of our mathematical, perfect life in the United State. If this be so, will not this derivative be a poem in itself, despite my limitations? It will. I believe it, I know it.

My cheeks still burn as I write this. I feel something similar to what a woman probably feels when for the first time she senses within herself the pulse of a tiny, blind, human being. It is I, and at the same time it is not I. And for many long months it will be necessary to feed it with my life, with my blood, and then with a pain at my heart, to tear it from myself and lay it at the feet of the United State.

From: Evgenii Zamiatin, *We* (New York: Dutton, 1952), pp. 3–10, 142–148, 217–218.

Yet I am ready, as everyone, or nearly everyone of us, is. I am ready.

Record 2

Ballet
Square Harmony
X

Spring. From behind the Green Wall, from some unknown plains the wind brings to us the yellow honeyed pollen of flowers. One's lips are dry from this sweet dust. Every moment one passes one's tongue over them. Probably all women whom I meet in the street (and certainly men also) have sweet lips today. This somewhat disturbs my logical thinking. But the sky! The sky is blue. Its limpidness is not marred by a single cloud. (How primitive was the taste of the ancients, since their poets were always inspired by these senseless, formless, stupidly rushing accumulations of vapor!) I love, I am sure it will not be an error if I say *we* love, only such a sky—a sterile, faultless sky. On such days the whole universe seems to be moulded of the same eternal glass, like the Green Wall, and like all our buildings. On such days one sees their wonderful equations, hitherto unknown. One sees these equations in everything, even in the most ordinary, everyday things.

Here is an example: this morning I was on the dock where the *Integral* is being built, and I saw the lathes; blindly, with abandon, the balls of the regulators were rotating; the cranks were swinging from side to side with a glimmer; the working beam proudly swung its shoulder; and the mechanical chisels were dancing to the melody of unheard tarantellas. I suddenly perceived all the music, all the beauty, of this colossal, this mechanical ballet, illumined by light blue rays of sunshine. Then the thought came: why beautiful? Why is the dance beautiful? Answer: because it is an *unfree* movement. Because the deep meaning of the dance is contained in its absolute, ecstatic submission, in the ideal *non-freedom.* If it is true that our ancestors would abandon themselves in dancing at the most inspired moments of their lives (religious mysteries, military parades), then it means only one thing: the instinct of non-freedom has been characteristic of human nature from ancient times, and we in our life of today, we are only consciously—

I was interrupted. The switchboard clicked. I raised my eyes—O-90, of course! In half a minute she will be here to take me for the walk.

Dear O-! She always seems to me to look like her name, O-. She is approximately ten centimeters shorter than the required Maternal Norm. Therefore she appears round all over; the rose-colored O of her lips is open to meet every word of mine. She has a round soft dimple on her wrist. Children have such dimples. As she came in, the logical flywheel was still buzzing in my head, and following its inertia, I began to tell her about my new formula which embraced the machines and the dancers and all of us.

"Wonderful, isn't it?" I asked.

"Yes, wonderful . . . Spring!" she replied, with a rosy smile.

You see? Spring! She talks about Spring! Females! . . . I became silent.

We were down in the street. The avenue was crowded. On days when the weather is so beautiful, the afternoon personal hour is usually the hour of the supplementary walk. As always, the big Musical Tower was playing the March of the United State with all its pipes. The Numbers, hundreds, thousands of Numbers in light blue unifs (probably a derivative of the ancient uniform) with golden badges on the chest—the State number of each one, male or female—the Numbers were walking slowly, four abreast, exaltedly keeping step. I, we four, were but one of the innumerable waves of a powerful torrent: to my left, O-90 (if one of my long-haired ancestors were writing this a thousand years ago he would probably call her by that funny word, *mine*); to my right, two unknown Numbers, a she-Number and a he-Number.

Blue sky, tiny baby suns in each one of our badges; our faces are unclouded by the insanity of thoughts. Rays. . . . Do you picture it? Everything seems to be made of a kind of smiling, a ray-like matter. And the brass measures: Tra-ta-ta-tam . . . Tra-ta-ta-tam . . . Stamping on the brassy steps that sparkle in the sun, with every step you rise higher and higher into the dizzy blue heights. . . . Then, as this morning on the dock, again I saw, as if for the first time in my life, the impeccably straight streets, the glistening glass of the pavement, the divine parallelepipeds of the transparent dwellings, the square harmony of the grayish-blue rows of Numbers. And it seemed to me that not past generations, but I myself, had won a victory over the old god and the old life, that I myself had created all this. I felt like a tower: I was afraid to move my elbow, lest the walls, the cupola, and the machines should fall to pieces.

Then without warning—a jump through centuries: I remembered (apparently through an association by contrast) a picture in the museum, a picture of an avenue of the twentieth century, a thundering, many-colored confusion of men, wheels, animals, billboards, trees, colors, and birds. . . . They say all this once actually existed!

It seemed to me so incredible, so absurd, that I lost control of myself and laughed aloud. A laugh, as if an echo of mine, reached my ear from the right. I turned. I saw white, very white, sharp teeth, and an unfamiliar female face.

"I beg your pardon," she said, "but you looked about you like an inspired mythological god on the seventh day of creation. You look as though you are sure that I, too, was created by you, by no one but you. It is very flattering."

All this without a smile, even with a certain degree of respect (she may know that I am the builder of the *Integral*). In her eyes, nevertheless, and on her brows, there was a strange irritating X, and I was unable to grasp it, to find an arithmetical expression for it. Somehow I was confused; with a somewhat hazy mind, I tried logically to explain my laughter.

"It was absolutely clear that this contrast, this impassable abyss, between the things of today and of years ago—"

"But why impassable?" (What bright, sharp teeth!) "One might throw a bridge over that abyss. Please imagine: a drum battalion, rows—all this existed before and consequently—"

"Oh, yes, it is clear," I exclaimed.

It was a remarkable intersection of thoughts. She said almost in the same words the things I had written down before the walk! Do you understand? Even the thoughts! It is because nobody is *one,* but *one of.* We are all so much alike—

"Are you sure?" I noticed her brows that rose to the temples in an acute angle—like the sharp corners of an X. Again I was confused, casting a glance to the right, then to the left. To my right—she, slender, abrupt, resistantly flexible like a whip, I-330 (I saw her number now). To my left, O—, totally different, all made of circles with a childlike dimple on her wrist; and at the very end of our row, an unknown he-Number, double-curved like the letter S. We were all so different from one another. . . .

The one to my right, I-330, apparently caught the confusion in my eye, for she said with a sigh, "Yes, alas!"

I don't deny that this exclamation was quite in place, but again there was something in her face or in her voice . . .

With an abruptness unusual for me, I said, "Why, 'alas'? Science is developing and if not now, then within fifty or one hundred years—"

"Even the noses will—"

"Yes, noses!" This time I almost shouted, "Since there is still a reason, no matter what, for envy. . . . Since my nose is button-like and someone else's is—"

"Well, your nose is rather classic, as they would have said in ancient days, although your hands—No, no, show me your hands!"

I hate to have anyone look at my hands; they are covered with long hair—a stupid atavism. I stretched out my hand and said as indifferently as I could, "Apelike."

She glanced at my hand, then at my face.

"No, a very curious harmony."

She weighed me with her eyes as though with scales. The little horns again appeared at the corners of her brows.

"He is registered in my name," exclaimed O-90 with a rosy smile.

I made a grimace. Strictly speaking, she was out of order. This dear O-, how shall I say it? The speed of her tongue is not correctly calculated; the speed per second of her tongue should be slightly less than the speed per second of her thoughts—at any rate not the reverse.

At the end of the avenue the big bell of the Accumulating Tower resounded seventeen. The personal hour was at an end. I-330 was leaving us with that S-like he-Number. He has such a respectable, and I noticed then, such a familiar, face. I must have met him somewhere, but where I could not remember. Upon leaving me I-330 said with the same X-like smile:

"Drop in day after tomorrow at auditorium 112."

I shrugged my shoulders: "If I am assigned to the auditorium you just named—"

She, with a peculiar, incomprehensible certainty: "You will be."

The woman had a disagreeable effect upon me, like an irrational component of an equation which you cannot eliminate. I was glad to remain alone with dear O-, at least for a short while. Hand in hand with her, I passed four lines of avenues; at the next corner she went to the right, I to the left. O-timidly raised her round blue crystalline eyes.

"I would like so much to come to you today and pull down the curtains, especially today, right now. . . ."

How funny she is. But what could I say to her? She was with me only yesterday and she knows as well as I that our next sexual day is day after tomorrow. It is merely another case in which her thoughts are too far ahead. It sometimes happens that the spark comes too early to the motor.

At parting I kissed her twice—no, I shall be exact, three times, on her wonderful blue eyes, such clear, unclouded eyes.

* * *

Record 27

No Headings. It Is Impossible!

I was alone in the endless corridors. In those same corridors . . . A mute, concrete sky. Water was dripping somewhere upon a stone. The familiar, heavy, opaque door—and the subdued noise from behind it.

She said she would come out at sixteen sharp. It was already five minutes, then ten, then fifteen past sixteen. No one appeared. For a second I was my former self, horrified at the thought that the door might open.

"Five minutes more, and if she does not come out . . ."

Water was dripping somewhere upon a stone. No one about. With melancholy pleasure I felt: "Saved," and slowly I turned and walked back along the corridor. The trembling dots of the small lamps on the ceiling became dimmer and dimmer. Suddenly a quick rattle of a door behind me. Quick steps, softly echoing from the ceiling and the walls. It was she, light as a bird, panting somewhat from running.

"I knew you would be here, you would come! I knew you—you . . ."

The spears of her eyelashes moved apart to let me in and . . . How can I describe what effect that ancient, absurd, and wonderful rite has upon me when her lips touch mine? Can I find a formula to express that whirlwind which sweeps out of my soul everything, everything save her? Yes, yes, from my *soul.* You may laugh at me if you will.

She made an effort to raise her eyelids, and her slow words, too, came with an effort:

"No. Now we must go."

The door opened. Old, worn steps. An unbearably multicolored noise, whistling and light. . . .

Twenty-four hours have passed since then and everything seems to have settled in me, yet it is most difficult for me to find words for even an approximate description. . . . It is as though a bomb had exploded in my head. . . . Open mouths, wings, shouts, leaves, words, stones, all these one after another in a heap. . . .

I remember my first thought was: "Fast—back!" For it was clear to me that while I was waiting there in the corridors, *they* somehow had blasted and destroyed the Green Wall, and from behind it, everything rushed in and splashed over our city which until then had been kept clean of that lower world. I must have said something of this sort to I-330. She laughed.

"No, we have simply come out *beyond the Green Wall.*"

Then I opened my eyes, and close to me, actually, I saw those very things which until then not a single living Number had ever seen except depreciated a thousand times, dimmed and hazy through the cloudy glass of the Wall.

The sun—it was no longer our light evenly diffused over the mirror surface of the pavements; it seemed an accumulation of living fragments, of incessantly oscillating, dizzy spots which blinded the eyes. And the trees! Like candles rising into the very sky, or like spiders that squatted upon the earth, supported by their clumsy paws, or like mute green fountains. And all this was moving, jumping, rustling. Under my feet some strange little ball was crawling. . . . I stood as though rooted to the ground. I was unable to take a step because under my foot there was not an even plane, but (imagine!) something disgustingly soft, yielding, living, springy, green! . . .

I was dazed; I was strangled—yes, strangled; it is the best word to express my state. I stood holding fast with both hands to a swinging branch.

"It is nothing. It is all right. It is natural, the first time. It will pass. Courage!"

At I-330's side, bouncing dizzily on a green net, someone's thinnest profile, cut out of paper. No, not "someone's." I recognized him. I remembered. It was the doctor. I understood everything very clearly. I realized that they both caught me beneath the arms and laughingly dragged me forward. My legs twisted and glided. . . . Terrible noise, cawing, stumps, yelling, branches, tree trunks, wings, leaves, whistling. . . .

The trees drew apart. A bright clearing. In the clearing, people, or perhaps, to be more exact, *beings.* Now comes the most difficult part to describe, for *this* was beyond any bounds of probability. It is clear to me now why I-330 was stubbornly silent about it before; I would not have believed it, would not have believed even her. It is even possible that tomorrow I shall not believe myself, shall not believe my own description in these pages.

In the clearing, around a naked, skull-like rock, a noisy crowd of three or four hundred . . . people. Well, let's call them people. I find it difficult to coin new words. Just as on the stands you recognize in the general accumulation of faces only those which are familiar to you, so at first I recognized only our grayish-blue unifs. But one second later and I saw distinctly and clearly among the unifs dark, red, golden, black, brown, and white humans—apparently they were humans. None of them had any clothes on, and their bodies were covered with short, glistening hair, like that which may be seen on the stuffed horse in the Prehistoric Museum. But their females had faces exactly, yes, exactly, like the faces of our women: tender, rosy, and not overgrown with hair. Also their breasts were free of hair, firm breasts of wonderful geometrical form. As to the males, only a part of their faces were free from hair, like our ancestors's, and the organs of reproduction were similar to ours.

All this was so unbelievable, so unexpected, that I stood there quietly (I assert positively that I stood quietly) and looked around. Like a scale: overload one side sufficiently and then you may gently put on the other as much as you will; the arrow will not move.

Suddenly I felt alone. I-330 was no longer with me. I don't know how or where she disappeared. Around me were only *those,* with their hair glistening like silk in the sunlight. I caught someone's warm, strong, dark shoulder.

"Listen, please, in the name of the Well-Doer, could you tell me where she went? A while, a minute ago, she . . ."

Long-haired, austere eyebrows turned to me.

"Sh . . . sh . . . silence!" He made a sign with his head toward the center of the clearing where there stood the yellow skull-like stone.

There above the heads of all I saw her. The sun beat straight into my eyes, and because of that she seemed coal-black, standing out on the blue cloth of the sky—a coal-black silhouette on a blue background. A little higher the clouds were floating. And it seemed that not the clouds but the rock itself, and she herself upon that rock, and the crowd and the clearing—all were silently floating like a ship, and the earth was light and glided away from under the feet. . . .

"Brothers!" (It was she.) "Brothers, you all know that there inside the Wall, in the City, they are building the *Integral.* And you know also that the day has come for us to destroy that Wall and all other walls, so that the green wind may blow over all the earth, from end to end. But the *Integral* is going to take these walls up, up into the heights, to the thousands of other worlds which every evening whisper to us with their lights through the black leaves of night . . . "

Waves and foam and wind were beating the rock:

"Down with the *Integral!* Down!"

"No, brothers, not 'down.' The *Integral* must be ours. And it *shall* be ours. On the day when it first sets sail into the sky *we* shall be on board. For the Builder of the *Integral* is with us. He left the walls, he came with me here in order to be with us. Long live the Builder!"

A second—and I was somewhere above everything. Under me: heads, heads, heads, wide-open, yelling mouths, arms rising and falling. . . . There was something strange and intoxicating in it all. I felt myself *above everybody;* I was, I, a separate world; I ceased to be the usual item; I became unity. . . .

Again I was below, near the rock, my body happy, shaken, and rumpled, as after an embrace of love. Sunlight, voices, and from above—the smiles of I-330. A golden-haired woman, her whole body silky-golden and diffusing an odor of different herbs, was nearby. She held a cup, apparently made of wood. She drank a little from it with her red lips, and then offered the cup to me. I closed my eyes and eagerly drank the sweet, cold, prickly sparks, pouring them down on the fire which burned within me.

Soon afterward my blood and the whole world began to circulate a thousand times faster; the earth seemed to be flying, light as dawn. And within me everything was simple, light, and clear. Only then I noticed on the rock the familiar, enormous letters: MEPHI, and for some reason the inscription seemed to me *necessary*. It seemed to be a simple thread binding everything together. A rather rough picture hewn in the rock—this, too, seemed comprehensible; it represented a youth with wings and a transparent body and, in the place ordinarily occupied by the heart, a blinding, red, blazing coal. Again I understood that coal—or no, I *felt* it as I felt without hearing every word of I-330's (she continued to speak from above, from the rock); and I felt that all of them breathed one breath, and that they were all ready to fly somewhere like the birds over the Wall.

From behind, from the confusion of breathing bodies, a loud voice:

"But this is folly!"

It seems to me it was I—yes, I am certain it was I who then jumped on the rock; from there I saw the sun, the heads, a green sea on a blue background, and I cried:

"Yes, yes, precisely. All must become insane; we must become insane as soon as possible! We must: I know it:"

I-330 was at my side. Her smile—two dark lines from the angles of her mouth directed upward. . . . And within me a blazing coal. It was momentary, light, a little painful, beautiful. . . . And later, only stray fragments that remained sticking in me. . . .

. . . Very low and slowly a bird was moving. I saw it was living, like me. It was turning its head now to the right and then to the left like a human being, and its round black eyes drilled themselves into me. . . .

. . . Then: a human back glistening with fur the color of ancient ivory; a mosquito crawling on that back, a mosquito with tiny transparent wings. The back twitched to chase the mosquito away; it twitched again. . . .

. . . And yet another thing: a shadow from the leaves, a woven, net-like shadow. Some humans lay in that shadow, chewing something, something similar to the legendary food of the ancients, a long yellow fruit and a piece of something dark. They put some of it in my hand, and it seemed strange to me for I did not know whether I might eat it or not. . . .

. . . And again: a crowd, heads, legs, arms, mouths, faces appearing for a second and disappearing like bursting bubbles. For a second (or perhaps it was only a hallucination?) the transparent, flying wing ears appeared. . . .

With all my might I pressed the hand of I-330. She turned to me.

"What is the matter?"

"He is here! I thought, I—"

"Who?"

"S-, a second ago, in the crowd."

The ends of the thin, coal-black brows moved to the temples—a smile like a sharp triangle. I could not see clearly why she smiled. How could she smile?

"But you understand, I-330, don't you, you understand what it means if he, or one of them, is here?"

"You are funny! How could it ever enter the heads of those within the Wall that we are here? Remember; take yourself. Did you ever think it was possible? They are busy hunting us *there*—let them! You are delirious!"

Her smile was light and cheerful and I, too, was smiling; the earth was drunken, cheerful, light, floating. . . .

* * *

Record 40

Facts
The Bell
I Am Certain

Daylight. It is clear. The barometer—760 mm. Is it possible that I, D-503, really wrote these—pages? Is it possible that I ever felt, or imagined I felt, all this?

The handwriting is mine. And what follows is all in my handwriting. Fortunately, only the handwriting. No more delirium, no absurd metaphors, no feelings—only facts. For I am healthy—perfectly, absolutely healthy . . . I am smiling; I cannot help smiling; a splinter has been taken out of my head, and I feel so light, so empty! To be more exact, not empty, but there is nothing foreign, nothing that prevents me from smiling. (Smiling is the normal state for a normal human being.)

The facts are as follows: That evening my neighbor who discovered the finiteness of the universe, and I, and all others who did not have a certificate showing that we had been operated on, all of us were taken to the nearest auditorium. (For some reason the number of the auditorium, 112, seemed familiar to me.) There they tied us to the tables and performed the great operation. Next day, I, D-503, appeared before the Well-Doer and told him everything known to me about the enemies of happiness. Why, before, it had seemed hard for me to go, I cannot understand. The only explanation seems to be my illness—my soul.

That same evening, sitting at the same table with Him, with the Well-Doer, I saw for the first time in my life the famous Gas Chamber. They brought in that woman. She was to testify in my presence. She remained stubbornly silent and smiling. I noticed that she had sharp and very white teeth which were very pretty.

Then she was brought under the Bell. Her face became very white, and as her eyes were large and dark, all was very pretty. When they began pumping the air from under the Bell she threw her head back and half-closed her eyes; her lips were pressed together. This reminded me of something. She looked at me, holding the arms of the chair firmly. She continued to look until her eyes closed. Then she was taken out and brought back to consciousness by means of electrodes, and again she was put under the Bell. The procedure was repeated three times, yet she did not utter a word.

The others who were brought in with that woman proved to be more honest; many of them began to speak after the first trial. Tomorrow they will all ascend the steps to the Machine of the Well-Doer. No postponement is possible, for there still is chaos, groaning, cadavers, beasts in the western section; and to our regret there are still quantities of Numbers who have betrayed Reason.

But on the transverse avenue Forty we have succeeded in establishing a temporary Wall of high-voltage waves. And I hope we win. More than that; I am certain we shall win. For Reason must prevail.

✧ PART TEN ✧

World War I

World War I, which all belligerents believed would be brief, turned into a war of attrition. Trench warfare, with all of its military, physical, and psychological destruction, became the rule. In this image, German soldiers await developments.

World War I

In August 1914, the Great War pitted Germany and Austria-Hungary against Great Britain, France, and Russia. A tangled system of alliances, competition among the Great Powers, and nationalism all contributed to the first major war in Europe since Napoleon's defeat. The assassination of Archduke Franz Ferdinand, successor to Emperor-King Franz Joseph of Austria-Hungary, set off, as though by trip wire, the activation of various military alliances, full mobilizations, and, ultimately, a world war. Initial enthusiasm among all belligerents soon waned as the war continued longer than anyone expected. The Germans advanced in the East against the Russians, who in turn pushed back the Austro-Hungarian forces. Drained and demoralized, Russia left the war after the Bolshevik Revolution. In the West, deadly but stable trench warfare yielded only to the joint American, British, and French juggernaut, which defeated the Germans and their allies in the autumn of 1918.

Friedrich von Bernhardi (1849–1930), a German general, believed that war was a biological imperative. Peace marked the "decay of spirit and political courage," whereas war had "its necessary place in historical development." Before World War I, many Germans shared these unofficial views and eagerly read Bernhardi's book, *Germany and the Next War* (1912). The organization behind Archduke Franz Ferdinand's assassination was the Serbian arch-nationalist organization, the Black Hand (Ujedinjenje ili Smrt), whose Constitution, written in 1911, suggests its extremity. One of its members, Gavrilo Princip, performed the act that set off the Great War. The young Englishman, Siegfried Sassoon (1886–1967), at first an enthusiast of the war, soon realized its harsh reality. His *War Poems* testify to his new antiwar convictions. *All Quiet on the Western Front* (1926) by Erich Maria Remarque (1898–1970) is also a powerful example of antiwar literature. Its depiction of ordinary soldiers' disillusionment sufficed to have it burned by the Nazis in 1933. Ernst Juenger (1895–1998), an officer in the German army during World War I, published his recollections of the conflict in 1920. As realistic as Remarque's account, *Storm of Steel* (1920) extolled the war experience and contributed to the "cult of action" that underlay fascism.

✦ **Reading 36** ✦

Germany and the Next War

Friedrich von Bernhardi

The Right to Make War

Since 1795, when Immanuel Kant published in his old age his treatise on "Perpetual Peace," many have considered it an established fact that war is the destruction of all good and the origin of all evil. In spite of all that history teaches, no conviction is felt that the struggle between nations is inevitable, and the growth of civilization is credited with a power to which war must yield. But, undisturbed by such human theories and the change of times, war has again and again marched from country to country with the clash of arms, and has proved its destructive as well as creative and purifying power. It has not succeeded in teaching mankind what its real nature is. Long periods of war, far from convincing men of the necessity of war, have, on the contrary, always revived the wish to exclude war, where possible, from the political intercourse of nations.

This wish and this hope are widely disseminated even to-day. The maintenance of peace is lauded as the only goal at which statesmanship should aim. This unqualified desire for peace has obtained in our days a quite peculiar power over men's spirits. This aspiration finds its public expression in peace leagues and peace congresses; the Press of every country and of every party opens its columns to it. The current in this direction is, indeed, so strong that the majority of Governments profess—outwardly, at any rate—that the necessity of maintaining peace is the real aim of their policy; while when a war breaks out the aggressor is universally stigmatized, and all Governments exert themselves, partly in reality, partly in pretence, to extinguish the conflagration.

Pacific ideals, to be sure, are seldom the real motive of their action. They usually employ the need of peace as a cloak under which to promote their own political aims. This was the real position of affairs at the Hague Congresses, and this is also the meaning of the action of the United States of America, who in recent times have earnestly tried to conclude treaties for the establishment of Arbitration Courts, first and foremost with England, but also with Japan, France, and Germany. No practical results, it must be said, have so far been achieved.

We can hardly assume that a real love of peace prompts these efforts. This is shown by the fact that precisely those Powers which, as the weaker, are exposed to aggression, and therefore were in the greatest need of international protection, have been completely passed over in the American proposals for Arbitration Courts. It must consequently be assumed that very matter-of-fact political motives led the Americans, with their commercial instincts, to take such steps, and induced "perfidious Albion" to accede to the proposals. We may suppose that England intended to protect her rear in event of a war with Germany, but that America wished to have a free hand in order to follow her policy of sovereignty in Central America without hindrance, and to carry out her plans regarding the Panama Canal in the exclusive interests of America. Both countries certainly entertained the hope of gaining advantage over the other signatory of the treaty, and of winning the lion's share for themselves. Theorists and fanatics imagine that they see in the efforts of President Taft a great step forward on the path to perpetual peace, and enthusiastically agree with him. Even the Minister for Foreign Affairs in England, with well-affected idealism, termed the procedure of the United States an era in the history of mankind.

This desire for peace has rendered most civilized nations anæmic, and marks a decay of spirit and

From: Friedrich von Bernhardi, *Germany and the Next War*, trans. Allen H. Powles (New York: Longmans, Green, and Co., 1914), pp. 16–19, 86, 103–104, 169–170, 172–175.

political courage such as has often been shown by a race of Epigoni. "It has always been," H. von Treitschke tells us, "the weary, spiritless, and exhausted ages which have played with the dream of perpetual peace."

Everyone will, within certain limits, admit that the endeavours to diminish the dangers of war and to mitigate the sufferings which war entails are justifiable. It is an incontestable fact that war temporarily disturbs industrial life, interrupts quiet economic development, brings widespread misery with it, and emphasizes the primitive brutality of man. It is therefore a most desirable consummation if wars for trivial reasons should be rendered impossible, and if efforts are made to restrict the evils which follow necessarily in the train of war, so far as is compatible with the essential nature of war. All that the Hague Peace Congress has accomplished in this limited sphere deserves, like every permissible humanization of war, universal acknowledgment. But it is quite another matter if the object is to abolish war entirely, and to deny its necessary place in historical development.

This aspiration is directly antagonistic to the great universal laws which rule all life. War is a biological necessity of the first importance, a regulative element in the life of mankind which cannot be dispensed with, since without it an unhealthy development will follow, which excludes every advancement of the race, and therefore all real civilization. "War is the father of all things." The sages of antiquity long before Darwin recognized this.

The struggle for existence is, in the life of Nature, the basis of all healthy development. All existing things show themselves to be the result of contesting forces. So in the life of man the struggle is not merely the destructive, but the life-giving principle. "To supplant or to be supplanted is the essence of life," says Goethe, and the strong life gains the upper hand. The law of the stronger holds good everywhere. Those forms survive which are able to procure themselves the most favourable conditions of life, and to assert themselves in the universal economy of Nature. The weaker succumb. This struggle is regulated and restrained by the unconscious sway of biological laws and by the interplay of opposite forces. In the plant world and the animal world this process is worked out in unconscious tragedy. In the human race it is consciously carried out, and regulated by social ordinances. The man of strong will and strong intellect tries by every means to assert himself, the ambitious strive to rise, and in this effort the individual is far from being guided merely by the consciousness of right. The life-work and the life-struggle of many men are determined, doubtless, by unselfish and ideal motives, but to a far greater extent the less noble passions—craving for possessions, enjoyment and honour, envy and the thirst for revenge—determine men's actions. Still more often, perhaps, it is the need to live which brings down even natures of a higher mould into the universal struggle for existence and enjoyment.

There can be no doubt on this point. The nation is made up of individuals, the State of communities. The motive whch influences each member is prominent in the whole body. It is a persistent struggle for possessions, power and sovereignty, which primarily governs the relations of one nation to another, and right is respected so far only as it is compatible with advantage. So long as there are men who have human feelings and aspirations, so long as there are nations who strive for an enlarged sphere of activity, so long will conflicting interests come into being and occasions for making war arise.

"The natural law, to which all laws of Nature can be reduced, is the law of struggle. All intrasocial property, all thoughts, inventions, and institutions, as, indeed, the social system itself, are a result of the intrasocial struggle, in which one survives and another is cast out. The extrasocial, the supersocial struggle which guides the external development of societies, nations, and races, is war. The internal development, the intrasocial struggle, is man's daily work—the struggle of thoughts, feelings, wishes, sciences, activities. The outward development, the supersocial struggle, is the sanguinary struggle of nations—war. In what does the creative power of this struggle consist? In growth and decay, in the victory of the one factor and in the defeat of the other! This struggle is a creator, since it eliminates."

* * *

We see the European Great Powers divided into two great camps.

On the one side Germany, Austria, and Italy have concluded a defensive alliance, whose sole object is to guard against hostile aggression. In this alliance the two first-named States form the solid, probably unbreakable, core, since by the nature of things they are intimately connected. The geographical conditions force this result. The two States combined form a compact series of territories from the Adriatic to the North Sea and the Baltic.

* * *

Under these conditions the position of Germany is extraordinarily difficult. We not only require for the full material development of our nation, on a scale corresponding to its intellectual importance, an extended political basis, but, as explained in the previous chapter, we are compelled to obtain space for our increasing population and markets for our growing industries. But at every step which we take in this direction England will resolutely oppose us. English policy may not yet have made the definite decision to attack us; but it doubtless wishes, by all and every means, even the most extreme, to hinder every further expansion of German international influence and of German maritime power. The recognized political aims of England and the attitude of the English Government leave no doubt on this point. But if we were involved in a struggle with England, we can be quite sure that France would not neglect the opportunity of attacking our flank. Italy, with her extensive coast-line, even if still a member of the Triple Alliance, will have to devote large forces to the defence of the coast to keep off the attacks of the Anglo-French Mediterranean Fleet, and would thus be only able to employ weaker forces against France. Austria would be paralyzed by Russia; against the latter we should have to leave forces in the East. We should thus have to fight out the struggle against France and England practically alone with a part of our army, perhaps with some support from Italy. It is in this double menace by sea and on the mainland of Europe that the grave danger to our political position lies, since all freedom of action is taken from us and all expansion barred.

Since the struggle is, as appears on a thorough investigation of the international question, necessary and inevitable, we must fight it out, cost what it may. Indeed, we are carrying it on at the present moment, though not with drawn swords, and only by peaceful means so far. On the one hand it is being waged by the competition in trade, industries and warlike preparations; on the other hand, by diplomatic methods with which the rival States are fighting each other in every region where their interests clash.

With these methods it has been possible to maintain peace hitherto, but not without considerable loss of power and prestige. This apparently peaceful state of things must not deceive us; we are facing a hidden, but none the less formidable, crisis—perhaps the most momentous crisis in the history of the German nation.

We have fought in the last great wars for our national union and our position among the Powers of *Europe;* we now must decide whether we wish to develop into and maintain a *World Empire,* and procure for German spirit and German ideas that fit recognition which has been hitherto withheld from them.

Have we the energy to aspire to that great goal? Are we prepared to make the sacrifices which such an effort will doubtless cost us? or are we willing to recoil before the hostile forces, and sink step by step lower in our economic, political, and national importance? That is what is involved in our decision.

"To be, or not to be," is the question which is put to us to-day, disguised, indeed, by the apparent equilibrium of the opposing interests and forces, by the deceitful shifts of diplomacy, and the official peace-aspirations of all the States; but by the logic of history inexorably demanding an answer, if we look with clear gaze beyond the narrow horizon of the day and the mere surface of things into the region of realities.

There is no standing still in the world's history. All is growth and development. It is obviously impossible to keep things in the *status quo,* as diplomacy has so often attempted. No true statesman will ever seriously count on such a possibility; he will only make the outward and temporary maintenance of existing conditions a duty when he wishes to gain time and deceive an opponent, or when he cannot see what is the trend of events. He will use such diplomatic means only as inferior tools; in reality he will only reckon with actual forces and with the powers of a continuous development.

We must make it quite clear to ourselves that there can be no standing still, no being satisfied for us, but only progress or retrogression, and that it is tantamount.

* * *

Since the crucial point is to safeguard our much-threatened position on the continent of Europe, we must first of all face the serious problem of the land war—by what means we can hope to overcome the great numerical superiority of our enemies. Such superiority will certainly exist if Italy ceases to be an active member of the Triple Alliance, whether nominally belonging to it, or politically going over to Irredentism. The preparations for the naval war are of secondary importance.

The first essential requirement, in case of a war by land, is to make the total fighting strength of the nation available for war, to educate the entire youth of the country in the use of arms, and to make universal service an existing fact.

The system of universal service, born in the hour of need, has by a splendid development of strength liberated us from a foreign yoke, has in long years of peace educated a powerful and well-armed people, and has brought us victory upon victory in the German wars of unification. Its importance for the social evolution of the nation has been discussed in a separate chapter. The German Empire would to-day have a mighty political importance if we had been loyal to the principle on which our greatness was founded.

France has at the present day a population of some 40,000,000; Russia in Europe, with Poland and the Caucasus, has a population of 140,000,000. Contrasted with this, Germany has only 65,000,000 inhabitants. But since the Russian military forces are, to a great extent, hampered by very various causes and cannot be employed at any one time or place, and are also deficient in military value, a German army which corresponded to the population would be certainly in a position to defend itself successfully against its two enemies, if it operated resolutely on the inner line, even though England took part in the war.

Disastrously for ourselves, we have become disloyal to the idea of universal military service, and have apparently definitely discontinued to carry it out effectively. The country where universal service exists is now France. With us, indeed, it is still talked about, but it is only kept up in pretence, for in reality 50 per cent., perhaps, of the able-bodied are called up for training. In particular, very little use has been made of the larger towns as recruiting-grounds for the army.

In this direction some reorganization is required which will energetically combine the forces of the nation and create a real army, such as we have not at the present time. Unless we satisfy this demand, we shall not long be able to hold our own against the hostile Powers.

Although we recognize this necessity as a national duty, we must not shut our eyes to the fact that it is impossible in a short time to make up our deficiencies. Our peace army cannot be suddenly increased by 150,000 men. The necessary training staff and equipment would not be forthcoming, and on the financial side the required expenditure could not all at once be incurred. The full effectiveness of an increased army only begins to be gradually felt when the number of reservists and Landwehr is correspondingly raised. We can therefore only slowly recur to the reinforcement of universal service. The note struck by the new Five Years Act cannot be justified on any grounds. But although we wish to increase our army on a more extensive scale, we must admit that, even if we strain our resources, the process can only work slowly, and that we cannot hope for a long time to equalize even approximately the superior forces of our opponents.

We must not, therefore, be content merely to strengthen our army; we must devise other means of gaining the upper hand of our enemies. These means can only be found in the spiritual domain.

History teaches us by countless examples that numbers in themselves have only been the decisive factor in war when the opponents have been equally matched otherwise, or when the superiority of the one party exceeds the proportion required by the numerical law.

* * *

In a future European war "masses" will be employed to an extent unprecedented in any previous one. Weapons will be used whose deadliness will exceed all previous experience. More effective and varied means of communication will be available than were known in earlier wars. These three momentous factors will mark the war of the future.

"Masses" signify in themselves an increase of strength, but they contain elements of weakness as well. The larger they are and the less they can be commanded by professional soldiers, the more their tactical efficiency diminishes. The less they are able to live on the country during war-time, especially when concentrated, and the more they are therefore dependent on the daily renewal of food-supplies, the slower and less mobile they become. Owing to the great space which they require for their deployment, it is extraordinarily difficult to bring them into effective action simultaneously. They are also far more accessible to morally depressing influences than compacter bodies of troops, and may prove dangerous to the strategy of their own leaders, if supplies run short, if discipline breaks down, and the commander loses his authority over the masses which he can only rule under regulated conditions.

The increased effectiveness of weapons does not merely imply a longer range, but a greater deadliness, and therefore makes more exacting claims on the *morale* of the soldier. The danger zone begins sooner than formerly; the space which must be crossed in an attack has become far wider; it must be passed by the attacking party creeping or running. The soldier must often use the spade in defensive operations, during which he is exposed to a far hotter fire than formerly; while under all circumstances he must shoot more than in bygone days. The quick firing which the troop encounters increases the losses at every incautious movement. All branches of arms have to suffer under these circumstances. Shelter and supplies will be more scanty than ever before. In short, while the troops on the average have diminished in value, the demands made on them have become considerably greater.

Improved means of communication, finally, facilitate the handling and feeding of large masses, but tie them down to railway systems and main roads, and must, if they fail or break down in the course of a campaign, aggravate the difficulties, because the troops were accustomed to their use, and the commanders counted upon them.

The direct conclusion to be drawn from these reflections is that a great superiority must rest with the troops whose fighting capabilities and tactical efficiency are greater than those of their antagonists.

The commander who can carry out all operations quicker than the enemy, and can concentrate and employ greater masses in a narrow space than they can, will always be in a position to collect a numerically superior force in the decisive direction; if he controls the more effective troops, he will gain decisive successes against one part of the hostile army, and will be able to exploit them against other divisions of it before the enemy can gain equivalent advantages in other parts of the field.

Since the tactical efficiency and the *morale* of the troops are chiefly shown in the offensive, and are then most needful, the necessary conclusion is that safety only lies in offensive warfare.

In an attack, the advantage, apart from the elements of moral strength which it brings into play, depends chiefly on rapidity of action. Inasmuch as the attacking party determines the direction of the attack to suit his own plans, he is able at the selected spot to collect a superior force against his surprised opponent. The initiative, which is the privilege of the attacking party, gives a start in time and place which is very profitable in operations and tactics. The attacked party can only equalize this advantage if he has early intimation of the intentions of the assailant, and has time to take measures which hold out promise of success. The more rapidly, therefore, the attacking General strikes his blow and gains his success, and the more capable his troops, the greater is the superiority which the attack in its nature guarantees.

This superiority increases with the size of the masses. If the advancing armies are large and unwieldy, and the distances to be covered great, it will be a difficult and tedious task for the defending commander to take proper measures against a surprise attack. On the other hand, the prospects of success of the attacking General will be very favourable, especially if he is in the fortunate position of having better troops at his disposal.

Finally, the initiative secures to the numerically weaker a possibility of gaining the victory, even when other conditions are equal, and all the more so the greater the masses engaged. In most cases it is impossible to bring the entire mass of a modern army simultaneously and completely into action. A victory, therefore, in the decisive direction—the direction, that is, which directly cuts the arteries of the opponents—is usually conclusive for the whole course of the war, and its effect is felt in the most distant parts of the field of operations. If the assailant, therefore, can advance in this direction with superior numbers, and can win the day, because the enemy cannot utilize his numerical superiority, there is a possibility of an ultimate victory over the arithmetically stronger army. In conformity to this law, Frederick the Great, through superior tactical capability and striking strength, had always the upper hand of an enemy far more powerful in mere numbers.

No further proof is required that the superiority of the attack increases in proportion to the rapidity with which it is delivered, and to the lack of mobility of the hostile forces. Hence the possibility of concealing one's own movements and damaging the effective tactics of the enemy secures an advantage which, though indirect, is yet very appreciable.

We arrive, then, at the conclusion that, in order to secure the superiority in a war of the future under otherwise equal conditions, it is incumbent on us: First, during the period of preparation to raise the tactical value and capabilities of the troops as much as possible, and especially to develop the means of concealing the attacking movements and damaging the enemy's tactical powers; secondly, in the war itself to act on the offensive and strike the first blow, and to exploit the manœuvring capacity of the troops as much as possible, in order to be superior in the decisive directions. Above all, a State which has objects to attain that cannot be relinquished, and is exposed to attacks by enemies more powerful than itself, is bound to act in this sense. It must, before all things, develop the attacking powers of its army, since a strategic defensive must often adopt offensive methods. This principle holds good pre-eminently for Germany.

✦ Reading 37 ✦

The Constitution of the Ujedinjenje ili Smrt—Unification or Death

I. Purpose and Name

Article 1. For the purpose of realising the national ideals—the Unification of Serbdom—an organization is hereby created, whose members may be any Serbian irrespective of sex, religion, place or birth, as well as anybody else who will sincerely serve this idea.

Article 2. The organisation gives priority to the revolutionary struggle rather than relies on cultural striving, therefore its institution is an absolutely secret one for wider circles.

Article 3. The organization bears the name: "Ujedinjenje ili Smrt".

Article 4. In order to carry into effect its task the organization will do the following things:

(1) Following the character of its raison d'etre it will exercise its influence over all the official factors in Serbia—which is the Piedmont of Serbdom—as also over all the strata of the State and over the entire social life in it:

(2) It will carry out a revolutionary organisation in all the territories where Serbians are living:

(3) Beyond the frontiers, it will fight with all means against all enemies of this idea:

(4) It will maintain friendly relations with all the States, nations, organisations, and individual persons who sympathise with Serbia and the Serbian race:

(5) It will give every assistance to those nations and organisations who are fighting for their own national liberation and unification.

From: Harold B. Lee Library, Brigham Young University, *The Constitution of the Ujedinjenje Smrt—Unification or Death* [Online], Available October 2001: http://www.lib.byu.edu/~rdh/wwi/1914m/blkcons.html.

II. Official Departments of the Organisation

Article 5. The supreme authority is vested in the Supreme Central Directorate with its headquarters at Belgrade. Its duty will be to see that the resolutions are carried into effect.

Article 6. The number of members of the Supreme Central Directorate is unlimited—but in principle it should be kept as low as possible.

Article 7. The Supreme Central Directorate shall include, in addition to the members from the Kingdom of Serbia, one accredited delegate from each of the organisations of all the Serbian regions: (1) Bosnia and Herzegovina, (2) Montenegro, (3) Old Serbia and Macedonia, (4) Croatia, Slovenia and Symria (Srem), (5) Voyvodina, (6) Sea-coasts.

Article 8. It will be the task of the Supreme Central Directorate to carry out the principles of the organisation within the territory of the Kingdom of Serbia.

Article 9. The duty of each individual Provincial Directorate will be to carry out the principles of the organisation within the respective territories of each Serbian region outside the frontiers of the Kingdom of Serbia. The Provincial Directorate will be the supreme authority of the organisation within its own territory.

Article 10. The subdivisions of the organisation into District Directorates and other units of authority shall be established by the By-Laws of the organisation which shall be laid down, and if need be, from time to time amended and amplified by the Supreme Central Directorate.

Article 11. Each Directorate shall elect, from amongst its own members, its President, Secretary and Treasures.

Article 12. By virtue of the nature of his work, the Secretary may act as a Deputy President. In order that he may devote himself entirely to the work of the organisation, the Secretary's salary and expenses shall be provided by the Supreme Central Directorate.

Article 13. The positions of President and Treasurers shall be unsalaried.

Article 14. All official business questions of the organisation shall be decided in the sessions of the Supreme Central Directorate by a majority of votes.

Article 15. For the execution of such decisions of the organisation, the absolute executive power shall be vested in the President and the Secretary.

Article 16. In exceptional and less important cases the President and the Secretary shall make the decisions and secure their execution, but they shall report accordingly at the next following session of the Supreme Central Directorate.

Article 17. For the purpose of ensuring a more efficient discharge of business, the Supreme Central Directorate shall be divided into sections, according to the nature of the work.

Article 18. The Supreme Central Directorate shall maintain its relations with the Provincial Directorates through the accredited delegates of the said provincial organisations, it being understood that such delegates shall be at the same time members of the Supreme Central Directorate; in exceptional cases, however, these relations shall be maintained through special delegates.

Article 19. Provincial Directorates shall have freedom of action. Only in cases of the execution of broader revolutionary movements will they depend upon the approval of the Supreme Central Directorate.

Article 20. The Supreme Central Directorate shall regulate all the signs and watchwords, necessary for the maintenance of secrecy in the organisation.

Article 21. It shall be the Supreme Central Directorate's duty punctually and officially to keep all the members of the organisation well posted about all the more important questions relative to the organisation.

Article 22. The Supreme Central Directorate shall from time to time control and inspect the work of its own departments. Analogically, the other Directorates shall do likewise with their own departments.

III. The Members of the Organisation

Article 23. The following rule, as a principle, shall govern all the detailed transactions of the organisation: All communications and conversations to be conducted only through specially appointed and authorised persons.

Article 24. It shall be the duty of every member to recruit new members, but it shall be understood that every introducing member shall vouch with his own life for all those whom he introduces into the organisation.

Article 25. The members of the organisation as amongst themselves shall not be known to one another. Only the members of Directorates shall be known personally to one another.

Article 26. In the organisation the members shall be registered and known by their respective numbers. But the Supreme Central Directorate must know them also by their respective names.

Article 27. The members of the organisation must unconditionally obey all the commands given by their respective Directorates, as also all the Directorates must obey unconditionally the commands which they receive direct from their superior Directorate.

Article 28. Every member shall be obliged to impart officially to the organisation whatever comes to his knowledge, either in his private life or in the discharge of his official duties, in as far as it may be of interest to the organisation.

Article 29. The interest of the organisation shall stand above all other interests.

Article 30. On entering into the organisation, every member must know that by joining the organisation he loses his own personality; he must not expect any glory for himself, nor any personal benefit, material or moral. Consequently the member who should dare to try to exploit the organisation for his personal, or class, or party interests shall be punished by death.

Article 31. Whosoever has once entered into the organisation can never by any means leave it, nor shall anybody have the authority to accept the resignation of a member.

Article 32. Every member shall support the organisation by his weekly contributions. The organisations, however, shall have the authority to procure money, if need be, by coercion. The permission to resort to these means may be given only by Supreme Central Directorate within the country, or by the regional Directorates within their respective region.

Article 33. In administering capital punishment the sole responsibility of the Supreme Central Directorate shall be to see that such punishment is safely and unfailingly carried into effect without any regard for the ways and means to be employed in the execution.

IV. The Seal and the Oath of Allegiance

Article 34. The Organisation's official seal is thus composed: In the centre of the seal there is a powerful arm holding in its hand an unfurled flag on which—as a coat of arms—there is a skull with crossed bones; by the side of the flag, a knife, a bomb and a phial of poison. Around, in a circle, there is the following inscription, reading from left to right: "Unification or Death", and in the base: "The Supreme Central Directorate".

Article 35. On entering into the organisation the joining member must pronounce the following oath of allegiance:

> *"I (the Christian name and surname of the joining member), by entering into the organisation "Unification or Death", do hereby swear by the Sun which shineth upon me, by the Earth which feedeth me, by God, by the blood of my forefathers, by my honour and by my life, that from this moment onward and until my death, I shall faithfully serve the task of this organisation and that I shall at all times be prepared to bear for it any sacrifice. I further swear by God, by my honour and by my life, that I shall unconditionally carry into effect all its orders and commands. I further swear by my God, by my honour and by my life, that I shall keep within myself all the secrets of this organisation and carry them with me into my grave. May God and my comrades in this organisation be my judges if at any time I should wittingly fail or break this oath!"*

V. Supplementary Orders

Article 36. The present Constitution shall come into force immediately.

Article 37. The present Constitution must not be altered.

Done at Belgrade this 9th day of May, 1911 A.D.

Signed:

Major Ilija Radivojevitch
Vice-Consul Bogdan Radenkovitch
Colonel Cedimilj A. Popovitch
Lt.-Col. Velimir Vemitch
Journalist Ljubomir S. Jovanovitch
Col. Dragutin T. Dimitrijevitch
Major Vojin P. Tanksoitch
Major Milan Vasitch
Col. Milovan Gr. Milovanovitch

✦ Reading 38 ✦

War Poems

Siegfried Sassoon

The Redeemer

Darkness: the rain sluiced down; the
mire was deep;
It was past twelve on a mid-winter night,
When peaceful folk in beds lay snug asleep;
There, with much work to do before the
light,
We lugged our clay-sucked boots as best
we might
Along the trench; sometimes a bullet sang,
And droning shells burst with a hollow
bang;
We were soaked, chilled and wretched,
every one;
Darkness; the distant wink of a huge gun.

I turned in the black ditch, loathing the
storm;
A rocket fizzed and burned with
blanching flare,
And lit the face of what had been a form
Floundering in mirk. He stood before me
there;
I say that He was Christ; stiff in the glare;
And leaning forward from His burdening
task,
Both arms supporting it; His eyes on mine
Stared from the woeful head that seemed a
mask
Of mortal pain in Hell's unholy shine.

No thorny crown, only a woollen cap
He wore—an English soldier, white and
strong,
Who loved his time like any simple chap,
Good days of work and sport and homely
song;
Now he has learned that nights are very
long,
And dawn a watching of the windowed sky.
But to the end, unjudging, he'll endure
Horror and pain, not uncontent to die
That Lancaster on Lune may stand secure.

He faced me, reeling in his weariness,
Shouldering his load of planks, so hard to
bear.
I say that He was Christ, who wrought to
bless
All groping things with freedom bright as
air,
And with His mercy washed and made
them fair.
Then the flame sank, and all grew black
as pitch,
While we began to struggle along the ditch;
And someone flung his burden in the muck,
Mumbling: "O Christ Almighty, now I'm
stuck!"

November 1915/March 1916

The Dragon and the Undying

All night the flares go up; the Dragon
sings
And beats upon the dark with furious wings;
And, stung to rage by his own darting fires,
Reaches with grappling coils from town to
town;
He lusts to break the loveliness of spires,

From: Siegfried Sassoon, *The War Poems of Siegfried Sassoon,* arranged and introduced by Rupert Hart-Davis (London: Faber and Faber, 1983), pp. 16, 17, 22, 23, 128.

And hurl their martyred music toppling
down.

Yet, though the slain are homeless as
the breeze,
Vocal are they, like storm-bewilder'd seas.
Their faces are the fair, unshrouded night,
And planets are their eyes, their ageless
dreams.
Tenderly stooping earthward from their
height,
They wander in the dusk with chanting
streams,
And they are dawn-lit trees, with arms
up-flung,
To hail the burning heavens they left
unsung.

February 1916

In the Pink

So Davies wrote: "This leaves me in
the pink."
Then scrawled his name: "Your loving
sweetheart, Willie."
With crosses for a hug. He'd had a drink
Of rum and tea; and, though the barn was
chilly,
For once his blood ran warm; he had pay
to spend.
Winter was passing; soon the year would
mend.

But he couldn't sleep that night; stiff in
the dark
He groaned and thought of Sundays at
the farm,
And how he'd go as cheerful as a lark
In his best suit, to wander arm in arm
With brown-eyed Gwen, and whisper in
her ear
The simple, silly things she liked to hear.

And then he thought: to-morrow night
we trudge
Up to the trenches, and my boots are rotten.
Five miles of stodgy clay and freezing sludge,
And everything but wretchedness
forgotten.
To-night he's in the pink; but soon he'll die.
And still the war goes on—he don't
know why.

10 February 1916

Battalion-Relief

"Fall in! Now get a move on." (Curse
the rain.)
We splash away along the straggling village,
Out to the flat rich country, green with
June . . .
And sunset flares across wet crops and
tillage,
Blazing with splendour-patches. (Harvest
soon,
Up in the Line.) "Perhaps the War'll be
done
"By Christmas-Day. Keep smiling then,
old son."

Here's the Canal: it's dusk; we cross
the bridge.
"Lead on there, by platoons." (The Line's
a-glare
With shell-fire through the poplars;
distant rattle
Of rifles and machine-guns.) "Fritz is there!
"Christ, ain't it lively, Sergeant? Is't a
battle?"
More rain: the lightning blinks, and
thunder rumbles.
"There's overhead artillery!" some chap
grumbles.

What's all this mob at the cross-roads?
Where are the guides? . . .
"Lead on with Number One." And off
they go.
"Three minute intervals." (Poor
blundering files,
Sweating and blindly burdened; who's to
know

If death will catch them in those two
dark miles?)
More rain. "Lead on, Headquarters."
(That's the lot.)
"*Who's that? . . . Oh, Sergeant-Major,*
don't get shot!
"*And tell me, have we won this war or*
not?"

July 1918

The Dug-Out

Why do you lie with your legs ungainly
huddled,
And one arm bent across your sullen, cold,
Exhausted face? It hurts my heart to watch
you,
Deep-shadow'd from the candle's guttering
gold;
And you wonder why I shake you by the
shoulder;
Drowsy, you mumble and sigh and turn
your head . . .
You are too young to fall asleep for ever;
And when you sleep you remind me of
the dead.

St Venant, July 1918

✦ Reading 39 ✦

All Quiet on the Western Front

Erich Maria Remarque

Paul Baumer, along with his classmates, enlists in the German Army when the Great War breaks out in 1914. Their youthful enthusiasm soon wanes, and Paul decides to fight against the principle of hate that has pitted him against other young men of his generation.

We travel for several days. The first aeroplanes appear in the sky. We roll on past transport lines. Guns, guns. The light railway picks us up. I search for my regiment. No one knows exactly where it lies. Somewhere or other I put up for the night, somewhere or other I receive provisions and a few vague instructions. And so with my pack and my rifle I set out again on the way.

By the time I come up they are no longer in the devastated place. I hear we have become one of the flying divisions that are pushed in wherever it is hottest. That does not sound cheerful to me. They tell me of heavy losses that we have been having. I inquire after Kat and Albert. No one knows anything of them.

I search farther and wander about here and there; it is a strange feeling. One night more and then another I camp out like a Red Indian. Then at last I get some definite information, and by the afternoon I am able to report to the Orderly Room.

The sergeant-major detains me there. The company comes back in two days' time. There is no object in sending me up now.

"What was it like on leave?" he asks, "pretty good, eh?"

"In parts," I say.

"Yes," he sighs, "yes, if a man didn't have to come away again. The second half is always rather messed up by that."

I loaf around until the company comes back in the early morning, grey, dirty, soured, and gloomy. Then I jump up, push in amongst them, my eyes searching. There is Tjaden, there is Müller blowing his nose, and there are Kat and Kropp. We arrange our sacks of straw side by side. I have an uneasy conscience when I look at them, and yet without any good reason. Before we turn in I bring out the rest of the potato-cakes and jam so that they can have some too.

The outer cakes are mouldy, still it is possible to eat them. I keep those for myself and give the fresh ones to Kat and Kropp.

Kat chews and says: "These are from your mother?"

I nod.

"Good," says he, "I can tell by the taste."

I could almost weep. I can hardly control myself any longer. But it will soon be all right again back here with Kat and Albert. This is where I belong.

"You've been lucky," whispers Kropp to me before we drop off to sleep, "they say we are going to Russia."

To Russia? It's not much of a war over there.

In the distance the front thunders. The walls of the hut rattle.

* * *

There's a great deal of polishing being done. We are inspected at every turn. Everything that is torn is exchanged for new. I score a spotless new tunic out of it and Kat, of course, an entire outfit. A rumour is going round that there may be peace, but the other story is more likely—that we are bound for Russia. Still, what do we need new things for in Russia? At last it leaks out—the Kaiser is coming to review us. Hence all the inspections.

For eight whole days one would suppose we were in a base-camp, there is so much drill and fuss.

From: Erich Maria Remarque, *All Quiet on the Western Front*, trans. by A. W. Wheen (Boston, Toronto: Little Brown and Co., 1975), pp. 171–196.

Everyone is peevish and touchy, we do not take kindly to all this polishing, much less to the full-dress parades. Such things exasperate a soldier more than the frontline.

At last the moment arrives. We stand to attention and the Kaiser appears. We are curious to see what he looks like. He stalks along the line, and I am really rather disappointed; judging from his pictures I imagined him to be bigger and more powerfully built, and above all to have a thundering voice.

He distributes Iron Crosses, speaks to this man and that. Then we march off.

Afterwards we discuss it. Tjaden says with astonishment:

"So that is the All-Highest! And everyone, bar nobody, has to stand up stiff in front of him!" He meditates: "Hindenburg too, he has to stand up stiff to him, eh?"

"Sure," says Kat.

Tjaden hasn't finished yet. He thinks for a while and then asks: "And would a king have to stand up stiff to an emperor?"

None of us is quite sure about it, but we don't suppose so. They are both so exalted that standing strictly to attention is probably not insisted on.

"What rot you do hatch out," says Kat. "The main point is that you have to stand stiff yourself."

But Tjaden is quite fascinated. His otherwise prosy fancy is blowing bubbles. "But look," he announces, "I simply can't believe that an emperor has to go to the latrine the same as I have."

"You can bet your boots on it."

"Four and a half-wit make seven," says Kat. "You've got a maggot in your brain, Tjaden, just you run along to the latrine quick, and get your head clear, so that you don't talk like a two-year-old."

Tjaden disappears.

"But what I would like to know," says Albert, "is whether there would not have been a war if the Kaiser had said No."

"I'm sure there would," I interject, "he was against it from the first."

"Well, if not him alone, then perhaps if twenty or thirty people in the world had said No."

"That's probable," I agree, "but they damned well said Yes."

"It's queer, when one thinks about it," goes on Kropp, "we are here to protect our fatherland. And the French are over there to protect their fatherland. Now who's in the right?"

"Perhaps both," say I without believing it.

"Yes, well now," pursues Albert, and I see that he means to drive me into a corner, "but our professors and parsons and newspapers say that we are the only ones that are right, and let's hope so;—but the French professors and parsons and newspapers say that the right is on their side, now what about that?"

"That I don't know," I say, "but whichever way it is there's war all the same and every month more countries coming in."

Tjaden reappears. He is still quite excited and again joins the conversation, wondering just how a war gets started.

"Mostly by one country badly offending another," answers Albert with a slight air of superiority.

Then Tjaden pretends to be obtuse. "A country? I don't follow. A mountain in Germany cannot offend a mountain in France. Or a river, or a wood, or a field of wheat."

"Are you really as stupid as that, or are you just pulling my leg?" growls Kropp, "I don't mean that at all. One people offends the other——"

"Then I haven't any business here at all," replies Tjaden, "I don't feel myself offended."

"Well, let me tell you," says Albert sourly, "it doesn't apply to tramps like you."

"Then I can be going home right away," retorts Tjaden, and we all laugh.

"Ach, man! he means the people as a whole, the State——" exclaims Müller.

"State, State"—Tjaden snaps his fingers contemptuously, "Gendarmes, police, taxes, that's your State;—if that's what you are talking about, no, thank you."

"That's right," says Kat, "you've said something for once, Tjaden. State and home-country, there's a big difference."

"But they go together," insists Kropp, "without the State there wouldn't be any home-country."

"True, but just you consider, almost all of us are simple folk. And in France, too, the majority of men are labourers, workmen, or poor clerks. Now just why would a French blacksmith or a French shoemaker want to attack us? No, it is merely the rulers. I had never seen a Frenchman before I came here, and it will be just the same with the majority of

Frenchmen as regards us. They weren't asked about it any more than we were."

"Then what exactly is the war for?" asks Tjaden.

Kat shrugs his shoulders. "There must be some people to whom the war is useful."

"Well, I'm not one of them," grins Tjaden.

"Not you, nor anybody else here."

"Who are they then?" persists Tjaden. "It isn't any use to the Kaiser either. He has everything he can want already."

"I'm not so sure about that," contradicts Kat, "he has not had a war up till now. And every full-grown emperor requires at least one war, otherwise he would not become famous. You look in your school books."

"And generals too," adds Detering, "they become famous through war."

"Even more famous than emperors," adds Kat.

"There are other people back behind there who profit by the war, that's certain," growls Detering.

"I think it is more of a kind of fever," says Albert. 'No one in particular wants it, and then all at once there it is. We didn't want the war, the others say the same thing—and yet half the world is in it all the same."

"But there are more lies told by the other side than by us," say I; "just think of those pamphlets the prisoners have on them, where it says that we eat Belgian children. The fellows who write those lies ought to go and hang themselves. They are the real culprits."

Müller gets up. "Anyway, it is better that the war is here instead of in Germany. Just you look at the shell-holes."

"True," assents Tjaden, "but no war at all would be better still."

He is quite proud of himself because he has scored for once over us volunteers. And his opinion is quite typical, here one meets it time and again, and there is nothing with which one can properly counter it, because that is the limit of their comprehension of the factors involved. The national feeling of the tommy resolves itself into this—here he is. But that is the end of it; everything else he criticizes from his own practical point of view.

Albert lies down on the grass and growls angrily: "The best thing is not to talk about the rotten business."

"It won't make any difference, that's sure," agrees Kat.

To make matters worse, we have to return almost all the new things and take back our old rags again. The good ones were merely for the inspection.

* * *

Instead of going to Russia, we go up the line again. On the way we pass through a devastated wood with the tree trunks shattered and the ground ploughed up.

At several places there are tremendous craters. "Great guns, something's hit that," I say to Kat.

"Trench mortars," he replies, and then points up at one of the trees.

In the branches dead men are hanging. A naked soldier is squatting in the fork of a tree, he still has his helmet on, otherwise he is entirely unclad. There is only half of him sitting up there, the top half, the legs are missing.

"What can that mean?" I ask.

"He's been blown out of his clothes," mutters Tjaden.

"It's funny," says Kat, "we have seen that several times now. If a mortar gets you it blows you clean out of your clothes. It's the concussion that does it."

I search around. And so it is. Here hang bits of uniform, and somewhere else is plastered a bloody mess that was once a human limb. Over there lies a body with nothing but a piece of the underpants on one leg and the collar of the tunic around its neck. Otherwise it is naked and the clothes are hanging up in the tree. Both arms are missing as though they had been pulled out. I discover one of them twenty yards off in a shrub.

The dead man lies on his face. There, where the arm wounds are, the earth is black with blood. Underfoot the leaves are scratched up as though the man had been kicking.

"That's no joke, Kat," say I.

"No more is a shell splinter in the belly," he replies, shrugging his shoulders.

"But don't get tender-hearted," says Tjaden.

All this can only have happened a little while ago, the blood is still fresh. As everybody we see there is dead we do not waste any more time, but report the affair at the next stretcher-bearers' post. After all it is not our business to take these stretcher-bearers' jobs away from them.

* * *

A patrol has to be sent out to discover just how strongly the enemy position is manned. Since my leave I feel a certain strange attachment to the other fellows, and so I volunteer to go with them. We agree on a plan, slip out through the wire and then divide and creep forward separately. After a while I find a shallow shell-hole and crawl into it. From here I peer forward.

There is moderate machine-gun fire. It sweeps across from all directions, not very heavy, but always sufficient to make one keep down.

A parachute star-shell opens out. The ground lies stark in the pale light, and then the darkness shuts down again blacker than ever. In the trenches we were told there were black troops in front of us. That is nasty, it is hard to see them; they are very good at patrolling, too. And oddly enough they are often quite stupid; for instance, both Kat and Kropp were once able to shoot down a black enemy patrol because the fellows in their enthusiasm for cigarettes smoked while they were creeping about. Kat and Albert had simply to aim at the glowing ends of the cigarettes.

A bomb or something lands close beside me. I have not heard it coming and am terrified. At the same moment a senseless fear takes hold on me. Here I am alone and almost helpless in the dark—perhaps two other eyes have been watching me for a long while from another shell-hole in front of me, and a bomb lies ready to blow me to pieces. I try to pull myself together. It is not my first patrol and not a particularly risky one. But it is the first since my leave, and besides, the lie of the land is still rather strange to me.

I tell myself that my alarm is absurd, that there is probably nothing at all there in the darkness watching me, otherwise they would not be firing so low.

It is in vain. In whirling confusion my thoughts hum in my brain—I hear the warning voice of my mother, I see the Russians with the flowing beards leaning against the wire fence, I have a bright picture of a canteen with stools, of a cinema in Valenciennes; tormented, terrified, in my imagination I see the grey, implacable muzzle of a rifle which moves noiselessly before me whichever way I try to turn my head. The sweat breaks out from every pore.

I still continue to lie in the shallow bowl. I look at the time; only a few minutes have passed. My forehead is wet, the sockets of my eyes are damp, my hands tremble, and I am panting softly. It is nothing but an awful spasm of fear, a simple animal fear of poking out my head and crawling on farther.

All my efforts subside like froth into the one desire to be able just to stay lying there. My limbs are glued to the earth. I make a vain attempt;—they refuse to come away. I press myself down on the earth, I cannot go forward, I make up my mind to stay lying there.

But immediately the wave floods over me anew, a mingled sense of shame, of remorse, and yet at the same time of security. I raise myself up a little to take a look round.

My eyes burn with staring into the dark. A star-shell goes up;—I duck down again.

I wage a wild and senseless fight, I want to get out of the hollow and yet slide back into it again; I say "You must, it is your comrades, it is not an idiotic command," and again: "What does it matter to me, I have only one life to lose——"

That is the result of all this leave, I plead in extenuation. But I cannot reassure myself; I become terribly faint. I raise myself slowly and reach forward with my arms, dragging my body after me and then lie on the edge of the shell-hole, half in and half out.

There I hear sounds and drop back. Suspicious sounds can be detected clearly despite the noise of the artillery-fire. I listen; the sound is behind me. They are our people moving along the trench. Now I hear muffled voices. To judge by the tone that might be Kat talking.

At once a new warmth flows through me. These voices, these quiet words, these footsteps in the trench behind me recall me at a bound from the terrible loneliness and fear of death by which I had been almost destroyed. They are more to me than life, these voices, they are more than motherliness and more than fear; they are the strongest, most comforting thing there is anywhere: they are the voices of my comrades.

I am no longer a shuddering speck of existence, alone in the darkness;—I belong to them and they to me; we all share the same fear and the same life, we are nearer than lovers, in a simpler, a harder way; I could bury my face in them, in these voices, these words that have saved me and will stand by me.

* * *

Cautiously I glide out over the edge and snake my way forward. I shuffle along on all fours a bit farther, I keep track of my bearings, look around me and observe the distribution of the gunfire so as to be able to find my way back. Then I try to get in touch with the others.

I am still afraid, but it is an intelligent fear, an extraordinarily heightened caution. The night is windy and shadows flit hither and thither in the flicker of the gunfire. It reveals too little and too much. Often I pause, stock still, motionless, and always for nothing. Thus I advance a long way and then turn back in a wide curve. I have not established touch with the others. Every yard nearer our trench fills me with confidence;—and with haste, too. It would be bad to get hit now.

Then a new fear lays hold of me. I can no longer remember the direction. Quiet, I squat in a shell-hole and try to locate myself. More than once it has happened that some fellow has jumped joyfully into a trench, only then to discover that it was the wrong one.

After a little time I listen again, but still I am not sure. The confusion of shell-holes now seems so bewildering that I can no longer tell in my agitation which way I should go. Perhaps I am crawling parallel to the lines, and that might go on for ever. So I crawl round once again in a wide curve.

These damned rockets! They seem to burn for an hour, and a man cannot make the least movement without bringing the bullets whistling round.

But there is nothing for it, I must get out. Falteringly I work my way farther; I move off over the ground like a crab and rip my hands sorely on the jagged splinters, as sharp as razorblades. Often I think that the sky is becoming lighter on the horizon, but it may be merely my imagination. Then gradually I realize that to crawl in the right direction is a matter of life or death.

A shell crashes. Almost immediately two others. And then it begins in earnest. A bombardment. Machine-guns rattle. Now there is nothing for it but to stay lying low. Apparently an attack is coming. Everywhere the rockets shoot up. Unceasing.

I lie huddled in a large shell-hole, my legs in the water up to the belly. When the attack starts I will let myself fall into the water, with my face as deep in the mud as I can keep it without suffocating. I must pretend to be dead.

Suddenly I hear the barrage lift. At once I slip down into the water, my helmet on the nape of my neck and my mouth just clear so that I can get a breath of air.

I lie motionless;—somewhere something clanks, it stamps and stumbles nearer—all my nerves become taut and icy. It clatters over me and away, the first wave has passed. I have but this one shattering thought: What will you do if someone jumps into your shell-hole?—Swiftly I pull out my little dagger, grasp it fast and bury it in my hand once again under the mud. If anyone jumps in here I will go for him. It hammers in my forehead; at once, stab him clean through the throat, so that he cannot call out; that's the only way; he will be just as frightened as I am; when in terror we fall upon one another, then I must be first.

Now our batteries are firing. A shell lands near me. That makes me savage with fury, all it needs now is to be killed by our own shells; I curse and grind my teeth in the mud; it is a raving frenzy; in the end all I can do is groan and pray.

The crash of the shells bursts in my ears. If our fellows make a counter-raid I will be saved. I press my head against the earth and listen to the muffled thunder, like the explosions of quarrying—and raise it again to listen for the sounds on top.

The machine-guns rattle. I know our barbed wire entanglements are strong and almost undamaged;—parts of them are charged with a powerful electric current. The rifle fire increases. They have not broken through; they have to retreat.

I sink down again, huddled, strained to the uttermost. The banging, the creeping, the clanging becomes audible. One single cry yelling amongst it all. They are raked with fire, the attack is repulsed.

* * *

Already it has become somewhat lighter. Steps hasten over me. The first. Gone. Again, another. The rattle of machine-guns becomes an unbroken chain. Just as I am about to turn round a little, something heavy stumbles, and with a crash a body falls over me into the shell-hole, slips down, and lies across me——

I do not think at all, I make no decision—I strike madly home, and feel only how the body suddenly convulses, then becomes limp, and collapses. When I recover myself, my hand is sticky and wet.

The man gurgles. It sounds to me as though he bellows, every gasping breath is like a cry, a thunder—but it is only my heart pounding. I want to stop his mouth, stuff it with earth, stab him again, he must be quiet, he is betraying me; now at last I regain control of myself, but have suddenly become so feeble that I cannot any more lift my hand against him.

So I crawl away to the farthest corner and stay there, my eyes glued on him, my hand grasping the knife—ready, if he stirs, to spring at him again. But he won't do so any more, I can hear that already in his gurgling.

I can see him indistinctly. I have but one desire, to get away. If it is not soon it will be too light; it will be difficult enough now. Then as I try to raise up my head I see it is impossible already. The machine-gunfire so sweeps the ground that I should be shot through and through before I could make one jump.

I test it once with my helmet, which I take off and hold up to find out the level of the shots. The next moment it is knocked out of my hand by a bullet. The fire is sweeping very low to the ground. I am not far enough from the enemy line to escape being picked off by one of the snipers if I attempt to get away.

The light increases. Burning I wait for our attack. My hands are white at the knuckles, I clench them so tightly in my longing for the fire to cease so that my comrades may come.

Minute after minute trickles away. I dare not look again at the dark figure in the shell-hole. With an effort I look past it and wait, wait. The bullets hiss, they make a steel net, never ceasing, never ceasing.

Then I notice my bloody hand and suddenly feel nauseated. I take some earth and rub the skin with it; now my hand is muddy and the blood cannot be seen any more.

The fire does not diminish. It is equally heavy from both sides. Our fellows have probably given me up for lost long ago.

* * *

It is early morning, clear and grey. The gurgling continues, I stop my ears, but soon take my fingers away again, because then I cannot hear the other sound.

The figure opposite me moves. I shrink together and involuntarily look at it. Then my eyes remain glued to it. A man with a small pointed beard lies there; his head is fallen to one side, one arm is half-bent, his head rests helplessly upon it. The other hand lies on his chest, it is bloody.

He is dead, I say to myself, he must be dead, he doesn't feel anything any more; it is only the body that is gurgling there. Then the head tries to raise itself, for a moment the groaning becomes louder, his forehead sinks back upon his arm. The man is not dead, he is dying, but he is not dead. I drag myself toward him, hesitate, support myself on my hands, creep a bit farther, wait, again a terrible journey of three yards, a long, a terrible journey. At last I am beside him.

Then he opens his eyes. He must have heard me, for he gazes at me with a look of utter terror. The body lies still, but in the eyes there is such an extraordinary expression of fright that for a moment I think they have power enough to carry the body off with them. Hundreds of miles away with one bound. The body is still perfectly still, without a sound, the gurgle has ceased, but the eyes cry out, yell, all the life is gathered together in them for one tremendous effort to flee, gathered together there in a dreadful terror of death, of me.

My legs give way and I drop on my elbows. "No, no," I whisper.

The eyes follow me. I am powerless to move so long as they are there.

Then his hand slips slowly from his breast, only a little bit, it sinks just a few inches, but this movement breaks the power of the eyes. I bend forward, shake my head and whisper: "No, no, no," I raise one hand, I must show him that I want to help him, I stroke his forehead.

The eyes shrink back as the hand comes, then they lose their stare, the eyelids droop lower, the tension is past. I open his collar and place his head more comfortably.

His mouth stands half open, it tries to form words. The lips are dry. My water bottle is not there. I have not brought it with me. But there is water in the mud, down at the bottom of the crater. I climb down, take out my handkerchief, spread it out, push it under and scoop up the yellow water that strains through into the hollow of my hand.

He gulps it down. I fetch some more. Then I unbutton his tunic in order to bandage him if it is possible. In any case I must do it, so that if the fellows over there capture me they will see that I wanted to help him, and so will not shoot me. He tries to resist, but his hand is too feeble. The shirt is stuck and will not come away, it is buttoned at the back. So there is nothing for it but to cut it open.

I look for the knife and find it again. But when I begin to cut the shirt the eyes open once more and the cry is in them again and the demented expression, so that I must close them, press them shut and whisper: "I want to help you, Comrade, camerade, camerade, camerade——" eagerly repeating the word, to make him understand.

There are three stabs. My field dressing covers them, the blood runs out under it, I press it tighter; there; he groans.

That is all I can do. Now we must wait, wait.

* * *

These hours. . . . The gurgling starts again—but how slowly a man dies! For this I know—he cannot be saved, I have, indeed, tried to tell myself that he will be, but at noon this pretence breaks down and melts before his groans. If only I had not lost my revolver crawling about, I would shoot him. Stab him I cannot.

By noon I am groping on the outer limits of reason. Hunger devours me, I could almost weep for something to eat, I cannot struggle against it. Again and again I fetch water for the dying man and drink some myself.

This is the first time I have killed with my hands, whom I can see close at hand, whose death is my doing. Kat and Kropp and Müller have experienced it already, when they have hit someone; it happens to many, in hand-to-hand fighting especially—

But every gasp lays my heart bare. This dying man has time with him, he has an invisible dagger with which he stabs me: Time and my thoughts.

I would give much if he would but stay alive. It is hard to lie here and to have to see and hear him.

In the afternoon, about three, he is dead.

I breathe freely again. But only for a short time. Soon the silence is more unbearable than the groans. I wish the gurgling were there again, gasping, hoarse, now whistling softly and again hoarse and loud.

It is mad, what I do. But I must do something. I prop the dead man up again so that he lies comfortably, although he feels nothing any more. I close his eyes. They are brown, his hair is black and a bit curly at the sides.

The mouth is full and soft beneath his moustache; the nose is slightly arched, the skin brownish; it is now not so pale as it was before, when he was still alive. For a moment the face seems almost healthy;—then it collapses suddenly into the strange face of the dead that I have so often seen, strange faces, all alike.

No doubt his wife still thinks of him; she does not know what has happened. He looks as if he would have often have written to her;—she will still be getting mail from him—Tomorrow, in a week's time—perhaps even a stray letter a month hence. She will read it, and in it he will he speaking to her.

My state is getting worse, I can no longer control my thoughts. What would his wife look like? Like the little brunette on the other side of the canal? Does she belong to me now? Perhaps by this act she becomes mine. I wish Kantorek were sitting here beside me. If my mother could see me——. The dead man might have had thirty more years of life if only I had impressed the way back to our trench more sharply on my memory. If only he had run two yards farther to the left, he might now be sitting in the trench over there and writing a fresh letter to his wife.

But I will get no further that way; for that is the fate of all of us: if Kemmerich's leg had been six inches to the right: if Haie Westhus had bent his back three inches further forward——

* * *

The silence spreads. I talk and must talk. So I speak to him and say to him: "Comrade, I did not want to kill you. If you jumped in here again, I would not do it, if you would be sensible too. But you were only an idea to me before, an abstraction that lived in my mind and called forth its appropriate response. It was that abstraction I stabbed. But now, for the first time, I see you are a man like me. I thought of your hand-grenades, of your bayonet, of your rifle; now I see your wife and your face and our fellowship. Forgive me, comrade. We always see it too late. Why do they never tell us that you are poor devils like us, that your mothers are just as anxious as ours, and that we have the same fear of death, and the same dying and the same agony—Forgive me, comrade; how could you be my enemy? If we threw away these rifles and this uniform you could be my brother just like Kat and Albert. Take twenty years of my life, comrade, and stand up—take more, for I do not know what I can even attempt to do with it now."

It is quiet, the front is still except for the crackle of rifle fire. The bullets rain over, they are not fired haphazard, hut shrewdly aimed from all sides. I cannot get out.

"I will write to your wife," I say hastily to the dead man, "I will write to her, she must hear it from me, I will tell her everything I have told you, she shall not suffer, I will help her, and your parents too, and your child——"

His tunic is half open. The pocket-book is easy to find. But I hesitate to open it. In it is the book with his name. So long as I do not know his name perhaps I may still forget him, time will obliterate it, this picture. But his name, it is a nail that will be hammered into me and never come out again. It has the power to recall this for ever, it will always come back and stand before me.

Irresolutely I take the wallet in my hand. It slips out of my hand and falls open. Some pictures and letters drop out. I gather them up and want to put them back again, but the strain I am under, the uncertainty, the hunger, the danger, these hours with the dead man have made me desperate, I want to hasten the relief, to intensify and to end the torture, as one strikes an unendurably painful hand against the trunk of a tree, regardless of everything.

There are portraits of a woman and a little girl, small amateur photographs taken against an ivy-clad wall. Along with them are letters. I take them out and try to read them. Most of it I do not understand, it is so hard to decipher and I scarcely know any French. But each word I translate pierces me like a shot in the chest;—like a stab in the chest.

My brain is taxed beyond endurance. But I realize this much, that I will never dare to write to these people as I intended. Impossible. I look at the portraits once more; they are clearly not rich people. I might send them money anonymously if I earn anything later on. I seize upon that, it is at least something to hold on to. This dead man is bound up with my life, therefore I must do everything, promise everything in order to save myself; I swear blindly that I mean to live only for his sake and his family, with wet lips I try to placate him—and deep down in me lies the hope that I may buy myself off in this way and perhaps even get out of this; it is a little stratagem: if only I am allowed to escape, then I will see to it. So I open the book and read slowly:—Gérard Duval, compositor.

With the dead man's pencil I write the address on an envelope, then swiftly thrust everything back into his tunic.

I have killed the printer, Gérard Duval. I must be a printer, I think confusedly, be a printer, printer——

* * *

By afternoon I am calmer. My fear was groundless. The name troubles me no more. The madness passes. "Comrade," I say to the dead man, but I say it calmly, "to-day you, to-morrow me. But if I come out of it, comrade, I will fight against this, that has struck us both down; from you, taken life—and from me—? Life also. I promise you, comrade. It shall never happen again."

The sun strikes low, I am stupefied with exhaustion and hunger. Yesterday is like a fog to me, there is no hope of ever getting out of this. I fall into a doze and do not at first realize that evening is approaching. The twilight comes. It seems to me to come quickly now. One hour more. If it were summer, it would be three hours more. One hour more.

Now suddenly I begin to tremble; something might happen in the interval. I think no more of the dead man, he is of no consequence to me now. With one bound the lust to live flares up again and everything that has filled my thoughts goes down before it. Now, merely to avert any ill-luck, I babble mechanically: "I will fulfil everything, fulfil everything I have promised you——" but already I know that I shall not do so.

Suddenly it occurs to me that my own comrades may fire on me as I creep up; they do not know I am coming. I will call out as soon as I can so that they will recognize me. I will stay lying in front of the trench until they answer me.

The first star. The front remains quiet. I breathe deeply and talk to myself in my excitement: "No foolishness now, Paul—Quiet, Paul, quiet—then you will be saved, Paul." When I use my Christian name it works as though someone else spoke to me, it has more power.

The darkness grows. My excitement subsides, I wait cautiously until the first rocket goes up. Then I crawl out of the shell-hole. I have forgotten the dead man. Before me lies the oncoming night and the pale gleaming field. I fix my eyes on a shell-hole; the moment the light dies I scurry over into it, grope farther, spring into the next, duck down, scramble onward.

I come nearer. There, by the light of a rocket I see something move in the wire, then it stiffens and I lie still. Next time I see it again, yes, they are men from our trench. But I am suspicious until I recognize our helmets. Then I call. And immediately an answer rings out, my name: "Paul—Paul——"

I call again in answer. It is Kat and Albert who have come out with a stretcher to look for me.

"Are you wounded?"

"No, no——"

We drop into the trench. I ask for something to eat and wolf it down. Müller gives me a cigarette. In a few words I tell what happened. There is nothing new about it; it happens quite often. The night attack is the only unusual feature of the business. In Russia Kat once lay for two days behind the enemy lines before he could make his way back.

I do not mention the dead printer.

But by next morning I can keep it to myself no longer. I must tell Kat and Albert. They both try to calm me. "You can't do anything about it. What else could you have done? That is what you are here for."

I listen to them and feel comforted, reassured by their presence. It was mere drivelling nonsense that I talked out there in the shell-hole.

"Look there for instance," points Kat.

On the fire-step stand some snipers. They rest their rifles with telescopic sights on the parapet and watch the enemy front. Once and again a shot cracks out.

Then we hear the cry: "That's found a billet!" "Did you see how he leapt in the air?" Sergeant Oellrich turns round proudly and scores his point. He heads the shooting list for to-day with three unquestionable hits.

"What do you say to that?" asks Kat. I nod.

"If he keeps that up he will get a little coloured bird for his buttonhole by this evening," says Albert.

"Or rather he will soon be made acting sergeant-major," says Kat.

We look at one another. "I would not do it," I say.

"All the same," says Kat, "It's very good for you to see it just now."

Sergeant Oellrich returns to the fire-step. The muzzle of his rifle searches to and fro.

"You don't need to lose any sleep over your affair," nods Albert.

And now I hardly understand it myself any more.

"It was only because I had to lie there with him so long," I say. "After all; war is war."

Oellrich's rifle cracks out sharply and dry.

✦ Reading 40 ✦

The Storm of Steel

Ernst Juenger

The Author's Preface to the English Edition

It is not impossible that among the English readers of this book there may be one who in 1915 and 1916 was in one of those trenches that were woven in a web among the ruins of Monchy-au-Bois. In that case he had opposite him at that time the 73rd Hanoverian Fusiliers, who wear as their distinctive badge a brassard with 'Gibraltar' inscribed on it in gold, in memory of the defence of that fortress under General Elliot; for this, besides Waterloo, has its place in the regiment's history.

At the time I refer to I was a nineteen-year-old lieutenant in command of a platoon, and my part of the line was easily recognizable from the English side by a row of tall shell-stripped trees that rose from the ruins of Monchy. My left flank was bounded by the sunken road leading to Berles-au-Bois, which was in the hands of the English; my right was marked by a sap running out from our lines, one that helped us many a time to make our presence felt by means of bombs and rifle-grenades.

I daresay this reader remembers, too, the white tom-cat, lamed in one foot by a stray bullet, who had his headquarters in No-man's-land. He used often to pay me a visit at night in my dugout. This creature, the sole living being that was on visiting terms with both sides, always made on me an impression of extreme mystery. This charm of mystery which lay over all that belonged to the other side, to that danger zone full of unseen figures, is one of the strongest impressions that the war has left with me. At that time, before the battle of the Somme, which opened a new chapter in the history of the war, the struggle had not taken on that grim and mathematical aspect which cast over its landscapes a deeper and deeper gloom. There was more rest for the soldier than in the later years when he was thrown into one murderous battle after another; and so it is that many of those days come back to my memory now with a light on them that is almost peaceful.

In our talks in the trenches, in the dugout, or on the fire-step, we often talked of the 'Tommy'; and, as any genuine soldier will easily understand, we spoke of him very much more respectfully than was commonly the case with the newspapers of those days. There is no one less likely to disparage the lion than the lion-hunter.

Indeed, the landscape in which we lived at that time had something about it of primeval Africa, with two mighty forces of nature locked in conflict there. It was only now and again that one caught sight of a brownish-yellow fleeting shadow against the desolate countryside that stretched on and on before one's eyes; or heard, after creeping through the wire at night, a whisper or a cough from a post. The distant sound of transport, a cloud of smoke from a fire hidden from view, fresh chalk spoil thrown out on the tortured ground, the monotonous duel of the guns stretching on from week to month—those were signs that we puzzled over as though they were the runes of a secret book or the spoor of some mighty and unknown beast that came nightly to drink.

As time went on, it grew more and more dangerous to lift a corner of the veil that fell like a magic hood over the spectre that was at once so near and so fatally far off. Raids undertaken to get a glimpse of the enemy's lines and some information about what was going on there became less frequent and more exacting as the volume and mass of war material increased. A more and more terrific barrage had to be put down before ten or twenty picked men, armed to the teeth, could make their occasional and

From: Ernst Juenger, *The Storm of Steel,* intro. by R. H. Mottram (New York: Howard Fertig, 1975), pp. ix–xiii, 244–256.

exceedingly brief appearances in the opposing trenches. What the survivors brought back with them was the memory of a rapid and frantic glance into Vulcan's white-hot cauldron.

Still, there were moments of another kind when the deep discord and the even deeper unity of this landscape came more clearly to one's mind. It was strange, for example, to hear at night the cry of the partridges from the waste fields, or at dawn the careless song of the lark as it rose high above the trenches. Did it not seem then that life itself was speaking out of the confidence of its savage and visionary heart, knowing very well that in its more secret and essential depths it had nothing to fear from even the deadliest of wars, and going its way quite unaffected by the superficial interchange of peace and war?

But then, too, did not this life, ruthless towards its creatures, superior to the pain and pleasure of the individual, looking on with indifference while its passive forces were melted down in the crucible of war, enter very clearly even into the soldier's simple mind? Many a time, in that quiet interlude after sunset before the first Verey light went up, this message was brought very near to the soul by the song of an outlying post waiting for the night relief. There was a deeper homesickness there than any peace in this world can set at rest.

Then the fire-step was manned once more, the relief moved off along the communication trenches, and the brisker rifle-fire of the night-time broke out; the ear was again on stretch to catch the pulse-beat of that other life under arms over there in the darkness. And often the Verey lights went up in dozens and the trench got lively when a patrol had crept up to our wire.

To-day there is no secret about what those trenches concealed, and a book such as this may, like a trench-map years after the event, be read with sympathy and interest by the other side. But here not only the blue and red lines of the trenches are shown, but the blood that beat and, the life that lay hid in them.

Time only strengthens my conviction that it was a good and strenuous life, and that the war, for all its destructiveness, was an incomparable schooling of the heart. The front-line soldier whose foot came down on the earth so grimly and harshly may claim this at least, that it came down cleanly. Warlike achievements are enhanced by the inherent worth of the enemy. Of all the troops who were opposed to the Germans on the great battlefields the English were not only the most formidable but the manliest and the most chivalrous. I rejoice, therefore, to have an opportunity of expressing in time of peace the sincere admiration which I never failed to make clear during the war whenever I came across a wounded man or a prisoner belonging to the British forces.

* * *

The Great Offensive

The battalion was quartered in the château of Brunemont. We were told that we were to march up the line on the night of March 19th–20th, and to occupy the dugouts in the line near Cagnicourt, ready to go over the top on the morning of March 21st. The task assigned to the regiment was to break through between the villages of Ecoust-St.-Mein and Noreuil, which we knew from 1915–16, on the first day. I sent Lieutenant Schmidt—who because of his amiability was never called anything but little Schmidt—on ahead to make sure of our quarters.

The regiment marched out of Brunemont at the appointed hour. Their morale was excellent in spite of pouring rain. I overlooked a drunken fellow who reeled bawling between the files of my company, for now any harsh words could only do harm. Training was over; and now we came to business, not a wheel of the machine was to be checked.

From some cross-roads where guides awaited us the companies went forward independently. When we got as far as the second line, where we were to be quartered, it came out that the guides had lost their way. Now begin a chase to and fro over the dim and sodden shell-hole area and a questioning of innumerable troops, who knew as little where they were as we did. To prevent the complete exhaustion of the men I called a halt and sent out the guides in all directions.

Sections piled arms and crowded into a gigantic crater, while I and Lieutenant Sprenger sat on the edge of a smaller one. There had been single shells falling about a hundred metres in front of us for some while. Then there was one nearer; the splinters struck the sides of the shell-hole. One of the men cried out and said he was hit in the foot. I shouted to the men to scatter among the surrounding shell-holes, and meanwhile I examined the man's boot to see if there was a hole. Then the whistle of another shell high in the air. Everybody had that clutching feeling: 'It's coming over!' There was a terrific stupefying crash . . . the shell had burst in the midst of us. . . .

I will make no secret of it that after a moment's blank horror I took to my heels like the rest and ran aimlessly into the night. It was not till I had fallen head over heels into a small shell-hole that I understood what had happened. Only to hear and see no more! Only to get away, far away, and creep into a hole! And yet the other voice was heard: 'You are the company commander, man!' Exactly so. I do not say it in self-praise. I might as well say: 'When God gives an office, He gives the understanding for it.' I have often observed in myself and others that an officer's sense of responsibility drowns his personal fears. There is a sticking-place, something to occupy the thoughts. So I forced myself back to the ghastly spot. On the way I ran into Fusilier Haller, he who had bagged the machine-gun on my November patrol, and took him along with me.

The wounded men never ceased to utter their fearful cries. Some came creeping to me when they heard my voice and whimpered, 'Sir . . . Sir!' One of my favourite recruits, Jasinski, whose leg was broken by a splinter, caught hold of me round the knees. Cursing my impotence to help, I vainly clapped him on the shoulder. Such moments can never be forgotten.

I had to leave the wretched creatures to the one surviving stretcher-bearer and lead the faithful few who remained and who collected round me away from the fatal spot. Half an hour before I had been at the head of a first-rate company at fighting strength. Now the few who followed me through the maze of trenches where I lost my way were utterly crestfallen. A young lad, a milksop, who a few days before had been jeered at by his companions because during training he had burst into tears over the weight of a box of ammunition, was now loyally hulking one along on our painful way after retrieving it from the scene of our disaster. When I saw that, I was finished. I threw myself on the ground and broke into convulsive sobs, while the men stood gloomily round me.

After we had hastened on for hours and to no purpose, and often menaced by shells, along the trench ankle-deep in mud and water, we crept, dead tired, into some ammunition bays in the side of the trench. My barman spread his ground-sheet over me, but the state of my nerves kept my eyes wide open, and thus, smoking cigars, I waited for daybreak.

The first light of dawn revealed an utterly incredible sight. Countless troops, all over the shelled area, were still in search of their appointed shelter. Artillerymen were humping ammunition; trench-mortar men were pulling their mortars along; signallers were laying wires. There was a regular fair a thousand metres in front of the enemy, who, incomprehensibly, appeared to observe nothing.

By good luck I ran across the commander of the 2nd Machine-gun Company, Lieutenant Fallenstein, an old front-line soldier, who was able to show me the way to our shelter. The first thing he said was: 'What makes you look like that, man?' I led my men to a large, deep dugout that we had passed a dozen times during the night. There I found little Schmidt, who knew nothing of our disaster. The guides, also, were there. After that day, whenever we moved into a new position I always chose the guides myself and with the greatest care. The lessons of the war are thorough but costly.

After settling-in the men who had come with me, I went back to the horrible scene of the night before. It was a ghastly sight. In a ring round the burst were lying over twenty charred corpses, nearly all of them unrecognizably mutilated. Some, indeed, we had to report as missing, as nothing of them was to be found.

I came on some soldiers of another unit busied in extracting the blood-stained possessions of the dead from out of the hideous mess, in the hope of booty. I chased the hyænas off, and told my orderly to collect the pocket-books and valuables, as far as could be done, so that we could send them to their people. We had, in any case, to leave them behind when next morning we went over the top.

I was delighted to see Lieutenant Sprenger come out of a dugout near by with a number of men who had spent the night there. I told the section leaders to report, and ascertained that I still disposed of sixty-three men. I had set out the night before in the best of spirits with a hundred and fifty! I succeeded in accounting for over twenty dead and over sixty wounded, some of whom died later from their injuries.

The only grain of comfort was that it might have been worse. Fusilier Rust, for example, was standing so close to the burst that the carrying strap of his box began to burn. The N.C.O. Peggau, who, it is true, was killed the next day, was standing between two men, both of whom were torn to bits, while he had not a scratch.

We spent the day in poor spirits, sleeping mostly. I had to go again and again to the C.O., as there was always something to do with the attack to arrange. Apart from this I lay on a bunk talking to my two officers about trifling matters, in order to escape the torture of our thoughts. The constant refrain was: 'Thank God, we can only die once.' I said a few words to the men, who crouched together in silence on the steps, with a view to cheering them up; but it seemed to have little effect. Nor was I myself in an encouraging mood.

At ten o'clock in the evening a runner brought orders to move into the first line. A wild beast dragged from its lair, or a sailor who sees the last plank swept from his grasp, may, perhaps, have feelings comparable to ours when we were compelled to leave the warmth and safety of the dugout. Yet not one of them was tempted to stay behind unobserved.

We hurried along the Felix trench under sharp shrapnel fire and got through without a casualty. While we passed along the trench below, guns crossed by bridges over our heads to take up forward positions. The section of the trench allotted to the battalion was quite narrow. Every dugout was filled with troops in a moment. The rest had to dig themselves holes in the sides of the trench so as to have some shelter at least during the bombardment preceding the attack. At last after much scrambling to and fro every one had found his hole. Once more Captain von Brixen assembled the company commanders for his last remarks. When we had synchronized watches for the last time we shook hands and separated.

I sat down on the steps of a dugout with my two officers to wait for 5.5 a.m., the moment when the artillery preparation was to begin. The atmosphere was slightly more cheerful, as the rain had left off and the clear, starry sky promised a fine morning. We passed the time eating and talking. Every one smoked hard, and the water-bottles went the round. In the early hours the enemy artillery was so lively that we were afraid the English had smelt a rat.

Just before zero the following flash signal was given us: 'H.M. the Kaiser and Hindenburg are on the scene of operations.' It was greeted with enthusiasm.

The hands crept on. We counted the last minutes as they marked them off. At last they stood at 5.5. At once the hurricane broke loose. A curtain of flames was let down, followed by a sudden impetuous tumult such as was never heard, a raging thunder that swallowed up the reports even of the heaviest guns in its tremendous reverberations and made the earth tremble. This gigantic roar of annihilation from countless guns behind us was so terrific that, compared with it, all preceding battles were child's-play. What we had not dared to hope came true. The enemy artillery was silenced, put out of action by one giant blow. We could not stay any longer in the dugouts. We got out on to the top and looked with wonder at the wall of fire towering over the English lines and the swaying blood-red clouds that hung above it.

Our delight was lessened by the tears and the burning of the mucous membrane caused by the fumes of our own gas-shells that the wind blew back on us. Many of the men were forced to pull off their masks when the unpleasant effects of our Blue Cross gas threw them into fits of choking and coughing. I was very uneasy, yet I felt sure that our command could not have made a miscalculation from which our destruction would necessarily follow. Meanwhile I exerted all my energy to keep the first cough back so as not to increase the irritation. After an hour we were able to take off our masks.

It was now daylight. The terrific tumult behind us rose higher and higher. In front stood a blind wall of smoke, dust, and gas. Men were running along the trench and shouting delightedly into each other's ears. Infantry and artillery, engineers and signallers, Prussians and Bavarians, officers and men, were all alike in transports over this elemental expression of German power and were burning with impatience for 9.40, when we were to advance to the attack. At 8.45 our heavy trench-mortars, that stood almost touching one another behind the front line, started up. We could see the great two-hundred-weight bombs fly in a steep trajectory through the air and fall to the earth on the other side with Hephaestean explosions. Their bursts made a close chain of craters in eruption.

The very laws of nature seemed to have lost their validity. The air shimmered as though on a day of summer heat. The changing index of refraction made fixed objects dance to and fro. Black streaks of shadow flitted across the mass of smoke. The roar had become a norm and one heard no longer. One could scarcely hear the thousands of machine-guns in our rear that swept the blue sky with swarm upon swarm of lead.

The last hour of the artillery preparation was unhealthier than all the four preceding ones, during which we had walked about unheeding on the top. The enemy brought a heavy battery into action that landed shell after shell into our crowded trench. I went to the left to avoid them, and ran into the adjutant, Lieutenant Heins, who asked me if I had seen Lieutenant Baron von Solemacher: 'He must take over the battalion at once. Captain von Brixen has just been killed.' I was shocked at this bad news, and went back and sat in a deep burrow in the earth. By the time I left there I had utterly forgotten the news I had heard. My brain had only one link with reality . . . 9.40. It seemed, though, that I was behaving very courageously, for everybody smiled approvingly when they looked at me.

The N.C.O. Dujesiefken, a comrade of the Regniéville patrol, came to a stop in front of my burrow and asked me to come out into the trench, as even a light shell bursting anywhere near might precipitate the whole mass of soil on my head. An explosion took the very words from his mouth. He fell to the ground with a leg torn off. I sprang over him and fled to the right, where I crept to earth again in a hole already occupied by two engineers.

The heavy shells were falling in a narrow circle all round us. Suddenly from a white cloud hurtled black lumps of soil; as for the detonation, it was lost in the general roar. Indeed, the sense of hearing was lost. In the piece of trench near us to our left three men of my company were torn to pieces. One of the last hits, a dud, killed poor little Schmidt, who had not left the dugout steps.

I was standing with Sprenger, with my watch in my hand, in front of my burrow, and waiting for the great moment. The rest of the company had collected round us. By jokes of a coarseness that unfortunately prevents me setting them down here, we succeeded in cheering and distracting them. Lieutenant Meyer, who peeped for a moment round the traverse, told me later that he thought us out of our minds.

The officer patrols who were to cover our advance left the trench at 9.10. As our front line and the enemy's were here eight hundred metres apart, we had to move forward even during the artillery preparation and to take up our position in No-man's-land in readiness to jump into the enemy's front line at 9.40. Sprenger and I climbed out on to the top after a few minutes, followed by the men.

'Now we'll show what the 7th Company can do!'

'I don't care for anything now.'

'Vengeance for the 7th Company.'

'Vengeance for Captain von Brixen.'

We drew our revolvers and crossed our wire, through which the first casualties were already trailing back.

I looked to the left and right. The distribution of the host presented a strange spectacle. In shell-holes in front of the enemy lines, churned and churned again by the utmost pitch of shell-fire, the attacking battalions were waiting massed in companies, as far as the eye could see. When I saw this massed might piled up, the break-through seemed to me a certainty. But was there strength in us to smash the enemy's reserves and hurl them to destruction? I was confident of it. The decisive battle, the final advance, had begun. The destiny of the nations drew to its iron conclusion, and the stake was the possession of the world. I was conscious, if only in feeling, of the significance of that hour; and I believe that on this occasion every man felt his personality fall away in the face of a crisis in which he had his part to play and by which history would be made. No one who has lived through moments like these can doubt that the course of nations in the last resort rises and falls with the destiny of war.

The atmosphere of intense excitement was amazing. Officers stood upright and shouted chaff nervously to each other. Often a heavy trench-mortar fired short and scattered us with its fountains of earth; and no one even bent his head. The roar of the battle had become so terrific that we were scarcely in our right senses. The nerves could register fear no longer. Every one was mad and beyond reckoning; we had gone over the edge of the world into superhuman perspectives. Death had lost its meaning and the will to live was made over to our country; and hence every one was blind and regardless of his personal fate.

Three minutes before the attack my batman, the faithful Vinke, beckoned to me, pointing to a full water-bottle. He recognized, in his own way, the need of the hour. I took a long pull. It was as though I drank water. There was only the cigar wanting, the usual one for such occasions. Three times the match was blown out by the commotion of the air. . . .

The great moment had come. The fire lifted over the first trenches. We advanced. . . .

The turmoil of our feelings was called forth by rage, alcohol, and the thirst for blood as we stepped out, heavily and yet irresistibly, for the enemy's lines. And therewith beat the pulse of heroism—the godlike and the bestial inextricably mingled. I was far in front of the company, followed by my batman and a man of one year's service called Haake. In my right hand I gripped my revolver, in my left a bamboo riding-cane. I was boiling with a fury now utterly inconceivable to me. The overpowering desire to kill winged my feet. Rage squeezed bitter tears from my eyes.

The tremendous force of destruction that bent over the field of battle was concentrated in our brains. So may men of the Renaissance have been locked in their passions, so may a Cellini have raged or werewolves have howled and hunted through the night on the track of blood. We crossed a battered tangle of wire without difficulty and at a jump were over the front line, scarcely recognizable any longer. The attacking waves of infantry bobbed up and down in ghostly lines in the white rolling smoke.

Against all expectation a machine-gun rattled at us from the second line. I and the men with me jumped for a shell-hole. A second later there was a frightful crack and I sank forward in a heap. Vinke caught me round the neck and turned me on my back: 'Are you hit, sir?' There was nothing to be seen. The one-year's-service fellow had a hole through his arm, and assured us, groaning, that he had a bullet in his back. We pulled off his uniform and bound him up. The churned-up earth showed that a shrapnel shell had burst at the level of our faces on the edge of the shell-hole. It was a wonder we were still alive.

Meanwhile the others were on beyond us. We scrambled after them, leaving the wounded man to his fate, after we had stuck a bit of wood in the ground near him with a strip of white muslin as a mark for the wave of stretcher-bearers that were following the fighting troops. Half-left of us the great railway embankment in the line Ecoust-Croisilles, which we had to cross, rose out of the mist. From loopholes and dugout windows built into the side of it rifles and machine-guns were rattling merrily.

Even Vinke had disappeared. I followed a sunken road, with its smashed-in shelters yawning in its banks. I strode on in a fury over the black and torn-up ground, from which rose the suffocating gas of our shells. I was entirely alone.

Then I caught sight of the first of the enemy. A figure crouched, wounded apparently, three metres in front of me in the middle of the pounded hollow of the road. I saw him start at the sight of me and stare at me with wide-open eyes as I walked slowly up to him holding out my revolver in front of me. A drama without an audience was ready. To me the mere sight of an enemy in tangible form was a release. Grinding my teeth, I pressed the muzzle to the temple of this wretch, whom terror now crippled, and with my other hand gripped hold of his tunic. With a beseeching cry he snatched a photograph from his pocket and held it before my eyes . . . himself, surrounded by a numerous family. . . .

I forced down my mad rage and walked past.

Revolution and Peacemaking

This photograph portrays Lenin as he addresses Red Army soldiers who are leaving for the civil war front. The Communist revolution promised hope for millions of Soviet citizens and for the downtrodden of the world, as yet unaware of the horrors the new regime would bring.

Revolution and Peacemaking

At the end of World War I, the victorious Western Allies pledged to construct an enduring peace that would ensure future prosperity and human rights. Yet these ideals ran afoul of British and French animosity toward Germany and the ideologically alien Soviet Russia. Diplomats at Versailles strove to outdo their predecessors at Vienna (1815), and many people came to believe, naively, that the Great War was the "war that ended all wars."

The original Allies had become the Western Allies when Russia, succumbing to the strains of war, experienced two profound revolutions. The first, in February 1917, overthrew the tsar, whereas the second brought to power a radical socialist group, the Bolsheviks (Communists). Under the leadership of Vladimir Ilich Lenin (1870–1924), Soviet Russia made peace with Germany in early 1918, further widening a rift between Russia and its former allies. Coming out of the war, Europe was already dividing into rival camps along several lines: the victors versus the pariahs, Communists versus non-Communists, supporters of democracy versus opponents. How would peace be maintained?

Russia's February Revolution produced a popular government that hoped to lead the wartime nation effectively. Overburdened by war-related tribulations, the new political consensus began to fracture by the spring of 1917. Symbolic of the new tensions were Lenin's famous April Theses (1917), which espoused a rapid deepening of the revolution toward a socialist state based upon the soviets. This set the stage for the October Revolution, a defining moment of twentieth-century European and global history. The novel *Doctor Zhivago* (1958) by the famous Russian poet and fiction writer Boris Pasternak (1890–1960) chronicles everyday people's fates in the midst of events that transform life even as they seem to hover at the edge of awareness. Perception and memory, implies the author, telescope vast events down to the level of human consciousness. The 1919 Versailles Peace Treaty, with the aim of leaving behind once and for all the horrors of war, oddly mixed liberal ideas with revenge. The consequences of the war and, ironically, the peace set the stage for endless problems and a new cataclysm.

✦ Reading 41 ✦

The April Theses

V. I. Lenin

(Issued upon his return to Russia on 16 April 1917)

1. In our attitude toward the war not the slightest concession must be made to "revolutionary defencism," for under the new government of Lvov and Co., owing to the capitalist nature of this government, the war on Russia's part remains a predatory imperialist war.

The class-conscious proletariat may give its consent to a revolutionary war actually justifying revolutionary defencism, only on condition (a) that all power be transferred to the proletariat and its ally, the poorest section of the peasantry; (b) that all annexations be renounced in deeds, not merely in words; (c) that there be a complete break, in practice, with all interests of capital.

In view of the undoubted honesty of the mass of rank and file representatives of revolutionary defencism who accept the war only as a necessity and not as a means of conquest, in view of their being deceived by the bourgeoisie, it is necessary most thoroughly, persistently, patiently to explain to them their error, to explain the inseparable connection between capital and the imperialist war, to prove that without the overthrow of capital it is *impossible* to conclude the war with a really democratic, non-oppressive peace.

This view is to be widely propagated among the army units in the field. Fraternisation.

2. The peculiarity of the present situation in Russia is that it represents a *transition* from the first stage of the revolution, which, because of the inadequate organization and insufficient class-consciousness of the proletariat, led to the assumption of power by the bourgeoisie,—to its second stage which is to place power in the hands of the proletariat and the poorest strata of the peasantry.

This transition is characterised, on the one band, by a maximum of legality (Russia is now the freest of all the belligerent countries of the world); on the other, by the absence of oppression of the masses, and, finally, by the trustingly ignorant attitude of the masses toward the capitalist government, the worst enemy of peace and Socialism.

This peculiar situation demands of us an ability to adapt ourselves to the specific conditions of party work amidst vast masses of the proletariat just awakened to political life.

3. No support to the Provisional Government; exposure of the utter falsity of all of its promises, particularly those relating to the renunciation of annexations. Unmasking, instead of admitting, the illusion-breeding "demand" that *this* government, a government of capitalists, cease being imperialistic.

4. Recognition of the fact that in most of the Soviets of Workers' Deputies our party constitutes a minority, and a small one at that, in the face of the *bloc* of all the petty-bourgeois opportunist elements, from the People's Socialists, Socialists-Revolutionists, down to the Organization Committee (Chkheidze, Tsereteli, etc., Steklov, etc.), who have yielded to the influence of the bourgeoisie and have been extending this influence to the proletariat as well.

It must be explained to the masses that the Soviet of Workers' Deputies is the only possible form of revolutionary government and that, therefore, our task is, while this government is submitting to the influence of the bourgeoisie, to present patient, systematic, and persistent analysis of its errors and tactics, an analysis especially adapted to the practical needs of the masses.

From: *The Russian Provisional Government 1917: Documents*, Vol. 3, eds. R. P. Browder and Alexander Kerensky (Stanford, CA: Stanford University Press, 1961), pp. 1205–1206.

While we are in the minority, we carry on the work of criticism and of exposing errors, advocating all long the necessity of transferring the entire power of state to the Soviets of Workers' Deputies, so that the masses might learn from experience how to rid themselves of errors.

5. Not a parliamentary republic,—a return to it from the Soviet of Workers' Deputies would be a step backward—but a republic of Soviets of Workers', Agricultural Labourers' and Peasants' Deputies throughout the land, from top to bottom.

Abolition of the police, the army, the bureaucracy.

All officers to be elected and to be subject to recall at any time, their salaries not to exceed the average wage of a competent worker.

6. In the agrarian programme, the emphasis must be shifted to the Soviets of Agricultural Labourers' Deputies.

Confiscation of all private lands.

Nationalisation of all lands in the country, and management of such lands by local Soviets of Agricultural Labourers' and Peasants' Deputies. A separate organisation of Soviets of Deputies of the poorest peasants. Creation of model agricultural establishments out of large estates (from one hundred to three hundred *desiatinas,* in accordance with local and other conditions and with the estimates of local institutions) under the control of the Soviet of Agricultural Labourers' Deputies, and at public expense.

7. Immediate merger of all the banks in the country into one general national bank, over which the Soviet of Workers' Deputies should have control.

8. Not the "introduction" of Socialism as an immediate task, but the immediate placing of the Soviet of Workers' Deputies in control of social production and distribution of goods.

9. Party tasks:

A. Immediate calling of a party convention.

B. Changing the party programme, mainly:

1. Concerning imperialism and the imperialist war.
2. Concerning our attitude toward the state, and our demand for a "commune state."
3. Amending our antiquated minimum programme.

C. Changing the name of the party.

10. Rebuilding the International.

Taking the initiative in the creation of a revolutionary International, an International against the social-chauvinists and against the "centre."

✦ Reading 42 ✦

Doctor Zhivago

Boris Pasternak

Doctor Zhivago and his nurse-assistant Lara Antipova are stationed at a military clinic behind the front. Although Zhivago has a wife and children back in St. Petersburg, his and Lara's mutual attraction eventually leads to a passionate love affair.

Farewell to the Old

1

The small town was called Meliuzeievo and lay in the fertile, black-soil country. Black dust hung over its roofs like a cloud of locusts. It was raised by the troops and convoys passing through the town; they moved in both directions, some going to the front and others away from it, and it was impossible to tell whether the war were still going on or had ceased.

Every day newly created offices sprang up like mushrooms. And they were elected to everything—Zhivago, Lieutenant Galiullin, and Nurse Antipova, as well as a few others from their group, all of them people from the big cities, well-informed and experienced.

They served as temporary town officials and as minor commissars in the army and the health department, and they looked upon this succession of tasks as an outdoor sport, a diversion, a game of blindman's buff. But more and more they felt that it was time to stop and to get back to their ordinary occupations and their homes.

Zhivago and Antipova were often brought together by their work.

2

The rain turned the black dust into coffee-colored mud and the mud spread over the streets, most of them unpaved.

The town was small. At the end of almost every street you could see the steppe, gloomy under the dark sky, all the vastness of the war, the vastness of the revolution.

Yurii Andreievich wrote to his wife:

"The disintegration and anarchy in the army continue. Measures are being taken to improve discipline and morale. I have toured units stationed in the neighborhood.

"By way of a postscript, though I might have mentioned it much earlier, I must tell that I do a lot of my work with a certain Antipova, a nurse from Moscow who was born in the Urals.

"You remember the girl student who shot at the public prosecutor on that terrible night of your mother's death? I believe she was tried later. I remember telling you that Misha and I had once seen her, when she was still a schoolgirl, at some sordid hotel where your father took us. I can't remember why we went, only that it was a bitterly cold night. I think it was at the time of the Presnia uprising. Well, that girl was Antipova.

"I have made several attempts to go home, but it is not so simple. It is not so much the work—we could hand that over easily enough—the trouble is the trip. Either there are no trains at all or else they are so overcrowded that there is no way of finding a seat.

"But of course it can't go on like this forever, and some of us, who have resigned or been discharged, including Antipova, Galiullin, and myself, have made up our minds that whatever happens we shall leave next week. We'll go separately; it gives us a better chance.

"So I may turn up any day out of the blue, though I'll try to send a telegram."

Before he left, however, he received his wife's reply. In sentences broken by sobs and with tear

---

From: Boris Pasternak, *Doctor Zhivago,* trans. Max Hayward and Manya Harari (New York: Pantheon, 1958), pp. 131–155.

stains and ink spots for punctuation, she begged him not to come back to Moscow but to go straight to the Urals with that wonderful nurse whose progress through life was marked by portents and coincidences so miraculous that her own, Tonia's, modest life could not possibly compete with it.

"Don't worry about Sasha's future," she wrote. "You will never need to be ashamed of him. I promise you to bring him up in those principles which as a child you saw practiced in our house."

Yurii Andreievich wrote back at once: "You must be out of your mind, Tonia! How could you imagine such a thing? Don't you know, don't you know well enough, that if it were not for you, if it were not for my constant, faithful thoughts of you and of our home, I would never have survived these two terrible, devastating years of war? But why am I writing this—soon well be together, our life will begin again, everything will be cleared up.

"What frightens me about your letter is something else. If I really gave you cause to write in such a way, my behavior must have been ambiguous and I am at fault not only before you but before that other woman whom I am misleading. I'll apologize to her as soon as she is back. She is away in the country. Local councils, which formerly existed only in provincial capitals and county seats, are being set up in the villages, and she has gone to help a friend of hers who is acting as instructor in connection with these legislative changes.

"It may interest you to know that although we live in the same house I don't know to this day which is Antipova's room. I've never bothered to find out."

3

Two main roads ran from Meliuzeievo, one going east, the other west. One was a mud track leading through the woods to Zybushino, a small grain center that was administratively a subdivision of Meliuzeievo although it was ahead of it in every way. The other was gravelled and went through fields, boggy in winter but dry in summer, to Biriuchi, the nearest railway junction.

In June Zybushino became an independent republic. It was set up by the local miller Blazheiko and supported by deserters from the 212th Infantry who had left the front at the time of the upheavals, kept their arms, and come to Zybushino through Biriuchi.

The republic refused to recognize the Provisional Government and split off from the rest of Russia. Blazheiko, a religious dissenter who had once corresponded with Tolstoy, proclaimed a new millennial Zybushino kingdom where all work and property were to be collectivized, and referred to the local administration as an Apostolic Seat.

Zybushino had always been a source of legends and exaggerations. It is mentioned in documents dating from the Times of Troubles and the thick forests surrounding it teemed with robbers even later. The prosperity of its merchants and the fabulous fertility of its soil were proverbial. Many popular beliefs, customs, and oddities of speech that distinguished this whole western region near the front originated in Zybushino.

Now amazing stories were told about Blazheiko's chief assistant. It was said that he was deaf and dumb, that he acquired the gift of speech at moments of inspiration, and then lost it again.

The republic lasted two weeks. In July a unit loyal to the Provisional Government entered the town. The deserters fell back on Biriuchi. Several miles of forest had once been cleared along the railway line on both sides of the junction, and there, among the old tree stumps overgrown with wild strawberries, the piles of timber depleted by pilfering, and the tumble-down mud huts of the seasonal laborers who had cut the trees, the deserters set up their camp.

4

The hospital in which Zhivago convalesced and later served as a doctor, and which he was now preparing to leave, was housed in the former residence of Countess Zhabrinskaia. She had offered it to the Red Cross at the beginning of the war.

It was a two-story house on one of the best sites of the town, at the corner or the main street and the square, known as the *Platz,* where soldiers had drilled in the old days and where meetings were held now.

Its position gave it a good view of the neighborhood; in addition to the square and the street it overlooked the adjoining farm (owned by a poor, provincial family who lived almost like peasants) as well as the Countess's old garden at the back.

The Countess had a large estate in the district, Razdolnoie, and had used the house only for occasional business visits to the town and as a rallying point for the guests who came from near and far to stay at Razdolnoie in summer.

Now the house was a hospital, and its owner was in prison in Petersburg, where she had lived.

Of the large staff, only two women were left, Ustinia, the head cook, and Mademoiselle Fleury, the former governess of the Countess's daughters, who were now married.

Gray-haired, pink-cheeked, and dishevelled, Mademoiselle Fleury shuffled about in bedroom slippers and a floppy, wornout housecoat, apparently as much at home in the hospital as she had been in the Zhabrinsky family. She told long stories in her broken Russian, swallowing the ends of her words in the French manner, gesticulated, struck dramatic poses, and burst into hoarse peals of laughter that ended in coughing fits.

She believed that she knew Nurse Antipova inside out and thought that the nurse and the doctor were bound to be attracted to each other. Succumbing to her passion for matchmaking, so deep-rooted in the Latin heart, she was delighted when she found them in each other's company, and would shake her finger and wink slyly at them. This puzzled Antipova and angered the doctor; but, like all eccentrics, Mademoiselle cherished her illusions and would not be parted from them at any price.

Ustinia was an even stranger character. Her clumsy, pear-shaped figure gave her the look of a brood hen. She was dry and sober to the point of maliciousness, but her sober-mindedness went hand in hand with an imagination unbridled in everything to do with superstition. Born in Zybushino and said to be the daughter of the local sorcerer, she knew countless spells and would never go out without first muttering over the stove and the keyhole to protect the house in her absence from Fire and the Evil One. She could keep quiet for years, but once she was roused nothing would stop her. Her passion was to defend the truth.

After the fall of the Zybushino republic, the Meliuzeievo Executive Committee launched a campaign against the local anarchistic tendencies. Every night peaceful meetings were held at the *Platz,* attended by small numbers of citizens who had nothing better to do and who, in the old days, used to gather for gossip outside the fire station. The Meliuzeievo cultural soviet encouraged them and invited local and visiting speakers to guide the discussions. The visitors believed the tales about the talking deaf-mute to be utter nonsense and were anxious to say so. But the small craftsmen, the soldiers' wives, and former servants of Meliuzeievo did not regard these stories as absurd and stood up in his defense.

One of the most outspoken of his defenders was Ustinia. At first held back by womanly reserve, she had gradually become bolder in heckling orators whose views were unacceptable in Meliuzeievo. In the end she developed into an expert public speaker.

The humming of the voices in the square could be heard through the open windows of the hospital, and on quiet nights even fragments of speeches. When Ustinia took the floor, Mademoiselle often rushed into any room where people were sitting and urged them to listen, imitating her without malice in her broken accent: "Disorder . . . Disorder . . . Tsarist, bandit . . . Zybushi- . . . deaf-mute . . . traitor! traitor!"

Mademoiselle was secretly proud of the spirited and sharp-tongued cook. The two women were fond of each other although they never stopped bickering.

5

Yurii Andreievich prepared to leave, visiting homes and offices where he had friends, and applying for the necessary documents.

At that time the new commissar of the local sector of the front stopped at Meliuzeievo on his way to the army. Everybody said he was completely inexperienced, a mere boy.

A new offensive was being planned and a great effort was made to improve the morale of the army masses. Revolutionary courts-martials were instituted, and the death penalty, which had recently been abolished, was restored.

Before leaving, the doctor had to obtain a paper from the local commandant.

Usually crowds filled his office, overflowing far out into the street. It was impossible to elbow one's way to the desks and no one could hear anything in the roar caused by hundreds of voices.

But this was not one of the reception days. The clerks sat writing silently in the peaceful office, disgruntled at the growing complication of their work, and exchanging ironic glances. Cheerful voices came from the commandant's room; it sounded as if, in there, people had unbuttoned their tunics and were having refreshments.

Galiullin came out of the inner room, saw Zhivago, and vigorously beckoned to him.

Since the doctor had in any case to see the commandant, he went in. He found the room in a state of artistic disorder.

The center of the stage was held by the new commissar, the hero of the day and the sensation of the town, who, instead of being at his post, was addressing the rulers of this paper kingdom quite unconnected with staff and operational matters.

"Here's another of our stars," said the commandant, introducing the doctor. The commissar, completely self-absorbed, did not look around, and the commandant turned to sign the paper that the doctor put in front of him and waved him politely to a low ottoman in the center of the room.

The doctor was the only person in the room who sat normally. All the rest were lolling eccentrically with an air of exaggerated and assumed ease. The commandant almost lay across his desk, his cheek on his fist, in a thoughtful, Byronic pose. His aide, a massive, stout man, perched on the arm of the sofa, his legs tucked on the seat as if he were riding side saddle. Galiullin sat astride a chair, his arms folded on its back and his head resting on his arms, and the commissar kept hoisting himself up by his wrists onto the window sill and jumping off and running up and down the room with small quick steps, buzzing about like a wound-up top, never still or silent for a moment. He talked continuously; the subject of the conversation was the problem of the deserters at Biriuchi.

The commissar was exactly as he had been described to Zhivago. He was thin and graceful, barely out of his teens, aflame with the highest ideals. He was said to come of a good family (the son of a senator, some people thought) and to have been one of the first to march his company to the Duma in February. He was called Gints or Gintse—the doctor had not quite caught the name—and spoke very distinctly, with a correct Petersburg accent and a slight Baltic intonation.

He wore a tight-fitting tunic. It probably embarrassed him to be so young, and in order to seem older he assumed a sneer and an artificial stoop, hunching his shoulders with their stiff epaulettes and keeping his hands deep in his pockets; this did in fact give him a cavalryman's silhouette which could be drawn in two straight lines converging downward from the angle of his shoulders to his feet.

"There is a Cossack regiment stationed a short distance down the railway," the commandant informed him. "It's Red, it's loyal. It will be called out, the rebels will be surrounded, and that will be the end of the business. The corps commander is anxious that they should be disarmed without delay."

"Cossacks? Out of the question!" flared the commissar. "This is not 1905. We're not going back to prerevolutionary methods. On this point we don't see eye to eye. Your generals have outsmarted themselves."

"Nothing has been done yet. This is only a plan, a suggestion."

"We have an agreement with the High Command not to interfere with operational matters. I am not cancelling the order to call out the Cossacks. Let them come. But I, for my part, will take such steps as are dictated by common sense. I suppose they have a bivouac out there?"

"I guess so. A camp, at any rate. Fortified."

"So much the better. I want to go there. I want to see this menace, this nest of robbers. They may be rebels, gentlemen, they may even be deserters, but remember, they are the people. And the people are children, you have to know them, you have to know their psychology. To get the best out of them, you must have the right approach, you have to play on their best, most sensitive chords.

"I'll go, and I'll have a heart-to-heart talk with them. You'll see, they'll go back to the positions they have deserted. You don't believe me? Want to bet?"

"I wonder. But I hope you're right."

"I'll say to them, 'Take my own case, I am an only son, the hope of my parents, yet I haven't spared myself. I've given up everything—name, family, position. I have done this to fight for your freedom, such freedom as is not enjoyed by any other people in the world. This I did, and so did many other young men like myself, not to speak of the old guard of our glorious predecessors, the champions of the people's rights who were sent to hard labor in Siberia or locked up in the Schlüsselburg Fortress. Did we do this for ourselves? Did we have to do it? And you, you who are no longer ordinary privates but the warriors of the first revolutionary army in the world, ask yourselves honestly: Have you lived up to your proud calling? At this moment when our country is being bled white and is making a supreme effort to shake off the encircling hydra of the enemy, you have allowed yourselves to be fooled by a gang of nobodies, you have become a rabble, politically unconscious, surfeited with freedom, hooligans for whom nothing is enough. You're like the proverbial pig that was allowed in the dining room and at once jumped onto the table.' Oh, I'll touch them to the quick, I'll make them feel ashamed of themselves."

"No, that would be risky," the commandant objected half-heartedly, exchanging quick, meaningful glances with his aide.

Galiullin did his best to dissuade the commissar from his insane idea. He knew the reckless men of the 212th, they had been in his division at the front. But the commissar refused to listen.

Yurii Andreievich kept trying to get up and go. The commissar's naïveté embarrassed him, but the sly sophistication of the commandant and his aide—two sneering and dissembling opportunists—was no better. The foolishness of the one was matched by the slyness of the others. And all this expressed itself in a torrent of words, superfluous, utterly false, murky, profoundly alien to life itself.

Oh, how one wishes sometimes to escape from the meaningless dullness of human eloquence, from all those sublime phrases, to take refuge in nature, apparently so inarticulate, or in the wordlessness of long, grinding labor, of sound sleep, of true music, or of a human understanding rendered speechless by emotion!

The doctor remembered his coming talk with Antipova. Though it was bound to be unpleasant, he was glad of the necessity of seeing her, even at such a price. She was unlikely to be back. But he got up as soon as he could and went out, unnoticed by the others.

6

She was back. Mademoiselle, who gave him the news, added that she was tired, she had had a quick meal and had gone up to her room saying she was not to be disturbed. "But I should go up and knock if I were you," Mademoiselle suggested. "I am sure she is not asleep yet."—"Which is her room?" the doctor asked. Mademoiselle was surprised beyond words by his question. Antipova lived at the end of the passage on the top floor, just beyond several rooms in which all of the Countess's furniture was kept locked, and where the doctor had never been.

It was getting dark. Outside, the houses and fences huddled closer together in the dusk. The trees advanced out of the depth of the garden into the light of the lamps shining from the windows. The night was hot and sticky. At the slightest effort one was drenched with sweat. The light of the kerosene lamps streaking into the yard went down the trees in a dirty, vaporous flow.

The doctor stopped at the head of the stairs. It occurred to him that even to knock on Antipova's door when she was only just back and tired from her journey would be discourteous and embarrassing. Better leave the talk for tomorrow. Feeling at a loss as one does when one changes one's mind, he walked to the other end of the passage, where a window overlooked the neighboring yard, and leaned out.

The night was full of quiet, mysterious sounds. Next to him, inside the passage, water dripped from the washbasin regularly and slowly. Somewhere outside the window people were whispering. Somewhere in the vegetable patch they were watering cucumber beds, clanking the chain of the well as they drew the water and poured it from pail to pail.

All the flowers smelled at once; it was as if the earth, unconscious all day long, were now waking to their fragrance. And from the Countess's centuries-old garden, so littered with fallen branches that it was impenetrable, the dusty aroma of old linden trees coming into bloom drifted in a huge wave as tall as a house.

Noises came from the street beyond the fence on the right—snatches of a song, a drunken soldier, doors banging.

An enormous crimson moon rose behind the crows' nests in the Countess's garden. At first it was the color of the new brick mill in Zybushino, then it turned yellow like the water tower at Biriuchi.

And just under the window, the smell of new-mown hay, as perfumed as jasmine tea, mixed with that of belladonna, Below there a cow was tethered; she had been brought from a distant village, she had walked all day, she was tired and homesick for the herd and would not yet accept food from her new mistress.

"Now, now, whoa there, I'll show you how to butt," her mistress coaxed her in a whisper, but the cow crossly shook her head and craned her neck, mooing plaintively, and beyond the black barns of Meliuzeievo the stars twinkled, and invisible threads of sympathy stretched between them and the cow as if there were cattle sheds in other worlds where She was pitied.

Everything was fermenting, growing, rising with the magic yeast of life. The joy of living, like a gentle wind, swept in a broad surge indiscriminately through fields and towns, through walls and fences, through wood and flesh. Not to be overwhelmed by this tidal wave, Yurii Andreievich went out into the square to listen to the speeches.

7

By now the moon stood high. Its light covered everything as with a thick layer of white paint. The broad shadows thrown by the pillared government buildings that surrounded the square in a semicircle spread on the ground like black rugs.

The meeting was being held across the square. Straining one's ears, one could hear every word. But the doctor was stunned by the beauty of the spectacle; he sat down on the bench outside the fire station and instead of listening looked about him.

Narrow dead-end streets ran off the square, as deep in mud as country lanes and lined with crooked little houses. Fences of plaited willows stuck out of the mud like bow nets in a pond, or lobster pots. You could see the weak glint of open windows. In the small front gardens, sweaty red heads of corn with oily whiskers reached out toward the rooms, and single pale thin hollyhocks looked out over the fences; like women in night clothes whom the heat had driven out of their stuffy houses for a breath of air.

The moonlit night was extraordinary, like merciful love or the gift of clairvoyance. Suddenly, into this radiant, legendary stillness, there dropped the measured, rhythmic sound of a familiar, recently heard voice. It was a fine ardent voice and it rang with conviction. The doctor listened and recognized it at once. Commissar Gints was addressing the meeting on the square.

Apparently the municipality had asked him to lend them the support of his authority. With great feeling he chided the people of Meliuzeievo for their disorganized ways and for giving in to the disintegrating influence of the Bolsheviks, who, he said, were the real instigators of the Zybushino disorders. Speaking in the same spirit as at the Commandant's, he reminded them of the powerful and ruthless enemy, and of their country's hour of trial. Then the crowd began to heckle.

Calls of protest alternated with demands for silence. The interruptions grew louder and more frequent. A man who had come with Gints, and who now assumed the role of chairman, shouted that speeches from the floor were not allowed and called the audience to order. Some insisted that a citizeness who wished to speak should be given leave.

A woman made her way through the crowd to the wooden box that served as a platform. She did not attempt to climb on the box but stood beside it. The woman was known to the crowd. Its attention was caught. There was a silence. This was Ustinia.

"Now you were saying, Comrade Commissar, about Zybushino," she began, "and about looking sharp—you told us to look sharp and not to be deceived—but actually, you yourself, I heard you, all you do is to play about with words like 'Bolsheviks, Mensheviks,' that's all you talk about—Bolsheviks, Mensheviks. Now all that about no more fighting and all being brothers, I call that being godly, not Menshevik, and about the works and factories going to the poor, that isn't Bolshevik, that's just human decency. And about that deaf-mute, we're fed up hearing about him. Everybody goes on and on about the deaf-mute. And what have you got against him?

Just that he was dumb all that time and then he suddenly started to talk and didn't ask your permission? As if that were so marvellous! Much stranger things than that have been known to happen. Take the famous she-ass, for instance. 'Balaam, Balaam,' she says, 'listen to me, don't go that way, I beg you, you'll be sorry.' Well, naturally, he wouldn't listen, he went on. Like you saying, 'A deaf-mute,' he thought, 'a she-ass, a dumb beast, what's the good of listening to her.' He scorned her. And look how sorry he was afterwards. You all know what the end of it was."

"What?" someone asked curiously.

"That's enough," snapped Ustinia. "If you ask too many questions you'll grow old before your time."

"That's no good. You tell us," insisted the heckler.

"All right, all right, I'll tell you, you pest. He was turned into a pillar of salt."

"You've got it wrong, that was Lot. That was Lot's wife," people shouted. Everyone laughed. The chairman called the meeting to order. The doctor went to bed.

8

He saw Antipova the following evening. He found her in the pantry with a pile of linen, straight out of the wringer; she was ironing.

The pantry was one of the back rooms at the top, looking out over the garden. There the samovars were got ready, food was dished out, and the used plates were stacked in the dumb-waiter to be sent down to the kitchen. There too the lists of china, silver, and glass were kept and checked, and there people spent their moments of leisure, using it as a meeting place.

The windows were open. In the room, the scent of linden blossoms mingled, as in an old park, with the caraway-bitter smell of dry twigs and the charcoal fumes of the two flatirons that Antipova used alternately, putting them each in him in the flue to keep them hot.

"Well, why didn't you knock last night? Mademoiselle told me. But it's a good thing you didn't. I was already in bed. I couldn't have let you in. Well, how are you? Look out for the charcoal, don't get it on your suit."

"You look as if you've been doing the laundry for the whole hospital."

"No, there's a lot of mine in there. You see? You keep on teasing me about getting stuck in Meliuzeievo. Well, this time I mean it, I'm going. I'm getting my things together, I'm packing. When I've finished I'll be off. I'll be in the Urals and you'll be in Moscow. Then one day somebody will ask you: 'Do you happen to know a little town called Meliuzeievo?' and you'll say: 'I don't seem to call it to mind.'—'And who is Antipova?'—'Never heard of her.' "

"That's unlikely. Did you have a good trip? What was it like in the country?"

"That's a long story. How quickly these irons cool! Do hand me the other, do you mind? It's over there, look, just inside the flue. And could you put this one back? Thanks. Every village is different, it depends on the villagers. In some the people are industrious, they work hard, then it isn't bad. And in others I suppose all the men are drunks. Then it's desolate. A terrible sight."

"Nonsense! Drunks? A lot you understand! It's just that there is no one there, all the men are in the army. What about the new councils?"

"You're wrong about the drunks, I don't agree with you at all. The councils? There's going to be a lot of trouble with the councils. The instructions can't be applied, there's nobody to work with. All the peasants care about at the moment is the land question. . . . I stopped at Razdolnoie. What a lovely place, you should go and see it. . . . It was burned a bit and looted last spring, the barn is burned down, the orchards are charred, and there are smoke stains on some of the houses. Zybushino I didn't see, I didn't get there. But they all tell you the deaf-mute really exists. They describe what he looks like, they say he's young and educated."

"Last night Ustinia stood up for him on the square."

"The moment I got back there was another lot of old furniture from Razdolnoie. I've asked them a hundred times to leave it alone. As if we didn't have enough of our own. And this morning the guard from the commandant's office comes over with a note—they must have the silver tea set and the crystal glasses, it's a matter of life and death, just for one night, they'll send it back. Half of it we'll never see again. It's always a loan—I know these loans. They're having a party—in honor of some visitor or something."

"I can guess who that is. The new commissar has arrived, the one who's appointed to our sector of the front. They want to tackle the deserters, have them surrounded and disarmed. The commissar is a greenhorn, a babe in arms. The local authorities want to call out the Cossacks, but not he—he's planning to speak to their hearts. The people, he says, are like children, and so on; he thinks it's a kind of game. Galiullin tried to argue with him, he told him to leave the jungle alone, not to rouse the wild beast. 'Leave us to deal with it,' he said. But you can't do anything with a fellow like that once he's got a thing in his head. I do wish you'd listen to me. Do stop ironing a minute. There will be an unimaginable mess here soon; it's beyond our power to avert it. I do wish you'd leave before it happens."

"Nothing will happen, you're exaggerating. And anyway, I am leaving. But I can't just snap my fingers and say goodbye. I have to hand in a properly checked inventory. I don't want it to look as if I've stolen something and run away. And who is to take over? That's the problem, I can't tell you what I've been through with that miserable inventory, and all I get is abuse. I listed Zhabrinskaia's things as hospital property, because that was the sense of the decree. Now they say I did it on purpose to keep them for the owner! What a dirty trick!"

"Do stop worrying about pots and rugs. To hell with them. What a thing to fuss about at a time like this! Oh, I wish I'd seen you yesterday. I was in such good form that I could have told you all about everything, explained the whole celestial mechanics, answered any accursed question! It's true, you know, I'm not joking, I really did want to get it all off my chest. And I, wanted to tell you about my wife, and my son, and myself. . . . Why the hell can't a grown-up man talk to a grown-up woman without being at once suspected of some ulterior motive? Damn all motives—ulterior ones and others.

"Please, go on with your ironing, make the linen nice and smooth, don't bother about me, I'll go on talking. I'll talk a long time.

"Just think what's going on around us! And that you and I should be living at such a time. Such a thing happens only once in an eternity. Just think of it, the whole of Russia has had its roof torn off, and you and I and everyone else are out in the open! And there's nobody to spy on us. Freedom! Real freedom, not just talk about it, freedom, dropped out of the sky, freedom beyond our expectations, freedom by accident, through a misunderstanding.

"And how great everyone is, and completely at sea! Have you noticed? As if crushed by his own weight, by the discovery of his greatness.

"Go on ironing, I tell you. Don't talk. You aren't bored. Let me change your iron for you.

"Last night I was watching the meeting in the square. An extraordinary sight! Mother Russia is on the move, she can't stand still, she's restless and she can't find rest, she's talking and she can't stop. And it isn't as if only people were talking. Stars and trees meet and converse, flowers talk philosophy at night, stone houses hold meetings. It makes you think of the Gospel, doesn't it? The days of the apostles. Remember St. Paul? You will speak with tongues and you will prophesy. Pray for the gift of understanding."

"I know what you mean about stars and trees holding meetings. I understand that. It's happened to me too."

"It was partly the war, the revolution did the rest. The war was an artificial break in life—as if life could be put off for a time—what nonsense! The revolution broke out willy-nilly, like a sigh suppressed too long. Everyone was revived, reborn, changed, transformed. You might say that everyone has been through two revolutions—his own personal revolution as well as the general one. It seems to me that socialism is the sea, and all these separate streams, these private, individual revolutions, are flowing into it—the sea of life, the sea of spontaneity. I said life, but I mean life as you see it in a great picture, transformed by genius, creatively enriched. Only now people have decided to experience it not in books and pictures but in themselves, not as an abstraction but in practice."

The sudden trembling of his voice betrayed his rising agitation. Antipova stopped ironing and gave him a grave, astonished look. It confused him and he forgot what he was saying. After a moment of embarrassed silence he rushed on, blurting out whatever came into his head.

"These days I have such a longing to live honestly, to be productive. I so much want to be a part of all this awakening. And then, in the middle of all this general rejoicing, I catch your mysterious, sad glance, wandering God knows where, far away.

How I wish it were not there! How I wish your face to say that you are happy with your fate and that you need nothing from anyone. If only someone who is really close to you, your friend or your husband—best of all if he were a soldier—would take me by the hand and tell me to stop worrying about your fate and not to weary you with my attentions. But I'd wrest my hand free and take a swing. . . . Ah, I have forgotten myself. Please forgive me."

Once again the doctor's voice betrayed him. He gave up struggling and, feeling hopelessly awkward, got up and went to the window. Leaning on the sill, his cheek on his hand, he stared into the dark garden with absent, unseeing eyes, trying to collect himself.

Antipova walked round the ironing board, propped between the table and the other window, and stopped in the middle of the room a few steps behind him. "That's what I've always been afraid of," she said softly, as if to herself. "I shouldn't have . . . Don't, Yurii Andreievich, you mustn't. Oh, now just look at what you've made me do!" she exclaimed. She ran back to the board, where a thin stream of acrid smoke came from under the iron that had burned through a blouse.

She thumped it down crossly on its stand. "Yurii Andreievich," she went on, "do be sensible, go off to Mademoiselle for a minute, have a drink of water and come back, please, as I've always known you till now and as I want you to be. Do you hear, Yurii Andreievich? I know you can do it. Please do it, I beg you."

They had no more talks of this kind, and a week later Larisa Feodorovna left.

9

Some time later, Zhivago too set out for home. The night before he left there was a terrible storm. The roar of the gale merged with that of the downpour, which sometimes crashed straight onto the roofs and at other times drove down the street with the changing wind as if lashing its way step by step.

The peels of thunder followed each other uninterruptedly, producing a steady rumble. In the blaze of continual flashes of lightning the street vanished into the distance, and the bent trees seemed to be running in the same direction.

Mademoiselle Fleury was waked up in the night by an urgent knocking at the front door. She sat up in alarm and listened. The knocking went on.

Could it be, she thought, that there wasn't a soul left in the hospital to get up and open the door? Did she always have to do everything, poor old woman, just because nature had made her reliable and endowed her with a sense of duty?

Well, admittedly, the house had belonged to rich aristocrats, but what about the hospital—didn't that belong to the people, wasn't it their own? Whom did they expect to look after it? Where, for instance, had the male nurses got to, she'd like to know. Everyone had fled—no more orderlies, no more nurses, no doctors, no one in authority. Yet there were still wounded in the house, two legless men in the surgical ward where the drawing room used to be, and downstairs next to the laundry the storeroom full of dysentery cases. And that devil Ustinia had gone out visiting. She knew perfectly well that there was a storm coming, but did that stop her? Now she had a good excuse to spend the night out.

Well, thank God the knocking had stopped, they realized that nobody would answer, they'd given it up. Why anybody should want to be out in the weather . . . Or could it be Ustinia? No, she had her key. Oh God, how terrible, they've started again.

What pigs, just the same! Not that you could expect Zhivago to hear anything, he was off tomorrow, his thoughts were already in Moscow or on the journey. But what about Galiullin? How could he sleep soundly or lie calmly through all this noise, expecting that in the end she, a weak, defenseless old woman, would go down and open for God knows whom, on this frightening night in this frightening country.

Galiullin!—she remembered suddenly. No, such nonsense could occur to her only because she was half asleep, Galiullin wasn't there, he should be a long way off by now. Hadn't she herself, with Zhivago, hidden him, and disguised him as a civilian, and then told him about every road and village in the district to help him to escape after that horrible lynching at the station when they killed Commissar Gints and chased Galiullin all the way from Biriuchi to Meliuzeievo, shooting at him and then hunting for him all over the town!

If it hadn't been for those automobiles, not a stone would have been left standing in the town. An armored division happened to be passing through, and stopped those evil men.

The storm was subsiding, moving away. The thunder was less continuous, duller, more distant. The rain stopped occasionally, when the water could be heard splashing softly off the leaves and down the gutters. Noiseless reflections of distant lightning lit up Mademoiselle's room, lingering as though looking for something.

Suddenly the knocking at the front door, which had long since stopped, was resumed. Someone was in urgent need of help and was knocking repeatedly, in desperation. The wind rose again and the rain came dawn.

"Coming," shouted Mademoiselle to whoever it was, and the sound of her own voice frightened her.

It had suddenly occurred to her who it might be. Putting down her feet and pushing them into slippers, she threw her dressing gown over her shoulders and hurried to wake up Zhivago, it would be less frightening if he came down with her. But he had heard the knocking and was already coming down with a lighted candle. The same idea had occurred to both of them.

"Zhivago, Zhivago, they're knocking on the front door, I'm afraid to go down alone," she called out in French, adding in Russian: "You will see, it's either Lar or Lieutenant Gaiul."

Roused by the knocking, Yurii Andreievich had also felt certain that it was someone he knew—either Galiullin, who had been stopped in his flight and was coming back for refuge, or Nurse Antipova, prevented from continuing her journey for some reason.

In the hallway the doctor gave the candle to Mademoiselle, drew the bolts, and turned the key. A gust of wind burst the door open, putting out the candle and showering them with cold raindrops.

"Who is it? Who is it? Anybody there?"

Mademoiselle and the doctor shouted in turn into the darkness but there was no reply. Suddenly the knocking started again in another piece—was it at the back door, or, as they now thought, at the French window into the garden?

"Must be the wind," said the doctor. "But just to make sure, perhaps you'd have a look at the back. I'll stay here in case there really is someone."

Mademoiselle disappeared into the house while the doctor went out and stood under the entrance roof. His eyes had become accustomed to the darkness, and he could make out the first signs of dawn.

Above the town, clouds raced dementedly as if pursued, so low that their tatters almost caught the tops of the trees, which bent in the same direction so that they looked like brooms sweeping the sky. The rain lashed the wooden wall of the house, turning it from gray to black.

Mademoiselle came back. "Well?" said the doctor.

"You were right. There's no one." She had been all around the house; a branch knocking on the pantry window had broken one of the panes and there were huge puddles on the floor, and the same thing in what used to be Lara's room—there was a sea, a real sea, an ocean. "And on this side, look, there's a broken shutter knocking on the casement, do you see it? That's all it was."

They talked a little, locked the door, and went back to their rooms, both regretting that the alarm had been a false one.

They had been sure that when they opened the door Antipova would come in, chilled through and soaked to the skin, and they would ask her dozens of questions while she took off her things, and she would go and change and come down and dry herself in front of the kitchen stove, still warm from last night, and would tell them her adventures, pushing back her hair and laughing.

They had been so sure of it that after locking the front door they imagined that she was outside the house in the form of a watery wraith, and her image continued to haunt them.

10

It was said that the Biriuchi telegrapher, Kolia Frolenko, was indirectly responsible for the trouble at the station.

Kolia, the son of a well-known Meliuzeievo clockmaker, had been a familiar figure in Meliuzeievo from his earliest childhood. As a small boy he had stayed with some of the servants at Razdolnoie and had played with the Countess's daughters. It was then that he learned to understand French. Mademoiselle Fleury knew him well.

Everyone in Meliuzeievo was used to seeing him on his bicycle, coatless, hatless, and in canvas summer shoes in any weather. Arms crossed on his chest, he free-wheeled down the road, glancing up at the poles and wires to check the condition of the network.

Some of the houses in Meliuzeievo were connected by a branch line with the exchange at the station. The calls were handled by Kolia at the station switchboard. There he was up to his ears in work, for not only the telephone and telegraph were in his charge, but, if the stationmaster Povarikhin was absent for a few moments, also the railway signals, which were operated from the same control room.

Having to look after several mechanical instruments at once, Kolia had evolved a special style of speech, obscure, abrupt, and puzzling, which enabled him, if he chose, to avoid answering questions or getting involved in a conversation. He was said to have abused the advantage this gave him on the day of the disorders.

It is true that, by suppressing information, he had defeated Galiullin's good intentions and, perhaps unwittingly, had given a fatal turn to the events.

Galiullin had called up from town and asked for Commissar Gints, who was somewhere at the station or in its vicinity, in order to tell him that he was on his way to join him and to ask him to wait for him and do nothing until he arrived. Kolia, on the pretext that he was busy signalling an approaching train, refused to call the commissar. At the same time he did his utmost to delay the train, which was bringing up the Cossacks summoned to Biriuchi.

When the troops arrived nevertheless he did not conceal his dismay.

The engine, crawling slowly under the dark roof of the platform, stopped in front of the huge window of the control room. Kolia drew the green serge curtain with the initials of the Company woven in yellow into the border, picked up the enormous water jug standing on the tray on the window ledge, poured some water into the plain, thick, straight-sided glass, drank a few mouthfuls, and looked out.

The engineer saw him from his cab and gave him a friendly nod.

"The stinker, the louse," Kolia thought with hatred. He stuck out his tongue and shook his fist. The engineer not only understood him but managed to convey by a shrug of the shoulders and a nod in the direction of the train: "What was I to do? I'd like to know what you'd have done in my place. He's the boss."—"You're a filthy brute all the same," Kolia replied by gestures.

The horses were taken, balking, out of the freight cars. The thud of their hoofs on the wooden gangways was followed by the ring of their shoes on the stone platform. They were led, rearing, across the tracks.

At the end of the tracks were two rows of derelict wooden coaches. The rain had washed them clean of paint, and worms and damp had rotted them from inside, so that now they were reverting to their original kinship with the wood of the forest, which began just beyond the rolling stock, with its lichen, its birches, and the clouds towering above it.

At the word of command, the Cossacks mounted their horses and galloped to the clearing.

The rebels of the 212th were surrounded. In woods, horsemen always seem taller and more formidable than in an open field. They impressed the infantrymen, although they had rifles in their mud huts. The Cossacks drew their swords.

Within the ring formed by the horses, some timber was piled. up. Gints mounted it and addressed the surrounded men.

As usual, he spoke of soldierly duty, of the fatherland, and many other lofty subjects. But these ideas found no sympathy among his listeners. There were too many of them. They had suffered a great deal in the war, they were thick-skinned and exhausted. They had long been fed up with the phrases Gints was giving them. Four months of wooing by the Left and Right had corrupted these unsophisticated men, who, moreover, were alienated by the speaker's foreign-sounding name and Baltic accent.

Gints felt that his speech was too long and was annoyed at himself, but he thought that he had to make himself clear to his listeners, who instead of being grateful rewarded him with expressions of indifference or hostile boredom. Gradually losing his temper, he decided to speak straight from the shoulder and to bring up the threats he had so far held in reserve. Heedless of the rising murmurs, he reminded the deserters that revolutionary courts-martial had been set up, and called on them, on pain of death, to disarm and give up their ringleaders. If they refused, he said, they would prove that they were common traitors, an irresponsible swollen-headed rabble. The men had become unused to being talked to in such a tone.

Several hundred voices rose in an uproar. Some were low-pitched and almost without anger: "All right, all right. Pipe down. That's enough." But hate-filled, hysterical trebles predominated:

"The nerve! Just like in the old days! These officers still treat us like dirt. So we're traitors, are we? And what about you yourself, Excellency? Why bother with him? Obviously he's a German, an infiltrator. Show us your papers, blueblood. And what are you gaping at, pacifiers?" They turned to the Cossacks. "You've come to restore order, go on, tie us up, have your fun."

But the Cossacks, too, liked Gints' unfortunate speech less and less. "They are all swine to him," they muttered. "Thinks himself the lord and master!" At first singly, and then in ever-growing numbers, they began to sheathe their swords. One after another they got off their horses. When most of them had dismounted, they moved in a disorderly crowd toward the center of the clearing, mixed with the men of the 212th, and fraternized.

"You must vanish quietly," the worried Cossack officers told Gints. "Your car is at the station, we'll send for it to meet you. Hurry."

Gints went, but he felt that to steal away was beneath his dignity, so he turned quite openly toward the station. He was terribly agitated but out of pride forced himself to walk calmly and unhurriedly.

He was close to the station. At the edge of the woods, within sight of the tracks, he looked back for the first time. Soldiers with rifles had followed him. "What do they want?" he wondered. He quickened his pace.

So did his pursuers. The distance between them remained unchanged. He saw the double wall of derelict coaches, stepped behind them, and ran. The train that had brought the Cossacks had been shunted. The lines were clear. He crossed them at a run and leapt onto the steep platform. At the same moment the soldiers ran out from behind the old coaches. Povarikhin and Kolia were shouting and waving to him to get into the station building, where they could save him.

But once again the sense of honor bred in him for generations, a city-bred sense of honor, which impelled him to self-sacrifice and was out of place here, barred his way to safety. His heart pounding wildly, he made a supreme effort to control himself. He told himself: "I must shout to them, 'Come to your senses, men, you know I'm not a spy.' A really heart-felt word or two will bring them to their senses."

In the course of the past months his feeling for a courageous exploit or a heart-felt speech had unconsciously become associated with stages, speakers' platforms, or just chairs onto which you jumped to fling an appeal or ardent call to the crowds.

At the very doors of the station, under the station bell, there stood a water butt for use in case of fire. It was tightly covered. Gints jumped up on the lid and addressed the approaching soldiers with an incoherent but gripping speech. His unnatural voice and the insane boldness of his gesture, two steps from the door where he could so easily have taken shelter, amazed them and stopped them in their tracks. They lowered their rifles.

But Gints, who was standing on the edge of the lid, suddenly pushed it in. One of his legs slipped into the water and the other hung over the edge of the butt.

Seeing him sitting clumsily astride the edge of the butt, the soldiers burst into laughter and the one in front shot Gints in the neck. He was dead by the time the others ran up and thrust their bayonets into his body.

11

Mademoiselle called up Kolia and told him to find Dr. Zhivago a good seat in the train to Moscow, threatening him with exposure if he did not.

Kolia was as usual conducting another conversation and, judging by the decimal fractions that punctuated his speech, transmitting a message in code over a third instrument.

"Pskov, Pskov, can you hear me? What rebels? What help? What are you talking about, Mademoiselle? Ring off, please. Pskov, Pskov, thirty-six point zero one five. Oh hell, they've cut me off. Hello, hello, I can't hear. Is that you again, Mademoiselle? I've told you, I can't. Ask Povarikhin. All lies, fictions. Thirty-six . . . Oh hell . . . Get off the line, Mademoiselle."

And Mademoiselle was saying:

"Don't you throw dust in my eyes, Pskov, Pskov, you liar, I can see right through you, tomorrow you'll put the doctor on the train, and I won't listen to another word from any murdering little Judases." . . .

✦ Reading 43 ✦
Versailles Peace Treaty

The Covenant of the League of Nations

The High Contracting Parties, in order to promote international cooperation and to achieve international peace and security

by the acceptance of obligations not to resort to war by the prescription of open, just and honourable relations between nations

by the firm establishment of the understandings of international law as the actual rule of conduct among Governments, and

by the maintenance of justice and a scrupulous respect for all treaty obligations in the dealings of organised peoples with one another

Agree to this Covenant of the League of Nations.

* * *

Article 8.

The Members of the League recognise that the maintenance of peace requires the reduction of national armaments to the lowest point consistent with national safety and the enforcement by common action of international obligations. The Council, taking account of the geographical situation and circumstances of each State, shall formulate plans for such reduction for the consideration and action of the several Governments. Such plans shall be subject to reconsideration and revision at least every ten years.

* * *

Article 10.

The Members of the League undertake to respect and preserve as against external aggression the territorial integrity and existing political independence of all Members of the League. . . .

Article 11.

Any war or threat of war, whether immediately affecting any of the Members of the League or not, is hereby declared a matter of concern to the whole League, and the League shall take any action that may be deemed wise and effectual to safeguard the peace of nations. . . .

Article 12.

The Members of the League agree that if there should arise between them any dispute likely to lead to a rupture, they will submit the matter either to arbitration or to inquiry by the Council, and they agree in no case to resort to war until three months after the award by the arbitrators or the report by the Council.

* * *

Article 16.

Should any Member of the League resort to war in disregard of its covenants . . . , it shall ipso facto be deemed to have committed an act of war against all other Members of the League, which hereby undertake immediately to subject it to the severance of all trade or financial relations, the prohibition of all intercourse between their nations and the nationals of the covenant-breaking State, and the prevention of all financial, commercial, or personal intercourse between the nationals of the covenant-breaking State and the nationals of any other State, whether a Member of the League or not. . . . Any Member of

---

From: *The Treaty of Versailles and After* (Washington: U.S. Government Printing Office, 1947), pp. 69, 72, 82, 83, 84, 88, 92, 93, 94, 104, 105, 159, 161, 162, 166, 183, 198, 202, 206, 208, 253, 272, 273, 276, 319, 320, 325, 329, 330, 331, 341, 342, 351, 371, 413, 425, 428, 695, 696, 697, 718, 719, 720, 725, 737.

the League which has violated any covenant of the League may be declared to be no longer a Member of the League by a vote of the Council concurred in by the Representatives of all the other Members of the League represented thereon.

* * *

Article 18.

Every treaty or international engagement entered into hereafter by any Member of the League shall be forthwith registered with the Secretariat and shall as soon as possible be published by it. No such treaty or international engagement shall be binding until so registered.

* * *

Article 22.

To those colonies and territories which as a consequence of the late war have ceased to be under the sovereignty of the States which formerly governed them and which are inhabited by peoples not yet able to stand by themselves under the strenuous conditions of the modern world, there should be applied the principle that the well-being and development of such peoples form a sacred trust of civilisation and that securities for the performance of this trust should be embodied in this Covenant. The best method of giving practical effect to this principle is that the tutelage of such peoples should be entrusted to advanced nations who by reason of their resources, their experience or their geographical position can best undertake this responsibility, and who are willing to accept it, and that this tutelage should be exercised by them as Mandatories on behalf of the League. The character of the mandate must differ according to the stage of the development of the people, the geographical situation of the territory, its economic conditions, and other similar circumstances. Certain communities formerly belonging to the Turkish Empire have reached a stage of development where their existence as independent nations can be provisionally recognised subject to the rendering of administrative advice and assistance by a Mandatory until such time as they are able to stand alone. The wishes of these communities must be a principal consideration in the selection of the Mandatory. Other peoples, especially those of Central Africa, are at such a stage that the Mandatory must be responsible for the administration of the territory under conditions which will guarantee freedom of conscience and religion, subject only to the maintenance of public order and morals, the prohibition of abuses such as the slave trade, the arms traffic, and the liquor traffic, and the prevention of the establishment of fortifications or military and naval bases and of military training of the natives for other than police purposes and the defence of territory, and will also secure equal opportunities for the trade and commerce of other Members of the League. There are territories, such as South-West Africa and certain of the South Pacific Islands, which, owing to the sparseness of their population, or their small size, or their remoteness from the centres of civilisation, or their geographical contiguity to the territory of the Mandatory, and other circumstances, can be best administered under the laws of the Mandatory as integral portions of its territory, subject to the safeguards above mentioned in the interests of the indigenous population. In every case of mandate, the Mandatory shall render to the Council an annual report in reference to the territory committed to its charge. . . .

Article 23.

. . . the Members of the League: (a) will endeavour to secure and maintain fair and humane conditions of labour for men, women, and children, both in their own countries and in all countries to which their commercial and industrial relations extend, and for that purpose will establish and maintain the necessary international organisations; (b) undertake to secure just treatment of the native inhabitants of territories under their control; (c) will entrust the League with the general supervision over the execution of agreements with regard to the traffic in women and children, and the traffic in opium and other dangerous drugs; (d) will entrust the League with the general supervision of the trade in arms and ammunition with the countries in which the control of this traffic is necessary in the common interest; (e) will make provision to secure and maintain freedom of communications and of transit and equitable treatment for the commerce of all Members of the League. In this connection, the special necessities of the regions devastated during the war of 1914–1918 shall be borne in mind; (f) will endeavour to take steps in matters of international concern for the prevention and control of disease.

* * *

Article 25.

The Members of the League agree to encourage and promote the establishment and cooperation of duly authorised voluntary national Red Cross organisations having as purposes the improvement of health, the prevention of disease, and the mitigation of suffering throughout the world.

* * *

Article 42.

Germany is forbidden to maintain or construct any fortifications either on the left bank of the Rhine or on the right bank to the west of a line drawn 50 kilometres to the East of the Rhine.

Article 43.

In the area defined above the maintenance and the assembly of armed forces, either permanently or temporarily, and military maneuvers of any kind, as well as the upkeep of all permanent works for mobilization, are in the same way forbidden.

Article 44.

In case Germany violates in any manner whatever the provisions of Articles 42 and 43, she shall be regarded as committing a hostile act against the Powers signatory of the present Treaty and as calculated to disturb the peace of the world.

Article 45.

As compensation for the destruction of the coal-mines in the north of France and as part payment towards the total reparation due from Germany for the damage resulting from the war, Germany cedes to France in full and absolute possession, with exclusive rights of exploitation, unencumbered and free from all debts and charges of any kind, the coal-mines situated in the Saar Basin . . .

Article 49.

. . . At the end of fifteen years from the coming into force of the present Treaty the inhabitants of the [Saar Basin] shall be called upon to indicate the sovereignty under which they desire to be placed.

* * *

Article 51.

The territories [of Alsace and Lorraine] which were ceded to Germany in accordance with the Preliminaries of Peace signed at Versailles on February 26, 1871, and the Treaty of Frankfort of May 10, 1871, are restored to French sovereignty as from the date of the Armistice of November 11, 1918. . . .

* * *

Article 80.

Germany acknowledges and will respect strictly the independence of Austria . . . ; she agrees that this independence shall be inalienable, except with the consent of the Council of the League of Nations.

Article 81.

Germany . . . recognises the complete independence of the Czecho-Slovak State. . . .

* * *

Article 84.

German nationals habitually resident in any of the territories recognised as forming part of the Czecho-Slovak State will obtain Czecho-Slovak nationality ipso facto and lose their German nationality.

* * *

Article 87.

Germany, in conformity with the action already taken by the Allied and Associated Powers, recognises the complete independence of Poland . . .

* * *

Article 102.

The Principal Allied and Associated Powers undertake to establish the town of Danzig, together with the rest of the territory described in Article 100, as a Free City. It will be placed under the protection of

s per-
ll the
ssian

ation
aties,
her

y re-
nany
es of

* * *

Article 119.

Germany renounces in favour of the Principal Allied and Associated Powers all her rights and titles over her oversea possessions.

* * *

Article 160.

. . . The total number of effectives in the Army of the States constituting Germany must not exceed one hundred thousand men, including officers and establishments of depots. The Army shall be devoted exclusively to the maintenance of order within the territory and to the control of the frontiers.

The total effective strength of officers, including the personnel of staffs, whatever their composition, must not exceed four thousand. . . .

* * *

Article 168.

The manufacture of arms, munitions, or any war material, shall only be carried out in factories or works the location of which shall be communicated to and approved by the Governments of the Principal Allied and Associated Powers, and the number of which they retain the right to restrict. . . .

* * *

Article 173.

Universal compulsory military service shall be abolished in Germany.

The German Army may only be constituted and recruited by means of voluntary enlistment.

* * *

Article 176.

On the expiration of two months from the coming into force of the present Treaty there must only exist in Germany the number of military schools which is absolutely indispensable for the recruitment of the officers of the units allowed. . . .

* * *

Article 181.

. . . The German naval forces in commission must not exceed:

6 battleships of the Deutschland or Lothringen type, 6 light cruisers, 12 destroyers, 12 torpedo boats. . . .

No submarines are to be included.

All other warships, except where there is provision to the contrary in the present Treaty, must be placed in reserve or devoted to commercial, purposes.

* * *

Article 198.

The armed forces of Germany must not include any military or naval air forces. . . .

* * *

Article 227.

The Allied and Associated Powers publicly arraign William II of Hohenzollern, formerly German Emperor, for a supreme offence against international morality and the sanctity of treaties. . . .

* * *

Article 231.

The Allied and Associated Governments affirm and Germany accepts the responsibility of Germany and her allies for causing all the loss and damage to which the Allied and Associated Governments and their nationals have been subjected as a consequence of the war imposed upon them by the aggression of Germany and her allies. . . .

Article 232.

The Allied and Associated Governments recognise that the resources of Germany are not adequate, after taking into account permanent diminutions of such resources which will result from other provisions of the present Treaty, to make complete reparation for all such loss and damage.

The Allied and Associated Governments, however, require, and Germany undertakes, that she will make compensation for all damage done to the civilian population of the Allied and Associated Powers and to their property during the period of the belligerency of each as an Allied or Associated Power against Germany . . .

Article 233.

The amount of the above damage for which compensation is to be made by Germany shall be determined by an Inter-Allied Commission . . .

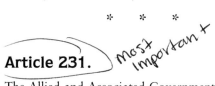

* * *

sire to secure the permanent peace of the world, agree to the following:

Article 387.

A permanent organisation is hereby established for the promotion of the objects set forth in the Preamble. . . .

* * *

Article 427.

[The High Contracting Parties] recognise that differences of climate, habits, and customs, of economic opportunity and industrial tradition, make strict uniformity in the conditions of labour difficult of immediate attainment. But, holding as they do, that labour should not be regarded merely as an Article of commerce, they think that there are methods and principles for regulating labour conditions which all industrial communities should endenvour to apply, so far as their special circumstances will permit.

Among these methods and principles, the following seem to the High Contracting Parties to be of special and urgent importance:

First.—The guiding principle above enunciated that labour should not be regarded merely as a commodity or article of commerce.

Second.—The right of association for all lawful purposes by the employed as well as by the employers.

Third.—The payment to the employed of a wage adequate to maintain a reasonable standard of life as this is understood in their time and country.

Fourth.—The adoption of an eight hours day or a forty-eight hours week as the standard to be aimed at where it has not already been attained.

Fifth.—The adoption of a weekly rest of at least twenty-four hours, which should include Sunday wherever practicable.

Sixth.—The abolition of child labour and the imposition of such limitations on the labour of young persons as shall permit the continuation of their education and assure their proper physical development.

Seventh.—The principle that men and women should receive equal remuneration for work of equal value.

Eighth.—The standard set by law in each country with respect to the conditions of labour should have due regard to the equitable economic treatment of all workers lawfully resident therein.

Ninth.—Each State should make provision for a system of inspection in which women should take part, in order to ensure the enforcement of the laws and regulations for the protection of the employed. . . .

Article 428.

As a guarantee for the execution of the present Treaty by Germany, the German territory situated to the west of the Rhine, together with the bridgeheads, will be occupied by Allied and Associated troops for a period of fifteen years from the coming into force of the present Treaty.

Article 430.

In case either during the occupation or after the expiration of the fifteen years referred to above the Reparation Commission finds that Germany refuses to observe the whole or part of her obligations under the present Treaty with regard to reparation, the whole or part of the areas specified in Article 429 will be reoccupied immediately by the Allied and Associated forces.

Article 431.

If before the expiration of the period of fifteen years Germany complies with all the undertakings resulting from the present Treaty, the occupying forces will be withdrawn immediately.

* * *

Article 434.

Germany undertakes to recognise the full force of the Treaties of Peace and Additional Conventions which may be concluded by the Allied and Associated Powers with the Powers who fought on the side of Germany and to recognise whatever dispositions nay be made concerning the territories of the former Austro-Hungarian Monarchy, of the Kingdom of Bulgaria and of the Ottoman Empire, and to recognise the new States within their frontiers as there laid down.

 PART TWELVE 

Early Twentieth Century Culture, 1900–1930

Cezanne's The Large Bathers *(1898–1905) illustrates his abandonment of realistic portrayals of human figures and the whole physical world in favor of impressions that had the goal of revealing underlying, sometimes disturbing truths.*

Early Twentieth Century Culture, 1900–1930

Just as before the Great War, the years following it were marked by sharp change and protracted political crises. Republics replaced the Central and Eastern European monarchies, but from the outset slow economic recovery from the war plagued the new governments. Even when political and economic stability finally returned to inter-war Europe by 1925, the sense of cultural unease that had characterized the prewar decades intensified. The cataclysm of war had not cleared the air. Radical change in both high and mass culture represented shifts that had begun before the war. According to the historian Peter Gay, within the formerly elite realms of art and literature, prewar "outsiders" simply became the new "insiders." In the realm of mass culture, the movies, already popular before the war, mesmerized millions and, along with radio, opened the way to manipulation through propaganda.

Franz Kafka (1883–1924), born in Prague of Jewish parents, lived a seemingly normal life, whereas his literary works reveal a more troubling picture. Although written before World War I, *The Metamorphosis* (1915) attained fame after the war. It narrates bizarre transformations in the lives of a middle-class family, suggesting Kafka's sense of the breakdown of traditional European civilization. *The Good Soldier Schweik* (1920–1923), written by Czech novelist Jaroslav Hasek (1883–1923) just before his untimely death, ostensibly portrays a humble soldier's often hilarious wartime experience. It shares Kafka's implied critique of existing society, although in a much lighter tone, with the barely perceived war serving as a handy backdrop. Whether at war or in peace, the supposedly simple-minded Schweik blithely subverts shaky values. Virginia Woolf (1882–1941) belonged to the "Bloomsbury Group," famed for its liveliness, innovation, and wit. Her *A Room of One's Own,* published in 1929, is an essay about society, art, and sexism, in which Woolf argued that financial freedom is necessary for intellectual freedom. In order to write, a woman must have money and a room of her own.

✦ Reading 44 ✦

The Metamorphosis

Franz Kafka

Gregor Samsa, a young traveling salesman, lives with and supports his parents and sister. At the beginning of the story Gregor awakes one morning to discover that he has become a "gigantic insect." Gregor's new identity disgraces him before his family, as he becomes an outsider in his own home.

As Gregor Samsa awoke one morning from uneasy dreams he found himself transformed in his bed into a gigantic insect. He was lying on his hard, as it were armor-plated, back and when he lifted his head a little he could see his domelike brown belly divided into stiff arched segments on top of which the bed quilt could hardly keep in position and was about to slide off completely. His numerous legs, which were pitifully thin compared to the rest of his bulk, waved helplessly before his eyes.

What has happened to me? he thought. It was no dream. His room, a regular human bedroom, only rather too small, lay quiet between the four familiar walls. Above the table on which a collection of cloth samples was unpacked and spread out—Samsa was a commercial traveler—hung the picture which he had recently cut out of an illustrated magazine and put into a pretty gilt frame. It showed a lady, with a fur cap on and a fur stole, sitting upright and holding out to the spectator a huge fur muff into which the whole of her forearm had vanished!

Gregor's eyes turned next to the window, and the overcast sky—one could hear raindrops beating on the window gutter—made him quite melancholy. What about sleeping a little longer and forgetting all this nonsense, he thought, but it could not be done, for he was accustomed to sleep on his right side and in his present condition he could not turn himself over. However violently he forced himself toward his right side he always rolled onto his back again. He tried it at least a hundred times, shutting his eyes to keep from seeing his struggling legs, and only desisted when he began to feel in his side a faint dull ache he had never experienced before.

Oh God, he thought, what an exhausting job I've picked on! Traveling about day in, day out. It's much more irritating work than doing the actual business in the office, and on top of that there's the trouble of constant traveling, of worrying about train connections, the bed and irregular meals, casual acquaintances that are always new and never become intimate friends. The devil take it all! He felt a slight itching up on his belly; slowly pushed himself on his back nearer to the top of the bed so that he could lift his head more easily; identified the itching place which was surrounded by many small white spots the nature of which he could not understand and made to touch it with a leg, but drew the leg back immediately, for the contact made a cold shiver run through him.

He slid down again into his former position. This getting up early, he thought, makes one quite stupid. A man needs his sleep. Other commercials live like harem women. For instance, when I come back to the hotel of a morning to write up the orders I've got, these others are only sitting down to the breakfast. Let me just try that with my chief; I'd be sacked on the spot. Anyhow, that might be quite a good thing for me, who can tell? If I didn't have to hold my hand because of my parents I'd have given notice long ago, I'd have gone to the chief and told him exactly what I think of him. That would knock him endways from his desk! It's a queer way of doing, too, this sitting on high at a desk and talking down to employees, especially when they have to come

From: Franz Kafka, *The Complete Stories,* ed. Nahum N. Glatzer (New York: Schocken Books, 1971), pp. 89–105.

quite near because the chief is hard of hearing. Well, there's still hope; once I've saved enough money to pay back my parents' debts to him—that should take another five or six years—I'll do it without fail. I'll cut myself completely loose then. For the moment, though, I'd better get up, since my train goes at five.

He looked at the alarm clock ticking on the chest. Heavenly Father! he thought. It was half-past six o'clock and the hands were quietly moving on, it was even past the half-hour, it was getting on toward a quarter to seven. Had the alarm clock not gone off? From the bed one could see that it had been properly set for four o'clock; of course it must have gone off. Yes, but was it possible to sleep quietly through that ear-splitting noise? Well, he had not slept quietly, yet apparently all the more soundly for that. But what was he to do now? The next train went at seven o'clock; to catch that he would need to hurry like mad and his samples weren't even packed up, and he himself wasn't feeling particularly fresh and active. And even if he did catch the train he wouldn't avoid a row with the chief, since the firm's porter would have been waiting for the five o'clock train and would have long since reported his failure to turn up. The porter was a creature of the chief's, spineless and stupid. Well, supposing he were to say he was sick? But that would be most unpleasant and would look suspicious, since during his five years' employment he had not been ill once. The chief himself would be sure to come with the sick-insurance doctor, would reproach his parents with their son's laziness, and would cut all excuses short by referring to the insurance doctor, who of course regarded all mankind as perfectly healthy malingerers. And would he be so far wrong on this occasion? Gregor really felt quite well, apart from a drowsiness that was utterly superfluous after such a long sleep, and he was even unusually hungry.

As all this was running through his mind at top speed without his being able to decide to leave his bed—the alarm clock had just struck a quarter to seven—there came a cautious tap at the door behind the head of his bed. "Gregor," said a voice—it was his mother's—"it's a quarter to seven. Hadn't you a train to catch?" That gentle voice! Gregor had a shock as he heard his own voice answering hers, unmistakably his own voice, it was true, but with a persistent horrible twittering squeak behind it like an undertone, which left the words in their clear shape only for the first moment and then rose up reverberating around them to destroy their sense, so that one could not be sure one had heard them rightly. Gregor wanted to answer at length and explain everything, but in the circumstances he confined himself to saying: "Yes, yes, thank you, Mother, I'm getting up now." The wooden door between them must have kept the change in his voice from being noticeable outside, for his mother contented herself with this statement and shuffled away. Yet this brief exchange of words had made the other members of the family aware that Gregor was still in the house, as they had not expected, and at one of the side doors his father was already knocking, gently, yet with his fist. "Gregor, Gregor," he called, "What's the matter with you?" And after a little while he called again in a deeper voice: "Gregor! Gregor!" At the other side door his sister was saying in a low, plaintive tone; "Gregor? Aren't you well? Are you needing anything?" He answered them both at once: "I'm just ready," and did his best to make his voice sound as normal as possible by enunciating the words very clearly and leaving long pauses between them. So his father went back to his breakfast, but his sister whispered: "Gregor, open the door, do." However, he was not thinking of opening the door, and felt thankful for the prudent habit he had acquired in traveling of locking all doors during the night, even at home.

His immediate intention was to get up quietly without being disturbed, to put on his clothes and above all eat his breakfast, and only then consider what else was to be done, since in bed, he was well aware, his meditations would come to no sensible conclusion. He remembered that often enough in bed he had felt small aches and pains, probably caused by awkward postures, which had proved purely imaginary once he got up, and he looked forward eagerly to seeing this morning's delusions gradually fall away. That the change in his voice was nothing but the precursor of a severe chill, a standing ailment of commercial travelers, he had not the least possible doubt.

To get rid of the quilt was quite easy; he had only to inflate himself a little and it fell off by itself. But the next move was difficult, especially because he was so uncommonly broad. He would have needed arms and hands to hoist himself up; instead he had only the numerous little legs which never stopped waving in all directions and which he could not control in the least. When he tried to bend one of them it was the first to stretch itself straight; and did he succeed at last in making it do what he wanted, all the other legs meanwhile waved the more wildly in a high degree of unpleasant agitation. "But what's the use of lying idle in bed," said Gregor to himself.

He thought that he might get out of bed with the lower part of his body first, but this lower part, which he had not yet seen and of which he could form no clear conception, proved too difficult to move; it shifted so slowly; and when finally, almost wild with annoyance, he gathered his forces together and thrust out recklessly, he had miscalculated the direction and bumped heavily against the lower end of the bed, and the stinging pain he felt informed him that precisely this lower part of his body was at the moment probably the most sensitive.

So he tried to get the top part of himself out first, and cautiously moved his head toward the edge of the bed. That proved easy enough, and despite its breadth and mass the bulk of his body at last slowly followed the movement of his head. Still, when he finally got his head free over the edge of the bed he felt too scared to go on advancing, for after all if he let himself fall in this way it would take a miracle to keep his head from being injured. And at all costs he must not lose consciousness now, precisely now; he would rather stay in bed.

But when after a repetition of the same efforts he lay in his former position again, sighing, and watched his little legs struggling against each other more wildly than ever, if that were possible, and saw no way of bringing any order into this arbitrary confusion, he told himself again that it was impossible to stay in bed and that the most sensible course was to risk everything for the smallest hope of getting away from it. At the same time he did not forget to remind himself occasionally that cool reflection, the coolest possible, was much better than desperate resolves. In such moments he focused his eyes as sharply as possible on the window, but, unfortunately, the prospect of the morning fog, which muffled even the other side of the narrow street, brought him little encouragement and comfort. "Seven o'clock already," he said to himself when the alarm clock chimed again, "seven o'clock already and still such a thick fog." And for a little while he lay quiet, breathing lightly, as if perhaps expecting such complete repose to restore all things to their real and normal condition.

But then he said to himself: "Before it strikes a quarter past seven I must be quite out of this bed, without fail. Anyhow, by that time someone will have come from the office to ask for me, since it opens before seven." And he set himself to rocking his whole body at once in a regular rhythm, with the idea of swinging it out of the bed. If he ripped himself out in that way he could keep his head from injury by lifting it at an acute angle when he fell. His back seemed to be hard and was not likely to suffer from a fall on the carpet. His biggest worry was the loud crash he would not be able to help making, which would probably cause anxiety, if not terror, behind all the doors. Still, he must take the risk.

When he was already half out of the bed—the new method was more a game than an effort, for he needed only to hitch himself across by rocking to and fro—it struck him how simple it would be if he could get help. Two strong people—he thought of his father and the servant girl—would be amply sufficient; they would only have to thrust their arms under his convex back, lever him out of the bed, bend down with their burden, and then be patient enough to let him turn himself right over onto the floor, where it was to be hoped his legs would then find their proper function. Well, ignoring the fact that the doors were all locked, ought he really to call for help? In spite of his misery he could not suppress a smile at the very idea of it.

He had got so far that he could barely keep his equilibrium when he rocked himself strongly, and he would have to nerve himself very soon for the final decision since in five minutes' time it would be quarter past seven—when the front doorbell rang. "That's someone from the office," he said to himself, and grew almost rigid, while his little legs only jigged about all the faster. For a moment everything stayed quiet. "They're not going to open the door," said Gregor to himself, catching at some kind of irrational hope. But then of course the servant girl went as usual to the door with her heavy tread, and opened it. Gregor needed only to hear the first good morning of the visitor to know immediately who it was—the chief clerk himself. What a fate, to be condemned to work for a firm where the smallest omission at once gave rise to the gravest suspicion! Were all employees in a body nothing but scoundrels, was there not among them one single loyal devoted man who, had he wasted only an hour or so of the firm's time in a morning, was so tormented by conscience as to be driven out of his mind and actually incapable of leaving his bed? Wouldn't it really have been sufficient to send an apprentice to inquire—if any inquiry were necessary at all—did the chief clerk himself have to come and thus indicate to the entire family, an innocent family, that this suspicious circumstance could be investigated by no one less versed in affairs than himself? And more through the agitation caused by these reflections than through any act of will Gregor swung himself out of bed with all his strength. There was a loud thump, but it was not really a crash. His fall was broken to some extent by the carpet, his back, too, was less stiff than he thought, and so there was merely a dull thud, not so very startling. Only he had not lifted his head carefully enough and had hit it; he turned it and rubbed it on the carpet in pain and irritation.

"That was something falling down in there," said the chief clerk in the next room to the left. Gregor tried to suppose to himself that something like what had happened to him today might someday happen to the chief clerk; one really could not deny that it was possible. But as if in brusque reply to this supposition the chief clerk took a couple of firm steps in the next-door room and his patent leather boots creaked. From the right-hand room his sister was whispering to inform him of the situation: "Gregor, the chief clerk's here." "I know," muttered Gregor to himself; but he didn't dare to make his voice loud enough for his sister to hear it.

"Gregor," said his father now from the left-hand room, "the chief clerk has come and wants to know why you didn't catch the early train. We don't know what to say to him. Besides, he wants to talk to you in person. So open the door, please. He will be good enough to excuse the untidiness of your room." "Good morning, Mr. Samsa," the chief clerk was calling amiably meanwhile. "He's not well," said his mother to the visitor, while his father was still speaking through the door, "he's not well, sir, believe me. What else would make him miss a train! The boy thinks about nothing but his work. It makes me almost cross the way he never goes out in the evenings; he's been here the last eight days and has stayed at home every single evening. He just sits there quietly at the table reading a newspaper or looking through railway timetables. The only amusement he gets is doing fretwork. For instance, he spent two or three evenings cutting out a little picture frame; you would be surprised to see how pretty it is; it's hanging in his room; you'll see it in a minute when Gregor opens the door. I must say I'm glad you've come, sir; we should never have got him to unlock the door by ourselves; he's so obstinate; and I'm sure he's unwell, though he wouldn't have it to be so this morning." "I'm just coming," said Gregor slowly and carefully, not moving an inch for fear of losing one word of the conversation. "I can't think of any other explanation, madame," said the chief clerk, "I hope it's nothing serious. Although on the other hand I must say that we men of business—fortunately or unfortunately—very often simply have to ignore any slight indisposition, since business must be attended to." "Well, can the chief clerk come in now?" asked Gregor's father impatiently, again knocking on the door. "No," said Gregor. In the left-hand room a painful silence followed this refusal, in the right-hand room his sister began to sob.

Why didn't his sister join the others? She was probably newly out of bed and hadn't even begun to put on her clothes yet. Well, why was she crying? Because he wouldn't get up and let the chief clerk in, because he was in danger of losing his job, and because the chief would begin dunning his parents again for the old debts? Surely these were things one didn't need to worry about for the present. Gregor was still at home and not in the least thinking of deserting the family. At the moment, true, he was lying on the carpet and no one who knew the condition he was in could seriously expect him to admit the chief clerk. But for such a small discourtesy, which could plausibly be explained away somehow later on, Gregor could hardly be dismissed on the spot. And it seemed to Gregor that it would be much more sensible to leave him in peace for the present than to trouble him with tears and entreaties. Still, of course, their uncertainty bewildered them all and excused their behavior.

"Mr. Samsa," the chief clerk called now in a louder voice, "what's the matter with you? Here you are, barricading yourself in your room, giving only 'yes' and 'no' for answers, causing your parents a lot of unnecessary trouble and neglecting—I mention this only in passing—neglecting your business duties in an incredible fashion. I am speaking here in the name of your parents and of your chief, and I beg you quite seriously to give me an immediate and precise explanation. You amaze me, you amaze me. I thought you were a quiet, dependable person, and now all at once you seem bent on making a disgraceful exhibition of yourself. The chief did hint to me early this morning a possible explanation for your disappearance—with reference to the cash payments that were entrusted to you recently—but I almost pledged my solemn word of honor that this could not be so. But now that I see how incredibly obstinate you are, I no longer have the slightest desire to take your part at all. And your position in the firm is not so unassailable. I came with the intention of telling you all this in private, but since you are wasting my time so needlessly I don't see why your parents shouldn't hear it too. For some time past your work has been most unsatisfactory; this is not the season of the year for a business boom, of course, we admit that, but a season of the year for doing no business at all, that does not exist, Mr. Samsa, must not exist."

"But, sir," cried Gregor, beside himself and in his agitation forgetting everything else, "I'm just going to open the door this very minute. A slight illness, an attack of giddiness, has kept me from getting up. I'm still lying in bed. But I feel all right again. I'm getting out of bed now. Just give me a moment or two longer! I'm not quite so well as I thought. But I'm all right, really. How a thing like that can suddenly strike one down! Only last night I was quite well, my parents can tell you, or rather I did have a slight presentiment. I must have showed some sign of it. Why didn't I report it at the office! But one always thinks that an indisposition can be got over without staying in the house. Oh sir, do spare my parents! All that you're reproaching me with now has no foundation; no one has ever said a word to me about it. Perhaps you haven't looked at the last orders I sent in. Anyhow, I can still catch the eight o'clock train, I'm much the better for my few hours' rest. Don't let me detain you here, sir; I'll be attending to business very soon, and do be good enough to tell the chief so and to make my excuses to him!"

And while all this was tumbling out pell-mell and Gregor hardly knew what he was saying, he had reached the chest quite easily, perhaps because of the practice he had had in bed, and was now trying to lever himself upright by means of it. He meant actually to open the door, actually to show himself and speak to the chief clerk; he was eager to find out what the others, after all their insistence, would say at the sight of him. If they were horrified then the responsibility was no longer his and he could stay quiet. But if they took it calmly, then he had no reason either to be upset, and could really get to the station for the eight o'clock train if he hurried. At first he slipped down a few times from the polished surface of the chest, but at length with a last heave he stood upright; he paid no more attention to the pains in the lower part of his body, however they smarted. Then he let himself fall against the back of a nearby chair, and clung with his little legs to the edges of it. That brought him into control of himself again and he stopped speaking, for now he could listen to what the chief clerk was saying.

"Did you understand a word of it?" the chief clerk was asking; "surely he can't be trying to make fools of us?" "Oh dear," cried his mother, in tears, "perhaps he's terribly ill and we're tormenting him. Grete! Grete!" she called out then. "Yes Mother?" called his sister from the other side. They were calling to each other across Gregor's room. "You must go this minute for the doctor. Gregor is ill. Go for the doctor, quick. Did you hear how he was speaking?" "That was no human voice," said the chief clerk in a voice noticeably low beside the shrillness of the mother's. "Anna! Anna!" his father was calling through the hall to the kitchen, clapping his hands, "get a locksmith at once!" And the two girls were already running through the hall with a swish of skirts—how could his sister have got dressed so quickly?—and were tearing the front door open. There was no sound of its closing again; they had evidently left it open, as one does in houses where some great misfortune has happened.

But Gregor was now much calmer. The words he uttered were no longer understandable, apparently, although they seemed clear enough to him, even clearer than before, perhaps because his ear had grown accustomed to the sound of them. Yet at any rate people now believed that something was wrong with him, and were ready to help him. The positive certainty with which these first measures had been taken comforted him. He felt himself drawn once more into the human circle and hoped for great and remarkable results from both the doctor and the locksmith, without really distinguishing precisely between them. To make his voice as clear as possible for the decisive conversation that was now imminent he coughed a little, as quietly as he could, of course, since this noise too might not sound like a human cough for all he was able to judge. In the next room meanwhile there was complete silence. Perhaps his parents were sitting at the table with the chief clerk, whispering, perhaps they were all leaning against the door and listening.

Slowly Gregor pushed the chair toward the door, then let go of it, caught hold of the door for support—the soles at the end of his little legs were somewhat sticky—and rested against it for a moment after his efforts. Then he set himself to turning the key in the lock with his mouth. It seemed, unhappily, that he hadn't really any teeth—what could he grip the key with?—but on the other hand his jaws were certainly very strong; with their help he did manage to set the key in motion, heedless of the fact that he was undoubtedly damaging them somewhere, since a brown fluid issued from his mouth, flowed over the key, and dripped on the floor. "Just listen to that," said the chief clerk next door; "he's turning the key." That was a great encouragement to Gregor; but they should all have shouted encouragement to him, his father and mother too: "Go on, Gregor," they should have called out, "keep going, hold on to that key!" And in the belief that they were all following his efforts intently, he clenched his jaws recklessly on the key with all the force at his command. As the turning of the key progressed he circled around the lock, holding on now only with his mouth, pushing on the key, as required, or pulling it down again with all the weight of his body. The louder click of the finally yielding lock literally quickened Gregor. With a deep breath of relief he said to himself: "So I didn't need the locksmith," and laid his head on the handle to open the door wide.

Since he had to pull the door toward him, he was still invisible when it was really wide open. He had to edge himself slowly around the near half of the double door, and to do it very carefully if he was not to fall plump upon his back just on the threshold. He was still carrying out this difficult maneuver, with no time to observe anything else, when he heard the chief clerk utter a loud "Oh!"—it sounded like a gust of wind—and now he could see the man, standing as he was nearest to the door, clapping one hand before his open mouth and slowly backing away as if driven by some invisible steady pressure. His mother—in spite of the chief clerk's being there her hair was still undone and sticking up in all directions—first clasped her hands and looked at his father, then took two steps toward Gregor and fell on the floor among her outspread skirts, her face quite hidden on her breast. His father knotted his fist with a fierce expression on his face as if he meant to knock Gregor back into his room, then looked uncertainly around the living room, covered his eyes with his hands, and wept till his great chest heaved.

Gregor did not go now into the living room, but leaned against the inside of the firmly shut wing of the door, so that only half his body was visible and his head above it bending sideways to look at the others. The light had meanwhile strengthened; on the other side of the street one could see clearly a section of the endlessly long, dark gray building opposite—it was a hospital—abruptly punctuated by its row of regular windows; the rain was still falling, but only in large singly discernible and literally singly splashing drops. The breakfast dishes were set out on the table lavishly, for breakfast was the most important meal of the day to Gregor's father, who lingered it out for hours over various newspapers. Right opposite Gregor on the wall hung a photograph of himself in military service, as a lieutenant, hand on sword, a carefree smile on his face, inviting one to respect his uniform and military bearing. The door leading to the hall was open, and one could see that the front door stood open too, showing the landing beyond and the beginning of the stairs going down.

"Well," said Gregor, knowing perfectly that he was the only one who had retained any composure, "I'll put my clothes on at once, pack up my samples, and start off. Will you only let me go? You see, sir, I'm not obstinate, and I'm willing to work; traveling is a hard life, but I couldn't live without it. Where are you going, sir? To the office? Yes? Will you give a true account of all this? One can be temporarily incapacitated, but that's just the moment for remembering former services and bearing in mind that later on, when the incapacity has been got over, one will certainly work with all the more industry and concentration. I'm loyally bound to serve the chief, you know that very well. Besides, I have to provide for my parents and my sister. I'm in great difficulties, but I'll get out of them again. Don't make things any worse for me than they are. Stand up for me in the firm. Travelers are not popular there, I know. People think they earn sacks of money and just have a good time. A prejudice there's no particular reason for revising. But you, sir, have a more comprehensive view of affairs than the rest of the staff, yes, let me tell you in confidence, a more comprehensive view than the chief himself, who, being the owner, lets his judgment easily be swayed against one of his employees. And you know very well that the traveler, who is never seen in the office almost the whole year around, can so easily fall a victim to gossip and ill luck and unfounded complaints, which he mostly knows nothing about, except when he comes back exhausted from his rounds, and only then suffers in person from their evil consequences, which he can no longer trace back to the original causes. Sir, sir, don't go away without a word to me to show that you think me in the right at least to some extent!"

But at Gregor's very first words the chief clerk had already backed away and only stared at him with parted lips over one twitching shoulder. And while Gregor was speaking he did not stand still one moment but stole away toward the door, without taking his eyes off Gregor, yet only an inch at a time, as if obeying some secret injunction to leave the room. He was already at the hall, and the suddenness with which he took his last step out of the living room would have made one believe he had burned the sole of his foot. Once in the hall he stretched his right arm before him toward the staircase, as if some supernatural power were waiting there to deliver him.

Gregor perceived that the chief clerk must on no account be allowed to go away in this frame of mind if his position in the firm were not to be endangered to the utmost. His parents did not understand this so well; they had convinced themselves in the course of years that Gregor was settled for life in this firm, and besides they were so preoccupied with their immediate troubles that all foresight had forsaken them. Yet Gregor had this foresight. The chief clerk must be detained, soothed, persuaded, and finally won over; the whole future of Gregor and his family depended on it! If only his sister had been there! She was intelligent; she had begun to cry while Gregor was still lying quietly on his back. And no doubt the chief clerk, so partial to ladies, would have been guided by her; she would have shut the door of the flat and in the hall talked him out of his horror. But she was not there, and Gregor would have to handle the situation himself. And without remembering that he was still unaware what powers of movement he possessed, without even remembering that his words in all possibility, indeed in all likelihood, would again be unintelligible, he let go the wing of the door, pushed himself through the opening, started to walk toward the chief clerk, who was already ridiculously clinging with both hands to the railing on the landing; but immediately, as he was feeling for a support, he fell down with a little cry upon all his numerous legs. Hardly was he down when he experienced for the first time this morning a sense of physical comfort; his legs had firm ground under them; they were completely obedient, as he noted with joy; they even strove to carry him forward in whatever direction he chose; and he was inclined to believe that a final relief from all his sufferings was at hand. But in the same moment as he found himself on the floor, rocking with suppressed eagerness to move, not far from his mother, indeed just in front of her, she, who had seemed so completely crushed, sprang all at once to her feet, her arms and fingers outspread, cried: "Help, for God's sake, help!" bent her head down as if to see Gregor better, yet on the contrary kept backing senselessly away; had quite forgotten that the laden table stood behind her; sat upon it hastily, as if in absence of mind, when she bumped into it; and seemed altogether unaware that the big coffeepot beside her was upset and pouring coffee in a flood over the carpet.

"Mother, Mother," said Gregor in a low voice, and looked up at her. The chief clerk, for the moment, had quite slipped from his mind; instead, he could not resist snapping his jaws together at the sight of the streaming coffee. That made his mother scream again, she fled from the table and fell into the arms of his father, who hastened to catch her. But

Gregor had now no time to spare for his parents; the chief clerk was already on the stairs; with his chin on the banisters he was taking one last backward look. Gregor made a spring, to be as sure as possible of overtaking him; the chief clerk must have divined his intention, for he leaped down several steps and vanished; he was still yelling "Ugh!" and it echoed through the whole staircase.

Unfortunately, the flight of the chief clerk seemed completely to upset Gregor's father, who had remained relatively calm until now, for instead of running after the man himself, or at least not hindering Gregor in his pursuit, he seized in his right hand the walking stick that the chief clerk had left behind on a chair, together with a hat and greatcoat, snatched in his left hand a large newspaper from the table, and began stamping his feet and flourishing the stick and the newspaper to drive Gregor back into his room. No entreaty of Gregor's availed, indeed no entreaty was even understood, however humbly he bent his head his father only stamped on the floor the more loudly. Behind his father his mother had torn open a window, despite the cold weather, and was leaning far out of it with her face in her hands. A strong draught set in from the street to the staircase, the window curtains blew in, the newspapers on the table fluttered, stray pages whisked over the floor. Pitilessly Gregor's father drove him back, hissing and crying "Shoo!" like a savage. But Gregor was quite unpracticed in walking backwards, it really was a slow business. If he only had a chance to turn around he could get back to his room at once, but he was afraid of exasperating his father by the slowness of such a rotation and at any moment the stick in his father's hand might hit him a fatal blow on the back or on the head. In the end, however, nothing else was left for him to do since to his horror he observed that in moving backwards he could not even control the direction he took; and so, keeping an anxious eye on his father all the time over his shoulder, he began to turn around as quickly as he could, which was in reality very slowly. Perhaps his father noted his good intentions, for he did not interfere except every now and then to help him in the maneuver from a distance with the point of the stick. If only he would have stopped making that unbearable hissing noise! It made Gregor quite lose his head. He had turned almost completely around when the hissing noise so distracted him that he even turned a little the wrong way again. But when at last his head was fortunately right in front of the doorway, it appeared that his body was too broad simply to get through the opening. His father, of course, in his present mood was far from thinking of such a thing as opening the other half of the door, to let Gregor have enough space. He had merely the fixed idea of driving Gregor back into his room as quickly as possible. He would never have suffered Gregor to make the circumstantial preparations for standing up on end and perhaps slipping his way through the door. Maybe he was now making more noise than ever to urge Gregor forward, as if no obstacle impeded him; to Gregor, anyhow, the noise in his rear sounded no longer like the voice of one single father; this was really no joke, and Gregor thrust himself—come what might—into the doorway. One side of his body rose up, he was tilted at an angle in the doorway, his flank was quite bruised, horrid blotches stained the white door, soon he was stuck fast and, left to himself, could not have moved at all, his legs on one side fluttered trembling in the air, those on the other were crushed painfully to the floor—when from behind his father gave him a strong push which was literally a deliverance and he flew far into the room, bleeding freely. The door was slammed behind him with the stick, and then at last there was silence. . . .

✦ Reading 45 ✦

The Good Soldier Schweik

Jaroslav Hasek

Drafted into the Austro-Hungarian army during World War I, Schweik, of Czech birth, has little interest in the war. Whether he is simple-minded or simply crafty is not clear as, in this episode, he "carries out" his duties as assistant to an army chaplain. Clearly, nothing is sacred either to Schweik or his creator, Hasek.

II.

Schweik had been the chaplain's orderly for three whole days, and during this period he had seen him only once. On the third day an orderly arrived from Lieutenant Helmich telling Schweik to come and fetch the chaplain.

On the way, the orderly told Schweik that the chaplain had had a row with the lieutenant, had smashed a piano, was dead drunk, and refused to go home. Lieutenant Helmich, who was also drunk, had thrown the chaplain into the passage, where he was dozing on the ground by the doorway.

When Schweik reached the spot, he shook the chaplain, and when the latter opened his eyes and began to mumble, Schweik saluted and said, "Beg to report, sir, I'm here."

"And what do you want here?"

"Beg to report, sir, I've come to fetch you."

"So you've come to fetch me, have you? And where are we going?"

"Home, sir."

"And what have I got to go home for? Aren't I at home?"

"Beg to report, sir, you're on the floor in somebody else's home."

"And—how—did—I get here?"

"Beg to report, sir, you were paying a call."

"Not—not—not paying a call. You're—you're—wrong there."

Schweik lifted the chaplain and propped him up against the wall. While Schweik was holding him, the chaplain floundered from side to side and clung to him, saying, "You're letting me fall." And then, once more, with a fatuous smile, he repeated, "You're letting me fall." At last Schweik managed to squeeze the chaplain up against the wall, whereupon he began to doze again in his new posture.

Schweik woke him up.

"What d'you want?" asked the chaplain, making a vain attempt to drag himself along by the wall and to sit up. "Who are you, anyway?"

"Beg to report, sir," replied Schweik, pushing the chaplain back against the wall, "I'm your batman, sir."

"I haven't got a batman," said the chaplain with some effort, making a fresh attempt to tumble on top of Schweik. There was a little tussle which ended in Schweik's complete victory. Schweik took advantage of this to drag the chaplain down the stairs into the entrance hall, where the chaplain tried to stop Schweik from taking him into the street. "I don't know you," he kept telling Schweik during their tussle. "Do you know Otto Katz? That's me.

"I've been to the Archbishop's," he yelled, catching hold of the door in the entrance hall. "The Vatican takes a great interest in me. Is that clear to you?"

Schweik assented and began to talk to the chaplain as man to man. "Let go of that, I tell you," he said, "or I'll give you such a wallop. We're going home; so now stow your gab."

The chaplain let go of the door and clung to Schweik, who pushed him aside and then carried him out into the street, where he drew him along the pavement in a homeward direction.

"Who's that bloke?" asked one of the onlookers in the street.

From: Jaroslav Hasek, *The Good Soldier Schweik* (New York: Signet Classics, 1963), pp. 111–123.

"That's my brother," replied Schweik. "He came home on leave and when he saw me, he was so happy that he got tight, because he thought I was dead."

The chaplain, who caught the last few words, stood up straight and faced the onlookers. "Any of you who are dead must report themselves to headquarters within three days so that their corpses can be consecrated."

And he lapsed into silence, endeavoring to fall nose-first onto the pavement, while Schweik held him under the arm and drew him along homeward. With his head thrust forward and his feet trailing behind and dangling like those of a cat with a broken back, the chaplain was muttering to himself, *"Dominus vobiscum—et cum spiritu tuo. Dominus vobiscum."*

When they reached a cab rank, Schweik propped the chaplain in a sitting posture up against a wall and went to negotiate with the cabmen about the fare. One of the cabmen declared that he knew the chaplain very well, that he'd driven him home once and would never do it again.

"He spewed all over my cab," he announced in plain terms, "and then he never paid his fare. I was carting him around for more than two hours before he found out where he lived. And a week later, when I'd been after him about three times, he paid me five crowns for the whole lot."

After long discussions, one of the cabmen agreed to take them.

Schweik went back to the chaplain, who had now fallen asleep. Somebody had removed his bowler hat (for he usually put on civilian clothing when he went for a walk) and taken it away.

Schweik woke him up and with the help of the cabman got him inside the cab. There the chaplain collapsed in a complete torpor and took Schweik for Colonel Just of the 75th Infantry Regiment. He kept muttering, "Don't be too hard on me, sir. I know I'm a bit of a cad." At one moment, it seemed as if the jolting of the cab against the curb was bringing him to his senses. He sat up straight and began to sing snatches from some unrecognizable song. But then he lapsed once again into a complete torpor and turning to Schweik with a wink he inquired, "How are you today, dear lady?"

Then, after a brief pause, "Where are you going for your summer holidays?"

Evidently he saw everything double, for he then remarked, "So you've got a grown-up son," and he pointed to Schweik. "Sit down," shouted Schweik, when the chaplain started trying to climb onto the seat, "or I'll teach you how to behave, see if I don't."

The chaplain thereupon became quiet and his little piglike eyes stared out of the cab in a state of complete bewilderment as to what was happening to him. Then, with a melancholy expression, he propped his head up in his hands and began to sing:

"I seem to be the only one
Whom nobody loves at all."

But he immediately broke off and remarked in German, "Excuse me, sir, you don't know what you're talking about. I can sing whatever I like." Whereupon he attempted to whistle some tune or other, but the noise which issued from his lips was so loud that the cab came to a standstill. Schweik told the cabman to drive on and the chaplain then tried to light his cigarette holder.

"It won't burn," he said despondently, when he had used up all his matches. "You keep on blowing at it."

But again he at once lost the thread of continuity and started laughing.

"This is no end of a lark. We're in a tram, aren't we?"

He began to search his pockets.

"I've lost my ticket," he shouted. "Stop the tram. I must find my ticket."

And with a gesture of resignation, "All right. Let them drive on."

Then he began to babble. "In the vast majority of cases . . . Yes, all right . . . In all cases . . . You're wrong . . . Second floor . . . That's only an excuse . . . That's your concern, not mine, dear lady . . . Bill, please . . . I've had a black coffee."

In a semidream he began to squabble with an imaginary adversary who was disputing his rights to a seat by the window in a restaurant. Then he began to take the cab for a train and leaning out, he yelled in Czech and German, "Nymburk, all change." Schweik thereupon pulled him back and the chaplain forgot about the train and began to imitate various farmyard noises. He kept up the cock crow longest and his clarion call was trumpeted forth in fine style from the cab. For a while he became altogether very active and restless, trying to get out of the cab and hurling terms of abuse at the people past whom they drove. After that he threw his handkerchief out of the cab and shouted to the cabman to stop, because he had lost his luggage. Next he started telling a story: "At Budejovice there was a drummer. He got married. A year later he died." He burst out laughing. "Isn't that screamingly funny?"

All this time Schweik treated the chaplain with relentless severity. Each time that he made various frolicsome attempts to get out of the cab, to smash the seat and so on, Schweik gave him one or two hard punches in the ribs, which treatment he accepted with remarkable lethargy. Only once did he put up any sort of resistance by trying to jump out of the cab. He said that he wouldn't go a step further, because he knew that they were on their way to Podmokly and not to Budejovice, as they ought to be. Within a minute Schweik had settled his attempt at mutiny and forced him to resume his previous posture on the seat, at the same time taking care to stop him from falling asleep. His mildest remark in this connection was, "Keep awake, or you'll be a dead'un."

All at once the chaplain was overcome by a fit of melancholy and he began to cry. Tearfully he asked Schweik whether he had a mother.

"I'm all alone in the world, my friends," he shouted from the cab. "Take pity on me!"

"Stop that row," said Schweik. "Shut up, or everybody'll say you're boozed."

"I've not drunk a thing, old boy," replied the chaplain. "I'm as sober as a judge."

But suddenly he stood up and saluted. "Beg to report, sir, I'm drunk," he said in German. And then he repeated ten times in succession, with a heartfelt accent of despair, "I'm a dirty dog." And turning to Schweik he persistently begged and entreated, "Throw me out of the cab. What are you taking me with you for?"

He sat down again and muttered, "Rings are forming around the moon. I say, Captain, do you believe in the immortality of the soul? Can a horse get into heaven?"

He started laughing heartily, but after a while he began to mope and gazed apathetically at Schweik, remarking, "I say, excuse me, but I've seen you before somewhere. Weren't you in Vienna? I remember you from the seminary."

For a while he amused himself by reciting Latin verses:

"Aurea prima satas aetas, qual vindice nullo."

"This won't do," he then said. "Throw me out. Why won't you throw me out? I shan't hurt myself.

"I want to fall on my nose," he declared in a resolute tone. Then, beseechingly, he continued, "I say, old chap, give me a smack in the eye."

"Do you want one or several?" inquired Schweik.

"Two."

"Well, there you are then."

The chaplain counted out aloud the smacks as he received them, beaming with delight.

"That does you good," he said, "it helps the digestion. Give me another on the mouth.

"Thanks awfully," he exclaimed, when Schweik had promptly complied with his request. "Now I'm quite satisfied. I say, tear my waistcoat, will you?"

He manifested the most diverse desires. He wanted Schweik to dislocate his foot, to throttle him for a while, to cut his nails, to pull out his front teeth. He exhibited a yearning for martyrdom, demanding that his head should be cut off, put in a bag, and thrown into the river.

"Stars around my head would suit me nicely," he said with enthusiasm. "I should need ten of them."

Then he began to talk about horse racing and rapidly passed on to the topic of the ballet, but that did not detain him for long, either.

"Can you dance the czardas?" he asked Schweik. "Can you do the bunny hug? It's like this. . . ."

He wanted to jump on top of Schweik, who accordingly began to use his fists on him and then laid him down on the seat.

"I want something," shouted the chaplain, "but I don't know what. Do you know what I want?" And he drooped his head in complete resignation.

"What's it matter to me what I want?" he said solemnly. "And it doesn't matter to you, either. I don't know you. How dare you stare at me like that? Can you fence?"

For a moment he became more aggressive and tried to push Schweik off the seat. Afterward, when Schweik had quieted him down by a frank display of his physical superiority, the chaplain asked, "Is today Monday or Friday?"

He was also anxious to know whether it was December or June and he exhibited a great aptitude for asking the most diverse questions, such as: "Are you married? Do you like Gorgonzola cheese? Have you got any bugs at home? Are you quite well? Has your dog had the mange?"

He became communicative. He said that he had not yet paid for his riding boots, whip, and saddle, that some years ago he had suffered from a certain disease which had been cured with permanganate.

"There was no time to think of anything else," he said with a belch. "You may think it's a nuisance, but, hm, hm, what am I to do? Hm, hm. Tell me that. So you must excuse me.

"Thermos flasks," he continued, forgetting what he had just been talking about, "are receptacles which will keep beverages and food stuffs at their original temperature. Which game do you think is fairer, bridge or poker?

"Oh yes, I've seen you somewhere before," he shouted, trying to embrace Schweik. "We used to go to school together.

"You're a good chap," he said tenderly, stroking his foot. "You've quite grown up since I saw you last. The pleasure of seeing you makes up for all my troubles."

He waxed poetic and began to talk about the return to the sunshine of happy faces and warm hearts.

Then he knelt down and began to pray, laughing the whole time.

When finally they reached their destination, it was very difficult to get him out of the cab.

"We aren't there yet," he shouted. "Help, help! I'm being kidnapped. I want to drive on."

He had to be wrenched out of the cab like a boiled snail from its shell. At one moment it seemed as if he were going to be pulled apart, because his legs got mixed up with the seat. At last, however, he was dragged through the entrance hall and up the stairs into his rooms, where he was thrown like a sack onto the sofa. He declared that he would not pay for the cab because he had not ordered it, and it took more than a quarter of an hour to explain to him that it was a cab. Even then he continued to argue the point.

"You're trying to do me down," he declared, winking at Schweik and the cabman. "We walked all the way here."

But suddenly, in an outburst of generosity, he threw his purse to the cabman. "Here, take the lot, *ich kann bezahlen.* A kreutzer more or less doesn't matter to me."

To be strictly accurate, he ought to have said that thirty-six kreutzers more or less didn't matter to him, for that was all the purse contained. Fortunately, the cabman submitted it to a close inspection, referring the while to smacks in the eye.

"All right, then, you give me one," replied the chaplain. "Do you think I couldn't stand it? I could stand five from you."

The cabman discovered a five-crown piece in the chaplain's waistcoat pocket. He departed, cursing his fate and the chaplain, who had wasted his time and reduced his takings.

The chaplain got to sleep very slowly, because he kept making fresh schemes. He was anxious to do all kinds of things, to play the piano, to have a dancing lesson, to fry some fish, and so on. But at last he fell asleep.

III.

When Schweik entered the chaplain's room in the morning, he found him reclining on the sofa in a very dejected mood.

"I can't remember," he said, "how I got out of bed and landed on the sofa."

"You never went to bed, sir. As soon as we got here, we put you on the sofa. That was as much as we could manage."

"And what sort of things did I do? Did I do anything at all? Was I drunk?"

"Not half you wasn't," replied Schweik. "Canned to the wide, sir. In fact, you had a little dose of the D.T.'s. It strikes me, sir, that a change of clothes and a wash wouldn't do you any harm."

"I feel as if someone had given me a good hiding," complained the chaplain, "and then I've got an awful thirst on me. Did I kick up a row yesterday?"

"Oh, nothing to speak of, sir. And as for your thirst, why, that's the result of the thirst you had yesterday. It's not so easy to get rid of. I used to know a cabinetmaker who got drunk for the first time in 1910 on New Year's Eve and the morning of January first he had such a thirst on him and felt so seedy that he bought a herring and then started drinking again. He did that every day for four years and nothing can be done for him because he always buys his herrings on a Saturday to last him the whole week. It's one of those vicious circles that our old sergeant major in the Ninety-first Regiment used to talk about."

The chaplain was thoroughly out of sorts and had a bad fit of the blues. Anyone listening to him at that moment would have supposed that he regularly attended those teetotal lectures, the gist of which was, "Let us proclaim a life-and-death struggle against alcohol which slaughters the best men," and that he was a reader of that edifying work *A Hundred Sparks From the Ethical Anvil.* It is true that he slightly modified the views expressed them. "If," he said, "a chap drank high-class beverages, such as arak, maraschino, or cognac, it'd be all right. But what I drank yesterday was gin. It's a marvel to me how I can swallow so much of the stuff. The taste of it's disgusting. It's got no color and it burns your throat. And if it was at least the real thing, distilled from the juniper like I've drunk in Moravia—but the gin I had yesterday was made of some sort of wood alcohol mixed with oily bilge. Just listen to the way I croak.

"Brandy's poison," he decided. "It must be the real original stuff and not produced at a low temperature in a factory by a pack of Jews. It's the same with rum. Good rum's a rarity. Now, if I only had some genuine cherry brandy here," he sighed, "it'd put my stomach right in no time. The sort of stuff that Captain Schnabel's got."

He began to search in his pockets and inspected his purse.

"Holy Moses! I've got thirty-six kreutzers. What about selling the sofa?" he reflected. "What do you think? Will anyone buy a sofa? I'll tell the landlord that I've lent it or that someone's pinched it from me. No, I'll leave the sofa. I'll send you to Captain Schnabel to see if you can get him to lend me a hundred crowns. He won some money at cards the day before yesterday. If he won't fork out, try Lieutenant Mahler in the barracks at Vrsovice. If that's no go, try Captain Fischer at Hradcany. Tell him I've got to pay for the horse's fodder and that I've blued the money on booze. And if he don't come up to scratch, why we'll have to pawn the piano, and be blowed to them. I'll write a note that'll do just as well for one as the other. Don't let them put you off. Say that I'm absolutely stony broke. You can pitch any yarn you please, but don't come back empty-handed or I'll send you to the front. And ask Captain Schnabel where he gets that cherry brandy, and then buy two bottles of it."

Schweik carried out his task in brilliant style. His simplicity and his honest countenance aroused complete confidence in what he said. He deemed it inexpedient to tell Captain Schnabel, Captain Fischer, and Lieutenant Mahler that the chaplain owed money for the horse's fodder, but he thought it best to support his application by stating that the chaplain was at his wit's end about a paternity order. And he got the money from all of them.

When he produced the 300 crowns on his victorious return from the expedition, the chaplain, who in the meanwhile had washed and changed, was very surprised.

"I got the whole lot at one go," said Schweik, "so as we shouldn't have to worry our heads about money again tomorrow or the next day. It was a fairly easy job, although I had to beg and pray of Captain Schnabel before I could get anything out of him. Oh, he's a brute. But when I told him about our paternity case—"

"Paternity case?" repeated the chaplain, horrified.

"Yes, paternity case, sir. You know, paying girls so much a week. You told me to pitch any yarn I pleased, and that's all I could think of. Down our way there was a cobbler who had to pay money like that to five different girls. It fairly drove him crazy and he had to go and borrow from people, but everyone took his word for it that he was in the deuce of a fix. They asked me what sort of a girl it was and I told them she was a very smart little bit, not fifteen yet. Then they wanted to have her address."

"You've made a nice mess of it, I must say," sighed the chaplain and began to pace the room.

"This is a pretty kettle of fish," he said, clutching at his head. "Oh, what a headache I've got."

"I gave them the address of a deaf old lady down our street," explained Schweik. "I wanted to do the thing properly, because orders are orders. I wasn't going to let them put me off and I had to think of something. And now there's some men waiting in the passage for that piano. I brought them along with me, so as they can take it to the pawnshop for us. It'll be a good thing when that piano's gone. We'll have more room and we'll have more money, too. That'll keep our minds easy for a few days. And if the landlord asks what we've done with the piano, I'll tell him some of the wires are broke and we've sent it to the factory to be repaired. I've already told that to the house porter's wife so as she won't think it funny when they take the piano away in a van. And I've found a customer for the sofa. He's a secondhand furniture dealer—a friend of mine, and he's coming here in the afternoon. You can get a good price for leather sofas nowadays."

"Is there anything else you've done?" inquired the chaplain, still holding his head and showing signs of despair.

"Beg to report, sir, I've brought five bottles of that cherry brandy like Captain Schnabel has, instead of the two you said. You see, now we'll have some in stock and we shan't be hard up for a drink. Shall I see about that piano before the pawnshop closes?"

The chaplain replied with a gesture signifying his hopeless plight. And in a trice the piano was being stowed away in the van.

When Schweik got back from the pawnshop he found the chaplain sitting with an open bottle of cherry brandy in front of him, and fuming because he had been given an underdone cutlet for lunch. He was again tipsy. He declared to Schweik that on the next day he would turn over a new leaf. Drinking alcoholic beverages was, he said, rank materialism and man was made to live the life of the spirit. He talked in a philosophical strain for about half an hour. When he had opened the third bottle, the secondhand furniture dealer arrived and the chaplain sold him the sofa for a mere song. He asked him to stop and have a chat and he was very disappointed when the dealer excused himself, as he had to go and buy a night commode.

"I'm sorry I haven't got one," said the chaplain regretfully, "but a man can't think of everything."

After the secondhand furniture dealer had gone, the chaplain started an affable little talk with Schweik, in the course of which he drank another bottle. A part of the conversation dealt with the chaplain's personal attitude toward women and cards. They sat there for a long time. And when evening came, it overtook Schweik and the chaplain in friendly discourse.

In the night, however, there was a change in the situation. The chaplain reverted to the state in which he had been on the previous day. He mixed Schweik up with somebody else and said to him, "Here, don't go away. Do you remember that redheaded cadet in the transport section?"

This idyllic interlude continued until Schweik said to the chaplain, "I've had enough of this. Now you're going to toddle along to bed and have a good snooze, see?"

"I'll toddle along, my dear boy, of course I will," babbled the chaplain. "Do you remember we were in the Fifth together and I used to do your Greek exercises for you? You've got a villa at Zbraslav. And you can go for the steamer trips on the Vltava. Do you know what the Vltava is?"

Schweik made him take his boots off and undress. The chaplain obeyed, but addressed a protest to unknown persons: "You see, gentlemen," he said to the cupboard, "how my relatives treat me.

"I refuse to asknowledge my relatives," he suddenly decided, getting into bed. "Even if heaven and earth conspire against me, I refuse to acknowledge them."

And the room resounded with the chaplain's snoring.

IV.

It was about this time that Schweik paid a visit to Mrs. Müller, his old charwoman. The door was opened to him by Mrs. Müller's cousin, who amid tears informed him that Mrs. Müller had been arrested on the same day on which she had taken Schweik in a Bath chair to the army medical board. They had tried the old lady before a court-martial, and as they had no evidence against her, they had taken her to the internment camp at Steinhof. There was a postcard from her. Schweik took this household relic and read:

Dear Aninka,

We are Very comfortable hear and are all well. The Woman on the bed next to mine has Spotted . . . and their are also some with small . . . Otherwise, all is well.

We have plenty to eat and collect Potato . . . for Soup, I have heard that Mr. Schweik is . . . so find out somehow wear he is berried so that after the War we can put some Flowers on his grave. I forgot to tell you that in the Attic in a dark corner there is a box with a little Dog, a terrier puppy, in it. But he has had nothing to eat for several Weeks ever since they came to fetch me to . . . So I think it must be to late and the littel Dog is also . . .

Across the letter had been stamped a pink inscription: "*Zensuriert k. k. Konzentrationslager, Steinhof.*

"And the little dog *was* dead," sobbed Mrs. Müller's cousin. "And you'd never recognize the place where you used to live. I've got some dressmakers lodging there. And they've turned the place into a regular drawing room. Fashion pictures on all the walls and flowers in the windows."

Mrs. Müller's cousin was thoroughly upset.

Amid continued sobbing and lamentation she finally expressed the fear that Schweik had run away from the army and wanted to bring about her downfall also and plunge her into misery. She wound up by talking to him as if he were an infamous adventurer.

"That's one of the best jokes I've heard," said Schweik. "I'm fairly tickled to death by it. Well, I don't mind telling you, Mrs. Kejr, you guessed it right, first go. I have done a bunk. But first of all I had to do in fifteen sergeants and sergeant majors. Only don't tell anyone. . . ."

And as Schweik departed from the home which had given him so chilly a welcome, he said, "Mrs. Kejr, there's some collars and shirt fronts of mine at the laundry. You might go and fetch them for me, so that when I come back from the army, I'll have some civilian togs to put on. And see that the moths don't get at my things in the wardrobe. Well, give me best respects to the young ladies who are sleeping in my bed."

Then Schweik went to see what was going on at The Flagon. When Mrs. Palivec saw him, she said that she wouldn't serve him with any drink, because he'd probably taken French leave.

"My husband," she said, beginning to harp upon a now ancient topic, "he was as careful as could be and there he is, poor fellow, in prison, though as innocent as a babe unborn. And yet there's people going about scot-free who've run away from the army. They were looking for you here again last week.

"We was more careful than you," she concluded her discourse, "and now look at the bad luck we've had. It ain't everyone who's as lucky as what you are."

An elderly man, a locksmith from Smichow, had overheard these remarks and he now came up to Schweik, saying, "Do you mind waiting for me outside? I'd like to have a word with you."

In the street it turned out that from what Mrs. Palivec had said he took Schweik for a deserter. He told him he had a son who had also run away from the army and was hiding with his grandmother. Although Schweik assured him that he was not a deserter, he pressed a ten-crown piece into his hand.

"Just to keep you going for a bit," he explained, taking him into a wineshop around the corner. "I know how things are with you. Don't you worry. I won't give you away."

It was late at night when Schweik got back, but the chaplain was not yet at home. He did not turn up till the morning, when he woke Schweik up and said, "Tomorrow we're going to celebrate Mass for the troops. Make some black coffee and put some rum into it. Or better still, brew some grog."

✦ Reading 46 ✦

A Room of One's Own

Virginia Woolf

Chapter One

But, you may say, we asked you to speak about women and fiction—what has that got to do with a room of one's own? I will try to explain. When you asked me to speak about women and fiction I sat down on the banks of a river and began to wonder what the words meant. They might mean simply a few remarks about Fanny Burney; a few more about Jane Austen; a tribute to the Brontës and a sketch of Haworth Parsonage under snow; some witticisms if possible about Miss Mitford; a respectful allusion to George Eliot; a reference to Mrs. Gaskell and one would have done. But at second sight the words seemed not so simple. The title women and fiction might mean, and you may have meant it to mean, women and what they are like; or it might mean women and the fiction that they write; or it might mean women and the fiction that is written about them; or it might mean that somehow all three are inextricably mixed together and you want me to consider them in that light. But when I began to consider the subject in this last way, which seemed the most interesting, I soon saw that it had one fatal drawback. I should never be able to come to a conclusion. I should never be able to fulfil what is, I understand, the first duty of a lecturer—to hand you after an hour's discourse a nugget of pure truth to wrap up between the pages of your notebooks and keep on the mantel-piece for ever. All I could do was to offer you an opinion upon one minor point—a woman must have money and a room of her own if she is to write fiction; and that, as you will see, leaves the great problem of the true nature of woman and the true nature of fiction unsolved. I have shirked the duty of coming to a conclusion upon these two questions—women and fiction remain, so far as I am concerned, unsolved problems. But in order to make some amends I am going to do what I can to show you how I arrived at this opinion about the room and the money. I am going to develop in your presence as fully and freely as I can the train of thought which led me to think this. Perhaps if I lay bare the ideas, the prejudices, that lie behind this statement you will find that they have some bearing upon women and some upon fiction. At any rate, when a subject is highly controversial—and any question about sex is that—one cannot hope to tell the truth. One can only show how one came to hold whatever opinion one does hold. One can only give one's audience the chance of drawing their own conclusions as they observe the limitations, the prejudices, the idiosyncrasies of the speaker. Fiction here is likely to contain more truth than fact. Therefore I propose, making use of all the liberties and licences of a novelist, to tell you the story of the two days that preceded my coming here—how, bowed down by the weight of the subject which you have laid upon my shoulders, I pondered it, and made it work in and out of my daily life. I need not say that what I am about to describe has no existence; Oxbridge is an invention; so is Fernham; "I" is only a convenient term for somebody who has no real being. Lies will flow from my lips, but there may perhaps be some truth mixed up with them; it is for you to seek out this truth and to decide whether any part of it is worth keeping. If not, you will of course throw the whole of it into the wastepaper basket and forget all about it.

Here then was I (call me Mary Beton, Mary Seton, Mary Carmichael or by any name you please—it is not a matter of any importance) sitting on the banks of a river a week or two ago in fine October weather, lost in thought. That collar I have

From: Virginia Woolf, *A Room of One's Own* (San Diego, New York, London: Harcourt Brace & Company, 1989), pp. 3–8, 25–40, 106–114.

spoken of, women and fiction, the need of coming to some conclusion on a subject that raises all sorts of prejudices and passions, bowed my head to the ground. To the right and left bushes of some sort, golden and crimson, glowed with the colour, even it seemed burnt with the heat, of fire. On the further bank the willows wept in perpetual lamentation, their hair about their shoulders. The river reflected whatever it chose of sky and bridge and burning tree, and when the undergraduate had oared his boat through the reflections they closed again, completely, as if he had never been. There one might have sat the clock round lost in thought. Thought—to call it by a prouder name than it deserved—had let its line down into the stream. It swayed, minute after minute, hither and thither among the reflections and the weeds, letting the water lift it and sink it, until—you know the little tug—the sudden conglomeration of an idea at the end of one's line: and then the cautious hauling of it in, and the careful laying of it out? Alas, laid on the grass how small, how insignificant this thought of mine looked; the sort of fish that a good fisherman puts back into the water so that it may grow fatter and be one day worth cooking and eating. I will not trouble you with that thought now, though if you look carefully you may find it for yourselves in the course of what I am going to say.

But however small it was, it had, nevertheless, the mysterious property of its kind—put back into the mind, it became at once very exciting, and important; and as it darted and sank, and flashed hither and thither, set up such a wash and tumult of ideas that it was impossible to sit still. It was thus that I found myself walking with extreme rapidity across a grass plot. Instantly a man's figure rose to intercept me. Nor did I at first understand that the gesticulations of a curious-looking object, in a cut-away coat and evening shirt, were aimed at me. His face expressed horror and indignation. Instinct rather than reason came to my help; he was a Beadle; I was a woman. This was the turf; there was the path. Only the Fellows and Scholars are allowed here; the gravel is the place for me. Such thoughts were the work of a moment. As I regained the path the arms of the Beadle sank, his face assumed its usual repose, and though turf is better walking than gravel, no very great harm was done. The only charge I could bring against the Fellows and Scholars of whatever the college might happen to be was that in protection of their turf, which has been rolled for 300 years in succession, they had sent my little fish into hiding.

What idea it had been that had sent me so audaciously trespassing I could not now remember. The spirit of peace descended like a cloud from heaven, for if the spirit of peace dwells anywhere, it is in the courts and quadrangles of Oxbridge on a fine October morning. Strolling through those colleges past those ancient halls the roughness of the present seemed smoothed away; the body seemed contained in a miraculous glass cabinet through which no sound could penetrate, and the mind, freed from any contact with facts (unless one trespassed on the turf again), was at liberty to settle down upon whatever meditation was in harmony with the moment. As chance would have it, some stray memory of some old essay about revisiting Oxbridge in the long vacation brought Charles Lamb to mind—Saint Charles, said Thackeray, putting a letter of Lamb's to his forehead. Indeed, among all the dead (I give you my thoughts as they came to me), Lamb is one of the most congenial; one to whom one would have liked to say, Tell me then how you wrote your essays? For his essays are superior even to Max Beerbohm's, I thought, with all their perfection, because of that wild flash of imagination, that lightning crack of genius in the middle of them which leaves them flawed and imperfect, but starred with poetry. Lamb then came to Oxbridge perhaps a hundred years ago. Certainly he wrote an essay—the name escapes me—about the manuscript of one of Milton's poems which he saw here. It was *Lycidas* perhaps, and Lamb wrote how it shocked him to think it possible that any word in *Lycidas* could have been different from what it is. To think of Milton changing the words in that poem seemed to him a sort of sacrilege. This led me to remember what I could of *Lycidas* and to amuse myself with guessing which word it could have been that Milton had altered, and why. It then occurred to me that the very manuscript itself which Lamb had looked at was only a few hundred yards away, so that one could follow Lamb's footsteps across the quadrangle to that famous library where the treasure is kept. Moreover, I recollected, as I put this plan into execution, it is in this famous library that the manuscript of Thackeray's *Esmond* is also preserved. The critics often say that *Esmond* is Thackeray's most perfect novel. But the affectation of the style, with its imitation of the eighteenth century, hampers one, so far as I remember; unless indeed the eighteenth-century style was natural to Thackeray—a fact that one might prove by looking at the manuscript and seeing whether the alterations were for the benefit of the style or of the sense. But then one would have to decide what is style and what is meaning, a question which—but here I was actually at the door which leads into the library itself. I must have opened it, for instantly there issued, like a guardian angel barring the way with a flutter of black gown instead of white wings, a deprecating, silvery, kindly gentleman, who regretted in a low voice as he waved me back that ladies are only admitted to the library if accompanied by a Fellow of the College or furnished with a letter of introduction. . . .

Chapter Two

The scene, if I may ask you to follow me, was now changed. The leaves were still falling, but in London now, not Oxbridge; and I must ask you to imagine a room, like many thousands, with a window looking across people's hats and vans and motor-cars to other windows, and on the table inside the room a blank sheet of paper on which was written in large letters WOMEN AND FICTION, but no more. The inevitable sequel to lunching and dining at Oxbridge seemed, unfortunately, to be a visit to the British Museum. One must strain off what was personal and accidental in all these impressions and so reach the pure fluid, the essential oil of truth. For that visit to Oxbridge and the luncheon and the dinner had started a swarm of questions. Why did men drink wine and women water? Why was one sex so prosperous and the other so poor? What effect has poverty on fiction? What conditions are necessary for the creation of works of art?—a thousand questions at once suggested themselves. But one needed answers, not questions; and an answer was only to be had by consulting the learned and the unprejudiced, who have removed themselves above the strife of tongue and the confusion of body and issued the result of their reasoning and research in books which are to be found in the British Museum. If truth is not to be found on the shelves of the British Museum, where, I asked myself, picking up a notebook and a pencil, is truth?

Thus provided, thus confident and enquiring, I set out in the pursuit of truth. The day, though not actually wet, was dismal, and the streets in the neighborhood of the Museum were full of open coal-holes, down which sacks were showering; four-wheeled cabs were drawing up and depositing on the pavement corded boxes containing, presumably, the entire wardrobe of some Swiss or Italian family seeking fortune or refuge or some other desirable commodity which is to be found in the boarding-houses of Bloomsbury in the winter. The usual hoarse-voiced men paraded the streets with plants on barrows. Some shouted; others sang. London was like a workshop. London was like a machine. We were all being shot backwards and forwards on this plain foundation to make some pattern. The British Museum was another department of the factory. The swing-doors swung open; and there one stood under the vast dome, as if one were a thought in the huge bald forehead which is so splendidly encircled by a band of famous names. One went to the counter; one took a slip of paper; one opened a volume of the catalogue, and . . . . . the five dots here indicate five separate minutes of stupefaction, wonder and bewilderment. Have you any notion how many books are written about women in the course of one year? Have you any notion how many are written by men? Are you aware that you are, perhaps, the most discussed animal in the universe? Here had I come with a notebook and a pencil proposing to spend a morning reading, supposing that at the end of the morning I should have transferred the truth to my notebook. But I should need to be a herd of elephants, I thought, and a wilderness of spiders, desperately referring to the animals that are reputed longest lived and most multitudinously eyed, to cope with all this. I should need claws of steel and beak of brass even to penetrate the husk. How shall I ever find the grains of truth embedded in all this mass of paper, I asked myself, and in despair began running my eye up and down the long list of titles. Even the names of the books gave me food for thought. Sex and its nature might well attract doctors and biologists; but what was surprising and difficult of explanation was the fact that sex—woman, that is to say—also attracts agreeable essayists, light-fingered novelists, young men who have taken the M.A. degree; men who have taken no degree; men who have no apparent qualification save that they are not women. Some of these books were, on the face of it, frivolous and facetious; but many, on the other hand, were serious and prophetic, moral and hortatory. Merely to read the titles suggested innumerable schoolmasters, innumerable clergymen mounting their platforms and pulpits and holding forth with a loquacity which far exceeded the hour usually allotted to such discourse on this one subject. It was a most strange phenomenon; and apparently—here I consulted the letter M—one confined to male sex. Women do not write books about men—a fact that I could not help welcoming with relief, for if I had first to read all that men have written about women, then all that women have written about men, the aloe that flowers once in a hundred years would flower twice before I could set pen to paper. So, making a perfectly arbitrary choice of a dozen volumes or so, I sent my slips of paper to lie in the wire tray, and waited in my stall, among the other seekers for the essential oil of truth.

What could be the reason, then, of this curious disparity, I wondered, drawing cart-wheels on the slips of paper provided by the British taxpayer for other purposes. Why are women, judging from this catalogue, so much more interesting to men than men are to women? A very curious fact it seemed, and my mind wandered to picture the lives of men who spend their time in writing books about women; whether they were old or young, married or unmarried, red-nosed or humpbacked—anyhow, it was flattering, vaguely, to feel oneself the object of such attention, provided that it was not entirely bestowed by the crippled and the infirm—so I pondered until all such frivolous thoughts were ended by an avalanche of books sliding down on to the desk in front of me. Now the trouble began. The student who has been trained in research at Oxbridge has no doubt some method of shepherding his question past all distractions till it runs into its answer as a sheep runs into its pen. The student by my side, for instance, who was copying assiduously from a scientific manual was, I felt sure, extracting pure nuggets of the essential ore every ten minutes or so. His little grunts of satisfaction indicated so much. But if, unfortunately, one has had no training in a university, the question far from being shepherded to its pen flies like a frightened flock hither and thither, helter-skelter, pursued by a whole pack of hounds. Professors, schoolmasters, sociologists, clergymen, novelists, essayists, journalists, men who had no qualification save that they were not women, chased my simple and single question—Why are women poor?—until it became fifty questions; until the fifty questions leapt frantically into mid-stream and were carried away. Every page in my notebook was scribbled over with notes. To show the state of mind I was in, I will read you a few of them, explaining that the page was headed quite simply, WOMEN AND POVERTY, in block letters; but what followed was something like this:

Condition in Middle Ages of,
Habits in the Fiji Islands of,
Worshipped as goddesses by,
Weaker in moral sense than,
Idealism of,
Greater conscientiousness of,
South Sea Islanders, age of puberty among,
Attractiveness of,
Offered as sacrifice to,
Small size of brain of,
Profounder sub-consciousness of,
Less hair on the body of,
Mental, moral and physical inferiority of,
Love of children of,
Greater length of life of,
Weaker muscles of,
Strength of affections of,
Vanity of,
Higher education of,
Shakespeare's opinion of,
Lord Birkenhead's opinion of,
Dean Inge's opinion of,
La Bruyère's opinion of,
Dr. Johnson's opinion of,
Mr. Oscar Browning's opinion of, . . .

Here I drew breath and added, indeed, in the margin, Why does Samuel Butler say, "Wise men never say what they think of women"? Wise men never say anything else apparently. But, I continued, leaning back in my chair and looking at the vast dome in which I was a single but by now somewhat harassed thought, what is so unfortunate is that wise men never think the same thing about women. Here is Pope:

Most women have no character at all.

And here is La Bruyère:

Les femmes sont extrêmes; elles sont meilleures ou pires que les hommes—

a direct contradiction by keen observers who were contemporary. Are they capable of education or incapable? Napoleon thought them incapable. Dr. Johnson thought the opposite. Have they souls or have they not souls? Some savages say they have none. Others, on the contrary, maintain that women are half divine and worship them on that account. Some sages hold that they are shallower in the brain; others that they are deeper in the consciousness. Goethe honoured them; Mussolini despises them. Wherever one looked men thought about women and thought differently. It was impossible to make head or tail of it all, I decided, glancing with envy at the reader next door who was making the neatest abstracts, headed often with an A or a B or a C, while my own notebook rioted with the wildest scribble of contradictory jottings. It was distressing, it was bewildering, it was humiliating. Truth had run through my fingers. Every drop had escaped.

I could not possibly go home, I reflected, and add as a serious contribution to the study of women and fiction that women have less hair on their bodies than men, or that the age of puberty among the South Sea Islanders is nine—or is it ninety?—even the handwriting had become in its distraction indecipherable. It was disgraceful to have nothing more weighty or respectable to show after a whole morning's work. And if I could not grasp the truth about W. (as for brevity's sake I had come to call her) in the past, why bother about W. in the future? It seemed pure waste of time to consult all those gentlemen who specialise in woman and her effect on whatever it may be—politics, children, wages, morality—numerous and learned as they are. One might as well leave their books unopened.

But while I pondered I had unconsciously, in my listlessness, in my desperation, been drawing a picture where I should, like my neighbour, have been writing a conclusion. I had been drawing a face, a figure. It was the face and the figure of Professor von X. engaged in writing his monumental work entitled *The Mental, Moral, and Physical Inferiority of the Female Sex*. He was not in my picture a man attractive to women. He was heavily built; he had a great jowl; to balance that he had very small eyes; he was very red in the face. His expression suggested that he was labouring under some emotion that made him jab his pen on the paper as if he were killing some noxious insect as he wrote, but even when he had killed it that did not satisfy him; he must go on killing it; and even so, some cause for anger and irritation remained. Could it be his wife, I asked, looking at my picture. Was she in love with a cavalry officer? Was the cavalry officer slim and elegant and dressed in astrachan? Had he been laughed at, to adopt the Freudian theory, in his cradle by a pretty girl? For even in his cradle the professor, I thought, could not have been an attractive child. Whatever the reason, the professor was made to look very angry and very ugly in my sketch, as he wrote his great book upon the mental, moral and physical inferiority of women. Drawing pictures was an idle way of finishing an unprofitable morning's work. Yet it is in our idleness, in our dreams, that the submerged truth sometimes comes to the top. A very elementary exercise in psychology, not to be dignified by the name of psycho-analysis, showed me, on looking at my notebook, that the sketch of the angry professor had been made in anger. Anger had snatched my pencil while I dreamt. But what was anger doing there? Interest, confusion, amusement, boredom—all these emotions I could trace and name as they succeeded each other throughout the morning. Had anger, the black snake, been lurking among them? Yes, said the sketch, anger had. It referred me unmistakably to the one book, to the one phrase, which had roused the demon; it was the professor's statement about the mental, moral and physical inferiority of women. My heart had leapt. My cheeks had burnt. I had flushed with anger. There was nothing specially remarkable, however foolish, in that. One does not like to be told that one is naturally the inferior of a little man—I looked at the student next me—who breathes hard, wears a ready-made tie, and has not shaved this fortnight. One has certain foolish vanities. It is only human nature, I reflected, and began drawing cart-wheels and circles over the angry professor's face till he looked like a burning bush or a flaming comet—anyhow, an apparition without human semblance or significance. The professor was nothing now but a faggot burning on the top of Hampstead Heath. Soon my own anger was explained and done with; but curiosity remained. How explain the anger of the professors? Why were they angry? For when it came to analysing the impression left by these books there was always an element of heat. This heat took many forms; it showed itself in satire, in sentiment, in curiosity, in reprobation. But there was another element which was often present and could not immediately be identified. Anger, I called it. But it was anger that had gone underground and mixed itself with all kinds of other emotions. To judge from its odd effects, it was anger disguised and complex, not anger simple and open.

Whatever the reason, all these books, I thought, surveying the pile on the desk, are worthless for my purposes. They were worthless scientifically, that is to say, though humanly they were full of instruction, interest, boredom, and very queer facts about the habits of the Fiji Islanders. They had been written in the red light of emotion and not in the white light of truth. Therefore they must be returned to the central desk and restored each to his own cell in the enormous honeycomb. All that I had retrieved from that morning's work had been the one facts of anger. The professors—I lumped them together thus—were angry. But why, I asked myself, having returned the books, why, I repeated, standing under the colonnade among the pigeons and the prehistoric canoes, why are they angry? And, asking myself this question, I strolled off to find a place for luncheon. What is the real nature of what I call for the moment their anger? I asked. Here was a puzzle that would last all the time that it takes to be served with food in a small restaurant somewhere near the British Museum. Some previous luncher had left the lunch edition of the evening paper on a chair, and, waiting to be served, I began idly reading the headlines. A ribbon of very large letters ran across the page. Somebody had made a big score in South Africa. Lesser ribbons announced that Sir Austen Chamberlain was at Geneva. A meat axe with human hair on it had been found in a cellar. Mr. Justice——commented in the Divorce Courts upon the Shamelessness of Women. Sprinkled about the paper were other pieces of news. A film actress had been lowered from a peak in California and hung suspended in mid-air. The weather was going to be foggy. The most transient visitor to this planet, I thought, who picked up this paper could not fail to be aware, even from this scattered testimony, that England is under the rule of a patriarchy. Nobody in their senses could fail to detect the dominance of the professor. His was the power and the money and the influence. He was the proprietor of the paper and its editor and sub-editor. He was the Foreign Secretary and the Judge. He was the cricketer; he owned the racehorses and the yachts. He was the director of the company that pays two hundred per cent to its shareholders. He left millions to charities and colleges that were ruled by himself. He suspended the film actress in mid-air. He will decide if the hair on the meat axe is human; he it is who will acquit or convict the murderer, and hang him, or let him go free. With the exception of the fog he seemed to control everything. Yet he was angry. I knew that he was angry by this token. When I read what he wrote about women I thought, not of what he was saying, but of himself. When an arguer argues dispassionately he thinks only of the argument; and the reader cannot help thinking of the argument too. If he had written dispassionately about women, had used indisputable proofs to establish his argument and had shown no trace of wishing that the result should be one thing rather than another, one would not have been angry either. One would have accepted the fact, as one accepts the fact that a pea is green or a canary yellow. So be it, I should have said. But I had been angry because he was angry. Yet it seemed absurd, I thought, turning over the evening paper, that a man with all this power should be angry. Or is anger, I wondered, somehow, the familiar, the attendant sprite on power? Rich people, for example, are often angry because they suspect that the poor want to seize their wealth. The professors, or patriarchs, as it might be more accurate to call them, might be angry for that reason partly, but partly for one that lies a little less obviously on the surface. Possibly they were not "angry" at all; often, indeed, they were admiring, devoted, exemplary in the relations of private life. Possibly when the professor insisted a little too emphatically upon the inferiority of women, he was concerned not with their inferiority, but with his own superiority. That was what he was protecting rather hot-headedly and with too much emphasis, because it was a jewel to him of the rarest price. Life for both sexes—and I looked at them, shouldering their way along the pavement—is arduous, difficult, a perpetual struggle. It calls for gigantic courage and strength. More than anything, perhaps, creatures of illusion as we are, it calls for confidence in oneself. Without self-confidence we are as babes in the cradle. And how can we generate this imponderable quality, which is yet so invaluable, most quickly? By thinking that other people are inferior to oneself. By feeling that one has some innate superiority—it may be wealth, or rank, a straight nose, or the portrait of a grandfather by Romney—for there is no end to the pathetic devices of the human imagination—over other people. Hence the enormous importance to a patriarch who has to conquer, who has to rule, of feeling that great numbers of people, half the human race indeed, are by nature inferior to himself. It must indeed be one of the chief sources of his power. But let me turn the light of this observation on to real life, I thought. Does it help to explain some of those psychological puzzles that one notes in the margin of daily life? Does it explain my astonishment the other day when Z, most humane, most modest of men, taking up some book by Rebecca West and reading a passage in it, exclaimed, "The arrant feminist! She says that men are snobs!" The exclamation, to me so surprising for why was Miss West an arrant feminist for making a possibly true if uncomplimentary statement about the other sex?—was not merely the cry of wounded vanity; it was a protest against some infringement of his power to believe in himself. Women have served all these centuries as looking-glasses possessing the magic and delicious power of reflecting the figure of man at twice its natural size. Without that power probably the earth would still be swamp and jungle. The glories of all our wars would be unknown. We should still be scratching the outlines of deer on the remains of mutton bones and bartering flints for sheepskins or whatever simple ornament took our unsophisticated taste. Supermen and Fingers of Destiny would never have existed. The Czar and the Kaiser would never have worn their crowns or lost them. Whatever may be their use in civilised societies, mirrors are essential to all violent and heroic action. That is why Napoleon and Mussolini both insist so emphatically upon the inferiority of women, for if they were not inferior, they would cease to enlarge. That serves to explain in part the necessity that women so often are to men. And it serves to explain how restless they are under her criticism; how impossible it is for her to say to them this book is bad, this picture is feeble, or whatever it may be, without giving far more pain and rousing far more anger than a man would do who gave the same criticism. For if she begins to tell the truth, the figure in the looking-glass shrinks; his fitness for life is diminished. How is he to go on giving judgement, civilising natives, making laws, writing books, dressing up and speechifying at banquets, unless he can see himself at breakfast and at dinner at least twice the size he really is? So I reflected, crumbling my bread and stirring my coffee and now and again looking at the people in the street. The looking-glass vision is of supreme importance because it charges the vitality; it stimulates the nervous system. Take it away and man may die, like the drug fiend deprived of his cocaine. Under the spell of that illusion, I thought, looking out of the window, half the people on the pavement are striding to work. They put on their hats and coats in the morning under its agreeable rays. They start the day confident, braced, believing themselves desired at Miss Smith's tea party; they say to themselves as they go into the room, I am the superior of half the people here, and it is thus that they speak with that self-confidence, that self-assurance, which have had such profound consequences in public life and lead to such curious notes in the margin of the private mind.

But these contributions to the dangerous and fascinating subject of the psychology of the other sex—it is one, I hope, that you will investigate when you have five hundred a year of your own—were interrupted by the necessity of paying the bill. It came to five shillings and ninepence. I gave the waiter a ten-shilling note and he went to bring me change. There was another ten-shilling note in my purse; I noticed it, because it is a fact that still takes my breath away—the power of my purse to breed ten-shilling notes automatically. I open it and there they are. Society gives me chicken and coffee, bed and lodging, in return for a certain number of pieces of paper which were left me by an aunt, for no other reason than that I share her name.

My aunt, Mary Beton, I must tell you, died by a fall from her horse when she was riding out to take the air in Bombay. The news of my legacy reached me one night about the same time that the act was passed that gave votes to women. A solicitor's letter fell into the post-box and when I opened it I found that she had left me five hundred pounds a year for ever. Of the two—the vote and the money—the money, I own, seemed infinitely the more important. Before that I had made my living by cadging odd jobs from newspapers, by reporting a donkey show here or a wedding there; I had earned a few pounds by addressing envelopes, reading to old ladies, making artificial flowers, teaching the alphabet to small children in a kindergarten. Such were the chief occupations that were open to women before 1918. I need not, I am afraid, describe in any detail the hardness of the work, for you know perhaps women who have done it; nor the difficulty of living on the money when it was earned, for you may have tried. But what still remains with me as a worse infliction than either was the poison of fear and bitterness which those days bred in me. To begin with, always to be doing work that one did not wish to do, and to do it like a slave, flattering and fawning, not always necessarily perhaps, but it seemed necessary and the stakes were too great to run risks; and then the thought of that one gift which it was death to hide—a small one but dear to the possessor—perishing and with it myself, my soul—all this became like a rust eating away the bloom of the spring, destroying the tree at its heart. However, as I say, my aunt died; and whenever I change a ten-shilling note a little of that rust and corrosion is rubbed off; fear and bitterness go. Indeed, I thought, slipping the silver into my purse, it is remarkable, remembering the bitterness of those days, what a change of temper a fixed income will bring about. No force in the world can take from me my five hundred pounds. Food, house and clothing are mine for ever. Therefore not merely do effort and labour cease, but also hatred and bitterness. I need not hate any man; he cannot hurt me. I need not flatter any man; he has nothing to give me. So imperceptibly I found myself adopting a new attitude towards the other half of the human race. It was absurd to blame any class or any sex, as a whole. Great bodies of people are never responsible for what they do. They are driven by instincts which are not within their control. They too, the patriarchs, the professors, had endless difficulties, terrible drawbacks to contend with. Their education had been in some ways as faulty as my own. It had bred in them defects as great. True, they had money and power, but only at the cost of harbouring in their breasts an eagle, a vulture, for ever tearing the liver out and plucking at the lungs—the instinct for possession, the rage for acquisition which drives them to desire other people's fields and goods perpetually; to make frontiers and flags; battleships and poison gas; to offer up their own lives and their children's lives. Walk through the Admiralty Arch (I had reached that monument), or any other avenue given up to trophies and cannon, and reflect upon the kind of glory celebrated there. Or watch in the spring sunshine the stockbroker and the great barrister going indoors to make money and more money and more money when it is a fact that five hundred pounds a year will keep one alive in the sunshine. These are unpleasant instincts to harbour, I reflected. They are bred of the conditions of life; of the lack of civilisation, I thought, looking at the statue of the Duke of Cambridge, and in particular at the feathers in his cocked hat, with a fixity that they have scarcely ever received before. And, as I realised these drawbacks, by degrees fear and bitterness modified themselves into pity and toleration; and then in a year or two, pity and toleration went, and the greatest release of all came, which is freedom to think of things in themselves. That building, for example, do I like it or not? Is that picture beautiful or not? Is that in my opinion a good book or a bad? Indeed my aunt's legacy unveiled the sky to me, and substituted for the large and imposing figure of a gentleman, which Milton recommended for my perpetual adoration, a view of the open sky.

So thinking, so speculating, I found my way back to my house by the river. Lamps were being lit and an indescribable change had come over London since the morning hour. It was as if the great machine after labouring all day had made with our help a few yards of something very exciting and beautiful—

a fiery fabric flashing with red eyes, a tawny monster roaring with hot breath. Even the wind seemed flung like a flag as it lashed the houses and rattled the hoardings.

In my little street, however, domesticity prevailed. The house painter was descending his ladder; the nursemaid was wheeling the perambulator carefully in and out back to nursery tea; the coal-heaver was folding his empty sacks on top of each other; the woman who keeps the green-grocer's shop was adding up the day's takings with her hands in red mittens. But so engrossed was I with the problem you have laid upon my shoulders that I could not see even these usual sights without referring them to one centre. I thought how much harder it is now than it must have been even a century ago to say which of these employments is the higher, the more necessary. Is it better to be a coal-heaver or a nursemaid; is the charwoman who has brought up eight children of less value to the world than the barrister who has made a hundred thousand pounds? It is useless to ask such questions; for nobody can answer them. Not only do the comparative values of charwomen and lawyers rise and fall from decade to decade, but we have no rods with which to measure them even as they are at the moment. I had been foolish to ask my professor to furnish me with "indisputable proofs" of this or that in his argument about women. Even if one could state the value of any one gift at the moment, those values will change; in a century's time very possibly they will have changed completely. Moreover, in a hundred years, I thought, reaching my own doorstep, women will have ceased to be the protected sex. Logically they will take part in all the activities and exertions that were once denied them. The nursemaid will heave coal. The shopwoman will drive an engine. All assumptions founded on the facts observed when women were the protected sex will have disappeared—as, for example (here a squad of soldiers marched down the street), that women and clergymen and gardeners live longer than other people. Remove that protection, expose them to the same exertions and activities, make them soldiers and sailors and engine-drivers and dock labourers, and will not women die off so much younger, so much quicker, than men that one will say, "I saw a woman today," as one used to say, "I saw an aeroplane." Anything may happen when womanhood has ceased to be a protected occupation, I thought, opening the door. But what bearing has all this upon the subject of my paper, Women and Fiction? I asked, going indoors.

* * *

Chapter Six

. . . Next I think that you may object that in all this I have made too much of the importance of material things. Even allowing a generous margin for symbolism, that five hundred a year stands for the power to contemplate, that a lock on the door means the power to think for oneself, still you may say that the mind should rise above such things; and that great poets have often been poor men. Let me then quote to you the words of your own Professor of Literature, who knows better than I do what goes to the making of a poet. Sir Arthur Quiller-Couch writes:

"What are the great poetical names of the last hundred years or so? Coleridge, Wordsworth, Byron, Shelley, Landor, Keats, Tennyson, Browning, Arnold, Morris, Rossetti, Swinburne—we may stop there. Of these, all but Keats, Browning, Rossetti were University men; and of these three, Keats, who died young, cut off in his prime, was the only one not fairly well to do. It may seem a brutal thing to say, and it is a sad thing to say: but, as a matter of hard fact, the theory that poetical genius bloweth where it listeth, and equally in poor and rich, holds little truth. As a matter of hard fact, nine out of those twelve were University men: which means that somehow or other they procured the means to get the best education England can give. As a matter of hard fact, of the remaining three you know that Browning was well to do, and I challenge you that, if he had not been well to do, he would no more have attained to write *Saul* or *The Ring and the Book* than Ruskin would have attained to writing *Modern Painters* if his father had not dealt prosperously in business. Rossetti had a small private income; and, moreover, he painted. There remains but Keats; whom Atropos slew young, as she slew John Clare in a mad-house, and James Thomson by the laudanum he took to drug disappointment. These are dreadful facts, but let us face them. It is—however dishonouring to us as a nation—certain that, by some fault in our commonwealth, the poor poet has not in these days, nor has had for two hundred years, a dog's chance. Believe me—and I have spent a great part of ten years in watching some three hundred and twenty elementary schools—we may prate of democracy, but actually, a poor child in England has little more hope than had the son of an Athenian slave to be emancipated into that intellectual freedom of which great writings are born."

Nobody could put the point more plainly. "The poor poet has not in these days, nor has had for two hundred years, a dog's chance . . . a poor child in England has little more hope than had the son of an Athenian slave to be emancipated into that intellectual freedom of which great writings are born." That is it. Intellectual freedom depends upon material things. Poetry depends upon intellectual freedom. And women have always been poor, not for two hundred years merely, but from the beginning of time. Women have had less intellectual freedom than the sons of Athenian slaves. Women, then, have not had a dog's chance of writing poetry. That is why I have laid so much stress on money and a room of one's own. However, thanks to the toils of those obscure women in the past, of whom I wish we knew more, thanks, curiously enough, to two wars, the Crimean which let Florence Nightingale out of her drawing-room, and the European War which opened the doors to the average woman some sixty years later, these evils are in the way to be bettered. Otherwise you would not be here tonight, and your chance of earning five hundred pounds a year, precarious as I am afraid that it still is, would be minute in the extreme.

Still, you may object, why do you attach so much importance to this writing of books by women when, according to you, it requires so much effort, leads perhaps to the murder of one's aunts, will make one almost certainly late for luncheon, and may bring one into very grave disputes with certain very good fellows? My motives, let me admit, are partly selfish. Like most uneducated Englishwomen, I like reading—I like reading books in the bulk. Lately my diet has become a trifle monotonous; history is too much about wars; biography too much about great men; poetry has shown, I think, a tendency to sterility, and fiction—but I have sufficiently exposed my disabilities as a critic of modern fiction and will say no more about it. Therefore I would ask you to write all kinds of books, hesitating at no subject however trivial or however vast. By hook or by crook, I hope that you will possess yourselves of money enough to travel and to idle, to contemplate the future or the past of the world, to dream over books and loiter at street corners and let the line of thought clip deep into the stream. For I am by no means confining you to fiction. If you would please me—and there are thousands like me—you would write books of travel and adventure; and research and scholarship, and history and biography, and criticism and philosophy and science. By so doing you will certainly profit the art of fiction. For books have a way of influencing each other. Fiction will be much the better for standing cheek by jowl with poetry and philosophy. Moreover, if you consider any great figure of the past, like Sappho, like the Lady Murasaki, like Emily Brontë, you will find that she is an inheritor as well as an originator, and has come into existence because women have come to have the habit of writing naturally; so that even as a prelude to poetry such activity on your part would be invaluable.

But when I look back through these notes and criticise my own train of thought as I made them, I find that my motives were not altogether selfish. There runs through these comments and discursions the conviction—or is it the instinct?—that good books are desirable and that good writers, even if they show every variety of human depravity, are still good human beings. Thus when I ask you to write more books I am urging you to do what will be for your good and for the good of the world at large. How to justify this instinct or belief I do not know, for philosophic words, if one has not been educated at a university, are apt to play one false. What is meant by "reality"? It would seem to be something very erratic, very undependable—now to be found in a dusty road, now in a scrap of newspaper in the street, now in a daffodil in the sun. It lights up a group in a room and stamps some casual saying. It overwhelms one walking home beneath the stars and makes the silent world more real than the world of speech—and then there it is again in an omnibus in the uproar of Piccadilly. Sometimes, too, it seems to dwell in shapes too far away for us to discern what their nature is. But whatever it touches, it fixes and makes permanent. That is what remains over when the skin of the day has been cast into the hedge; that is what is left of past time and of our loves and hates. Now the writer, as I think, has the chance to live more than other people in the presence of this reality. It is his business to find it and collect it and communicate it to the rest of us. So at least I infer from reading *Lear* or *Emma* or *La Recherche du Temps Perdu.* For the reading of these books seems to perform a curious couching operation on the senses; one sees more intensely afterwards; the world seems bared of its covering and given an intenser life. Those are the enviable people who live at enmity with unreality; and those are the pitiable who are knocked on the head by the thing done without knowing or caring. So that when I ask you to earn money and have a room of your own, I am asking you to live in the presence of reality, an invigorating life, it would appear, whether one can impart it or not.

Here I would stop, but the pressure of convention decrees that every speech must end with a peroration. And a peroration addressed to women should have something, you will agree, particularly exalting and ennobling about it. I should implore you to remember your responsibilities, to be higher, more spiritual; I should remind you how much depends upon you, and what an influence you can exert upon the future. But those exhortations can safely, I think, be left to the other sex, who will put them, and indeed have put them, with far greater eloquence than I can compass. When I rummage in my own mind I find no noble sentiments about being companions and equals and influencing the world to higher ends. I find myself saying briefly and prosaically that it is much more important to be oneself than anything else. Do not dream of influencing other people, I would say, if I knew how to make it sound exalted Think of things in themselves.

And again I am reminded by dipping into newspapers and novels and biographies that when a woman speaks to women she should have something very unpleasant up her sleeve. Women are hard on women. Women dislike women. Women—but are you not sick to death of the word? I can assure you that I am. Let us agree, then, that a paper read by a woman to women should end with something particularly disagreeable.

But how does it go? What can I think of? The truth is, I often like women. I like their unconventionality. I like their subtlety. I like their anonymity. I like—but I must not run on in this way. That cupboard there,—you say it holds clean table-napkins only; but what if Sir Archibald Bodkin were concealed among them? Let me then adopt a sterner tone. Have I; in the preceding words, conveyed to you sufficiently the warnings and reprobation of mankind? I have told you the very low opinion in which you were held by Mr. Oscar Browning. I have indicated what Napoleon once thought of you and what Mussolini thinks now. Then, in case any of you aspire to fiction, I have copied out for your benefit the advice of the critic about courageously acknowledging the limitations of your sex. I have referred to Professor X and given prominence to his statement that women are intellectually, morally and physically inferior to men. I have handed on all that has come my way without going in search of it, and here is a final warning—from Mr. John Langdon Davies. Mr. John Langdon Davies warns women "that when children cease to be altogether desirable, women cease to be altogether necessary." I hope you will make a note of it.

How can I further encourage you to go about the business of life? Young women, I would say, and please attend, for the peroration is beginning, you are, in my opinion, disgracefully ignorant. You have never made a discovery of any sort of importance. You have never shaken an empire or led an army into battle. The plays of Shakespeare are not by you, and you have never introduced a barbarous race to the blessings of civilisation. What is your excuse? It is all very well for you to say, pointing to the streets and squares and forests of the globe swarming with black and white and coffee-coloured inhabitants, all busily engaged in traffic and enterprise and love-making, we have had other work on our hands. Without our doing, those seas would be unsailed and those fertile lands a desert. We have borne and bred and washed and taught, perhaps to the age of six or seven years, the one thousand six hundred and twenty-three million human beings who are, according to statistics, at present in existence, and that, allowing that some had help, takes time.

There is truth in what you say—I will not deny it. But at the same time may I remind you that there have been at least two colleges for women in existence in England since the year 1866; that after the year 1880 a married woman was allowed by law to possess her own property; and that in 1919—which is a whole nine years ago—she was given a vote? May I also remind you that the most of the professions have been open to you for close on ten years now? When you reflect upon these immense privileges and the length of time during which they have been enjoyed, and the fact that there must be at this moment some two thousand women capable of earning over five hundred a year in one way or another, you will agree that the excuse of lack of opportunity, training, encouragement, leisure and money no longer holds good. Moreover, the economists are telling us that Mrs. Seton has had too many children. You must, of course, go on bearing children, but, so they say, in twos and threes, not in tens and twelves.

Thus, with some time on your hands and with some book learning in your brains—you have had enough of the other kind, and are sent to college partly, I suspect, to be uneducated—surely you should embark upon another stage of your very long, very laborious and highly obscure career. A thousand pens are ready to suggest what you should do and what effect you will have. My own suggestion is a little fantastic, I admit; I prefer, therefore, to put it in the form of fiction.

I told you in the course of this paper that Shakespeare had a sister; but do not look for her in Sir Sidney Lee's life of the poet. She died young—alas, she never wrote a word. She lies buried where the omnibuses now stop, opposite the Elephant and Castle. Now my belief is that this poet who never wrote a word and was buried at the crossroads still lives. She lives in you and in me, and in many other women who are not here tonight, for they are washing up the dishes and putting the children to bed. But she lives; for great poets do not die; they are continuing presences; they need only the opportunity to walk among us in the flesh. This opportunity, as I think, it is now coming within your power to give her. For my belief is that if we live another century or so—I am talking of the common life which is the real life and not of the little separate lives which we live as individuals—and have five hundred a year each of us and rooms of our own; if we have the habit of freedom and the courage to write exactly what we think; if we escape a little from the common sitting-room and see human beings not always in their relation to each other but in relation to reality; and the sky, too, and the trees or whatever it may be in themselves; if we look past Milton's bogey, for no human being should shut out the view; if we face the fact, for it is a fact, that there is no arm to cling to, but that we go alone and that our relation is to the world of reality and not only to the world of men and women, then the opportunity will come and the dead poet who was Shakespeare's sister will put on the body which she has so often laid down. Drawing her life from the lives of the unknown who were her forerunners, as her brother did before her, she will be born. As for her coming without that preparation, without that effort on our part, without that determination that when she is born again she shall find it possible to live and write her poetry, that we cannot expect, for that would be impossible. But I maintain that she would come if we worked for her, and that so to work, even in poverty and obscurity, is worth while.

✧ PART THIRTEEN ✧

The Rise of Fascism

Fascism in all its varieties became a popular movement in the 1930s. Its leaders used oratorical skills and visual propaganda. This photograph of Hitler speaking to Nazi youth reveals propagandistic techniques in which layers of people provide an illusion of a crowded room.

The Rise of Fascism

After World War I, the Western Allies encouraged democratic government, which at first arose throughout much of Europe. During the 1920s, though, the fascist movement in various forms, playing on fears of communism, established a foothold in many countries. When Benito Mussolini (1883–1945) and his Fascist Party came to power in Italy in 1922, fascism had its first test case. The post-1925 general European recovery offered a reprieve to democracy, whereas fascism and authoritarian government, whether left- or right-wing, seemed on the wane. Economic depression altered the course of history, bringing Adolf Hitler (1889–1945) to power in Germany in 1933. By the end of the decade, fascist governments also ruled in Spain, Portugal, Hungary, Romania, Slovakia, and Bulgaria, and right-wing authoritarian regimes governed the remainder of non-Soviet Eastern Europe.

Except for its anticommunist and antidemocratic tendencies, fascist ideology was notoriously flexible. Benito Mussolini summarized his theories in *Fascism: Doctrine and Institutions* (1932). For him fascism was more than a mere political doctrine. It was an all-encompassing ideology and culture, a civilization. It was the action and thought of an entire people, with the state at the center. Borrowing heavily from the ideas of Mussolini, Adolf Hitler penned his views of Nazism in *Mein Kampf,* written while he was in prison in 1923–1924. Hitler added racial and anti-Semitic components to Mussolini's concept of an omnipotent state. In the face of the spread of Fascist ideologies, opposition to authoritarian regimes was disorganized and ineffective. During the Spanish Civil War (1936–1939), Hitler and Mussolini supported the fascist-aligned Franco against the Spanish Republic, which at first had to rely for support on individual liberals and leftists, who came to fight fascism. As the democracies stood inexplicably aside, the Spanish Republic received aid only from Stalinist Soviet Russia, worse than no help at all. In *Homage to Catalonia* (1938), George Orwell (1903–1950) wrote an account of his confused experiences in this war.

✦ Reading 47 ✦

Fascism

Benito Mussolini

Fundamental Ideas

Like all sound political conceptions, Fascism is action and it is thought; action in which doctrine is immanent, and doctrine arising from a given system of historical forces in which it is inserted, and working on them from within. It has therefore a form correlated to contingencies of time and space; but it has also an ideal content which makes it an expression of truth in the higher region of the history of thought. There is no way of exercising a spiritual influence in the world as a human will dominating the will of others, unless one has a conception both of the transient and the specific reality on which that action is to be exercised, and of the permanent and universal reality in which the transient dwells and has its being. To know men one must know man; and to know man one must be acquainted with reality and its laws. There can be no conception of the State which is not fundamentally a conception of life: philosophy or intuition, system of ideas evolving within the framework of logic or concentrated in a vision or a faith, but always, at least potentially, an organic conception of the world.

Thus many of the practical expressions of Fascism—such as party organisation, system of education, discipline—can only be understood when considered in relation to its general attitude toward life. A spiritual attitude. Fascism sees in the world not only those superficial, material aspects in which man appears as an individual, standing by himself, self-centred, subject to natural law which instinctively urges him toward a life of selfish momentary pleasure; it sees not only the individual but the nation and the country; individuals and generations bound together by a moral law, with common traditions and a mission which suppressing the instinct for life closed in a brief circle of pleasure, builds up a higher life, founded on duty, a life free from the limitations of time and space, in which the individual, by self-sacrifice, the renunciation of self-interest, by death itself, can achieve that purely spiritual existence in which his value as a man consists.

The conception is therefore a spiritual one, arising from the general reaction of the century against the fiacid materialistic positivism of the XIXth century. Anti-positivistic but positive; neither sceptical nor agnostic; neither pessimistic nor supinely optimistic as are, generally speaking, the doctrines (all negative) which place the centre of life outside man; whereas, by the exercise of his free will, man can and must create his own world.

Fascism wants man to be active and to engage in action with all his energies; it wants him to be manfully aware of the difficulties besetting him and ready to face them. It conceives of life as a struggle in which it behoves a man to win for himself a really worthy place, first of all by fitting himself (physically, morally, intellectually) to become the implement required for winning it. As for the individual, so for the nation, and so for mankind. Hence the high value of culture in all its forms (artistic, religious, scientific), and the outstanding importance of education. Hence also the essential value of work, by which man subjugates nature and creates the human world (economic, political, ethical, intellectual).

This positive conception of life is obviously an ethical one. It invests the whole field of reality as well as the human activities which master it. No action is exempt from moral judgement; no activity can be despoiled of the value which a moral purpose confers on all things. Therefore life, as conceived of by the Fascist, is serious, austere, religious; all its manifestations are poised in a world sustained by

From: Benito Mussolini, *Fascism: Doctrine and Institutions* (New York: Howard Fertig, 1968), pp. 7–14, 18–26.

moral forces and subject to spiritual responsabilities. The Fascist disdains an "easy" life.

The Fascist conception of life is a religious one, in which man is viewed in his immanent relation to a higher law, endowed with an objective will transcending the individual and raising him to conscious membership of a spiritual society. Those who perceive nothing beyond opportunistic considerations in the religious policy of the Fascist régime fail to realise that Fascism is not only a system of government but also and above all a system of thought.

In the Fascist conception of history, man is man only by virtue of the spiritual process to which he contributes as a member of the family, the social group, the nation, and in function of history to which all nations bring their contribution. Hence the great value of tradition in records, in language, in customs, in the rules of social life. Outside history man is a nonentity. Fascism is therefore opposed to all individualistic abstractions based on eighteenth century materialism; and it is opposed to all Jacobinistic utopias and innovations. It does not believe in the possibility of "happiness" on earth as conceived by the economistic literature of the XVIIIth century, and it therefore rejects the teleological notion that at some future time the human family will secure a final settlement of all its difficulties. This notion runs counter to experience which teaches that life is in continual flux and in process of evolution. In politics Fascism aims at realism; in practice it desires to deal only with those problems which are the spontaneous product of historic conditions and which find or suggest their own solutions. Only by entering in to the process of reality and taking possession of the forces at work within it, can man act on man and on nature.

Anti-individualistic, the Fascist conception of life stresses the importance of the State and accepts the individual only in so far as his interests coincide with those of the State, which stands for the conscience and the universal will of man as a historic entity. It is opposed to classical liberalism which arose as a reaction to absolutism and exhausted its historical function when the State became the expression of the conscience and will of the people. Liberalism denied the State in the name of the individual; Fascism reasserts the rights of the State as expressing the real essence of the individual. And if liberty is to be the attribute of living men and not of abstract dummies invented by individualistic liberalism, then Fascism stands for liberty, and for the only liberty worth having, the liberty of the State and of the individual within the State. The Fascist conception of the State is all-embracing; outside of it no human or spiritual values can exist, much less have value. Thus understood, Fascism, is totalitarian, and the Fascist State—a synthesis and a unit inclusive of all values—interprets, develops, and potentiates the whole life of a people.

No individuals or groups (political parties, cultural associations, economic unions, social classes) outside the State. Fascism is therefore opposed to Socialism to which unity within the State (which amalgamates classes into a single economic and ethical reality) is unknown, and which sees in history nothing but the class struggle. Fascism is likewise opposed to trade-unionism as a class weapon. But when brought within the orbit of the State, Fascism recognises the real needs which gave rise to socialism and trade-unionism, giving them due weight in the guild or corporative system in which divergent interests are coordinated and harmonised in the unity of the State.

Grouped according to their several interests, individuals form classes; they form trade-unions when organised according to their several economic activities; but first and foremost they form the State, which is no mere matter of numbers, the sum of the individuals forming the majority. Fascism is therefore opposed to that form of democracy which equates a nation to the majority, lowering it to the level of the largest number; but it is the purest form of democracy if the nation be considered—as it should be—from the point of view of quality rather than quantity, as an idea, the mightiest because the most ethical, the most coherent, the truest, expressing itself in a people as the conscience and will of the few, if not, indeed, of one, and ending to express itself in the conscience and the will of the mass, of the whole group ethnically moulded by natural and historical conditions into a nation, advancing, as one conscience and one will, along the self-same line of development and spiritual formation. Not a race, nor a geographically defined region, but a people, historically perpetuating itself; a multitude unified by an idea and imbued with the will to live, the will to power, self-consciousness, personality.

In so far as it is embodied in a State, this higher personality becomes a nation. It is not the nation which generates the State; that is an antiquated naturalistic concept which afforded a basis for XIXth century publicity in favor of national governments. Rather is it the State which creates the nation, conferring volition and therefore real life on a people made aware of their moral unity.

The right to national independence does not arise from any merely literary and idealistic form of self-consciousness; still less from a more or less passive and unconscious *de facto* situation, but from an active, self-conscious, political will expressing itself in action and ready to prove its rights. It arises, in short, from the existence, at least *in fieri,* of a State. Indeed, it is the State which, as the expression of a universal ethical will, creates the right to national independence.

A nation, as expressed in the State, is a living, ethical entity only in so far as it is progressive. Inactivity is death. Therefore the State is not only Authority which governs and confers legal form and spiritual value on individual wills, but it is also Power which makes its will felt and respected beyond its own frontiers, thus affording practical proof of the universal character of the decisions necessary to ensure its development. This implies organisation and expansion, potential if not actual. Thus the State equates itself to the will of man, whose development cannot be checked by obstacles and which, by achieving self-expression, demonstrates its own infinity.

The Fascist State, as a higher and more powerful expression of personality, is a force, but a spiritual one. It sums up all the manifestations of the moral and intellectual life of man. Its functions cannot therefore be limited to those of enforcing order and keeping the peace, as the liberal doctrine had it. It is no mere mechanical device for defining the sphere within which the individual may duly exercise his supposed rights. The Fascist State is an inwardly accepted standard and rule of conduct, a discipline of the whole person; it permeates the will no less than the intellect. It stands for a principle which becomes the central motive of man as a member of civilised society, sinking deep down into his personality; it dwells in the heart of the man of action and of the thinker, of the artist and of the man of science: soul of the soul.

Fascism, in short, is not only a law-giver and a founder of institutions, but an educator and a promoter of spiritual life. It aims at refashioning not only the forms of life but their content—man, his character, and his faith. To achieve this purpose it enforces discipline and uses authority, entering into the soul and ruling with undisputed sway. Therefore it has chosen as its emblem the Lictor's rods, the symbol of unity, strength, and justice.

* * *

Fascism is now clearly defined not only as a régime but as a doctrine. This means that Fascism, exercising its critical faculties on itself and on others, has studied from its own special standpoint and judged by its own standards all the problems affecting the material and intellectual interests now causing such grave anxiety to the nations of the world, and is ready to deal with them by its own policies.

First of all, as regards the future development of mankind,—and quite apart from all present political considerations—Fascism does not, generally speaking, believe in the possibility or utility of perpetual peace. It therefore discards pacifism as a cloak for cowardly supine renunciation in contra-distinction to self-sacrifice. War alone keys up all human energies to their maximum tension and sets the seal of nobility on those peoples who have the courage to face it. All other tests are substitutes which never place a man face to face with himself before the alternative of life or death. Therefore all doctrines which postulate peace at all costs are incompatible with Fascism. Equally foreign to the spirit of Fascism, even if accepted as useful in meeting special political situations—are all internationalistic or League superstructures which, as history shows, crumble to the ground whenever the heart of nations is deeply stirred by sentimental, idealistic or practical considerations. Fascism carries this anti-pacifistic attitude into the life of the individual. "I don't care a damn" (*me ne frego*)—the proud motto of the fighting squads scrawled by a wounded man on his bandages, is not only an act of philosophic stoicism, it sums up a doctrine which is not merely political: it is evidence of a fighting spirit which accepts all risks. It signifies a new style of Italian life. The Fascist accepts and loves life; he rejects and despises suicide as cowardly. Life as he understands it means duty, elevation, conquest; life must be lofty and full, it must be lived for oneself but above all for others, both near bye and far off, present and future.

The population policy of the régime is the consequence of these premises. The Fascist loves his neighbor, but the word "neighbor" does not stand for some vague and unseizable conception. Love of one's neighbor does not exclude necessary educational severity; still less does it exclude differentiation and rank. Fascism will have nothing to do with universal embraces; as a member of the community of nations it looks other peoples straight in the eyes; it is vigilant and on its guard; it follows others in all their manifestations and notes any changes in their interests; and it does not allow itself to be deceived by mutable and fallacious appearances.

Such a conception of life makes Fascism the resolute negation of the doctrine underlying so-called scientific and Marxian socialism, the doctrine of historic materialism which would explain the history of mankind in terms of the class-struggle and by changes in the processes and instruments of production, to the exclusion of all else.

That the vicissitudes of economic life—discoveries of raw materials, new technical processes, scientific inventions—have their importance, no one denies; but that they suffice to explain human history to the exclusion of other factors is absurd. Fascism believes now and always in sanctity and heroism, that is to say in acts in which no economic motive—remote or immediate—is at work. Having denied historic materialism, which sees in men mere puppets on the surface of history, appearing and disappearing on the crest of the waves while in the depths the real directing forces move and work, Fascism also denies the immutable and irreparable character of the class struggle which is the natural outcome of this economic conception of history; above all it denies that the class struggle is the preponderating agent in social transformations. Having thus struck a blow at socialism in the two main points of its doctrine, all that remains of it is the sentimental aspiration—old as humanity itself—toward social relations in which the sufferings and sorrows of the humbler folk will be alleviated. But here again Fascism rejects the economic interpretation of felicity as something to be secured socialistically, almost automatically, at a given stage of economic evolution when all will be assured a maximum of material comfort. Fascism denies the materialistic conception of happiness as a possibility, and abandons it to the economists of the mid-eighteenth century. This means that Fascism denies the equation: well-being = happiness, which sees in men mere animals, content when they can feed and fatten, thus reducing them to a vegetative existence pure and simple.

After socialism, Fascism trains its guns on the whole block of democratic ideologies, and rejects both their premises and their practical applications and implements. Fascism denies that numbers, as such, can be the determining factor in human society; it denies the right of numbers to govern by means of periodical consultations; it asserts the irremediable and fertile and beneficent inequality of men who cannot be levelled by any such mechanical and extrinsic device as universal suffrage. Democratic régimes may be described as those under which the people are, from time to time, deluded into the belief that they exercise sovereignty, while all the time real sovereignty resides in and is exercised by other and sometimes irresponsible and secret forces. Democracy is a kingless régime infested by many kings who are sometimes more exclusive, tyrannical, and destructive than one, even if he be a tyrant. This explains why Fascism—although, for contingent reasons, it was republican in tendency prior to 1922—abandoned that stand before the March on Rome, convinced that the form of government is no longer a matter of preeminent importance, and because the study of past and present monarchies and past and present republics shows that neither monarchy nor republic can be judged *sub specie aeternitatis,* but that each stands for a form of government expressing the political evolution, the history, the traditions, and the psychology of a given country.

Fascism has outgrown the dilemma: monarchy v. republic, over which democratic régimes too long dallied, attributing all insufficiences to the former and proning the latter as a régime of perfection, whereas experience teaches that some republics are inherently reactionary and absolutist while some monarchies accept the most daring political and social experiments.

In one of his philosophic Meditations Renan—who had pre-fascist intuitions—remarks:

"Reason and science are the products of mankind, but it is chimerical to seek reason directly for the people and through the people. It is not essential to the existence of reason that all should be familiar with it; and even if all had to be initiated, this could not be achieved through democracy which seems fated to lead to the extinction of all arduous forms of culture and all highest forms of learning. The maxim that society exists only for the well-being and freedom of the individuals composing it does not seem to be in conformity with nature's plans, which care only for the species and seem ready to sacrifice the individual. It is much to be feared that the last word of democracy thus understood (and let me hasten to add that it is susceptible of a different interpretation) would be a form of society in which a degenerate mass would have no thought beyond that of enjoying the ignoble pleasures of the vulgar".

So far Renan. In rejecting democracy Fascism rejects the absurd conventional lie of political equalitarianism, the habit of collective irresponsibility, the myth of felicity and indefinite progress. But if democracy be understood as meaning a régime in which the masses are not driven back to the margin of the State, then the writer of these pages has already defined Fascism as an organised, centralised, authoritarian democracy.

Fascism is definitely and absolutely opposed to the doctrines of liberalism, both in the political and the economic sphere. The importance of liberalism in the XIXth century should not be exaggerated for present-day polemical purposes, nor should we make of one of the many doctrines which flourished in that century a religion for mankind for the present and for all time to come. Liberalism really flourished for fifteen years only. It arose in 1830 as a reaction to the Holy Alliance which tried to force Europe to recede further back than 1789; it touched its zenith in 1848 when even Pius IXth was a liberal. Its decline began immediately after that year. If 1848 was a year of light and poetry, 1849 was a year of darkness and tragedy. The Roman Republic was killed by a sister republic, that of France. In that same year Marx, in his famous Communist Manifesto, launched the gospel of socialism. In 1851 Napoleon III made his illiberal *coup d'état* and ruled France until 1870 when he was turned out by a popular rising following one of the severest military defeats known to history. The victor was Bismarck who never even knew the whereabouts of liberalism and its prophets. It is symptomatic that throughout the XIXth century the religion of liberalism was completely unknown to so highly civilised a people as the Germans but for one parenthesis which has been described as the "ridiculous parliament of Frankfort" which lasted just one season. Germany attained her national unity outside liberalism and in opposition to liberalism, a doctrine which seems foreign to the German temperament, essentially monarchical, whereas liberalism is the historic and logical anteroom to anarchy. The three stages in the making of German unity were the three wars of 1864, 1866, and 1870, led by such "liberals" as Moltke and Bismarck. And in the upbuilding of Italian unity liberalism played a very minor part when compared to the contribution made by Mazzini and Garibaldi who were not liberals. But for the intervention of the illiberal Napoleon III we should not have had Lombardy, and without that of the illiberal Bismarck at Sadowa and at Sedan very probably we should not have had Venetia in 1866 and in 1870 we should not have entered Rome. The years going from 1870 to 1915 cover a period which marked, even in the opinion of the high priests of the new creed, the twilight of their religion, attacked by decadentism in literature and by activism in practice. Activism: that is to say nationalism, futurism, fascism.

The liberal century, after piling up innumerable Gordian knots, tried to cut them with the sword of the world war. Never has any religion claimed so cruel a sacrifice. Were the Gods of liberalism thirsting for blood?

Now liberalism is preparing to close the doors of its temples, deserted by the peoples who feel that the agnosticism it professed in the sphere of economics and the indifferentism of which it has given proof in the sphere of politics and morals, would lead the world to ruin in the future as they have done in the past.

This explains why all the political experiments of our day are antiliberal, and it is supremely ridiculous to endeavor on this account to put them outside the pale of history, as though history were a preserve set aside for liberalism and its adepts; as though liberalism were the last word in civilisation beyond which no one can go.

The Fascist negation of socialism, democracy, liberalism, should not, however, be interpreted as implying a desire to drive the world backwards to positions occupied prior to 1789, a year commonly referred to as that which opened the demo-liberal century. History does not travel backwards. The Fascist doctrine has not taken De Maistre as its prophet. Monarchical absolutism is of the past, and so is ecclesiolatry. Dead and done for are feudal privileges and the division of society into closed, uncommunicating casts. Neither has the Fascist conception of authority anything in common with that of a police-ridden State.

A party governing a nation "totalitarianly" is a new departure in history. There are no points of reference nor of comparison. From beneath the ruins of liberal, socialist, and democratic doctrines, Fascism extracts those elements which are still vital. It preserves what may be described as "the acquired facts" of history; it rejects all else. That is to say, it rejects the idea of a doctrine suited to all times and to all people. Granted that the XIXth century was the century of socialism, liberalism, democracy, this does not mean that the XXth century must also be the century of socialism, liberalism, democracy. Political doctrines pass; nations remain. We are free to believe that this is the century of authority, a century tending to the "right", a Fascist century. If the XIXth century was the century of the individual (liberalism implies individualism) we are free to believe that this is the "collective" century, and therefore the century of the State. It is quite logical for a new doctrine to make use of the still vital elements of other doctrines. No doctrine was ever born quite new and bright and unheard of. No doctrine can boast absolute originality. It is always connected, if only historically, with those which preceded it and those which will follow it. Thus the scientific socialism of Marx links up to the utopian socialism of the Fouriers, the Owens, the Saint-Simons; thus the liberalism of the XIXth century traces its origin back to the illuministic movement of the XVIIIth, and the doctrines of democracy to those of the Encyclopaedists. All doctrines aim at directing the activities of men towards a given objective; but these activities in their turn react on the doctrine, modifying and adjusting it to new needs, or outstripping it. A doctrine must therefore be a vital act and not a verbal display. Hence the pragmatic strain in Fascism, its will to power, its will to live, its attitude toward violence, and its value.

✦ Reading 48 ✦

Mein Kampf

Adolf Hitler

Nation and Race

There are some truths which are so obvious that for this very reason they are not seen or at least not recognized by ordinary people. They sometimes pass by such truisms as though blind and are most astonished when someone suddenly discovers what everyone really ought to know. Columbus's eggs lie around by the hundreds of thousands, but Columbuses are met with less frequently.

Thus men without exception wander about in the garden of Nature; they imagine that they know practically everything and yet with few exceptions pass blindly by one of the most patent principles of Nature's rule: the inner segregation of the species of all living beings on this earth.

Even the most superficial observation shows that Nature's restricted form of propagation and increase is an almost rigid basic law of all the innumerable forms of expression of her vital urge. Every animal mates only with a member of the same species. The titmouse seeks the titmouse, the finch the finch, the stork the stork, the field mouse the field mouse, the dormouse the dormouse, the wolf the she-wolf, etc.

Only unusual circumstances can change this, primarily the compulsion of captivity or any other cause that makes it impossible to mate within the same species. But then Nature begins to resist this with all possible means, and her most visible protest consists either in refusing further capacity for propagation to bastards or in limiting the fertility of later offspring; in most cases, however, she takes away the power of resistance to disease or hostile attacks.

This is only too natural.

Any crossing of two beings not at exactly the same level produces a medium between the level of the two parents. This means: the offspring will probably stand higher than the racially lower parent, but not as high as the higher one. Consequently, it will later succumb in the struggle against the higher level. Such mating is contrary to the will of Nature for a higher breeding of all life. The precondition for this does not lie in associating superior and inferior, but in the total victory of the former. The stronger must dominate and not blend with the weaker, thus sacrificing his own greatness. Only the born weakling can view this as cruel, but he after all is only a weak and limited man; for if this law did not prevail, any conceivable higher development of organic living beings would be unthinkable.

The consequence of this racial purity, universally valid in Nature, is not only the sharp outward delimitation of the various races, but their uniform character in themselves. The fox is always a fox, the goose a goose, the tiger a tiger, etc., and the difference can lie at most in the varying measure of force, strength, intelligence, dexterity, endurance, etc., of the individual specimens. But you will never find a fox who in his inner attitude might, for example, show humanitarian tendencies toward geese, as similarly there is no cat with a friendly inclination toward mice.

Therefore, here, too, the struggle among themselves arises less from inner aversion than from hunger and love. In both cases, Nature looks on calmly, with satisfaction, in fact. In the struggle for daily bread all those who are weak and sickly or less determined succumb, while the struggle of the males for the female grants the right or opportunity to propagate only to the healthiest. And struggle is always a means for improving a species' health and power of resistance and, therefore, a cause of its higher development.

From: Adolf Hitler, *Mein Kampf,* trans. Ralph Manheim (Boston: Houghton Mifflin Company, 1943), pp. 284–286, 288, 290–296, 300–306, 316–324, 327–329.

If the process were different, all further and higher development would cease and the opposite would occur. For, since the inferior always predominates numerically over the best, if both had the same possibility of preserving life and propagating, the inferior would multiply so much more rapidly that in the end the best would inevitably be driven into the background, unless a correction of this state of affairs were undertaken. Nature does just this by subjecting the weaker part to such severe living conditions that by them alone the number is limited, and by not permitting the remainder to increase promiscuously, but making a new and ruthless choice according to strength and health.

No more than Nature desires the mating of weaker with stronger individuals, even less does she desire the blending of a higher with a lower race, since, if she did, her whole work of higher breeding, over perhaps hundreds of thousands of years, might be ruined with one blow.

Historical experience offers countless proofs of this. It shows with terrifying clarity that in every mingling of Aryan blood with that of lower peoples the result was the end of the cultured people. North America, whose population consists in by far the largest part of Germanic elements who mixed but little with the lower colored peoples, shows a different humanity and culture from Central and South America, where the predominantly Latin immigrants often mixed with the aborigines on a large scale. By this one example, we can clearly and distinctly recognize the effect of racial mixture. The Germanic inhabitant of the American continent, who has remained racially pure and unmixed, rose to be master of the continent; he will remain the master as long as he does not fall a victim to defilement of the blood.

The result of all racial crossing is therefore in brief always the following:

(a) Lowering of the level of the higher race;

(b) Physical and intellectual regression and hence the beginning of a slowly but surely progressing sickness.

To bring about such a development is, then, nothing else but to sin against the will of the eternal creator.

* * *

Everything we admire on this earth today—science and art, technology and inventions—is only the creative product of a few peoples and originally perhaps of *one* race. On them depends the existence of this whole culture. If they perish, the beauty of this earth will sink into the grave with them.

* * *

If we were to divide mankind into three groups, the founders of culture, the bearers of culture, the destroyers of culture, only the Aryan could be considered as the representative of the first group. From him originate the foundations and walls of all human creation, and only the outward form and color are determined by the changing traits of character of the various peoples. He provides the mightiest building stones and plans for all human progress and only the execution corresponds to the nature of the varying men and races. In a few decades, for example, the entire east of Asia will possess a culture whose ultimate foundation will be Hellenic spirit and Germanic technology, just as much as in Europe. Only the *outward* form—in part at least—will bear the features of Asiatic character. It is not true, as some people think, that Japan adds European technology to its culture; no, European science and technology are trimmed with Japanese characteristics. The foundation of actual life is no longer the special Japanese culture, although it determines the color of life—because outwardly, in consequence of its inner difference, it is more conspicuous to the European—but the gigantic scientific-technical achievements of Europe and America; that is, of Aryan peoples. Only on the basis of these achievements can the Orient follow general human progress. They furnish the basis of the struggle for daily bread, create weapons and implements for it, and only the outward form is gradually adapted to Japanese character.

If beginning today all further Aryan influence on Japan should stop, assuming that Europe and America should perish, Japan's present rise in science and technology might continue for a short time; but even in a few years the well would dry up, the Japanese special character would gain, but the present culture would freeze and sink back into the slumber from which it was awakened seven decades ago by the wave of Aryan culture. Therefore, just as the present Japanese development owes its life to Aryan origin, long ago in the gray past foreign influence and foreign spirit awakened the Japanese culture of that time. The best proof of this is furnished by the fact of its subsequent sclerosis and total petrifaction. This can occur in a people only when the original creative racial nucleus has been lost, or if the external influence which furnished the impetus and the material for the first development in the cultural field was later lacking. But if it is established that a people receives the most essential basic materials of its culture from foreign races, that it assimilates and adapts them, and that then, if further external influence is lacking, it rigidifies again and again, such a race may be designated as *'culture-bearing,'* but never as *'culture-creating.'* An examination of the various peoples from this standpoint points to the fact that practically none of them were originally *culture-founding,* but almost always *culture-bearing.*

Approximately the following picture of their development always results:

Aryan races—often absurdly small numerically—subject foreign peoples, and then, stimulated by the special living conditions of the new territory (fertility, climatic conditions, etc.) and assisted by the multitude of lower-type beings standing at their disposal as helpers, develop the intellectual and organizational capacities dormant within them. Often in a few millenniums or even centuries they create cultures which originally bear all the inner characteristics of their nature, adapted to the above-indicated special qualities of the soil and subjected beings. In the end, however, the conquerors transgress against the principle of blood purity, to which they had first adhered; they begin to mix with the subjugated inhabitants and thus end their own existence; for the fall of man in paradise has always been followed by his expulsion.

After a thousand years and more, the last visible trace of the former master people is often seen in the lighter skin color which its blood left behind in the subjugated race, and in a petrified culture which it had originally created. For, once the actual and spiritual conqueror lost himself in the blood of the subjected people, the fuel for the torch of human progress was lost! Just as, through the blood of the former masters, the color preserved a feeble gleam in their memory, likewise the night of cultural life is gently illumined by the remaining creations of the former light-bringers. They shine through all the returned barbarism and too often inspire the thoughtless observer of the moment with the opinion that he beholds the picture of the present people before him, whereas he is only gazing into the mirror of the past.

It is then possible that such a people will a second time, or even more often in the course of its history, come into contact with the race of those who once brought it culture, and the memory of former encounters will not necessarily be present. Unconsciously the remnant of the former master blood will turn toward the new arrival, and what was first possible only by compulsion can now succeed through the people's own will. A new cultural wave makes its entrance and continues until those who have brought it are again submerged in the blood of foreign peoples.

It will be the task of a future cultural and world history to carry on researches in this light and not to stifle in the rendition of external facts, as is so often, unfortunately, the case with our present historical science.

This mere sketch of the development of 'culture-bearing' nations gives a picture of the growth, of the activity, and—the decline—of the true culture-founders of this earth, the Aryans themselves.

As in daily life the so-called genius requires a special cause, indeed, often a positive impetus, to make him shine, likewise the genius-race in the life of peoples. In the monotony of everyday life even significant men often seem insignificant, hardly rising above the average of their environment; as soon, however, as they are approached by a situation in which others lose hope or go astray, the genius rises manifestly from the inconspicuous average child, not seldom to the amazement of all those who had hitherto seen him in the pettiness of bourgeois life—and that is why the prophet seldom has any honor in his own country. Nowhere have we better occasion to observe this than in war. From apparently harmless children, in difficult hours when others lose hope, suddenly heroes shoot up with death-defying determination and an icy cool presence of mind. If this hour of trial had not come, hardly anyone would ever have guessed that a young hero was hidden in this beardless boy. It nearly always takes some stimulus to bring the genius on the scene. The hammer-stroke of Fate which throws one man to the ground suddenly strikes steel in another, and when the shell of everyday life is broken, the previously hidden kernel lies open before the eyes of the astonished world. The world then resists and does not want to believe that the type which is apparently identical with it is suddenly a very different being; a process which is repeated with every eminent son of man.

Though an inventor, for example, establishes his fame only on the day of his invention, it is a mistake to think that genius as such entered into the man only at this hour—the spark of genius exists in the brain of the truly creative man from the hour of his birth. True genius is always inborn and never cultivated, let alone learned.

As already emphasized, this applies not only to the individual man but also to the race. Creatively active peoples always have a fundamental creative gift, even if it should not be recognizable to the eyes of superficial observers. Here, too, outward recognition is possible only in consequence of accomplished deeds, since the rest of the world is not capable of recognizing genius in itself, but sees only its visible manifestations in the form of inventions, discoveries, buildings, pictures, etc.; here again it often takes a long time before the world can fight its way through to this knowledge. Just as in the life of the outstanding individual, genius or extraordinary ability strives for practical realization only when spurred on by special occasions, likewise in the life of nations the creative forces and capacities which are present can often be exploited only when definite preconditions invite.

We see this most distinctly in connection with the race which has been and is the bearer of human cultural development—the Aryans. As soon as Fate leads them toward special conditions, their latent abilities begin to develop in a more and more rapid sequence and to mold themselves into tangible forms. The cultures which they found in such cases are nearly always decisively determined by the existing soil, the given climate, and—the subjected people. This last item, to be sure, is almost the most decisive. The more primitive the technical foundations for a cultural activity, the more necessary is the presence of human helpers who, organizationally assembled and employed, must replace the force of the machine. Without this possibility of using lower human beings, the Aryan would never have been able to take his first steps toward his future culture; just as without the help of various suitable beasts which he knew how to tame, he would not have arrived at a technology which is now gradually permitting him to do without these beasts. The saying, 'The Moor has worked off his debt, the Moor can go,' unfortunately has only too deep a meaning. For thousands of years the horse had to serve man and help him lay the foundations of a development which now, in consequence of the motor car, is making the horse superfluous. In a few years his activity will have ceased, but without his previous collaboration man might have had a hard time getting where he is today.

Thus, for the formation of higher cultures the existence of lower human types was one of the most essential preconditions, since they alone were able to compensate for the lack of technical aids without which a higher development is not conceivable. It is certain that the first culture of humanity was based less on the tamed animal than on the use of lower human beings.

Only after the enslavement of subjected races did the same fate strike beasts, and not the other way around, as some people would like to think. For first the conquered warrior drew the plow—and only after him the horse. Only pacifistic fools can regard this as a sign of human depravity, failing to realize that this development had to take place in order to reach the point where today these sky-pilots could force their drivel on the world.

The progress of humanity is like climbing an endless ladder; it is impossible to climb higher without first taking the lower steps. Thus, the Aryan had to take the road to which reality directed him and not the one that would appeal to the imagination of a modern pacifist. The road of reality is hard and difficult, but in the end it leads where our friend would like to bring humanity by dreaming, but unfortunately removes more than bringing it closer.

Hence it is no accident that the first cultures arose in places where the Aryan, in his encounters with lower peoples, subjugated them and bent them to his will. They then became the first technical instrument in the service of a developing culture.

Thus, the road which the Aryan had to take was clearly marked out. As a conqueror he subjected the lower beings and regulated their practical activity under his command, according to his will and for his aims. But in directing them to a useful, though arduous activity, he not only spared the life of those he subjected; perhaps he gave them a fate that was better than their previous so-called 'freedom.' As long as he ruthlessly upheld the master attitude, not only did he really remain master, but also the preserver and increaser of culture. For culture was based exclusively on his abilities and hence on his actual survival. As soon as the subjected people began to raise themselves up and probably approached the conqueror in language, the sharp dividing wall between master and servant fell. The Aryan gave up the purity of his blood and, therefore, lost his sojourn in the paradise which he had made for himself. He became submerged in the racial mixture, and gradually, more and more, lost his cultural capacity, until at last, not only mentally but also physically, he began to resemble the subjected aborigines more than his own ancestors. For a time he could live on the existing cultural benefits, but then petrifaction set in and he fell a prey to oblivion.

Thus cultures and empires collapsed to make place for new formations.

Blood mixture and the resultant drop in the racial level is the sole cause of the dying out of old cultures; for men do not perish as a result of lost wars, but by the loss of that force of resistance which is contained only in pure blood.

All who are not of good race in this world are chaff.

And all occurrences in world history are only the expression of the races' instinct of self-preservation in the good or bad sense.

* * *

The mightiest counterpart to the Aryan is represented by the Jew. In hardly any people in the world is the instinct of self-preservation developed more strongly than in the so-called 'chosen.' Of this, the mere fact of the survival of this race may be considered the best proof. Where is the people which in the last two thousand years has been exposed to so slight changes of inner disposition, character, etc., as the Jewish people? What people, finally, has gone through greater upheavals than this one—and nevertheless issued from the mightiest catastrophes of mankind unchanged? What an infinitely tough will to live and preserve the species speaks from these facts!

The mental qualities of the Jew have been schooled in the course of many centuries. Today he passes as 'smart,' and this in a certain sense he has been at all times. But his intelligence is not the result of his own development, but of visual instruction through foreigners. For the human mind cannot climb to the top without steps; for every step upward he needs the foundation of the past, and this in the comprehensive sense in which it can be revealed only in general culture. All thinking is based only in small part on man's own knowledge, and mostly on the experience of the time that has preceded. The general cultural level provides the individual man, without his noticing it as a rule, with such a profusion of preliminary knowledge that, thus armed, he can more easily take further steps of his own. The boy of today, for example, grows up among a truly vast number of technical acquisitions of the last centuries, so that he takes for granted and no longer pays attention to much that a hundred years ago was a riddle to even the greatest minds, although for following and understanding our progress in the field in question it is of decisive importance to him. If a very genius from the twenties of the past century should suddenly leave his grave today, it would be harder for him even intellectually to find his way in the present era than for an average boy of fifteen today. For he would lack all the infinite preliminary education which our present contemporary unconsciously, so to speak, assimilates while growing up amidst the manifestations of our present general civilization.

Since the Jew—for reasons which will at once become apparent—was never in possession of a culture of his own, the foundations of his intellectual work were always provided by others. His intellect at all times developed through the cultural world surrounding him.

The reverse process never took place.

For if the Jewish people's instinct of self-preservation is not smaller but larger than that of other peoples, if his intellectual faculties can easily arouse the impression that they are equal to the intellectual gifts of other races, he lacks completely the most essential requirement for a cultured people, the idealistic attitude.

In the Jewish people the will to self-sacrifice does not go beyond the individual's naked instinct of self-preservation. Their apparently great sense of solidarity is based on the very primitive herd instinct that is seen in many other living creatures in this world. It is a noteworthy fact that the herd instinct leads to mutual support only as long as a common danger makes this seem useful or inevitable. The same pack of wolves which has just fallen on its prey together disintegrates when hunger abates into its individual beasts. The same is true of horses which try to defend themselves against an assailant in a body, but scatter again as soon as the danger is past.

It is similar with the Jew. His sense of sacrifice is only apparent. It exists only as long as the existence of the individual makes it absolutely necessary. However, as soon as the common enemy is conquered, the danger threatening all averted and the booty, hidden, the apparent harmony of the Jews among themselves ceases, again making way for their old causal tendencies. The Jew is only united when a common danger forces him to be or a common booty entices him; if these two grounds are lacking, the qualities of the crassest egoism come into their own, and in the twinkling of an eye the united people turns into a horde of rats, fighting bloodily among themselves.

If the Jews were alone in this world, they would stifle in filth and offal; they would try to get ahead of one another in hate-filled struggle and exterminate one another, in so far as the absolute absence of all sense of self-sacrifice, expressing itself in their cowardice, did not turn battle into comedy here too.

So it is absolutely wrong to infer any ideal sense of sacrifice in the Jews from the fact that they stand together in struggle, or, better expressed, in the plundering of their fellow men.

Here again the Jew is led by nothing but the naked egoism of the individual.

That is why the Jewish state—which should be the living organism for preserving and increasing a race—is completely unlimited as to territory. For a state formation to have a definite spatial setting always presupposes an idealistic attitude on the part of the state-race, and especially a correct interpretation of the concept of work. In the exact measure in which this attitude is lacking, any attempt at forming, even of preserving, a spatially delimited state fails. And thus the basis on which alone culture can arise is lacking.

Hence the Jewish people, despite all apparent intellectual qualities, is without any true culture, and especially without any culture of its own. For what sham culture the Jew today possesses is the property of other peoples, and for the most part it is ruined in his hands.

In judging the Jewish people's attitude on the question of human culture, the most essential characteristic we must always bear in mind is that there has never been a Jewish art and accordingly there is none today either; that above all the two queens of all the arts, architecture and music, owe nothing original to the Jews. What they do accomplish in the field of art is either patchwork or intellectual theft. Thus, the Jew lacks those qualities which distinguish the races that are creative and hence culturally blessed.

To what an extent the Jew takes over foreign culture, imitating or rather ruining it, can be seen from the fact that he is mostly found in the art which seems to require least original invention, the art of acting. But even here, in reality, he is only a 'juggler,' or rather an ape; for even here he lacks the last touch that is required for real greatness; even here he is not the creative genius, but a superficial imitator, and all the twists and tricks that he uses are powerless to conceal the inner lifelessness of his creative gift. Here the Jewish press most lovingly helps him along by raising such a roar of hosannahs about even the most mediocre bungler, just so long as he is a Jew, that the rest of the world actually ends up by thinking that they have an artist before them, while in truth it is only a pitiful comedian.

No, the Jew possesses no culture-creating force of any sort, since the idealism, without which there is no true higher development of man, is not present in him and never was present. Hence his intellect will never have a constructive effect, but will be destructive, and in very rare cases perhaps will at most be stimulating, but then as the prototype of the 'force which always wants evil and nevertheless creates good.' Not through him does any progress of mankind occur, but in spite of him.

Since the Jew never possessed a state with definite territorial limits and therefore never called a culture his own, the conception arose that this was a people which should be reckoned among the ranks of the *nomads*. This is a fallacy as great as it is dangerous. The nomad does possess a definitely limited living space, only he does not cultivate it like a sedentary peasant, but lives from the yield of his herds with which he wanders about in his territory. The outward reason for this is to be found in the small fertility of a soil which simply does not permit of settlement. The deeper cause, however, lies in the disparity between the technical culture of an age or people and the natural poverty of a living space. There are territories in which even the Aryan is enabled only by his technology, developed in the course of more than a thousand years, to live in regular settlements, to master broad stretches of soil and obtain from it the requirements of life. If he did not possess this technology, either he would have to avoid these territories or likewise have to struggle along as a nomad in perpetual wandering, provided that his thousand-year-old education and habit of settled residence did not make this seem simply unbearable to him. We must bear in mind that in the time when the American continent was being opened up, numerous Aryans fought for their livelihood as trappers, hunters, etc., and often in larger troops with wife and children, always on the move, so that their existence was completely like that of the nomads. But as soon as their increasing number and better implements permitted them to clear the wild soil and make a stand against the natives, more and more settlements sprang up in the land.

Probably the Aryan was also first a nomad, settling in the course of time, but for that very reason he was never a Jew! No, the Jew is no nomad; for the nomad had also a definite attitude toward the concept of work which could serve as a basis for his later development in so far as the necessary intellectual premises were present. In him the basic idealistic view is present, even if in infinite dilution, hence in his whole being he may seem strange to the Aryan peoples, but not unattractive. In the Jew, however, this attitude is not at all present; for that reason he was never a nomad, but only and always a *parasite* in the body of other peoples. That he sometimes left his previous living space has nothing to do with his own purpose, but results from the fact that from time to time he was thrown out by the host nations he had misused. His spreading is a typical phenomenon for all parasites; he always seeks a new feeding ground for his race.

This, however, has nothing to do with nomadism, for the reason that a Jew never thinks of leaving a territory that he has occupied, but remains where he is, and he sits so fast that even by force it is very hard to drive him out. His extension to ever-new countries occurs only in the moment in which certain conditions for his existence are there present, without which—unlike the nomad—he would not change his residence. He is and remains the typical parasite, a sponger who like a noxious bacillus keeps spreading as soon as a favorable medium invites him. And the effect of his existence is also like that of spongers: wherever he appears, the host people dies out after a shorter or longer period.

Thus, the Jew of all times has lived in the states of other peoples, and there formed his own state, which, to be sure, habitually sailed under the disguise of 'religious community' as long as outward circumstances made a complete revelation of his nature seem inadvisable. But as soon as he felt strong enough to do without the protective cloak, he always dropped the veil and suddenly became what so many of the others previously did not want to believe and see: the Jew.

The Jew's life as a parasite in the body of other nations and states explains a characteristic which once caused Schopenhauer, as has already been mentioned, to call him the 'great master in lying.' Existence impels the Jew to lie, and to lie perpetually, just as it compels the inhabitants of the northern countries to wear warm clothing.

His life within other peoples can only endure for any length of time if he succeeds in arousing the opinion that he is not a people but a 'religious community,' though of a special sort.

And this is the first great lie.

In order to carry on his existence as a parasite on other peoples, he is forced to deny his inner nature. The more intelligent the individual Jew is, the more he will succeed in this deception. Indeed, things can go so far that large parts of the host people will end by seriously believing that the Jew is really a Frenchman or an Englishman, a German or an Italian, though of a special religious faith. Especially state authorities, which always seem animated by the historical fraction of wisdom, most easily fall a victim to this infinite deception. Independent thinking sometimes seems to these circles a true sin against holy advancement, so that we may not be surprised if even today a Bavarian state ministry, for example, still has not the faintest idea that the Jews are members of a *people* and not of a '*religion*' though a glance at the Jew's own newspapers should indicate this even to the most modest mind. The *Jewish Echo* is not yet an official organ, of course, and consequently is unanthoritative as far as the intelligence of one of these government potentates is concerned.

The Jew has always been a people with definite racial characteristics and never a religion; only in order to get ahead he early sought for a means which could distract unpleasant attention from his person. And what would have been more expedient and at the same time more innocent than the 'embezzled' concept of a religious community? For here, too, everything is borrowed or rather stolen. Due to his own original special nature, the Jew cannot possess a religious institution, if for no other reason because he lacks idealism in any form, and hence belief in a hereafter is absolutely foreign to him. And a religion in the Aryan sense cannot be imagined which lacks the conviction of survival after death in some form. Indeed, the Talmud is not a book to prepare a man for the hereafter, but only for a practical and profitable life in this world.

* * *

Since, however, his whole being still has too strong a smell of the foreign for the broad masses of the people in particular to fall readily into his nets, he has his press give a picture of him which is as little in keeping with reality as conversely it serves his desired purpose. His comic papers especially strive to represent the Jews as a harmless little people, with their own peculiarities, of course—like other peoples as well—but even in their gestures, which seem a little strange, perhaps, giving signs of a possibly ludicrous, but always thoroughly honest and benevolent, soul. And the constant effort is to make him seem almost more 'insignificant' than *dangerous.*

His ultimate goal in this stage is the victory of 'democracy,' or, as he understands it: the rule of parliamentarianism. It is most compatible with his requirements; for it excludes the personality—and puts in its place the majority characterized by stupidity, incompetence, and last but not least, cowardice.

The final result will be the overthrow of the monarchy, which is now sooner or later bound to occur.

(j) The tremendous economic development leads to a change in the social stratification of the people. The small craftsman slowly dies out, and as a result the worker's possibility of achieving an independent existence becomes rarer and rarer; in consequence the worker becomes visibly proletarianized. There arises the industrial 'factory worker' whose most essential characteristic is to be sought in the fact that he hardly ever is in a position to found an existence of his own in later life. He is propertyless in the truest sense of the word. His old age is a torment and can scarcely be designated as living.

Once before, a similar situation was created, which pressed urgently for a solution and also found one. The peasants and artisans had slowly been joined by the officials and salaried workers—particularly of the state—as a new class. They, too, were propertyless in the truest sense of the word. The state finally found a way out of this unhealthy condition by assuming the care of the state employee who could not himself provide for his old age; it introduced the pension. Slowly, more and more enterprises followed this example, so that nearly every regularly employed brain-worker draws a pension in later life, provided the concern he works in has achieved or surpassed a certain size. Only by safeguarding the state official in his old age could he be taught the selfless devotion to duty which in the pre-War period was the most eminent quality of German officialdom.

In this way a whole class that had remained propertyless was wisely snatched away from social misery and articulated with the body of the people.

Now this question again, and this time on a much larger scale, faced the state and the nation. More and more masses of people, numbering millions, moved from peasant villages to the larger cities to earn their bread as factory workers in the newly established industries. The working and living conditions of the new class were more than dismal. If nothing else, the more or less mechanical transference of the old artisan's or even peasant's working methods to the new form was by no means suitable. The work done by these men could not be compared with the exertions which the industrial factory worker has to perform. In the old handicraft, this may not have been very important, but in the new working methods it was all the more so. The formal transference of the old working hours to the industrial large-scale enterprise was positively catastrophic, for the actual work done before was but little in view of the absence of our present intensive working methods. Thus, though previously the fourteen-or even fifteen-hour working day had been bearable, it certainly ceased to be bearable at a time when every minute was exploited to the fullest. The result of this senseless transference of the old working hours to the new industrial activity was really unfortunate in two respects: the worker's health was undermined and his faith in a higher justice destroyed. To this finally was added the miserable wages on the one hand and the employer's correspondingly and obviously so vastly superior position on the other.

In the country there could be no social question, since master and hired hand did the same work and above all ate out of the same bowls. But this, too, changed.

The separation of worker and employer now seems complete in all fields of life. How far the inner Judaization of our people has progressed can be seen from the small respect, if not contempt, that is accorded to manual labor. This is not German. It took the foreignization of our life, which was in truth a Jewification, to transform the old respect for manual work into a certain contempt for all physical labor.

Thus, there actually comes into being a new class enjoying very little respect, and one day the question must arise whether the nation would possess the strength to articulate the new class into general society, or whether the social difference would broaden into a classlike cleavage.

But one thing is certain: the new class did not count the worst elements in its ranks, but on the contrary definitely the most energetic elements. The overrefinements of so-called culture had not yet exerted their disintegrating and destructive effects. The broad mass of the new class was not yet infected with the poison of pacifist weakness; it was robust and if necessary even brutal.

While the bourgeoisie is not at all concerned about this all important question, but indifferently lets things slide, the Jew seizes the unlimited opportunity it offers for the future; while on the one hand he organizes capitalistic methods of human exploitation to their ultimate consequence, he approaches the very victims of his spirit and his activity and in a short time becomes the leader of their struggle against himself. 'Against himself' is only figuratively speaking; for the great master of lies understands as always how to make himself appear to be the pure one and to load the blame on others. Since he has the gall to lead the masses, it never even enters their heads that this might be the most infamous betrayal of all times.

And yet it was.

Scarcely has the new class grown out of the general economic shift than the Jew, clearly and distinctly, realizes that it can open the way for his own further advancement. First, he used the bourgeoisie as a battering-ram against the feudal world, then the worker against the bourgeois world. If formerly he knew how to swindle his way to civil rights in the shadow of the bourgeoisie, now he hopes to find the road to his own domination in the worker's struggle for existence.

From now on the worker has no other task but to fight for the future of the Jewish people. Unconsciously he is harnessed to the service of the power which he thinks he is combating. He is seemingly allowed to attack capital, and this is the easiest way of making him fight for it. In this the Jew keeps up an outcry against international capital and in truth he means the national economy which must be demolished in order that the international stock exchange can triumph over its dead body.

Here the Jew's procedure is as follows:

He approaches the worker, simulates pity with his fate, or even indignation at his lot of misery and poverty, thus gaining his confidence. He takes pains to study all the various real or imaginary hardships of his life—and to arouse his longing for a change in such an existence. With infinite shrewdness be fans the need for social justice, somehow slumbering in every Aryan man, into hatred against those who have been better favored by fortune, and thus gives the struggle for the elimination of social evils a very definite philosophical stamp. He establishes the Marxist doctrine.

By presenting it as inseparably bound up with a number of socially just demands, he promotes its spread and conversely the aversion of decent people to fulfill demands which, advanced in such form and company, seem from the outset unjust and impossible to fulfill. For under this cloak of purely social ideas truly diabolic purposes are hidden, yes, they are publicly proclaimed with the most insolent frankness. This theory represents an inseparable mixture of reason and human madness, but always in such a way that only the lunacy can become reality and never the reason. By the categorical rejection of the personality and hence of the nation and its racial content, it destroys the elementary foundations of all human culture which is dependent on just these factors. This is the true inner kernel of the Manxist philosophy in so far as this figment of a criminal brain can be designated as a 'philosophy.' With the shattering of the personality and the race, the essential obstacle is removed to the domination of the inferior being—and this is the Jew.

Precisely in political and economic madness lies the sense of this doctrine. For this prevents all truly intelligent people from entering its service, while those who are intellectually less active and poorly educated in economics hasten to it with flying colors. The intellectuals for this movement—for even this movement needs intellectuals for its existence—are 'sacrificed' by the Jew from his own ranks.

Thus there arises a pure movement entirely of manual workers under Jewish leadership, apparently aiming to improve the situation of the worker, but in truth planning the enslavement and with it the destruction of all non-Jewish peoples.

The general pacifistic paralysis of the national instinct of self-preservation begun by Freemasonry in the circles of the so-called intelligentsia is transmitted to the broad masses and above all to the bourgeoisie by the activity of the big papers which today are always Jewish. Added to there two weapons of disintegration comes a third and by far the most terrible, the organization of brute force. As a shock and storm troop, Marxism is intended to finish off what the preparatory softening up with the first two weapons has made ripe for collapse.

Here we have teamwork that is positively brilliant—and we need really not be surprised if in confronting it those very institutions which always like to represent themselves as the pillars of a more or less legendary state authority hold up least. It is in our high and highest state officialdom that the Jew has at all times (aside from a few exceptions) found the most compliant abettor of his work of disintegration. Cringing submissiveness to superiors and high-handed arrogance to inferiors distinguish this class to the same degree as a narrow-mindedness that often cries to high Heaven and is only exceeded by a self-conceit that is sometimes positively amazing.

And these are qualities that the Jew needs in our authorities and loves accordingly.

The practical struggle which now begins, sketched in broad outlines, takes the following course:

In keeping with the ultimate aims of the Jewish struggle, which are not exhausted in the mere economic conquest of the world, but also demand its political subjugation, the Jew divides the organization of his Marxist world doctrine into two halves which, apparently separate from one another, in truth form an inseparable whole: the political and the trade-union movement.

The trade-union movement does the recruiting. In the hard struggle for existence which the worker must carry on, thanks to the greed and shortsightedness of many employers, it offers him aid and protection, and thus the possibility of winning better living conditions. If, at a time when the organized national community, the state, concerns itself with him little or not at all, the worker does not want to hand over the defense of his vital human rights to the blind caprice of people who in part have little sense of responsibility and are often heartless to boot, he must take their defense into his own hands. In exact proportion as the so-called national bourgeoisie, blinded by financial interests, sets the heaviest obstacles in the path of this struggle for existence and not only resists all attempts at shortening the inhumanly long working day, abolishing child labor, safeguarding and protecting the woman, improving sanitary conditions in the workshops and homes, but often actually sabotages them, the shrewder Jew takes the oppressed people under his wing. Gradually he becomes the leader of the trade-union movement, all the more easily as he is not interested in really eliminating social evils in an honest sense, but only in training an economic storm troop, blindly devoted to him, with which to destroy the national economic independence. For while the conduct of a healthy social policy will consistently move between the aims of preserving the national health on the one hand and safeguarding an independent national economy on the other, for the Jew in his struggle these two criteria not only cease to exist, but their elimination, among other things, is his life goal. He desires, not the preservation of an independent national economy, but its destruction. Consequently, no pangs of conscience can prevent him as a leader of the trade-union movement from raising demands which not only overshoot the goal, but whose fulfillment is either impossible for practical purposes or means the ruin of the national economy. Moreover, he does not want to have a healthy, sturdy race before him, but a rickety herd capable of being subjugated. This desire again permits him to raise demands of the most senseless kind whose practical fulfillment he himself knows to be impossible and which, therefore, could not lead to any change in things, but at most to a wild incitement of the masses. And that is what he is interested in and not a true and honest improvement of social conditions.

Hence the Jewish leadership in trade-union affairs remains uncontested until an enormous work of enlightenment influences the broad masses and sets them right about their never-ending misery, or else the state disposes of the Jew and his work. For as long as the insight of the masses remains as slight as now and the state as indifferent as today, these masses will always be first to follow the man who in economic matters offers the most shameless promises. And in this the Jew is a master. For in his entire activity he is restrained by no moral scruples!

And so he inevitably drives every competitor in this sphere from the field in a short time. In keeping with all his inner rapacious brutality, he at once teaches the trade-union movement the most brutal use of violence. If anyone by his intelligence resists the Jewish lures, his defiance and understanding are broken by terror. The success of such an activity is enormous.

Actually the Jew by means of the trade union, which could be a blessing for the nation, shatters the foundations of the national economy.

Parallel with this, the political organization advances.

It plays hand in glove with the trade-union movement, for the latter prepares the masses for political organization, in fact, lashes them into it with violence and coercion. Furthermore, it is the permanent financial source from which the political organization feeds its enormous apparatus. It is the organ controlling the political activity of the individual and does the pandering in all big demonstrations of a political nature. In the end it no longer comes out for political interests at all, but places its chief instrument of struggle, the cessation of work in the form of a mass and general strike, in the service of the political idea.

By the creation of a press whose content is adapted to the intellectual horizon of the least educated people, the political and trade-union organization finally obtains the agitational institution by which the lowest strata of the nation are made ripe for the most reckless acts. Its function is not to lead people out of the swamp of a base mentality to a higher stage, but to cater to their lowest instincts. Since the masses are as mentally lazy as they are sometimes presumptuous, this is a business as speculative as it is profitable.

It is this press, above all, which wages a positively fanatical and slanderous struggle, tearing down everything which can be regarded as a support of national independence, cultural elevation, and the economic independence of the nation.

Above all, it hammers away at the characters of all those who will not bow down to the Jewish presumption to dominate, or whose ability and genius in themselves seem a danger to the Jew. For to be hated by the Jew it is not necessary to combat him; no, it suffices if he suspects that someone might even conceive the idea of combating him some time or that on the strength of his superior genius he is an augmenter of the power and greatness of a nationality hostile to the Jew.

His unfailing instinct in such things scents the original soul in everyone, and his hostility is assured to anyone who is not spirit of his spirit. Since the Jew is not the attacked but the attacker, not only anyone who attacks passes as his enemy, but also anyone who resists him. But the means with which he seeks to break such reckless but upright souls is not honest warfare, but lies and slander.

Here he stops at nothing, and in his vileness he becomes so gigantic that no one need be surprised if among our people the personification of the devil as the symbol of all evil assumes the living shape of the Jew.

The ignorance of the broad masses about the inner nature of the Jew, the lack of instinct and narrow-mindedness of our upper classes, make the people an easy victim for this Jewish campaign of lies.

While from innate cowardice the upper classes turn away from a man whom the Jew attacks with lies and slander, the broad masses from stupidity or simplicity believe everything. The state authorities either cloak themselves in silence or, what usually happens, in order to put an end to the Jewish press campaign, they persecute the unjustly attacked, which, in the eyes of such an official ass, passes as the preservation of state authority and the safeguarding of law and order.

Slowly fear of the Marxist weapon of Jewry descends like a nightmare on the mind and soul of decent people.

They begin to tremble before the terrible enemy and thus have become his final victim.

* * *

If we pass all the causes of the German collapse in review, the ultimate and most decisive remains the failure to recognize the racial problem and especially the Jewish menace.

The defeats on the battlefield in August, 1918, would have been child's play to bear. They stood in no proportion to the victories of our people. It was not they that caused our downfall; no, it was brought about by that power which prepared these defeats by systematically over many decades robbing our people of the political and moral instincts and forces which alone make nations capable and hence worthy of existence.

In heedlessly ignoring the question of the preservation of the racial foundations of our nation, the old Reich disregarded the sole right which gives life in this world. Peoples which bastardize themselves, or let themselves be bastardized, sin against the will of eternal Providence, and when their ruin is encompassed by a stronger enemy it is not an injustice done to them, but only the restoration of justice. If a people no longer wants to respect the Nature-given qualities of its being which root in its blood, it has no further right to complain over the loss of its earthly existence.

Everything on this earth is capable of improvement. Every defeat can become the father of a subsequent victory, every lost war the cause of a later resurgence, every hardship the fertilization of human energy, and from every oppression the forces for a new spiritual rebirth can come—as long as the blood is preserved pure.

The lost purity of the blood alone destroys inner happiness forever, plunges man into the abyss for all time, and the consequences can never more be eliminated from body and spirit.

Only by examining and comparing all other problems of life in the light of this one question shall we see how absurdly petty they are by this standard. They are all limited in time—but the question of preserving or not preserving the purity of the blood will endure as long as there are men.

All really significant symptoms of decay of the pre-War period can in the last analysis be reduced to racial causes.

Whether we consider questions of general justice or cankers of economic life, symptoms of cultural decline or processes of political degeneration, questions of faulty schooling or the bad influence exerted on grown-ups by the press, etc., everywhere and always it is fundamentally the disregard of the racial needs of our own people or failure to see a foreign racial menace.

And that is why all attempts at reform, all works for social relief and political exertions, all economic expansion and every apparent increase of intellectual knowledge were futile as far as their results were concerned. The nation, and the organism which enables and preserves its life on this earth, the state, did not grow inwardly healthier, but obviously languished more and more. All the illusory prosperity of the old Reich could not hide its inner weakness, and every attempt really to strengthen the Reich failed again and again, due to disregarding the most important question.

It would be a mistake to believe that the adherents of the various political tendencies which were tinkering around on the German national body—yes, even a certain section of the leaders—were bad or malevolent men in themselves. Their activity was condemned to sterility only because the best of them saw at most the forms of our general disease and tried to combat them, but blindly ignored the virus. Anyone who systematically follows the old Reich's line of political development is bound to arrive, upon calm examination, at the realization that even at the time of the unification, hence the rise of the German nation, the inner decay was already in full swing, and that despite all apparent political successes and despite increasing economic wealth, the general situation was deteriorating from year to year. If nothing else, the elections for the Reichstag announced, with their outward swelling of the Marxist vote, the steadily approaching inward and hence also outward collapse. All the successes of the so-called bourgeois parties were worthless, not only because even with so-called bourgeois electoral victories they were unable to halt the numerical growth of the Marxist flood, but because they themselves above all now bore the ferments of decay in their own bodies. Without suspecting it, the bourgeois world itself was inwardly infected with the deadly poison of Marxist ideas and its resistance often sprang more from the competitor's envy of ambitious leaders than from a fundamental rejection of adversaries determined to fight to the utmost. In these long years there was only one who kept up an imperturbable, unflagging fight, and this was the *Jew.* His Star of David rose higher and higher in proportion as our people's will for self-preservation vanished.

Therefore, in August, 1914, it was not a people resolved to attack which rushed to the battlefield; no, it was only the last flicker of the national instinct of self-preservation in face of the progressing pacifist-Marxist paralysis of our national body. Since even in these days of destiny, our people did not recognize the inner enemy, all outward resistance was in vain and Providence did not bestow her reward on the victorious sword, but followed the law of eternal retribution.

On the basis of this inner realization, there took form in our new movement the leading principles as well as the tendency, which in our conviction were alone capable, not only of halting the decline of the German people, but of creating the granite foundation upon which some day a state will rest which represents, not an alien mechanism of economic concerns and interests, but a national organism:

A Germanic State of the German Nation

✦ Reading 49 ✦

Homage to Catalonia

George Orwell

On the eastern side of Huesca, until late March, nothing happened—almost literally nothing. We were twelve hundred metres from the enemy. When the Fascists were driven back into Huesca the Republican Army troops who held this part of the line had not been over-zealous in their advance, so that the line formed a kind of pocket. Later it would have to be advanced—a ticklish job under fire—but for the present the enemy might as well have been non-existent; our sole preoccupation was keeping warm and getting enough to eat. As a matter of fact there were things in this period that interested me greatly, and I will describe some of them later. But I shall be keeping nearer to the order of events if I try here to give some account of the internal political situation on the Government side.

At the beginning I had ignored the political side of the war, and it was only about this time that it began to force itself upon my attention. If you are not interested in the horrors of party politics, please skip; I am trying to keep the political parts of this narrative in separate chapters for precisely that purpose. But at the same time it would be quite impossible to write about the Spanish war from a purely military angle. It was above all things a political war. No event in it, at any rate during the first year, is intelligible unless one has some grasp of the inter-party struggle that was going on behind the Government lines.

When I came to Spain, and for some time afterwards, I was not only uninterested in the political situation but unaware of it. I knew there was a war on, but I had no notion what kind of a war. If you had asked me why I had joined the militia I should have answered: 'To fight against Fascism,' and if you had asked me what I was fighting *for,* I should have answered: 'Common decency.' I had accepted the *News Chronicle-New Statesman* version of the war as the defence of civilization against a maniacal outbreak by an army of Colonel Blimps in the pay of Hitler. The revolutionary atmosphere of Barcelona had attracted me deeply, but I had made no attempt to understand it. As for the kaleidoscope of political parties and trade unions, with their tiresome names—P.S.U.C., P.O.U.M., F.A.I., C.N.T., U.G.T., J.C.I., J.S.U., A.I.T.—they merely exasperated me. It looked at first sight as though Spain were suffering from a plague of initials. I knew that I was serving in something called the P.O.U.M. (I had only joined the P.O.U.M. militia rather than any other because I happened to arrive in Barcelona with I.L.P. papers), but I did not realize that there were serious differences between the political parties. At Monte Pocero, when they pointed to the position on our left and said: 'Those are the Socialists' (meaning the P.S.U.C.), I was puzzled and said: 'Aren't we all Socialists?' I thought it idiotic that people fighting for their lives should *have* separate parties; my attitude always was, 'Why can't we drop all this political nonsense and get on with the war?' This of course was the correct 'anti-Fascist' attitude which had been carefully disseminated by the English newspapers, largely in order to prevent people from grasping the real nature of the struggle. But in Spain, especially in Catalonia, it was an attitude that no one could or did keep up indefinitely. Everyone, however unwillingly, took sides sooner or later. For even if one cared nothing for the political parties and their conflicting 'lines,' it was too obvious that one's own destiny was involved. As a militiaman one was a soldier against Franco, but one was also a pawn in an enormous struggle that was being fought out between two political theories. When I scrounged for firewood on the mountain-side and wondered whether this was really a war or whether the *News Chronicle* had made it up, when I dodged the Com-

From: George Orwell, *Homage to Catalonia* (New York: Harcourt Brace Jovanovich, Publishers, 1952), pp. 46–48, 72–85.

munist machine-guns in the Barcelona riots, when I finally fled from Spain with the police one jump behind me—all these things happened to me in that particular way because I was serving in the P.O.U.M. militia and not in the P.S.U.C. So great is the difference between two sets of initials! . . .

* * *

Meanwhile, the daily—more particularly nightly—round, the common task. Sentry-go, patrols, digging; mud, rain, shrieking winds, and occasional snow. It was not till well into April that the nights grew noticeably warmer. Up here on the plateau the March days were mostly like an English March, with bright blue skies and nagging winds. The winter barley was a foot high, crimson buds were forming on the cherry trees (the line here ran through deserted orchards and vegetable gardens), and if you searched the ditches you could find violets and a kind of wild hyacinth like a poor specimen of a bluebell. Immediately behind the line there ran a wonderful, green, bubbling stream, the first transparent water I had seen since coming to the front. One day I set my teeth and crawled into the river to have my first bath in six weeks. It was what you might call a brief bath, for the water was mainly snow-water and not much above freezing-point.

Meanwhile nothing happened, nothing ever happened. The English had got into the habit of saying that this wasn't a war, it was a bloody pantomime. We were hardly under direct fire from the Fascists. The only danger was from stray bullets, which, as the lines curved forward on either side, came from several directions. All the casualties at this time were from strays. Arthur Clinton got a mysterious bullet that smashed his left shoulder and disabled his arm, permanently, I am afraid. There was a little shell-fire, but it was extraordinarily ineffectual. The scream and crash of the shells was actually looked upon as a mild diversion. The Fascists never dropped their shells on our parapet. A few hundred yards behind us there was a country house, called La Granja, with big farm-buildings, which was used as a store, headquarters, and cook-house for this sector of the line. It was this that the Fascist gunners were trying for, but they were five or six kilometres away and they never aimed well enough to do more than smash the windows and chip the walls. You were only in danger if you happened to be coming up the road when the firing started, and the shells plunged into the fields on either side of you. One learned almost immediately the mysterious art of knowing by the sound of a shell how close it will fall. The shells the Fascists were firing at this period were wretchedly bad. Although they were 150 mm. they only made a crater about six feet wide by four deep, and at least one in four failed to explode. There were the usual romantic tales of sabotage in the Fascist factories and unexploded shells in which, instead of the charge, there was found a scrap of paper saying 'Red Front,' but I never saw one. The truth was that the shells were hopelessly old; someone picked up a brass fuse-cap stamped with the date, and it was 1917. The Fascist guns were of the same make and calibre as our own, and the unexploded shells were often reconditioned and fired back. There was said to be one old shell with a nickname of its own which travelled daily to and fro, never exploding.

At night small patrols used to be sent into no man's land to lie in ditches neat the Fascist lines and listen for sounds (bugle-calls, motor-horns, and so forth) that indicated activity in Huesca. There was a constant come-and-go of Fascist troops, and the numbers could be checked to some extent from listeners' reports. We always had special orders to report the ringing of church bells. It seemed that the Fascists always heard mass before going into action. In among the fields and orchards there were deserted mud-walled huts which it was safe to explore with a lighted match when you had plugged up the windows. Sometimes you came on valuable pieces of loot such as a hatchet or a Fascist water-bottle (better than ours and greatly sought after). You could explore in the daytime as well, but mostly it had to be done crawling on all fours. It was queer to creep about in those empty, fertile fields where everything had been arrested just at the harvest-moment. Last year's crops had never been touched. The unpruned vines were snaking across the ground, the cobs on the standing maize had gone as hard as stone, the mangels and sugar-beets were hypertrophied into huge woody lumps. How the peasants must have cursed both armies! Sometimes parties of men went spud-gathering in no man's land. About a mile to the right of us, where the lines were closer together, there was a patch of potatoes that was frequented both by the Fascists and ourselves. We went there in the daytime, they only at night, as it was commanded by our machine-guns. One night to our annoyance they turned out *en masse* and cleared up the whole patch. We discovered another patch farther on, where there was practically no cover and you had to lift the potatoes lying on your belly—a fatiguing job. If their machine-gunners spotted you, you had to flatten yourself out like a rat when it squirms under a door, with the bullets cutting up the clods a few yards behind you. It seemed worth it at the time. Potatoes were getting very scarce. If you got a sackful you could take them down to the cookhouse and swap them for a water-bottleful of coffee.

And still nothing happened, nothing ever looked like happening. 'When are we going to attack? Why don't we attack?' were the questions you heard night and day from Spaniard and Englishman alike. When you think what fighting means it is queer that soldiers want to fight, and yet undoubtedly they do. In stationary warfare there are three things that all soldiers long for: a battle, more cigarettes, and a week's leave. We were somewhat better armed now than before. Each man had a hundred and fifty rounds of ammunition instead of fifty, and by degrees we were being issued with bayonets, steel helmets, and a few bombs. There were constant rumours of forthcoming battles, which I have since thought were deliberately circulated to keep up the spirits of the troops. It did not need much military knowledge to see that there would be no major action on this side of Huesca, at any rate for the time being. The strategic point was the road to Jaca, over on the other side. Later, when the Anarchists made their attacks on the Jaca road, our job was to make 'holding attacks' and force the Fascists to divert troops from the other side.

During all this time, about six weeks, there was only one action on our part of the front. This was when our Shock Troopers attacked the Manicomio, a disused lunatic asylum which the Fascists had converted into a fortress. There were several hundred refugee Germans serving with the P.O.U.M. They were organized in a special battalion called the Battallon de Choque, and from a military point of view they were on quite a different level from the rest of the militia—indeed, were more like soldiers than anyone I saw in Spain, except the Assault Guards and some of the International Column. The attack was mucked up, as usual. How many operations in this war, on the Government side, were *not* mucked up, I wonder? The Shock Troops took the Manicomio by storm, but the troops, of I forget which militia, who were to support them by seizing the neighbouring hill that commanded the Manicomio, were badly let down. The captain who led them was one of those Regular Army officers of doubtful loyalty whom the Government persisted in employing. Either from fright or treachery he warned the Fascists by flinging a bomb when they were two hundred yards away. I am glad to say his men shot him dead on the spot. But the surprise-attack was no surprise, and the militiamen were mown down by heavy fire and driven off the hill, and at nightfall the Shock Troops had to abandon the Manicomio. Through the night the ambulances filed down the abominable road to Sietamo, killing the badly wounded with their joltings.

All of us were lousy by this time; though still cold it was warm enough for that. I have had a big experience of body vermin of various kinds, and for sheer beastliness the louse beats everything I have encountered. Other insects, mosquitoes for instance, make you suffer more, but at least they aren't *resident* vermin. The human louse somewhat resembles a tiny lobster, and he lives chiefly in your trouser. Short of burning all your clothes there is no known way of getting rid of him. Down the seams of your trousers he lays his glittering white eggs, like tiny grains of rice, which hatch out and breed families of their own at horrible speed. I think the pacifists might find it helpful to illustrate their pamphlets with enlarged photographs of lice. Glory of war, indeed! In war *all* soldiers are lousy, at least when it is warm enough. The men who fought at Verdun, at Waterloo, at Flodden, at Senlac, at Thermopylae—every one of them had lice crawling over his testicles. We kept the brutes down to some extent by burning out the eggs and by bathing as often as we could face it. Nothing short of lice could have driven me into that ice-cold river.

Everything was running short—boots, clothes, tobacco, soap, candles, matches, olive oil. Our uniforms were dropping to pieces, and many of the men had no boots, only rope-soled sandals. You came on piles of worn-out boots everywhere. Once we kept a dug-out fire burning for two days mainly with boots, which are not bad fuel. By this time my wife was in Barcelona and used to send me tea, chocolate, and even cigars when such things were procurable; but even in Barcelona everything was running short, especially tobacco. The tea was a godsend, though we had no milk and seldom any sugar. Parcels were constantly being sent from England to men in the contingent, but they never arrived; food, clothes, cigarettes—everything was either refused by the Post Office or seized in France. Curiously enough, the only firm that succeeded in sending packets of tea—even, on one memorable occasion, a tin of biscuits—to my wife was the Army and Navy Stores. Poor old Army and Navy! They did their duty nobly, but perhaps they might have felt happier if the stuff had been going to Franco's side of the barricade. The shortage of tobacco was the worst of all. At the beginning we had been issued with a packet of cigarettes a day, then it got down to eight cigarettes a day, then to five. Finally there were ten deadly days when there was no issue of tobacco at all. For the first time, in Spain, I saw something that you see every day in London—people picking up fag-ends.

Towards the end of March I got a poisoned hand that had to be lanced and put in a sling. I had to go into hospital, but it was not worth sending me to Sietamo for such a petty injury, so I stayed in the so-called hospital at Monflorite, which was merely a casualty clearing station. I was there ten days, part of the time in bed. The *practicantes* (hospital assistants) stole practically every valuable object I possessed, including my camera and all my photographs. At the front everyone stole, it was the inevitable effect of shortage, but the hospital people were always the worst. Later, in the hospital at Barcelona, an American who had come to join the International Column on a ship that was torpedoed by an Italian submarine, told me how he was carried ashore wounded, and how, even as they lifted him into the ambulance, the stretcher-bearers pinched his wrist-watch.

While my arm was in the sling I spent several blissful days wandering about the countryside. Monflorite was the usual huddle of mud and stone houses, with narrow tortuous alleys that had been churned by lorries till they looked like the craters of the moon. The church had been badly knocked about but was used as a military store. In the whole neighbourhood there were only two farm-houses of any size, Torre Lorenzo and Torre Fabian, and only two really large buildings, obviously the houses of the landowners who had once lorded it over the countryside; you could see their wealth reflected in the miserable huts of the peasants. Just behind the river, close to the front line, there was an enormous flour-mill with a country-house attached to it. It seemed shameful to see the huge costly machine rusting useless and the wooden flour-chutes torn down for firewood. Later on, to get firewood for the troops farther back, parties of men were sent in lorries to wreck the place systematically. They used to smash the floorboards of a room by bursting a hand-grenade in it. La Granja, our store and cookhouse, had possibly at one time been a convent. It had huge courtyards and outhouses, covering an acre or more, with stabling for thirty or forty horses. The country-houses in that part of Spain are of no interest architecturally, but their farm-buildings, of lime-washed stone with round arches and magnificent roof-beams, are noble places, built on a plan that has probably not altered for centuries. Sometimes it gave you a sneaking sympathy with the Fascist ex-owners to see the way the militia treated the buildings they had seized. In La Granja every room that was not in use had been turned into a latrine—a frightful shambles of smashed furniture and excrement. The little church that adjoined it, its walls perforated by shell-holes, had its floor inches deep in dung. In the great courtyard where the cooks ladled out the rations the litter of rusty tins, mud, mule dung, and decaying food was revolting. It gave point to the old army song:

There are rats, rats,
Rats as big as cats,
In the quartermaster's store!

The ones at La Granja itself really were as big as cats, or nearly; great bloated brutes that waddled over the beds of muck, too impudent even to run away unless you shot at them.

Spring was really here at last. The blue in the sky was softer, the air grew suddenly balmy. The frogs were mating noisily in the ditches. Round the drinking-pool that served for the village mules I found exquisite green frogs the size of a penny, so brilliant that the young grass looked dull beside them. Peasant lads went out with bucket hunting for snails, which they roasted alive on sheets of tin. As soon as the weather improved the peasants had turned out for the spring ploughing. It is typical of the utter vagueness in which the Spanish agrarian revolution is wrapped that I could not even discover for certain whether the land here was collectivized or whether the peasants had simply divided it up among themselves. I fancy that in theory it was collectivized, this being P.O.U.M. and Anarchist territory. At any rate the landowners were gone, the fields were being cultivated, and people seemed satisfied. The friendliness of the peasants towards ourselves never ceased to astonish me. To some of the older ones the war must have seemed meaningless, visibly it produced a shortage of everything and a dismal dull life for everybody, and at the best of times peasants hate having troops quartered upon them. Yet they were invariably friendly—I suppose reflecting that, however intolerable we might be in other ways, we did stand between them and their one-time landlords. Civil war is a queer thing. Huesca was not five miles away, it was these people's market town, all of them had relatives there, every week of their lives they had gone there to sell their poultry and vegetables. And now for eight months an impenetrable barrier of barbed wire and machine-guns had lain between. Occasionally it slipped their memory. Once I was talking to an old woman who was carrying one of those tiny iron lamps in which the Spaniards burn olive oil. "Where can I buy a lamp like that?" I said. "In Huesca," she said without thinking, and then we both laughed. The village girls were splendid vivid creatures with coal-black hair, a swinging walk, and a straightforward, man-to-man demeanour which was probably a by-product of the revolution.

Men in ragged blue shirts and black corduroy breeches, with broad-brimmed straw hats, were ploughing the fields behind team of mules with rhythmically flopping ears. Their ploughs were wretched things, only stirring the soil, not cutting anything we should regard as a furrow. All the agricultural implements were pitifully antiquated, everything being governed by the expensiveness of metal. A broken ploughshare, for instance, was patched, and then patched again, till sometimes it was mainly patches. Rakes and pitchforks were made of wood. Spades, among a people who seldom possessed boots, were unknown; they did their digging with a clumsy hoe like those used in India. There was a kind of harrow that took one straight back to the later Stone Age. It was made of boards joined together, to about the size of a kitchen table; in the boards hundreds of holes were morticed, and into each hole was jammed a piece of flint which had been chipped into shape exactly as men used to chip them ten thousand years ago. I remember my feeling almost of horror when I first came upon one of these things in a derelict hut in no man's land. I had to puzzle over it for a long while before grasping that it was a harrow. It made me sick to think of the work that must go into the making of such a thing, and the poverty that was obliged to use flint in place of steel. I have felt more kindly towards industrialism ever since. But in the village there were two up-to-date farm tractors, no doubt seized from some big landowner's estate.

Once or twice I wandered out to the little walled graveyard that stood a mile or so from the village. The dead from the front were normally sent to Sietamo; these were the village dead. It was queerly different from an English graveyard. No reverence for the dead here! Everything overgrown with bushes and coarse grass, human bones littered everywhere. But the really surprising thing was the almost complete lack of religious inscriptions on the gravestones, though they all dated from before the revolution. Only once, I think, I saw the 'Pray for the soul of so-and-so' which is usual on Catholic graves. Most of the inscriptions were purely secular, with ludicrous poems about the virtues of the deceased. On perhaps one grave in four or five there was a small cross or a perfunctory reference to Heaven; this had usually been chipped off by some industrious atheist with a chisel.

It struck me that the people in this part of Spain must be genuinely without religious feeling—religious feeling, I mean, in the orthodox sense. It is curious that all the time I was in Spain I never once saw a person cross himself; yet you would think such a movement would become instinctive, revolution or no revolution. Obviously the Spanish Church will come back (as the saying goes, night and the Jesuits always return), but there is no doubt that at the outbreak of the revolution it collapsed and was smashed up to an extent that would be unthinkable even for the moribund C. of E. in like circumstances. To the Spanish people, at any rate in Catalonia and Aragon, the Church was a racket pure and simple. And possibly Christian belief was replaced to some extent by Anarchism, whose influence is widely spread and which undoubtedly has a religious tinge.

It was the day I came back from hospital that we advanced the line to what was really its proper position, about a thousand yards forward, along the little stream that lay a couple of hundred yards in front of the Fascist line. This operation ought to have been carried out months earlier. The point of doing it now was that the Anarchists were attacking on the Jaca road, and to advance on this side made them divert troops to face us.

We were sixty or seventy hours without sleep, and my memories go down into a sort of blur, or rather a series of pictures. Listening-duty in no man's land, a hundred yards from the Casa Francesa, a fortified farm-house which was part of the Fascist line. Seven hours lying in a horrible marsh, in reedy-smelling water into which one's body subsided gradually deeper and deeper: the reedy smell, the numbing cold, the stars immovable in the black sky, the harsh croaking of the frogs. Though this was April it was the coldest night that I remember in Spain. Only a hundred yards behind us the working-parties were hard at it, but there was utter silence except for the chorus of the frogs. Just once during the night I heard a sound—the familiar noise of a sand-bag being flattened with a spade. It is queer how, just now and again, Spaniards can carry out a brilliant feat of organization. The whole move was beautifully planned. In seven hours six hundred men constructed twelve hundred metres of trench and parapet, at distances of from a hundred and fifty to three hundred yards from the Fascist line, and all so silently that the Fascists heard nothing, and during the night there was only one casualty. There were more next day, of course. Every man had his job assigned to him, even to the cook-house orderlies who suddenly arrived when the work was done with buckets of wine laced with brandy.

And then the dawn coming up and the Fascists suddenly discovering that we were there. The square white block of the Casa Francesa, though it was two hundred yards away, seemed to tower over us, and the machine-guns in its sand-bagged upper windows seemed to be pointing straight down into the trench. We all stood gaping at it, wondering why the Fascists didn't see us. Then a vicious swirl of bullets, and everyone had flung himself on his knees and was frantically digging, deepening the trench and scooping out small shelters in the side. My arm was still in bandages, I could not dig, and I spent most of that day reading a detective story—*The Missing Moneylender* its name was. I don't remember the plot of it, but I remember very clearly the feeling of sitting there reading it; the dampish clay of the trench bottom underneath me, the constant shifting of my legs out of the way as men hurried stooping down the trench, the crack-crack-crack of bullets a foot or two overhead. Thomas Parker got a bullet through the top of his thigh, which, as he said, was nearer to being a D.S.O. than he cared about. Casualties were happening all along the line, but nothing to what there would have been if they had caught us on the move during the night. A deserter told us afterwards that five Fascist sentries were shot for negligence. Even now they could have massacred us if they had had the initiative to bring up a few mortars. It was an awkward job getting the wounded down the narrow, crowded trench. I saw one poor devil, his breeches dark with blood, flung out of his stretcher and gasping in agony. One had to carry wounded men a long distance, a mile or more, for even when a road existed the ambulances never came very near the front line. If they came too near the Fascists had a habit of shelling them—justifiably, for in modern war no one scruples to use an ambulance for carrying ammunition.

And then, next night, waiting at Torre Fabian for an attack that was called off at the last moment by wireless. In the barn where we waited the floor was a thin layer of chaff over deep beds of bones, human bones and cows' bones mixed up, and the place was alive with rats. The filthy brutes came swarming out of the ground on every side. If there is one thing I hate more than another it is a rat running over me in the darkness. However, I had the satisfaction of catching one of them a good punch that sent him flying.

And then waiting fifty or sixty yards from the Fascist parapet for the order to attack. A long line of men crouching in an irrigation ditch with their bayonets peeping over the edge and the whites of their eyes shining through the darkness. Kopp and Benjamin squatting behind us with a man who had a wireless receiving-box strapped to his shoulders. On the western horizon rosy gun-flashes followed at intervals of several seconds by enormous explosions. And then a pip-pip-pip noise from the wireless and the whispered order that we were to get out of it while the going was good. We did so, but not quickly enough. Twelve wretched children of the J.C.I. (the Youth League of the P.O.U.M., corresponding to the J.S.U. of the P.S.U.C.) who had been posted only about forty yards from the Fascist parapet, were caught by the dawn and unable to escape. All day they had to lie there, with only tufts of grass for cover, the Fascists shooting at them every time they moved. By nightfall seven were dead, then the other five managed to creep away in the darkness.

And then, for many mornings to follow, the sound of the Anarchist attacks on the other side of Huesca. Always the same sound. Suddenly, at some time in the small hours, the opening crash of several score bombs bursting simultaneously—even from miles away a diabolical, rending crash—and then the unbroken roar of massed rifles and machine-guns, a heavy rolling sound curiously similar to the roll of drums. By degrees the firing would spread all round the lines that encircled Huesca, and we would stumble out into the trench to lean sleepily against the parapet while a ragged meaningless fire swept overhead.

In the daytime the guns thundered fitfully. Torre Fabian, now our cook-house; was shelled and partially destroyed. It is curious that when you are watching artillery-fire from a safe distance you always want the gunner to hit his mark, even though the mark contains your dinner and some of your comrades. The Fascists were shooting well that morning; perhaps there were German gunners on the job. They bracketed neatly on Torre Fabian. One shell beyond it, one shell short of it, then whizz-BOOM! Burst rafters leaping upwards and a sheet of uralite skimming down the air like a flicked playing-card. The next shell took off the corner of a building as neatly as a giant might do it with a knife. But the cooks produced dinner on time—a memorable feat.

As the days went on the unseen but audible guns began each to assume a distinct personality. There were the two batteries of Russian 75-mm. guns which fired from close in our rear and which somehow evoked in my mind the picture of a fat man hitting a golf-ball. These were the first Russian guns I had seen—or heard, rather. They had a low trajectory and a very high velocity, so that you heard the cartridge explosion, the whizz and the shell-burst almost simultaneously. Behind Monflorite were two very heavy guns which fired a few times a day, with a deep, muffled roar that was like the baying of distant chained-up monsters. Up at Mount Aragon, the medieval fortress which the Government troops had stormed last year (the first time in its history, it was said), and which guarded one of the approaches to Huesca, there was a heavy gun which must have dated well back into the nineteenth century. Its great shells whistled over so slowly that you felt certain you could run beside them and keep up with them. A shell from this gun sounded like nothing so much as a man riding along on a bicycle and whistling. The trench-mortars, small though they were, made the most evil sound of all. Their shells are really a kind of winged torpedo, shaped like the darts thrown in public-houses and about the size of a quart bottle; they go off with a devilish metallic crash, as of some monstrous globe of brittle steel being shattered on an anvil. Sometimes our aeroplanes flew over and let loose the aerial torpedoes whose tremendous echoing roar makes the earth tremble even at two miles' distance. The shell-bursts from the Fascist anti-aircraft guns dotted the sky like cloudlets in a bad water-colour, but I never saw them get within a thousand yards of an aeroplane. When an aeroplane swoops down and uses its machine-gun the sound, from below, is like the fluttering of wings.

On our part of the line not much was happening. Two hundred yards to the right of us, where the Fascists were on higher ground, their snipers picked off a few of our comrades. Two hundred yards to the left, at the bridge over the stream, a sort of duel was going on between the Fascist mortars and the men who were building a concrete barricade across the bridge. The evil little shells whizzed over, zwing-crash! zwing-crash!, making a doubly diabolical noise when they landed on the asphalt road. A hundred yards away you could stand in perfect safety and watch the columns of earth and black smoke leaping into the air like magic trees. The poor devils round the bridge spent much of the daytime cowering in the little man-holes they had scooped in the side of the trench. But there were less casualties than might have been expected, and the barricade rose steadily, a wall of concrete two feet thick, with embrasures for two machine-guns and a small field-gun. The concrete was being reinforced with old bedsteads, which apparently was the only iron that could be found for the purpose.

PART FOURTEEN

THE SECOND WORLD WAR

The Second World War allied Britain, the United States, and the Soviet Union in the effort against Nazi Germany. During February 1945, Churchill, Roosevelt, and Stalin met at Yalta to discuss the future of Europe. Although the Yalta conference has come to symbolize the division of Europe, it actually represented the high point of wartime cooperation.

The Second World War

Germany invaded Poland on September 1, 1939, and two days later Britain and France declared war on Germany. The Second World War, for which Hitler had long been preparing, had begun. When Hitler had annexed Austria and Czechoslovakia the previous year, the impotent League of Nations had done nothing and the liberal democracies had actively appeased the aggressor. Now with the Nazi-Soviet Pact of August 1939 in his pocket, Hitler was on the move. After Poland, he turned first to Scandinavia and then, in June 1940, to France, both of which succumbed quickly to the onslaught. In the West, only Britain remained unconquered by the Germans, who, misjudging the Soviet Union's military capabilities, invaded that country in June 1941. After the Japanese attack on Pearl Harbor, the United States entered the war. The Western Allies defeated Fascist Italy in September 1943 and invaded Normandy in June 1944. In May 1945 Germany, again trapped in a two-front vise and exhausted by its lengthy, desperate struggle with the resilient Soviet Army, finally surrendered. On the eve of the surrender, Hitler committed suicide. Germany and much of Europe lay in bleak ruins.

The clearest early evidence for Hitler's expansionist and warlike goals is the Hossbach Memorandum. This report, written by Hitler's military adjutant, Colonel Friedrich Hossbach, reflects the author's notes and recollections of a top-level Nazi meeting in 1937. Although not accurate in all expectations, the memorandum discloses Hitler's clear intention to wage an all-European war. Victor Klemperer (1881–1960), a Jewish citizen of Germany at the time of Hitler's 1939 invasion of Poland, provides an acutely critical analysis of the events in his *I Will Bear Witness*. Before his death, the French historian Marc Bloch (1886–1944) described his country's 1940 collapse in the face of the Nazi invasion in *Strange Defeat,* which was published in 1949. Bloch characterized the shattering event as a moral and psychological rather than a military defeat. Famous Russian writers such as Anna Akhmatova (1889–1966), Konstantin Simonov (1915–1979), and Olga Berggolts (1910–1975) used poems to capture their heartrending wartime experiences.

✦ Reading 50 ✦

Hossbach Memorandum

Memorandum

BERLIN, November 10, 1937.
Minutes of a Conference in the Reich Chancellery, Berlin, November 5, 1937, FROM 4:15 to 8:30 P.M.

Present:
The Fuehrer and Chancellor, Field Marshal von Blomberg, War Minister, Colonel General Baron von Fritsch, Commander in Chief, Army, Admiral Dr. h. c. Raeder, Commander in Chief, Navy, Colonel General Goring, Commander in Chief, Luftwaffe, Baron von Neurath, Foreign Minister, Colonel Hossbach.

The Fuehrer began by stating that the subject of the present conference was of such importance that its discussion would, in other countries, certainly be a matter for a full Cabinet meeting, but he—the Fuehrer—had rejected the idea of making it a subject of discussion before the wider circle of the Reich Cabinet just because of the importance of the matter. His exposition to follow was the fruit of thorough deliberation and the experiences of his 41/2 years of power. He wished to explain to the gentlemen present his basic ideas concerning the opportunities for the development of our position in the field of foreign affairs and its requirements, and he asked, in the interests of a long-term German policy, that his exposition be regarded, in the event of his death, as his last will and testament.

The Fuehrer then continued:

The aim of German policy was to make secure and to preserve the racial community [Volksmasse] and to enlarge it. It was therefore a question of space.

The German racial community comprised over 85 million people and, because of their number and the narrow limits of habitable space in Europe, constituted a tightly packed racial core such as was not to be met in any other country and such as implied the right to a greater living space than in the case of other peoples. If, territorially speaking, there existed no political result corresponding to this German racial core, that was a consequence of centuries of historical development, and in the continuance of these political conditions lay the greatest danger to the preservation of the German race at its present peak. To arrest the decline of Germanism [Deutschtum] in Austria and Czechoslovakia was as little possible as to maintain the present level in Germany itself. Instead of increase, sterility was setting in, and in its train disorders of a social character must arise in course of time, since political and ideological ideas remain effective only so long as they furnish the basis for the realization of the essential vital demands of a people. Germany's future was therefore wholly conditional upon the solving of the need for space, and such a solution could be sought, of course, only for a foreseeable period of about one to three generations.

Before turning to the question of solving the need for space, it had to be considered whether a solution holding promise for the future was to be reached by means of autarchy or by means of an increased participation in world economy.

Autarchy

Achievement only possible under strict National Socialist leadership of the State, which is assumed; accepting its achievement as possible, the following could be stated as results:—

A. In the field of raw materials only limited, not total, autarchy.

1) In regard to coal, so far as it could be considered as a source of raw materials, autarchy was possible;

Source: http://www.yale.edu/lawweb/avalon/imt/document/hossbach.htm. Yale University Law School, Avalon Project, November 2000.

2) But even as regards ores, the position was much more difficult. Iron requirements can be met from home resources and similarly with light metals, but with other raw materials—copper, tin—this was not the case.
3) Synthetic textile requirements can be met from home resources to the limit of timber supplies. A permanent solution impossible.
4) Edible fats—possible.

B. In the field of food the question of autarchy was to be answered by a flat "No."

With the general rise in the standard of living compared with that of 30 to 40 years ago, there has gone hand in hand an increased demand and an increased home consumption even on the part of the producers, the farmers. The fruits of the increased agricultural production had all gone to meet the increased demand, and so did not represent an absolute production increase. A further increase in production by making greater demands on the soil, which already, in consequence of the use of artificial fertilizers, was showing signs of exhaustion, was hardly possible, and it was therefore certain that even with the maximum increase in production, participation in world trade was unavoidable. The not inconsiderable expenditure of foreign exchange to insure food supplies by imports, even when harvests were good, grew to catastrophic proportions with bad harvests. The possibility of a disaster grew in proportion to the increase in population, in which, too, the excess of births of 560,000 annually produced, as a consequence, an even further increase in bread consumption, since a child was a greater bread consumer than an adult.

It was not possible over the long run, in a continent enjoying a practically common standard of living, to meet the food supply difficulties by lowering that standard and by rationalization. Since, with the solving of the unemployment problem, the maximum consumption level had been reached, some minor modifications in our home agricultural production might still, no doubt, be possible, but no fundamental alteration was possible in our basic food position. Thus autarchy was untenable in regard both to food and to the economy as a whole.

Participation in World Economy

To this there were limitations which we were unable to remove. The establishment of Germany's position on a secure and sound foundation was obstructed by market fluctuations, and commercial treaties afforded no guarantee for actual execution. In particular it had to be remembered that since the World War, those very countries which had formerly been food exporters had become industrialized. We were living in an age of economic empires in which the primitive urge to colonization was again manifesting itself; in the cases of Japan and Italy economic motives underlay the urge for expansion, and with Germany, too, economic need would supply the stimulus. For countries outside the great economic empires, opportunities for economic expansion were severely impeded.

The boom in world economy caused by the economic effects of rearmament could never form the basis of a sound economy over a long period, and the latter was obstructed above all also by the economic disturbances resulting from Bolshevism. There was a pronounced military weakness in those states which depended for their existence on foreign trade. As our foreign trade was carried on over the sea routes dominated by Britain, it was more a question of security of transport than one of foreign exchange, which revealed, in time of war, the full weakness of our food situation. The only remedy, and one which might appear to us as visionary, lay in the acquisition of greater living space—a quest which has at all times been the origin of the formation of states and of the migration of peoples. That this quest met with no interest at Geneva or among the satiated nations was understandable. If, then, we accept the security of our food situation as the principal question, the space necessary to insure it can only be sought in Europe, not, as in the liberal-capitalist view, in the exploitation of colonies. It is not a matter of acquiring population but of gaining space for agricultural use. Moreover, areas producing raw materials can be more usefully sought in Europe in immediate proximity to the Reich, than overseas; the solution thus obtained must suffice for one or two generations. Whatever else might prove necessary later must be left to succeeding generations to deal with. The development of great world political constellations progressed but slowly after all, and the German people with its strong racial core would find the most favorable prerequisites for such achievement in the heart of the continent of Europe. The history of all ages—the Roman Empire and the British Empire—had proved that expansion could only be carried out by breaking down resistance and taking risks; setbacks were inevitable. There had never in former times been spaces without a master, and there were none today; the attacker always comes up against a possessor.

The question for Germany ran: where could she achieve the greatest gain at the lowest cost.

German policy had to reckon with two hate-inspired antagonists, Britain and France, to whom a German colossus in the center of Europe was a thorn in the flesh, and both countries were opposed to any further strengthening of Germany's position either in Europe or overseas; in support of this opposition they were able to count on the agreement of all their political parties. Both countries saw in the establishment of German military bases overseas a threat to their own communications, a safeguarding of German commerce, and, as a consequence, a strengthening of Germany's position in Europe.

Because of opposition of the Dominions, Britain could not cede any of her colonial possessions to us. After England's loss of prestige through the passing of Abyssinia into Italian possession, the return of East Africa was not to be expected. British concessions could at best be expressed in an offer to satisfy our colonial demands by the appropriation of colonies which were not British possessions—e.g., Angola. French concessions would probably take a similar line.

Serious discussion of the question of the return of colonies to us could only be considered at a moment when Britain was in difficulties and the German Reich armed and strong. The Fuehrer did not share the view that the Empire was unshakable. Opposition to the Empire was to be found less in the countries conquered than among her competitors. The British Empire and the Roman Empire could not be compared in respect of permanence; the latter was not confronted by any powerful political rival of a serious order after the Punic Wars. It was only the disintegrating effect of Christianity, and the symptoms of age which appear in every country, which caused ancient Rome to succumb to the onslaught of the Germans.

Beside the British Empire there existed today a number of states stronger than she. The British motherland was able to protect her colonial possessions not by her own power, but only in alliance with other states. How, for instance, could Britain alone defend Canada against attack by America, or her Far Eastern interests against attack by Japan!

The emphasis on the British Crown as the symbol of the unity of the Empire was already an admission that, in the long run, the Empire could not maintain its position by power politics. Significant indications of this were:

(a) The struggle of Ireland for independence.

(b) The constitutional struggles in India, where Britain's half measures had given to the Indians the opportunity of using later on as a weapon against Britain, the nonfulfillment of her promises regarding a constitution.

(c) The weakening by Japan of Britain's position in the Far East.

(d) The rivalry in the Mediterranean with Italy who—under the spell of her history, driven by necessity and led by a genius was expanding her power position, and thus was inevitably coming more and more into conflict with British interests. The outcome of the Abyssinian War was a loss of prestige for Britain which Italy was striving to increase by stirring up the in the Mohammeden world.

To sum up, it could be stated that, with 45 million Britons, in spite of its theoretical soundness, the position of the Empire could not in the long run be maintained by power politics. The ratio of the population of the Empire to that of the motherland of 9:1, was a warning to us not, in our territorial expansion to allow the foundation constituted by the numerical strength of our own people to become too weak.

France's position was more favorable than that of Britain. The French Empire was better placed territorially; the inhabitants of her colonial possessions represented a supplement to her military strength. But France was going to be confronted with internal political difficulties. In a nation's life about 10 percent of its span is taken up by parliamentary forms of government and about 90 percent by authoritarian forms. Today, nonetheless, Britain, France, Russia, and the smaller states adjoining them, must be included as factors [Machtfaktoren] in our political calculations.

Germany's problem could only be solved by means of force and this was never without attendant risk. The campaigns of Frederick the Great for Silesia and Bismarck's wars against Austria and France had involved unheard-of risk, and the swiftness of the Prussian action in 1870 had kept Austria from entering the war. If one accepts as the basis of the following exposition the resort to force with its attendant risks, then there remain still to be answered the questions "when" and "how." In this matter there were three cases [Falle] to be dealt with:

Case 1: Period 1943–1945

After this date only a change for the worse, from our point of view, could be expected.

The equipment of the army, navy, and luftwaffe, as well as the formation of the officer corps, was nearly completed. Equipment and armament were modern; in further delay there lay the danger of their obsolescence. In particular, the secrecy of "special weapons" could not be preserved forever. The recruiting of reserves was limited to current age groups; further drafts from older untrained age groups were no longer available.

Our relative strength would decrease in relation to the rearmament which would by then have been carried out by the rest of the world. If we did not act by 1943–45 any year could, in consequence of a lack of reserves, produce the food crisis, to cope with which the necessary foreign exchange was not available, and this must be regarded as a "waning point of the regime." Besides, the world was expecting our attack and was increasing its counter-measures from year to year. It was while the rest of the world was still preparing its defenses [sich abriegele] that we were obliged to take the offensive.

Nobody knew today what the situation would be in the years 1943–45. One thing only was certain, that we could not wait longer.

On the one hand there was the great Wehrmacht, and the necessity of maintaining it at its present level, the aging of the movement and of its leaders; and on the other, the prospect of a lowering of the standard of living and of a limitation of the birth rate, which left no choice but to act. If the Fuehrer was still living, it was his unalterable resolve to solve Germany's problem of space at the latest by 1943–45. The necessity for action before 1943–45 would arise in cases 2 and 3.

Case 2

If internal strife in France should develop into such a domestic crisis as to absorb the French Army completely and render it incapable of use for war against Germany, then the time for action against the Czechs had come.

Case 3

If France is so embroiled by a war with another state that she cannot "proceed" against Germany.

For the improvement of our politico-military position our first objective, in the event of our being embroiled in war, must be to overthrow Czechoslovakia and Austria simultaneously in order to remove the threat to our flank in any possible operation against the West. In a conflict with France it was hardly to be regarded as likely that the Czechs would declare war on us on the very same day as France. The desire to join in the war would, however, increase among the Czechs in proportion to any weakening on our part and then her participation could clearly take the form of an attack toward Silesia, toward the north or toward the west.

If the Czechs were overthrown and a common German-Hungarian frontier achieved, a neutral attitude on the part of Poland could be the more certainly counted on in the event of a Franco-German conflict. Our agreements with Poland only retained their force as long as Germany's strength remained unshaken. In the event of German setbacks a Polish action against East Prussia, and possibly against Pomerania and Silesia as well, had to be reckoned with.

On the assumption of a development of the Situation leading to action: on our part as planned, in the years 1943–45, the attitude of France, Britain, Italy, Poland, and Russia could probably be estimated as follows:

Actually, the Fuehrer believed that almost certainly Britain, and probably France as well, had already tacitly written off the Czechs and were reconciled to the fact that this question could be cleared up in due course by Germany. Difficulties connected with the Empire, and the prospect of being once more entangled in a protracted European war, were decisive considerations for Britain against participation in a war against Germany. Britain's attitude would certainly not be without influence on that of France. An attack by France without British support, and with the prospect of the offensive being brought to a standstill on our western fortifications, was hardly probable. Nor was a French march through Belgium and Holland without British support to be expected; this also was a course not to be contemplated by us in the event of a conflict with France, because it would certainly entail the hostility of Britain. It would of course be necessary to maintain a strong defense [eine Abriegelung] on our western frontier during the prosecution of our attack on the Czechs and Austria. And in this connection it had to be remembered that the defense measures of the Czechs were growing in strength from year to year, and that the actual worth of the Austrian Army also was increasing in the course of time. Even though the populations concerned, especially of Czechoslovakia, were not sparse, the annexation of Czechoslovakia and Austria would mean an acquisition of foodstuffs for 5 to 6 million people, on the assumption that the compulsory emigration of 2 million people from Czechoslovakia and 1 million people from Austria was practicable. The incorporation of these two States with Germany meant, from the politico-military point of view, a substantial advantage because it would mean shorter and better frontiers, the freeing of forces for other purposes, and the possibility of creating new units up to a level of about 12 divisions, that is, 1 new division per million inhabitants.

Italy was not expected to object to the elimination of the Czechs, but it was impossible at the moment to estimate what her attitude on the Austrian question would be; that depended essentially upon whether the Duce were still alive.

The degree of surprise and the swiftness of our action were decisive factors for Poland's attitude. Poland with Russia at her rear will have little inclination to engage in war against a victorious Germany.

Military intervention by Russia must be countered by the swiftness of our operations; however, whether such an intervention was a practical contingency at all was, in view of Japan's attitude, more than doubtful.

Should case 2 arise—the crippling of France by civil war—the situation thus created by the elimination of the most dangerous opponent must he seized upon whenever it occurs for the blow against the Czechs.

The Fuehrer saw case 3 coming definitely nearer; it might emerge from the present tensions in the Mediterranean, and he was resolved to take advantage of it whenever it happened, even as early as 1938.

In the light of past experience, the Fuehrer did not see any early end to the hostilities in Spain. If one considered the length of time which Franco's offensives had taken up till now, it was fully possible that the war would continue another 3 years. On the other hand, a 100 percent victory for Franco was not desirable either, from the German point of view; rather were we interested in a continuance of the war and in the keeping up of the tension in the Mediterranean. Franco in undisputed possession of the Spanish Peninsula precluded the possibility of any further intervention on the part of the Italians or of their continued occupation of the Balearic Islands. As our interest lay more in the prolongation of the war in Spain, it must be the immediate aim of our policy to strengthen Italy's rear with a view to her remaining in the Balearics. But the permanent establishment of the Italians on the Balearics would be intolerable both to France and Britain, and might lead to a war of France and England against Italy—a war in which Spain, should she be entirely in the hands of the Whites, might make her appearance on the side of Italy's enemies. The probability of Italy's defeat in such a war was slight, for the road from Germany was open for the supplementing of her raw materials. The Fuehrer pictured the military strategy for Italy thus: on her western frontier with France she would remain on the defensive, and carry on the war against France from Libya against the French North African colonial possessions.

As a landing by Franco-British troops on the coast of Italy could be discounted, and a French offensive over the Alps against northern Italy would be very difficult and would probably come to a halt before the strong Italian fortifications, the crucial point [Schwerpunkt] of the operations lay in North Africa. The threat to French lines of communication by the Italian Fleet would to a great extent cripple the transportation of forces from North Africa to France, so that France would have only home forces at her disposal on the frontiers with Italy and Germany.

If Germany made use of this war to settle the Czech and Austrian questions, it was to be assumed that Britain—herself at war with Italy—would decide not to act against Germany. Without British support, a warlike action by France against Germany was not to be expected.

The time for our attack on the Czechs and Austria must be made dependent on the course of the Anglo-French-Italian war and would not necessarily coincide with the commencement of military operations by these three States. Nor had the Fuehrer in mind military agreements with Italy, but wanted, while retaining his own independence of action, to exploit this favorable situation, which would not occur again, to begin and carry through the campaign against the Czechs. This descent upon the Czechs would have to be carried out with "lightning speed."

In appraising the situation Field Marshal von Blomberg and Colonel General von Fritsch repeatedly emphasized the necessity that Britain and France must not appear in the role of our enemies, and stated that the French Army would not be so committed by the war with Italy that France could not at the same time enter the field with forces superior to ours on our western frontier. General von Fritsch estimated the probable French forces available for use on the Alpine frontier at approximately twenty divisions, so that a strong French superiority would still remain on the western frontier, with the role, according to the German view, of invading the Rhineland. In this matter, moreover, the advanced state of French defense preparations [Mobiolmachung] must be taken into particular account, and it must be remembered apart from the insignificant value of our present fortifications—on which Field Marshal von Blomberg laid special emphasis—that the four motorized divisions intended for the West were still more or less incapable of movement. In regard to our offensive toward the southeast, Field Marshal von Blomberg drew particular attention to the strength of the Czech fortifications, which had acquired by now a structure like a Maginot Line and which would gravely hamper our attack.

General von Fritsch mentioned that this was the very purpose of a study which he had ordered made this winter, namely, to examine the possibility of conducting operations against the Czechs with special reference to overcoming the Czech fortification system; the General further expressed his opinion, that under existing circumstances he must give up his plan to go abroad on his leave, which was due to begin on November 10. The Fuehrer dismissed this idea on the ground that the possibility of a conflict need not yet be regarded as imminent. To the Foreign Minister's objection that an Anglo-French-Italian conflict was not yet within such a measurable distance as the Fuehrer seemed to assume, the Fuehrer put the summer of 1938 as the date which seemed to him possible for this. In reply to considerations offered by Field Marshal von Blomberg and General von Fritsch regarding the attitude of Britain and France, the Fuehrer repeated his previous statements that he was convinced of Britain's nonparticipation, and therefore he did not believe in the probability of belligerent action by France against Germany. Should the Mediterranean conflict under discussion lead to a general mobilization in Europe, then we must immediately begin action against the Czechs. On the other hand, should the powers not engaged in the war declare themselves disinterested, then Germany would have to adopt a similar attitude to this for the time being.

Colonel General Goring thought that, in view of the Fuehrer's statement, we should consider liquidating our military undertakings in Spain. The Fuehrer agrees to this with the limitation that he thinks he should reserve a decision for a proper moment.

The second part of the conference was concerned with concrete questions of armament.

HOSSBACH
Certified Correct:
Colonel (General Staff)

✦ Reading 51 ✦

I Will Bear Witness

Victor Klemperer

June 27, Tuesday

The manuscript of the sixth-form chapter is complete; the next 10 or 12 days set aside for typewritten copy. I will not ask how far I can take the Curriculum, nor what its fate will be. Only keep going—Poetry and Truth; I respect inner truth completely, writing is not much more than shaping and arranging, sometimes condensing, sometimes leaving out. The work is much harder than might have been assumed, my diaries often let me down.

The 16 brilliant Romains volumes finished. Began the more classical and weaker *Thibaults*. Unfortunately only the German translation to hand for the earlier parts. [. . .]

The propaganda against England more vociferous every day, even more vociferous than against Poland; every day new emphasis on the absolute defenselessness and helplessness of England, its humiliation by Japan, its prostrations before Russia, its songs of hate against Germany. I absolutely want to believe, I really do 75 percent believe, that the catastrophe will come before autumn, but everyone (Natscheff and all of Juda) around me doubts it. Either England will back down, or Germany will back down, or the hostile powers will calmly sit back and watch Germany partition Poland. Always with the same arguments, the references to everything that has already happened.

Yesterday I received a very nice letter from Max Sebba in London, to which I want to reply today. A type of emigrant letter is taking shape: Our relatives are in Uruguay, in New York, in Sydney, etc., our eighty-year-old mother remained in Germany . . . And always: I can't complain, things are much worse for so many others . . . And always the helpless pity for those still in Germany.

July 4, Wednesday

June 29 was especially moving for us this time. 35 years, and now this situation, this loneliness, this enormous tension. But on the whole we were cheerful and almost optimistic. In the evening we drank a whole bottle of Haut Sauternes.

Today I said to Vogel, who collects his orders in Dölzschen on Wednesday morning: One always hears three things at once: First there are those who say, he will not dare do anything. Then there are those who say, there have been such tremendous preparations that he will overrun Poland in the next few weeks, it will happen as quickly and smoothly as with Czechoslovakia. Finally those who say, this time it will be the big war. What is your opinion? Vogel, a calm man, not at all a Nazi, answered immediately and with conviction: He'll probably bring it off again. And that is the most widespread opinion, the true vox populi. Yesterday Frau Bonheim, she had spoken to her divorced husband (which only takes place in secret and at the risk of prison). He said: Only Jews and Communists believe in war, Poland will be swallowed up as quickly and bloodlessly as Czechoslovakia; the Western powers will not raise a finger. Beresin, the cigarette man and stateless, was here yesterday. He dug for six weeks as a laborer, with very many others he is being expelled from August 2 and has no idea where to go. He is learning photography, his hopes are pinned on Shanghai. A civil servant told him: Don't worry about August 2—by that time there will be war. I can no longer believe it. Disappointed too often. It will all go smoothly for him this time too. The newspapers ever more excited, even though one would think any further increase impossible. Hess, the Führer's deputy, in a speech at the West Wall: Everything that comes from the Führer cannot be surpassed by anything in the world, this Wall is his

From: Victor Klemperer, *I Will Bear Witness: A Diary of the Nazi Years, 1933–1941*, trans. Martin Chalmers (New York: Random House, 1998), pp. 302–309.

work, it would mean suicide for any nation that attacked it.

July 14

We wanted to celebrate Eva's birthday as we had celebrated June 29. In the afternoon her nerves failed her; it was not nice, it is not nice. The self-induced optimism of recent weeks can no longer hold up. It is increasingly evident that Germany is negotiating with Russia.

Language: An article recently bore the headline: Heartland Bulgaria (state visit of a Bulgarian to Berlin, the usual courting of the Balkans, the usual crooked double game of the Balkanese). What is interesting about it: In itself heartland is a geographical expression referring to a central location and does not correspond to Bulgaria's position; but it becomes infected in National Socialist language, its original emotional meaning is restored, becomes the country in which the heart of the Balkans beats, in which Balkanese heroism, nobility, etc. has its home. In which no usually hook-nosed intellectualism rules. (Hook-nosed intellectualism from an article yesterday about art in Germany and Munich before the seizure of power and now.)

Max Sebba wrote to us from London, where things are going badly for him and his family. [. . .]

Curriculum: Sixth form in good. Student chapter very difficult. Despite looking everywhere I can find nothing about the Sorbonne in 1903. Nothing in my diary, no memories, no lecture notes, no document. For the other semesters everything is there. Puzzling.

July 25

Time stands still: nothing changes; always the same deadly, lethargic uncertainty and imprisonment.

[. . .] Georg has been silent for months.—At the beginning of August Grete leaves Strausberg for an old people's home in Friedrichshagen (Berlin).

A young tram driver, at first I thought him in his early twenties, but he must have been a couple of years older: Do you know why they made the changes at Bismarckplatz?—?—The lawns were divided differently before.—?—The paths marked out the lines of the English flag, the diagonals.—Are you joking or serious?—Serious and really true. My mother-in-law told me. She's English. She has gone back to England; she doesn't like it here anymore.—You should not say that out loud.—There are many things one should not say out loud.—Are you in trouble?—My two boys have English first names, I'm supposed to change them.—Here a man with a Party badge got on. End of the conversation. And I got off at the corner of Waisenhausstrasse. Such little incidents always give me hope for a quarter of an hour. No more.

August 14, Monday

The same tension for weeks, always growing and always unchanged. Vox populi: He attacks in September, partitions Poland with Russia, England-France are impotent. Natscheff and some others: He does not dare attack, keeps the peace and stays in power for years. Jewish opinion: bloody pogrom on the first day of the war. Whichever of these three things may happen: Our situation is desperate.

We go on living, reading, working, but in an ever more depressed state.

[. . .]

Yesterday afternoon a Herr Schroeter, whom we do not know, was here. From Leipzig for the Naval Day, with greetings from Trude Öhlmann, who asks us to write to her—she herself dare not get in touch with us. The man had a fixed, gloomy stare, sat there as if made of stone, had difficulty speaking, long gaps—he had suffered greatly. We were glad when he was gone. [. . .] Then there was a letter from the Confessing Christians, Pastor Grüber's Office. I should inform the National Association of Jews, they would deal with it. So today I went to their office in Johann Georgen Allee. I no longer need to pay the church tax, without thereby losing my Protestantism: But I shall have to pay twice as much to the National Association as I previously paid to the Church. [. . .]

August 29, Tuesday

It has become tremendously difficult for me to finish the section Paris 1903, these last few days pulled and still pull too much at my nerves. The unconcealed mobilization without any mobilization being announced (people, cars, horses), the pact with the Russians and the incredible turnabout, confusion, the incalculable situation, the balance of forces after this volte-face. (Where does popular opinion stand? to what effect? what is the mood? etc., etc. Endless, agonizing conversations.) Incalculable danger for all Jews here. From Friday to Monday constantly increasing tension. Masses of people called up for military service during the night, horses gone from the market hall. Moral came unexpectedly on Sunday morning: He wanted to go underground in the home of an Aryan friend in Berlin, he is expecting the outbreak of war and in that case being shot down, perhaps not in some wild pogrom, but properly rounded up and put up against a barracks wall. Then in the afternoon food ration cards were distributed; that prevented him leaving and going underground. In the evening I went to the station, the people there looked considerably depressed (later Eva told me that up here too, all the people streaming home from the open-air swimming pool had spoken quietly, without laughing and fooling around as usual). There was a crowd around the notice announcing the reduction in rail traffic. The ten-day postal ban for all troops out of garrison was already published on Saturday. What particularly depressed us on Sunday was the suggestion that we should give our little tomcat an easy death by injection, since he eats only meat and we really need a quarter pound for him every day, for him alone, and all three of us are now supposed to get one pound per week. Since then we have switched him to fish and accustomed ourselves to the never ending crisis. The prospects of war and peace, the prospects and groupings in a possible war appear to fluctuate from hour to hour. Everyone guesses, waits, the tension is too great and is already giving way to apathy once more. At the moment what seems most likely to me is that Hitler wins the game yet again, through sheer pressure and without a battle. But how long can he then remain an ally of the Bolshevists . . . , etc., etc.?

Leave the broad lines to history, note down my own little observations for the Curriculum. Memories of the last war coming to the surface: the ration card. The way it fell upon people on Sunday afternoon, it must have had a terrible effect on their mood. A joke had just been going around: The war will last three days, begin after the Tannenberg celebrations, that is, on the twenty-eighth, and the Poles (they alone) will fight to the last. The celebrations, already announced on a postmark, are canceled, likewise the Party Rally. It's possible that optimism is already on the rise again. Or just indifference. Who can judge the mood of 80 million people, with the press bound and everyone afraid of opening their mouth? The maddest thing was the hand-in-hand picture of Ribbentrop and Stalin. Machiavelli is a babe in arms by comparison. It is always said that the separation of morality and politics was his discovery. But a politics that is too immoral turns into political stupidity.

[. . .]

It had been a difficult decision, but we had decided to travel to Friedrichshagen to see Grete last Sunday; then she wrote to cancel: heart attack, in the Jewish Hospital, Berlin N, Iranische Strasse, 20 people in the ward, no conversation possible. According to Trude Scherk, Grete is not seriously ill, only wanted to get away from the home, which she does not like. But do they have room in the Jewish Hospital nowadays for people who are not seriously ill? My conscience is not quite clear. Then again: Travel now, when there is no certainty of getting a train back? To chat for a couple of minutes in the general ward? And perhaps make Grete feel that things must really be looking bad for her, if we come all that way to see her for half an hour?

Lingua: [. . .] There is now no longer any talk of Bolshevists, but instead of the Russian people. However, in his last speech Hess said: Jews and freemasons want war against us.—In the newspaper just now: Nothing decided, but no matter how hardened one is, it does seem as if war must begin in the next few hours, all measures in Germany, France and Britain point to it. A relaxation had been expected as a result of the visit of the British ambassador. Not a word about it and new war measures everywhere.

Especially exciting and kept under a cloak of secrecy the news of the guarantees of neutrality to Holland and Belgium. [. . .]

September 3, Sunday afternoon

This torture of one's nerves ever more unbearable. On Friday morning blackout ordered until further notice. We sit in the tiny cellar, the terrible damp closeness, the constant sweating and shivering, the smell of mold, the food shortage, makes everything even more miserable. I try to save butter and meat for Eva and Muschel, to make do myself as far as possible with still unrationed bread and fish. This in itself would all be trivial, but it is all only by the way. What will happen? From hour to hour we tell ourselves, now is the moment when everything is decided, whether Hitler is all-powerful, whether his rule will last indefinitely, or whether it falls now, *now*.

On Friday morning, September I, the young butcher's lad came and told us: There had been a radio announcement, we already held Danzig and the Corridor, the war with Poland was under way, England and France remained neutral. I said to Eva, then a morphine injection or something similar was the best thing for us, our life was over. But then we said to one another, *that* could not possibly be the way things were, the boy had often reported absurd things (he was a perfect example of the way in which people take in news reports). A little later we heard Hitler's agitated voice, then the usual roaring, but could not make anything out. We said to ourselves, if the report were even only half true they must already be putting out the flags Then down in town the dispatch of the outbreak of war. I asked several people whether English neutrality had already been declared. Only an intelligent salesgirl in a cigar shop on Chemnitzer Platz said: No—that would really be a joke! At the baker's, at Vogel's, they all said, as good as declared, all over in a few days! A young man in front of the newspaper display: The English are cowards, they won't do anything! And thus with variations the general mood, vox populi (butter seller, newspaper man, bill collector of the gas company etc., etc.). In the afternoon read the Führer's speech. It seemed to me pessimistic as far as the external and the internal position was concerned. Also all the regulations pointed and still point to more than a mere punitive expedition against Poland. And now this is the third day like this, it feels as if it has been three years: the waiting, the despairing, hoping, weighing up, not knowing. The newspaper yesterday, Saturday, vague and in fact anticipating a general outbreak of war: England, the attacker—English mobilization, French mobilization, they will bleed to death! etc., etc. But still no declaration of war on their side. Is it coming or will they fail to resist and merely demonstrate weakness?

The military bulletin is also unclear. Talks of successes everywhere, reports no serious opposition anywhere and yet also shows that German troops have nowhere advanced far beyond the frontiers. How does it all fit together? All in all: Reports and measures taken are serious, popular opinion absolutely certain of victory, ten thousand times more arrogant than in '14. The consequence will either be an overwhelming, almost unchallenged victory, and England and France are castrated minor states, or a catastrophe ten thousand times worse than '18. And the two of us right in the middle, helpless and probably lost in either case . . . And yet we force ourselves, and sometimes it even succeeds for a couple of hours, to go on with our everyday life: reading aloud, eating (as best we can), writing, garden. But as I lie down to sleep I think: Will they come for me tonight? Will I be shot, will I be put in a concentration camp?

Waiting in peaceful Dölzschen, cut off from the world, is particularly bad. One listens to every sound, watches every face, pays attention to everything. One learns nothing. One waits for the newspaper and can make nothing of it. At the moment I do tend to think that there will be war with the great powers.

At the butcher an old dear puts her hand on my shoulder and says in a voice full of tears: *He* has said that he will put on a soldier's coat again and be a soldier himself, and if he falls, then Goering. . . . A young lady brings me my ration card, looks at me with a friendly expression: Do you still remember me? I studied under you, I've married into the family here.—An old gentleman, very friendly, brings the blackout order: Terrible, that it's war again—but yet one is so patriotic, when I saw a battery leaving yesterday, I wanted more than anything to go with them! No one is outraged by the Russian alliance, people think it is brilliant or an excellent joke—Vogel's optimism (yesterday: We've almost finished off the Poles, the others won't stir themselves!) is to our benefit in coffee, sausage, tea, soap etc.—Is this the general mood in Germany? Is it founded on facts or on hubris? [. . .]

The Jewish Community in Dresden inquires whether I want to join it, since it represents the National Association of Jews locally; the Confessing Christians inquire whether I shall remain with them. I replied to the Grüber people that I was and will remain Protestant, I would not reply to the Jewish Community at all.

Note how on September 1 the Führer declared lasting friendship with Russia in two words. Is there really no one in Germany who does not feel a pang of conscience? Once more: Machiavelli was mistaken; there is a line beyond which the separation of morality and politics is unpolitical and has to be paid for. Sooner or later. But can *we* wait until the later?

We invited Moral for a discussion of the situation and received no reply. Evidently he really has left for his Berlin mousehole.

On Thursday Natscheff claimed that Himmler is against war because he mistrusts the mood at home. Despite the pact with Russia Hitler is lost in a general war.—??

September 4, Monday afternoon

Yesterday, Sunday, September 3, after a big washing up, went to the Plauen station. I bought a bar of chocolate and asked the elderly assistant about broadcast news. She reported the English-French ultimatum. I asked: Rejected? She smiled, as if I were a bit simple, shrugged her shoulders: But of course. I could ask the two gentlemen there, if I liked, they had heard it themselves. They were two fitters. They confirmed it. I asked: France too?—Reply: Yes, but now Italy will get involved too. At home we were doubtful again.—This morning we got confirmation from the mailman. The man was dismayed: I was buried alive in 1914, and now I have to serve again as a reservist. Was it necessary, is it human? You should see the gloomy faces on the troop transports—different from '14. And did we start off with food shortages in '14? We will be defeated, it can't last four years again.—In Bienert Park, Berger, the grocer, a soldier in '14, now a radio operator: You've got it easy now!—I? I expect to be beaten to death.—You're well out of it—it's us poor swine who have to do it all again!—Notices and newspapers in town, likewise the *Dresdener NN* which has just arrived, trivialize, virtually *suppress* the fact that France has been at war with us since five o'clock, and talk only of French support for Poland, are full of the successes on all fronts (i.e., Poland), report on approval of the German victories in the Italian press and do not *once* mention Italian neutrality. Only in the *Basler Zeitung*, which curiously enough was also displayed, did I see the headline: Italy neutral for the time being. Striking in Hitler's three proclamations: (1) Now the enemy is the *Jewish plutocracy* instead of Jewish Bolshevism, and it battles against the government of the German people. (2) The constant insistence: Traitors will be exterminated. (That is, they are expecting there will be traitors. As in the speech on September 1.) (3) Not a word about Italy. (4) Friendship with the Russian people. (5) Poland will be defeated in a few weeks, and *then* we shall turn on the West, the West Wall will hold that long.—The mailman said, Dresden and the whole of Germany was under military dictatorship. If that is the case, then we probably do not need to fear a pogrom.

Annemarie brought two bottles of sparkling wine for Eva's birthday. We drank one, and decided to save the other for the day of the English declaration of war. So today it's the turn of the second one. During the day I was full of hope, now I am depressed again.

Little peace of mind, but not much time to work either. Increasing difficulties with food supply. I try to leave meat and butter for Eva and the cat, but eating so much bread and fish gives me stomach pains, and now preserved meats are also increasingly in short supply. Everywhere: Only one tin! Or: No longer available! E.g., smoked herrings have disappeared.—Hampered by constant blackout. The last two days I killed time. (We can only black out the kitchen and the dining cellar and so have the light on there.) Today I intend to choose a Florian volume and read it. After our meal I read aloud downstairs. Early to bed. Until now the moonlight has helped up here. But only for a few more days. Lack of air downstairs, to smoke I have to sit in the dark behind the study door. Eva's cigarette glows less conspicuously.

Half of the Paris chapter copied and read out. Eva says, the page about the enmity with Georg should be left in autumn '03 where it actually belongs. I shall change it.

England has already violated Dutch neutrality.

Reading 52

Strange Defeat

Marc Bloch

One of the Vanquished Gives Evidence

We have just suffered such a defeat as no one would have believed possible. On whom or on what should the blame be laid? On the French system of parliamentary government, say our generals; on the rank and file of the fighting services, on the English, on the fifth column—in short, on any and everybody except themselves. Old Joffre was wiser. 'Whether I was responsible for the winning of the Battle of the Marne', he said, 'I do not know. But of this I feel pretty certain, that, had it been lost, the failure would have been laid at my door.' He intended, by that remark, to remind us that a commanding officer is responsible for everything that happens while he is in supreme charge of events. Whether the initiative for each separate decision comes directly from him, whether in each instance he knows what is being done, is beside the point. The mere fact that he has accepted the position of 'Chief' means that he must take upon his shoulders the burden of failure as well as the panoply of success. The great truth which that simple man expressed so unequivocably is seen to-day to have an even deeper meaning. When the Army was disbanded after the final campaign, it would have been hard to find a single officer among those with whom I was in daily contact who had the slightest doubt on the subject. Whatever the deep-seated causes of the disaster may have been, the immediate occasion (as I shall attempt to explain later) was the utter incompetence of the High Command.

I very much fear that this brutally frank assertion may shock many in whose minds certain prejudices are deeply rooted. Almost the whole of our national Press, and the more academic portions of our national literature, have, as I see it, consistently upheld the conventional view in these matters. For a great many journalists and for a considerable number of 'patriotic' authors, any general is, by definition, a *great* general. If he leads his men to disaster, he is duly rewarded with a high class of the Legion of Honour. No doubt the argument runs that only by drawing a decent veil over the more glaring indiscretions of our public men can the morale of the country be kept at a high level. In fact, the only result of this method is to sow the seeds of a dangerous irritation in the minds of those who make up the fighting forces. But there are other motives, too; some of them, perhaps, not quite so discreditable.

A somewhat odd historical law seems to control the relations existing between States and their military chiefs. Successful soldiers are almost always kept from exercising any political power, though the failures receive it as a free gift from the hands of those very citizens whom they have been unable to lead to victory. MacMahon in spite of Sedan, Hindenburg after the collapse of 1918, were both chosen to preside over the régimes which emerged from defeat. It is not the Pétain of Verdun or the Weygand of Rethondes whom France to-day has promoted or accepted. I realize, of course, that recent events did not result wholly from a spontaneous movement of the popular will. Still, they do stand in some sort of relation to what is, in effect, a form of collective psychosis. In the eyes of the defeated, uniforms bristling with badges of rank and smothered in decorations symbolize not only sacrifices willingly endured on the field of battle, but also the glories of our past and, quite possibly, of our future. When a widely held opinion is glaringly at odds with the truth, we are bound in honesty, I think, to attack it. I share Pascal's view that 'it is a very strange kind of enthusiasm that is roused to fury against those who point out the errors of our public men, rather than against

---

From: Marc Bloch, *Strange Defeat: A Statement of Evidence Written in 1940*, trans. Gerard Hopkins (New York: Oxford University Press, 1949), pp. 25–27, 126–127, 134–145.

the men themselves . . .'. 'The Saints', he writes elsewhere, 'have never kept silent.' It is not my intention to use the phrase as a general justification for every kind of fault-finding. Nevertheless, it should be carefully pondered by all who—without, alas, being able to lay claim to sanctity—try to govern their lives by the standards of the normal decent man. Those who genuinely respect these will find that it is impossible, with an easy conscience, to avoid doing their duty.

I referred a while back to the 'High Command'. But scarcely had my pen written the words than the historian in me was shocked by their use. For the ABC of my trade consists in avoiding big-sounding abstract terms. Those who teach history should be continually concerned with the task of seeking the solid and the concrete behind the empty and the abstract. In other words, it is on men rather than functions that they should concentrate their attention. The errors of the High Command were, fundamentally, the errors of a specific group of human beings.

* * *

A Frenchman Examines His Conscience

In no nation is any professional group ever entirely responsible for its own actions. The solidarity of society as a whole is too strong to permit the existence of the sort of moral autonomy, existing in isolation, which any such total responsibility would seem to imply. The staffs worked with tools which were put into their hands by the nation at large. The psychological conditions in which they lived were not altogether of their own making, and they themselves, through their members, were as their origins had moulded them. They could be only what the totality of the social *fact,* as it existed in France, permitted them to be. That is why I cannot rest content with what I have so far written. I trust that I am honest: certainly, I have done my best to describe, in the terms of my own experience, what I believe to have been the vices of our military system, and the part played by them in the defeat of my country. But, unless I am to be guilty of betraying a trust, I must go farther. The very nature of my inquiry makes it necessary that the evidence of the soldier be balanced and completed by the self-examination of the Frenchman.

I do not joyfully or lightly embark on this part of my task. As a Frenchman I feel constrained, in speaking of my country, to say of her only what is good. It is a harsh duty that compels a man to make a public show of his mother's weaknesses when she is in misery and despair. As an historian, I know better than do most men how difficult it is to conduct an analysis which, if it is to have any value, must be concerned with a complex of causes, remote, involved, and, in the present state of sociological science, extremely difficult to uncover. But personal scruples are, in this matter, wholly unimportant. My children, when they read this balance-sheet of history, the unknown friends into whose hands it may some day come, must not be allowed to reproach its author with having played tricks with truth, of having condemned a number of glaring faults, while, at the same time, maintaining a deliberate silence about errors for which every citizen was, in part, responsible.

* * *

But this very question of the 'governing class' raises questions which need very careful consideration. In the France of 1939 the members of the upper middle class were never sick of declaring that they had lost all power. This was an exaggeration. Solidly supported by the banks and the Press, the régime of the *élite* was not, to that extent, 'finished'. But it *is* true that the great industrialists no longer held a monopoly in the running of the country. The leaders of the principal trade unions, and, to a smaller extent, the mass of the wage-earners, had risen to a position of power in the affairs of the Republic. That had been obvious in 1938, when a certain minister—a 'Man of Munich' if ever there was one—used them as intermediaries when he set about spreading an atmosphere of panic in order to cover up his own weakness. There can be no denying that if much heavy responsibility in this war rested on the shoulders of the military authorities, a considerable amount of blame must also be laid at the door of the trade unions.

I am about to speak of matters of which I have no first-hand knowledge. I need hardly stress the fact that the life of the factory, both before and during the period of hostilities, lay far outside my normal field of operations. But the evidence which I have amassed is so unanimous, and comes from so many different sources, ranging in variety from chief engineers to machine-minders, that I am forced to accept its conclusions as valid. The output of our war factories was insufficient. We were not turning out enough aeroplanes, engines, or tanks. I do not for a moment believe that it was only, or even principally, the wage-earners who were to blame for this state of affairs. On the other hand, it would ill become them to plead complete innocence. Forgetful of the fact that they too, in their own way, were just as much soldiers as the men in uniform, they thought first and foremost about selling their labour at the highest price: in other words, about doing as little as possible, for the shortest time possible, in return for as much money as possible. In normal times that would be a perfectly natural attitude. 'Sordid materialism!' once exclaimed a certain politician whose own enthusiasm for the spiritual was not, I should have said, particularly obvious. But that, of course, is sheer nonsense. The manual worker is out to sell the strength of his arms. The men who sell textiles, sugar, or armaments are scarcely in a position to be shocked if he applies to his own case the great law of trade, which is to give little and to receive much. But however legitimate that point of view may be at other times, it is cruelly out of place when the very existence of one's country is at stake, and when those at the front are risking their lives. The plumber of the village where I live told me that when he was called up to work in a war factory the other men used to hide his tools to prevent him from turning out more, or working more quickly, than was permitted by the unwritten 'law' of the shop. That is an undeniable fact, and it provides a terrible indictment. But to suppose for a moment that that kind of indifference to the interests of the nation was general in one whole class of the population would be the height of injustice. I am more than ready to admit that there were honourable exceptions. Still, this attitude was quite widely enough spread for its consequences to weigh heavily in the scales of war. How it arose at all needs to be explained.

It has been said again and again, and by all sorts of people, that this war failed to rouse the deepest feelings of the nation to a much larger extent than did the last one. I believe that view to be entirely wrong. Our people are temperamentally disinclined actively to *want* any war. No Frenchman in 1939 burned with the desire to 'die for Danzig'. But then it is equally true to say that in 1914 none of them was particularly anxious to 'die for Belgrade'. The *camarilla* which hatched its plots around the Serbian throne was no more familiar to our workers and peasants than was, twenty years later, the corrupt government of Polish colonels; nor if it had been would it have fanned them to a white heat of enthusiasm. As to Alsace-Lorraine, though it is, no doubt, true that when the actual fighting began in 1914, a picture of the martyred provinces did suddenly emerge in men's minds from that decent obscurity which, only a few days earlier, had still shrouded it, but that was merely under the pressure of a necessity which, for quite other reasons, had already been accepted by the nation. Since we had been forced to take up arms, it was difficult to imagine that we should lay them down before we had delivered our lost brothers. Certainly, the beautiful Alsatian eyes, which the popular prints of the time were so fond of depicting, would never, of themselves, have had sufficient influence, in peace-time, on a public opinion which was concerned only to maintain the security of the nation's homes; would never have persuaded men lightly to launch their country on an adventure bristling with the most appalling dangers, with the sole object of drying those bewitching tears.

The truth of the matter is that on both occasions the national response drew its vigour from the same source. '*They're* always picking a quarrel with the rest of the world. The more we give 'em, the more they'll want. It just can't go on like this.' That was what one of my neighbours in a little village of the Creuse said to me shortly before I left for Strasbourg. A peasant of 1914 would have expressed himself in much the same words. As a matter of fact, if either of the two wars was more likely than the other to appeal to the deepest instincts of the masses, and especially of the industrial masses, it was undoubtedly the second, and that because of the very 'ideological' complexion which so many have blamed, but which did succeed in giving a touch of beauty to the sacrifices entailed. The men of the factories and the fields would no more, in 1939, have *deliberately* shed their blood for the overthrow of the dictators than would their elders of 1914 for the liberation of Alsace-Lorraine. But once the battle had been joined against those same dictators, and as a result of *their* action, they felt that by fighting they were helping forward one of the great tasks of humanity. To believe otherwise is to show complete ignorance of the high nobility which lies unexpressed in the hearts of a people which, like ours, has behind it a long history of political action. The absurd ineptitude of our official propaganda, its irritating and crude optimism, its timidity, and, above all, the inability of our rulers to give a frank definition of their war aims, may well, during the long months of inaction, have muddied to some extent what, in the early days, had been so crystal-clear. In May 1940 the spirit that had animated the men when they were first mobilized was not yet dead. Those for whom the *Marseillaise* was still a rallying-song had not ceased to link it with the cult of patriotism and the hatred of tyrants.

The trouble was that among the wage-earners these instincts, which were still strong, and which a less pusillanimous government would have known how to encourage, were at variance with certain other, and more recent, tendencies which were at work within the collective mind. I, with most of the men of my generation, had built enormous hopes, when we were young, on the trade-union movement. But we made no allowance for the narrowness of outlook which, little by little, choked the enthusiasm of the early, epic struggles. What was the cause of this failure? Partly, no doubt, an inevitable preoccupation with wage-claims, and a consequent scaling-down of interest and policy; partly, too, the fact that Labour's leaders allowed themselves to get tangled up in the old political game of electoral propaganda and lobbying. However that may be, it is true to say that the trade-union movement has shown a growing tendency everywhere to diverge from the road on which its feet were originally set, as though dogged by some ineluctable Fate.

Everyone knows that word *kleinbürgerlich* with which Marx stigmatized all politico-social movements which confined themselves to the narrow field of partial interests. Could anything have been more *kleinbürgerlich*, more *petit bourgeois,* than the attitude adopted in the last few years, and even during the war, by most of the big unions, and especially by those which included civil servants in their ranks? I have attended not a few meetings of my own professional organization. Its members were drawn from the intellectual class, but it is true to say that scarcely ever did they show real concern for anything except—not money on a large scale, but what I may call the small change of remuneration. They seemed to be blissfully unaware of such problems as the rôle which our corporation might play in the life of the country; nor were they ever prepared to discuss the bigger question of France's material future. Their vision was limited to immediate issues of petty profit, and I am afraid that this blindness marked the conduct of most of the big unions. I saw something of the way in which the Post Office workers and the railwaymen behaved both during and after the war, and the spectacle was not a very edifying one. Most of them, I am sure, were very decent fellows; a few, as events showed, could on occasion conduct themselves like heroes. But is it by any means certain that the rank and file, and, what is more important, their representatives, ever really understood that the days through which we were living called for more than parish-pump politics? Did they, I mean, fully realize what was demanded of them in pursuance of their daily work? That, after all, is the touchstone of the professional conscience. In most of the cities of western France during the month of June I saw hordes of wretched men wandering about the streets in an effort to get back to their homes. All of them were carrying loads far heavier than they could cope with, and why? Simply because the railway stations had seen fit to close their left-luggage offices for fear of imposing on their staffs a few hours of overtime, or of rather heavier work than usual. It was this kind of short-sightedness, this kind of administrative bumbledom, the effect of petty rivalry and a refusal to get the last ounce out of their members—so different from the dynamic energy of a Pelloutier—which explains the nervelessness of the trade-union movement all over Europe, and not least in France, when confronted by the first aggressive moves of the dictator states. It accounts for their war record. What did a few noisy 'resolutions', aimed at the gallery, matter? The point is that the general run of organized labour never got it into their heads that the only thing that counted was as complete and as rapid a victory as possible for their country, and the defeat, not only of Nazism, but of all those elements of its philosophy which its imitators, in the event of success, would inevitably borrow. They had not been taught, as they should have been by leaders worthy of the name, to look above, beyond, and around the petty problems of every day. By concentrating attention on matters concerned with the earning of their daily bread, they ran the risk of discovering that there might be no daily bread to earn. And now the hour of doom has sounded. Seldom has short-sightedness been more harshly punished.

Then, too, there was the ideology of international pacifism. I flatter myself that I am a good citizen of the world, and among the least chauvinistic of men. As an historian, I know that there is a good deal of truth in Karl Marx's slogan of 'Workers of the World Unite!' I have seen too much of war not to know that it is both horrible and senseless. But the narrowness of outlook which I have just been denouncing consists precisely in a refusal to bring these sentiments into harmonious relation with other forms of enthusiasm which are no less worthy of respect. I have never believed that because a man loves his country he cannot also love his children, nor can I see why any form of internationalism, whether of the intellect or of class interests, should be irreconcilable with patriotism. I go farther, and say, after carefully searching my own conscience, that this presumed antinomy has no real existence at all. It is a poor heart that cannot find room for more than one kind of affection.

But let us not linger in this world of the emotions. Those of us who have a certain degree of self-respect, who hate big words which have become so popularly debased that they no longer express the intimate truths of mind and heart, find it difficult to breathe its atmosphere for long without a sensation of nausea. Besides, that particular world is one into which the pacifists did not as a rule ask us to follow them. What they primarily invoked was the sentiment of self-interest; and it was because they made of this presumed self-interest an image woefully at variance with any true knowledge of their fellow men, that they overweighted with error the minds of the somewhat sheep-like disciples who trusted them. They said that French capitalism was a hard task-master; and in that they were certainly not wrong. But what they forgot was that victory for the authoritarian régimes would be bound to lead to the complete enslavement of the workers. Were they really blind to the fact that the profiteers-to-be of our defeat were already on the prowl ready to seize upon it—nay, actually hoping that it would occur? They taught, not without reason, that war builds up a mass of useless destruction. But they omitted to distinguish between a war which men have deliberately planned, and a war imposed from without; between murder and legitimate self-defence. To those who asked them whether they did not think it was one's duty to wring the neck of the executioner, they replied: 'No one's attacking us'—for they loved to play with words. Maybe, having lost the habit of looking their own thoughts fairly and squarely in the face, they had allowed themselves to be caught in the tangle of their own equivocations. The highwayman does not say to his victim, 'It's your blood I'm after'; he offers him a choice—'Your money or your life'. Similarly, when an aggressor nation sets out to oppress its neighbours it says: 'Either abdicate your liberty or take the consequence of massacre.' They maintained that war is the concern of the rich and powerful, that the poor should have nothing to do with it. As though, in an old society, cemented by centuries of a shared culture, the humble are not always, for good or ill, constrained to make common cause with the mighty. They whispered—I have heard them—that Hitler was not nearly so black as he was painted; that the nation would save itself a great deal of suffering by opening its gates to the enemy, instead of setting itself to oppose invasion by force of arms. How, I wonder, do these noble apostles feel to-day in that occupied zone which lies in starvation beneath the jack-boot of tyranny?

Since the gospel they preached was one of seeming convenience, their sermons found an easy echo in those lazy, selfish instincts which exist in all men's hearts side by side with nobler potentialities. These enthusiasts, many of whom were not, as individuals, lacking in courage, worked unconsciously to produce a race of cowards. For it is an undoubted truth that unless virtue is accompanied by severe self-criticism, it always runs the risk of turning against its own most dearly held convictions. Dear fellow teachers—when it came to the point, you did, for the most part, put up a magnificent fight. It was your goodwill which managed to create in many a sleepy secondary school, in many a tradition-ridden university, the only form of education of which, perhaps, we can feel genuinely proud. I only hope that a day will come, and come soon, a day of glory and of happiness for France, when, liberated from the enemy, and freer than ever in our intellectual life, we may meet again for the mutual discussion of ideas. And when that happens, do you not think that, having learned from an experience so dearly purchased, you will find much to alter in the things you were teaching only a few years back?

But what is really remarkable is that these extremist lovers of the human race showed no surprise at all when, on the road that led to capitulation, they found themselves walking arm in arm with the born enemies of their class, the sworn foes of their ideals. As a matter of fact, odd though such an alliance may seem, its intellectual basis is to be found in conditions long antecedent to a supervening political hostility. Among those with whom they had more than once crossed swords on the battlefield of the hustings, with whom now they were prepared to collaborate in the work of securing peace at any price, were many who had the same social background as themselves, though they had taken early flight to richer feeding-grounds. These turncoats had long hidden away all that might remind people of their earlier enthusiasm for revolution. Old clothes of just that cut, they thought, might prove a shade embarrassing in the circumstances of their new lives. But, in their onward march, they had passed through many political parties, and something of what they had found there had remained indelibly impressed upon them. They had lost all sense of national values, and were quite incapable of finding them again. It is no accident that the collapse of our country brought to power a minister who was once at Kienthal, nor will it be one if the Germans, wishing to elevate to a position of influence some gutter-agitator, should pick on a man who, before assuming in the years before the war a wash of sham patriotism, had been a Communist leader. Against one particular school of politics no more terrible charge can be brought than this: that once a man has been formed by it, he may forget everything it taught him, including much that was fine, much that was noble, save only this—the denial of his country.

Thus it came about that though the general needs of our national defence were more inextricably than ever bound up with the interests of the wage-earners, they made demands upon the working class which, however legitimately obvious they may have been, were compromised by a spirit of uncertainty and gloom in the factories. This vague lack of purpose was bad enough: it was made far worse by the incredible contradictions of French Communism.

But here I find myself coming to grips with an entirely different order of problems which belong, strictly, to the world of thought.

It was not only in the field that intellectual causes lay at the root of our defeat. As a nation we had been content with incomplete knowledge and imperfectly thought-out ideas. Such an attitude is not a good preparation for military success. Our system of government demands the participation of the masses. The destiny of the People is in their own hands, and I see no reason for believing that they are not perfectly capable of choosing rightly. But what effort had been made to supply them with that minimum of clear and definite information without which no rational conduct is possible? To that question the answer is 'None'. In no way did our so-called democratic system so signally fail. That particular dereliction of duty constituted the most heinous crime of our self-styled democrats. The matter would be less serious if what we had to deplore were merely the lies and half-truths inspired by party loyalties openly avowed. Wicked these may be, but, on the whole, they can be fairly easily discounted. Far graver is the fact that our national Press, claiming to provide an impartial news-service, was sailing under false colours. Many newspapers, even those which openly wore the livery of party beliefs, were secretly enslaved to unavowed and, often, squalid interests. Some of them were controlled by foreign influences. I do not deny that the common sense of the ordinary reader did, to some extent, counterbalance this, but only at the cost of developing an attitude of scepticism to *all* propaganda, printed and broadcast alike. It would be a great mistake to think that the elector always votes as 'his' paper tells him to. I have known more than one humble citizen who votes almost automatically *against* the views expressed by his chosen rag, and it may be that this refusal to be stampeded by printed insincerities is among the more consoling elements of our contemporary national life. It does, at least, offer some hope for the future. Still, it must be admitted that such an attitude provides a poor intellectual training for those who are called upon to understand what is at stake in a vast world struggle, to judge rightly of the coming storm, and to arm themselves adequately against its violence. Quite deliberately—as one can see by reading *Mein Kampf* or the records of Rauschning's conversations—Hitler kept the truth from his servile masses. Instead of intellectual persuasion he gave them emotional suggestion. For us there is but one set of alternatives. Either, like the Germans, we must turn our people into a keyboard on which a few leaders can play at will (but who are those leaders? The playing of those at present on the stage is curiously lacking in resonance); or we can so train them that they may be able to collaborate to the full with the representatives in whose hands they have placed the reins of government. At the present stage of civilization this dilemma admits of no middle term. . . . The masses no longer obey. They *follow,* either because they have been hypnotized or because they *know.*

✦ Reading 53 ✦

Courage

Anna Akhmatova

We know what today lies in the scales
And what is happening now.
The hour of courage has struck on the clock
And courage will not desert us.
It is not frightening to fall dead under enemy bullets
It is not bitter to remain homeless,
But we shall preserve you, our Russian speech,
Our great Russian word.
We shall carry you to the end, free and pure,
And give you to our grandchildren and save you from bondage,
For ever.

From: Alexander Werth, *Russia at War, 1941–1945* (New York: Carroll & Graf Publishers, 1984), pp. 410–411.

✦ Reading 54 ✦

Wait for Me

Konstantin Simonov

Wait for me, and I'll return, only wait very hard.
Wait, when you are filled with sorrow as you watch the yellow rain;
Wait, when the winds sweep the snowdrifts,
Wait in the sweltering heat,
Wait when others have stopped waiting, forgetting their yesterdays.
Wait even when from afar, no letters come to you,
Wait even when others are tired of waiting . . .
Wait even when my mother and son think I am no more,
And when friends sit around the fire, drinking to my memory.
Wait, and do not hurry to drink to my memory, too;
Wait, for I'll return, defying every death.
And let those who did not wait say that I was lucky;
They will never understand that in the midst of death,
You, with your waiting, saved me.
Only you and I will know how I survived:
It's because you waited, as no one else did.

From: Alexander Werth, *Russia at War 1941–1945* (New York: Carroll & Graf Publishers, 1984), p. 273.

✦ Reading 55 ✦

Second Letter to the Kama

Olga Berggolts

Here I am writing again to the Kama,
I place the date: 20 December.
How happy I am to see how hot and clear
  the stamp "Leningrad"
  gleams on the envelope.
The stamp "Leningrad"! You have to
  understand.
All defenders of the city understand me—
A Leningrader, comrade, glancing
  backward,
  a half year into the war, amazes herself:
We have looked death in the eyes.
We prepared for the last struggle.
Leningrad in September, Leningrad in
  September . . .
Dark golden, glorious falling leaves,
The crash of the first bombs, the wailing
  sirens,
Dark-rusty contours of the barricades.
All that I wrote about back then to the
  Kama,
All that I now so blithely describe—
Leningrader, you know—
Was only the beginning, only the first
  small step
  toward your December!
Leningrad in December, Leningrad in
  December!
Oh how the windows rattle in the dark
  dawn,
How gloomy is your icy home,
How wounded your body by enemies . . .
Mother, bright Homeland, from behind
  the encirclement
  you endlessly assure us:
  "Every hour we take pride in you."
Yes, we won't again turn away from
  death,
We accept starving, slow battle.
Leningrader, my fellow traveler,
  my seasoned friend,
For us the December days are heavier than
  September.
All the same we will not unclasp our
  enfeebled hands:
We must overcome even this, even this.
It will come, the solemn Leningrad
  half-day,
  filled with quiet, and peace,
  and fragrant bread.
Oh, what joy, what enormous pride to
  know
  that you will reply to everyone:
"I lived in Leningrad in December of '41,
and there received the first news of
  victory."
. . . No, there is no second letter to the
  far Kama!
Instead a hymn to Leningraders—starved,
  obstinate, dear.
I will send beyond the ring a telegram in
  their name:
"We are alive. We will hold out.
  We will win!"

20 December 1941

From: Ol'ga Berggol'ts, *Proshlogo—Net! Stikhi, Poemy, Iz rabochikh tetradei,* trans. Michael Melancon and Boris Gorshkov (Moscow: Russkaia kniga, 1999), pp. 37–39.

THE PURGES AND THE HOLOCAUST

The 1930s and 1940s witnessed virtual wars against civilians in Europe. Stalin's purges sent millions to work camps or to their deaths. Nazi Germany legalized persecution against Jews and other "undesirables," leading to the extermination of millions. This photograph shows Nazi soldiers rounding up Jewish men, women, and children in Warsaw for "resettlement" to the death camps.

THE PURGES AND THE HOLOCAUST

Totalitarian regimes use terror to intimidate the public and eliminate class, racial, or other perceived enemies. Even though it is impossible to equate any two totalitarian systems, the two most destructive during the 1930s and 1940s were Stalinist Communism and National Socialism. Both Joseph Stalin and Adolf Hitler perpetrated massive crimes against other human beings. During the 1930s Stalin sent off resisters, misfits, and political opponents to forced labor camps in Siberia. After 1933 the Nazi regime implemented racial laws against Germany's Jews and sent political opponents to concentration camps. By the mid-1930s Stalin began purging his own party, culminating in the show trials of the late 1930s in which Bolshevik leaders confessed to unlikely crimes before being executed. By 1942 Hitler's racial laws turned into a war of annihilation against the Jews. The Nazis built death camps in the East as part of the Final Solution for their "Jewish Problem."

Eugenia Semyonovna Ginzburg (1896–1977), who saw herself as an ordinary Communist woman, described the terror of Stalin's regime in *Journey into the Whirlwind* (1967). Engaged in party work in the Volga city of Kazan during 1937, she was arrested for allegedly collaborating with the "enemies of the people" and spent eighteen years in exile and prison camps. Primo Levi (1919–1987), an Italian Jew, was arrested by the Germans in 1943 and sent to Auschwitz. He recorded his horrendous experience in *Survival in Auschwitz* (1986). Elie Wiesel (1928–) describes life and death in Auschwitz in his book, *Night* (1958). Wiesel asks the question: where is God? He answers himself: "Here He is—He is hanging here on this gallows . . ." Wiesel's work discloses the moral responsibility to fight hatred, racism, and genocide.

✦ Reading 56 ✦

Journey into the Whirlwind

Eugenia Semyonovna Ginzburg

Life Counted in Minutes

From that moment, events rushed on with breathtaking speed. I spent the two and a half months until my arrest in tormented conflict between reason and the kind of foreboding which Lermontov called "prophetic anguish."

My mind told me that there was absolutely nothing for which I could be arrested. It was true, of course, that in the monstrous accusations which the newspapers daily hurled at "enemies of the people" there was something clearly exaggerated, not quite real. All the same, I thought to myself, there must be something in it, however little—they must at least have voted the wrong way on some occasion or other. I, on the other hand, had never belonged to the opposition, nor had I ever had the slightest doubt as to the rightness of the Party line.

"If they arrested people like you they'd have to lock up the whole Party," my husband encouraged me in my line of reasoning.

Yet, in spite of all these rational arguments, I could not shake off a feeling of approaching disaster. I seemed to be at the center of an iron ring which was all the time contracting and would soon crush me.

The journey back to Moscow at Yaroslavsky's summons was terrible. I was very near to suicide.

I shared the first-class compartment with a woman doctor I knew, a children's doctor, Makarova, who had been to Kazan to defend her university thesis. She was a pleasant woman, not given to many words, gentle in her movements and with an attentive, thoughtful expression.

I thought that by talking about trifles I had more or less succeeded in hiding the state I was in. But suddenly—it had nothing to do with our conversation—she stroked my hand and said quietly:

"I'm very sorry for all the Communists I know. It's a very hard time for you. Anyone can be accused."

That night I was overwhelmed by such unspeakable misery that, as quietly as I could, I stole out of the compartment and along the corridor to the platform at the end of the carriage. My mind was empty of thought, except for some verses by Nekrasov which fitted themselves to the rhythm of the train. Their theme was that those whose lives had been broken could still assert their courage by dying. The beat was hammered out by the wheels and the pulse throbbing in my temples. It was to escape from it that I had left the compartment. The November wind blew open my light dressing gown and for a moment distracted me. Then my wretchedness beset me again.

I opened the carriage door slightly. The cold air rushed in my face. I looked down into the noisy blackness, my mind finally invaded by a torturing vision. One step . . . one instant . . . and I wouldn't have to go to Yaroslavsky. I would never need to be afraid of anything.

I felt a strong but gentle grip on my arm. Makarova should have been a psychiatrist. Without any exclamations, without showering me with words, she led me back to the compartment and made me lie down. All she said as she stroked my hair was:

"All this will be over one day, and you've only got one life."

I would never have thought that Yaroslavsky, who was known as the "conscience of the Party," could have woven such a web of lying syllogisms. It was he who first explained to me the theory which became popular in 1937, that "when you get down to it, there is no difference between 'subjective' and 'objective.' " Whether you had committed a crime or, out of inadvertence or lack of vigilance, "added

From: Eugenia Semyonovna Ginzburg, *Journey into the Whirlwind,* trans. Paul Stevenson and Max Hayward (New York: Harcourt, Brace & World, 1967), pp. 30–34, 41–47, 83–88, 273–279.

grist" to the criminal's mill, you were equally guilty. Even if you had not the slightest idea of what was going on, it was the same. The chain of "logical" reasoning in my case was as follows: "Elvov's article contained theoretical errors. Whether he intended them or not is beside the point. You who worked with him and knew he had written the article failed to denounce him. This is collusion with the enemy."

The charge of "relaxation of vigilance," formulated by the kindly and conscientious Sidorov, was replaced by one even harsher than Beylin's: Yaroslavsky accused me of "collaborating with enemies of the people."

So the i's were dotted—"collaboration with the enemy" was a specific, punishable, criminal offense.

My composure left me. I shouted and stamped my feet at that venerable old man. I might have gone for him with my fists if the wide, glossy surface of the desk had not been between us. I no longer remember exactly what I said to him, but it amounted to a counter-accusation. Yes, I was driven to such despair that I asked him plain questions, dictated by common sense. This was the height of bad form, for we were all supposed to pretend that syllogisms invented by sadists reflected the normal processes of the human mind. If anyone asked a question which showed up this lunacy for what it was, his hearers were either outraged or smiled condescendingly and treated him as an idiot.

But in my state of excitement that day in Yaroslavsky's office I actually shouted at him:

"All right, so I didn't denounce Elvov's article. But you—you not only didn't denounce it, you edited it and published it in your four-volume history of the Party. Why are you judging me and not I you? I'm thirty, you're sixty. I am a young member of the Party, while you are its 'conscience.' Why must I be torn to pieces and you left sitting behind that desk? It's a disgrace!"

I saw a glimmer of fright in his eyes. He must have thought I was mad. How otherwise could I have dared to say such things in this room, a cross between a shrine and a court of justice? But he at once resumed his stern mask of bigoted righteousness. He said with an almost natural tremor in his voice:

"No one knows my mistakes better than I do. Yes, I have wronged the Party—I, a man whose very existence is unthinkable outside its ranks."

It was on the tip of my tongue to ask another insanely daring question:

"Why can you redeem your mistake by merely being conscious of it, while I must pay for mine with my blood, my life, my children?"

But I didn't say it. My excitement was over. Instead, I felt horror. What had I said? What would they do to me now? Then the horror too died down and was replaced by a merciless clarity of vision: nothing would make any difference, nothing was any use. The time had come either to die silently or to tread the path to Golgotha along with others, thousands of others. When I was finally told to go back to Kazan where I would soon be notified of the decision, I could not wait to begin my journey. I knew for certain now that what was left of my life could not be measured in years or months but in minutes and I must hurry back to my children. What would become of them?

* * *

That Day

After my expulsion from the Party, eight days went by before my arrest. All those days I sat at home, shut in my room and not answering the telephone. I was waiting; so were all my family. What for? We told each other that we were waiting for the leave my husband had been promised at this unusual time. When it came we would go again to Moscow and try to get people to help me. We would ask Razumov, who was a member of the Central Committee, to help us.

In our hearts we knew perfectly well that none of this would happen, that we were waiting for something quite different. My mother and my husband took turns watching over me. My mother sometimes fried some potatoes. "Do have some, darling. Remember how you liked them done this way when you were little?" Every time my husband had been out and came home he rang in a special way and shouted through the door:

"It's only me, open up!"

It was as if he were saying:

"It's still only me, not them."

We started a purge of our books. Our old nurse carried out pail after pailful of ashes. We burned Radek's *Portraits and Pamphlets*, the *History of*

Western Europe by Friedland and Slutsky, Bukharin's *Political Economy*.

The "Index" grew longer and longer, and the scale of our *auto da fé* grander and grander. We even had to burn Stalin's *On the Opposition*. This too had become illegal under the new dispensation.

A few days before my arrest, Biktagirov, second secretary of the Party municipal committee, was summarily removed from a meeting at which he was presiding. His secretary came in:

"Comrade Biktagirov, you are wanted."

"In the middle of a meeting? What nonsense. Tell them I'm busy."

But the secretary came back:

"They insist."

So he went, and was invited to put on his coat and go "for a short drive."

My husband was even more puzzled and shaken by this event than by my own expulsion from the Party. A secretary of the municipal committee! And he too had "turned out to be an enemy of the people". . .

"Really, the Cheka is getting a bit above itself. They'll have to let a good many of these people out again."

He was trying to convince himself that it was all no more than a checkup, or a misunderstanding of some sort, temporary and almost ludicrous. Surely on our next free day we would find Biktagirov sitting once more at table at Livadia, telling with a smile how he had almost been mistaken for an enemy of the people.

But the nights were very unpleasant. The windows of our bedroom faced the street and cars drove past all the time. And how we listened in fear and trembling when it seemed as though one of them might be pulling up in front of our house. At night, even my husband's optimism would give way to terror—the great terror that gripped our whole country by the throat.

"Paul! A car!"

"Well, what of it, darling? It's a big town, there are plenty of cars."

"It's stopped. I'm sure it has."

My husband, barefooted, would leap across to the window. He was pale but spoke with exaggerated calm:

"There, you see, it's only a truck." "Don't they use trucks sometimes?"

We would fall asleep only after six, and when we woke there was the latest news about who had been "exposed."

"Have you heard? Petrov has turned out to be an enemy of the people! How cunning he must have been to get away with it for so long."

This meant that Petrov had been arrested overnight.

Sheaves of newspapers would arrive, and by now there was no telling which was the *Literary Gazette* and which, say, *Soviet Art*. They all ranted and raved in the same way about enemies, conspiracies, shootings. . . .

The nights were terrifying. But what we were waiting for actually happened in the daytime.

We were in the dining room, my husband, Alyosha, and I. My stepdaughter Mayka was out skating. Vasya was in the nursery. I was ironing some laundry. I often felt like doing manual work; it distracted me from my thoughts. Alyosha was having breakfast, and my husband was reading a story by Valeria Gerasimova aloud to him. Suddenly the telephone rang. It sounded as shrill as on that day in December 1934.

For a few moments, none of us picked it up. We hated telephone calls in those days. Then my husband said in that unnaturally calm voice he so often used now:

"It must be Lukovnikov. I asked him to call."

He took the receiver, listened, went as white as a sheet, and said even more quietly:

"It's for you, Genia. Vevers, of the NKVD."

Vevers, the head of the NKVD department for special political affairs, could not have been more amiable and charming. His voice burbled on like a brook in spring.

"Good morning, dear comrade. Tell me, how are you fixed for time today?"

"I'm always free now. Why?"

"Oh, dear, always free, how depressing. Never mind, these things will pass. So anyway, you'd have time to come and see me for a moment. The thing is, we'd like some information about that fellow Elvov . . . some additional information. My word, he did land you in a mess, didn't he! Oh, well, we'll soon sort it all out."

"When shall I come?"

"Whenever it suits you best. Now, if you like, or if it's more convenient, after lunch."

"How long is it likely to take?"

"Oh, say forty minutes, perhaps an hour."

My husband, who was standing beside me and could hear, was making signs and whispering to me to go at once, so that Vevers shouldn't think I was afraid—there was nothing to be afraid of.

I told Vevers I'd go at once.

"Perhaps I'll just stop at Mother's on the way," I said to my husband.

"No, don't. Go at once. The sooner it's all cleared up, the better."

He helped me to get quickly into my things. I sent Alyosha off to the skating rink. He went without saying good-by. I never saw him again.

For some strange reason, little Vasya, who was used to my going and coming and always took it perfectly calmly, ran out into the hall after me and kept asking insistently:

"Where are you going, Mother, where? Tell me. I don't want you to go!"

But I could not so much as look at the children or kiss them—if I had, I would have died then and there. I turned away and called out to the nurse:

"Fima, do take him. I haven't time for him now."

Perhaps it was just as well not to see my mother either. What must be must be, and there's no point in trying to postpone it. The door banged shut. I still remember the sound. That was all . . . I was never again to open that door behind which I had lived with my dear children.

On the stairs we met Mayka, back from the skating rink. She was a child who understood everything intuitively. She said nothing, and didn't seem to wonder where we could be going at that unusual hour. Her enormous blue eyes wide open, she pressed herself against the wall, and so deep an understanding of pain and horror showed in her twelve-year-old face that I dreamed of it for years afterward.

Our old nurse Fima caught up with us at the front door. She had run down to tell me something. But she looked at me and said nothing. She only made the sign of the cross after us as we moved away.

"Let's walk, shall we."

"Yes, let's, while we still can."

"Don't be silly. That's not the way they arrest people. They want some information, that's all."

We walked for a long time in silence. It was a lovely, bright February day. Snow had fallen that morning and was still very clean.

"It's our last walk together, Paul darling. I'm a state criminal now."

"Don't talk nonsense, Genia. I told you before, if they arrested people like you they'd have to lock up the whole Party."

"I sometimes have the crazy idea that that's what they mean to do."

I waited for my husband's usual reaction, thinking he would scold me for my blasphemous words. But instead, he himself gave way to "heresy" and said he was sure of the innocence of many of those who had been arrested as enemies, and he talked indignantly about very highly placed people indeed.

I was glad we were once again of one mind. I imagined then that everything was quite clear to me, though in fact many bitter discoveries still lay before me.

But here we were at the well-known address in Black Lake Street.

"Well, Genia, we'll expect you home for lunch."

How pathetic he looked, all of a sudden, how his lips trembled! I thought of his assured, masterful tone in the old days, the tone of an old Communist, an experienced Party worker.

"Good-by, Paul dear. We've had a good life together."

I didn't even say "Look after the children." I knew he would not be able to take care of them. He was again trying to comfort me with commonplaces—I could no longer catch what he was saying. I walked quickly toward the reception room, and suddenly heard his broken cry:

"Genia!"

He had the haunted look of a baited animal, of a harried and exhausted human being—it was a look I was to see again and again, *there.*

* * *

The "Conveyor Belt"

They started on me again. I was put on the "conveyor belt"—uninterrupted questioning by a changing team of examiners. Seven days without sleep or food, without even returning to my cell. Relaxed and fresh, they passed before me as in a dream—Livanov, Tsarevsky, Krokhichev, Vevers, Yelshin and his assistant, Lieutenant Bikchentayev, a chubby, curly-haired, pink-checked young man who looked like a fattened turkey cock.

The object of the conveyor belt is to wear out the nerves, weaken the body, break resistance, and force the prisoner to sign whatever is required. The first day or two I still noticed the individual characteristics of the interrogators—Livanov, calm and bureaucratic as before, urging me to sign some monstrous piece of nonsense, as though it were no more than a perfectly normal, routine detail; Tsarevsky and Vevers always shouting and threatening—Vevers sniffing cocaine and giggling as well as shouting.

"Ha-ha-ha! What's become of our university beauty now! You look at least forty. Aksyonov wouldn't recognize his sweetheart. And if you go on being stubborn we'll turn you into a real grandma. You haven't been in the rubber cell yet, have you? You haven't? Oh well, the best is still to come."

Major Yelshin was invariably courteous and "humane." He liked to talk about my children. He had heard I was a good mother, yet it didn't look as if I cared what happened to them. He asked me why I was so "becomingly pale" and was "amazed" to hear that I had been questioned without food or sleep for four or five days on end:

"Is it really worth torturing yourself like that rather than signing a purely formal, unimportant record? Come on now, get it over and go to sleep. Right here, on this sofa. I'll see you're not disturbed."

The "unimportant record" stated that, on Elvov's instructions, I had organized a Tartar writers' branch of the terrorist group of which I was a member; there followed a list of Tartar writers I had "recruited," starting with Kavi Nadzhimi.

"Anxious to spare Nadzhimi? He didn't spare you," said the Major enigmatically.

"That's between him and his conscience."

"What are you, an Evangelist or something?"

"Just honest."

Again the Major couldn't miss the chance to display his learning, and gave me a lecture on the Marxist-Leninist view of ethics. "Honest" meant useful to the proletariat and its state.

"It can't be useful to the proletarian state to wipe out the first generation of Tartar writers, who are all Communists at that."

"We know for a fact that these people are traitors."

"Then why do you need my evidence?"

"Just for the record."

"I can't put on record what I don't know."

"Don't you trust us?"

"How can I do that when you arrest me without cause, keep me in jail, and use illegal methods of interrogation?"

"What are we doing that's illegal?"

"You've kept me without sleep, drink, or food for several days to force me to give false evidence."

"Have your dinner, I'm not stopping you. They'll bring it this minute. Just sign here. You're only torturing yourself."

Lieutenant Bikchentayev, who now always accompanied the Major, evidently as a trainee, stood by "in readiness," repeating the final words of Yelshin's sentences like an infant learning to talk.

"It's all your own fault," said the Major.

"Your own fault," echoed the Lieutenant.

One day the Major prepared a questionnaire on my contacts with Tartar intellectuals.

"You're an educated woman, you speak French and German, why should you have wanted to learn Tartar?"

"So that I could do translations."

"But it's an uncivilized language. . . ."

"Is it? Is that what you think too, Lieutenant?"

The turkey cock smiled sheepishly and said nothing.

After this preamble I was invited to sign a statement to the effect that, on the orders of Trotskyist headquarters, I had tried to organize an opportunist alliance with bourgeois-nationalist elements of the Tartar intelligentsia.

I ventured on irony: "That's right! All my life it's been my dream to unite the Moslem world for the greater glory of Islam!"

The Major laughed, but he didn't give me anything to eat or drink, or let me go away to sleep.

It seemed to me then that my suffering was beyond measure. But in a few months' time I was to realize that my spell on the conveyor belt had been child's play compared with what was meted out to others, from June 1937 on. I was deprived of sleep and food but allowed to sit down and, occasionally, given a sip of water from the jug on the interrogator's desk. I was not beaten.

It is true that once Vevers nearly killed me, but that was under the influence of cocaine, when he was not responsible for his actions, and it gave him a great fright.

It happened, I think, on the fifth or sixth night. By then I was half delirious. As a means of "psychological pressure," the prisoner was customarily made to sit a long way off from the interrogator, sometimes at the opposite end of the room. On this occasion Vevers sat me down against the far wall and shouted his questions at me right across the vast office. He asked me in what year I had first met Professor Korbut, who had joined the Trotskyist opposition in 1927.

"I don't remember the exact year but it was a long time ago, before he voted for the opposition."

"Wha-at!" Excited by cocaine and my stubbornness, Vevers was beside himself with rage. "Opposition d'you call it, that gang of spies and murderers? Why, you . . ."

A large marble paperweight flew straight at me. Only when I saw the hole in the wall half an inch from where my temple had been did I realize what a narrow escape I had had.

Vevers was so frightened that he actually brought me a glass of water. His hands were shaking. Killing prisoners under interrogation was not yet allowed. His feelings had run away with him.

On the seventh day I was taken to the floor below, to a colonel whose name I cannot remember. Here, for the first time, I was made to stand throughout the interrogation. As I kept falling asleep on my feet, the guards placed on either side of me had continuously to shake me awake, saying: "You're not allowed to sleep."

A similar scene from a film called *Palace and Fortress* floated through my mind. The hero, Karakozov, was interrogated in exactly this way; he, too, was deprived of sleep. Then my head began to swim. As through a thick fog, I saw the Colonel's disgusted expression, and the revolver on his desk, evidently put there to frighten me. What particularly annoyed me, I remember, were the circles on the wallpaper, the same as in Vevers's office. They kept dancing before my eyes.

I have no idea what answers I gave the Colonel. I think I was silent most of the time, only repeating occasionally: "I won't sign." He alternated threats and persuasion, promising that I would see my husband, my children. Finally I blacked out.

I must have been unconscious for so long that they had to stop the "belt." When I awoke I was on my bunk and saw Lyama's dear, tear-stained face bending over me. She was feeding me drops of orange juice, which Ira had just received in a parcel.

Soon I heard anxious inquiries from Garey and Abdullin next door.

"Thank heaven she's come around. Splendid. Kiss her for us."

Supper was brought, and I ate two portions of the disgusting slop that passed for fish stew. By way of dessert, Ira triumphantly produced two small squares of chocolate from her parcel.

I had only just enough time to think how kind people were when I was called out for another spell on the conveyor belt.

* * *

Car Number 7

Before we got into the car I had noticed the inscription "Special equipment." I thought at first, naturally enough, that this had been left on it from its previous journey. But I began to have doubts—and so did the rest of us—after the officer in charge of the convoy had told us the rules to be observed during the journey.

"The 'special equipment' must be us," said Tanya Stankovskaya, climbing onto one of the wooden bunks. "That's why they tell us that we can talk while the train's moving but not to make a sound at stations. He said we'd be put in irons if we so much as whispered."

From behind, Tanya looked like a sprightly, mischievous girl. The movements with which she folded her prison coat into a pillow were carefree and youthful. Her voice, too, sounded young as she cried from above our heads:

"Look at me! I've taken the top bunk—there's social consciousness for you. At least there's room for me here—there wouldn't be for any of you plumper ones!"

No one replied; very few of the women even heard her. Car Number 7 was full of no less than seventy-six women, all talking at once, jostling one another and thrown about by the motion of the train. All wore the same dirty-gray uniform with the brown "convict's" stripes on the jacket and skirt.

None of us stopped talking for a single moment. No one listened to anyone else, and there was no common theme: each of us talked about her own affairs from the moment the train left Yaroslavl. Some began to recite verses, sing, and tell stories even before installing themselves on the wooden bunks. It was the first time for two years that we had been surrounded by fellow human beings, and every one of us was rejoicing in the sound of her own voice. In Yaroslavl, where the prisoners came from all over the Soviet Union, those in solitary confinement had virtually not spoken for seven hundred and thirty days. For all that time they had heard some six or seven words a day: Get up, hot water, walk, washroom, dinner, lights out. . . .

In the general crush I found myself on one of the lower bunks. There was scarcely room to move, but with my experience of such matters I realized that I had got one of the better spots. In the first place, I was at the end of a row, so that I could be pushed from one side only; and secondly, I was near the high, barred window, which let through a thin stream of air. I stopped talking for a moment, raised myself on my elbows, and breathed in deeply. Yes, I could smell open fields. It was the month of June—the glorious, sweltering June of 1939.

Then, like the others, I went on talking and talking—in a hoarse voice which faltered every now and then, trying to tell everything at once and occasionally making an effort to hear and understand others. . . . My head spun painfully as I caught fragmentary sentences:

"Well, whatever happens we're lucky to be out of that stone morgue."

"Ten years' imprisonment and five years' deprivation of rights. Everyone here's got the same."

"Could you eat that soup they gave us yesterday? I couldn't, it made me sick."

"Have you heard that Anna's supposed to be here, the partisan girl, one of Chapayev's machine gunners?"

"D'you think we get anything to eat on this trip?"

Tanya Stankovskaya dangled her incredibly thin legs from the upper bunk—she had no calves, and her enormous prison boots were many sizes too big. To my amazement I saw that from the front she did not look like a girl but like an old woman, with unkempt gray hair and a bony face, and her skin was dry and peeling. To my question, she replied that she was thirty-five.

"That surprises you, does it? I mean, of course, thirty-five ordinary, calendar years. If you count the two Yaroslavl ones as twenty, that makes fifty-five. Plus at least ten for the interrogation, so I'm sixty-five really. . . . Could you make room for a minute? I'm coming down for a breath of air."

She climbed down and sat on the floor next to the car door, which was open by about a hand's breadth. However, at that moment the clatter of the wheels slowed down and the guards ran up hastily, slamming the doors to and fastening the heavy wooden bar, which remained in position except when the guards had to enter the car.

"We're stopping!" At once there was dead silence, as though the carload of women had been gagged. All seventy-six of us—excited, disheveled, still afraid to believe in the change in our fortunes—became absolutely silent, doing our best to express in looks what we had been about to say. Only the more impatient ones tried to continue their conversations by means of gestures, pantomime, or even the prisoner's wall alphabet.

When the train moved on half an hour later, we found that we had all lost our voices and were speaking in hoarse whispers.

"Laryngitis—acute laryngitis," laughed Musya Lyubinskaya, who was a doctor and one of the youngest of our company. Her black braids were familiar to many of us from Butyrki.

The only person whose voice had not given out was a strapping girl from the Urals called Fisa Korkodinova. She had a metallic contralto voice with occasional bass notes, which now boomed out like a trumpet amid the confused squeaks of an amateur orchestra. This was one reason that prompted us to choose her as our starosta*—this, together with her composed manner, her rich Ural accent, and the ruddy complexion which she had not lost even at Yaroslavl. Presently we each received from her generous hands an earthenware mug without a handle, a tin bowl, and a chipped wooden spoon.

"Do you mean to say we can't smoke? Yaroslavl was bad enough, but at least they let us do that sometimes." This was Nadya Korolyova, a forty-year-old woman from Leningrad, who was almost as emaciated as Tanya but more trim in appearance, with smoothly combed hair.

Everyone began to explain that it was because of the paper. We might unroll it and write messages, and "they" were terrified of our doing so and throwing them out of the train.

I had acquired the habit of smoking in prison, and I was secretly glad that it was not allowed now—otherwise how should we have been able to breathe?

The officer in charge made his appearance, and we were relieved to see that he was a different type from the Yaroslavl warders, who spoke six words a day and stalked about the carpeted corridors like tigers. This was a cheerful rogue whom we nicknamed the Brigand, with a lock of hair brushed back stylishly and a fund of racy expressions.

"Starosta of Number 7—stand up and be counted!" he roared, scanning the benches with piercing eyes and grunting with pleasure when the plump Fisa rose before him and boomed in her Ural accent: "Starosta of Number 7 reporting, Citizen Officer." Then, with relish, he repeated the various prohibitions:

"Whenever the train stops, not a squeak out of you, or you'll be put in irons. No books on the journey—you've done enough reading in the last two years. Tell each other fairy tales if you like. As to food—we-ell, you might say we're on iron rations. Back there you got two hot meals a day, here you'll get one. There's enough bread, but we're a bit short of water. You'll get a mugful a day, do what you like with it—drink, wash, brush your teeth. . . ."

"Why did you let him look at you like that?" growled a voice as the Brigand moved off. It was that of Tamara Varazashvili, "Queen Tamara," who now tossed her proud head even higher. She had been arrested in 1935; her father, an expert on Georgian literature, had been accused of nationalism. She was guilty of nothing more than being her father's daughter, but she considered herself a "genuine political" and coldly despised the "1937 lot" for their lack of independence, their wheedling tone with the guards, and the fact that they asked for things instead of demanding them.

"Like what?" asked Fisa in a puzzled tone.

"You know perfectly well—he was ogling you. And how could you smile back at him? It shows lack of self-respect."

Seventy-six hoarse voices began arguing at once, as usual paying no attention to one another. Then the voice of Polya Shvyrkova prevailed:

"After all, some of them are human beings. Why shouldn't he make eyes at her? She's a good-looking girl, and I think it's a good sign if he wants to—it means he sees us as human beings, even as women. And it's better to be any sort of woman than a number, isn't it?"

At these words the rest of us fell silent for a moment. It was as though we who had been buried alive in a dank dungeon till yesterday, who only this morning had been given back our names instead of numbers, had once again felt a cold breath from the tomb.

"Bravo, Polya! You're quite right—anything but a number!"

"I'm sorry if I've spoken out of turn—you're all clever people and Party members, and I'm only a cook. They arrested me because of my relations—I don't know why they had to think up anything as fancy as counter-revolutionary Trotskyist activity."

Somehow or other the day wore to a close. A new moon was visible through the barred window. There were two or three more bursts of conversation, and then silence.

I lay down on the bunk. It was not uncomfortable—in this heat one was glad of bare boards, and the prison coat made an excellent pillow.

"Tell you one thing," said Tanya's voice from above, "if I were a queen, I'd make sure I got the bottom bunk every time."

My neighbor introduced herself to me: Zinaida Tulub, a Ukrainian writer of historical novels. When she asked who I was and what I did, I could not reply at once. Until today I had been "Cell 3, north side." Finally I told her my name and said I had been a teacher and journalist. As I heard my own voice I felt bewildered, as though I were speaking of someone else. Could it really be me? A girl at Butyrki called Sonya used to reply to questions about her past: "It was long ago and it never happened anyway."

I was almost asleep, oblivious at last to the excitements of this incredible day, when I felt something furry brush my face. What was this? Was I back in the punishment cell with the rats? Was Car Number 7 boldly marked "Special equipment" just a dream after all?

"I'm sorry, comrade, my hair brushed against you."

Zinaida Tulub looked like a great lady of the last century. Her hair was magnificent, bedraggled and dirty though it was.

"Did I frighten you, comrade? You're crying!"

No, I was not crying, but my heart was pounding with excitement. I so wanted her to go on and on calling me "comrade." To think that such a word still existed and that someone could use it to me! So I was not just Cell Number 3, north side, after all. The train was bound eastward, toward the camps. "Penal servitude—what bliss!"

✦ Reading 57 ✦

Survival in Auschwitz

Primo Levi

The Journey

I was captured by the Fascist Militia on 13 December 1943. I was twenty-four, with little wisdom, no experience and a decided tendency—encouraged by the life of segregation forced on me for the previous four years by the racial laws—to live in an unrealistic world of my own, a world inhabited by civilized Cartesian phantoms, by sincere male and bloodless female friendships. I cultivated a moderate and abstract sense of rebellion.

It had been by no means easy to flee into the mountains and to help set up what, both in my opinion and in that of friends little more experienced than myself, should have become a partisan band affiliated with the Resistance movement *Justice and Liberty*. Contacts, arms, money and the experience needed to acquire them were all missing. We lacked capable men, and instead we were swamped by a deluge of outcasts, in good or bad faith, who came from the plain in search of a non-existent military or political organization, of arms, or merely of protection, a hiding place, a fire, a pair of shoes.

At that time I had not yet been taught the doctrine I was later to learn so hurriedly in the Lager: that man is bound to pursue his own ends by all possible means, while he who errs but once pays dearly. So that I can only consider the following sequence of events justified. Three Fascist Militia companies, which had set out in the night to surprise a much more powerful and dangerous band than ours, broke into our refuge one spectral snowy dawn and took me down to the valley as a suspect person.

During the interrogations that followed, I preferred to admit my status of 'Italian citizen of Jewish race'. I felt that otherwise I would be unable to justify my presence in places too secluded even for an evacuee; while I believed (wrongly as was subsequently seen) that the admission of my political activity would have meant torture and certain death. As a Jew, I was sent to Fossoli, near Modena, where a vast detention camp, originally meant for English and American prisoners-of-war, collected all the numerous categories of people not approved of by the new-born Fascist Republic.

At the moment of my arrival, that is, at the end of January 1944, there were about one hundred and fifty Italian Jews in the camp, but within a few weeks their number rose to over six hundred. For the most part they consisted of entire families captured by the Fascists or Nazis through their imprudence or following secret accusations. A few had given themselves up spontaneously, reduced to desperation by the vagabond life, or because they lacked the means to survive, or to avoid separation from a captured relation, or even—absurdly—'to be in conformity with the law'. There were also about a hundred Jugoslavian military internees and a few other foreigners who were politically suspect.

The arrival of a squad of German SS men should have made even the optimists doubtful; but we still managed to interpret the novelty in various ways without drawing the most obvious conclusions. Thus, despite everything, the announcement of the deportation caught us all unawares.

On 20 February, the Germans had inspected the camp with care and had publicly and loudly upbraided the Italian commissar for the defective organization of the kitchen service and for the scarce amount of wood distribution for heating; they even said that an infirmary would soon be opened. But on the morning of the 21st we learned that on the following day the Jews would be leaving. All the Jews, without exception. Even the children, even the old,

From: Primo Levi, *Survival in Auschwitz: The Nazi Assault on Humanity*, trans. Stuart Woolf (New York: Collier, 1961), pp. 13–22.

even the ill. Our destination? Nobody knew. We should be prepared for a fortnight of travel. For every person missing at the roll-call, ten would be shot.

Only a minority of ingenuous and deluded souls continued to hope; we others had often spoken with the Polish and Croat refugees and we knew what departure meant.

For people condemned to death, tradition prescribes an austere ceremony, calculated to emphasize that all passions and anger have died down, and that the act of justice represent only a sad duty towards society which moves even the executioner to pity for the victim. Thus the condemned man is shielded from all external cares, he is granted solitude and, should he want it, spiritual comfort; in short, care is taken that he should feel around him neither hatred nor arbitrariness, only necessity and justice, and by means of punishment, pardon.

But to us this was not granted, for we were many and time was short. And in any case, what had we to repent, for what crime did we need pardon? The Italian commissar accordingly decreed that all services should continue to function until the final notice: the kitchens remained open, the corvées for cleaning worked as usual, and even the teachers of the little school gave lessons until the evening, as on other days. But that evening the children were given no homework.

And night came, and it was such a night that one knew that human eyes would not witness it and survive. Everyone felt this: not one of the guards, neither Italian nor German, had the courage to come and see what men do when they know they have to die.

All took leave from life in the manner which most suited them. Some praying, some deliberately drunk, others lustfully intoxicated for the last time. But the mothers stayed up to prepare the food for the journey with tender care, and washed their children and packed the luggage; and at dawn the barbed wire was full of children's washing hung out in the wind to dry. Nor did they forget the diapers, the toys, the cushions and the hundred other small things which mothers remember and which children always need. Would you not do the same? If you and your child were going to be killed tomorrow, would you not give him to eat today?

In hut 6A old Gattegno lived with his wife and numerous children and grandchildren and his sons-and daughters-in-law. All the men were carpenters; they had come from Tripoli after many long journeys, and had always carried with them the tools of their trade, their kitchen utensils and their accordions and violins to play and dance to after the day's work. They were happy and pious folk. Their women were the first to silently and rapidly finish the preparations for the journey in order to have time for mourning. When all was ready, the food cooked, the bundles tied together, they unloosened their hair, took off their shoes, placed the Yahrzeit candles on the ground and lit them according to the customs of their fathers, and sat on the bare soil in a circle for the lamentations, praying and weeping all the night. We collected in a group in front of their door, and we experienced within ourselves a grief that was new for us, the ancient grief of the people that has no land, the grief without hope of the exodus which is renewed every century.

Dawn came on us like a betrayer; it seemed as though the new sun rose as an ally of our enemies to assist in our destruction. The different emotions that overcame us, of resignation, of futile rebellion, of religious abandon, of fear, of despair, now joined together after a sleepless night in a collective, uncontrolled panic. The time for meditation, the time for decision was over, and all reason dissolved into a tumult, across which flashed the happy memories of our homes, still so near in time and space, as painful as the thrusts of a sword.

Many things were then said and done among us; but of these it is better that there remain no memory.

With the absurd precision to which we later had to accustom ourselves, the Germans held the roll-call. At the end the officer asked '*Wieviel Stück?*' The corporal saluted smartly and replied that there were six hundred and fifty 'pieces' and that all was in order. They then loaded us on to the buses and took us to the station of Carpi. Here the train was waiting for us, with our escort for the journey. Here we received the first blows: and it was so new and senseless that we felt no pain, neither in body nor in spirit. Only a profound amazement: how can one hit a man without anger?

There were twelve goods wagons for six hundred and fifty men; in mine we were only forty-five, but it was a small wagon. Here then, before our very eyes, under our very feet, was one of those notorious transport trains, those which never return, and of which, shuddering and always a little incredulous, we had so often heard speak. Exactly like this, detail for detail: goods wagons closed from the outside, with men, women and children pressed together without pity, like cheap merchandise, for a journey towards nothingness, a journey down there, towards the bottom. This time it is us who are inside.

Sooner or later in life everyone discovers that perfect happiness is unrealizable, but there are few who pause to consider the antithesis: that perfect unhappiness is equally unattainable. The obstacles preventing the realization of both these extreme states are of the same nature: they derive from our human condition which is opposed to everything infinite. Our ever-insufficient knowledge of the future opposes it: and this is called, in the one instance, hope, and in the other, uncertainty of the following day. The certainty of death opposes it: for it places a limit on every joy, but also on every grief. The inevitable material cares oppose it: for as they poison every lasting happiness, they equally assiduously distract us from our misfortunes and make our consciousness of them intermittent and hence supportable.

It was the very discomfort, the blows, the cold, the thirst that kept us aloft in the void of bottomless despair, both during the journey and after. It was not the will to live, nor a conscious resignation; for few are the men capable of such resolution, and we were but a common sample of humanity.

The doors had been closed at once, but the train did not move until evening. We had learnt of our destination with relief. Auschwitz: a name without significance for us at that time, but it at least implied some place on this earth.

The train travelled slowly, with long, unnerving halts. Through the slit we saw the tall pale cliffs of the Adige Valley and the names of the last Italian cities disappear behind us. We passed the Brenner at midday of the second day and everyone stood up, but no one said a word. The thought of the return journey stuck in my heart, and I cruelly pictured to myself the inhuman joy of that other journey, with doors open, no one wanting to flee, and the first Italian names . . . and I looked around and wondered how many, among that poor human dust, would be struck by fate. Among the forty-five people in my wagon only four saw their homes again; and it was by far the most fortunate wagon.

We suffered from thirst and cold; at every stop we clamoured for water, or even a handful of snow, but we were rarely heard; the soldiers of the escort drove off anybody who tried to approach the convoy. Two young mothers, nursing their children, groaned night and day, begging for water. Our state of nervous tension made the hunger, exhaustion and lack of sleep seem less of a torment. But the hours of darkness were nightmares without end.

There are few men who know how to go to their deaths with dignity, and often they are not those whom one would expect. Few know how to remain silent and respect the silence of others. Our restless sleep was often interrupted by noisy and futile disputes, by curses, by kicks and blows blindly delivered to ward off some encroaching and inevitable contact. Then someone would light a candle, and its mournful flicker would reveal an obscure agitation, a human mass, extended across the floor, confused and continuous, sluggish and aching, rising here and there in sudden convulsions and immediately collapsing again in exhaustion.

Through the slit, known and unknown names of Austrian cities, Salzburg, Vienna, then Czech, finally Polish names. On the evening of the fourth day the cold became intense: the train ran through interminable black pine forests, climbing perceptibly. The snow was high. It must have been a branch line as the stations were small and almost deserted. During the halts, no one tried any more to communicate with the outside world: we felt ourselves by now 'on the other side'. There was a long halt in open country. The train started up with extreme slowness, and the convoy stopped for the last time, in the dead of night, in the middle of a dark silent plain.

On both sides of the track rows of red and white lights appeared as far as the eye could see; but there was none of that confusion of sounds which betrays inhabited places even from a distance. By the wretched light of the last candle, with the rhythm of the wheels, with every human sound now silenced, we awaited what was to happen.

Next to me, crushed against me for the whole journey, there had been a woman. We had known each other for many years, and the misfortune had struck us together, but we knew little of each other.

Now, in the hour of decision, we said to each other things that are never said among the living. We said farewell and it was short; everybody said farewell to life through his neighbour. We had no more fear.

The climax came suddenly. The door opened with a crash, and the dark echoed with outlandish orders in that curt, barbaric barking of Germans in command which seems to give vent to a millennial anger. A vast platform appeared before us, lit up by reflectors. A little beyond it, a row of lorries. Then everything was silent again. Someone translated: we had to climb down with our luggage and deposit it alongside the train. In a moment the platform was swarming with shadows. But we were afraid to break that silence: everyone busied himself with his luggage, searched for someone else, called to somebody, but timidly, in a whisper.

A dozen SS men stood around, legs akimbo, with an indifferent air. At a certain moment they moved among us, and in a subdued tone of voice, with faces of stone, began to interrogate us rapidly, one by one, in bad Italian. They did not interrogate everybody, only a few: 'How old? Healthy or ill?' And on the basis of the reply they pointed in two different directions.

Everything was as silent as an aquarium, or as in certain dream sequences. We had expected something more apocalyptic: they seemed simple police agents. It was disconcerting and disarming. Someone dared to ask for his luggage: they replied, 'luggage afterwards'. Someone else did not want to leave his wife: they said, 'together again afterwards'. Many mothers did not want to be separated from their children: they said 'good, good, stay with child'. They behaved with the calm assurance of people doing their normal duty of every day. But Renzo stayed an instant too long to say good-bye to Francesca, his fiancée, and with a single blow they knocked him to the ground. It was their everyday duty.

In less than ten minutes all the fit men had been collected together in a group. What happened to the others, to the women, to the children, to the old men, we could establish neither then nor later: the night swallowed them up, purely and simply. Today, however, we know that in that rapid and summary choice each one of us had been judged capable or not of working usefully for the Reich; we know that of our convoy no more than ninety-six men and twenty-nine women entered the respective camps of Monowitz-Buna and Birkenau, and that of all the others, more than five hundred in number, not one was living two days later. We also know that not even this tenuous priciple of discrimination between fit and unfit was always followed, and that later the simpler method was often adopted of merely opening both the doors of the wagon without warning or instructions to the new arrivals. Those who by chance climbed down on one side of the convoy entered the camp; the others went to the gas chamber.

This is the reason why three-year-old Emilia died: the historical necessity of killing the children of Jews was self-demonstrative to the Germans. Emilia, daughter of Aldo Levi of Milan, was a curious, ambitious, cheerful, intelligent child; her parents had succeeded in washing her during the journey in the packed car in a tub with tepid water which the degenerate German engineer had allowed them to draw from the engine that was dragging us all to death.

Thus, in an instant, our women, our parents, our children disappeared. We saw them for a short while as an obscure mass at the other end of the platform; then we saw nothing more.

Instead, two groups of strange individuals emerged into the light of the lamps. They walked in squads, in rows of three, with an odd, embarrassed step, head dangling in front, arms rigid. On their heads they wore comic berets and were all dressed in long striped overcoats, which even by night and from a distance looked filthy and in rags. They walked in a large circle around us, never drawing near, and in silence began to busy themselves with our luggage and to climb in and out of the empty wagons.

We looked at each other without a word. It was all incomprehensible and mad, but one thing we had understood. This was the metamorphosis that awaited us. Tomorrow we would be like them.

Without knowing how I found myself loaded on to a lorry with thirty others; the lorry sped into the night at full speed. It was covered and we could not see outside, but by the shaking we could tell that the road had many curves and bumps. Are we unguarded? Throw ourselves down? It is too late, too late, we are all 'down'. In any case we are soon aware that we are not without guard. He is a strange guard, a German soldier bristling with arms. We do not see him because of the thick darkness, but we feel the hard contact every time that a lurch of the lorry throws us all in a heap. At a certain point he switches on a pocket torch and instead of shouting threats of damnation at us, he asks us courteously, one by one, in German and in pidgin language, if we have any money or watches to give him, seeing that they will not be useful to us any more. This is no order, no regulation: it is obvious that it is a small private initiative of our Charon. The matter stirs us to anger and laughter and brings relief.

On the Bottom

The journey did not last more than twenty minutes. Then the lorry stopped, and we saw a large door, and above it a sign, brightly illuminated (its memory still strikes me in my dreams): *Arbeit Macht Frei,* work gives freedom.

We climb down, they make us enter an enormous empty room that is poorly heated. We have a terrible thirst. The weak gurgle of the water in the radiators makes us ferocious; we have had nothing to drink for four days. But there is also a tap—and above it a card which says that it is forbidden to drink as the water is dirty. Nonsense. It seems obvious that the card is a joke, 'they' know that we are dying of thirst and they put us in a room, and there is a tap, and *Wassertrinken Verboten.* I drink and I incite my companions to do likewise, but I have to spit it out, the water is tepid and sweetish, with the smell of a swamp.

This is hell. . . .

✦ Reading 58 ✦

Night

Elie Wiesel

There were two boys attached to our group: Yossi and Tibi, two brothers. They were Czechs whose parents had been exterminated at Birkenau. They lived, body and soul, for each other.

They and I very soon became friends. Having once belonged to a Zionist youth organization, they knew innumerable Hebrew chants. Thus we would often hum tunes evoking the calm waters of Jordan and the majestic sanctity of Jerusalem. And we would often talk of Palestine. Their parents, like mine, had lacked the courage to wind up their affairs and emigrate while there was still time. We decided that, if we were granted our lives until the liberation, we would not stay in Europe a day longer. We would take the first boat for Haifa.

Still lost in his cabbalistic dreams, Akiba Drumer had discovered a verse in the Bible which, interpreted in terms of numerology, enabled him to predict that the deliverance was due within the coming weeks.

We had left the tents for the musicians' block. We were entitled to a blanket, a wash bowl, and a bar of soap. The head of the block was a German Jew.

It was good to be under a Jew. He was called Alphonse. A young man with an extraordinarily aged face, he was entirely devoted to the cause of "his" block. Whenever he could, he would organize a cauldron of soup for the young ones, the weak, all those who were dreaming more about an extra plateful than of liberty.

One day when we had just come back from the warehouse, I was sent for by the secretary of the block.

"A-7713?"

"That's me."

"After eating, you're to go to the dentist."

"But I haven't got toothache."

"After eating. Without fail."

I went to the hospital block. There were about twenty prisoners waiting in a queue in front of the door. It did not take long to discover why we had been summoned: it was for the extraction of our gold teeth.

The dentist, a Jew from Czechoslovakia, had a face like a death mask. When he opened his mouth, there was a horrible sight of yellow, decaying teeth. I sat in the chair and asked him humbly: "Please, what are you going to do?"

"Simply take out your gold crown," he replied, indifferently.

I had the idea of pretending to be ill.

"You couldn't wait a few days, Doctor? I don't feel very well. I've got a temperature. . . ."

He wrinkled his brow, thought for a moment, and took my pulse.

"All right, son. When you feel better, come back and see me. But don't wait till I send for you!"

I went to see him a week later. With the same excuse: I still did not feel any better. He did not seem to show any surprise, and I do not know if he believed me. He was probably glad to see that I had come back of my own accord, as I had promised. He gave me another reprieve.

A few days after this visit of mine, they closed the dentist's surgery, and he was thrown into prison. He was going to be hanged. It was alleged that he had been running a private traffic of his own in the prisoners' gold teeth. I did not feel any pity for him. I was even pleased about what had happened. I had saved my gold crown. It might be useful to me one day to buy something—bread or life. I now took little interest in anything except my daily plate of soup and my crust of stale bread. Bread, soup—these were my whole life. I was a body. Perhaps less than

---

From: Elie Wiesel, *Night,* trans. Stella Rodway (New York: Bantam Books, 1960), pp. 48–62.

that even: a starved stomach. The stomach alone was aware of the passage of time.

At the warehouse I often worked next to a young French girl. We did not speak to one another, since she knew no German and I did not understand French.

She seemed to me to be a Jewess, though here she passed as Aryan. She was a forced labor deportee.

One day when Idek was seized with one of his fits of frenzy, I got in his way. He leapt on me, like a wild animal, hitting me in the chest, on the head, throwing me down and pulling me up again, his blows growing more and more violent, until I was covered with blood. As I was biting my lips to stop myself from screaming with pain, he must have taken my silence for defiance, for he went on hitting me even harder.

Suddenly he calmed down. As if nothing had happened, he sent me back to work. It was as though we had been taking part together in some game where we each had our role to play.

I dragged myself to my corner. I ached all over. I felt a cool hand wiping my blood-stained forehead. It was the French girl. She gave me her mournful smile and slipped a bit of bread into my hand. She looked into my eyes. I felt that she wanted to say something but was choked by fear. For a long moment she stayed like that, then her face cleared and she said to me in almost perfect German:

"Bite your lip, little brother. . . . Don't cry. Keep your anger and hatred for another day, for later on. The day will come, but not now. . . . Wait. Grit your teeth and wait. . . ."

Many years later, in Paris, I was reading my paper in the Metro. Facing me was a very beautiful woman with black hair and dreamy eyes. I had seen those eyes before somewhere. It was she.

"You don't recognize me?"

"I don't know you."

"In 1944 you were in Germany, at Buna, weren't you?"

"Yes. . . ."

"You used to work in the electrical warehouse. . . ."

"Yes," she said, somewhat disturbed. And then, after a moment's silence: "Wait a minute . . . I do remember. . . ."

"Idek, the Kapo . . . the little Jewish boy . . . your kind words. . . ."

We left the Metro together to sit down on the terrace of a café. We spent the whole evening reminiscing.

Before I parted from her, I asked her: "May I ask you a question?"

"I know what it will be—go on."

"What?"

"Am I Jewish . . . ? Yes, I am Jewish. From a religious family. During the occupation I obtained forged papers and passed myself off as an Aryan. That's how I was enlisted in the forced labor groups, and when I was deported to Germany, I escaped the concentration camp. At the warehouse, no one knew I could speak German. That would have aroused suspicions. Saying those few words to you was risky: but I knew you wouldn't give me away. . . ."

Another time we had to load Diesel engines onto trains supervised by German soldiers. Idek's nerves were on edge. He was restraining himself with great difficulty. Suddenly, his frenzy broke out. The victim was my father.

"You lazy old devil!" Idek began to yell. "Do you call that work?"

And he began to beat him with an iron bar. At first my father crouched under the blows, then he broke in two, like a dry tree struck by lightning, and collapsed.

I had watched the whole scene without moving. I kept quiet. In fact I was thinking of how to get farther away so that I would not be hit myself. What is more, any anger I felt at that moment was directed, not against the Kapo, but against my father. I was angry with him, for not knowing how to avoid Idek's outbreak. That is what concentration camp life had made of me.

Franek, the foreman, one day noticed the gold-crowned tooth in my mouth.

"Give me your crown, kid."

I told him it was impossible, that I could not eat without it.

"What do they give you to eat, anyway?"

I found another answer; the crown had been put down on a list after the medical inspection. This could bring trouble on us both.

"If you don't give me your crown, you'll pay for it even more."

This sympathetic, intelligent youth was suddenly no longer the same person. His eyes gleamed with desire. I told him I had to ask my father's advice.

"Ask your father, kid. But I want an answer by tomorrow."

When I spoke to my father about it, he turned pale, was silent a long while, and then said:

"No, son, you mustn't do it."

"He'll take it out on us!"

"He won't dare."

But alas, Franek knew where to touch me; he knew my weak point. My father had never done military service, and he never succeeded in marching in step. Here, every time we moved from one place to another in a body, we marched in strict rhythm. This was Franek's chance to torment my father and to thrash him savagely every day. Left, right: punch! Left, right: clout!

I decided to give my father lessons myself, to teach him to change step, and to keep to the rhythm. We began to do exercises in front of our block. I would give the commands: "Left, right!" and my father would practice. Some of the prisoners began to laugh at us.

"Look at this little officer teaching the old chap to march. . . . Hey, general, how many rations of bread does the old boy give you for this?"

But my father's progress was still inadequate, and blows continued to rain down on him.

"So you still can't march in step, you lazy old devil?"

These scenes were repeated for two weeks. We could not stand any more. We had to give in. When the day came, Franek burst into wild laughter.

"I knew it, I knew quite well I would win. Better late than never. And because you've made me wait, that's going to cost you a ration of bread. A ration of bread for one of my pals, a famous dentist from Warsaw, so that he can take your crown out."

"What? *My* ration of bread so that you can have *my* crown?"

Franek grinned.

"What would you like then? Shall I break your teeth with my fist?"

That same evening, in the lavatory, the dentist from Warsaw pulled out my crowned tooth, with the aid of a rusty spoon.

Franek grew kinder. Occasionally, he even gave me extra soup. But that did not last long. A fortnight later, all the Poles were transferred to another camp. I had lost my crown for nothing.

A few days before the Poles left, I had a new experience.

It was a Sunday morning. Our unit did not need to go to work that day. But all the same Idek would not hear of our staying in the camp. We had to go to the warehouse. This sudden enthusiasm for work left us stunned.

At the warehouse, Idek handed us over to Franek, saying, "Do what you like. But do something. If not, you'll hear from me. . . ."

And he disappeared.

We did not know what to do. Tired of squatting down, we each in turn went for a walk through the warehouse, looking for a bit of bread some civilian might have left behind.

When I came to the back of the building. I heard a noise coming from a little room next door. I went up and saw Idek with a young Polish girl, half-naked, on a mattress. Then I understood why Idek had refused to let us stay in the camp. Moving a hundred prisoners so that he could lie with a girl! It struck me as so funny that I burst out laughing.

Idek leapt up, turned around, and saw me, while the girl tried to cover up her breasts. I wanted to run away, but my legs were glued to the ground. Idek seized me by the throat.

Speaking in a low voice, he said, "You wait and see, kid. . . . You'll soon find out what leaving your work's going to cost you. . . . You're going to pay for this pretty soon. . . . And now, go back to your place."

Half an hour before work usually ended, the Kapo collected together the whole unit. Roll call. Nobody knew what had happened. Roll call at this time of day? Here? But I knew. The Kapo gave a short speech.

"An ordinary prisoner has no right to meddle in other people's affairs. One of you does not seem to have understood this. I'm obliged, therefore, to make it very clear to him once and for all."

I felt the sweat run down my back.

"A-7713!"

I came forward.

"A box!" he ordered.

They brought him a box.

"Lie down on it! On your stomach!"

I obeyed.

Then I was aware of nothing but the strokes of the whip.

"One . . . two . . . ," he counted.

He took his time between each stroke. Only the first ones really hurt me. I could hear him counting:

"Ten . . . eleven . . ."

His voice was calm and reached me as through a thick wall.

"Twenty-three . . ."

Two more, I thought, half conscious. The Kapo waited.

"Twenty-four . . . twenty-five!"

It was over. But I did not realize it, for I had fainted. I felt myself come round as a bucket of cold water was thrown over me. I was still lying on the box. I could just vaguely make out the wet ground surrounding me. Then I heard someone cry out. It must have been the Kapo. I began to distinguish the words he was shouting.

"Get up!"

I probably made some movement to raise myself, because I felt myself falling back onto the box. How I longed to get up!

"Get up!" he yelled more loudly.

If only I could have answered him, at least; if only I could have told him that I could not move! But I could not manage to open my lips.

At Idek's command, two prisoners lifted me up and led me in front of him.

"Look me in the eye!"

I looked at him without seeing him. I was thinking of my father. He must have suffered more than I did.

"Listen to me, you bastard!" said Idek, coldly. "That's for your curiosity. You'll get five times more if you dare tell anyone what you saw! Understand?"

I nodded my head, once, ten times. I nodded ceaselessly, as if my head had decided to say yes without ever stopping.

One Sunday, when half of us—including my father—were at work, the rest—including myself—were in the block, taking advantage of the chance to stay in bed late in the morning.

At about ten o'clock, the air-raid sirens began to wail. An alert. The leaders of the block ran to assemble us inside, while the SS took refuge in the shelters. As it was relatively easy to escape during a warning—the guards left their lookout posts and the electric current was cut off in the barbed-wire fences—the SS had orders to kill anyone found outside the blocks.

Within a few minutes, the camp looked like an abandoned ship. Not a living soul on the paths. Near the kitchen, two cauldrons of steaming hot soup had been left, half full. Two cauldrons of soup, right in the middle of the path, with no one guarding them! A feast for kings, abandoned, supreme temptation! Hundreds of eyes looked at them, sparkling with desire. Two lambs, with a hundred wolves lying in wait for them. Two lambs without a shepherd—a gift. But who would dare?

Terror was stronger than hunger. Suddenly, we saw the door of Block 37 open imperceptibly. A man appeared, crawling like a worm in the direction of the cauldrons.

Hundreds of eyes followed his movements. Hundreds of men crawled with him, scraping their knees with his on the gravel. Every heart trembled, but with envy above all. This man had dared.

He reached the first cauldron. Hearts raced: he had succeeded. Jealousy consumed us, burned us up like straw. We never thought for a moment of admiring him. Poor hero, committing suicide for a ration of soup! In our thoughts we were murdering him.

Stretched out by the cauldron, he was now trying to raise himself up to the edge. Either from weakness or fear he stayed there, trying, no doubt, to muster up the last of his strength. At last he succeeded in hoisting himself onto the edge of the pot. For a moment, he seemed to be looking at himself, seeking his ghost-like reflection in the soup. Then, for no apparent reason, he let out a terrible cry, a rattle such as I had never heard before, and, his mouth open, thrust his head toward the still steaming liquid. We jumped at the explosion. Falling back onto the ground, his face stained with soup, the man writhed for a few seconds at the foot of the cauldron, then he moved no more.

Then we began to hear the airplanes. Almost at once, the barracks began to shake.

"They're bombing Buna!" someone shouted.

I thought of my father. But I was glad all the same. To see the whole works go up in fire—what revenge! We had heard so much talk about the defeats of German troops on various fronts, but we did not know how much to believe. This, today, was real!

We were not afraid. And yet, if a bomb had fallen on the blocks, it alone would have claimed hundreds of victims on the spot. But we were no longer afraid of death; at any rate, not of that death. Every bomb that exploded filled us with joy and gave us new confidence in life.

The raid lasted over an hour. If it could only have lasted ten times ten hours! . . . Then silence fell once more. The last sound of an American plane was lost on the wind, and we found ourselves back again in the cemetery. A great trail of black smoke was rising up on the horizon. The sirens began to wail once more. It was the end of the alert.

Everyone came out of the blocks. We filled our lungs with the fire- and smoke-laden air, and our eyes shone with hope. A bomb had fallen in the middle of the camp, near the assembly point, but it had not gone off. We had to take it outside the camp.

The head of the camp, accompanied by his assistant and the chief Kapo, made a tour of inspection along the paths. The raid had left traces of terror on his face.

Right in the middle of the camp lay the body of the man with the soup-stained face, the only victim. The cauldrons were taken back into the kitchen.

The SS had gone back to their lookout posts, behind their machine guns. The interlude was over.

At the end of an hour, we saw the units come back, in step, as usual. Joyfully, I caught sight of my father.

"Several buildings have been flattened right out," he said, "but the warehouse hasn't suffered."

In the afternoon we went cheerfully to clear away the ruins.

A week later, on the way back from work, we noticed in the center of the camp, at the assembly place, a black gallows.

We were told that soup would not be distributed until after roll call. This took longer than usual. The orders were given in a sharper manner than on other days, and in the air there were strange undertones.

"Bare your heads!" yelled the head of the camp, suddenly.

Ten thousand caps were simultaneously removed.

"Cover your heads!"

Ten thousand caps went back onto their skulls, as quick as lightning.

The gate to the camp opened. An SS section appeared and surrounded us: one SS at every three paces. On the lookout towers the machine guns were trained on the assembly place.

"They fear trouble," whispered Juliek.

Two SS men had gone to the cells. They came back with the condemned man between them. He was a youth from Warsaw. He had three years of concentration camp life behind him. He was a strong, well-built boy, a giant in comparison with me.

His back to the gallows, his face turned toward his judge, who was the head of the camp, the boy was pale, but seemed more moved than afraid. His manacled hands did not tremble. His eyes gazed coldly at the hundreds of SS guards, the thousands of prisoners who surrounded him.

The head of the camp began to read his verdict, hammering out each phrase:

"In the name of Himmler . . . prisoner Number . . . stole during the alert. . . . According to the law . . . paragraph . . . prisoner Number . . . is condemned to death. May this be a warning and an example to all prisoners."

No one moved.

I could hear my heart beating. The thousands who had died daily at Auschwitz and at Birkenau in the crematory ovens no longer troubled me. But this one, leaning against his gallows—he overwhelmed me.

"Do you think this ceremony'll be over soon? I'm hungry. . . . " whispered Juliek.

At a sign from the head of the camp, the Lagerkapo advanced toward the condemned man. Two prisoners helped him in his task—for two plates of soup.

The Kapo wanted to bandage the victim's eyes, but he refused.

After a long moment of waiting, the executioner put the rope round his neck. He was on the point of motioning to his assistants to draw the chair away from the prisoner's feet, when the latter cried, in a calm, strong voice:

"Long live liberty! A curse upon Germany! A curse . . . ! A cur—"

The executioners had completed their task.

A command cleft the air like a sword.

"Bare your heads."

Ten thousand prisoners paid their last respects.

"Cover your heads!"

Then the whole camp, block after block, had to march past the hanged man and stare at the dimmed eyes, the lolling tongue of death. The Kapos and heads of each block forced everyone to look him full in the face.

After the march, we were given permission to return to the blocks for our meal.

I remember that I found the soup excellent that evening. . . .

I witnessed other hangings. I never saw a single one of the victims weep. For a long time those dried-up bodies had forgotten the bitter taste of tears.

Except once. The Oberkapo of the fifty-second cable unit was a Dutchman, a giant, well over six feet. Seven hundred prisoners worked under his orders, and they all loved him like a brother. No one had ever received a blow at his hands, nor an insult from his lips.

He had a young boy under him, a *pipel,* as they were called—a child with a refined and beautiful face, unheard of in this camp.

(At Buna, the *pipel* were loathed; they were often crueller than adults. I once saw one of thirteen beating his father because the latter had not made his bed properly. The old man was crying softly while the boy shouted: "If you don't stop crying at once I shan't bring you any more bread. Do you understand?" But the Dutchman's little servant was loved by all. He had the face of a sad angel.)

One day, the electric power station at Buna was blown up. The Gestapo, summoned to the spot, suspected sabotage. They found a trail. It eventually led to the Dutch Oberkapo. And there, after a search, they found an important stock of arms.

The Oberkapo was arrested immediately. He was tortured for a period of weeks, but in vain. He would not give a single name. He was transferred to Auschwitz. We never heard of him again.

But his little servant had been left behind in the camp in prison. Also put to torture, he too would not speak. Then the SS sentenced him to death, with two other prisoners who had been discovered with arms.

One day when we came back from work, we saw three gallows rearing up in the assembly place, three black crows. Roll call. SS all round us, machine guns trained: the traditional ceremony. Three victims in chains—and one of them, the little servant, the sad-eyed angel.

The SS seemed more preoccupied, more disturbed than usual. To hang a young boy in front of thousands of spectators was no light matter. The head of the camp read the verdict. All eyes were on the child. He was lividly pale, almost calm, biting his lips. The gallows threw its shadow over him.

This time the Lagerkapo refused to act as executioner. Three SS replaced him.

The three victims mounted together onto the chairs.

The three necks were placed at the same moment within the nooses.

"Long live liberty!" cried the two adults.

But the child was silent.

"Where is God? Where is He?" someone behind me asked.

At a sign from the head of the camp, the three chairs tipped over.

Total silence throughout the camp. On the horizon, the sun was setting.

"Bare your heads!" yelled the head of the camp. His voice was raucous. We were weeping.

"Cover your heads!"

Then the march past began. The two adults were no longer alive. Their tongues hung swollen, blue-tinged. But the third rope was still moving; being so light, the child was still alive. . . .

For more than half an hour he stayed there, struggling between life and death, dying in slow agony under our eyes. And we had to look him full in the face. He was still alive when I passed in front of him. His tongue was still red, his eyes were not yet glazed.

Behind me, I heard the same man asking:

"Where is God now?"

And I heard a voice within me answer him:

"Where is He? Here He is—He is hanging here on this gallows. . . ."

That night the soup tasted of corpses.

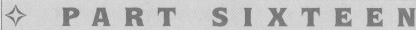

PART SIXTEEN

THE COLD WAR AND DECOLONIZATION

In 1934, Gandhi, disenchanted with the reception given to his philosophy of nonviolence, quit the Congress party. Decrying industrialization's negative influences, he embarked on a national "constructive programme" to encourage traditional village industries such as hand spinning and weaving, increase access to education and sanitation, and eradicate the doctrine of untouchability. Spinning regularly at public gatherings and wearing only hand-spun clothes, Ghandi came to see the craft as an integral part of the nationalist mantra: "Here is an industry which will enable the Indian people not only to live as a nation, but to live as a nation producing real wealth."

THE COLD WAR AND DECOLONIZATION

By its end, the combat of World War II had slaughtered tens of millions, displaced millions of others, and devastated cities and property. The United States decided to help rebuild. The wary Soviet Union preferred establishing friendly states on its borders to receiving aid, which the United States now tied to a Soviet pullback. Europe's future was decided by *fait accompli,* as Soviet troops stayed put in Eastern Europe. Western Europe and Eastern Europe grew apart and tension increased between the United States and the Soviet Union. By 1950 both were full-fledged nuclear powers. The hot war had turned into a cold war between former allies. The growing tension led to a semipermanent division of Europe and a bipolar world. The immediate post-World War II decades also witnessed burgeoning African and Asian liberation movements, as nationalism inspired the peoples of Europe's colonies to evict their colonizers by persuasion or, if needed, force. Especially in France withdrawal from colonies spurred sharp political conflict. Completed by 1970, the decolonialization process set off a chain of events still felt in Europe and in the newly independent states. New African and Asian nations have experienced extreme economic hardship and political discord. In an ironic reversal of expectations, the colonial episode has resulted in transfers of populations from Africa and Asia to Europe, as turmoil in the newly independent nations has induced many inhabitants to migrate to European capitals.

Symbolizing Europe's division was the so-called "Iron Curtain," a phrase introduced by Winston Churchill (1874–1965) in a 1946 speech, "The Sinews of Peace." The super powers' intense mutual distrust led to spying on both sides. *The Spy Who Came in from the Cold,* a suspense novel by John le Carré (1931–), portrays the mentality of the spy game in which both sides resort to the same methods. The *Wretched of the Earth* by Frantz Fanon (1925–1961) provided a spiritual blueprint for the black liberation movement. Born in Martinique, Fanon staunchly supported Algerian resistance to French colonialism. Within a Marxist framework, Fanon suggests to colonial peoples that they find their own non-European path of development. His fame reminds us of the economic and cultural vitality, as well as political unease, promoted by the continued reverse transfer of Asian and African populations to former colonial powers.

✦ Reading 59 ✦

The Sinews of Peace

Winston Churchill

I am very glad, indeed, to come to Westminister College this afternoon, and I am complimented that you should give me a degree from an institution whose reputation has been so solidly accepted. It is the name Westminister, somehow or other, which seems familiar to me. I feel as if I'd heard of it before. Indeed, now that I come to think of it, it was at Westminster that I received a very large part of my education in politics, dialectics, rhetoric, and one or two other things. In fact, we have both been educated at the same, or similar, or at any rate kindred, establishments.

It is also an honor, ladies and gentlemen, perhaps almost unique, for a private visitor to be introduced to an academic audience by the president of the United States. Amid his heavy burdens, duties, and responsibilities—unsought but not recoiled from—the president has traveled a thousand miles to dignify and magnify our meeting here today and to give me an opportunity of addressing this kindred nation, as well as my own countrymen across the ocean and perhaps some other countries too.

The president has told you that it is his wish, as I am sure it is yours, that I should have full liberty to give my true and faithful counsel in these anxious and baffling times. I shall certainly avail myself of this freedom and feel the more right to do so because any private ambitions I may have cherished in my younger days have been satisfied beyond my wildest dreams.

Let me, however, make it clear that I have no official mission or status of any kind and that I speak only for myself. There is nothing here but what you see. I can, therefore, allow my mind, with the experience of a lifetime, to play over the problems which beset us on the morrow of our absolute victory in arms, and to try to make sure, with what strength I have, that what has been gained with so much sacrifice and suffering shall be preserved for the future glory and safety of mankind.

Ladies and gentlemen, the United States stands at this time at the pinnacle of world power. It is a solemn moment for the American democracy. For with this primacy in power is also joined an awe-inspiring accountability to the future. As you look around you, you must feel not only the sense of duty done, but also you must feel anxiety lest you fall below the level of achievement. Opportunity is here now, clear and shining, for both our countries. To reject it or ignore it or fritter it away will bring upon us all the long reproaches of the aftertime.

It is necessary that constancy of mind, persistency of purpose, and the grand simplicity of decision shall rule and guide the conduct of the English-speaking peoples in peace as they did in war. We must—and I believe we shall—prove ourselves equal to this severe requirement.

President McCluer, when American military men approach some serious situation, they are wont to write at the head of their directive the words "Overall Strategic Concept." There is wisdom in this, as it leads to clarity of thought. What, then, is the overall strategic concept which we should inscribe today? It is nothing less than the safety and welfare, the freedom and progress, of all the homes and families of all the men and women in all the lands. And here I speak particularly of the myriad cottage or apartment homes where the wage earner strives, amid the accidents and difficulties of life, to guard his wife and children from privation and bring the family up in the fear of the Lord or upon ethical conceptions which often play their potent part.

To give security to these countless homes they must be shielded from the two gaunt marauders—

From: Winston Churchill, "The Sinews of Peace," in *Lend Me Your Ears: Great Speeches in History,* ed. William Safire (New York: W.W. Norton & Company, 1992), pp. 785–795.

war and tyranny. We all know the frightful disturbance in which the ordinary family is plunged when the curse of war swoops down upon the breadwinner and those for whom he works and contrives.

The awful ruin of Europe, with all its vanished glories, and of large parts of Asia, glares us in the eyes.

When the designs of wicked men or the aggressive urge of mighty states dissolve, over large areas, the frame of civilized society, humble folk are confronted with difficulties with which they cannot cope. For them all is distorted, all is broken or is even ground to pulp.

When I stand here this quiet afternoon, I shudder to visualize what is actually happening to millions now and what is going to happen in this period when famine stalks the earth. None can compute what has been called "the unestimated sum of human pain." Our supreme task and duty is to guard the homes of the common people from the horrors and miseries of another war. We are all agreed on that.

Our American military colleagues, after having proclaimed their "overall strategic concept" and computed available resources, always proceed to the next stop—namely, the method. Here again there is widespread agreement.

A world organization has already been erected for the prime purpose of preventing war. UNO, the successor of the League of Nations, with the decisive addition of the United States and all that that means, is already at work.

We must make sure that its work is fruitful, that it is a reality and not a sham, that it is a force for action and not merely a frothing of words, that it is a true temple of peace, in which the shields of many nations can someday be hung up, and not merely a cockpit in a tower of Babel.

Before we cast away the solid assurances of national armaments for self-preservation, we must be certain that our temple is built not upon shifting sands or quagmires but upon the rock. Anyone can see, with his eyes open, that our path will be difficult and also long, but if we persevere together as we did in the two world wars—though not, alas, in the interval between them—I cannot doubt that we shall achieve our common purpose in the end.

I have, however, a definite and practical proposal to make for action. Courts and magistrates may be set up, but they cannot function without sheriffs and constables. The United Nations Organization must immediately begin to be equipped with an international armed force. In such a matter we can only go step by step: but we must begin now.

I propose that each of the powers and states should be invited to dedicate a certain number of air squadrons to the service of the world organization. These squadrons would be trained and prepared in their own countries but would move around in rotation from one country to another. They would wear the uniform of their own countries with different badges. They would not be required to act against their own nation but in other respects they would be directed by the world organization.

This might be started on a modest scale, and it would grow as confidence grew.

I wished to see this done after the First World War, and I devoutly trust that it may be done forthwith.

It would, nevertheless, ladies and gentlemen, be wrong and imprudent to entrust the secret knowledge or experience of the atomic bomb, which the United States, Great Britain, and Canada now share, to the world organization while it is still in its infancy. It would be criminal madness to cast it adrift in this still agitated and un-united world.

No one in any country has slept less well in their beds because this knowledge and the method and the raw materials to apply it are at present largely retained in American hands.

I do not believe we should all have slept so soundly had the positions been reversed and some Communist or neo-Fascist state monopolized, for the time being, these dread agents. The fear of them alone might easily have been used to enforce totalitarian systems upon the free democratic world, with consequences appalling to human imagination.

God has willed that this shall not be, and we have at least a breathing space to set our house in order, before this peril has to be encountered, and even then, if no effort is spared, we should still possess so formidable a superiority as to impose effective deterrents upon its employment or threat of employment by others.

Ultimately, when the essential brotherhood of man is truly embodied and expressed in a world organization, with all the necessary practical safeguards to make it effective, these powers would naturally be confided to that organization.

Now I come to the second of the two marauders, to the second danger which threatens the cottage home and ordinary people—namely, tyranny. We cannot be blind to the fact that the liberties enjoyed by individual citizens throughout the United States and throughout the British Empire are not valid in a considerable number of countries, some of which are very powerful.

In these states, control is enforced upon the common people by various kinds of all embracing police governments, to a degree which is overwhelming and contrary to every principle of democracy. The power of the state is exercised without restraint, either by dictators or by compact oligarchies operating through a privileged party and a political police.

It is not our duty at this time, when difficulties are so numerous, to interfere forcibly in the internal affairs of countries which we have not conquered in war, but we must never cease to proclaim in fearless tones the great principles of freedom and the rights of man, which are the joint inheritance of the English-speaking world and which, through Magna Carta, the Bill of Rights, the habeas corpus, trial by jury, and the English common law, find their most famous expression in the American Declaration of Independence.

All this means that the people of any country have the right and should have the power by constitutional action, by free, unfettered elections, with secret ballot, to choose or change the character or form of government under which they dwell, that freedom of speech and thought should reign, that courts of justice independent of the executive, unbiased by any party, should administer laws which have received the broad assent of large majorities or are consecrated by time and custom. Here are the title deeds of freedom, which should lie in every cottage home. Here is the message of the British and American peoples to mankind. Let us preach what we practice; let us practice what we preach.

I have stated the two great dangers which menace the homes of the people: war and tyranny. I have not yet spoken of poverty and privation, which are in many cases the prevailing anxiety. But if the dangers of war and tyranny are removed, there is no doubt that science and cooperation can bring in the next few years, certainly in the next few decades, to the world, newly taught in the sharpening school of war, an expansion of material well-being beyond anything that has yet occurred in human experience.

Now, at this sad and breathless moment, we are plunged in the hunger and distress which are the aftermath of our stupendous struggle; but this will pass and may pass quickly, and there is no reason except human folly or subhuman crime which should deny to all the nations the inauguration and enjoyment of an age of plenty.

I have often used words which I learned fifty years ago from a great Irish-American orator, a friend of mine, Mr. Bourke Cochran. "There is enough for all. The earth is a generous mother; she will provide in plentiful abundance food for all her children if they will but cultivate her soil in justice and in peace." So far I feel that we are in full agreement.

Now, while still pursuing the method of realizing our overall strategic concept, I come to the crux of what I have traveled here to say.

Neither the sure prevention of war nor the continuous rise of world organization will be gained without what I have called the fraternal association of the English-speaking peoples. This means a special relationship between the British Commonwealth and Empire and the United States of America.

Ladies and gentlemen, this is no time for generalities, and I will venture to be precise.

Fraternal association requires not only the growing friendship and mutual understanding between our two vast but kindred systems of society but the continuance of the intimate relationships between our military advisers, leading to common study of potential dangers, the similarity of weapons and manuals of instruction, and the interchange of officers and cadets at technical colleges.

It should carry with it the continuance of the present facilities for mutual security by the joint use of all naval and air force bases in the possession of either country all over the world.

This would perhaps double the mobility of the American navy and air force. It would greatly expand that of the British Empire forces, and it might well lead, if and as the world calms down, to important financial savings.

Already we use together a large number of islands; more may well be entrusted to our joint care in the near future. The United States has already a permanent defense agreement with the Dominion of

Canada, which is so devotedly attached to the British Commonwealth and Empire. This agreement is more effective than many of those which have often been made under formal alliances. This principle should be extended to all the British Commonwealths with full reciprocity.

Thus, whatever happens, and thus only, shall we be secure ourselves and able to work together for the high and simple causes that are dear to us and bode no ill to any. Eventually there may come, I feel eventually there will come, the principle of common citizenship, but that we may be content to leave to destiny, whose outstretched arm so many of us can already clearly see.

There is, however, an important question we must ask ourselves. Would a special relationship between the United States and the British Commonwealth be inconsistent with our overriding loyalties to the world organization? I reply that, on the contrary, it is probably the only means by which that organization will achieve its full stature and strength. There are already the special United States relations with Canada, which I just mentioned, and there are the relations between the United States and the South American republics.

We British have also our twenty years' treaty of collaboration and mutual assistance with Soviet Russia. I agree with Mr. Bevin, the foreign secretary of Great Britain, that it might well be a fifty years' treaty so far as we are concerned. We aim at nothing but mutual assistance and collaboration with Russia. We have an alliance, the British, with Portugal, unbroken since the year 1384 and which produced fruitful results at a critical moment in the recent war. None of these clash with the general interest of a world agreement or a world organization. On the contrary, they help it.

"In my father's house are many mansions." Special associations between members of the United Nations which have no aggressive point against any other country, which harbor no design incompatible with the Charter of the United Nations, far from being harmful, are beneficial, and, as I believe, indispensable.

I spoke earlier, ladies and gentlemen, of the temple of peace. Workmen from all countries must build that temple. If two of the workmen know each other particularly well and are old friends, if their families are intermingled and if they have faith in each other's purpose, hope in each other's future, and charity toward each other's shortcomings, to quote some good words I read here the other day, why cannot they work together at the common task as friends and partners?

Why can they not share their tools and thus increase each other's working powers? Indeed they must do so, or else the temple may not be built, or, being built, it may collapse, and we shall all be proved again unteachable and have to go and try to learn again for a third time, in a school of war, incomparably more rigorous than that from which we have just been released.

The Dark Ages may return, the Stone Age may return on the gleaming wings of science, and what might now shower, shower immeasurable material blessings upon mankind, may even bring about its total destruction. Beware, I say; time is plenty short. Do not let us take the course of allowing events to drift along until it is too late.

If there is to be a fraternal association of the kind I have described, with all the extra strength and security which both our countries can derive from it, let us make sure that that great fact is known to the world, and that it plays its part in steadying and stabilizing the foundations of peace. There is the path of wisdom. Prevention is better than cure.

A shadow has fallen upon the scenes so lately lightened, lighted by the Allied victory. Nobody knows what Soviet Russia and its Communist international organization intends to do in the immediate future, or what are the limits, if any, to their expansive and proselytizing tendencies.

I have a strong admiration and regard for the valiant Russian people and for my wartime comrade Marshal Stalin. There is deep sympathy and good will in Britain—and I doubt not here also—toward the peoples of all the Russias and a resolve to persevere through many differences and rebuffs in establishing lasting friendships.

We understand the Russian need to be secure on her western frontiers from the removal, by the removal of all possibility of German aggression. We welcome Russia to her rightful place among the leading nations of the world. We welcome her flag upon the seas. Above all, we welcome or should welcome constant, frequent, and growing contacts between the Russian people and our own peoples on both sides of the Atlantic.

It is my duty, however—and I am sure you would not wish me not to state the facts as I see them to you—it is my duty to place before you certain facts about the present position in Europe.

From Stettin in the Baltic to Trieste in the Adriatic, an iron curtain has descended across the Continent. Behind that line lie all the capitals of the ancient states of Central and Eastern Europe. Warsaw, Berlin, Prague, Vienna, Budapest, Belgrade, Bucharest, and Sofia; all these famous cities and the populations around them lie in what I might call the Soviet sphere, and all are subject, in one form or another, not only to Soviet influence but to a very high and in some cases increasing measure of control from Moscow.

Police governments are pervading from Moscow. But Athens alone, with its immortal glories, is free to decide its future at an election under British, American, and French observation.

The Russian-dominated Polish government has been encouraged to make enormous and wrongful inroads upon Germany, and mass expulsions of millions of Germans on a scale grievous and undreamed-of are now taking place.

The Communist parties, which were very small in all these eastern states of Europe, have been raised to preeminence and power far beyond their numbers and are seeking everywhere to obtain totalitarian control.

Police governments are prevailing in nearly every case, and so far, except in Czechoslovakia, there is no true democracy. Turkey and Persia are both profoundly alarmed and disturbed at the claims which are being made upon them and at the pressure being exerted by the Moscow government.

An attempt is being made by the Russians, in Berlin, to build up a quasi-Communist party in their zone of occupied Germany by showing special favors to groups of left-wing German leaders. At the end of the fighting last June, the American and British armies withdrew westward, in accordance with an earlier agreement, to a depth at some points of 150 miles upon a front of nearly 400 miles, in order to allow our Russian allies to occupy this vast expanse of territory which the Western democracies had conquered.

If now the Soviet government tries, by separate action, to build up a pro-Communist Germany in their areas, this will cause new serious difficulties in the American and British zones, and will give the defeated Germans the power of putting themselves up to auction between the Soviets and the Western democracies. Whatever conclusions may be drawn from these facts—and facts they are—this is certainly not the liberated Europe we fought to build up. Nor is it one which contains the essentials of permanent peace.

The safety of the world, ladies and gentlemen, requires a unity in Europe from which no nation should be permanently outcast. It is from the strong parent races in Europe that the world wars we have witnessed, or which occurred in former times, have sprung.

Twice in our own lifetime we have—the United States against her wishes and her traditions, against arguments the force of which it is impossible not to comprehend—twice we have seen them drawn by irresistible forces into these wars in time to secure the victory of the good cause, but only after frightful slaughter, and devastation have occurred.

Twice the United States has had to send several millions of its young men across the Atlantic to fight the wars. But now we all can find any nation, wherever it may dwell, between dusk and dawn. Surely we should work with conscious purpose for a grand pacification of Europe within the structure of the United Nations and in accordance with our Charter.

That, I feel, opens a course of policy of very great importance.

In front of the iron curtain which lies across Europe are other causes for anxiety. In Italy the Communist party is seriously hampered by having to support the Communist-trained Marshal Tito's claims to former Italian territory at the head of the Adriatic. Nevertheless, the future of Italy hangs in the balance.

Again one cannot imagine a regenerated Europe without a strong France. All my public life I have worked for a strong France and I have never lost faith in her destiny, even in the darkest hours. I will not lose faith now.

However, in a great number of countries, far from the Russian frontiers and throughout the world, Communist fifth columns are established and work in complete unity and absolute obedience to directions they receive from the Communist center. Except in the British Commonwealth and in the United States, where communism is in its infancy, the Communist parties or fifth columns constitute a growing challenge and peril to Christian civilization. These are somber facts for anyone to have to recite on the morrow of a victory gained by so much splendid comradeship in arms and in the cause of freedom and democracy, but we should be most unwise not to face them squarely while time remains.

The outlook is also anxious in the Far East and especially in Manchuria. The agreement which was made at Yalta, to which I was party, was extremely favorable to Soviet Russia, but it was made at a time when no one could say that the German war might not extend all through the summer and autumn of 1945 and when the Japanese war was expected by the best judges to last for a further eighteen months from the end of the German war. In this country you are so well informed about the Far East, and such devoted friends of China. that I do not need expatiate on the situation there.

I had, however, felt bound to portray the shadow which, alike in the West and in the East, falls upon the world. I was a minister at the time of the Versailles treaty and a close friend of Mr. Lloyd George, who was the head of the British delegation at that time. I did not myself agree with many things that were done, but I have a very vague impression in my mind of that situation, and I find it painful to contrast it with that which prevails now. In those days there were high hopes and unbounded confidence that the wars were over, and that the League of Nations would become all-powerful. I do not see or feel that same confidence or even the same hopes in the haggard world at the present time.

On the other hand, ladies and gentlemen, I repulse the idea that a new war is inevitable—still more that it is imminent. It is because I am sure that our fortunes are still in our hands, in our own hands, and that we hold the power to save the future, that I feel the duty to speak out now that I have the occasion and opportunity to do so.

I do not believe that Soviet Russia desires war. What they desire is the fruits of war and the indefinite expansion of their power and doctrines.

But what we have to consider here today while time remains, is the permanent prevention of war and the establishment of conditions of freedom and democracy as rapidly as possible in all countries. Our difficulties and dangers will not be removed by closing our eyes to them. They will not be removed by mere waiting to see what happens: nor will they be removed by a policy of appeasement.

What is needed is a settlement, and the longer this is delayed, the more difficult it will be and the greater our dangers will become.

From what I have seen of our Russian friends and allies during the war, I am convinced that there is nothing they admire so much as strength, and there is nothing for which they have less respect than for weakness, especially military weakness.

For that, for that reason, the old doctrine of a balance of power is unsound. We cannot afford, if we can help it, to work on narrow margins, offering temptations to a trial of strength.

If the Western democracies stand together in strict adherence to the principles of the United Nations Charter, their influence for furthering those principles will be immense and no one is likely to molest them. If, however, they become divided or falter in their duty, and if these all-important years are allowed to slip away, then indeed catastrophe may overwhelm us all.

Last time I saw it all coming and cried aloud to my own fellow countrymen and to the world, but no one paid any attention. Up till the year 1933 or even 1935, Germany might have been saved from the awful fate which has overtaken her, and we might all have been spared the miseries Hitler let loose upon mankind.

There never was a war in history easier to prevent by timely action than the one which has just desolated such great areas of the globe. It could have been prevented, in my belief, without the firing of a single shot, and Germany might be powerful, prosperous, and honored today; but no one would listen and one by one we were all sucked into the awful whirlpool.

We surely, ladies and gentlemen, I put it to you, but surely we must not let that happen again. This can only be achieved by reaching now, in 1946, this year 1946, by reaching a good understanding on all points with Russia under the general authority of the United Nations Organization and by the maintenance of that good understanding through many peaceful years, by the world instrument, supported by the whole strength of the English-speaking world and all its connections.

There is the solution which I respectfully offer to you in this address to which I have given the title "The Sinews of Peace."

Let no man underrate the abiding power of the British Empire and Commonwealth. Because you see, because you see the forty-six millions in our island harassed about their food supply, of which they only grow one-half, even in wartime, or because we have difficulty in restarting our industries and export trade after six years of passionate war effort, do not suppose that we shall not come through these dark years of privation as we have come through the glorious years of agony, or that half a century from now. you will not see seventy or eighty millions of Britons spread about the world and united in defense of our traditions, and our way of life, and of the world causes which you and we espouse.

If the population of the English-speaking Commonwealth be added to that of the United States, with all such cooperation implies in the air, on the sea, all over the globe, and in science and in industry, and in moral force, there will be no quivering, precarious balance of power to offer its temptation to ambition or adventure. On the contrary, there will be an overwhelming assurance of security.

If we adhere faithfully to the Charter of the United Nations and walk forward in sedate and sober strength, seeking no one's land or treasure, seeking to lay no arbitrary control upon the thoughts of men, if all British moral and material forces and convictions are joined with your own in fraternal association, the high roads of the future will be clear, not only for us but for all, not only for our time but for a century to come.

✦ Reading 60 ✦

The Spy Who Came in from the Cold

John le Carré

British agent Alec Leamas, is responsible for double agents in East Germany. When the rival spy organization begins killing off the double agents, Leamas is called back to London. In London he has a love affair with a lonely librarian as part of his assignment to play a disgraced agent, a failure. He is then sent back into the cold to destroy the leader of the rival spy organization and is double-crossed by his own people.

Checkpoint

The American handed Leamas another cup of coffee and said, "Why don't you go back and sleep? We can ring you if he shows up."

Leamas said nothing, just stared through the window of the checkpoint, along the empty street.

"You can't wait forever, sir. Maybe he'll come some other time. We can have the *Polizei* contact the Agency: you can be back here in twenty minutes."

"No," said Leamas, "it's nearly dark now."

"But you can't wait forever; he's nine hours over schedule."

"If you want to go, go. You've been very good," Leamas added. "I'll tell Kramer you've been damn good."

"But how long will you wait?"

"Until he comes." Leamas walked to the observation window and stood between the two motionless policemen. Their binoculars were trained on the Eastern checkpoint.

"He's waiting for the dark," Leamas muttered, "I know he is."

"This morning you said he'd come across with the workmen."

Leamas turned on him.

"Agents aren't airplanes. They don't have schedules. He's blown, he's on the run, he's frightened. Mundt's after him, now, at this moment. He's got only one chance. Let him choose his time."

The younger man hesitated, wanting to go and not finding the moment.

A bell rang inside the hut. They waited, suddenly alert. A policeman said in German, "Black Opel Rekord, Federal registration."

"He can't see that far in the dusk, he's guessing," the American whispered and then he added: "How did Mundt know?"

"Shut up," said Leamas from the window.

One of the policemen left the hut and walked to the sandbag emplacement two feet short of the white demarkation which lay across the road like the base line of a tennis court. The other waited until his companion was crouched behind the telescope in the emplacement, then put down his binoculars, took his black helmet from the peg by the door and carefully adjusted it on his head. Somewhere high above the checkpoint the arclights sprang to life, casting theatrical beams onto the road in front of them.

The policeman began his commentary. Leamas knew it by heart.

"Car halts at the first control. Only one occupant, a woman. Escorted to the Vopo hut for document check." They waited in silence.

"What's he saying?" said the American. Leamas didn't reply. Picking up a spare pair of binoculars, he gazed fixedly toward the East German controls.

"Document check completed. Admitted to the second control."

"Mr. Leamas, is this your man?" the American persisted. "I ought to ring the Agency."

"Wait."

"Where's the car now? What's it doing?"

"Currency check, Customs," Leamas snapped.

From: John le Carré, *The Spy Who Came in from the Cold* (New York: Coward-McCann, 1963), pp. 7–27, 167–179, 232–253.

Leamas watched the car. There were two Vopos at the driver's door, one doing the talking, the other standing off, waiting. A third was sauntering around the car. He stopped at the trunk, then walked back to the driver. He wanted the key. He opened the trunk, looked inside, closed it, returned the key and walked thirty yards up the road to where, midway between the two opposing checkpoints, a solitary East German sentry was standing, a squat silhouette in boots and baggy trousers. The two stood together talking, self-conscious in the glare of the arclight.

With a perfunctory gesture they waved the car on. It reached the two sentries in the middle of the road and stopped again. They walked around the car, stood off and talked again; finally, almost unwillingly, they let it continue across the line to the Western sector.

"It is a man you're waiting for, Mr. Leamas?" asked the American.

"Yes, it's a man."

Pushing up the collar of his jacket, Leamas stepped outside into the icy October wind. He remembered the crowd then. It was something you forgot inside the hut, this group of puzzled faces. The people changed but the expressions were the same. It was like the helpless crowd that gathers around a traffic accident, no one knowing how it happened, whether you should move the body. Smoke or dust rose through the beams of the arc lamps, a constant shifting pall between the margins of light.

Leamas walked over to the car and said to the woman, "Where is he?"

"They came for him and he ran. He took the bicycle. They can't have known about me."

"Where did he go?"

"We had a room near Brandenburg, over a pub. He kept a few things there, money, papers. I think he'll have gone there. Then he'll come over."

"Tonight?"

"He said he would come tonight. The others have all been caught—Paul, Viereck, Ländser, Salomon. He hasn't got long."

Leamas stared at her for a moment in silence.

"Ländser too?"

"Last night."

A policeman was standing at Leamas' side.

"You'll have to move away from here," he said. "It's forbidden to obstruct the crossing point."

Leamas half turned. "Go to hell," he snapped. The German stiffened, but the woman said, "Get in. We'll drive down to the corner."

He got in beside her and they drove slowly until they reached a side road.

"I didn't know you had a car," he said.

"It's my husband's," she replied indifferently. "Karl never told you I was married, did he?" Leamas was silent. "My husband and I work for an optical firm. They let us over to do business. Karl only told you my maiden name. He didn't want me to be mixed up with . . . you."

Leamas took a key from his pocket.

"You'll want somewhere to stay," he said. His voice sounded flat. "There's an apartment in the Albrecht-Dürer-Strasse, next to the Museum. Number 28A. You'll find everything you want. I'll telephone you when he comes."

"I'll stay here with you."

"I'm not staying here. Go to the flat. I'll ring you. There's no point in waiting here now."

"But he's coming to this crossing point."

Leamas looked at her in surprise.

"He told you that?"

"Yes. He knows one of the Vopos there, the son of his landlord. It may help. That's why he chose this route."

"And he told *you* that?"

"He trusts me. He told me everything."

"Christ."

He gave her the key and went back to the checkpoint hut, out of the cold. The policemen were muttering to each other as he entered; the larger one ostentatiously turned his back.

"I'm sorry," said Leamas. "I'm sorry I bawled you out." He opened a tattered briefcase and rummaged in it until he found what he was looking for: a half bottle of whisky. With a nod the elder man accepted it, half filled each coffee mug and topped them up with black coffee.

"Where's the American gone?" asked Leamas.

"Who?"

"The CIA boy. The one who was with me."

"Bedtime," said the elder man and they all laughed.

Leamas put down his mug and said, "What are your rules for shooting to protect a man coming over? A man on the run."

"We can only give covering fire if the Vopos shoot into our sector."

"That means you can't shoot until a man's over the boundary?"

The older man said, "We can't give covering fire, Mr. . . ."

"Thomas," Leamas replied. "Thomas." They shook hands, the two policemen pronouncing their own names as they did so.

"We can't give covering fire. That's the truth. They tell us there'd be war if we did."

"It's nonsense," said the younger policeman, emboldened by the whisky. "If the allies weren't here the Wall would be gone by now."

"So would Berlin," muttered the elder man.

"I've got a man coming over tonight," said Leamas abruptly.

"Here? At this crossing point?"

"It's worth a lot to get him out. Mundt's men are looking for him."

"There are still places where you can climb," said the younger policeman.

"He's not that kind. He'll bluff his way through; he's got papers, if the papers are still good. He's got a bicycle."

There was only one light in the checkpoint, a reading lamp with a green shade, but the glow of the arclights, like artificial moonlight, filled the cabin. Darkness had fallen, and with it silence. They spoke as if they were afraid of being overheard. Leamas went to the window and waited, in front of him the road and to either side the Wall, a dirty, ugly thing of breeze blocks and strands of barbed wire, lit with cheap yellow light, like the backdrop for a concentration camp. East and west of the Wall lay the unrestored part of Berlin, a half-world of ruin, drawn in two dimensions, crags of war.

That damned woman, thought Leamas, and that fool Karl, who'd lied about her. Lied by omission, as they all do, agents the world over. You teach them to cheat, to cover their tracks, and they cheat you as well. He'd only produced her once, after that dinner in the Schürzstrasse last year. Karl had just had his big scoop and Control had wanted to meet him. Control always came in on success. They'd had dinner together—Leamas, Control and Karl. Karl loved that kind of thing. He turned up looking like a Sunday school boy, scrubbed and shining, doffing his hat and all respectful.

Control had shaken his hand for five minutes and said: "I want you to know how pleased we are, Karl, damn pleased." Leamas had watched and thought, That'll cost us another couple of hundred a year.

When they'd finished dinner Control pumped their hands again, nodded significantly and, implying that he had to go off and risk his life somewhere else, got back into his chauffeur-driven car. Then Karl had laughed, and Leamas had laughed with him, and they'd finished the champagne, still laughing about Control. Afterwards they'd gone to the Alter Fass; Karl had insisted on it and there Elvira was waiting for them, a forty-year-old blonde, tough as nails.

"This is my best kept secret, Alec," Karl had said, and Leamas was furious. Afterwards they'd had a row.

"How much does she know? Who is she? How did you meet her?" Karl sulked and refused to say. After that things went badly. Leamas tried to alter the routine, change the meeting places and the catchwords, but Karl didn't like it. He knew what lay behind it and he didn't like it.

"If you don't trust her it's too late anyway," he'd said, and Leamas took the hint and shut up. But he went carefully after that, told Karl much less, used more of the hocus-pocus of espionage technique. And there she was, out there in her car, knowing everything, the whole network, the safe house, everything; and Leamas swore, not for the first time, never to trust an agent again.

He went to the telephone and dialed the number of his flat. Frau Martha answered.

"We've got guests at the Dürer Strasse," said Leamas, "a man and a woman."

"Married?" asked Martha.

"Near enough," said Leamas, and she laughed that frightful laugh. As he put down the receiver one of the policemen turned to him.

"Herr Thomas! Quick!" Leamas stepped to the observation window.

"A man, Herr Thomas," the younger policeman whispered, "with a bicycle." Leamas picked up the binoculars.

It was Karl, the figure was unmistakable even at that distance, shrouded in an old Wehrmacht mackintosh, pushing his bicycle. He's made it, thought Leamas, he must have made it, he's through the document check, only currency and customs to go. Leamas watched Karl lean his bicycle against the railing, walk casually to the customs hut. Don't overdo it, he thought. At last Karl came out, waved cheerfully to the man on the barrier, and the red and white pole swung slowly upwards. He was through, he was coming toward them, he had made it. Only the Vopo in the middle of the road, the line and safety.

At that moment Karl seemed to hear some sound, sense some danger; he glanced over his shoulder, began to pedal furiously, bending low over the handlebars. There was still the lonely sentry on the bridge, and he had turned and was watching Karl. Then, totally unexpected, the searchlights went on, white and brilliant, catching Karl and holding him in their beam like a rabbit in the headlights of a car. There came the seesaw wail of a siren, the sound of orders wildly shouted. In front of Leamas the two policemen dropped to their knees, peering through the sandbagged slits, deftly flicking the rapid load on their automatic rifles.

The East German sentry fired, quite carefully, away from them, into his own sector. The first shot seemed to thrust Karl forward, the second to pull him back. Somehow he was still moving, still on the bicycle, passing the sentry, and the sentry was still shooting at him. Then he sagged, rolled to the ground, and they heard quite clearly the clatter of the bike as it fell. Leamas hoped to God he was dead.

The Circus

He watched the Templehof runway sink beneath him.

Leamas was not a reflective man and not a particularly philosophical one. He knew he was written off—it was a fact of life which he would henceforth live with, as a man must live with cancer or imprisonment. He knew there was no kind of preparation which could have bridged the gap between then and now. He met failure as one day he would probably meet death, with cynical resentment and the courage of a solitary. He'd lasted longer than most; now he was beaten. It is said a dog lives as long as its teeth; metaphorically, Leamas' teeth had been drawn; and it was Mundt who had drawn them.

Ten years ago he could have taken the other path—there were desk jobs in that anonymous government building in Cambridge Circus which Leamas could have taken and kept till he was God knows how old; but Leamas wasn't made that way. You might as well have asked a jockey to become a betting clerk as expect Leamas to abandon operational life for the tendentious theorizing and clandestine self-interest of Whitehall. He had stayed on in Berlin, conscious that Personnel had marked his file for review at the end of every year—stubborn, willful, contemptuous of instruction, telling himself that something would turn up. Intelligence work has one moral law—it is justified by results. Even the sophistry of Whitehall paid court to that law, and Leamas got results. Until Mundt came.

It was odd how soon Leamas had realized that Mundt was the writing on the wall.

Hans-Dieter Mundt, born forty-two years ago in Leipzig. Leamas knew his dossier, knew the photograph on the inside of the cover, the blank, hard face beneath the flaxen hair; knew by heart the story of Mundt's rise to power as second man in the Abteilung and effective head of operations. Mundt was hated even within his own department. Leamas knew that from the evidence of defectors, and from Riemeck, who as a member of the SED Praesidium sat on security committees with Mundt, and dreaded him. Rightly as it turned out, for Mundt had killed him.

Until 1959 Mundt had been a minor functionary of the Abteilung, operating in London under the cover of the East German Steel Mission. He returned to Germany in a hurry after murdering two of his own agents to save his skin and was not heard of for more than a year. Quite suddenly he reappeared at the Abteilung's headquarters in Leipzig as head of the Ways and Means Department, responsible for allocating currency, equipment and personnel for special tasks. At the end of that year came the big struggle for power within the Abteilung. The number and influence of Soviet liaison officers were drastically reduced, several of the old guard were dismissed on ideological grounds and three men emerged: Fiedler as head of counterintelligence, Jahn took over from Mundt as head of facilities, and Mundt himself got the plum—deputy director of operations—at the age of forty-one. Then the new style began. The first agent Leamas lost was a girl. She was only a small link in the network; she was used for courier jobs. They shot her dead in the street as she left a West Berlin cinema. The police never found the murderer and Leamas was at first inclined to write the incident off as unconnected with her work. A month later a railroad porter in Dresden, a discarded agent from Peter Guillam's network, was found dead and mutilated beside a railroad track. Leamas knew it wasn't coincidence any longer. Soon after that two members of another network under Leamas' control were arrested and summarily sentenced to death. So it went on: remorseless and unnerving.

And now they had Karl, and Leamas was leaving Berlin as he had come—without a single agent worth a farthing. Mundt had won.

Leamas was a short man with close-cropped, iron-gray hair, and the physique of a swimmer. He was very strong. This strength was discernible in his back and shoulders, in his neck, and in the stubby formation of his hands and fingers.

He had a utilitarian approach to clothes, as he did to most other things, and even the spectacles he occasionally wore had steel rims. Most of his suits were of artificial fiber, none of them had waistcoats. He favored shirts of the American kind with buttons on the points of the collars, and suede shoes with rubber soles.

He had an attractive face, muscular, and a stubborn line to his thin mouth. His eyes were brown and small; Irish, some said. It was hard to place Leamas. If he were to walk into a London club the porter would certainly not mistake him for a member; in a Berlin night club they usually gave him the best table. He looked like a man who could make trouble, a man who looked after his money; a man who was not quite a gentleman.

The stewardess thought he was interesting. She guessed that he was North of England, which he might well have been, and rich, which he was not. She put his age at fifty, which was about right. She guessed he was single, which was half true. Somewhere long ago there had been a divorce; somewhere there were children, now in their teens, who received their allowance from a rather odd private bank in the City.

"If you want another whisky," said the stewardess, "you'd better hurry. We shall be at London airport in twenty minutes."

"No more." He didn't look at her; he was looking out of the window at the gray-green fields of Kent.

Fawley met him at the airport and drove him to London.

"Control's pretty cross about Karl," he said, looking sideways at Leamas. Leamas nodded.

"How did it happen?" asked Fawley.

"He was shot. Mundt got him."

"Dead?"

"I should think so, by now. He'd better be. He nearly made it. He should never have hurried, they couldn't have been sure. The Abteilung got to the checkpoint just after he'd been let through. They started the siren and a Vopo shot him twenty yards short of the line. He moved on the ground for a moment, then lay still."

"Poor bastard."

"Precisely," said Leamas.

Fawley didn't like Leamas, and if Leamas knew he didn't care. Fawley was a man who belonged to clubs and wore representative ties, pontificated on the skills of sportsmen and assumed a service rank in office correspondence. He thought Leamas suspect, and Leamas thought him a fool.

"What section are you in?" asked Leamas.

"Personnel."

"Like it?"

"Fascinating."

"Where do I go now? On ice?"

"Better let Control tell you, old boy."

"Do you know?"

"Of course."

"Then why the hell don't you tell me?"

"Sorry, old man," Fawley replied, and Leamas suddenly very nearly lost his temper. Then he reflected that Fawley was probably lying anyway.

"Well, tell me one thing, do you mind? Have I got to look for a bloody flat in London?"

Fawley scratched at his ear: "I don't think so, old man, no."

"No? Thank God for that."

They parked near Cambridge Circus, at a parking meter, and went together into the hall.

"You haven't got a pass, have you? You'd better fill in a slip, old man."

"Since when have we had passes? McCall knows me as well as his own mother."

"Just a new routine. Circus is growing, you know."

Leamas said nothing, nodded at McCall and got into the lift without a pass.

Control shook his hand rather carefully, like a doctor feeling the bones.

"You must be awfully tired," he said apologetically, "do sit down." That same dreary voice, the donnish bray.

Leamas sat down in a chair facing an olive-green electric fire with a bowl of water balanced on the top of it.

"Do you find it cold?" Control asked. He was stooping over the fire rubbing his hands together. He wore a cardigan under his black jacket, a shabby brown one. Leamas remembered Control's wife, a stupid little woman called Mandy who seemed to think her husband was on the Coal Board. He supposed she had knitted it.

"It's so dry, that's the trouble." Control continued. "Beat the cold and you parch the atmosphere. Just as dangerous." He went to the desk and pressed some button. "Well try and get some coffee," he said. "Ginnie's on leave, that's the trouble. They've given me some new girl. It really is too bad." He was shorter than Leamas remembered him; otherwise, just the same. The same affected detachment, the same fusty conceits; the same horror of drafts; courteous according to a formula miles removed from Leamas' experience. The same milk-and-water smile, the same elaborate diffidence, the same apologetic adherence to a code of behavior which he pretended to find ridiculous. The same banality.

He brought a pack of cigarettes from the desk and gave one to Leamas.

"You're going to find these more expensive," he said and Leamas nodded dutifully. Slipping the cigarettes into his pocket, Control sat down.

There was a pause; finally Leamas said: "Riemeck's dead."

"Yes, indeed," Control declared, as if Leamas had made a good point. "It is very unfortunate. Most. . . . I suppose that girl blew him—Elvira?"

"I suppose so." Leamas wasn't going to ask him how he knew about Elvira.

"And Mundt had him shot," Control added.

"Yes."

Control got up and drifted around the room looking for an ashtray. He found one and put it awkwardly on the floor between their two chairs.

"How did you feel? When Riemeck was shot, I mean? You saw it, didn't you?"

Leamas shrugged. "I was bloody annoyed," he said.

Control put his head to one side and half closed his eyes. "Surely you felt more than that? Surely you were upset? That would be more natural."

"I was upset. Who wouldn't be?"

"Did you like Riemeck—as a man?"

"I suppose so," said Leamas helplessly. "There doesn't seem much point in going into it," he added.

"How did you spend the night, what was left of it, after Riemeck had been shot?"

"Look, what is this?" Leamas asked hotly; "what are you getting at?"

"Riemeck was the last," Control reflected, "the last of a series of deaths. If my memory is right it began with the girl, the one they shot in Wedding, outside the cinema. Then there was the Dresden man, and the arrests at Jena. Like the ten little niggers. Now Paul, Viereck and Ländser—all dead. And finally Riemeck." He smiled deprecatingly. "That is quite a heavy rate of expenditure. I wondered if you'd had enough."

"What do you mean—enough?"

"I wondered whether you were tired. Burned out" There was long silence.

"That's up to you," Leamas said at last.

"We have to live without sympathy, don't we? That's impossible of course. We act it to one another, all this hardness; but we aren't like that really. I mean . . . one can't be out in the cold all the time; one has to come in from the cold . . . do you see what I mean?"

Leamas saw. He saw the long road outside Rotterdam, the long straight road beside the dunes, and the stream of refugees moving along it; saw the little airplane miles away, the procession stop and look toward it; and the plane coming in, neatly over the dunes; saw the chaos, the meaningless hell, as the bombs hit the road.

"I can't talk like this, Control," Leamas said at last. "What do you want me to do?"

"I want you to stay out in the cold a little longer." Leamas said nothing, so Control went on: "The ethic of our work, as I understand it, is based on a single assumption. That is, we are never going to be aggressors. Do you think that's fair?"

Leamas nodded. Anything to avoid talking.

"Thus we do disagreeable things, but we are *defensive*. That, I think, is still fair. We do disagreeable things so that ordinary people here and elsewhere can sleep safely in their beds at night. Is that too romantic? Of course, we occasionally do very wicked things." He grinned like a schoolboy. "And in weighing up the moralities, we rather go in for dishonest comparisons; after all, you can't compare the ideals of one side with the methods of the other, can you now?"

Leamas was lost. He'd heard the man talked a lot of drivel before getting the knife in, but he'd never heard anything like this before.

"I mean, you've got to compare method with method, and ideal with ideal. I would say that since the war, our methods—ours and those of the opposition—have become much the same. I mean you can't be less ruthless than the opposition simply because your government's *policy* is benevolent, can you now?" He laughed quietly to himself. "That would *never* do," he said.

For God's sake, thought Leamas, it's like working for a bloody clergyman. What *is* he up to?

"That is why," Control continued, "I think we ought to try and get rid of Mundt. . . . Oh really," he said, turning irritably toward the door, "where is that damned coffee?"

Control crossed to the door, opened it and talked to some unseen girl in the outer room. As he returned he said: "I really think we *ought* to get rid of him if we can manage it."

"Why? We've got nothing left in East Germany, nothing at all. You just said so—Riemeck was the last. We've nothing left to protect."

Control sat down and looked at his hands for a while.

"That is not altogether true," he said finally; "but I don't think I need to bore you with the details."

Leamas shrugged.

"Tell me," Control continued, "are you tired of spying? Forgive me if I repeat the question. I mean that is a phenomenon we understand here, you know. Like aircraft designers . . . metal fatigue, I think the term is. Do say if you are."

Leamas remembered the flight home that morning and wondered.

"If you were," Control added, "we would have to find some other way of taking care of Mundt. What I have in mind is a little out of the ordinary."

The girl came in with the coffee. She put the tray on the desk and poured out two cups. Control waited till she had left the room.

"Such a *silly* girl," he said, almost to himself. "It seems extraordinary they can't find good ones any more. I do wish Ginnie wouldn't go on holiday at times like this." He stirred his coffee disconsolately for a while.

"We really must discredit Mundt," he said. "Tell me, do you drink a lot? Whisky and that kind of thing?"

Leamas had thought he was used to Control.

"I drink a bit. More than most, I suppose."

Control nodded understandingly. "What do you know about Mundt?"

"He's a killer. He was here a year or two back with the East German Steel Mission. We had an adviser here then: Maston."

"Quite so."

"Mundt was running an agent, the wife of an F.O. man. He killed her."

"He tried to kill George Smiley. And of course he shot the woman's husband. He is a very distasteful man. Ex Hitler-Youth and all that kind of thing. Not at all the intellectual kind of Communist. A practitioner of the cold war."

"Like us," Leamas observed drily.

Control didn't smile. "George Smiley knew the case well. He isn't with us any more, but I think you ought to ferret him out. He's doing things on seventeenth-century Germany. He lives in Chelsea, just behind Sloane Square. Bywater Street, do you know it?"

"Yes."

"And Guillam was on the case as well. He's in Satellites Four, on the first floor. I'm afraid everything's changed since your day."

"Yes."

"Spend a day or two with them. They know what I have in mind. Then I wondered if you'd care to stay with me for the weekend. My wife," he added hastily, "is looking after her mother, I'm afraid. It will be just you and I."

"Thanks. I'd like to."

"We can talk about things in comfort then. It would be very nice. I think you might make a lot of money out of it. You can have whatever you make."

"Thanks."

"That is, of course, if you're *sure you want* to . . . no metal fatigue or anything?"

"If it's a question of killing Mundt, I'm game."

"Do you really feel that?" Control inquired politely. And then, having looked at Leamas thoughtfully for a moment, he observed, "Yes, I really think you do. But you mustn't feel you *have* to say it. I mean in our world we pass so quickly out of the register of hate or love—like certain sounds a dog can't hear. All that's left in the end is a kind of nausea; you never want to cause suffering again. Forgive me, but isn't that rather what you felt when Karl Riemeck was shot? Not hate for Mundt, nor love for Karl, but a sickening jolt like a blow on a numb body. . . . They tell me you walked all night—just walked through the streets of Berlin. Is that right?"

"It's right that I went for a walk."

"All night?"

"Yes."

"What happened to Elvira?"

"God knows. . . . I'd like to take a swing at Mundt," he said.

"Good . . . good. Incidentally, if you should meet any old friends in the meantime, I don't think there's any point in discussing this with them. In fact," Control added after a moment, "I should be rather short with them. Let them think we've treated you badly. It's as well to begin as one intends to continue, isn't it?"

* * *

Arrest

Fiedler and Leamas drove back the rest of the way in silence. In the dusk the hills were black and cavernous, the pinpoint lights struggling against the gathering darkness like the lights of distant ships at sea.

Fiedler parked the car in a shed at the side of the house and they walked together to the front door. They were about to enter the lodge when they heard a shout from the direction of the trees, followed by someone calling Fiedler's name. They turned, and Leamas distinguished in the twilight twenty yards away three men standing, apparently waiting for Fiedler.

"What do you want?" Fiedler called.

"We want to talk to you. We're from Berlin."

Fiedler hesitated. "Where's that damn guard?" Fiedler asked Leamas. "There should be a guard on the front door."

Leamas shrugged.

"Why aren't the lights on in the hall?" he asked again; then, still unconvinced, he began walking slowly toward the men.

Leamas waited a moment, then, hearing nothing, made his way through the unlit house to the annex behind it. This was a shoddy barrack hut attached to the back of the building and hidden from all sides by close plantations of young pine trees. The hut was divided into three adjoining bedrooms; there was no corridor. The center room had been given to Leamas, and the room nearest to the main building was occupied by two guards. Leamas never knew who occupied the third. He had once tried to open the connecting door between it and his own room, but it was locked. He had only discovered it was a bedroom by peering through a narrow gap in the lace curtains early one morning as he went for a walk. The two guards, who followed him everywhere at fifty yards' distance, had not rounded the corner of the hut, and he looked in at the window. The room contained a single bed, made, and a small writing desk with papers on it. He supposed that someone, with what passes for German thoroughness, watched him from that bedroom. But Leamas was too old a dog to allow himself to be bothered by surveillance. In Berlin it had been a fact of life—if you couldn't spot it, so much the worse: it only meant they were taking greater care, or you were losing your grip. Usually, because he was good at that kind of thing, because he was observant and had an accurate memory—because, in short, he was good at his job—he spotted them anyway. He knew the formations favored by a shadowing team, he knew the tricks, the weaknesses, the momentary lapses that could give them away. It meant nothing to Leamas that he was watched, but as he walked through the improvised doorway from the lodge to the hut and stood in the guards' bedroom, he had the distinct feeling that something was wrong.

The lights in the annex were controlled from some central point. They were put on and off by an unseen hand. In the mornings he was often awakened by the sudden blaze of the single overhead light in his room. At night he would be hastened to bed by perfunctory darkness. It was only nine o'clock as he entered the annex, and the lights were already out. Usually they stayed on till eleven, but now they were out and the shutters had been lowered. He had left the connecting door from the house open, so that the pale twilight from the hallway reached, but scarcely penetrated, the guards' bedroom, and by it he could just see the two empty beds. As he stood there peering into the room, surprised to find it empty, the door behind him closed. Perhaps by itself, but Leamas made no attempt to open it. It was pitch-dark. No sound accompanied the closing of the door, no click nor footstep. To Leamas, his instinct suddenly alert, it was as if the sound track had stopped. Then he smelled the cigar smoke, It must have been hanging in the air but he had not noticed it till now. Like a blind man, his senses of touch and smell were sharpened by the darkness.

There were matches in his pocket but he did not use them. He took one pace sideways, pressed his back against the wall and remained motionless. To Leamas there could only be one explanation—they were waiting for him to pass from the guards' room to his own and therefore he determined to remain where he was. Then from the direction of the main building whence he had come he heard clearly the sound of a footstep. The door which had just closed was tested, the lock turned and made fast. Still Leamas did not move. Not yet. There was no pretense: he was a prisoner in the hut. Very slowly, Leamas now lowered himself into a crouch, putting his hand in the side pocket of his jacket as he did so. He was quite calm, almost relieved at the prospect of action, but memories were racing through his mind. "You've nearly always got a weapon: an ashtray, a couple of coins, a fountain pen—anything that will gouge or cut." It was the favorite dictum of the mild little Welsh sergeant at that house near Oxford in the war: "Never use both hands at once, not with a knife, a stick or a pistol; keep your left arm free, and hold it across the belly. If you can't find anything to hit with, keep the hands open and the thumbs stiff." Taking the box of matches in his right hand, he clasped it longways and deliberately crushed it, so that the small, jagged edges of boxwood protruded from between his fingers. This done, he edged his way along the wall until he came to a chair which he knew was in the corner of the room. Indifferent now to the noise he made, he shoved the chair into the center of the floor. Counting his footsteps as he moved back from the chair, he positioned himself in the angle of the two walls. As he did so, he heard the door of his own bedroom flung open. Vainly he tried to discern the figure that must be standing in the doorway, but there was no light from his own room either. The darkness was impenetrable. He dared not move forward to attack, for the chair was now in the middle of the room; it was his tactical advantage, for he knew where it was, and they did not. They must come for him, they must; he could not let them wait until their helper outside had reached the master switch and put on the lights.

"Come on, you windy bastards," he hissed in German. "I'm here, in the corner. Come and get me, can't you?" Not a move, not a sound.

"I'm here, can't you see me? What's the matter then? What's the matter, children, come on, can't you?"

And then he heard one stepping forward, and another following; and then the oath of a man as he stumbled against the chair, and that was the sign that Leamas was waiting for. Tossing away the box of matches he slowly, cautiously crept forward, pace by pace, his left arm extended in the attitude of a man warding off twigs in a wood until, quite gently, he had touched an arm and felt the warm prickly cloth of a military uniform. Still with his left hand Leamas deliberately tapped the arm twice—two distinct taps—and heard a frightened voice whisper close to his ear in German:

"Hans, is it you?"

"Shut up, you fool," Leamas whispered in reply, and in that same moment reached out and grasped the man's hair, pulling his head forward and down, then in a terrible cutting blow drove the side of his right hand into the nape of the neck, pulled him up again by the arm, hit him in the throat with an upward thrust of his open fist, then released him to fall where the force of gravity took him. As the man's body hit the ground, the lights went on.

In the doorway stood a young captain of the People's Police smoking a cigar, and behind him two men. One was in civilian clothes, quite young. He held a pistol in his hand. Leamas thought it was the Czech kind with a loading lever on the spine of the butt. They were all looking at the man on the floor. Somebody unlocked the outer door and Leamas turned to see who it was. As he turned, there was a shout—Leamas thought it was the captain—telling him to stand still. Slowly he turned back and faced the three men.

His hands were still at his side as the blow came. It seemed to crush his skull. As he fell, drifting warmly into unconsciousness, he wondered whether he had been hit with a revolver, the old kind with a swivel on the butt where you fastened the lanyard.

He was wakened by the lag singing and the warder yelling at him to shut up. He opened his eyes and like a brilliant light the pain burst upon his brain. He lay quite still, refusing to close them, watching the sharp, colored fragments racing across his vision. He tried to take stock of himself: his feet were icy cold and he was aware of the sour stench of prison denims. The singing had stopped and suddenly Leamas longed for it to start again, although he knew it never would. He tried to raise his hand and touch the blood that was caked on his cheek, but his hands were behind him, locked together. His feet too must be bound: the blood had left them, that was why they were cold. Painfully he looked about him, trying to lift his head an inch or two from the floor. To his surprise he saw his own knees in front of him. Instinctively he tried to stretch his legs and as he did so his whole body was seized with a pain so sudden and terrible that he screamed out a sobbing agonized cry of self-pity, like the last cry of a man upon the rack. He lay there panting, attempting to master the pain, then through the sheer perversity of his nature he tried again, quite slowly, to straighten his legs. At once the agony returned, but Leamas had found the cause: his hands and feet were chained together behind his back. As soon as he attempted to stretch his legs the chain tightened, forcing his shoulders down and his damaged head onto the stone floor. They must have beaten him up while he was unconscious, his whole body was stiff and bruised and his groin ached. He wondered if he'd killed the guard. He hoped so.

Above him shone the light, large, clinical and fierce. No furniture, just whitewashed walls, quite close all around, and the gray steel door, a smart charcoal gray, the color you see on clever London houses. There was nothing else. Nothing at all. Nothing to think about, just the savage pain.

He must have lain there hours before they came. It grew hot from the light; he was thirsty but he refused to call out. At last the door opened and Mundt stood there. He knew it was Mundt from the eyes. Smiley had told him about them.

Mundt

They untied him and let him try to stand. For a moment he almost succeeded, then, as the circulation returned to his hands and feet, and as the joints of his body were released from the contraction to which they had been subject, he fell. They let him lie there, watching him with the detachment of children looking at an insect. One of the guards pushed past Mundt and yelled at Leamas to get up. Leamas crawled to the wall and put the palms of his throbbing hands against the white brick. He was half-way up when the guard kicked him and he fell again. He tried once more and this time the guard let him stand with his back against the wall. He saw the guard move his weight onto his left leg and he knew he would kick him again. With all his remaining strength. Leamas thrust himself forward, driving his lowered head into the guard's face. They fell together, Leamas on top. The guard got up and Leamas lay there waiting for the payoff. But Mundt said something to the guard and Leamas felt himself being picked up by the shoulders and feet and heard the door of his cell close as they carried him down the corridor. He was terribly thirsty.

They took him to a small comfortable room, decently furnished with a desk and armchairs. Swedish blinds half covered the barred windows. Mundt sat at the desk and Leamas in an armchair, his eyes half closed. The guards stood at the door.

"Give me a drink," said Leamas.

"Whisky?"

"Water."

Mundt filled a carafe from a basin in the corner, and put it on the table beside him with a glass.

"Bring him something to eat," he ordered, and one of the guards left the room, returning with a mug of soup and some sliced sausage. He drank and ate, and they watched him in silence.

"Where's Fiedler?" Leamas asked finally.

"Under arrest," Mundt replied curtly.

"What for?"

"Conspiring to sabotage the security of the people."

Leamas nodded slowly. "So you won," he said. "When did you arrest him?"

"Last night."

Leamas waited a moment, trying to focus again on Mundt.

"What about me?" he asked.

"You're a material witness. You will of course stand trial yourself later."

"So I'm part of a put-up job by London to frame Mundt, am I?"

Mundt nodded, lit a cigarette and gave it to one of the sentries to pass to Leamas. "That's right, he said. The sentry came over, and with a gesture of grudging solicitude, put the cigarette between Leamas' lips.

"A pretty elaborate operation," Leamas observed, and added stupidly, "Clever chaps these Chinese."

Mundt said nothing. Leamas became used to his silences as the interview progressed. Mundt had rather a pleasant voice, that was something Leamas hadn't expected, but he seldom spoke. It was part of Mundt's extraordinary self-confidence, perhaps, that he did not speak unless he specifically wished to, that he was prepared to allow long silences to intervene rather than exchange pointless words. In this he differed from professional interrogators who set store by initiative, by the evocation of atmosphere and the exploitation of that psychological dependency of a prisoner upon his inquisitor. Mundt despised technique: he was a man of fact and action. Leamas preferred that.

Mundt's appearance was fully consistent with his temperament. He looked an athlete. His fair hair was cut short. It lay mat and neat. His young face had a hard, clean line, and a frightening directness; it was barren of humor or fantasy. He looked young but not youthful; older men would take him seriously. He was well built. His clothes fitted him because he was an easy man to fit. Leamas found no difficulty in recalling that Mundt was a killer. There was a coldness about him, a rigorous self-sufficiency which perfectly equipped him for the business of murder. Mundt was a very hard man.

"The other charge on which you will stand trial, if necessary," Mundt added quietly, "is murder."

"So the sentry died, did he?" Leamas replied.

A wave of intense pain passed through his head.

Mundt nodded. "That being so," he said, "your trial for espionage is somewhat academic. I propose that the case against Fiedler should be publicly heard. That is also the wish of the Praesidium."

"And you want my confession?"

"Yes."

"In other words you haven't any proof."

"We shall have proof. We shall have your confession." There was no menace in Mundt's voice. There was no style, no theatrical twist. "On the other hand, there could be mitigation in your case. You were blackmailed by British Intelligence; they accused you of stealing money and then coerced you into preparing a *revanchist* trap against myself. The court would have sympathy for such a plea."

Leamas seemed to be taken off his guard.

"How did you know they accused me of stealing money?" But Mundt made no reply.

"Fiedler has been very stupid," Mundt observed. "As soon as I read the report of our friend Peters I knew why you had been sent, and I knew that Fiedler would fall into the trap. Fiedler hates me so much." Mundt nodded, as if to emphasize the truth of his observation. "Your people knew that of course. It was a very clever operation. Who prepared it, tell me. Was it Smiley? Did he do it?" Leamas said nothing.

"I wanted to see Fiedler's report of his own interrogation of you, you see. I told him to send it to me. He procrastinated and I knew I was right. Then yesterday he circulated it among the Praesidium, and did not send me a copy. Someone in London has been very clever."

Leamas said nothing.

"When did you last see Smiley?" Mundt asked casually. Leamas hesitated, uncertain of himself. His head was aching terribly.

"When did you last see him?" Mundt repeated.

"I don't remember," Leamas said at last; "he wasn't really in the outfit any more. He'd drop in from time to time."

"He is a great friend of Peter Guillam, is he not?"

"I think so, yes."

"Guillam, you thought, studied the economic situation in the GDR. Some odd little section in your Service; you weren't quite sure what it did."

"Yes." Sound and sight were becoming confused in the mad throbbing of his brain. His eyes were hot and painful. He felt sick.

"Well, when did you last see Smiley?"

"I don't remember . . . I don't remember."

Mundt shook his head.

"You have a very good memory—for anything that incriminates me. We can all remember when we *last* saw somebody. Did you, for instance, see him after you returned from Berlin?"

"Yes, I think so. I bumped into him . . . in the Circus once, in London." Leamas had closed his eyes and he was sweating. "I can't go on, Mundt . . . not much longer, Mundt . . . I'm sick," he said.

"After Ashe had picked you up, after he had walked into the trap that had been set for him, you had lunch together, didn't you?"

"Yes. Lunch together."

"Lunch ended at about four o'clock. Where did you go then?"

"I went down to the City, I think. I don't remember for sure . . . For Christ's sake, Mundt," he said holding his head with his hand, "I can't go on. My bloody head's . . ."

"And after that where did you go? Why did you shake off your followers, why were you so keen to shake them off?"

Leamas said nothing: he was breathing in sharp gasps, his head buried in his hands.

"Answer this one question, then you can go. You shall have a bed. You can sleep if you want. Otherwise you must go back to your cell, do you understand? You will be tied up again and fed on the floor like an animal, do you understand? Tell me where you went."

The wild pulsation of his brain suddenly increased, the room was dancing; he heard voices around him and the sound of footsteps; spectral shapes passed and repassed, detached from sound and gravity; someone was shouting, but not at him; the door was open, he was sure someone had opened the door. The room was full of people, all shouting now, and then they were going, some of them had gone, he heard them marching away, the stamping of their feet was like the throbbing of his head; the echo died and there was silence. Then like the touch of mercy itself, a cool cloth was laid across his forehead, and kindly hands carried him away.

He woke on a hospital bed, and standing at the foot of it was Fiedler, smoking a cigarette.

* * *

The Commissar

Liz stood at the window, her back to the wardress, and stared blankly into the tiny yard outside. She supposed the prisoners took their exercise there. She was in somebody's office; there was food on the desk beside the telephones but she couldn't touch it. She felt sick and terribly tired; physically tired. Her legs ached, her face felt stiff and raw from weeping. She felt dirty and longed for a bath.

"Why don't you eat?" the woman asked again. "It's all over now." She said this without compassion, as if the girl were a fool not to eat when the food was there.

"I'm not hungry."

The wardress shrugged. "You may have a long journey," she observed, "and not much at the other end."

"What do you mean?"

"The workers are starving in England," she declared complacently. "The capitalists let them starve."

Liz thought of saying something but there seemed no point. Besides, she wanted to know; she had to know, and this woman could tell her.

"What is this place?"

"Don't you know?" The wardress laughed. "You should ask them over there." She nodded toward the window. "They can tell you what it is."

"Who are they?"

"Prisoners."

"What kind of prisoners?"

"Enemies of the state," she replied promptly. "Spies, agitators."

"How do you know they are spies?"

"The Party knows. The Party knows more about people than they know themselves. Haven't you been told that?" The wardress looked at her, shook her head and observed, "The English! The rich have eaten your future and your poor have given them the food—that's what's happened to the English."

"Who told you that?"

The woman smiled and said nothing. She seemed pleased with herself.

"And this is a prison for spies?" Liz persisted.

"It is a prison for those who fail to recognize socialist reality; for those who think they have the right to err; for those who slow down the march. Traitors," she concluded briefly.

"But what have they done?"

"We cannot build Communism without doing away with individualism. You cannot plan a great building if some swine builds his sty on your site."

Liz looked at her in astonishment.

"Who told you all this?"

"I am Commissar here," she said proudly. "I work in the prison."

"You are very clever," Liz observed, approaching her.

"I am a worker," the woman replied acidly. "The concept of brain workers as a higher category must be destroyed. There are no categories, only workers; no antithesis between physical and mental labor. Haven't you read Lenin?"

"Then the people in this prison are intellectuals?"

The woman smiled. "Yes," she said, "they are reactionaries who call themselves progressive: they defend the individual against the state. Do you know what Khrushchev said about the counterrevolution in Hungary?"

Liz shook her head. She must show interest, she must make the woman talk.

"He said it would never have happened if a couple of writers had been shot in time."

"Who will they shoot now?" Liz asked quickly. "After the trial?"

"Leamas," she replied indifferently, "and the Jew, Fiedler." Liz thought for a moment she was going to fall but her hand found the back of a chair and she managed to sit down.

"What has Leamas done?" she whispered. The woman looked at her with her small, cunning eyes. She was very large; her hair was scant, stretched over her head to a bun at the nape of her thick neck. Her face was heavy, her complexion flaccid and watery.

"He killed a guard," she said.

"Why?"

The woman shrugged.

"As for the Jew," she continued, "he made an accusation against a loyal comrade."

"Will they shoot Fiedler for that?" asked Liz incredulously.

"Jews are all the same," the woman commented. "Comrade Mundt knows what to do with Jews. We don't need their kind here. If they join the Party they think it belongs to them. If they stay out, they think it is conspiring against them. It is said that Leamas and Fiedler plotted together against Mundt. Are you going to eat that?" she inquired, indicating the food on the desk. Liz shook her head. "Then I must," she declared, with a grotesque attempt at reluctance. "They have given you a potato. You must have a lover in the kitchen." The humor of this observation sustained her until she had finished the last of Liz's meal.

Liz went back to the window.

In the confusion of Liz's mind, in the turmoil of shame and grief and fear, there predominated the appalling memory of Leamas as she had last seen him in the courtroom, sitting stiffly in his chair, his eyes averted from her own. She had failed him and he dared not look at her before he died; would not let her see the contempt, the fear perhaps, that was written on his face.

But how could she have done otherwise? If Leamas had only told her what he had to do—even now it wasn't clear to her—she would have lied and cheated for him, anything, if he had only told her! Surely he understood that; surely he knew her well enough to realize that in the end she would do whatever he said, that she would take on his form and being, his will, life, his image, his pain, if she could; that she prayed for nothing more than the chance to do so. But how could she have known, if she was not told, how to answer those veiled, insidious questions? There seemed no end to the destruction she had caused. She remembered, in the fevered condition of her mind, how, as a child, she had been horrified to learn that with every step she made, thousands of minute creatures were destroyed beneath her foot; and now, whether she had lied or told the truth—or even, she was sure, had kept silent—she had been forced to destroy a human being; perhaps two, for was there not also the Jew, Fiedler, who had been gentle with her, taken her arm and told her to go back to England? They would shoot Fiedler; that's what the woman said. Why did it have to be Fiedler—why not the old man who asked the questions, or the fair one in the front row between the soldiers, the one who smiled all the time? Whenever she turned around she had caught sight of his smooth, blond head and his smooth, cruel face smiling as if it were all a great joke. It comforted her that Leamas and Fiedler were on the same side.

She turned to the woman again and asked, "Why are we waiting here?"

The wardress pushed the plate aside and stood up.

"For instructions," she replied. "They are deciding whether you must stay."

"Stay?" repeated Liz blankly.

"It is a question of evidence. Fiedler may be tried. I told you: they suspect conspiracy between Fiedler and Leamas."

"But who against? How could he conspire in England? How did he come here? He's not in the Party."

The woman shook her head.

"It is secret," she replied. "It concerns only the Praesidium. Perhaps the Jew brought him here."

"But *you* know," Liz insisted, a note of blandishment in her voice, "*you* are Commissar at the prison. Surely they told *you?*"

"Perhaps," the woman replied complacently. "It is very secret," she repeated.

The telephone rang. The woman lifted the receiver and listened. After a moment she glanced at Liz.

"Yes, Comrade. At once," she said, and put down the receiver. "You are to stay," she said shortly. "The Praesidium will consider the case of Fiedler. In the meantime you will stay here. That is the wish of Comrade Mundt."

"Who is Mundt?"

The woman looked cunning.

"It is the wish of the Praesidium," she said.

"I don't want to stay," Liz cried. "I want—"

"The Party knows more about us than we know ourselves," the woman interrupted. "You must stay here. It is the Party's wish."

"Who is Mundt?" Liz asked again, but still she did not reply.

Slowly Liz followed her along endless corridors, through grilles manned by sentries, past iron doors from which no sound came, down endless stairs, across whole courtyards far beneath the ground, until she thought she had descended to the bowels of hell itself, and no one would even tell her when Leamas was dead.

She had no idea what time it was when she heard the footsteps in the corridor outside her cell. It could have been five in the evening—it could have been midnight. She had been awake—staring blankly into the pitch-darkness, longing for a sound. She had never imagined that silence could be so terrible. Once she had cried out, and there had been no echo, nothing. Just the memory of her own voice. She had visualized the sound breaking against the solid darkness like a fist against a rock. She had moved her hands about her as she sat on the bed, and it seemed to her that the darkness made them heavy, as if she were groping in the water. She knew the cell was small; that it contained the bed on which she sat, a handbasin without taps, and a crude table: she had seen them when she first entered. Then the light had gone out, and she had run wildly to where she knew the bed had stood, had struck it with her shins, and had remained there, shivering with fright. Until she heard the footstep, and the door of her cell was opened abruptly.

She recognized him at once, although she could only discern his silhouette against the pale blue light in the corridor. The trim, agile figure, the clear line of the cheek and the short fair hair just touched by the light behind him.

"It's Mundt," he said. "Come with me, at once." His voice was contemptuous yet subdued, as if he were not anxious to be overheard.

Liz was suddenly terrified. She remembered the wardress: "Mundt knows what to do with Jews." She stood by the bed, staring at him, not knowing what to do.

"Hurry, you fool." Mundt had stepped forward and seized her wrist. "Hurry." She let herself be drawn into the corridor. Bewildered, she watched Mundt quietly relock the door of her cell. Roughly he took her arm and forced her quickly along the first corridor, half running, half walking. She could hear the distant whirr of air conditioners; and now and then the sound of other footsteps from passages branching from their own. She noticed that Mundt hesitated, drew back even, when they came upon other corridors, would go ahead and confirm that no one was coming, then signal her forward. He seemed to assume that she would follow, that she knew the reason. It was almost as if he were treating her as an accomplice.

And suddenly he had stopped, was thrusting a key into the keyhole of a dingy metal door. She waited, panic-stricken. He pushed the door savagely outwards and the sweet, cold air of a winter's evening blew against her face. He beckoned to her again, still with the same urgency, and she followed him down two steps onto a gravel path which led through a rough kitchen garden.

They followed the path to an elaborate Gothic gateway which gave on to the road beyond. Parked in the gateway was a car. Standing beside it was Alec Leamas.

"Keep your distance," Mundt warned her as she started to move forward. "Wait here."

Mundt went forward alone and for what seemed an age she watched the two men standing together, talking quietly between themselves. Her heart was beating madly, her whole body shivering with cold and fear. Finally Mundt returned.

"Come with me," he said, and led her to where Leamas stood. The two men looked at one another for a moment.

"Good-bye," said Mundt indifferently. "You're a fool, Leamas," he added. "She's trash, like Fiedler." And he turned without another word and walked quickly away into the twilight.

She put her hand out and touched him, and he half turned from her, brushing her hand away as he opened the car door. He nodded to her to get in, but she hesitated.

"Alec," she whispered, "Alec, what are you doing? Why is he letting you go?"

"Shut up!" Leamas hissed. "Don't even think about it, do you hear? Get in."

"What was it he said about Fiedler? Alec, why is he letting us go?"

"He's letting us go because we've done our job. Get into the car; quick!" Under the compulsion of his extraordinary will she got into the car and closed the door. Leamas got in beside her.

"What bargain have you struck with him?" she persisted, suspicion and fear rising in her voice. "They said you had tried to conspire against him, you and Fiedler. Then why is he letting you go?"

Leamas had started the car and was soon driving fast along the narrow road. On either side, bare fields; in the distance, dark monotonous hills were mingling with the gathering darkness. Leamas looked at his watch.

"Were five hours from Berlin," he said. "We've got to make Köpenick by quarter to one. We should do it easily."

For a time Liz said nothing; she stared through the windshield down the empty road, confused and lost in a labyrinth of half-formed thoughts. A full moon had risen and the frost hovered in long shrouds across the fields. They turned onto an autobahn.

"Was I on your conscience, Alec?" she said at last. "Is that why you made Mundt let me go?"

Leamas said nothing.

"You and Mundt are enemies, aren't you?"

Still he said nothing. He was driving fast now, the speedometer showed a hundred and twenty kilometers; the autobahn was pitted and bumpy. He had his headlights on full, she noticed, and didn't bother to dip for oncoming traffic on the other lane. He drove roughly, learning forward, his elbows almost on the wheel.

"What will happen to Fiedler?" Liz asked suddenly and this time Leamas answered.

"He'll be shot."

"Then why didn't they shoot you?" Liz continued quickly. "You conspired with Fiedler against Mundt, that's what they said. You killed a guard. Why has Mundt let you go?"

"All right!" Leamas shouted suddenly. "I'll tell you. I'll tell you what you were never, never to know, neither you nor I. Listen: Mundt is London's man, their agent; they bought him when he was in England. We are witnessing the lousy end to a filthy, lousy operation to save Mundt's skin. To save him from a clever little Jew in his own Department who had begun to suspect the truth. They made us kill him, do you see, kill the Jew. Now you know, and God help us both."

The Wall

"If that is so, Alec," she said at last, "what was my part in all this?" Her voice was quite calm, almost matter-of-fact.

"I can only guess, Liz, from what I know and what Mundt told me before we left. Fiedler suspected Mundt; had suspected him ever since Mundt came back from England; he thought Mundt was playing a double game. He hated him, of course—why shouldn't he—but he was right, too: Mundt was London's man. Fiedler was too powerful for Mundt to eliminate alone, so London decided to do it for him. I can see them working it out, they're so damned academic; I can see them sitting around a fire in one of their smart bloody clubs. They knew it was no good just eliminating Fiedler—he might have told friends, published accusations: they had to eliminate *suspicion*. Public rehabilitation, that's what they organized for Mundt."

He swung into the left-hand lane to overtake a lorry and trailer. As he did so the lorry unexpectedly pulled out in front of him, so that he had to brake violently on the pitted road to avoid being forced into the crash-fence on his left.

"They told me to frame Mundt," he said simply, "they said he had to be killed, and I was game. It was going to be my last job. So I went to seed, and punched the grocer—You know all that."

"And made love?" she asked quietly.

Leamas shook his head. "But this is the point, you see," he continued. "Mundt knew it all, he knew the plan, he had me picked up, he and Fiedler. Then he let Fiedler take over, because he knew in the end Fiedler would hang himself. My job was to let them think what in fact was the truth: that Mundt was a British spy." He hesitated. "Your job was to discredit me. Fiedler was shot and Mundt was saved, mercifully delivered from a fascist plot. It's the old principle of love on the rebound.

"But how could they know about me; how could they know we would come together?" Liz cried. "Heavens above, Alec, can they even tell when people will fall in love?"

"It didn't matter—it didn't depend on that. They chose you because you were young and pretty and in the Party, because they knew you would come to Germany if they rigged an invitation. That man in the Labour Exchange, Pitt, he sent me up there, they knew I'd work at the library. Pitt was in the Service during the war and they squared him, I suppose. They only had to put you and me in contact, even for a day, it didn't matter, then afterwards they could call on you, send you the money, make it look like an affair even if it wasn't, don't you see? Make it look like an infatuation, perhaps. The only material point was that after bringing us together they should send you money as if it came at my request. As it was, we made it very easy for them. . . ."

"Yes, we did." And then she added, "I feel dirty, Alec, as if I'd been put out to stud."

Leamas said nothing.

"Did it ease your Department's conscience at all? Exploiting . . . somebody in the Party, rather than just anybody?" Liz continued.

Leamas said, "Perhaps. They don't really think in those terms. It was an operational convenience."

"I might have stayed in that prison, mightn't I? That's what Mundt wanted, wasn't it? He saw no point in taking the risk—I might have heard too much, guessed too much. After all, Fiedler was innocent, wasn't he? But then he's a Jew," she added excitedly, "so that doesn't matter so much, does it?"

"Oh, for God's sake!" Leamas exclaimed.

"It seems odd that Mundt let me go, all the same—even as part of the bargain with you," she mused. "I'm a risk now, aren't I? When we get back to England, I mean: a Party member knowing all this. . . . It doesn't seem logical that he should let me go."

"I expect," Leamas replied, "he is going to use our escape to demonstrate to the Praesidium that there are other Fiedlers in his Department who must be hunted down."

"And other Jews?"

"It gives him a chance to secure his position," Leamas replied curtly.

"By killing more innocent people? It doesn't seem to worry you much."

"Of course it worries me. It makes me sick with shame and anger and . . . But I've been brought up differently, Liz; I can't see it in black and white. People who play this game take risks. Fiedler lost and Mundt won. London won—that's the point. It was a foul, foul operation. But it's paid off, and that's the only rule." As he spoke his voice rose, until finally he was nearly shouting.

"You're trying to convince yourself," Liz cried. "They've done a wicked thing. How can you kill Fiedler? He was good, Alec; I know he was. And Mundt—"

"What the hell are you complaining about?" Leamas demanded roughly. "Your Party's always at war, isn't it? Sacrificing the individual to the mass. That's what it says. Socialist reality: fighting night and day—the relentless battle—that's what they say, isn't it? At least you've survived. I never heard that Communists preached the sanctity of human life—perhaps I've got it wrong," he added sarcastically. "I agree, yes I agree, you might have been destroyed. That was in the cards. Mundt's a vicious swine; he saw no point in letting you survive. His promise—I suppose he gave a promise to do his best by you—isn't worth a great deal. So you might have died—today, next year or twenty years from now—in a prison in the worker's paradise. And so might I. But I seem to remember the Party is aiming at the destruction of a whole class. Or have I got it wrong?" Extracting a packet of cigarettes from his jacket he handed her two, together with a box of matches. Her fingers trembled as she lit them and passed one back to Leamas.

"You've thought it all out, haven't you?" she asked.

"We happened to fit the mold," Leamas persisted, "and I'm sorry. I'm sorry for the others too—the others who fit the mold. But don't complain about the terms, Liz; they're Party terms. A small price for a big return. One sacrificed for many. It's not pretty, I know, choosing who it'll be—turning the plan into people."

She listened in the darkness, for a moment scarcely conscious of anything except the vanishing road before them, and the numb horror in her mind.

"But they let me love you," she said at last. "And you let me believe in you and love you."

"They used us," Leamas replied pitilessly. "They cheated us both because it was necessary. It was the only way. Fiedler was bloody nearly home already, don't you see? Mundt would have been caught; can't you understand that?"

"How can you turn the world upside down?" Liz shouted suddenly. "Fiedler was kind and decent, he was only doing his job, and now you've killed him. Mundt is a spy and a traitor and you protect him. Mundt is a Nazi, do you know that? He hates Jews. What side are you on? How can you . . . ?"

"There's only one law in this game," Leamas retorted. "Mundt is their man; he gives them what they need. That's easy enough to understand, isn't it? Leninism—the expediency of temporary alliances. What do you think spies are: priests, saints and martyrs? They're a squalid procession of vain fools, traitors too, yes; pansies, sadists and drunkards, people who play cowboys and Indians to brighten their rotten lives. Do you think they sit like monks in London, balancing the rights and wrongs? I'd have killed Mundt if I could, I hate his guts; but not now. It so happens that they need him. They need him so that the great moronic mass you admire can sleep soundly in their beds at night. They need him for the safety of ordinary, crummy people like you and me."

"But what about Fiedler—don't you feel anything for him?"

"This is a war," Leamas replied. "It's graphic and unpleasant because it's fought on a tiny scale, at close range; fought with a wastage of innocent life sometimes, I admit. But it's nothing, nothing at all beside other wars—the last or the next."

"Oh God," said Liz softly. "You don't understand. You don't want to. You're trying to persuade yourself. It's far more terrible, what they are doing; to find the humanity in people, in me and whoever else they use, to turn it like a weapon in their hands, and use it to hurt and kill—"

"Christ Almighty!" Leamas cried. "What else have men done since the world began? I don't believe in anything, don't you see—not even destruction or anarchy. I'm sick, sick of killing but I don't see what else they can do. They don't proselytize; they don't stand in pulpits or on party platforms and tell us to fight for Peace or for God or whatever it is. They're the poor sods who try to keep the preachers from blowing each other sky high."

"You're wrong," Liz declared hopelessly; "they're more wicked than all of us."

"Because I made love to you when you thought I was a tramp?" Leamas asked savagely.

"Because of their contempt," Liz replied; "contempt for what is real and good; contempt for love, contempt for . . ."

"Yes," Leamas agreed, suddenly weary. "That is the price they pay; to despise God and Karl Marx in the same sentence. If that is what you mean."

"It makes you the same," Liz continued; "the same as Mundt and all the rest. . . . I should know, I was the one who was kicked about, wasn't I? By them, by you because you don't care. Only Fiedler didn't. . . . But the rest of you . . . you all treated me as if I was . . . nothing . . . just currency to pay with. . . . You're all the same, Alec."

"Oh Liz," he said desperately, "for God's sake believe me. I hate it, I hate it all, I'm tired. But it's the world, it's mankind that's gone mad. We're a tiny price to pay . . . but everywhere's the same, people cheated and misled, whole lives thrown away, people shot and in prison, whole groups and classes of men written off for nothing. And you, your Party—God knows it was built on the bodies of ordinary people. You've never seen men die as I have, Liz. . . ."

As he spoke Liz remembered the drab prison courtyard, and the wardress saying, "It is a prison for those who slow down the march . . . for those who think they have the right to err."

Leamas was suddenly tense, peering forward through the windshield. In the headlights of the car Liz discerned a figure standing in the road. In his hand was a tiny light which he turned on and off as the car approached. "That's him," Leamas muttered; switched off the headlights and engine, and coasted silently forward. As they drew up, Leamas leaned back and opened the rear door.

Liz did not turn around to look at him as he got in. She was staring stiffly forward, down the street at the falling rain.

"Drive at thirty kilometers," the man said. His voice was taut, frightened. "I'll tell you the way. When we reach the place you must get out and run to the wall. The searchlight be shining at the point where you must climb. Stand in the beam of the searchlight. When the beam moves away begin to climb. You will have ninety seconds to get over. You go first," he said to Leamas, "and the girl follows. There are iron rungs in the lower part—after that you must pull yourself up as best you can. You'll have to sit on top and pull the girl up. Do you understand?"

"We understand," said Leamas. "How long have we got?"

"If you drive at thirty kilometers we shall be there in about nine minutes. The searchlight will be on the wall at five past one exactly. They can give you ninety seconds. Not more."

"What happens after ninety seconds?" Leamas asked.

"They can only give you ninety seconds," the man repeated; "otherwise it is too dangerous. Only one detachment has been briefed. They think you are being infiltrated into West Berlin. They've been told not to make it too easy. Ninety seconds are enough."

"I bloody well hope so," said Leamas drily. "What time do you make it?"

"I checked my watch with the sergeant in charge of the detachment," the man replied. A light went on and off briefly in the back of the car. "It is twelve forty-eight. We must leave at five to one. Seven minutes to wait."

They sat in total silence save for the rain pattering on the roof. The cobblestone road reached out straight before them, staged by dingy streetlights every hundred meters. There was no one about. Above them the sky was lit with the unnatural glow of arclights. Occasionally the beam of a searchlight flickered overhead, and disappeared. Far to the left Leamas caught sight of a fluctuating light just above the skyline, constantly altering in strength, like the reflection of a fire.

"What's that?" he asked, pointing toward it.

"Information Service," the man replied. "A scaffolding of lights. It flashes news headlines into East Berlin."

"Of course," Leamas muttered. They were very near the end of the road.

"There is no turning back," the man continued. "He told you that? There is no second chance."

"I know," Leamas replied.

"If something goes wrong—if you fall or get hurt—don't turn back. They shoot on sight within the area of the wall. You *must* get over."

"We know," Leamas repeated; "he told me."

"From the moment you get out of the car you are in the area."

"We know. Now shut up," Leamas retorted. And then he added, "Are you taking the car back?"

"As soon as you get out of the car I shall drive it away. It is a danger for me, too," the man replied.

"Too bad," said Leamas drily.

Again there was silence. Then Leamas asked, "Do you have a gun?"

"Yes," said the man, "but I can't give it to you; he said I shouldn't give it to you . . . that you were sure to ask for it."

Leamas laughed quietly. "He would," he said.

Leamas pulled the starter. With a noise that seemed to fill the street the car moved slowly forward.

They had gone about three hundred yards when the man whispered excitedly, "Go right here, then left." They swung into a narrow side street. There were empty market stalls on either side so that the car barely passed between them.

"Left here, now!"

They turned again, fast, this time between two tall buildings into what looked like a cul-de-sac. There was washing strung across the street, and Liz wondered whether they would pass under it. As they approached what seemed to be the dead end the man said, "Left again—follow the path." Leamas mounted the curb, crossed the pavement and they followed a broad footpath bordered by a broken fence to their left, and a tall, windowless building to their right. They heard a shout from somewhere above them, a woman's voice, and Leamas muttered "Oh, shut up" as he steered clumsily around a right-angle bend in the path and came almost immediately upon a major road.

"Which way?" he demanded.

"Straight across—past the chemist—between the chemist and the post office—there!" The man was leaning so far forward that his face was almost level with theirs. He pointed now, reaching past Leamas, the tip of his finger pressed against the windshield.

"Get back," Leamas hissed. "Get your hand away. How the hell can I see if you wave your hand around like that?" Slamming the car into first gear, he drove fast across the wide road. Glancing to his left, he was astonished to glimpse the plump silhouette of the Brandenburg Gate three hundred yards away, and the sinister grouping of military vehicles at the foot of it.

"Where are we going?" asked Leamas suddenly.

"We're nearly there. Go slowly now—left, left, go *left!*" he cried, and Leamas jerked the wheel in the nick of time; they passed under a narrow archway into a courtyard. Half the windows were missing or boarded up; the empty doorways gaped sightlessly at them. At the other end of the yard was an open gateway. "Through there," came the whispered command, urgent in the darkness; "then hard right. You'll see a streetlamp on your right. The one beyond it is broken. When you reach the second lamp, switch off the engine and coast until you see a fire hydrant. That's the place."

"Why the hell didn't you drive yourself?"

"He said you should drive; he said it was safer."

They passed through the gate and turned sharply to the right. They were in a narrow street, pitch-dark.

"Lights out!"

Leamas switched off the car lights, drove slowly forward toward the first streetlamp. Ahead, they could just see the second. It was unlit. Switching off the engine they coasted silently past it, until, twenty yards ahead of them, they discerned the dim outline of the fire hydrant. Leamas braked; the car rolled to a standstill.

"Where are we?" Leamas whispered. "We crossed the Leninallee, didn't we?"

"Greifswalder Strasse. Then we turned north. We're north of Bernauerstrasse."

"Pankow?"

"Just about. Look." The man pointed down a side street to the left. At the far end they saw a brief stretch of wall, gray-brown in the weary arclight. Along the top ran a triple strand of barbed wire.

"How will the girl get over the wire?"

"It is already cut where you climb. There is a small gap. You have one minute to reach the wall. Good-bye."

They got out of the car, all three of them. Leamas took Liz by the arm, and she started from him as if he had hurt her.

"Good-bye," said the German.

Leamas just whispered, "Don't start that car till we're over."

Liz looked at the German for a moment in the pale light: she had a brief impression of a young, anxious face; the face of a boy trying to be brave.

"Good-bye," said Liz. She disengaged her arm and followed Leamas across the road and into the narrow street that led toward the wall.

As they entered the street they heard the car start up behind them, turn and move quickly away in the direction they had come.

"Pull up the ladder, you bastard," Leamas muttered, glancing back at the retreating car.

Liz hardly heard him.

✦ Reading 61 ✦

The Wretched of the Earth

Frantz Fanon

National liberation, national renaissance, the restoration of nationhood to the people, commonwealth: whatever may be the headings used or the new formulas introduced, decolonisation is always a violent phenonomen. At whatever level we study it—relationships between individuals, new names for sports clubs, the human admixture at cocktail parties, in the police, on the directing boards of national or private banks—decolonisation is quite simply the replacing of a certain "species" of men by another "species" of men. Without any period of transition, there is a total, complete and absolute substitution. It is true that we could equally well stress the rise of a new nation, the setting up of a new State, its diplomatic relations, and its economic and political trends. But we have precisely chosen to speak of that kind of *tabula rasa* which characterises at the outset all decolonisation. Its unusual importance is that it constitutes, from the very first day, the minimum demands of the colonised. To tell the truth, the proof of success lies in a whole social structure being changed from the bottom up. The extraordinary importance of this change is that it is willed, called for, demanded. The need for this change exists in its crude state, impetuous and compelling, in the consciousness and in the lives of the men and women who are colonised. But the possibility of this change is equally experienced in the form of a terrifying future in the consciousness of another "species" of men and women: the colonisers.

Decolonisation, which sets out to change the order of the world, is, obviously, a programme of complete disorder. But it cannot come as a result of magical practices, nor of a natural shock, nor of a friendly understanding. Decolonisation, as we know, is a historical process: that is to say that it cannot be understood, it cannot become intelligible nor clear to itself except in the exact measure that we can discern the movements which give it historical form and content. Decolonisation is the meeting of two forces, opposed to each other by their very nature, which in fact owe their originality to that sort of substantification which results from and is nourished by the situation in the colonies. Their first encounter was marked by violence and their existence together—that is to say the exploitation of the native by the settler—was carried on by dint of a great array of bayonets and cannon. The settler and the native are old acquaintances. In fact, the settler is right when he speaks of knowing "them" well. For it is the settler who has brought the native into existence and who perpetuates his existence. The settler owes the fact of his very existence, that is to say his property, to the colonial system.

Decolonisation never takes place un-noticed, for it influences individuals and modifies them fundamentally. It transforms spectators crushed with their inessentiality into privileged actors, with the grandiose glare of history's floodlights upon them. It brings a natural rhythm into existence, introduced by new men, and with it a new language and a new humanity. Decolonisation is the veritable creation of new men. But this creation owes nothing of its legitimacy to any supernatural power; the "thing" which has been colonised becomes man during the same process by which it frees itself.

In decolonisation, there is therefore the need of a complete calling in question of the colonial situation. If we wish to describe it precisely, we might find it in the well-known words: "The last shall be first and the first last." Decolonisation is the putting into practice of this sentence. That is why, if we try to describe it, all decolonisation is successful.

From: Frantz Fanon, *The Wretched of the Earth,* trans. Constance Farrington (New York: Grove Press, Inc., 1963), pp. 29–34, 121–123, 252–255.

The naked truth of decolonisation evokes for us the searing bullets and bloodstained knives which emanate from it. For if the last shall be first, this will only come to pass after a murderous and decisive struggle between the two protagonists. That affirmed intention to place the last at the head of things, and to make them climb at a pace (too quickly, some say) the well-known steps which characterise an organised society, can only triumph if we use all means to turn the scale, including, of course, that of violence.

You do not turn any society, however primitive it may be, upside-down with such a programme if you are not decided from the very beginning, that is to say from the actual formulation of that programme, to overcome all the obstacles that you will come across in so doing. The native who decides to put the programme into practice, and to become its moving force, is ready for violence at all times. From birth it is clear to him that this narrow world, strewn with prohibitions, can only be called in question by absolute violence.

The colonial world is a world divided into compartments. It is probably unnecessary to recall the existence of native quarters and European quarters, of schools for natives and schools for Europeans; in the same way we need not recall Apartheid in South Africa. Yet, if we examine closely this system of compartments, we will at least be able to reveal the lines of force it implies. This approach to the colonial world, its ordering and its geographical lay-out will allow us to mark out the lines on which a decolonised society will be reorganised.

The colonial world is a world cut in two. The dividing line, the frontiers are shown by barracks and police stations. In the colonies it is the policeman and the soldier who are the official, instituted go-betweens, the spokesmen of the settler and his rule of oppression. In capitalist societies the educational system, whether lay or clerical, the structure of moral reflexes handed down from father to son, the exemplary honesty of workers who are given a medal after fifty years of good and loyal service, and the affection which springs from harmonious relations and good behaviour—all these esthetic expressions of respect for the established order serve to create around the exploited person an atmosphere of submission and of inhibition which lightens the task of policing considerably. In the capitalist countries a multitude of moral teachers, counsellors and "bewilderers" separate the exploited from those in power. In the colonial countries, on the contrary, the policeman and the soldier, by their immediate presence and their frequent and direct action maintain contact with the native and advise him by means of rifle-butts and napalm not to budge. It is obvious here that the agents of government speak the language of pure force. The intermediary does not lighten the oppression, nor seek to hide the domination; he shows them up and puts them into practice with the clear conscience of an upholder of the peace; yet he is the bringer of violence into the home and into the mind of the native.

The zone where the natives live is not complementary to the zone inhabited by the settlers. The two zones are opposed, but not in the service of a higher unity. Obedient to the rules of pure Aristotelian logic, they both follow the principle of reciprocal exclusivity. No conciliation is possible, for of the two terms, one is superfluous. The settlers' town is a strongly-built town, all made of stone and steel. It is a brightly-lit town; the streets are covered with asphalt, and the garbage-cans swallow all the leavings, unseen, unknown and hardly thought about. The settler's feet are never visible, except perhaps in the sea; but there you're never close enough to see them. His feet are protected by strong shoes although the streets of his town are clean and even, with no holes or stones. The settler's town is a well-fed town, an easy-going town; its belly is always full of good things. The settler's town is a town of white people, of foreigners.

The town belonging to the colonised people, or at least the native town, the negro village, the medina, the reservation, is a place of ill fame, peopled by men of evil repute. They are born there, it matters little where or how; they die there, it matters not where, nor how. It is a world without spaciousness; men live there on top of each other, and their huts are built one on top of the other. The native town is a hungry town, starved of bread, of meat, of shoes, of coal, of light. The native town is a crouching village, a town on its knees, a town wallowing in the mire. It is a town of niggers and dirty arabs. The look that the native turns on the settler's town is a look of lust, a look of envy; it expresses his dreams of possession—all manner of possession: to sit at the settler's table, to sleep in the settler's bed, with his wife if possible. The colonised man is an envious man. And this the settler knows very well; when their glances meet he ascertains bitterly, always on the defensive "They want to take our place." It is true, for there is no native who does not dream at least once a day of setting himself up in the settler's place.

This world divided into compartments, this world cut in two is inhabited by two different species. The originality of the colonial context is that economic reality, inequality and the immense difference of ways of life never come to mask the human realities. When you examine at close quarters the colonial context, it is evident that what parcels out the world is to begin with the fact of belonging to or not belonging to a given race, a given species. In the colonies the economic substructure is also a superstructure. The cause is the consequence; you are rich because you are white, you are white because you are rich. This is why Marxist analysis should always be slightly stretched every time we have to do with the colonial problem.

Everything up to and including the very nature of precapitalist society, so well explained by Marx, must here be thought out again. The serf is in essence different from the knight, but a reference to divine right is necessary to legitimise this statutory difference. In the colonies, the foreigner coming from another country imposed his rule by means of guns and machines. In defiance of his successful transplantation, in spite of his appropriation, the settler still remains a foreigner. It is neither the act of owning factories, nor estates, nor a bank balance which distinguishes the governing classes. The governing race is first and foremost those who come from elsewhere, those who are unlike the original inhabitants, "the others."

The violence which has ruled over the ordering of the colonial world, which has ceaselessly drummed the rhythm for the destruction of native social forms and broken up without reserve the systems of reference of the economy, the customs of dress and external life, that same violence will be claimed and taken over by the native at the moment when, deciding to embody history in his own person, he surges into the forbidden quarters. To wreck the colonial world is henceforward a mental picture of action which is very clear, very easy to understand and which may be assumed by each one of the individuals which constitute the colonised people. To break up the colonial world does not mean that after the frontiers have been abolished lines of communication will be set up between the two zones. The destruction of the colonial world is no more and no less that the abolition of one zone, its burial in the depths of the earth or its expulsion from the country.

The natives' challenge to the colonial world is not a rational confrontation of points of view. It is not a treatise on the universal, but the untidy affirmation of an original idea propounded as an absolute. The colonial world is a Manichean world. It is not enough for the settler to delimit physically, that is to say with the help of the army and the police force, the place of the native. As if to show the totalitarian character of colonial exploitation the settler paints the native as a sort of quintessence of evil. Native society is not simply described as a society lacking in values. It is not enough for the colonist to affirm that those values have disappeared from, or still better never existed in, the colonial world. The native is declared insensible to ethics; he represents not only the absence of values, but also the negation of values. He is, let us dare to admit, the enemy of values, and in this sense he is the absolute evil. He is the corrosive element, destroying all that comes near him; he is the deforming element, defiguring all that has to do with beauty or morality; he is the depository of maleficent powers, the unconscious and irretrievable instrument of blind forces. Monsieur Meyer could thus state seriously in the French National Assembly that the Republic must not be prostituted by allowing the Algerian people to become part of it. All values, in fact are irrevocably poisoned and diseased as soon as they are allowed in contact with the colonised race. The customs of the colonised people, their traditions, their myths—above all, their myths—are the very sign of that poverty of spirit and of their constitutional depravity. That is why we must put the DDT which destroys parasites, the bearers of disease, on the same level as the Christian religion which wages war on embryonic heresies and instincts, and on evil as yet unborn. The recession of yellow fever and the advance of evangelisation form part of the same balance-sheet. But the triumphant *communiqués* from the missions are in fact a source of information concerning the implantation of foreign influences in the core of the colonised people. I speak of the Christian religion, and no one need be astonished. The Church in the colonies is the white people's Church, the foreigner's Church. She does not call the native to God's ways but to the ways of the white man, of the master, of the oppressor. And as we know, in this matter many are called but few chosen.

* * *

History teaches us clearly that the battle against colonialism does not run straight away along the lines of nationalism. For a very long time the native devotes his energies to ending certain definite abuses: forced labour, corporal punishment, inequality of salaries, limitation of political rights, etc. This fight for democracy against the oppression of mankind will slowly leave the confusion of neoliberal universalism to emerge, sometimes laboriously, as a claim to nationhood. It so happens that the unpreparedness of the educated classes, the lack of practical links between them and the mass of the people, their laziness, and, let it be said, their cowardice at the decisive moment of the struggle will give rise to tragic mishaps.

National consciousness, instead of being the all-embracing crystallization of the innermost hopes of the whole people, instead of being the immediate and most obvious result of the mobilisation of the people, will be in any case only an empty shell, a crude and fragile travesty of what it might have been. The faults that we find in it are quite sufficient explanation of the facility with which, when dealing with young and independent nations, the nation is passed over for the race, and the tribe is preferred to the state. These are the cracks in the edifice which show the process of retrogression, that is so harmful and prejudicial to national effort and national unity. We shall see that such retrograde steps with all the weaknesses and serious dangers that they entail are the historical result of the incapacity of the national middle-class to rationalise popular action, that is to say their incapacity to see into the reasons for that action.

This traditional weakness, which is almost congenital to the national consciousness of under-developed countries, is not solely the result of the mutilation of the colonised people by the colonial regime. It is also the result of the intellectual laziness of the national middle-class, of its spiritual penury, and of the profoundly cosmopolitan mould that its mind is set in.

The national middle-class which takes over power at the end of the colonial regime is an under-developed middle-class. It has practically no economic power, and in any case it is in no way commesurate with the bourgeoisie of the mother country which it hopes to replace. In its wilful narcissism, the national middle-class is easily convinced that it can advantageously replace the middle-class of the mother country. But that same independence which literally drives it into a corner will give rise within its ranks to catastrophic reactions, and will oblige it to send out frenzied appeals for help to the former mother country. The university and merchant classes which make up the most enlightened section of the new state are in fact characterised by the smallness of their number and their being concentrated in the capital, and the type of activities in which they are engaged: business, agriculture and the liberal professions. Neither financiers nor industrial magnates are to be found within this national middle-class. The national bourgeoisie of under-developed countries is not engaged in production, nor in invention, nor building, nor labour: it is completely canalised into activities of the intermediary type. Its innermost vocation seems to be to keep in the running and to be part of the racket. The psychology of the national bourgeoisie is that of the business-man, not that of a captain of industry; and it is only too true that the greed of the settlers and the system of embargoes set up by colonialism has hardly left them any other choice.

Under the colonial system, a middle-class which accumulates capital is an impossible phenomenon. Now, precisely, it would seem that the historical vocation of an authentic national middle-class in an under-developed country is to repudiate its own nature in so far it as it is bourgeois, that is to say in so far as it is the tool of capitalism, and to make itself the willing slave of that revolutionary capital which is the people.

In an under-developed country an authentic national middle-class ought to consider as its bounden duty to betray the calling fate has marked out for it, and to put itself to school with the people: in other words to put at the people's disposal the intellectual and technical capital that it has snatched when going through the colonial universities. But unhappily we shall see that very often the national middle-class does not follow this heroic, positive, fruitful and just path; rather, it disappears with its soul set at peace into the shocking ways—shocking because anti-national—of a traditional bourgeoisie, of a bourgeoisie which is stupidly, contemptibly, cynically bourgeois.

* * *

Conclusion

Come, then, comrades; it would be as well to decide at once to change our ways. We must shake off the heavy darkness in which we were plunged, and leave it behind. The new day which is already at hand must find us firm, prudent and resolute.

We must leave our dreams and abandon our old beliefs and friendships of the time before life began. Let us waste no time in sterile litanies and nauseating mimicry. Leave this Europe where they are never done talking of Man, yet murder men everywhere they find them, at the corner of every one of their own streets, in all the corners of the globe. For centuries they have stifled almost the whole of humanity in the name of a so-called spiritual experience. Look at them today swaying between atomic and spiritual disintegration.

And yet it may be said that Europe has been successful in as much as everything that she has attempted has succeeded.

Europe undertook the leadership of the world with ardour, cynicism and violence. Look at how the shadow of her palaces stretches out ever further! Every one of her movements has burst the bounds of space and thought. Europe has declined all humility and all modesty; but she has also set her face against all solicitude and all tenderness.

She has only shown herself parsimonious and niggardly where men are concerned; it is only men that she has killed and devoured.

So, my brothers, how is it that we do not understand that we have better things to do than to follow that same Europe?

That same Europe where they were never done talking of Man, and where they never stopped proclaiming that they were only anxious for the welfare of Man: today we know with what sufferings humanity has paid for every one of their triumphs of the mind.

Come, then, comrades, the European game has finally ended; we must find something different. We today can do everything, so long as we do not imitate Europe, so long as we are not obsessed by the desire to catch up with Europe.

Europe now lives at such a mad, reckless pace that she has shaken off all guidance and all reason, and she is running headlong into the abyss; we would do well to avoid it with all possible speed.

Yet it is very true that we need a model, and that we want blueprints and examples. For many among us the European model is the most inspiring. We have therefore seen in the preceding pages to what mortifying set-backs such an imitation has led us. European achievements, European techniques and the European style ought no longer to tempt us and to throw us off our balance.

When I search for Man in the technique and the style of Europe, I see only a succession of negations of man, and an avalanche of murders.

The human condition, plans for mankind and collaboration between men in those tasks which increase the sum total of humanity are new problems, which demand true inventions.

Let us decide not to imitate Europe; let us combine our muscles and our brains in a new direction. Let us try to create the whole man, whom Europe has been incapable of bringing to triumphant birth.

Two centuries ago, a former European colony decided to catch up with Europe. It succeeded so well that the United States of America became a monster, in which the taints, the sickness and the inhumanity of Europe have grown to appalling dimensions.

Comrades, have we not other work to do than to create a third Europe? The West saw itself as a spiritual adventure. It is in the name of the spirit, in the name of the spirit of Europe, that Europe has made her encroachments, that she has justified her crimes and legitimised the slavery in which she holds the four-fifths of humanity.

Yes, the European spirit has strange roots. All European thought has unfolded in places which were increasingly more deserted and more encircled by precipices; and thus it was that the custom grew up in those places of very seldom meeting man.

A permanent dialogue with oneself and an increasingly obscene narcissism never ceased to prepare the way for a half delirious state, where intellectual work became suffering and the reality was not at all that of a living man, working and creating himself, but rather words, different combinations of words, and the tensions springing from the meanings contained in words. Yet some Europeans were found to urge the European workers to shatter this narcissism and to break with this unreality.

But in general, the workers of Europe have not replied to these calls; for the workers believe, too, that they are part of the prodigious adventure of the European spirit.

All the elements of a solution to the great problems of humanity have, at different times, existed in European thought. But the action of European men has not carried out the mission which fell to them, and which consisted of bringing their whole weight to bear violently to bear upon these elements, of modifying their arrangement and their nature, of changing them and finally of bringing the problem of mankind to an infinitely higher plane.

Today, we are present at the stasis of Europe. Comrades, let us flee from this motionless movement where gradually dialectic is changing into the logic of equilibrium. Let us reconsider the question of mankind. Let us reconsider the question of cerebral reality and of the cerebral mass of all humanity, whose connections must be increased, whose channels must be diversified and whose messages must be re-humanised.

Come, brothers, we have far too much work to do for us to play the game of rear-guard. Europe has done what she set out to do and on the whole she has done it well; let us stop blaming her, but let us say to her firmly that she should not make such a song and dance about it. We have no more to fear; so let us stop envying her.

The Third World today faces Europe like a colossal mass whose aim should be to try to resolve the problems to which Europe has not been able to find the answers.

But let us be clear: what matters is to stop talking about output, and intensification, and the rhythm of work.

No, there is no question of a return to Nature. It is simply a very concrete question of not dragging men towards mutilation, of not imposing upon the brain rhythms which very quickly obliterate it and wreck it. The pretext of catching up must not be used to push man around, to tear him away from himself or from his privacy, to break and kill him.

No, we do not want to catch up with anyone. What we want to do is to go forward all the time, night and day, in the company of Man, in the company of all men. The caravan should not be stretched out, for in that case each line will hardly see those who precede it; and men who no longer recognise each other meet less and less together, and talk to each other less and less.

It is a question of the Third World starting a new history of Man, a history which will have regard to the sometimes prodigious theses which Europe has put forward, but which will also not forget Europe's crimes, of which the most horrible was committed in the heart of man, and consisted of the pathological tearing apart of his functions and the crumbling away of his unity. And in the framework of the collectivity there were the differentiations, the stratification and the bloodthirsty tensions fed by classes; and finally, on the immense scale of humanity, there were racial hatreds, slavery, exploitation and above all the bloodless genocide which consisted in the setting aside of fifteen thousand millions of men.

So, comrades, let us not pay tribute to Europe by creating states, institutions and societies which draw their inspiration from her.

Humanity is waiting for something other from us than such an imitation, which would be almost an obscene caricature.

If we want to turn Africa into a new Europe, and America into a new Europe, then let us leave the destiny of our countries to Europeans. They will know how to do it better than the most gifted among us.

But if we want humanity to advance a step further, if we want to bring it up to a different level than that which Europe has shown it, then we must invent and we must make discoveries.

If we wish to live up to our peoples' expectations, we must seek the response elsewhere than in Europe.

Moreover, if we wish to reply to the expectations of the people of Europe, it is no good sending them back a reflection, even an ideal reflection, of their society and their thought with which from time to time they feel immeasurably sickened.

For Europe, for ourselves and for humanity, comrades, we must turn over a new leaf, we must work out new concepts, and try to set afoot a new man.

PART SEVENTEEN

THE NEW EUROPE

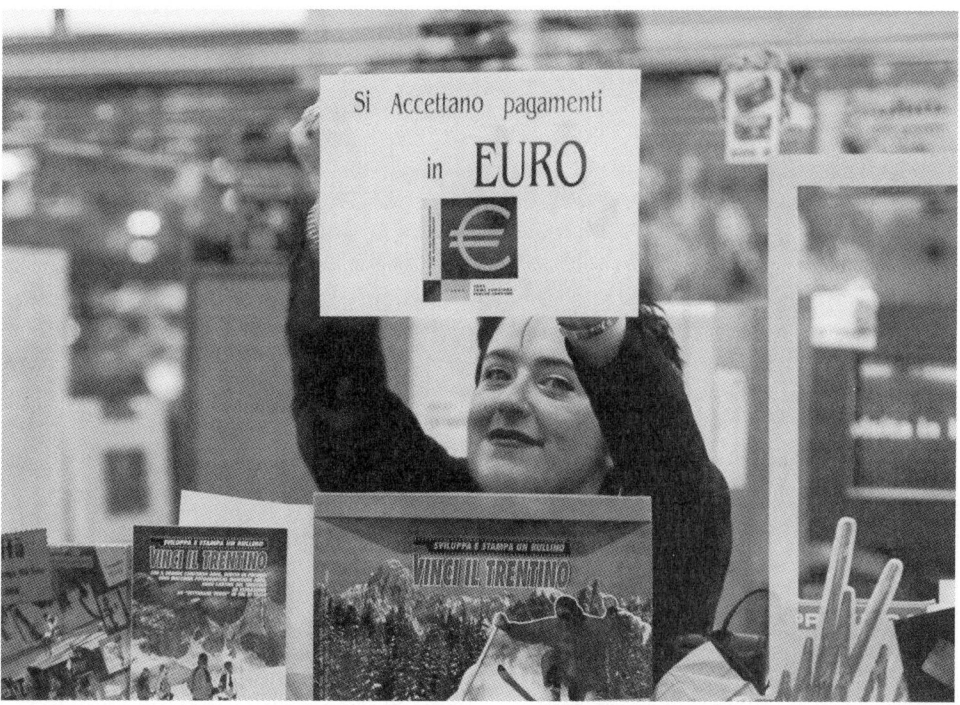

This Italian proclamation of the Euro, which in 1999 united the currencies of eleven European nations, suggests the high hopes for integrated economic and political activity.

The New Europe

Despite the Cold War, Europe emerged from World War II's devastation. With generous U.S. aid, the western nations prospered, whereas the eastern states had to rely on their own resources. Still, memories of the recent past, a dawning awareness of something awry on the other side of the Iron Curtain, the trauma of decolonialization, and a sense of malaise at the untrammeled pursuit of wealth all cast shadows on Western Europe. As many citizens pursued the good life, intellectuals engaged in tortured self-examination and joined some students and workers in strident criticism of existing society. Despite material backwardness and cultural hindrances, in Eastern Europe spiritual and cultural values thrived: In the West, as some observed, everything is possible and nothing is important; in the East, nothing is possible and everything is important. Europe remained divided and unsure of its role, with centers of gravity in the United States and Soviet Union rather than in traditional capitals.

Post-war incertitude received its classic expression in existentialism, a philosophy of personal introspection and independent decision making in a morally uncertain world. For Jean-Paul Sartre (1905–1980) and other French intellectuals, recent horrendous experience annihilated hope in religion or progressive ideologies. Existence's meaning—without God or Marx—resided in unrewarded personal commitment. Sartre's story, *The Wall* (1939), with its absurdist narrative, became the virtual theme song of post-war existentialism. Material well-being brought to the fore other unfinished agendas such as the women's question. A prominent women's spokesperson was Simone de Beauvoir (1908–1986), long-time partner of Sartre and writer of equal fame. De Beauvoir's *The Second Sex* outlined the case for women's liberation from male servitude. *Anti-Politics* by Georg Konrad (1933–), an Eastern European intellectual's response to post-war Europe's alleged political bankruptcy, assumes the moral equivalency between the democratic and communist states. The writings of Daniel Cohn-Bendit (1945–) and the Red Army Faction reflect strains of 1960s radicalism, whereas the Green proclamation by Petra Kelley (1947–1992) offers a moderate critique of unchecked economic growth. As their comments reveal, members of the National Front in France and other similar current movements resort to naked racism in answer to migrations from Africa and Asia as persons of color seek work and relief from post-colonial strife at home.

✦ Reading 62 ✦

The Wall

Jean-Paul Sartre

The story takes place during the Spanish Civil War. Arrested by the Falangists (supporters of Franco), the narrator is jailed with other anti-Franco prisoners awaiting their likely fate—the firing squad.

The Wall

They pushed us into a big white room and I began to blink because the light hurt my eyes. Then I saw a table and four men behind the table, civilians, looking over the papers. They had bunched another group of prisoners in the back and we had to cross the whole room to join them. There were several I knew and some others who must have been foreigners. The two in front of me were blond with round skulls; they looked alike. I supposed they were French. The smaller one kept hitching up his pants; nerves.

It lasted about three hours; I was dizzy and my head was empty; but the room was well heated and I found that pleasant enough: for the past 24 hours we hadn't stopped shivering. The guards brought the prisoners up to the table, one after the other. The four men asked each one his name and occupation. Most of the time they didn't go any further—or they would simply ask a question here and there: "Did you have anything to do with the sabotage of munitions?" Or "Where were you the morning of the 9th and what were you doing?" They didn't listen to the answers or at least didn't seem to. They were quiet for a moment and then looking straight in front of them began to write. They asked Tom if it were true he was in the International Brigade; Tom couldn't tell them otherwise because of the papers they found in his coat. They didn't ask Juan anything but they wrote for a long time after he told them his name.

"My brother José is the anarchist," Juan said, "you know he isn't here any more. I don't belong to any party, I never had anything to do with politics."

They didn't answer. Juan went on, "I haven't done anything. I don't want to pay for somebody else."

His lips trembled. A guard shut him up and took him away. It was my turn.

"Your name is Pablo Ibbieta?"

"Yes."

The man looked at the papers and asked me, "Where's Ramon Gris?"

"I don't know."

"You hid him in your house from the 6th to the 19th."

"No."

They wrote for a minute and then the guards took me out. In the corridor Tom and Juan were waiting between two guards. We started walking. Tom asked one of the guards, "So?"

"So what?" the guard said.

"Was that the cross-examination or the sentence?"

"Sentence," the guard said.

"What are they going to do with us?"

The guard answered dryly, "Sentence will be read in your cell."

As a matter of fact, our cell was one of the hospital cellars. It was terrifically cold there because of the drafts. We shivered all night and it wasn't much better during the day. I had spent the previous five days in a cell in a monastery, a sort of hole in the wall that must have dated from the middle ages: since there were a lot of prisoners and not much room, they locked us up anywhere. I didn't miss my cell; I hadn't suffered too much from the cold but I was alone; after a long time it gets irritating. In the cellar

---

From: *Existentialism from Dostoevsky to Sartre,* ed. Walter Kaufmann (Cleveland and New York: The World Publishing Company, 1956), pp. 223–240.

I had company. Juan hardly ever spoke: he was afraid and he was too young to have anything to say. But Tom was a good talker and he knew Spanish well.

There was a bench in the cellar and four mats. When they took us back we sat and waited in silence. After a long moment, Tom said, "We're screwed."

"I think so too," I said, "but I don't think they'll do anything to the kid."

"They don't have a thing against him," said Tom. "He's the brother of a militiaman and that's all."

I looked at Juan: he didn't seem to hear. Tom went on, "You know what they do in Saragossa? They lay the men down on the road and run over them with trucks. A Moroccan deserter told us that. They said it was to save ammunition."

"It doesn't save gas," I said.

I was annoyed at Tom: he shouldn't have said that.

"Then there's officers walking along the road," he went on, "supervising it all. They stick their hands in their pockets and smoke cigarettes. You think they finish off the guys? Hell no. They let them scream. Sometimes for an hour. The Moroccan said he damned near puked the first time."

"I don't believe they'll do that here," I said. "Unless they're really short on ammunition."

Day was coming in through four airholes and a round opening they had made in the ceiling on the left, and you could see the sky through it. Through this hole, usually closed by a trap, they unloaded coal into the cellar. Just below the hole there was a big pile of coal dust; it had been used to heat the hospital, but since the beginning of the war the patients were evacuated and the coal stayed there, unused; sometimes it even got rained on because they had forgotten to close the trap.

Tom began to shiver. "Good Jesus Christ, I'm cold," he said. "Here it goes again."

He got up and began to do exercises. At each movement his shirt opened on his chest, white and hairy. He lay on his back, raised his legs in the air and bicycled. I saw his great rump trembling. Tom was husky but he had too much fat. I thought how rifle bullets or the sharp points of bayonets would soon be sunk into this mass of tender flesh as in a lump of butter. It wouldn't have made me feel like that if he'd been thin.

I wasn't exactly cold, but I couldn't feel my arms and shoulders any more. Sometimes I had the impression I was missing something and began to look around for my coat and then suddenly remembered they hadn't given me a coat. It was rather uncomfortable. They took our clothes and gave them to their soldiers leaving us only our shirts—and those canvas pants that hospital patients wear in the middle of summer. After a while Tom got up and sat next to me, breathing heavily.

"Warmer?"

"Good Christ, no. But I'm out of wind."

Around eight o'clock in the evening a major came in with two *falangistas*. He had a sheet of paper in his hand. He asked the guard, "What are the names of those three?"

"Steinbock, Ibbieta and Mirbal," the guard said.

The major put on his eyeglasses and scanned the list: "Steinbock . . . Steinbock . . . Oh yes . . . You are sentenced to death. You will be shot tomorrow morning." He went on looking. "The other two as well."

"That's not possible," Juan said. "Not me."

The major looked at him amazed. "What's your name?"

"Juan Mirbal," he said.

"Well, your name is there," said the major. "You're sentenced."

"I didn't do anything," Juan said.

The major shrugged his shoulders and turned to Tom and me.

"You're Basque?"

"Nobody is Basque."

He looked annoyed. "They told me there were three Basques. I'm not going to waste my time running after them. Then naturally you don't want a priest?"

We didn't even answer.

He said, "A Belgian doctor is coming shortly. He is authorized to spend the night with you." He made a military salute and left.

"What did I tell you," Tom said. "We get it."

"Yes," I said, "it's a rotten deal for the kid."

I said that to be decent but I didn't like the kid. His face was too thin and fear and suffering had disfigured it, twisting all his features. Three days before he was a smart sort of kid, not too bad; but now he looked like an old fairy and I thought how he'd never be young again, even if they were to let him go. It wouldn't have been too hard to have a little pity for him but pity disgusts me, or rather it horrifies me. He hadn't said anything more but he had turned grey; his face and hands were both grey. He sat down again and looked at the ground with round eyes. Tom was good hearted, he wanted to take his arm, but the kid tore himself away violently and made a face.

"Let him alone," I said in a low voice, "you can see he's going to blubber."

Tom obeyed regretfully; he would have liked to comfort the kid, it would have passed his time and he wouldn't have been tempted to think about himself. But it annoyed me: I'd never thought about death because I never had any reason to, but now the reason was here and there was nothing to do but think about it.

Tom began to talk. "So you think you've knocked guys off, do you?" he asked me. I didn't answer. He began explaining to me that he had knocked off six since the beginning of August; he didn't realize the situation and I could tell he didn't *want* to realize it. I hadn't quite realized it myself, I wondered if it hurt much, I thought of bullets, I imagined their burning hail through my body. All that was beside the real question; but I was calm: we had all night to understand. After a while Tom stopped talking and I watched him out of the corner of my eye; I saw he too had turned grey and he looked rotten; I told myself "Now it starts." It was almost dark, a dim glow filtered through the airholes and the pile of coal and made a big stain beneath the spot of sky; I could already see a star through the hole in the ceiling: the night would be pure and icy.

The door opened and two guards came in, followed by a blonde man in a tan uniform. He saluted us. "I am the doctor," he said. "I have authorization to help you in these trying hours."

He had an agreeable and distinguished voice. I said, "What do you want here?"

"I am at your disposal. I shall do all I can to make your last moments less difficult."

"What did you come here for? There are others, the hospital's full of them."

"I was sent here," he answered with a vague look. "Ah! Would you like to smoke?" he added hurriedly, "I have cigarettes and even cigars."

He offered us English cigarettes and *puros,* but we refused. I looked him in the eyes and he seemed irritated. I said to him, "You aren't here on an errand of mercy. Besides, I know you. I saw you with the fascists in the barracks yard the day I was arrested."

I was going to continue, but something surprising suddenly happened to me; the presence of this doctor no longer interested me. Generally when I'm on somebody I don't let go. But the desire to talk left me completely; I shrugged and turned my eyes away. A little later I raised my head; he was watching me curiously. The guards were sitting on a mat. Pedro, the tall thin one, was twiddling his thumbs, the other shook his head from time to time to keep from falling asleep.

"Do you want a light?" Pedro suddenly asked the doctor. The other nodded "Yes": I think he was about as smart as a log, but he surely wasn't bad. Looking in his cold blue eyes it seemed to me that his only sin was lack of imagination. Pedro went out and came back with an oil lamp which he set on the corner of the bench. It gave a bad light but it was better than nothing: they had left us in the dark the night before. For a long time I watched the circle of light the lamp made on the ceiling. I was fascinated. Then suddenly I woke up, the circle of light disappeared and I felt myself crushed under an enormous weight. It was not the thought of death, or fear; it was nameless. My cheeks burned and my head ached.

I shook myself and looked at my two friends. Tom had hidden his face in his hands. I could only see the fat white nape of his neck. Little Juan was the worst, his mouth was open and his nostrils trembled. The doctor went to him and put his hand on his shoulder to comfort him: but his eyes stayed cold. Then I saw the Belgian's hand drop stealthily along Juan's arm, down to the wrist. Juan paid no attention. The Belgian took his wrist between three fingers, distractedly, the same time drawing back a little and turning his back to me. But I leaned backward and saw him take a watch from his pocket and look at it for a moment, never letting go of the wrist. After a minute he let the hand fall inert and went and leaned his back against the wall, then, as if he suddenly remembered something very important which had to be jotted down on the spot, he took a notebook from his pocket and wrote a few lines. "Bastard," I thought angrily, "let him come and take my pulse. I'll shove my fist in his rotten face."

He didn't come but I felt him watching me. I raised my head and returned his look. Impersonally, he said to me, "Doesn't it seem cold to you here?" He looked cold, he was blue.

"I'm not cold," I told him.

He never took his hard eyes off me. Suddenly I understood and my hands went to my face: I was drenched in sweat. In this cellar, in the midst of winter, in the midst of drafts, I was sweating. I ran my hands through my hair, gummed together with perspiration; at the same time I saw my shirt was damp and sticking to my skin: I had been dripping for an hour and hadn't felt it. But that swine of a Belgian hadn't missed a thing; he had seen the drops rolling down my cheeks and thought: this is the manifestation of an almost pathological state of terror; and he had felt normal and proud of being alive because he was cold. I wanted to stand up and smash his face but no sooner had I made the slightest gesture than my rage and shame were wiped out; I fell back on the bench with indifference.

I satisfied myself by rubbing my neck with my handkerchief because now I felt the sweat dropping from my hair onto my neck and it was unpleasant. I soon gave up rubbing, it was useless; my handkerchief was already soaked and I was still sweating. My bullocks were sweating too and my damp trousers were glued to the bench.

Suddenly Juan spoke. "You're a doctor?"

"Yes," the Belgian said.

"Does it hurt . . . very long?"

"Huh? When . . . ? Oh, no," the Belgian said paternally. "Not at all. It's over quickly." He acted as though he were calming a cash customer.

"But I . . . they told me . . . sometimes they have to fire twice."

"Sometimes," the Belgian said, nodding. "It may happen that the first volley reaches no vital organs."

"Then they have to reload their rifles and aim all over again?" He thought for a moment and then added hoarsely, "That takes time!"

He had a terrible fear of suffering, it was all he thought about: it was his age. I never thought much about it and it wasn't fear of suffering that made me sweat.

I got up and walked to the pile of coal dust. Tom jumped up and threw me a hateful look: I had annoyed him because my shoes squeaked. I wondered if my face looked as frightened as his: I saw he was sweating too. The sky was superb, no light filtered into the dark corner and I had only to raise my head to see the Big Dipper. But it wasn't like it had been: the night before I could see a great piece of sky from my monastery cell and each hour of the day brought me a different memory. Morning, when the sky was a hard, light blue, I thought of beaches on the Atlantic; at noon I saw the sun and I remembered a bar in Seville where I drank *manzanilla* and ate olives and anchovies; afternoons I was in the shade and I thought of the deep shadow which spreads over half a bull-ring leaving the other half shimmering in sunlight; it was really hard to see the whole world reflected in the sky like that. But now I could watch the sky as much as I pleased, it no longer evoked anything in me. I liked that better. I came back and sat near Tom. A long moment passed.

Tom began speaking in a low voice. He had to talk, without that he wouldn't have been able to recognize himself in his own mind. I thought he was talking to me but he wasn't looking at me. He was undoubtedly afraid to see me as I was, grey and sweating: we were alike and worse than mirrors of each other. He watched the Belgian, the living.

"Do you understand?" he said. "I don't understand."

I began to speak in a low voice too. I watched the Belgian. "Why? What's the matter?"

"Something is going to happen to us that I can't understand."

There was a strange smell about Tom. It seemed to me I was more sensitive than usual to odors. I grinned. "You'll understand in a while."

"It isn't clear," he said obstinately. "I want to be brave but first I have to know . . . Listen, they're going to take us into the courtyard. Good. They're going to stand up in front of us. How many?"

"I don't know. Five or eight. Not more."

"All right. There'll be eight. Someone'll holler 'aim!' and I'll see eight rifles looking at me. I'll think how I'd like to get inside the wall, I'll push against it with my back . . . with every ounce of strength I have, but the wall will stay, like in a nightmare. I can imagine all that. If you only knew how well I can imagine it."

"All right, all right!" I said, "I can imagine it too."

"It must hurt like hell. You know, they aim at the eyes and the mouth to disfigure you," he added mechanically. "I can feel the wounds already; I've had pains in my head and in my neck for the past hour. Not real pains. Worse. This is what I'm going to feel tomorrow morning. And then what?"

I well understood what he meant but I didn't want to act as if I did. I had pains too, pains in my body like a crowd of tiny scars. I couldn't get used to it. But I was like him, I attached no importance to it. "After," I said, "you'll be pushing up daisies."

He began to talk to himself: he never stopped watching the Belgian. The Belgian didn't seem to be listening. I knew what he had come to do; he wasn't interested in what we thought; he came to watch our bodies, bodies dying in agony while yet alive.

"It's like a nightmare," Tom was saying. "You want to think something, you always have the impression that it's all right, that you're going to understand and then it slips, it escapes you and fades away. I tell myself there will be nothing afterwards. But I don't understand what it means. Sometimes I almost can . . . and then it fades away and I start thinking about the pains again, bullets, explosions. I'm a materialist, I swear it to you; I'm not going crazy. But something's the matter. I see my corpse; that's not hard but *I'm* the one who sees it, with *my* eyes. I've got to think . . . think that I won't see anything anymore and the world will go on for the others. We aren't made to think that, Pablo. Believe me: I've already stayed up a whole night waiting for something. But this isn't the same: this will creep up behind us, Pablo, and we won't be able to prepare for it."

"Shut up," I said, "Do you want me to call a priest?"

He didn't answer. I had already noticed he had the tendency to act like a prophet and call me Pablo, speaking in a toneless voice. I didn't like that: but it seems all the Irish are that way. I had the vague impression he smelled of urine. Fundamentally, I hadn't much sympathy for Tom and I didn't see why, under the pretext of dying together, I should have any more. It would have been different with some others. With Ramon Gris, for example. But I felt alone between Tom and Juan. I liked that better, anyhow: with Ramon I might have been more deeply moved. But I was terribly hard just then and I wanted to stay hard.

He kept on chewing his words, with something like distraction. He certainly talked to keep himself from thinking. He smelled of urine like an old prostate case. Naturally, I agreed with him, I could have said everything he said: it isn't *natural* to die. And since I was going to die, nothing seemed natural to me, not this pile of coal dust, or the bench, or Pedro's ugly face. Only it didn't please me to think the same things as Tom. And I knew that, all through the night, every five minutes, we would keep on thinking things at the same time. I looked at him sideways and for the first time he seemed strange to me: he wore death on his face. My pride was wounded: for the past 24 hours I had lived next to Tom, I had listened to him, I had spoken to him and I knew we had nothing in common. And now we looked as much alike as twin brothers, simply because we were going to die together. Tom took my hand without looking at me.

"Pablo, I wonder . . . I wonder if it's really true that everything ends."

I took my hand away and said, "Look between your feet, you pig."

There was a big puddle between his feet and drops fell from his pants-leg.

"What is it," he asked, frightened.

"You're pissing in your pants" I told him.

"It isn't true," he said furiously. "I'm not pissing. I don't feel anything."

The Belgian approached us. He asked with false solicitude, "Do you feel ill?"

Tom did not answer. The Belgian looked at the puddle and said nothing.

"I don't know what it is," Tom said ferociously. "But I'm not afraid. I swear I'm not afraid."

The Belgian did not answer. Tom got up and went to piss in a corner. He came back buttoning his fly, and sat down without a word. The Belgian was taking notes.

All three of us watched him because he was alive. He had the motions of a living human being, the cares of a living human being; he shivered in the cellar the way the living are supposed to shiver; he had an obedient, well-fed body. The rest of us hardly felt ours—not in the same way anyhow. I wanted to feel my pants between my legs but I didn't dare; I watched the Belgian, balancing on his legs, master of his muscles, someone who could think about tomorrow. There we were, three bloodless shadows; we watched him and we sucked his life like vampires.

Finally he went over to little Juan. Did he want to feel his neck for some professional motive or was he obeying an impulse of charity? If he was acting by charity it was the only time during the whole night.

He caressed Juan's head and neck. The kid let himself be handled, his eyes never leaving him, then suddenly, he seized the hand and looked at it strangely. He held the Belgian's hand between his own two hands and there was nothing pleasant about them, two grey pincers gripping this fat and reddish hand. I suspected what was going to happen and Tom must have suspected it too: but the Belgian didn't see a thing, he smiled paternally. After a moment the kid brought the fat red hand to his mouth and tried to bite it. The Belgian pulled away quickly and stumbled back against the wall. For a second he looked at us with horror, he must have suddenly understood that we were not men like him. I began to laugh and one of the guards jumped up. The other was asleep, his wide open eyes were blank.

I felt relaxed and over-excited at the same time. I didn't want to think any more about what would happen at dawn, at death. It made no sense. I only found words or emptiness. But as soon as I tried to think of anything else I saw rifle barrels pointing at me. Perhaps I lived through my execution twenty times; once I even thought it was for good: I must have slept a minute. They were dragging me to the wall and I was struggling; I was asking for mercy. I woke up with a start and looked at the Belgian: I was afraid I might have cried out in my sleep. But he was stroking his moustache, he hadn't noticed anything. If I had wanted to, I think I could have slept a while; I had been awake for 48 hours. I was at the end of my rope. But I didn't want to lose two hours of life: they would come to wake me up at dawn, I would follow them, stupefied with sleep and I would have croaked without so much as an "Oof!"; I didn't want that, I didn't want to die like an animal, I wanted to understand. Then I was afraid of having nightmares. I got up, walked back and forth, and, to change my ideas, I began to think about my past life. A crowd of memories came back to me pell-mell. There were good and bad ones—or at least I called them that *before*. There were faces and incidents. I saw the face of a little *novillero* who was gored in Valencia during the *Feria*, the face of one of my uncles, the face of Ramon Gris. I remembered my whole life: how I was out of work for three months in 1926, how I almost starved to death. I rememberd a night I spent on a bench in Granada: I hadn't eaten for three days. I was angry, I didn't want to die. That made me smile. How madly I ran after happiness, after women, after liberty. Why? I wanted to free Spain, I admired Pi y Margall, I joined the anarchist movement, I spoke in public meetings: I took everything as seriously as if I were immortal.

At that moment I felt that I had my whole life in front of me and I thought, "It's a damned lie." It was worth nothing because it was finished. I wondered how I'd been able to walk, to laugh with the girls: I wouldn't have moved so much as my little finger if I had only imagined I would die like this. My life was in front of me, shut, closed, like a bag and yet everything inside of it was unfinished. For an instant I tried to judge it. I wanted to tell myself, this is a beautiful life. But I couldn't pass judgment on it; it was only a sketch; I had spent my time counterfeiting eternity, I had understood nothing. I missed nothing: there were so many things I could have missed, the taste of *manzanilla* or the baths I took in summer in a little creek near Cadiz; but death had disenchanted everything.

The Belgian suddenly had a bright idea. "My friends," he told us, "I will undertake—if the military administration will allow it—to send a message for you, a souvenir to those who love you . . ."

Tom mumbled, "I don't have anybody."

I said nothing. Tom waited an instant then looked at me with curiosity. "You don't have anything to say to Concha?"

"No."

I hated this tender complicity: it was my own fault, I had talked about Concha the night before, I should have controlled myself. I was with her for a year. Last night I would have given an arm to see her again for five minutes. That was why I talked about her, it was stronger than I was. Now I had no more desire to see her, I had nothing more to say to her. I would not even have wanted to hold her in my arms: my body filled me with horror because it was grey and sweating—and I wasn't sure that her body didn't fill me with horror. Concha would cry when she found out I was dead, she would have no taste for life for months afterward. But I was still the one who was going to die. I thought of her soft, beautiful eyes. When she looked at me something passed from her to me. But I knew it was over: if she looked at me *now* the look would stay in her eyes, it wouldn't reach me. I was alone.

Tom was alone too but not in the same way. Sitting cross-legged, he had begun to stare at the bench with a sort of smile, he looked amazed. He put out his hand and touched the wood cautiously as if he were afraid of breaking something, then drew back his hand quickly and shuddered. If I had been Tom I wouldn't have amused myself by touching the bench; this was some more Irish nonsense, but I too found that objects had a funny look: they were more obliterated, less dense than usual. It was enough for me to look at the bench, the lamp, the pile of coal dust, to feel that I was going to die. Naturally I couldn't think clearly about my death but I saw it everywhere, on things, in the way things fell back and kept their distance, discreetly, as people who speak quietly at the bedside of a dying man. It was *his* death which Tom had just touched on the bench.

In the state I was in, if someone had come and told me I could go home quietly, that they would leave me my life whole, it would have left me cold: several hours or several years of waiting is all the same when you have lost the illusion of being eternal. I clung to nothing, in a way I was calm. But it was a horrible calm—because of my body; my body, I saw with its eyes, I heard with its ears, but it was no longer me; it sweated and trembled by itself and I didn't recognize it any more. I had to touch it and look at it to find out what was happening, as if it were the body of someone else. At times I could still feel it, I felt sinkings, and fallings, as when you're in a plane taking a nose-dive, or I felt my heart beating. But that didn't reassure me. Everything that came from my body was all cockeyed. Most of the time it was quiet and I felt no more than a sort of weight, a filthy presence against me; I had the impression of being tied to an enormous vermin. Once I felt my pants and I felt they were damp; I didn't know whether it was sweat or urine, but I went to piss on the coal pile as a precaution.

The Belgian took out his watch, looked at it. He said, "It is three-thirty."

Bastard! He must have done it on purpose. Tom jumped; we hadn't noticed time was running out; night surrounded us like a shapeless, somber mass, I couldn't even remember that it had begun.

Little Juan began to cry. He wrung his hands, pleaded, "I don't want to die. I don't want to die."

He ran across the whole cellar waving his arms in the air then fell sobbing on one of the mats. Tom watched him with mournful eyes, without the slightest desire to console him. Because it wasn't worth the trouble: the kid made more noise than we did, but he was less touched: he was like a sick man who defends himself against his illness by fever. It's much more serious when there isn't any fever.

He wept: I could clearly see he was pitying himself; he wasn't thinking about death. For one second, one single second, I wanted to weep myself, to weep with pity for myself. But the opposite happened: I glanced at the kid, I saw his thin sobbing shoulders and I felt inhuman: I could pity neither the others nor myself. I said to myself, "I want to die cleanly."

Tom had gotten up, he placed himself just under the round opening and began to watch for daylight. I was determined to die cleanly and I only thought of that. But ever since the doctor told us the time, I felt time flying, flowing away drop by drop.

It was still dark when I heard Tom's voice: "Do you hear them?"

Men were marching in the courtyard.

"Yes."

"What the hell are they doing? They can't shoot in the dark."

After a while we heard no more. I said to Tom, "It's day."

Pedro got up, yawning, and came to blow out the lamp. He said to his buddy, "Cold as hell."

The cellar was all grey. We heard shots in the distance.

"It's starting," I told Tom. "They must do it in the court in the rear."

Tom asked the doctor for a cigarette. I didn't want one; I didn't want cigarettes or alcohol. From that moment on they didn't stop firing.

"Do you realize what's happening," Tom said.

He wanted to add something but kept quiet, watching the door. The door opened and a lieutenant came in with four soldiers. Tom dropped his cigarette.

"Steinbock?"

Tom didn't answer. Pedro pointed him out.

"Juan Mirbal?"

"On the mat."

"Get up," the lieutenant said.

Juan did not move. Two soldiers took him under the arms and set him on his feet. But he fell as soon as they released him.

The soldiers hesitated.

"He's not the first sick one," said the lieutenant. "You two carry him; they'll fix it up down there."

He turned to Tom. "Let's go."

Tom went out between two soldiers. Two others followed, carrying the kid by the armpits. He hadn't fainted; his eyes were wide open and tears ran down his cheeks. When I wanted to go out the lieutenant stopped me.

"You Ibbieta?"

"Yes."

"You wait here; they'll come for you later."

They left. The Belgian and the two jailers left too, I was alone. I did not understand what was happening to me but I would have liked it better if they had gotten it over with right away. I heard shots at almost regular intervals; I shook with each one of them. I wanted to scream and tear out my hair. But I gritted my teeth and pushed my hands in my pockets because I wanted to stay clean.

After an hour they came to get me and led me to the first floor, to a small room that smelt of cigars and where the heat was stifling. There were two officers sitting smoking in the armchairs, papers on their knees.

"You're Ibbieta?"

"Yes."

"Where is Ramon Gris?"

"I don't know."

The one questioning me was short and fat. His eyes were hard behind his glasses. He said to me, "Come here."

I went to him. He got up and took my arms, staring at me with a look that should have pushed me into the earth. At the same time he pinched my biceps with all his might. It wasn't to hurt me, it was only a game: he wanted to dominate me. He also thought he had to blow his stinking breath square in my face. We stayed for a moment like that, and I almost felt like laughing. It takes a lot to intimidate a man who is going to die; it didn't work. He pushed me back violently and sat down again. He said, "It's his life against yours. You can have yours if you tell us where he is."

These men dolled up with their riding crops and boots were still going to die. A little later than I, but not too much. They busied themselves looking for names in their crumpled papers, they ran after other men to imprison or suppress them; they had opinions on the future of Spain and on other subjects. Their little activities seemed shocking and burlesqued to me; I couldn't put myself in their place, I thought they were insane. The little man was still looking at me, whipping his boots with the riding crop. All his gestures were calculated to give him the look of a live and ferocious beast.

"So? You understand?"

"I don't know where Gris is," I answered. "I thought he was in Madrid."

The other officer raised his pale hand indolently. This indolence was also calculated. I saw through all their little schemes and I was stupefied to find there were men who amused themselves that way.

"You have a quarter of an hour to think it over," he said slowly. "Take him to the laundry, bring him back in fifteen minutes. If he still refuses he will be executed on the spot."

They knew what they were doing: I had passed the night in waiting; then they had made me wait an hour in the cellar while they shot Tom and Juan and now they were locking me up in the laundry; they must have prepared their game the night before. They told themselves that nerves eventually wear out and they hoped to get me that way.

They were badly mistaken. In the laundry I sat on a stool because I felt very weak and I began to think. But not about their proposition. Of course I knew were Gris was; he was hiding with his cousins, four kilometers from the city. I also knew that I would not reveal his hiding place unless they tortured me (but they didn't seem to be thinking about that). All that was perfectly regulated, definite and in no way interested me. Only I would have liked to understand the reasons for my conduct. I would rather die than give up Gris. Why? I didn't like Ramon Gris any more. My friendship for him had died a little while before dawn at the same time as my love for Concha, at the same time as my desire to live. Undoubtedly I thought highly of him: he was tough. But it was not for this reason that I consented to die in his place; his life had no more value than mine; no life had value. They were going to slap a man up against a wall and shoot at him till he died, whether it was I or Gris or somebody else made no difference. I knew he was more useful than I to the cause of Spain but I thought to hell with Spain and anarchy; nothing was important. Yet I was there, I could save my skin and give up Gris and I refused to do it. I found that somehow comic; it was obstinacy. I thought, "I must be stubborn!" And a droll sort of gaiety spread over me.

They came for me and brought me back to the two officers. A rat ran out from under my feet and that amused me. I turned to one of the *falangistas* and said, "Did you see the rat?"

He didn't answer. He was very sober, he took himself seriously. I wanted to laugh but I held myself back because I was afraid that once I got started I wouldn't be able to stop. The *falangista* had a moustache. I said to him again, "You ought to shave off your moustache, idiot." I thought it funny that he would let the hairs of his living being invade his face. He kicked me without great conviction and I kept quiet.

"Well," said the fat officer, "have you thought about it?"

I looked at them with curiosity, as insects of a very rare species. I told them, "I know where he is. He is hidden in the cemetery. In a vault or in the gravediggers' shack."

It was a farce. I wanted to see them stand up, buckle their belts and give orders busily.

They jumped to their feet. "Let's go. Molés, go get fifteen men from Lieutenant Lopez. You," the fat man said, "I'll let you off if you're telling the truth, but it'll cost you plenty if you're making monkeys out of us."

They left in a great clatter and I waited peacefully under the guard of *falangistas*. From time to time I smiled, thinking about the spectacle they would make. I felt stunned and malicious. I imagined them lifting up tombstones, opening the doors of the vaults one by one. I represented this situation to myself as if I had been someone else: this prisoner obstinately playing the hero, these grim falangistas with their moustaches and their men in uniform running among the graves; it was irresistibly funny.

After half an hour the little fat man came back alone. I thought he had come to give the orders to execute me. The others must have stayed in the cemetery.

The officer looked at me. He didn't look at all sheepish. "Take him into the big courtyard with the others," he said. "After the military operations a regular court will decide what happens to him."

"Then they're not . . . not going to shoot me? . . . "

"Not now, anyway. What happens afterwards is none of my business."

I still didn't understand. I asked, "But why . . . ?"

He shrugged his shoulders without answering and the soldiers took me away. In the big courtyard there were about a hundred prisoners, women, children and a few old men. I began walking around the central grass-plot, I was stupefied. At noon they let us eat in the mess hall. Two or three people questioned me. I must have known them, but I didn't answer: I didn't even know where I was.

Around evening they pushed about ten new prisoners into the court. I recognized Garcia, the baker. He said, "What damned luck you have! I didn't think I'd see you alive."

"They sentenced me to death," I said, "and then they changed their minds. I don't know why."

"They arrested me at two o'clock," Garcia said.

"Why?" Garcia had nothing to do with politics.

"I don't know," he said. "They arrest everybody who doesn't think the way they do. He lowered his voice. "They got Gris."

I began to tremble. "When?"

"This morning. He messed it up. He left his cousin's on Tuesday because they had an argument. There were plenty of people to hide him but he didn't want to owe anything to anybody. He said, 'I'd go and hide in Ibbieta's place, but they got him, so I'll go hide in the cemetery.' "

"In the cemetery?"

"Yes. What a fool. Of course they went by there this morning, that was sure to happen. They found him in the grave-digger's shack. He shot at them and they got him."

"In the cemetery!"

Everything began to spin and I found myself sitting on the ground: I laughed so hard I cried.

✦ Reading 63 ✦

The Second Sex

Simone de Beauvoir

Woman is the victim of no mysterious fatality; the peculiarities that identify her as specifically a woman get their importance from the significance placed upon them. They can be surmounted, in the future, when they are regarded in new perspectives. Thus, as we have seen, through her erotic experience woman feels—and often detests—the domination of the male; but this is no reason to conclude that her ovaries condemn her to live forever on her knees. Virile aggressiveness seems like a lordly privilege only within a system that in its entirety conspires to affirm masculine sovereignty; and woman *feels* herself profoundly passive in the sexual act only because she already *thinks* of herself as such. Many modern women who lay claim to their dignity as human beings still envisage their erotic life from the standpoint of a tradition of slavery since it seems to them humiliating to lie beneath the man, to be penetrated by him, they grow tense in frigidity. But if the reality were different, the meaning expressed symbolically in amorous gestures and postures would be different, too: a woman who pays and dominates her lover can, for example, take pride in her superb idleness and consider that she is enslaving the male who is actively exerting himself. And here and now there are many sexually well balanced couples whose notions of victory and defeat are giving place to the idea of an exchange.

As a matter of fact, man, like woman, is flesh, therefore passive, the plaything of his hormones and of the species, the restless prey of his desires. And she, like him, in the midst of the carnal fever, is a consenting, a voluntary gift, an activity; they live out in their several fashions the strange ambiguity of existence made body. In those combats where they think they confront one another, it is really against the self that each one struggles, projecting into the partner that part of the self which is repudiated; instead of living out the ambiguities of their situation, each tries to make the other bear the abjection and tries to reserve the honor for the self. If, however, both should assume the ambiguity with a clear-sighted modesty, correlative of an authentic pride, they would see each other as equals and would live out their erotic drama in amity. The fact that we are human beings is infinitely more important than all the peculiarities that distinguish human beings from one another; it is never the given that confers superiorities: "virtue," as the ancients called it, is defined at the level of "that which depends on us." In both sexes is played out the same drama of the flesh and the spirit of finitude and transcendence; both are gnawed away by time and laid in wait for by death, they have the same essential need for one another; and they can gain from their liberty the same glory. If they were to taste it, they would no longer be tempted to dispute fallacious privileges, and fraternity between them could then come into existence.

I shall be told that all this is utopian fancy, because woman cannot be made over unless society has first made her really the equal of man. Conservatives have never failed in such circumstances to refer to that vicious circle; history, however, does not revolve. If a caste is kept in a state of inferiority, no doubt it remains inferior; but liberty can break the circle. Let the Negroes vote and they become worthy of having the vote; let woman be given responsibilities and she is able to assume them. The fact is that oppressors cannot be expected to make a move of gratuitous generosity; but at one time the revolt of the oppressed, at another time even the very evolution of the privileged caste itself, creates new situations; thus men have been led, in their own interest, to give partial emancipation to women: it remains only for women to continue their ascent,

From: Simone de Beauvoir, *The Second Sex*, ed. and trans. H. M. Pashley (New York: Bantam Books, 1961), pp. 675–677.

and the successes they are obtaining are an encouragement for them to do so. It seems almost certain that sooner or later they will arrive at complete economic and social equality, which will bring about an inner metamorphosis.

However this may be, there will be some to object that if such a world is possible it is not desirable. When woman is "the same" as her male, life will lose its salt and spice. This argument, also, has lost its novelty: those interested in perpetuating present conditions are always in tears about the marvelous past that is about to disappear, without having so much as a smile for the young future. It is quite true that doing away with the slave trade meant death to the great plantations, magnificent with azaleas and camellias, it meant ruin to the whole refined Southern civilization. The attics of time have received its rare odd laces along with the clear pure voices of the Sistine *castrati,* and there is a certain "feminine charm" that is also on the way to the same dusty repository. I agree that he would be a barbarian indeed who failed to appreciate exquisite flowers, rare lace, the crystal-clear voice of eunuch, and feminine charm.

When the "charming woman" shows herself in all her splendor, she is a much more exalting object than the idiotic paintings, overdoors, scenery, showman's garish signs, popular chromos," that excited Rimbaud; adorned with the most modern artifices, beautified according to the newest techniques, she comes down from the remoteness of the ages, from Thebes, from Crete, from Chichén-Itzá and she is also the totem set up deep in the African jungle; she is a helicopter and she is a bird; and there is this the greatest wonder of all: under her tinted hair the forest murmur becomes a thought, and words issue from her breasts. Men stretch forth avid hands toward the marvel, but when they grasp it it is gone; the wife, the mistress, speak like everybody else through their mouths: their words are worth just what they are worth; their breasts also. Does such a fugitive miracle—and one so rare—justify us in perpetuating a situation that is baneful for both sexes? One can appreciate the beauty of flowers, the charm of women, and appreciate them at their true value; if these treasures cost blood or misery, they must be sacrificed.

✦ Reading 64 ✦

Antipolitics

George Konrad

Peace: Anti-Yalta

To find the main reason for today's threat of war, we must go back to the year 1945, to Yalta. It was there that a helpless Europe was divided; it was there that agreements were reached for military zones of occupation that would become political spheres of interest as well. Yalta gave birth to a system of international relations based upon a state of rivalry and equilibrium between the Soviet Union and the United States. Whether the three old gentlemen who met there knew it or not, the idea of the Iron Curtain was born at Yalta, a symbol of great-power logic. Three old men—Roosevelt, Stalin, and Churchill—decided the fate of hundreds of millions for decades to come, the hundreds of millions having to respect their decision.

What a dirty trick of history! The allies who were defending mankind from fascist inhumanity hastened, on the very eve of victory, to strike an imperialist bargain, a pact between Anglo-Saxon and Soviet imperialism. They were able to do it because they commanded the biggest battalions, and went ahead and did it because—despite all the universalist rhetoric—nationalism, the ideology of the expansive nationstate, impelled them to. They thought it their historic right as victors to dictate the terms of peace. They made the mistake of thinking—whether in good faith or bad, we don't know—that on the will of the victor can be based the peace of a continent. A mistake with a long history, to be sure: for thousands of years, an unjust peace following one war has led to the next conflict. A powerful victor makes an arbitrary peace that the vanquished cannot accept.

The implication of Yalta is that the military status quo determines the political status quo. The morality of Yalta is simple: those who have the bombs and tanks decide the social and political system. Since the United States and the Soviet Union had the most bombs and tanks, they were called to lead the world. Later—by the fearful light of Hiroshima—their calling was confirmed, for only these two giant nation-states had the resources to build arsenals of nuclear weapons.

Thus whoever has the power of annihilation is called to lead the world. The Soviet and American presidents have more power than all the tyrants of history combined. Jehovah had power because he could destroy the world. I look at those two faces and I blanch. I wouldn't entrust the fate of humanity to even Aristotle and Kant. Is it possible that the destiny of mankind will be a parody? Is it possible that the Lord means to put an end to our species through a second Fall? Did He put the button of the Last Judgment under the fingers of two vain, frail old men? If they are human, like all the sons and daughters of Cain, their fingers must weigh heavily on the button. I don't trust in their wisdom, only in their fear of death.

The present status quo in Europe represents the petrifaction of an exceptional state of postwar occupation. Diplomatic declarations and the political consensus of nations agree in presenting this exceptional situation as a normal state of affairs. At Helsinki all the states involved solemnly declared that henceforward this absurdity would be law.

Why does the West refuse to accept the presence of Soviet troops in Afghanistan? Because they haven't been there very long. Their presence in East Central Europe is reasonable and acceptable by now, because they have been there nearly forty years. And it is all the more acceptable because American forces are present in Western Europe.

From: George Konrad, *Antipolitics: An Essay,* trans Richard E. Allen (San Diego, New York, London: Harcourt Brace Jovanovich, 1984), pp. 1–23.

Limited national sovereignty, as circumscribed by the terms of the Warsaw Pact, is bearable because the rather more loosely restricted national sovereignty defined by NATO is bearable. Indeed, both sets of limitations are geopolitical givens, respected by every rational politician. To question the partition of Europe is dangerous and misleading, because it fosters the illusion that it is possible to question it.

The West is not strong enough to compel the Soviet forces stationed in other countries to return home. At most, it can protest their expansion, however little impact that may make on Soviet military conduct. If, however, the West really wants to see those forces return home, why not make the Russians an offer advantageous to both sides? One might, for example, propose a mutual and balanced withdrawal of forces—not reduction, but withdrawal. Is it a mad fancy to enunciate the principle that no country should keep soldiers on the territory of another? I remember how, on October 23, 1956, the young men and women of Budapest chanted their new rhyme:

Soldiers from everywhere,
Go home and stay there.

I have liked this little verse ever since; a quarter of a century later, it seems more timely than ever.

A hard rule to follow, granted! There are always reasons for offering hospitality to foreign troops. A great power easily finds cooperative local politicians who will call in its forces, set up a client government, and then legalize the presence of the great power's troops, claiming it is the will of the occupied nation. There is always some mounting danger to avert, of course, always something sacred to defend—humanitarian interests, revolutionary achievements, democratic principles; the people's welfare must be defended from the people themselves.

I don't know of a single instance where one of the great powers occupied a small country in order to topple a local dictatorship and thereby free the people. If it is only a matter of a tyrannical regime oppressing a people, then—regrettably—national sovereignty must be respected and interference in internal affairs avoided. Idi Amin's grotesque depredations were tolerated by both great powers. They both have their share of client dictatorships, picturesque and absurd, but no one will trouble these petty dictators as long as they don't go against the interests of their patrons.

The interests of the great powers, and theirs alone, demand that they keep troops on the soil of other countries. The United States keeps 350,000 soldiers as a tripwire in Europe; it has accepted responsibility for West Berlin; in what is increasingly a symbolic gesture, it maintains conventional forces in Western Europe, on a soil that more and more is shifting beneath their feet. The ground is shaky beneath the Russians' feet, too, simply because they are here in Europe and not at home in the Soviet Union. Eastern Europe's nationalisms have reawakened, and it will be more and more difficult to put them to sleep again.

What is needed is not so much a radical change in the relations of military power as some way for normal social, economic, and cultural conditions to assert themselves freely and fully. It is not at all certain that the two superpowers must come to blows. Let them go on demonstrating that they can spend ever increasing sums on sophisticated weaponry; they will not gain much by it.

At the present time no one has a comprehensive strategy for peace. There is no theory about how the present system of international relations might be transformed. Neither West nor East has been able to make a broad, historic proposal to the other. No recommendations have appeared on positive ways to bring about coexistence and greater partnership. Only broad proposals are worth making, since partial ones invariably founder amid mutual suspicion. It is worthwhile thinking only in terms of the alternatives of war and peace, not in terms of the ebb and flow of détente and the Cold War.

It might seem easier for the West, which is less inflexible, to offer a useful alternative proposal to tame the bear. It is remarkable that the West, with its knack for achieving sensible compromises, has as yet made no concrete and comprehensive proposal to the Soviet Union. Not only has no government done so; no Western society has offered a rational plan which would carry advantages for the power elite and hence be acceptable to them, which would afford some scope in the world to the Russian people's pride, and which would not link peace to the humiliation of the Russian elite. The world is big enough for their abilities to find a place in it, too.

It is possible to imagine the gradual, controlled transformation of the Soviet empire—the U.S.S.R. and its dependent allies—into a community of nations capable of behaving like a partner toward the countries of Western Europe. Such a development, while making greater demands on the intelligence of the Soviet intellectual community, would also assure them of more initiative in world affairs. Today that is not the case: there are more Soviet agents in the world than scholars and students. The Russians must be afforded tranquillity so they can reform their economy and administrative system. They must have help if they are to put their fear of attack behind them and turn their faces toward the West. For if the Soviet Union doesn't want war, it must accept the pluralism which spans the northern hemisphere from Europe to America and on to Japan (and which may one day continue on across China and Russia to complete the circle).

To date the West has had no positive strategy of peace; it has merely rejected with suspicion the more or less propagandistic proposals of the Soviets. But the West doesn't lack the political capacity to take a creative initiative. Standing by Yalta is not a long-term strategy, but merely a ratification of the status quo, which is an impossibility in any longer perspective. The peoples of Central Europe should ponder this carefully; twice already, unsettled conditions in their region have led to world war.

If the West wants Yalta, the Soviet Union will move beyond Yalta—by moving westward. If the West wants Yalta, it can have November 4, 1956, in Budapest, August 21, 1968, in Prague, and December 13, 1981, in Warsaw. After every such aggression the West laments, protests, and looks on with alarm. Then by and by it signs a new agreement, largely for public relations purposes, while in the background the arms race goes on undisturbed.

The Americans and the Russians both demonstrate what they can do. The more they demonstrate it, the more threatened they feel. Disarmament has never yet been mutual, and so it has never been successful. Technical agreements about the size of arsenals don't lead to peace. It is difficult to dissuade any leadership from arming, if it feels threatened.

The Soviet Union has less room for maneuver because the tensions are building up within its empire; yet the leaders want to maintain that empire because they identify the empire's survival with their own. Anxious about their own power, they try to reassure themselves by overarming. As long as they will not negotiate about a German peace treaty and reunification, their troops will remain in Hungary and missiles will be pointed at Hungarian cities.

The present situation is unnatural and unsettling. The Iron Curtain gives rise to fears on both sides that the other will try to breach it, and provokes efforts by both sides to prevent that through military superiority. We have every reason to demand a general settlement; addressing the great questions of the day should not wait upon petty party squabbles. Deciding how to maintain the military balance following a mutual troop withdrawal would be a technical matter. Before that, however, political agreement must be reached on the questions that can profitably be taken up. So long as Russian and American troops glare at each other across the Elbe, there must be a better alternative. But what is it?

A United States of Europe based on the transcendence of a common European undertaking is the only possibility. A United States of *Western* Europe simply won't work in the present political context, since some Western European states belong to the Atlantic alliance while others have chosen neutrality. And Western European unity is being eroded still further by the divisive ideological struggles that surface as more and more Western Europeans, faced with a bipolar world, are drawn to neutrality. Today's Western Europe has no independent political philosophy, and so it offers none of the transcendence that would give meaning to a common enterprise like integration.

America perhaps refuses to concert its strategy with its European allies because the allies have no consistent strategy. Those allies want to preserve the status quo, but events are running ahead of them. There are independent national policies; these differ from the overall Atlantic course, however, less as creative initiatives than in their greater indulgence toward the Soviet bloc.

Not a single European government has made the cardinal peace proposal: an appeal for the removal of the Iron Curtain. Europe's politicians have no bold, incisive peace strategy and don't seek to launch any useful debate. This intellectual passivity is simply a retreat before Soviet peace propaganda, which uses military force to make Europeans and the whole world acknowledge that what the Soviets acquired in World War II is theirs. From the Pacific Ocean to the Iron Curtain, their empire is a seamless whole; to contest it from within is counterrevolution, while to contest it from without is to meddle in their internal affairs. The Helsinki Declaration only confirmed, three decades afterward, the validity of the agreements reached at Yalta and, later in 1945, at Potsdam.

It is pleasant to commiserate with the unfortunate Eastern European cousins, but let no one think the West is going to make any trouble on their account. They got détente, they got credits, what more do they want? What more? They want a creative initiative, a concrete, tangible peace proposal, a plan to take down the Iron Curtain. They want Western Europeans to understand that while Eastern Europe remains under occupation, Western Europeans cannot live in security. Western Europe is moving toward neutrality of its own accord, without even trying to demand that Eastern Europe be neutralized in exchange. It takes little intelligence to cling to the ideology either of blind loyalty to NATO or of unilateral concessions. Western Europe will find a worthy place for itself in the world only when it no longer allows the U.S.-Soviet dichotomy to determine its place.

To prevent a third world war, all foreign troops must be withdrawn from Europe. The fundamental guarantee of peace is a mutual agreement among the European states to withdraw from the two military blocs and abolish the Iron Curtain. Through a process of gradual integration, the western corner of the Eurasian land mass might then develop into a European confederation.

Does it make sense to ask whether there are any proposals for a nonviolent solution that might prevent Europe from becoming the scene of a third and final world war? It is we who are at stake, we Europeans. It is because of us that the two greatest nation-states in the world confront each other. Our intellectual failings brought about the baleful situation in which our continent is cut in two. European nation-states, European political doctrines, and the collective short-sightedness of respected European politicians are responsible for the Iron Curtain. No European political class is blameless; no European nation is exempt. Nowhere in Europe can a realistic public opinion pretend that it remains unaffected by the Iron Curtain, by its influence today and its possible consequences tomorrow.

It is an unobservant European who fails to notice that the Iron Curtain is made of explosive material. Western Europe rests its back against a wall of dynamite, while blithely gazing out over the Atlantic. I consider Western Europe's good fortune as uncertain as our misfortune. Caught between the United States and the Soviet Union, we Europeans can assure peace only if we detach ourselves from them militarily by mutual agreement, and then go on to draw the two parts of a divided Europe together again.

The International Ideological War: A Contest of National Political Elites

If we were to consider carefully, as a student of contemporary history might, what concrete conflicts of interests divide the Soviet and American people today, we would be surprised to find how few there are. And if we looked to see how many opportunities for mutually beneficial cooperation between the two there are, if they suspended the ideological war, we would be surprised at how many there are.

The ideological war is a fact, but far from an unalterable fact. It is the only war against which ideas have a chance of success, of building bridges between Moscow and Washington. It is precisely this hope that should spur independent people everywhere to apply the closest ethical scrutiny to those intellectuals who, under the Damocles' sword of multiple overkill, go on pursuing the intellectually sterile operations of ideological war, fraying the slender cord by which the sword is suspended. Intellectual cheerleaders are more dangerous today than ever before.

Ideology is a cloud that obscures as much as it explains; it confers upon the world whatever shape we like. Ideological competition follows from the existence of ideologies, but it doesn't follow that the competition must also be a nuclear one. It follows from the nature of ideology that our age has a certain style. More and more, the style of our time is to treat our human situation as a game—a game with ever more precise rules. It is an immanent, relativistic, understanding approach, dialectical, ironic, and critical of ideology. Part of this game is to subject to close intellectual and moral scrutiny those feverish laborers in the vineyard of ideological war as they pursue, with staggering conscientiousness, their labors of obfuscation.

In point of fact, it is not ideologies that contend today, nor is it systems like capitalism and communism. Anyone who believes that two systems and two ideologies are pitted against each other today has fallen victim to the secularized metaphysics of our civilization, which looks for a duel between God and Satan in what is, after all, only a game. Russians and Americans—their political classes, that is—circle each other in the ring. Each of the two world heavyweight champions would like to show he is the strongest in the world; they are playing a game with each other whose paraphernalia include nuclear missiles. Yet it is impossible to construct from the Soviet-American conflict an ideological dichotomy along whose axis the values of our continent can be ranged. The antitheses which fill our mental horizon—capitalism versus state socialism, democracy versus totalitarianism, market economy versus planned economy—are forced mythologies which the intelligentsias of East and West either confuse with reality or else, being aware that they are not very precise appellations, seek to square with the real facts.

What is basic and decisive is the strategy of the nation-state, which the political class of every nation devises and then declares to be identical with their country's interest. The various universalist appeals to the working class or to Christianity, to freedom or to socialism, are merely weapons in the strategy of the nation-state. We stand close to a third world war today because the American and Russian political classes have chosen a strategy of confrontation and of a prestige fight for world supremacy.

Politicians do the things they do because they want to do them, and for no other reason. If they didn't want to do them, they wouldn't. They would step down and cease to be politicians. If politicians make war, then the war has happened because the politicians wanted to make war. We too are at fault when these men take us into war, because, from stupidity or cowardice, we let them play with fire. I consider the demythologizing of politics to be the first duty of grown, thinking people. It is our business because it is the only way we can save our lives.

Europe suffered two world wars because of Franco-German rivalry, which once appeared so fateful but today seems quite contrived. The question of who should be master in Europe played a larger role in their contest than any concrete economic, demographic, or territorial conflict of interest. The game ended both times with the far-from-glorious triumph of France, and along the way Europe fell under the domination of the two peripheral powers, the Soviet Union and the United States. The question was answered: the strongest nation in Europe (or Eurasia) was neither France nor Germany, but Russia.

Ideologies played their part, too, but the struggle of nations was the essential thing, and the result was what might have been expected: the biggest nation was the strongest one. A race for prestige between two middle-sized European nations delivered up our continent to two enormous extra-European nation-states. Neither ideology nor any continental community of interest was able to prevent the struggle of the political classes of those two states for the hegemony of Europe. If there had been no Franco-German rivalry, there would have been no World War I; if there had been no World War I, there would have been no Hitler. If there had been no Hitler, there would have been no Yalta.

Yet all of European culture bore responsibility for World War I, philosophies as well as historical theories, poetic myths as well as formulations of interest. The fundamental values of the European intelligentsia were to blame as well as the bluster of the nation-state.

All three universal spiritual currents—Christianity, liberalism, and socialism—subordinated themselves to the ethos of particularism, the sentimental belligerence of the nation-state's bureaucracy—nationalism. Army chaplains rendered abundantly unto Caesar the things that were his; they exalted the murderous heroic deed. Liberals, according to their nineteenth-century custom, identified the conquest or defense of markets and sources of raw materials with the defense of civilization. Socialists looked into their hearts and discovered that they were no worse patriots than the others; they too could shoot at their comrades of other nationalities. From Zurich, meanwhile, Lenin saw that war economy offered a royal road to a system of redistributive state communism.

The romanticism of the nation-state triumphed everywhere. Overrefined poets prattled of redemption by fire; impotence identified vigor with bloodshed. And what has happened since? Nothing. Another world war, with three times as many dead, then the preparation of the physical and spiritual arsenal for a third. And the cream of our culture is complicitous in that labor of preparation, by virtue of their feckless impotence in the face of it.

It was totally senseless that so many people should perish over the foolish question of who should rule in Europe—Germans or Frenchmen—for the question was answerable in advance: neither would rule. Nor was it a novel notion even then that each and every people should take care of its own affairs, cooperating with the others in linking together the cultures and institutions of the continent to create a better society.

Today too, it is completely senseless for us to die over the foolish question of who is to rule the world—Russia or America. Neither is going to rule. Neither has a right or a mission to lead the world, nor indeed even the potential to do so. To be sure, both superpowers have an interest in justifying their egotism by appealing to some universal, international, and majoritarian principle of legitimacy. A powerful nation-state can found its claims to quasi-global authority only on supranational values in the second half of the twentieth century, following the collapse of the German bid for world hegemony with its heavy reliance on nationalistic ideas. For world dominion, universalist ideas are required today; and the real interests of the inhabitants of every country must be linked with those ideas.

The driving force behind the struggle for world power is not an ideological commitment to any social and political system, or to the values of a given culture; it is the craving of the strongest national elites for world dominion as found primarily in their political class, and in their military and technical elites as well. It is likely that the representatives of both the Russian and American power elite fancy the idea that they have a mission to lead the world. Men can invent few libidinous fantasies more enjoyable than those of world domination. For the power professional, power on a worldwide scale is the greatest earthly good.

The alternatives to the ideal of world power can only be metaphysical, ethical, aesthetic, and scientific; but statesmen, by reason of their occupation, are necessarily more interested in political power than in metaphysics or ethics, aesthetics or scientific knowledge. The medium of politics is power over people—power backed up by weapons. The not very cultivated intelligentsia that forms the political, military, and bureaucratic elite of every nation-state is too red-blooded and too commonplace to find any pleasure more voluptuous than the sensual experience of power.

Advocate of Human Rights: Which Superpower?

The Russians say that their conflict with America is a class struggle, that the contest of nation-states has a class character in which they represent the international working class, and America the international bourgeoisie. Yet an American worker might well wonder what advantages the Russian workers have that need to be defended, by force of arms if necessary. The working class holds power in neither America nor Russia, and by whatever name one characterizes the power elites of these two great states, no workers are to be found in their ranks.

In the one country as in the other it is politicians, high-level bureaucrats, industrial and military leaders, influential experts and ideologues, diplomats, and leading academics who are in the saddle. No doubt there are differences between the two countries in the composition of their power-elites, but they are not great enough to explain in sociological terms the present nuclear confrontation.

Unquestionably, these two elites are engaged in an international competition. We would like, however, to narrow the circle of competitors somewhat. It is not at all certain that the top-level managers of the Russian and American economies feel that they are involved in a life-and-death struggle with each other. They can find as many reasons for cooperation as for conflict. Nor do I see any reason why there shouldn't be room on earth for Russia's writers, artists, and scholars and for their American counterparts as well. Even Russian and American boxers, it seems to me, have little desire to aim nuclear missiles at each other, tough customers though they undoubtedly are.

In the Soviet world, Marxism-Leninism provides an explanation for the missiles: the irreconcilable, unrelenting struggle between bourgeoisie and proletariat, between the capitalist and socialist world systems. Peaceful coexistence is only an ideological concession, justified as a more effective form of international class struggle that demands less sacrifice of human life. It's even possible to manipulate the clichés of Marxist-Leninist literature in such a way that nuclear missiles follow from peaceful coexistence itself.

On the Russian side the conflict is the work of politicians, military men, ideologues, and journalists, while the rest of society, bewildered and beguiled by propaganda, has little choice but to go along, though many certainly believe that the imperialists seriously threaten them and that America is the source of the biggest trouble. However rapidly Russian national sentiment and a neo-Slavophile sense of mission may be gaining ground in their society, the Russian political elite still need Marxism-Leninism, if only because it holds together their empire and assures them supporters elsewhere in the world.

Why should other nations be enthusiastic about the Russians being the dominant nation in Europe, or even indeed in the world? The expansionist rhetoric of one nation is not enough to assure the integrity of a multinational empire. Russophilism may be useful to make Russian hearts swell with pride; for the Ukrainians, Estonians, and Tadzhiks, however, a Soviet ideology is needed. Yet it is no secret in Kiev and Tbilisi, I think, that this ideology comes labeled "Made in Moscow." It is the ideology of Russian domination.

For those outside the Soviet Union, something else is required: the ideology of the world socialist movement, in which belonging to the Soviet camp is a source of pride and not misfortune.

Here in Budapest it's perfectly clear that Marxism-Leninism is needed to explain why Soviet troops are still here, almost forty years after the end of World War II. The legitimacy of Marxism-Leninism is reinforced also by feelings of respect for the hundreds of thousands of Russian soldiers who fell on Hungarian, Polish, and Czech soil during World War II. Even today their sacrifice is often emphasized in the private conversation of Soviet leaders to explain why they regard our western (rather than our eastern) borders as their own frontier. The Soviet dead and the socialist world system are reason enough why we should go on living the way we do and not the way that would be proper and natural for us.

What is at stake are Russian interests, but the Russians act as if it were the interests of socialism. And they are wise to do so: the fascist experiments demonstrated that radical nationalism, with its mythology of an exclusive ruling nation, can never offer a permanent basis for dominion over other peoples. Soviet Marxism, on the other hand, is an export commodity. There is a demand for it in the developing countries, where it may come in handy for those destined to be the intellectuals, military leaders, and officials of the local dictatorships, and where it may be needed as a source of hope by the workers who toil on the periphery of the capitalist world, where there is neither consumer abundance nor democracy. And of course Marxism-Leninism has its followers, loyal to Moscow, beyond the confines of the Soviet bloc. Their relationship to the Soviet Union can be complex and indirect, but for the most part it is direct enough and not very complicated.

First comes Soviet Marxism, then come arms exports, advisers to help introduce the Soviet model, organizational experience with secret police and state culture. State-socialist dictatorship may not be perfect, but it offers a simple working model and is at least as exportable as liberal market economy and pluralist democracy. State society can be created quickly, but civil society takes a long time to build. Martial law can be proclaimed within hours. In one day, a whole host of things can be forbidden. One can nationalize easily, quickly, and decisively. The know-how and technology are ready at hand; the advisers know exactly how to apply them. It would be ungracious to expect them to know how to assure the freedom and well-being of a country as well.

It would be all the more ungracious because the Americans don't dispatch experts on freedom and well-being to the Third World either. To their Central American neighbors they send the same goods as the Russians, it seems: weapons and police experts. There are and will be pro-Soviet societies in the Third World to whom America can offer no better alternative than competition on the open world market—a competition in which those societies, unless unusually rich in natural resources, have a very small chance of coming out ahead.

In Vietnam, America suffered a sociological, cultural, and ideological defeat even before the failure of its military effort. It proved unable to offer South Vietnam any sort of reform outweighing the lure of communism. Since then, it appears, the American elite has learned little from its defeat. However prodigally it may give out money for weapons, it is as parsimonious as ever with the world's poor countries when it comes to giving out knowledge and democratic rights.

Like the Soviet Union in Eastern Europe, the United States cannot make itself loved in Latin America. In both places, crude national interest and great-power arrogance show through only too clearly. Nationalism in Eastern Europe is anti-Soviet, and in Latin America anti-American. The arrogance of power so blinds the Soviet and American elites that they can only take offense at this without being able to do anything about it. They are incapable of dealing with small nations in the way they should and the way those nations expect: on a footing of equality.

For Vietnam, things were different after the whole of that country came within the Soviet sphere of influence. The millennium did not dawn then and there for Vietnam, and the Vietnamese had to learn that the world they had fought for was a hard, hard world indeed. Little by little, the small nations are learning that it is not well to pay homage to either great power, and that the enemy of one's enemy is far from being one's friend. This accumulating experience may very well set bounds to the spread of Soviet Marxism and the Soviet model. The markets know the merchandise now, and the demand for it is falling off. The Great Russian exporter has to find a fresh packaging and a new marketing strategy.

It has been even easier for the American elite to cloak an itch for world power in the form of an ethic of global responsibility, in part perhaps because the Americans remained isolationist for so long, well past the time when their Russian counterparts had become frank expansionists. The American elite has a global responsibility to democracy and perhaps even to God as well. God and democracy: there you have America's Marxism-Leninism. And if, in the defense of those two sacred values, corporations acquire superprofits, generals acquire bases, and diplomats and propagandists acquire extraordinary influence, perhaps that is only a manifestation of the Biblical truth that to him who hath shall be given.

The leaders of a great nation-state need more than power; they also need the comfortable conviction that they represent the noblest possible ideas. The Protestant ethic regards with blue-eyed astonishment those cynics who smile ironically at this marriage of good conscience and material advantage. Perhaps that is why America's self-image (both popular and intellectual) is so pervaded by liberal moralism. Seen from here in Budapest, America's democracy and its versatile liberal economy seem rather attractive. At the same time, it is remarkable how little America has done for the spread of democracy. Democracy is found today in those places where it would have existed anyway—where, after the collapse of fascism, internal political dynamics would themselves have vindicated the democratic alternative, or where the European idea of freedom was able to build upon local traditions and society's demands.

In those place, however, where the Americans found undemocratic regimes of various kinds—monarchies, fascistoid military dictatorships, and the like—they were content with military and economic cooperation, and regarded the poverty and oppression of the people as an internal affair of their clients. Indeed, in those countries where democratic popular movements or political elites mobilized autonomous forces—where the nationalism of the poor nations struggled to win independence from both superpowers—the Americans strove for no less than the suppression of those aspirations for autonomy.

So far as we East Central Europeans are concerned, we have learned that de facto America recognizes Soviet hegemony over our area. It supports strivings for autonomy (whether successful or unsuccessful) only insofar as they can be exploited for propaganda purposes to counter centrifugal tendencies in the American camp.

Dissidents—autonomous intellectuals—are the same the world over, irrespective of their political philosophies. Whenever they chance to meet, they know one another by instinct. But I would think twice about exchanging the position of a Hungarian dissident for that of a Turkish or Southeast Asian or Latin American dissenter. It is possible that, in their shoes, I might long ago have been turned over for torture or even killed. No doubt American liberals are aware of this and no doubt they deplore it as well.

Recently we witnessed an attempt to make defense of human rights the ideological leading edge of American foreign policy, as a dramatic response to the limitation of human rights in the Soviet-type countries. Today, however, the American government is gradually removing human rights from the agenda; *Realpolitik* has triumphed over idealism. Meanwhile the ideologues declare that human rights violations are less serious if they happen in friendly countries rather than communist ones.

As I write these lines, American politicians are being moved to profound moral indignation by the violation of human rights in Poland, while Soviet politicians are being moved to profound moral indignation by the violation of human rights in El Salvador. This all-too-evident selectivity can only move the observer to profound cynicism about the moral rhetoric of the superpowers. It also suggests that we cannot expect our freedom from either of them, for neither one is particularly interested in our freedom. We can expect freedom only from ourselves, from our own patient, stubborn efforts to win it.

Move to socialism

Politically
- make them aware of the situation + they need to know that Govt. = enemy
- Create a nation where the people handle their own affairs + participate in the struggles
- Make a new political party that's different from all the other
- May Day can turn into an overthrow of capitalism + make a socialist state
- Revolution during elections because the workers aren't being treated fair

✦ Reading 65 ✦

Obsolete Communism

Daniel and Gabriel Cohn-Bendit

When the workers realize that they are being swindled out of their wage increases by rising prices, when they see that the same docile parliamentarians cannot stop playing their game of endlessly discussing decisions they themselves have never taken, when the top brass get round to imposing on students the educational reforms that have been worked out by some official in the Ministry of Education to ensure ever-better NCO's for the future:

We Must be Ready with the Answer

The Action Committees propose:

—to inform the population of the real political and social situation and the prospects opened up by the May crisis:

—to explain that the elections merely divert the struggle of the masses into the parliamentary field, mined by the enemy, and in which the political parties will once again prove their ineffectuality;

—to help the people to organize themselves, to construct a political system in which they themselves will take charge of the management and administration of their own affairs;

—to participate in all the struggles which are being waged and to support the factory strikes by fighting the repressive measures of the authorities (expulsion of foreigners, Gestapo style raids, banning of revolutionary groups, etc. . . .) and by organizing for self-defence.

The Action Committees want:

—to oppose the creation of any new political party on the lines of those we know already, all of which must sooner or later fit into the existing system;

—to unite in the streets, in the factories, and in the suburban communes, all those who agree with the above analysis and who realize that the struggle begun on 3 May can end in the overthrow of the capitalist system and the installation of a socialist state;

—to coordinate resistance at the Paris level and then at the national one, to fight in the front lines of the revolutionary movement.

This, then, is the current position of the Action Committees.

It is on this basis that they will intervene during and after the election campaign.

Now More than Ever the Struggle Continues

Today the Action Committees have to lie low, but in May and June they were the highest expression of our movement. They showed how simple it is to bypass the trade union and political bosses, how workers can spontaneously unite in action, without a 'vanguard' or a party.

Special mention should here be made of CLEOP (Committee for Student-Worker-Peasant Liaison) which saw to the provisioning of the strikers, above all in the smaller factories. One of the first of these committees originated in the Agricultural School of Nantes, most of the others, too, were started in Brittany. They made contact with agricultural cooperatives and unions, and bought directly from the farmers and smallholders who were only too glad to cock a snook at the hated government. CLEOP also organized public discussions and published bulletins to fill in the gaps which were deliberately left in the official communiqués—in short, CLEOP played much the same part in the countryside that the Action Committees played in Paris. Meeting places sprang up, the committees became a network for

From: Daniel Cohn-Bendit and Gabriel Cohn-Bendit, *Obsolete Communism* (New York: McGraw Hill Book Company, 1968), pp. 85–89.

disseminating information and ideas, and helped to cement solidarity between town and country workers in battles with the police and in organizing food transports.

At the end of the day, CLEOP, like the rest of the revolutionary student movement, became exhausted by fifty days of constant skirmishes with the police, and as the workers' struggle abated in its turn, the authorities moved in quickly to crush the last pockets of resistance.

But our temporary defeat is only the end of a chapter. When the movement takes the offensive again, its dynamism will return, and this time the battle will be on a field chosen by the students and workers themselves. The days of May and June will never be forgotten, and one day the barricades will surely be raised again. There is no better way to end this chapter than with the manifesto put out by one of that group of revolutionary students, known as the *Enragés de Caen.*

(1) The students have ushered in a university revolution. By their action they have made clear to one and all how basically repressive our educational institutions really are. They began by questioning the authority of their professors and the university administration and pretty soon they found themselves face to face with the CRS (riot police). They have proved that their Rector derives his powers from the Prefect of Police. Their action at the same time revealed the unity of interest of all the exploited and oppressed classes. It is in response to the movement born at Nanterre and continued at the Sorbonne in the face of police aggression, that the workers, the ordinary soldiers, the journalists, the research workers and the writers, have joined the battle.

(2) However, as soon as the workers came out on strike and the students tried to show their active solidarity with them, they came up against the CGT, which asked them not to interfere. While many students tell themselves that this is not the attitude of the majority of workers, they nevertheless feel rejected as 'middle class'. Quite a few students who were only too anxious to follow the lead of the working class are becoming disenchanted as the workers scorn them and refuse to take them seriously. Disenchantment is particularly strong among those students who were last to join the movement, and are really more interested in achieving a few concessions than in changing society as a whole. The more progressive students, by contrast, realize that, unless the revolution finishes off capitalism and the old universities with it, there can be no real change for the better. Hence they persist, often without hope, in offering their services to the workers, beginning to feel ashamed of being students.

(3) Students must rid themselves of these false feelings of guilt. Although their action sprang from the university, it has a validity that far transcends the narrow academic walls.

First of all, and most important, students must realize that the problems of the university are not irrelevant to the problems of industry. True, in industry, the workers carry the main weight of exploitation, the ownership of the means of production is in the hands of a hostile class, and the decisive struggle is played out within the productive process. But a mere change of ownership, such as the transfer of economic power from private to State enterprise, will in no way put an end to exploitation. What characterizes the structure of modern industry is not only the division between capital and labour, but also the division between supervisors and supervised, the skilled and the unskilled. The workers are exploited economically but also they are reduced to the role of mere pawns, by having no say in the running of their factories, no part in decisions that affect their own fate.

The monopoly of capital invariably goes hand in hand with a monopoly of power and knowledge.

Now, this is precisely where the students can show the way. They attack the self-styled custodians of authority and of wisdom; those who, on the pretext of dispensing knowledge, preach obedience and conformism.

Rather than waste their time analyzing the connexion between the university and other social sectors, students must proclaim that the same repressive structures are weighing down on them and the workers alike, that the same mentality thwarts the creative intelligence of individuals and groups everywhere. It is in the universities that this mentality structure is elaborated and maintained, and to shake it, we must shake the entire society—even though we still do not know the quickest path to that goal.

That shaking will surely come: we can already see its signs in the protests which are rising now, not only from the working but also from the middle class, from the press, radio and television, from artists and writers, and from Catholic, Jewish and Protestant youth who have suddenly rebelled against an oppressive theology.

The struggle of the students has opened the floodgates; it matters little that this struggle was born in a petty bourgeois environment—its effects involve the whole of society.

Moreover, it is a far too literal and ill-digested Marxism that tries to explain everything in terms of the antagonism between the workers and the middle class. This antagonism itself springs from an economic, social and political basis. Every attack against this basis, no matter from what source, has a revolutionary bearing.

(4) Students must not fear to make themselves heard and instead of searching for leaders where none can be found, boldly proclaim their principles—principles that are valid for all industrial societies, and for all the oppressed of our time.

These principles are:

To take collective responsibility for one's own affairs, that is, self-government;

To destroy all hierarchies which merely serve to paralyze the initiative of groups and individuals;

To make all those in whom any authority is vested permanently responsible to the people;

To spread information and ideas throughout the movement;

To put an end to the division of labour and of knowledge, which only serves to isolate people one from the others;

To open the university to all who are at present excluded;

To defend maximum political and intellectual freedom as a basic democratic right.

In affirming these principles, the students are in no way opposing themselves to the workers. They do not pretend that theirs is a blueprint for the reconstruction of society, even less a political programme, in the conventional sense of the word. They do not set themselves up as teachers. They recognize that each group has the right to lay down its own claims and its own methods of struggle. The students speak in the universal language of revolution. They do not deny that they have learned much of it from the workers; but they can also make a contribution of their own.

✦ Reading 66 ✦

The Concept of the Urban Guerilla

The Red Army Fraction

RAF (Baader-Meinhof Group)

The Concept of the Urban Guerrilla

If we are correct in saying that American imperialism is a paper tiger, i.e., that it can ultimately be defeated, and if the Chinese Communists are correct in their thesis that victory over American imperialism has become possible because the struggle against it is now being waged in all four corners of the earth, with the result that the forces of imperialism are fragmented, a fragmentation which makes them possible to defeat—if this is correct, then there is no reason to exclude or disqualify any particular country or any particular region from taking part in the anti-imperialist struggle because the forces of revolution are especially weak there and the forces of reaction especially strong.

As it is wrong to discourage the forces of revolution by underestimating their power, so it is wrong to suggest they should seek confrontations in which these forces cannot but be squandered or annihilated. The contradiction between the sincere comrades in the organizations—let's forget about the prattlers—and the Red Army Fraction, is that we charge them with discouraging the forces of revolution and they suspect us of squandering the forces of revolution. Certainly, this analysis does indicate the directions in which the fraction of those comrades working in the factories and at local level and the Red Army Fraction are overdoing things, if they are overdoing things. Dogmatism and adventurism have since time immemorial been characteristic deviations in periods of revolutionary weakness in all countries. Anarchists having since time immemorial been the sharpest critics of opportunism, anyone criticizing the opportunists exposes himself to the charge of anarchism. This is something of an old chestnut.

The concept of the "urban guerrilla" originated in Latin America. Here, the urban guerrilla can only be what he is there: the only revolutionary method of intervention available to what are on the whole weak revolutionary forces.

The urban guerrilla starts by recognizing that there will be no Prussian order of march of the kind in which so many so-called revolutionaries would like to lead the people into battle. He starts by recognizing that by the time the moment for armed struggle arrives, it will already be too late to start preparing for it; that in a country whose potential for violence is as great and whose revolutionary traditions are as broken and feeble as the Federal Republic's, there will not—without revolutionary initiative—even be a revolutionary orientation when conditions for revolutionary struggle are better than they are at present—which will happen as an inevitable consequence of the development of late capitalism itself.

To this extent, the "urban guerrilla" is the logical consequence of the negation of parliamentary democracy long since perpetrated by its very own representatives; the only and inevitable response to emergency laws and the rule of the hand grenade; the readiness to fight with those same means the system has chosen to use in trying to eliminate its opponents. The "urban guerrilla" is based on a recognition of the facts instead of an apologia of the facts.

The student movement, for one, realized something of what the urban guerrilla can do. He can make concrete the agitation and propaganda which remain the sum total of left-wing activity. One can imagine the concept being applied to the Springer Campaign at that time or to the Heidelberg students' Cabora Bassa Campaign, to the squads in Frankfurt,

---

From: *The Terrorism Reader: A Historical Anthology,* eds. Walter Laquer and Yonah Alexander (New York: New American Library, 1978), pp. 176–179.

or in relation to the Federal Republic's military aid to the *comprador* regimes in Africa, in relation to criticism of prison sentences and class justice, of safety legislation at work and injustice there.

The urban guerrilla can concretize verbal internationalism as the requisition of guns and money. He can blunt the state's weapon of a ban on communists by organizing an underground beyond the reach of the police. The urban guerrilla is a weapon in the class war.

The "urban guerrilla" signifies armed struggle, necessary to the extent that it is the police which make indiscriminate use of firearms, exonerating class justice from guilt and burying our comrades alive unless we prevent them. To be an "urban guerrilla" means not to let oneself be demoralized by the violence of the system.

The urban guerrilla's aim is to attack the state's apparatus of control at certain points and put them out of action, to destroy the myth of the system's omnipresence and invulnerability.

The "urban guerrilla" presupposes the organization of an illegal apparatus, in other words apartments, weapons, ammunition, cars, and papers. A detailed description of what is involved is to be found in Marighella's *Minimanual for the Urban Guerrilla.* As for what else is involved, we are ready at any time to inform anyone who needs to know because he intends to do it. We do not know a great deal yet, but we do know something.

What is important is that one should have had some political experience in legality before deciding to take up armed struggle. Those who have joined the revolutionary left just to be trendy had better be careful not to involve themselves in something from which there is no going back.

The Red Army Fraction and the "urban guerrilla" are that fraction and praxis which, because they draw a clear dividing line between themselves and the enemy, are combatted most intensively. This presupposes a political identity, presupposes that one or two lessons have already been learned.

In our original concept, we planned to combine urban guerrilla activity with grass-roots work. What we wanted was for each of us to work simultaneously within existing socialist groups at the work place and in local districts, helping to influence the discussion process, learning, gaining experience. It has become clear that this cannot be done. These groups are under such close surveillance by the political police, their meetings, timetables, and the content of their discussions so well monitored, that it is impossible to attend without being put under surveillance oneself. We have learned that individuals cannot combine legal and illegal activity.

Becoming an "urban guerrilla" presupposes that one is clear about one's own motivation, that one is sure of being immune to "Bild-Zeitung" methods, sure that the whole anti-Semite-criminal-subhuman-murderer-arsonist syndrome they use against revolutionaries, all that shit that they alone are able to abstract and articulate and that still influences some comrades' attitude to us, that none of this has any effect on us.

Reading 67

Thinking Green!

Petra K. Kelly

"Never doubt that a small group of thoughtful, committed citizens can change the world. Indeed, it's the only thing that ever has."—Margaret Mead

When we founded the West German Green Party, we used the term "anti-party party" to describe our approach to politics based on a new understanding of power, a "counter-power" that is natural and common to all, to be shared by all, and used by all for all. This is the power of transformation, rooted in the discovery of our own strength and ability to be active participants in society. This kind of power stands in stark contrast to the power of domination, terror, and oppression, and is the best remedy for powerlessness.

Using power to dominate humans and nature has brought us to an impasse and can never take us beyond it. We must learn to think and act from our hearts, to recognize the interconnectedness of all living creatures, and to respect the value of each thread in the vast web of life. This is a spiritual perspective, and it is the foundation of all Green politics. It entails the radical, nonviolent transformation of the structures of society and of our way of thinking, so that domination is no longer the primary *modus operandi.* At the root of all Green political action is nonviolence, starting with how we live our lives, taking small, unilateral steps towards peace in everything we do. Green politics requires us to be both tender and subversive. Affirming tenderness as a political value is already subversive. In Green politics, we practice tenderness in relations with others; in caring for ideas, art, language, and culture; and in cherishing and protecting the Earth.

To think Green is to build solidarity with those working for social justice and human rights everywhere, not bound by ideologies. The problems that threaten life on Earth were produced collectively, they affect us collectively, and we must act collectively to change them. We cannot retreat into isolation. The Green vision of a just society is one in which economic, social, and individual rights are guaranteed and protected, and everyone is free from exploitation, violence, and oppression.

Politicians give speeches about these values while working to undermine them. The benefits of the current political and economic systems are reserved for the privileged; therefore, any meaningful movement for social justice must focus on systemic change, on transforming both the oppressive state and economic structures that concentrate wealth and power in the hands of a few. The Green methodology is not to work from the top down, but to begin at the grassroots, empowering ourselves to direct our own destinies through the cultivation of civil space and democratic social forms.

First and foremost, Green politics is grassroots politics. Politics from the top is almost always corrupt and compromised. To bring about change from below is to challenge the moral authority of those who make decisions on our behalf. Through grassroots organization, education, and empowerment, we work to reverse the state-orientation of politics and instead open up a civil space in which we are active subjects, not passive objects of those in power. Substantive change in politics at the top will come only when there is enough pressure from below. The essence of Green politics is to live our values. We in the West German Green Party hurt ourselves over and over again by failing to maintain tenderness with each other as we gained power. We need to rededicate ourselves to our values, respect each other, be tolerant of differences, and stop trying to coerce and control one another.

Nonviolence, ecology, social justice, and feminism are the key principles of Green politics, and

From: Petra K. Kelly, *Thinking Green: Essays on Environmentalism, Feminism, and Nonviolence* (Berkeley: Parallax Press, 1994), pp. 38–44.

they are inseparably linked. We know, for example, that the wasteful patterns of production and consumption in the industrial North deplete and ravage the environment and furnish the motive and means for the violent appropriation of materials from the weaker nations in the South and for the wasteful process of militarization throughout the world. In both capitalist and state socialist countries, human beings are reduced to economic entities, with little or no regard for the human or ecological costs. Politics from the top, the pattern of hierarchical domination, is the characteristic of patriarchy. It is not a coincidence that power rests in the hands of men, benefits accrue first and foremost to men, and that women are exploited at all levels of society.

The Green approach to politics is a kind of celebration. We recognize that each of us is part of the world's problems, and we are also part of the solution. The dangers and the potentials for healing are not just outside us. We begin to work exactly where we are. There is no need to wait until conditions become ideal. We can simplify our lives and live in ways that affirm ecological and humane values. Better conditions will come because we have begun.

We have found so many ways to think each other to death—neutron warheads, nuclear reactors, Star Wars defense systems, and many other methods of mass destruction. We are killing each other with our euphemisms and abstractions. In warfare, we accept the deaths of thousands and millions of people we call our "enemy." When we dehumanize people, devalue nature, and exalt narrowly defined serf-interests, destruction is sure to follow. The healing of our planet requires a new way of thinking about politics and about life. At the heart of this is the understanding that all things are intimately interconnected in the complex web of life. It can therefore be said that the primary goal of Green politics is an inner revolution. Joanna Macy calls this "the greening of the self."

Politics needs spirituality. The profound political changes we need in order to heal our planet will not come about through fragmented problem solving or intellectual analyses that overlook the deepest yearnings and intuitions of the heart. Some of my fellow Greens have maintained their dogmatic leftist perspectives and remain suspicious of spirituality, confusing it with organized religion. I share many of their criticisms of religious institutions, but I firmly disagree with their dismissing spiritual concerns and wisdom. The long work of bringing harmony to the Earth requires a holistic vision based on mature values and deep intuitions.

Today's politics are based on the mechanistic worldview that prefers assertion to integration, analysis over synthesis, rational knowledge over intuitive wisdom, competition over cooperation, and expansionism over conservation. A few new ideas are not enough. We need an entirely new way of thinking. As we begin to cultivate a rich inner life and experience our connection with all of life, we realize how little of what society tells us we need is actually important for our well-being. We must reduce consumption and not cooperate with any practices that harm the natural world or other humans. This is not a sacrifice. It is the way to sustain ourselves.

Green politics must address the spiritual vacuum of industrial society, the alienation that is pervasive in a society where people have grown isolated from nature and from themselves. We in the Greens must also address our own alienation. Our social structures shape this alienation, and they themselves are shaped by it. It is a vicious cycle, and our work of healing must address the whole process. We have forgotten our historical rootedness in an integrated way of life. We must learn from those cultures that have maintained their traditions of wisdom and harmony with nature—Australian Aborigines, American Indians, and others. Tragically, many of these societies are threatened by the same forces that threaten the environment. We must join them in their struggles to preserve their values and traditions.

One such endangered society, Tibet, has been ruthlessly exploited and its people violently oppressed. The exiled leader of the Tibetan people, His Holiness the Dalai Lama, is, for me, a living example of how spiritual vision can influence politics:

Peace starts within each one of us. When we have inner peace, we can be at peace with those around us. When our community is in a state of peace, it can share that peace with neighboring communities. . . . What is important is that we each make a sincere effort to take seriously our responsibility for each other and for the natural environment.

We have little reason to place our hope in governments or established political parties, for their primary interest is always in extending their own power. But we can find hope in the strength and imagination of people working at the grassroots to create positive change. We Greens work within the political system solely for the benefit and empowerment of those at the grassroots. Our efforts within the halls of government are not to replace work at the grassroots. Our commitments are, first and foremost, to those who elected us. We must work with them, nonviolently, for life-affirming solutions to the problems of our day.

Green politics is based on direct democracy—our effort is to redefine and reorganize power so that it flows from the bottom up. We seek to decentralize power and maximize the freedom and self-determination of individuals, communities, and societies. This means moving power out of the hands of centralized bureaucracies—above all, the military-industrial complex—and empowering people on the local level. It also means reaching across national borders and ideologies to build alliances with others also working for peace and ecology. It means moving government power away from the state towards smaller and smaller units of organization. In economics, grassroots democracy means a production system that maximizes workers' self-management and minimizes corporate or government control. It means units of production scaled to a comprehensible human dimension and that are locally responsive and globally responsible. The day may come when the Greens find a truly democratic and ecological partner among the established political parties, but until then, we must work in government as an anti-party party, an experiment in radical parliamentary opposition unwilling to compromise fundamental values for the sake of expediency.

Thinking green—to think with the heart—is the solution to many if not all of our political dead-ends. To continue increasing production, consumption, and the depletion of our natural resources will only lead us further down the path of suffering. Albert Einstein said that with the splitting of the atom everything changed except the way people think. A new way of thinking must come soon, or the damage will be irreparable. Means and ends cannot be separated. "There is no way to peace. Peace is the way."*

*A. J. Muste, *The Essays of A. J. Muste,* edited by Nat Hentoff (New York: Simon & Schuster, 1970).

✦ Reading 68 ✦

Excerpts from Interviews

The National Front

[F]or centuries France and Europe have fought back the invasion. France, Europe, and Christianity fought back the Muslim invasion. We were successful for a thousand years, more than a thousand years, for fifteen hundred years in pushing them back, and now in fifty years Europe will be conquered by Muslims.

I believe that there is a major problem in France today and that is the immigration problem. Understanding it from abroad is hard. France has a social welfare system that is very attractive as well as a language that is equally attractive for the countries of the Maghrib and black Africa because they know how to speak French and therefore they have a tendency to come here quite easily. Previously, France was able to absorb, historically, immigrants coming from Poland, from Italy, and from quite a few other countries. [This previous immigration] was accomplished without problems, in small doses, because those people had the same culture as our own. The Maghrib problem is very different. This Islamic problem is quite different, because Islam mixes together religion and politics.

Law is a product of religion in Islam. They don't know how to adapt to the laws of French society. They are unable to be integrated. Previous immigrations were accomplished in a more normal manner in small doses and these people were very quickly integrated into the country. We have a flood of Islamic immigrants that it's just impossible to absorb. They create ghettos, and in my opinion they create the racial phenomenon. I fear that in Marseilles there will be an explosion. You must understand that people are witnessing their surroundings fall into disrepair, they no longer can find their heritage, and in certain neighborhoods of their city they are just no longer allowed in.

Certainly, the most important problem has to be the issue of immigration because around this revolves all the other problems. Immigration is a problem with our national identity. France is swamped by immigrants and it risks losing its soul, its culture, its heritage—simply put, its identity. It's also a problem of security. Domestic security, because the people who come from these other countries, often African countries, come generally to find here what they can't find at home: much more favorable working conditions, salaries which are evidently a lot higher, and the whole social welfare system.

* * *

We are going to have a profound transformation of our national identity. You see it every day. I can tell you that in the district where I have campaigned . . . certain parts of the city are populated by no one but foreigners. When I say a foreign city, I mean a city where you see Islamic butcher shops, where you see mosques, or where you see people dressed as they would be in the Maghrib, etcetera.

* * *

I would say that the primary problem is a cultural problem, and that French culture and the French nation are threatened. I'm a strong supporter of the defense of French culture. I also support the National Front's positions on immigration, the nationality code, and national identity because these are essentially questions of culture rather than legal or political issues. I'm not one of those who is going to accept a multiracial or a multicultural France.

From: Edward G. DeClair, *Politics on the Fringe: The People, Policies and Organization of the French National Front* (Durham, NC: Duke University Press, 1999), pp. 125–133.

French culture +
nation are
threatened.

 PART EIGHTEEN 

The End of the Cold War and Globalization

This photograph of a warm agreement between the reformist Mikhail Gorbachev and President Ronald Reagan, who earlier on had criticized the U.S.S.R. as an "evil empire," captures the melting away of the cold war.

The End of the Cold War and Globalization

By the 1960s, Eastern European dissidents began to express opposition to Communist rule, with few results except harassment, arrest, and, occasionally, enforced expulsion to the West. During the mid-1980s, the dynamic Mikhail Gorbachev (1931–) undertook a drastic reshaping of the failing Soviet system. Using the Communist Party's vast power, Gorbachev opened realms of political freedom and urged economic restructuring. He also began withdrawing Soviet troops from Eastern Europe, thus unilaterally ending the Cold War. The Berlin Wall came down and Germany reunited, as massive demonstrations swept away East Bloc Communist governments. After winning the Nobel Peace Prize, Gorbachev watched helplessly as his internal reforms floundered on unforeseen economic and political problems, including resurgent nationalism in some Soviet republics. In 1991 the Soviet Union broke up and an independent Russian Republic arose under the leadership of Boris Yeltsin (1931–), a reformer determined to construct liberal capitalism.

Former Communist states face enormous problems in reviving entrepreneurship, building appropriate infrastructure, and maintaining work and welfare support for their populations. Many also confront long-festering ethnic conflicts. The former Czechoslovakia divided peacefully into Czech and Slovak republics, whereas the various peoples of Yugoslavia have already witnessed a decade of warfare and strife along a perilous path toward ethnically defined small independent states. In Chechnya, Russia too has experienced ethnic conflict, as have the newly independent states of the Caucasus. Even as ethnic hostility and the anti-emigrant racism noted in an earlier section sound a note of caution on the European scene, global economic integration, whose chief symbol and tool is the Internet, open vistas hard to calculate. Europe's generally favorable economic, educational, and political situations bode well for the future in the globalized world.

The Soviet dissident Alexander Zinoviev (1922–) satirized certain realities of life under Communism in his novel, *Homo Sovieticus. The Magic Lantern,* written by British journalist Timothy Garton Ash (1955–), documents the demolition of the infamous Berlin Wall and other signal events of the Cold War's demise. In his article "The Last Ambassador," former American ambassador to Yugoslavia Warren Zimmermann blames this once prosperous nation's wanton destruction on abysmally failed leadership. The Russian Federation's 1993 Constitution suggests the tightrope walked by leaders of former Communist states as they attempt to balance society's needs and the prerequisites of building market economies within the context of free elections. Those who err in any direction can be voted out of office. No easy path to reform exists. The article "Stop Signs on the Web" reminds readers of the Internet's malign and benign potential and of the complete lack of dependable knowledge about how and whether to control it.

✦ Reading 69 ✦

Homo Sovieticus

Alexander Zinoviev

This bitter satire of post-Stalinist Soviet life focuses on the experiences of an unnamed antihero, an intellectual who compromises with repressive authority to survive.

Denunciations

The mechanism of my wishes is very cunningly constructed. As soon as I began to think of writing a novel my *arrière-pensée* whispered: why a novel? Perhaps it would be better to write a denunciation? That's more like it, you'll say. After all, it's more your style. But here I must disappoint you: I have never written a denunciation in my life. You don't believe me? An acquaintance of mine (not the one I mentioned earlier, but another), never wrote denunciations either. But then he was a KGB officer and people wrote denunciations to him. I wasn't a KGB officer. But I had occasion to study denunciations as part of my work, so I have some experience of them. I'm a specialist in denunciations, but not a denouncer. I am a theorist in the field, not a practitioner.

It is undeniable that we have lost the reverent and tremulous attitude to denunciations that we used to have. They have lost their revolutionary-romantic tinge. And it's no longer possible to say what their role in the history of our times has been. But the denunciation has retained a very great epistemological significance. It is the only branch of human culture in which people can achieve some competence without any training or literary ability. To write denunciations there is no need to be a member of the Soviet Writers' Union. And, as they sing in a popular opera, all ages are susceptible to denunciation.

At one time there was such a spate of denunciations to the KGB that its officers couldn't keep up with them on their own. They had to call in outside specialists to help. Hundreds of them, including myself, were brought in. You cannot imagine the size of the piles of *unread* denunciations alone in the central offices of the organs of State security, nor how many had piled up in the republics, provinces and districts and in the files and safes of individual operatives. And how many had been readied for action! How many perished in the war! How many were destroyed! What a mighty amount of human energy, feeling and thought went into the whole business of denunciation!

My task was to select from many thousands the ones which deserved attention and chuck away the rest; or, as it was then called, "write them off". I read the denunciations of innocent children in the morning of their lives; of decrepit old men wise with experience; of sober young careerists; of alcoholics out of their mind in their hopelessness; of prominent academics, of housewives, of young and pure virgins, of old debauchees, of Party officials, illiterate cretins, professors, pensioners and artists. They were all as alike as coins of the same value, or bugs. It was just as if denunciation was lodged in our genes from the start, instead of being, as we know, the most elevated product of human history. And then I realized that the denunciation is the most profound, comprehensive and sincere form of personal self-expression.

It is a pity that thousands of tons of denunciations were destroyed during the years of liberalism. The *oeuvre* of a vast population in its most interesting historical period disappeared without trace. Of course, denunciations will continue to be written in the future. But not on the same scale, nor with such an expenditure of intellect and passion, nor with such ingenuity of invention as there was then; it is sad indeed that this will never be repeated!

From: Alexander Zinoviev, *Homo Sovieticus,* translated by Charles Janson (Boston and New York: Atlantic Monthly Press, 1982), pp. 12–13.

✦ Reading 70 ✦
The Magic Lantern
Timothy Garton Ash

Berlin: Wall's End

Once upon a time, and a very bad time it was, there was a famous platform in West Berlin where distinguished visitors would be taken to stare at the Wall. American Presidents from Kennedy to Reagan stood on that platform looking out over the no man's land beyond. They were told that this, the Potsdamer Platz, had once been Berlin's busiest square, its Piccadilly Circus. Their hosts pointed out a grassy mound on the far side: the remains of Hitler's bunker. East German border-guards watched impassively, or rode up and down the death strip on their army motorbikes.

On the morning of Sunday, 12 November I walked through the Wall and across that no man's land with a crowd of East Berliners, a watchtower to our left, Hitler's bunker to our right. Bewildered border-guards waved us through. (As recently as February their colleagues had shot dead a man trying to escape.) Vertical segments of the wall stood at ease where the crane had just dumped them, their multicoloured graffiti facing east for the first time. A crowd of West Berliners applauded as we came through, and a man handed out free city plans. Then I turned round and walked back again, past more bewildered borderguards and customs officers. Ahead of me I noticed a tall man in an unfamiliar green uniform. He turned out to be the US commandant in Berlin, one General Haddock.

By nightfall, West Berlin workers had dismantled the famous platform, like an unneeded prop. Europe's *Mousetrap* had ended its twenty-eight-year run. Clear the stage for another show.

Everyone has seen the pictures of joyful celebration in West Berlin, the vast crowds stopping the traffic on the Kürfurstendamm, *Sekt* corks popping, strangers tearfully embracing—the greatest street-party in the history of the world. Yes, it was like that. But it was not only like that. Most of the estimated two million East Germans who flooded into West Berlin over the weekend simply walked the streets in quiet family groups, often with toddlers in pushchairs. They queued up at a bank to collect the 100 Deutschmarks 'greeting money' (about thirty-five pounds) offered to visiting East Germans by the West German government, and then they went, very cautiously, shopping. Generally they bought one or two small items, perhaps some fresh fruit, a Western newspaper and toys for the children. Then, clasping their carrier-bags, they walked quietly back through the Wall, through the grey, deserted streets of East Berlin, home.

It is very difficult to describe the quality of this experience because what they actually did was so stunningly ordinary. In effect, they just took a bus from Hackney or Dagenham to Piccadilly Circus, and went shopping in the West End. Berliners walked the streets of Berlin. What could be more normal? And yet, what could be more fantastic! 'Twenty-eight years and ninety-one days,' says one man in his late thirties strolling back up Friedrichstrasse. Twenty-eight years and ninety-one days since the building of the Wall. On that day, in August 1961, his parents had wanted to go to a late-night Western in a West Berlin cinema, but their eleven-year-old son had been too tired. In the early hours they woke to the sound of tanks. He had never been to West Berlin from that day to this. A taxi-driver asks me, with a sly smile: 'How much is the ferry to England?' The day before yesterday his question would have been unthinkable.

Everyone, but everyone, on the streets of East Berlin has just been, or is just going to West Berlin. A breathless, denim-jacketed couple stop me to ask,

From: Timothy Garton Ash, *The Magic Lantern* (New York: Random House, 1990), pp. 61–69.

'Is this the way out?' They have come hot-foot from Leipzig. 'Our hearts are going pitter-pat,' they say, in broad Saxon dialect. Everyone looks the same as they make their way home—except for the tell-tale Western carrier-bag. But everyone is inwardly changed, changed utterly. 'Now people are standing up straight,' says a hotel porter. 'They are speaking their minds. Even work is more fun. I think the sick will get up from their hospital beds.' And it was in East rather than West Berlin that this weekend had the magic, pentecostal quality which I last experienced in Poland in autumn 1980. Ordinary men and women find their voice and their courage—*Lebensmut,* as the porter puts it. These are moments when you feel that somewhere an angel has opened his wings.

They may have been ordinary people doing very ordinary things, but the Berliners immediately grasped the historical dimensions of the event. 'Of course the real villain was Hitler,' said one. A note stuck to a remnant of the Wall read: 'Stalin is dead, Europe lives.' The man who counted twenty-eight years and ninety-one days told me he had been most moved by an improvised poster saying: 'Only today is the war really over.'

Bild newspaper—West Germany's *Sun*—carried a black-red-gold banner headline declaring 'Good Morning, Germany', and underneath it an effusive thank-you letter from the editors to Mikhail Gorbachev. The East Germans also felt grateful to Gorbachev. But more important, they felt they had won this opening for themselves. For it was only the pressure of their massive, peaceful demonstrations that compelled the Party leadership to take this step. 'You see, it shows Lenin was wrong,' observed one worker. 'Lenin said a revolution could succeed only with violence. But this was a peaceful revolution.' And even the Party's Central Committee acknowledged at the beginning of its hastily drafted Action Programme that 'a revolutionary people's movement has set in motion a process of profound upheavals.'

Why did it happen? And why so quickly? No one in East Germany predicted it. To be sure in July, when I was finally allowed back by the GDR authorities, after applying in vain for several years, officials would say that the situation was *sehr kompliziert,* and shake their heads. But Church and opposition activists remained deeply pessimistic. The State Security Service—the 'Stasi'—still seemed all-powerful, the population at large not prepared to risk its modest prosperity. Above all, the ranks of the opposition had been continuously thinned by emigration to West Germany. For taking part in a demonstration, a young man would be threatened with a long prison term; then he would be taken into another room of the police station where another officer would present him with a neatly completed application to emigrate. Prison or the West. As one friend put it: 'It's like being asked to choose between heaven and hell.' 'Soon,' he added bitterly, 'there'll be nobody left in this country but a mass of stupid philistines and a few crazy idealists.'

Immigration

With hindsight we may be a little wiser. At the very least, one can list in order some factors that brought the cup of popular discontent to overflowing. In the beginning was the Wall itself: the Wall and the system it both represented and preserved. The Wall was not round the periphery of East Germany, it was at its very centre. And it ran through every heart. It was difficult even for people from other East European countries to appreciate the full psychological burden it imposed. An East Berlin doctor wrote a book describing the real sicknesses—and of course the suicides—that resulted. He called it *The Wall Sickness.* In a sense, the mystery was always why the people of East Germany did not revolt.

The second causal factor, both in time and importance, was Gorbachev. The 'Gorbachev effect' was strongest in East Germany because it was more strongly oriented towards—and ultimately dependent on—the Soviet Union than any other East European state. It was not for nothing that a 1974 amendment to the constitution proclaimed: 'The German Democratic Republic is for ever and irrevocably allied with the Union of Soviet Socialist Republics.' East Germany's young people had for years been told, *Von der Sowjetunion lernen heisst siegen lernen*—'To learn from the Soviet Union is to learn how to win.' So they did! For several years East Germans had been turning the name of Gorbachev, and the Soviet example, against their rulers. And Gorbachev personally gave the last push—on his visit to join the fortieth-anniversary celebrations of the GDR on 7 October—with his carefully calculated utterance that 'Life itself punishes those who delay', the leaked

Gorbachev

news that he had told Honecker Soviet troops would not be used for internal repression and (according to well-informed West German sources) his direct encouragement to the likes of Egon Krenz and the Berlin Party chief Günter Schabowski, to move to depose Honecker.

The Polish and Hungarian examples were not so important. To be sure, everyone learned about them, in great detail, from the West German television they watched nightly. To be sure, developments in those two countries demonstrated that fundamental changes were possible. But for most people the economic misery in Poland more than cancelled out the political example. Hungary—a favoured holiday destination for East Germans, with a better economic situation and a history (and, dare one say, national character) less fatefully at odds with Germany's—Hungary perhaps had a greater impact. Yet the crucial Hungarian input was not the example of its internal reforms, but the opening of its frontier with Austria.

As soon as the Hungarians starting cutting the barbed wire of the 'iron curtain', in May, East Germans began to escape across it. As the numbers grew, and East Germans gathered in refugee camps in Budapest, the Hungarian authorities decided, in early September, to let them leave officially (suspending a bilateral consular agreement with the GDR). The trickle turned into a flood: some 15,000 crossed the border in the first three days, 50,000 by the end of October. Others sought an exit route via the West German embassies in Prague and Warsaw. This was the final catalyst for internal change in East Germany.

Church-protected opposition activity had been increasing through the summer. There had been independent monitoring of the local elections in May, which clearly showed that they were rigged. In June, the East German authorities' emphatic endorsement of the repression in China brought another round of protests. It is important to recall that right up to, and during, the fortieth-anniversary celebrations on 7 October, the police used force, indeed gratuitous brutality, to disperse these protests and intimidate any who might have contemplated joining in. Young men were dragged along the cobbled streets by their hair. Women and children were thrown into prison. Innocent bystanders were beaten.

If one can identify a turning-point it was perhaps Monday, 9 October, the day after Gorbachev left. Since the late summer, the regular Monday evening 'prayers for peace' in Leipzig's Church of St Nicholas had been followed by small demonstrations on the adjacent Karl-Marx-Platz. At the outset, most of the demonstrators were people who wanted to emigrate. But on 25 September there were between 5,000 and 8,000 people, with the would-be emigrants now in a minority, and on 2 October, as the emigration crisis deepened, there were perhaps 15,000 to 20,000—the largest spontaneous demonstration in East Germany since the uprising of 17 June 1953. They sung the Internationale and demanded the legalization of the recently founded 'citizens' initiative', New Forum. The police were baffled, and in places peacefully overwhelmed.

On Monday, 9 October, however, following the violent repression during the fortieth anniversary celebrations two days earlier, riot police, army units, and factory 'combat groups' stood ready to clear the Karl-Marx-Platz, East Germany's Tiananmen Square. An article in the local paper by the commander of one of these 'combat groups' said they were prepared to defend socialism 'if need be, with weapon in hand.' But in the event some 70,000 people came out to make their peaceful protest, and this time force was not used to disperse them. (The figure of 70,000, like all the other crowd figures, can only be taken as a very crude estimate, at best an order of magnitude.) It was claimed, by sources close to the Politburo member responsible for internal security, Egon Krenz, that he, being in overall political control of internal security, had taken the brave, Gorbachevian decision not to use force. It was even claimed that he had personally gone to Leipzig to prevent bloodshed.

Subsequent accounts by those actually involved in Leipzig gave a quite different picture. By these accounts, the crucial action was taken by the famous Leipzig conductor, Kurt Masur, together with a well-known cabaret artist, Bernd-Lutz Lange, and a priest, Peter Zimmermann. They managed to persuade three local Party leaders to join them in a dramatic, last-minute appeal for non-violence, which was read in the churches, broadcast over loudspeakers—and relayed to the police by the acting Party chief in

Leipzig. This made the difference between triumph and disaster. It was, it seems, only later in the evening that Krenz telephoned to ask what was happening. The moment was, none the less, decisive for Krenz's bid for power. Nine days later he replaced Honecker as Party leader. But in those nine days the revolution had begun.

To say the growth of popular protest was exponential would be an understatement. It was a non-violent explosion. Those extraordinary, peaceful, determined Monday evening demonstrations in Leipzig—always starting with 'peace prayers' in the churches—grew week-by-week, from 70,000 to double that, to 300,000, to perhaps half a million. The whole of East Germany suddenly went into labour, an old world—to recall Marx's image—pregnant with the new. From that time forward the people acted and the Party reacted. 'Freedom!' demanded the Leipzig demonstrators, and Krenz announced a new travel law. 'Free travel!' said the crowds, and Krenz reopened the frontier to Hungary. 'A suggestion for May Day: let the leadership parade past the people,' said a banner, quoted by the writer Christa Wolf in the massive, peaceful demonstration in East Berlin on 4 November. And more leaders stepped down. 'Free elections!' demanded the people, and the Council of Ministers resigned *en masse*. 'We are the people!' they chanted, and the party leadership opened the Wall.

The cup of bitterness was already full to the brim. The years of Wall Sickness, the lies, the stagnation, the Soviet and Hungarian examples, the rigged elections, the police violence—all added their dose. The instant that repression was lifted, the cup flowed over. And then, with amazing speed, the East Germans discovered what the Poles had discovered ten years earlier, during the Pope's visit in 1979. They discovered their solidarity. 'Long live the October Revolution of 1989' proclaimed another banner on the Alexanderplatz. And so it was: the first peaceful revolution in German history.

✦ Reading 71 ✦

The Last Ambassador

Warren Zimmermann

A Memoir of the Collapse of Yugoslavia

In early 1989, shortly after I was confirmed as the new—and as it turned out the last—U.S. ambassador to Yugoslavia, I sought out Lawrence Eagleburger. Eagleburger had been named deputy secretary of state for the incoming Bush administration but had not yet been approved by the Senate. His temporary office was in the small back room adjoining the opulent deputy secretary's office, and there he could be found inhaling a cigarette, which, as an asthma sufferer, he was not supposed to have.

Larry Eagleburger remains one of the foremost American experts on the Balkans. Like an unusually large number of Foreign Service officers—myself included—he served twice in Yugoslavia. He and I shared a love of the country and its people. As we talked, we discovered a mutual view that the traditional American approach to Yugoslavia no longer made sense, given the revolutionary changes sweeping Europe.

By 1989 the world had changed dramatically. The Cold War was over and the Soviet Union was breaking up. The East European countries had already slipped Moscow's leash, and Poland and Hungary had achieved quasi-Western political systems, with Czechoslovakia soon to follow. In such circumstances, Eagleburger and I agreed that in my introductory calls in Belgrade and the republican capitals, I would deliver a new message: Yugoslavia no longer enjoyed the geopolitical importance that the United States had given it during the Cold War. Then, Marshal Josip Tito had made Yugoslavia a model for independence from the Soviet Union as well as for a brand of communism that was more open politically and less centralized economically.

Now Yugoslavia had been surpassed by both Poland and Hungary in economic and political openness. In addition, human rights had become a major element of U.S. policy, and Yugoslavia's record on that issue was not good—particularly in the province of Kosovo, where an authoritarian Serbian regime was systematically depriving the Albanian majority of its basic civil liberties.

Finally, I was to reassert the traditional mantra of U.S. support for Yugoslavia's unity, independence, and territorial integrity. But I would add that the United States could only support unity in the context of democracy; it would strongly oppose unity imposed or preserved by force.

Thus equipped, my wife and I arrived in Belgrade on March 9, 1989, after an absence of 21 years. The city had not changed much from the dusty half-Slav, half-Turkish town we remembered. Everybody still talked politics in the outdoor cafés, shaded by splendid chestnut trees. Belgrade was an acquired taste, and I had acquired it. What had changed was the character of the Serbian politics that people were busy discussing. Slobodan Milošević, an ambitious and ruthless communist party official, had clawed his way to power several years before. In early 1989, his efforts were focused on Kosovo.

Kosovo is to Serbs what Jerusalem is to Jews—a sacred ancestral homeland. In the postwar period, the Albanians in Kosovo—about 90 percent of the population—had carved out a dominant position in the province. Milošević was intent on wresting back that control, and he had no qualms about doing it unconstitutionally. Working through the intimidating powers of the communist apparatus, he took over or suspended Kosovo's governing bodies. He replaced bureaucratic and party incumbents with Serbs or pliant Albanians, one of whom, party chief

From: Warren Zimmermann, "The Last Ambassador of Yugoslavia," *Foreign Affairs,* March/April 1995, pp. 2–20.

Rahman Morina, sweated through his shirt during each of my meetings with him. Morina was later carried off prematurely by a heart attack brought on, no doubt, by stress.

On Kosovo, the message that Eagleburger and I had worked out was simple: if Yugoslavia wanted to continue its close relations with the United States, it would have to curb human rights abuses in the province. The point was naturally welcomed by the Albanians in Kosovo and also by Slovenia, an already democratic republic, which was proclaiming that Kosovo was the most egregious example of Milošević's dictatorial rule. Milošević, on the other hand, took my criticism personally; he later cited it as the reason he waited nearly a year before agreeing to meet me.

An Obsession with History

Milošević's Serbia was at the heart of the complex of issues that destroyed Yugoslavia. Serbs are a naturally talented and ebullient people with an instinctive liking for Americans that is based partly on a shared garrulity and partly on a military alliance spanning both world wars. Their tragic defect is an obsession with their own history; their hearts are in the past, not the future. In the Balkans, intellectuals tend to be the standard-bearers of nationalism; in Serbia, this is carried to fetishistic lengths.

A lugubrious, paranoid, and Serbocentric view of the past enables the Serbs to blame everyone but themselves for whatever goes wrong. They had a real grievance against Tito, in some measure justified, for creating a postwar Yugoslavia that denied them a role that they believed their large population (40 percent of the nation—similar to Russians in the old Soviet Union) and historical mission entitled them. When Tito died, leaving a Yugoslavia too decentralized for any ethnic group to dominate, it became inevitable that a Serbian nationalist would rise up to redress the perceived wrongs dealt his people. It was a tragedy for Serbia, its neighbors, and Europe as a whole that the nationalist turned out to be Slobodan Milošević.

After the year from the spring of 1989 to 1990 in which Milošević left me cooling my heels, I grew to know him well. We had many long conversations, all of them contentious but none of them shouting matches. "You see, Mr. Zimmermann," he would say, "only we Serbs really believe in Yugoslavia. We're not trying to secede like the Croats and Slovenes and we're not trying to create an Islamic state like the Muslims in Bosnia. They all fought against you in World War II. We were your allies." On Kosovo, Milošević painted a picture without shadings: "Kosovo has always been Serbian, except for a brief period during World War II. Yet we have given the Albanians their own government, their own parliament, their own national library, and their own schools [none of these assertions was true at the time he made them to me]. We have even given them their own academy of sciences. Have you Americans given your blacks their own academy of sciences?"

Milošević makes a stunning first impression on those who do not have the information to refute his often erroneous assertions. Many is the U.S. senator or congressman who has reeled out of his office exclaiming, "Why, he's not nearly as bad as I expected!" One congressman even invited him to a White House prayer breakfast. Milošević knows how to act with Americans. He dresses in the Western style (he spent considerable time in New York in his banking days), drinks Scotch on the rocks, and smokes Italian cigarillos. His cherubic cheeks do not fit the strongman image; in fact, he has to work hard at looking tough for his public posters. His manner is affable and displays his light side. Unfortunately, the man is almost totally dominated by his dark side.

Milošević began his career as a communist apparatchik of extremely authoritarian mien, even for Serbia. He rose to the leadership of the Serbian party by betraying the man who gave him his chance in politics, Ivan Stambolić, whose purge Milošević organized. Milošević is an opportunist, not an ideologue, a man driven by power rather than nationalism. He has made a Faustian pact with nationalism as a way to gain and hold power.

He is a man of extraordinary coldness. I never saw him moved by an individual case of human suffering; for him, people are groups (Serbs, Muslims) or simply abstractions. Nor did I ever hear him say a charitable or generous word about any human being, not even a Serb. This chilling personality trait made it possible for Milošević to condone, encourage, and even organize the unspeakable atrocities committed by Serbian citizens in the Bosnian war. It also accounts for his habitual mendacity, as in his outrageous distortion of Serbian behavior in Kosovo. For Milošević, truth has only a relative value. If it serves his objectives, it is employed; if not, it can be discarded.

When the unity of Yugoslavia was threatened in the late 1980s by Slovenia—Yugoslavia's only Serbless republic—Milošević cast himself as the apostle of unity. Not interested in unity per se, he wanted a unity that Serbia could dominate, working through the Yugoslav People's Army, whose officer corps was over 50 percent Serbian. Milošević's concept of unity did not extend to democracy or power-sharing with other national groups.

In fact, in his verbal attacks on Slovenia and Croatia and his subsequent trade sanctions against them, he became the major wrecker of Yugoslavia. When the Slovenian and Croatian independence movements, together with Milošević's own disruptive actions in the name of unity, made the preservation of Yugoslavia impossible, he fell back on an even more aggressive approach. If Yugoslavia could not encompass all Serbs, then Serbia would. The Serbian populations of Croatia, Bosnia, Montenegro, and possibly Macedonia would be incorporated—along with generous pieces of territory—into a Milošević-dominated "Yugoslavia." His rallying cry was that all Serbs have the right to live in a single state—a doctrine that, if applied globally, would cause the disintegration of dozens of multinational states.

Worst-Case Scenarios

From the beginning of my ambassadorship in Yugoslavia, I pressed the talented and highly professional group of political and economic officers in the U.S. embassy in Belgrade and the consulate general in Zagreb, Croatia, to consider worst-case scenarios for Yugoslavia. The worst case we could think of was the breakup of the country. We reported to Washington that no breakup of Yugoslavia could happen peacefully. The ethnic hatred sown by Milošević and his ilk and the mixture of ethnic groups in every republic except Slovenia meant that Yugoslavia's shattering would lead to extreme violence, perhaps even war. Thus we favored at least a loose unity while encouraging democratic development. The new Yugoslav prime minister, Ante Marković, a dynamic Croatian committed to economic reform and other Western policies, was pressing for both these objectives. The United States supported him and persuaded the West European governments to do so as well.

The U.S. policy of unity and democracy was not controversial within the Bush administration or initially in Western Europe. But it faced vehement criticism, led by Senator Robert Dole (R-Kans.), in the U.S. Congress. Critics of the policy charged that our efforts to hold together a country that was falling apart helped Milošević and hurt the democratic forces in Slovenia and Croatia. The critics did not understand that democratic unity favored Marković, not Milošević, who had no interest in unity on a democratic reformist basis. In the end, the dissolution of Yugoslavia did lead to war (and to Serbian territorial gains), and thus confirmed that unity and democracy were the Siamese twins of Yugoslavia's fate. The loss of one meant that the other would die.

In January 1990, the communist party created by Tito breathed its last; a party congress split by quarreling was adjourned, never to meet again. Yugoslavia lurched into its first democratic elections. The two most anti-Yugoslav republics, Slovenia and Croatia, were the first to vote. By the end of the year the four southern republics had voted as well. Even the Serbian government held elections, despite Milošević's occasional assertions to me that Serbia's needs were much better met by a one-party system.

The republican elections turned out to be a disaster for those who hoped to keep Yugoslavia together in a democratic framework. People had no opportunity to vote on a Yugoslavia-wide level once Prime Minister Marković failed to win approval for federal elections. They vented their pent-up frustrations by voting for nationalists who hammered on ethnic themes. The elections became a test of ethnic loyalty. Ethnic parties won power in five of the six republics, all but Macedonia.

Nationalism Unleashed

By bringing nationalism to power almost everywhere, the elections helped snuff out the very flame of democracy that they had kindled. Nationalism is by nature uncivil, antidemocratic, and separatist because it empowers one ethnic group over all others. If the elections weakened the democratic element so necessary for Yugoslavia, they also weakened the necessary unifying element. I visited all six republics to evaluate the new leaders. I found that not only was the country breaking up into different power centers, but each local region was developing a nationalist ideology, each different from the other. The age of naked nationalism had begun.

Slovenian nationalists, now in power, quickly broke almost all Slovenia's remaining political and economic ties with the Yugoslav government. The Slovenes' separatist nationalism was unique in Yugoslavia—it had no victims and no enemies; while the Slovenes hated Milošević, they built no ideology against him. They practiced a "Garbo nationalism"—they just wanted to be left alone. Their virtue was democracy and their vice was selfishness. In their drive to separate from Yugoslavia they simply ignored the 22 million Yugoslavs who were not Slovenes. They bear considerable responsibility for the bloodbath that followed their secession.

No Yugoslav republic was more transformed by the elections of 1990 than Croatia. The decisive victory of the Croatian Democratic Union in May brought to the presidency an implacable nationalist, Franjo Tudjman. I first met Tudjman in Zagreb on the morning of his victory; before then I had avoided him because of the extreme nature of some of his campaign statements. If Milošević recalls a slick con man, Tudjman resembles an inflexible schoolteacher. He is a former general and communist, expelled from the party under Tito and twice jailed for nationalism. Prim steel eyeglasses hang on a square face whose natural expression is a scowl. His mouth occasionally creases into a nervous chuckle or mirthless laugh. In our first meeting, he treated the colleagues who accompanied him with extreme disdain. Then, on the spot, he appointed two of them to high-ranking positions—to their surprise, since the venue for this solemn act was the breakfast table of the American consul general.

Tudjman's temper flared when I asked him about his remark during the campaign that he was glad his wife was neither a Serb nor a Jew. He launched into a ten-minute defense of his ethnic humanity, claiming, among other things, that some of his best friends were Serbs. While he didn't profess similar affinities with Jews (and his earlier writings had denigrated the Holocaust), he did promise to make restitution to the Zagreb Jewish community for the destruction of its synagogue by Croatian fascists during World War II. He kept that promise.

Unlike Milošević, who is driven by power, Tudjman is obsessed by nationalism. His devotion to Croatia is of the most narrow-minded sort, and he has never shown much understanding of or interest in democratic values. He presided over serious violations of the rights of Serbs, who made up 12 percent of the population of Croatia. They were dismissed from work, required to take loyalty oaths, and subjected to attacks on their homes and property. I have sat at Tudjman's lunch table and listened to several of his ministers revile Serbs in the most racist terms. He didn't join in, but he didn't stop them either. He has also stifled the independence of the press as much as Milošević, and maybe even more.

Tudjman's saving grace, which distinguishes him from Milošević, is that he really wants to be a Western statesman. He therefore listens to Western expressions of concern and criticism and often does something about them. For better or worse, Croatian nationalism is defined by Tudjman—intolerant, anti-Serb, and authoritarian. These attributes—together with an aura of wartime fascism, which Tudjman has done nothing to dispel—help explain why many Serbs in Croatia reject Croatian rule and why the core hostility in the former Yugoslavia is still between Serbs and Croats.

During 1990, Serbian nationalism under Milošević became even more aggressive. No longer was it enough for Serbs living outside Serbia to have their rights protected. They also had to own and control the territory they inhabited, regardless of prior sovereignty. These Serbian claims had no consistent principles behind them. Where Serbs were a minority, as in Kosovo, they asserted a historical, rather than a numerical, right to rule. Where no such historical right was plausible, as in the Krajina area of Croatia, they claimed self-determination on the majority principle. Revealingly, Milošević was unwilling to give the Albanians in Kosovo the same right of self-determination that he demanded for Serbs in Croatia and Bosnia.

In the Serbian elections of December 1990, Milošević made nationalism the litmus test: if you didn't vote for him, you were not a good Serb. The Serbian opposition, overwhelmed by the superior organization of Milošević's still-intact communist apparatus and a near-total media blackout, foundered on whether to play the nationalist game or reject it. Milošević won in a tainted but convincing landslide. The one-party system, beloved by the Serbian leader, survived. Milošević simply modernized it by giving it multiparty trimmings.

Albanian nationalism was, like Croatian nationalism, to some degree a reaction to Milošević's aggressive tactics. As the Serbs pressed, the Albanians stiffened. They boycotted the Serbian elections, despite U.S. counsel that a determined parliamentary minority could wield much political leverage. Milošević's strong-arm approach had launched the Albanians on a path of no return toward complete independence from the Serbs.

By December 1990, there were few Kosovo Albanians who did not insist either on an independent Kosovo or a Kosovo linked with Albania. The psychological break was complete. Any provocation launched by either side had the potential to blow the province apart. In these volatile circumstances, I urged Milošević to meet with the disciplined and impressive Albanian leader Ibrahim Rugova, who was urging a policy of peaceful resistance. Rugova agreed. Milošević refused, saying of the leader of some two million Albanian subjects of Serbia, "Who does he represent?"

The most interesting opposition figure in Serbia was Vuk Drašković, a flamboyant and talented novelist, who leaped onto the political stage as a pro-Serbian extremist, complete with Old Testament beard, racist ideas, and the persona of a Serbian peasant. Once he found his political sea legs, however, Drašković turned into a staunch defender of an open political system and free press. On March 9, 1991, he used his talent for motivating people to stage a mass rally in Belgrade against Milošević's control of the press. Clumsy handling by the police and the army led to two deaths—a demonstrator and a policeman—and to Drašković's arrest and brief detention. Many observers felt that the rally, which has now entered Serbian folklore, came close to dethroning Milošević. While this is doubtful, the courage of nearly 100,000 spontaneous demonstrators was a moving tribute to the democratic vibrancy of many Serbs.

Many new opposition figures within the former republics of Yugoslavia took a clear stand against nationalism. In speaking out, they paid a price in ransacked offices, bombings, death threats, beatings, and arrests. With my strong support, Western human rights groups helped many opposition organizations and publications to survive. The investment, however long-term, will pay off one day. The people being helped, and those who will succeed them, are part of the "other Serbia" and the "other Croatia"—the core of the democratic revival that in time must replace the current nationalist hysteria.

Neither Milošević nor Tudjman could understand why we cared so much about people who were murdered, tortured, abused, or harassed. Milošević would listen patiently, then ask, "Why do you waste time on these individuals, who are mostly criminals anyway, when Serbs as a nation have been abused for years?" Tudjman would often erupt in fury when I had the temerity to suggest that Croatian authorities were not always model democrats. When it came to results, however, Milošević almost never delivered; Tudjman sometimes did.

Eleventh-Hour Maneuvers

The last year of Yugoslavia's existence—1991—saw the unfolding of unilateral and conflicting nationalist strategies. Slovenia, where a December 1990 referendum showed overwhelming popular support for independence, announced its decision to secede in June 1991 if a loose confederal solution was not found. Wittingly making his republic a hostage to Slovenian policy, Tudjman said Croatia would do what Slovenia did. Milošević countered that the breakup of Yugoslavia would lead to Serbia's incorporating all Serbs into a single state. Bosnian leader Alija Izetbegović argued that the survival of Yugoslavia in some form was essential to Bosnia's survival as well.

Izetbegović was mild-mannered, deferential, and perpetually anxious; he wore the mantle of leadership with great discomfort. A devout Muslim but no extremist, he consistently advocated the preservation of a multinational Bosnia. Ironically, it was Milošević and Tudjman, in their professed desire for Bosnian Serbs and Bosnian Croats to live apart from Muslims, who laid the philosophical groundwork for a separate Muslim entity. Bosnia had a strong multiethnic character and the highest percentage of ethnically mixed marriages of any republic. While its history since the fifteenth-century Turkish occupation was no more bloody than the history of England or France, Bosnia was the major Balkan killing ground during World War II. Izetbegović was succinct with me: "If Croatia goes independent, Bosnia will be destroyed."

In early 1991, the supporters of a unified and democratic Yugoslavia were becoming marginalized. The leaders of the two republics with the most to lose from the breakup of Yugoslavia—Alija Izetbegović of Bosnia and Kiro Gligorov of Macedonia—proposed to hold it together in an even weaker configuration. Milošević gave their plan lip service; the Croats and Slovenes rejected it flatly for leaving too many powers with the central government.

During this period the Yugoslav People's Army (JNA in its Serbo-Croatian acronym) emerged as a major political player, an unusual role for a communist army. I met regularly with the defense minister, General Veljko Kadijević, a brooding, humorless officer who spoke with antipathy about Slovenes and Croats and with paranoia about Germans, whom he saw as bent on incorporating the Balkans into a Fourth Reich. The JNA enjoyed a proud tradition, with roots in Tito's Partisan fighters, who stood up to the Germans in World War II. The fifth-largest army in Europe, well supplied by the Soviet Union and an enormous domestic arms industry, it was seen by many as the most important unifying institution in Yugoslavia. Its officer corps, however, had a Serbian majority who, when events forced them to choose, followed Milošević.

The JNA was soon on a collision course with the breakaway republics. Both Croatia and Slovenia were trying to create their own military forces by calling on their young men to desert the JNA and by weakening the JNA's control over the republican Territorial Defense Forces, a sort of national guard. The JNA went berserk over this proliferation of armies. "How many armies does the United States have?" Kadijević stormed at me. In early 1991, the JNA tried to force the Yugoslav presidency—a comically weak, collective, eight-person chief of state—to declare a national emergency and authorize the army to disarm the Slovenian and Croatian militaries. This bid, which amounted to a military coup, was frustrated politically by the democratically inclined presidency members from Macedonia and Slovenia, Vasil Tupurkovski and Janez Drnovšek. The defeat led Milošević to use the four votes he controlled in the eight-member presidency to subvert the scheduled rotation of its "president" from a Serb to a Croat. I asked Milošević several days before the May 15 election by the presidency if he would block the accession of the Croat Stipe Mesić, even though it was called for by constitutional precedent. "Serbia will always act in the spirit of the highest democratic principles," replied Milošević, who was always at his most mellifluous when expatiating on his devotion to democracy. "There will be a democratic vote in the presidency."

"But are you going to accept a fair transition from a Serb to a Croat president?" I pursued. "Mr. Zimmermann," he said, "you can tell your government that it has absolutely nothing to worry about." I cabled Washington that Mesić was not a sure thing. Two days later Milošević's allies on the presidency blocked Mesić's ascension, throwing Yugoslavia into a constitutional crisis. When I accused Milošević later of lying to me, he asserted that he had not actually promised that Mesić would be named. The incident illustrated three important traits of Milošević's character: his cynicism about Yugoslavia's unity and institutions, his natural mendacity, and the pains he always took to avoid direct responsibility for aggressive actions. The third trait was to become particularly relevant to Milošević's hidden hand in the Bosnia crisis.

Enter Baker

It was in the context of Milošević's move against the Yugoslav presidency and its Croatian president-designate, Croatian actions against the jobs and property of Serbs in Croatia, growing violence between Serbs and Croats, and the threat by both Slovenia and Croatia to withdraw from Yugoslavia at midyear that Secretary of State James Baker arrived in Belgrade on June 21, 1991.

During his one-day visit Baker had nine consecutive meetings: with the Albanian leaders from Kosovo, with all six republican leaders, and twice with Yugoslav Prime Minister Ante Marković and

Foreign Minister Budimir Lončar. Listening to Baker deal with these complex and irascible personalities, I felt that I had rarely, if ever, heard a secretary of state make a more skillful or reasonable presentation. Baker's failure was due not to his message but to the fact that the different parts of Yugoslavia were on a collision course.

Baker expressed the American hope that Yugoslavia would hold together behind the reformist Marcović, who by that time was seen increasingly as a figurehead or, even worse, a fig leaf. Baker said that it was up to the people of Yugoslavia to determine their future governing structures; the United States would support any arrangement on which they could peacefully agree. Baker told Croatian President Franjo Tudjman and Slovene President Milan Kučan that the United States would not encourage or support unilateral secession; he hoped they would not secede, but if they had to leave, he urged them to leave by negotiated agreement. He argued that self-determination cannot be unilateral but must be pursued by dialogue and peaceful means. To Milošević and (indirectly) the army, Baker made clear that the United States strongly opposed any use of force, intimidation, or incitement to violence that would block democratic change. Yugoslavia could not be held together at gunpoint. In his encounter with Milošević—the most contentious of the nine meetings—Baker hammered the Serb leader on his human rights violations in Kosovo, urged his acquiescence to a looser constitutional arrangement for Yugoslavia, and pressed him to stop destabilizing the Yugoslav presidency.

Never was a green light given or implied to Milošević or the army to invade the seceding republics, as has since been alleged in some press accounts. But was there a red light? Not as such, because the United States had given no consideration to using force to stop a Serbian/JNA attack on Slovenia or Croatia. Nor, at that point, had a single member of Congress, as far as I know, advocated the introduction of American military power. Baker did, however, leave a strong political message. He said to Prime Minister Marcović, a conduit to the army, "If you force the United States to choose between unity and democracy, we will always choose democracy."

Baker's message was the right one, but it came too late. If a mistake was made, it was that the secretary of state had not come six months earlier, a time that unfortunately coincided with the massive American preparations for the Persian Gulf War. By June 1991, Baker was making a last-ditch effort. Even so, it is not clear that an earlier visit by Baker would have made a difference. The aggressive nationalism emanating like noxious fumes from the leaders of Serbia and Croatia and their even more extreme advisers, officials, media manipulators, and allies had cast the die for disintegration and violence.

The breakup of Yugoslavia is a classic example of nationalism from the top down—a manipulated nationalism in a region where peace has historically prevailed more than war and in which a quarter of the population were in mixed marriages. The manipulators condoned and even provoked local ethnic violence in order to engender animosities that could then be magnified by the press, leading to further violence. Milošević gave prime television time to fanatic nationalists like Vojislav Šešelj, who once said that the way to deal with the Kosovo Albanians was to kill them all. Tudjman also used his control of the media to sow hate. Nationalist "intellectuals," wrapped in the mantle of august academies of sciences, expounded their pseudo-history of the victimization of Serbs (or Croats) through the ages. One of them seriously asserted to me that Serbs had committed no crimes or moral transgressions at any point in their long history. Worst of all, the media, under the thumb of most republican regimes, spewed an endless daily torrent of violence and enmity. As a reporter for *Vreme,* one of the few independent magazines left in the former Yugoslavia, said, "You Americans would become nationalists and racists too if your media were totally in the hands of the Ku Klux Klan."

Secession and War

In late June 1991, just a few days after Baker's departure from Belgrade and almost exactly according to their timetable, Croatia and Slovenia declared independence. Fighting began in Slovenia almost immediately. Contrary to the general view, it was the Slovenes who started the war. Their independence declaration, which had not been preceded by even the most token effort to negotiate, effectively put under their control all the border and customs posts between Slovenia and its two neighbors, Italy and Austria. This meant that Slovenia, the only international gateway between the West and Yugoslavia, had unilaterally appropriated the right to goods destined for other republics, as well as customs revenues estimated at some 75 percent of the Yugoslav federal budget. Even an army less primitive than the JNA would have reacted. Worst of all, the Slovenes' understandable desire to be independent condemned the rest of Yugoslavia to war.

The Yugoslav generals, thinking they could intimidate the Slovenes, roared their tanks through peaceful Slovenian streets, slapping aside compact cars as they lumbered through. The Slovenes, trained by the JNA itself in territorial defense, fought back. After ten days, at Milošević's direction or with his acquiescence, the JNA withdrew from Slovenia, leaving the republic effectively independent. Compared to the Croatian and Bosnian wars that followed, the casualty figures in Slovenia seem ludicrously small: 37 JNA and 12 Slovenes killed. They do not bear out the generally held assumption that the Yugoslav army waged an extermination campaign in Slovenia. In provoking war, the Slovenes won the support of the world's television viewers and consolidated their entire population behind independence. Unlike the JNA, they welcomed foreign journalists, to whom they retailed the epic struggle of their tiny republic against the Yugoslav colossus. It was the most brilliant public relations coup in the history of Yugoslavia.

It was no surprise to me that Milošević was willing to let Slovenia go. His policy since 1989 provoked the Slovenes to secede by making it clear that he would not tolerate their liberal, independent ways. With Slovenia out of the game, he and the JNA were now free to take on a Croatia no longer able to count on Slovenia's support.

The fighting in Croatia began with the illusion of evenhandedness. The Yugoslav army would step in to separate the Serbian and Croatian combatants. During the summer of 1991, however, it soon became clear that the JNA, while claiming neutrality, was in fact turning territory over to Serbs. The war in Croatia had become a war of aggression.

As the war grew more bitter through the summer of 1991, the European Community (EC) and the United Nations launched a joint effort to achieve a cease-fire and an agreement among all the Yugoslav republics. Special U.N. envoys Cyrus Vance and Lord Peter Carrington, two former foreign ministers and old friends, shared the Sisyphean task of achieving a peaceful outcome. The determined Vance won the trust of the JNA and succeeded on January 3, 1992, in producing a cease-fire that froze both the military and political status quo in Croatia. The fighting stopped, but the Serbs were left holding about a quarter of the republic. The freeze was unwittingly stabilized by U.N. peacekeepers who arrived in March 1992.

Carrington's job was to get the feuding Yugoslav republics to define the relationship they were prepared to have with each other. He and Vance both argued—as did the U.S. government—that there should be no Western recognition of the independence of any Yugoslav republic until all had agreed on their mutual relationships. If this simple principle had been maintained, less blood would have been shed in Bosnia.

During the fall of 1991, while Vance and Carrington were launching their diplomatic efforts, the JNA shelled the Croatian cities of Vukovar and Dubrovnik, the first major war crimes in Yugoslavia since World War II. The pretty Croatian city of Vukovar, with a mixed population, of which over a third was Serb, first came under JNA shelling in August, apparently because of its location on the Danube River between Serbia and Croatia. For three months the army, shrinking from an attack that might have cost it casualties, sat outside the city and shelled it to pieces. The civilian population of the city—Serbs and Croats alike—huddled in cellars. Over 2,000 civilians were killed before the JNA finally "liberated" the city.

One of the employees in our embassy residence, a young Croatian woman named Danijela Hajnal, was from Vukovar; her mother was trapped in a cellar during the siege. During her stay with my wife and me after Vukovar fell, Danijela's mother described the relations between Serbs and Croats during the attack: "There were a hundred people in that cellar," she said, "half of us Croats and half Serbs. We were friends when we went into the cellar, and three months later when we came out, we were still friends." About the same time I asked Danijela how many Serbs and Croats were in her high school class in Vukovar. She replied that she didn't have the faintest idea. These vignettes, which could be multiplied thousands of times over, show how natural it was for Yugoslavs to get along with each other, despite the ranting of their leaders.

Notwithstanding solemn guarantees by General Kadijević, the JNA in October 1991 also shelled Dubrovnik from the hills and the sea. This medieval town, which glowed in the Adriatic like a piece of pink marble, had withstood the depredations of Turks, Venetians, and many other would-be conquerors. Now it was falling under the guns of an army whose constitutional duty was to defend it. Dubrovnik was not destroyed, but the damage inflicted by the Yugoslav army exceeded the best efforts of any previous marauder. Only Milošević pretended that there was any military objective in Dubrovnik. Denying, as usual, any personal responsibility for what the army did, he told me with a straight face that there were foreign mercenaries hiding in the city. Kadijević didn't even pretend that Dubrovnik was a military target. "I give you my word," he told me, "that the shelling of Dubrovnik was unauthorized. Those who did it will be punished." My repeated requests for the details of their punishment went unanswered.

Shelling civilian populations is a war crime. Vukovar and Dubrovnik led directly to the merciless attacks on Sarajevo and other Bosnian cities. Yet no Western government at the time called on NATO's military force to get the JNA to stop shelling Dubrovnik, although NATO's supreme commander, General John Galvin, had prepared contingency plans for doing so. The use of force was simply too big a step to consider in late 1991. I did not recommend it myself—a major mistake. The JNA's artillery on the hills surrounding Dubrovnik and its small craft on the water would have been easy targets. Not only would damage to the city have been averted, but the Serbs would have been taught a lesson about Western resolve that might have deterred at least, some of their aggression against Bosnia. As it was, the Serbs learned another lesson—that there was no Western resolve, and that they could push about as far as their power could take them.

A Tar Baby in Washington

Secretary of State Baker's failure to head off the Slovenian and Croatian declarations of independence cooled whatever ardor he may have had for projecting the United States into the Yugoslav imbroglio. During the summer of 1991, it had been fair enough to give the EC a chance to deal with what it called a "European problem." But by autumn, the Serbian/JNA plan for taking over parts of Croatia had crystallized in the attacks on Vukovar and Dubrovnik. Threats to the integrity of Bosnia were growing, and the EC, under German cajoling, was stumbling toward recognition of the breakaway republics. Even without threatening force, the United States could have thrown more weight behind the effort to prevent greater violence. However, between July 1991 and March 1992, the United States was not a major factor in the Yugoslav crisis. In the fall of 1991, at a U.S. ambassadors' meeting in Berlin, a friend from the State Department's European Bureau told me that Yugoslavia had become a tar baby in Washington. Nobody wanted to touch it. With the American presidential election just a year away, it was seen as a loser.

Unfortunately, American immobility coincided with growing pressure on Bosnia. Neither Milošević nor Tudjman made any effort to conceal their designs on Bosnia from me. As a place where Serbs, Croats, and Muslims had coexisted more or less peacefully for centuries, Bosnia was an affront and a challenge to these two ethnic supremacists.

At the end of a long meeting with me, Tudjman erupted into a diatribe against Izetbegović and the Muslims of Bosnia. "They're dangerous fundamentalists," he charged, "and they're using Bosnia as a beachhead to spread their ideology throughout Europe and even to the United States. The civilized nations should join together to repel this threat. Bosnia has never had any real existence. It should be divided between Serbia and Croatia."

I was flabbergasted at this outburst and got the impression that Tudjman's aides who were present were equally surprised. With some heat I asked, "Mr. President, how can you expect the West to help you get back the parts of Croatia taken by the Serbs when you yourself are advancing naked and unsupported claims on a neighboring republic?" There was no answer. I added, "And how can you expect Milošević to respect a deal with you to divide Bosnia when he's trying to annex part of Croatia?" Amazingly, Tudjman answered, "Because I can trust

Milošević." On the way down the stairs after this surreal discussion, I asked one of Tudjman's aides if I had gotten too emotional in defending the integrity of Bosnia. "Oh no," he said, "You were just fine."

Milošević's strategy for Bosnia, unlike Tudjman's, was calculating rather than emotional. When Slovenia and Croatia declared independence and stopped participating in the Yugoslav government, Milošević, notwithstanding all he had done to destroy Yugoslavia, now claimed to be its heir. He contended that all those who wanted to "remain" in Yugoslavia should have the right to do so. This included, of course, the Serbs of Croatia and the Serbs of Bosnia. As Milošević explained this to me, he added that while the Muslims in Bosnia tended to live in cities, the Serbs were a rural people living on 70 percent of the land, to which they therefore had a right. Thus, at least six months before the Bosnian Serb army and the irregulars from Serbia shattered the peace in Bosnia, Milošević was laying the groundwork for a Serbian claim. From that moment, in every conversation I had with him I emphasized the strong U.S. opposition to any Serbian power play in Bosnia.

Fatal Recognition

When Croatia opted for independence in mid-1991, Bosnian President Izetbegović saw the writing on the wall for his republic. He scurried throughout Europe and the United States looking for ways to head off disaster. He pushed, without success, the dying Izetbegović-Gligorov plan for a loosely connected Yugoslavia. He asked for and got EC observers in Bosnia. He asked for, but did not get, U.N. peacekeepers there. Vance and the U.N. leadership in New York took the traditional if puzzling line that peacekeepers are used after a conflict, not before. The U.S. government did not support Izetbegović on the request for peacekeepers either. In a cable to Washington I urged this innovative step, but did not press for it as hard as I should have. As an unsatisfactory compromise, when the U.N. peacekeepers arrived in Croatia in March 1992, they set up their headquarters in Sarajevo.

In the fall of 1991, German Foreign Minister Hans-Dietrich Genscher pressed his EC colleagues to recognize Slovenia and Croatia and to offer recognition to Bosnia and Macedonia. Izetbegović, briefed by the German ambassador to Yugoslavia on how to make his point with Genscher that EC recognition would bring violence to Bosnia, unaccountably failed to do so in his November meeting with the German foreign minister. The omission can only have led Genscher to assume that he had a green light from Izetbegović for recognition.

I was urging Washington to defer recognition, as the EC ambassadors in Belgrade were urging their governments. Although Washington was opposed to premature recognition, U.S. appeals to EC governments were perfunctory. On December 17, 1991, an EC summit decided to grant recognition. Carrington and Vance both complained loudly and publicly. The State Department's statement, to avoid ruffling the EC, was nuanced. War in Bosnia, which had until then been probable, now became virtually inevitable.

A few days after the EC's decision, I had lunch in Belgrade with Izetbegović's deputy, Ejup Ganić, a Muslim hard-liner who had trained at MIT. I asked him, "Is Bosnia really going to ask for recognition in the face of all the dangers Izetbegović has repeatedly warned about? Wouldn't it be better to tell the European Community that you need more time to work out the political issues involved?" Ganić looked at me as if I had just dropped out of the sky. He said, "Of course we're going to move ahead on recognition. With Croatia and Slovenia now gone, we can't consign Bosnia to a truncated Yugoslavia controlled by Serbia."

I concluded from the abrupt change of tack by Ganić that Izetbegović was now playing a double game. With the European Community heading toward recognition, he thought he could get away with it under the guns of the Serbs. Perhaps he counted on Western military support, though nobody had promised him that. Whatever his motives, it was a disastrous political mistake. Serbia, Bosnia's vastly more powerful neighbor, now had the pretext it needed to strike—the claim that 1.3 million Serbs were being taken out of "Yugoslavia" against their will. I believe that Milošević and Bosnian Serb leader Radovan Karadžić had already decided to annex the majority of Bosnia by military force (Milošević had spoken to me of 70 percent). The EC's irresponsibility, the United States' passivity, and Izetbegović's miscalculation made their job easier.

Events took their inexorable course following the EC's recognition décision. Hardly anybody noticed the December 20 resignation of Marković, so powerless had Yugoslavia's last prime minister become. Although defeated by an ad hoc cabal of nationalists, from the liberal Slovenes to the neo-communist Serbs, Marković still departed as a symbol of everything his country needed: a modern, stable economy, the rule of law, and ethnic tolerance. He had treated Yugoslavia like a patient with a serious cancer—nationalism. A semi-heroic, semi-tragic figure, Marković failed, but at least he had fought the cancer instead of adjusting to it. He had aspired to be Yugoslavia's savior. Instead, he turned out to be the Yugoslavian equivalent of Russia's last leader before the Bolshevik deluge, Aleksandr Kerensky. The war in Croatia, the impending war in Bosnia, and a future that promised a generation of violence in the Balkans were the results of Yugoslavia's demise.

Partners in Crime

During the first few months of 1992, events in Bosnia careened down two parallel tracks. On one, the Izetbegović government, following the EC lead, prepared for independence. Its referendum on February 29 and March 1 produced predictable results. Practically all the Muslims and Croats voted for independence, yielding a 64-percent majority, while practically all the Serbs boycotted the election. On the other track, the leaders of the Serbian minority prepared for secession and war. Since the 1990 Bosnian election, I had paid periodic visits to Karadžić. The Bosnian Serb leader is a large man with flamboyant hair, an outwardly friendly manner, and the unlikely profession of psychiatry. In the great tradition of nationalists who do not come from their nation (Hitler, Napoleon, Stalin), Karadžić is from Montenegro, not Bosnia. I learned from experience that his outstanding characteristics were his stubbornness and deep-seated hostility to Muslims, Croats, and any other non-Serb ethnic group in his neighborhood.

I was startled to hear the extravagance of Karadžić's claims on behalf of the Serbs. He told me that "Serbs have a right to territory not only where they're now living but also where they're buried, since the earth they lie in was taken unjustly from them." When I asked whether he would accept parallel claims on behalf of Croats or Muslims, he answered, "No, because Croats are fascists and Muslims are Islamic fanatics." His disdain for the truth was absolute; he insisted that "Sarajevo is a Serbian city," which it has never been. His apartheid philosophy was as extreme as anything concocted in South Africa. He was the architect of massacres in the Muslim villages, ethnic cleansing, and artillery attacks on civilian populations. In his fanaticism, ruthlessness, and contempt for human values, he invites comparison with a monster from another generation, Heinrich Himmler.

Karadžić and Milošević both made an elaborate pretense to me of not knowing each other very well and having no operational contacts. Milošević always reacted with cherubic innocence when I accosted him over Bosnia. "But why do you come to me, Mr. Zimmermann? Serbia has nothing to do with Bosnia. It's not our problem." This fiction suited each leader— Milošević to escape responsibility for aggression, Karadžić to avoid the charge that he was a henchman of Milošević's rather than a Serbian folk hero in his own right.

There is no doubt, however, that the two were partners in war crimes. Copying Milošević's strategy in Croatia, Karadžić's followers—beginning a year before the Bosnian war broke out—declared three "Serb Autonomous Regions" in Bosnia, began an arms supply relationship with the JNA, and accepted JNA intervention in September to define their borders. They established artillery positions around Sarajevo and other towns, created a "Bosnian Serb" army (effectively a branch of the JNA, commanded by a JNA general and using JNA-supplied heavy artillery, tanks, and air power), established their own parliament, and attempted a putsch in Sarajevo on March 2, 1992. In March 1992—before any country had recognized the independence of Bosnia—they declared a "Serbian Republic." These steps, particularly those involving the JNA, would not have been possible with out Milošević's direct involvement.

In response to the evidence of Serbian collusion and the results of the Bosnian referendum, and in hopes that recognition might deter a Serbian attack, the United States and other NATO countries recognized Bosnia in early April 1992. However, a few days before, Serbs had launched an attack from Serbia across the Drina River which forms the border between Serbia and Bosnia. Milošević, Karadžić, and their spokesmen have asserted that the Western recognition of Bosnia had forced the Serbs to move. I doubt this. The two Serbian leaders already had a joint strategy for dividing Bosnia and they were going to carry it out, regardless of what the rest of the world did.

The attack on Bosnia showed that Milošević and Karadžić are apostles of the most aggressive form of nationalism. Milošević-style nationalism has proven singularly resistant to economic inducements, penalties, or any other pressures short of force. Unfortunately, neither the Bush nor the Clinton administration was willing to step up to the challenge of using force in Bosnia, despite significant American interests in the Balkans. Moreover, the two Serbian strongmen behind their propaganda, espouse the doctrine of the single nation-state, a deeply uncivilized concept. Nation-states have nothing to unify them but their nationalism, and power within them will naturally gravitate to the most strident nationalists. Multinational states, a majority in the world, can be deeply conflicted, as Yugoslavia proves. But they can also be schools of tolerance, since the need to take account of minority interests moderates behavior. Yugoslavia had its democrats as well as is demagogues. The attackers across the Drina, however, were barbarians, pure and simple.

The Serbian attack was directed at towns with large Muslim majorities. Gangsters from Serbia proper, including the notorious Arkan, who had left a trail of murder and pillage during the Croatian war, were displayed on Belgrade television swaggering on the debris of Bijeljina and other Muslim towns. Those Serbia-based marauders accounted for the high volume of atrocities committed in the early days of the war—the gang rapes, ethnic cleansing, and wanton murder of Muslim villagers. The presence in Bosnia of irregulars from Serbia drained all credibility from Milošević's assertion that Serbia had nothing to do with what was going on there.

During one of the meetings in which, on Washington's instructions, I accused Milošević of aggression in Bosnia, he asserted, "There isn't a single Serb from Serbia involved in the fighting in Bosnia."

"But," I said, "I saw Arkan on your own Belgrade television boasting about his capture of Bosnian villages."

"Our television is free to broadcast whatever it wants," said Milošević. "You shouldn't take it so seriously. Besides, you needn't worry about trouble in Bosnia. Serbs have no serious grievances in Bosnia; they're not being abused there. This is a big difference with Serbs in Croatia." Via this backhanded compliment to the Izetbegović government, Milošević reduced the Serbian argument for naked aggression to the assumption that Serbs had a right to murder, torture, and expel simply because they did not want to live under an independent multiethnic government that was not abusing them.

Last Words

Just a few weeks before I was recalled in protest against the Serbian aggression in Bosnia, I had my last talk with Karadžić in Belgrade, where he was pretending not to see Milošević. He came to the U.S. embassy, bringing with him as usual his deputy and pilot fish, Nikola Koljević, a Bosnian Serb who had taught in the United States and was an expert on Shakespeare. Koljević's specialty was sidling up to me after my meetings with Karadžić and portraying himself as the humane influence on Bosnian Serb policy. Several months after my departure from Belgrade, I saw a photograph of Koljević directing artillery fire on the civilian population of Sarajevo from a hill above the city.

Perhaps it was fitting that I should have one of my last meetings in doomed Yugoslavia with this macabre pair, the professor of English literature and the psychiatrist. At least Shakespeare and Freud would have understood the power of the irrational that provoked these and other madmen to destroy the human fabric of Yugoslavia.

Karadžić began the conversation by running down his usual litany of criticisms of the Europeans, attacks on Izetbegović's character and ideology, and laments that the United States should be so blind as to abandon its traditional Serbian allies. He then launched into a stream-of-consciousness justification for everything he was doing. "You have to understand Serbs, Mr. Zimmermann. They have been betrayed for centuries. Today they cannot live with other nations. They must have their own separate existence. They are a warrior race and they can trust only themselves to take by force what is their due.

But this doesn't mean that Serbs can hate. Serbs are incapable of hatred."

I sought to pin him down. "What sort of Bosnian Serb republic do you have in mind?" I asked. "Will it be a part of Serbia?"

"That will be for the Bosnian Serb people to decide," he said. "But our first goal is independence, so we can live separately from others."

"Where will your capital be?" I asked.

"Why, Sarajevo, of course."

"But how can a city which is nearly 50 percent Muslim and only 30 percent Serb be the capital for the Serbs alone?"

Karadžić had a ready answer. "The city will be divided into Muslim, Serbian, and Croatian sections, so that no ethnic groups will have to live or work together."

"Just how will it be divided?"

"By walls," he said matter-of-factly. "Of course people will be able to pass from one part of the city to another, as long as they have permission and go through the checkpoints."

I thought of Sarajevo, which for centuries had been a moving symbol of the civility that comes from a people of different ethnicities living in harmony. Then I thought of Berlin, where the wall, which had symbolized all the hatreds and divisions of the Cold War, had been torn down just over a year before.

"Do you mean," I asked, "that Sarajevo will be like Berlin before the wall was destroyed?"

"Yes," he answered, "our vision of Sarajevo is like Berlin when the wall was still standing."

- U.S. Ambassador to Yugoslavia 1989-1992
- Breakup/Civil War:
  - Nationalism from top-down
  - Peace has usually prevailed
    - mixed marriages too

✦ Reading 72 ✦

Constitution of the Russian Federation

Part One

Chapter 1

The Principles of the Constitutional System

Article 1

1. The Russian Federation—Russia shall be a democratic, federative, law-based state with a republican form of government.

2. The names Russian Federation and Russia shall have one and the same meaning.

Article 2

Human beings and human rights and freedoms shall be of the highest value. Recognition of, respect for, and protection of the human and civil rights and freedoms shall be the duty of the state.

Article 3

1. The multi-ethnic people of the Russian Federation shall be the bearers of its sovereignty and the sole source of authority in the Russian Federation.

2. The people shall exercise their power directly and also through bodies of state authority and bodies of local self-government.

3. Referendums and free elections shall be the highest expression of the people's authority.

4. No person shall have the right to appropriate power in the Russian Federation. Seizure of power or appropriation of authority shall be prosecuted in accordance with federal law.

Article 4

1. The sovereignty of the Russian Federation shall extend to its entire territory.

2. The Constitution of the Russian Federation and federal laws shall have priority throughout the territory of the Russian Federation.

3. The Russian Federation shall ensure the integrity and inviolability of its territory.

Article 5

1. The Russian Federation shall be made up of republics, territories, regions, cities with federal status, the autonomous region and autonomous areas, all of which are equal members of the Russian Federation.

2. The republics (states) shall have their own constitutions and laws. Territories, regions, cities with federal status, the autonomous region and autonomous areas shall have their own statutes and laws.

3. The federative make-up of the Russian Federation shall be based upon its state integrity, a uniform system of state authority, the separation of jurisdiction and powers between the bodies of state authority of the Russian Federation and bodies of state authority of the members of the Russian Federation, and the equality and self-determination of the peoples within the Russian Federation.

4. All members of the Russian Federation shall be equal in their relations with federal bodies of state authority.

Article 6

1. Citizenship in the Russian Federation shall be acquired and revoked in accordance with federal law and shall be uniform and equal regardless of how it was obtained

2. Each citizen of the Russian Federation shall have, throughout its territory, all rights and freedoms and shall carry equal duties as provided for in the Constitution of the Russian Federation.

3. No citizen of the Russian Federation shall be deprived of citizenship or of the right to change it.

Article 7

1. The Russian Federation shall be a social state, the policies of which shall aim to create conditions ensuring adequate living standards and the free development of every individual.

From: *Constitution of the Russian Federation,* eds. Vladimir V. Belyakov and Walter J. Raymond (Lawrenceville, Va., and Moscow: Brunswick and Novosti, 1994), pp. 16–35.

2. Citizens of the Russian Federation shall be guaranteed the protection of: their work and health, a minimum wage; state support for the family, motherhood, fatherhood, childhood, invalids, and aged people; the development of a system of social services; and the provision of state pensions, allowances and other social security guarantees.

Article 8

1. A unified economic space, the free movement of commodities, services and finances, and support for competition and freedom of economic activity shall be guaranteed in the Russian Federation.

2. Private, state, municipal and other forms of property shall be equally recognized and protected in the Russian Federation

Article 9

1. Land and other natural resources shall be used and protected in the Russian Federation as the foundation of life and the activity of the peoples living in the corresponding territory.

2. Land and other natural resources may become private, state, municipal and other forms of property.

Article 10

State power in the Russian Federation shall be exercised on the basis of its separation into legislative, executive and judicial branches. The bodies of legislative, executive and judicial power shall be independent from one another.

Article 11

1. State power in the Russian Federation shall be exercised by the President of the Russian Federation, the Federal Assembly (Federation Council and State Duma), the Government of the Russian Federation and the courts of law of the Russian Federation.

2. State power in the members of the Russian Federation shall be exercised by the bodies of state authority established by them.

3. The jurisdiction and powers between the bodies of state authority of the Russian Federation and the bodies of state authority of the members of the Russian Federation shall be delineated by this Constitution, the Federation Treaty and other treaties on the delineation of jurisdiction and powers.

Article 12

Local self-government shall be recognized and guaranteed in the Russian Federation. Local self-government shall be independent within the limits of its powers. The bodies of local self-government shall not be part of the system of the bodies of state authority.

Article 13

1. Ideological pluralism shall be recognized in the Russian Federation.

2. No ideology shall be established as a state or compulsory ideology.

3. Political diversity and a multi-party system shall be recognized in the Russian Federation.

4. All public associations shall be equal before the law

5. The creation and activity of public associations whose purposes or actions are directed at forcibly changing the foundations of the constitutional system, disrupting the integrity of the Russian Federation, subverting the security of the state, creating armed units, or inciting social, racial, ethnic or religious strife, shall be prohibited.

Article 14

1. The Russian Federation shall be a secular state. No religion shall be declared an official or compulsory religion.

2. All religious associations shall be separate from the state and shall be equal before the law.

Article 15

1. The Constitution of the Russian Federation shall be the supreme law and shall be in force throughout the territory of the Russian Federation. No laws or other legislative acts passed in the Russian Federation shall contravene the Constitution of the Russian Federation.

2. Bodies of state authority and bodies of local self-government, officials, citizens and their associations shall abide by the Constitution of the Russian Federation.

3. All laws shall be made public on an official basis. No law shall be passed if it has not been made public. No regulatory legal acts affecting human or civil rights, freedoms and duties shall be effective if they have not been made public officially.

4. Universally acknowledged principles and standards of international law and international treaties of the Russian Federation shall be a part of its legal system. Should an international treaty of the Russian Federation establish rules other than those established by law, the rules of the international treaty shall be applied.

Article 16

1. The provisions of this Chapter of the Constitution shall constitute the fundamental principles of the constitutional system of the Russian Federation and shall not be changed except in accordance with the procedure established by this Constitution.

2. No other provisions of this Constitution shall contradict the fundamental principles of the constitutional system of the Russian Federation.

Chapter 2. Human and Civil Rights and Freedoms

Article 17

1. Within the Russian Federation human and civil rights and freedoms shall be recognized and guaranteed under universally acknowledged principles and rules of international law and in accordance with this Constitution.

2. Basic human rights and freedoms are inalienable and belong to each person from birth.

3. The exercise of human and civil rights and freedoms may not infringe on the rights and freedoms of other persons.

Article 18

Human and civil rights and freedoms shall be instituted directly. They shall determine the purpose, content and application of the laws, the work of legislative and executive authority and local self-government and shall be guaranteed by the justice system.

Article 19

1. All people shall be equal before the law and the court.

2. The state shall guarantee equal human and civil rights and freedoms without regard to sex, race, nationality language, origin, property or official status, place of residence, attitude toward religion, persuasions, affiliation with social associations or other circumstances. Any form of restriction of civil rights on the basis of social, racial, national, language or religious affiliation shall be prohibited.

3. Men and women shall have equal rights and freedoms and equal opportunities to exercise them.

Article 20

1. Each person shall have the right to life.

2. The death penalty, until its abolition, may be prescribed by federal law as an exceptional penalty for particularly grave crimes against life with the granting to the accused of the right to have the case heard by a court with the participation of jurors.

Article 21

1. The dignity of the individual shall be protected by the state. Nothing may serve as a justification for its diminution.

2. No person shall be subjected to torture, violence or other cruel or degrading treatment or punishment. No person may be subjected to medical, scientific or other experiments without his/her voluntary consent.

Article 22

1. Each person shall have the right to freedom and personal inviolability.

2. Arrest, taking into custody and holding in custody shall only be authorized by a judicial decision. Without a judicial decision no person may be subjected to detention for a period of more than 48 hours.

Article 23

1. Each person shall have the right to the inviolability of private life, personal and family secrecy, and the protection of honor and good reputation.

2. Each person shall have the right to privacy of correspondence, telephone conversations, postal, telegraph and other messages. The restriction of this right shall only be allowed on the basis of a judicial decision.

Article 24

1. The gathering, storage, use and dissemination of information concerning the private life of an individual without the individual's consent shall not be allowed.

2. The bodies of state authority, the bodies of local self-government and their officials shall be obliged to provide each person access to documents

and materials that directly affect his rights and freedoms unless otherwise specified in the law.

Article 25
The home shall be inviolable. No person shall have the right to enter a home against the will of the person(s) residing in it except in cases determined by federal law or on the basis of a judicial decision.

Article 26
1. Each person shall have the right to determine and indicate his nationality. No person may be forced to determine or indicate his nationality.
2. Each person shall have the right to use his native tongue and to choose freely the language of communication, upbringing, education, and artistic creation.

Article 27
1. Each person who is legitimately within the territory of the Russian Federation shall have the right to move freely and to choose where to live temporarily or permanently.
2. Each person may freely leave the boundaries of the Russian Federation. A citizen of the Russian Federation shall have the right to return to the Russian Federation without hindrance.

Article 28
Each person shall be guaranteed freedom of conscience and freedom of religion, including the right to profess individually or jointly with others any religion or to profess none, to freely choose, hold and propagate religious and other beliefs and to act in accordance with them.

Article 29
1. Each person shall be guaranteed freedom of thought and speech.
2. No propaganda or agitation inciting social, racial, national or religious hatred and enmity shall be allowed. The propaganda of social, racial, national, religious or language supremacy shall be prohibited.
3. Nobody may be forced to express his opinions and persuasions or renounce them.
4. Each person shall have the right to freely seek, receive, transmit, produce and disseminate information in any legitimate way. The list of data that constitute state secrets shall be fixed by federal law.
5. Freedom of the mass media shall be guaranteed. Censorship shall he prohibited.

Article 30
1. Each person shall have the right to association, including the right to establish trade unions to safeguard his/her interests. Freedom of activity of public associations shall be guaranteed.
2. No person may be forced to join, or to maintain membership in, any association.

Article 31
Citizens of the Russian Federation shall have the right to assemble peacefully without arms, to hold meetings, rallies, demonstrations, processions, and to picket.

Article 32
1. Citizens of the Russian Federation shall have the right to participate in the management of state affairs both directly and through their representatives.
2. Citizens of the Russian Federation shall have the right to elect and be elected to bodies of state authority and bodies of local self-government and to participate in referendums.
3. Citizens found by a court not to be sui juris or held in places of detention under a court sentence shall not have the right to elect or be elected.
4. Citizens of the Russian Federation shall have equal access to state employment.
5. Citizens of the Russian Federation shall have the right to participate in the administration of justice.

Article 33
Citizens of the Russian Federation shall have the right to appeal personally and to send individual and collective appeals to state bodies and bodies of local self-government.

Article 34
1. Each person shall have the right to freely use his abilities and property for entrepreneurial or any other economic activity not prohibited by law.
2. No economic activities aimed at monopolization or unfair competition shall be allowed.

Article 35

1. The right of private ownership shall be protected by law.

2. Each person shall have the right to own property and to possess, use and dispose of it both individually and jointly with other persons.

3. No person may be deprived of property except by a judicial decision. Compulsory alienation of property for state needs may only be carried out on the condition of prior and equal compensation.

4. The right of inheritance shall be guaranteed.

Article 36

1. Citizens and their associations shall be entitled to have land in private ownership.

2. The possession, use and disposal of land and other natural resources shall be exercised by the owners freely unless this inflicts damage on the environment and/or infringes the rights and legitimate interests of other persons.

3. The conditions or procedures for land use shall be determined on the basis of federal law.

Article 37

1. Labor shall be free. Each person shall have the right freely to dispose of his abilities to work and to choose an occupation.

2. Compulsory labor shall be prohibited.

3. Each person shall have the right to work in conditions that meet the requirements of safety and hygiene, to remuneration for labor without any discrimination and not below the minimum wage established by federal law, as well as the right to protection against unemployment.

4. The right to individual and collective labor disputes with the employment of methods specified by federal law for their resolution, including the right to strike, shall be recognized.

5. Each person shall have the right to rest and leisure. A person working under a labor contract shall be guaranteed the length of working time, days off, holidays, and paid annual leave prescribed by federal law.

Article 38

1. Motherhood, childhood, and the family are under state protection.

2. The care of children and their upbringing shall be the equal right and duty of parents.

3. Able-bodied children who have reached the age of eighteen years shall take care of parents who are unable to work.

Article 39

1. Each person shall be guaranteed social security in old age, in the event of sickness, disability or loss of a family's primary provider, for the raising of children and in other cases specified by law.

2. State pensions and social benefits shall be established by law.

3. Voluntary social insurance, the creation of additional forms of social security and charity shall be encouraged.

Article 40

1. Each person shall have the right to housing. No person may be arbitrarily deprived of housing.

2. Bodies of state authority and bodies of local self-government shall encourage housing construction and create conditions for the exercise of the right to housing.

3. Housing shall be provided free or for a reasonable charge out of state, municipal and other housing stocks to low-income and other persons indicated in the law who are in need of housing in accordance with procedures set by law.

Article 41

1. Each person shall have the right to health protection and medical assistance. Medical assistance in state and municipal health-care institutions shall be provided to citizens free of charge out of the resources of the appropriate budget, insurance premiums and other receipts.

2. Federal programs for the protection and improvement of the health of the population shall be financed. Measures to promote state, municipal and private systems of public health shall be taken. Activities conducive to improving the health of the individual, the development of physical culture and sports, and environmental, hygienic and epidemiological well-being shall be encouraged in the Russian Federation.

3. The withholding by officials of facts and circumstances that pose a threat to a person's life or

health shall entail responsibility in accordance with federal law.

Article 42
Each person shall have the right to a favorable environment, reliable information on its condition and compensation for damage inflicted on his/her health or property by violations of environmental laws.

Article 43
1. Each person shall have the right to education.
2. Preschool, basic general and secondary vocational education in state or municipal educational institutions and at enterprises shall be guaranteed to be accessible to all citizens free of charge.
3. Each person shall be entitled on a competitive basis and free of charge to receive a higher education in a state or municipal educational institution or at an enterprise.
4. Basic general education shall be compulsory. Parents or guardians shall ensure that children obtain a basic general education.
5. The Russian Federation shall establish federal state educational standards and support various forms of education and self-education.

Article 44
1. Each person shall be guaranteed freedom of literary, artistic, scientific, technical and other types of creative work and teaching. Intellectual property shall be protected by law.
2. Each person shall have the right to participate in cultural life, to make use of cultural institutions, and to enjoy access to cultural activities and values.
3. Each person shall be obliged to care for the preservation of the historical and cultural heritage and cherish historical and cultural monuments.

Article 45
1. The state protection of human and civil rights and freedoms in the Russian Federation shall be guaranteed.
2. Each person shall be entitled to defend his/her rights and freedoms in every way not prohibited by law.

Article 46
1. Each person shall be guaranteed the judicial protection of his/her rights and freedoms.
2. Decisions and actions (or inaction) by bodies of state authority or bodies of local self-government, public associations or officials may be appealed in court.
3. Each person shall be entitled, in accordance with international treaties of the Russian Federation, to apply to inter-state bodies involved in the protection of human rights and freedoms if all available internal means of legal protection have been exhausted.

Article 47
1. No person may be deprived of the right to have a case examined in the court or by the judge to whose jurisdiction it is referred by law.
2. A person accused of committing a crime shall have the right to have a case heard by a court with the participation of jurors in the cases provided for by federal law.

Article 48
1. Each person shall be guaranteed the right to receive qualified legal assistance. In cases provided for by law legal assistance shall be provided free of charge.
2. Each person arrested, taken into custody or accused of committing a crime shall have the right to use the assistance of a lawyer (defense attorney) from the moment of arrest, being taken into custody, or the bringing of a charge, respectively.

Article 49
1. Each person accused of committing a crime shall be presumed innocent until his/her culpability is proved in the manner specified by federal law and established by a court sentence which has become effective.
2. Defendants shall not be obliged to prove their innocence.
3. Irreconcilable doubts about the culpability of a person shall be interpreted in the defendant's favor.

Article 50
1. No person may be tried twice for the same crime.
2. Using evidence elicited in violation of federal law shall be inadmissible in administering justice.
3. Each person convicted of a crime shall have the right to a review of the sentence by a higher court in the manner specified by federal law, as well

as the right to ask for a pardon or the lessening of a sentence.

Article 51

1. Citizens shall not be obliged to testify against themselves, their spouses or close relatives as specified by federal law.

2. Federal law may establish other cases in which citizens are relieved of the duty to give testimony.

Article 52

The rights of victims of crimes or abuses of authority shall be protected by law. The state shall provide victims access to justice and compensation for damage inflicted.

Article 53

Each person shall have the right to compensation by the state for damage inflicted by illegal actions (or inaction) of bodies of state authority or their officials.

Article 54

1. Laws establishing or heightening responsibility shall not have retroactive force.

2. No person may be held responsible for an act which at the time of its commission was not considered to be a violation of the law. If after the commission of a violation of the law the criminal responsibility for it has been abolished or mitigated, the new law shall apply.

Article 55

1. The enumeration in the Constitution of the Russian Federation of fundamental rights and freedoms shall not be interpreted as a denial or diminution of other generally recognized human and civil rights and freedoms.

2. Laws abolishing or diminishing human and civil rights and freedoms shall not be issued in the Russian Federation.

3. Human and civil rights and freedoms may be restricted by federal law only to the extent necessary for upholding the foundations of the constitutional system, morality, or the health, rights and lawful interests of other persons or for ensuring the defense of the country and state security.

Article 56

1. Individual restrictions on rights and freedoms, with an indication of the scope and time limits of their operation, may be imposed during a state of emergency to safeguard citizens' safety and uphold the constitutional system in accordance with federal constitutional law.

2. A state of emergency throughout the Russian Federation and in its individual areas may be declared under circumstances and in the manner specified by federal constitutional law.

3. The rights and freedoms specified in Articles 20, 21, 23 (Part 1), 24, 28, 34 (Part 1), 40 (Part 1) and 46–54 of the Constitution of the Russian Federation shall not be subject to restriction.

Article 57

Each person shall be obliged to pay statutory taxes and levies. Laws imposing new taxes or worsening the position of the taxpayers shall not have retroactive force.

Article 58

Each person shall be obliged to protect nature and the environment and to treat natural wealth with care.

Article 59

1. Defense of the Fatherland shall be the duty and responsibility of citizens of the Russian Federation.

2. Citizens of the Russian Federation shall perform military service in accordance with federal law.

3. In cases where the performance of military service runs counter to a citizen's persuasions or religion, and also in other cases specified by federal law, a citizen of the Russian Federation shall have the right to replace military service with alternative civilian service.

Article 60

A citizen of the Russian Federation may independently exercise his/her rights and duties in full from the age of eighteen.

Article 61

1. A citizen of the Russian Federation may not be expelled from the Russian Federation or extradited to another state.

2. The Russian Federation shall guarantee its citizens defense and protection outside its boundaries.

Article 62

1. A citizen of the Russian Federation may have the citizenship of a foreign state (dual citizenship) in accordance with federal law or an international treaty of the Russian Federation.

2. A Russian Federation citizen's possession of the citizenship of a foreign state shall not detract from his/ her rights or freedoms and shall not release him/her from the duties arising from Russian citizenship unless otherwise specified in federal law or an international treaty of the Russian Federation.

3. Foreign citizens and stateless persons in the Russian Federation shall enjoy rights and bear responsibilities on a par with the citizens of the Russian Federation, except in cases specified by federal law or an international treaty of the Russian Federation.

Article 63

1. The Russian Federation shall grant political asylum to foreign citizens and stateless persons in accordance with universally acknowledged rules of international law.

2. Extradition from the Russian Federation to other countries of persons being pursued for their political persuasions, or for actions (or inaction) that are not recognized as a crime in the Russian Federation, shall not be allowed. The extradition of persons accused of committing a crime, and the transfer of convicts for serving their punishment in other states, shall be carried out on the basis of federal law or an international treaty of the Russian Federation.

Article 64

The provisions of this Chapter shall be the basis of the legal status of the individual in the Russian Federation and may not be changed except in the manner specified in this Constitution.

✦ Reading 73 ✦

Stop Signs on the Web

The Economist

In 1967 Roy Bates, a retired British army major, occupied an island fortress six miles off the English coast and declared it a sovereign nation. He was never sure what to do with his Principality of Sealand. Now, however, the fortress may have found its calling. For several months, a firm called HavenCo has been operating a data centre there. Anyone who wants to keep a website or other data out of the reach of national governments can rent space on the servers that hum in one of the concrete pillars. In the mid-1990s, Sealand would have been seen as yet more proof that the Internet cannot be regulated. If a country tried to censor digital content, the data would simply hop to a more liberal jurisdiction. These days, the data principality symbolizes just the opposite: the days of unrestricted freedom on the Internet are numbered, except, perhaps, in odd places like Sealand.

It seems likely that 2000 will be remembered as the year when governments started to regulate cyberspace in earnest, and forgot, in the process, that the reason the worldwide network became such an innovative force at all was a healthy mix of self-regulation and no regulation. In Britain, the Regulation of Investigatory Powers Act now gives the police broad access to e-mail and other online communications. South Korea has outlawed access to gambling websites. The United States has passed a law requiring schools and libraries that receive federal funds for Internet connections to install software on their computers to block material harmful to the young.

This year, governments are turning their attention to the many jurisdictional problems created by the Internet. These have been emphasized by a French ruling against Yahoo! on November 20th. The French court ordered the Internet portal firm to find some way of banning French users from seeing the Nazi memorabilia posted on its American sites, or face a daily fine of Ffr 100,000 ($13,000) from the end of February. Yahoo! is fighting the case, even though it has now stopped sales of Nazi memorabilia.

The case could be a taste of things to come. Under a new EU law, for example, European consumers may now sue EU-based Internet sites in their own countries, and the rule may well be extended internationally. The United States has just endorsed the gist of the Council of Europe's cybercrime treaty, which aims to harmonize laws against hacking, Internet fraud and child pornography. All this is a far cry from what leading Internet thinkers prophesied only five years ago. "You [governments] have no moral right to rule us nor do you possess any methods of enforcement we have true reason to fear," proclaimed John Perry Barlow in his 1996 "Declaration of Independence of Cyberspace." Libertarian thinking also ran through early Internet scholarship. David Post and David Johnson, law professors at Temple University in Philadelphia and Georgetown University respectively, argued in that same year that cyberspace was a distinct place that needed laws and legal institutions entirely of its own.

To treat cyberspace differently seemed logical. Because data are sent around the Internet in small packets, each of which can take a different route, the flow of information is hard to stop, even if much of the network is destroyed. It was this built-in resilience that appealed to the Internet's original sponsor, America's Defense Department, and made it the medium of choice for civil libertarians. "The Internet," runs their favourite motto, "interprets censorship as damage and routes around it."

Many online experts argue that, since the Internet does away with geographical boundaries, it also does away with territorially based laws. The transmission of data is almost instant, regardless of where sender

From: "Stop Signs on the Web," *The Economist,* January 13, 2001, pp. 8–12.

and receiver are. Today individuals, as well as multinational companies, can decide in which country to base their websites, thus creating competition between jurisdictions. For example, the United States, thanks to its constitutional guarantee of the right to free speech, has become a safe haven for hundreds of German neo-Nazi sites that are illegal under German law.

Yet, for all that, governments are not completely helpless in cyberspace. They have some potentially powerful tools at their disposal. Filtering is one. Software installed on a PC, in an Internet service provider's equipment or in gateways that link one country with the rest of the online world can block access to certain sites.

Less well known, but potentially more important, is the fact that websites themselves can block users. They do so by employing the same technology that serves up tailored banner advertisements to visitors from another country. They track the Internet service provider's "IP address," the number that identifies computers on the Internet and, in many cases, reveals where a user is.

This technology was the basis for the French ruling against Yahoo! The firm had argued that it was technically impossible to prevent French users from reaching auctions of illegal Nazi memorabilia on its sties. But a panel of three technical experts argued that IP-address tracking could spot more than 60% of French surfers.

Both filtering and IP-address tracking are far from perfect. Filters generally block too much—and too little. And surfers can block IP-address tracking by using services such as Zero Knowledge's Freedom or anonymizer.com. In any case, knowing where a user is is only part of the solution. In the case of Yahoo!, the firm would still have to work out which auctions to block.

But do these shortcomings matter? Jack Goldsmith, a law professor at the University of Chicago, argues that the real world is full of imperfect filtering and identification techniques: criminals crack safes, 15-year-olds visit bars with fake IDs, secret information is leaked to the press. To Mr. Goldsmith, there is little doubt that filtering and identification technologies will help to make cyberspace more regulated, because they will allow governments to raise the cost of getting certain information.

China, for instance, has essentially covered its territory with an Internet isolated from the rest of the online world by software that blocks access to sites with unwanted content. Although clever surfers can find ways to tunnel through the "Great Firewall," it keeps the majority from straying too far online. Most Chinese, in any case, get on the Internet from work or a public place, where the state can control the software and track what users do, and where they risk being seen if they go to an illegal site.

These technologies are likely to become more efficient. The demands of e-commerce, rather than governments, are driving improvements. Alkamai, an Internet firm which speeds up delivery by using a network of computers to store online content closer to consumers, recently started offering a new service called EdgeScape. This allows websites to determine exactly where a visitor is, at the time he visits, in order to customize content by region or country.

Online companies will certainly also make use in future of a controversial feature called IPv6, designed by the Internet Engineering Task Force (IETF). At present, the anonymity of most Internet users is more or less protected because service providers generally assign a different IP address each time someone logs on. But IPv6 includes a new, expanded IP address, part of which is the unique serial number of each computer's network-connection hardware. Every data packet sent will carry a user's electronic fingerprints.

The holy grail for e-commerce, however, would be a system in which users had permanent digital certificates on their computers containing details of age, citizenship, sex, professional credentials, and so on. Such technology would not only allow websites to aim their services at individuals, but would let governments reclaim their authority. These solutions to Internet regulation are far off, if they fly at all. But Lawrence Lessign, a law professor at Stanford University, warns that e-commerce firms will push for such certificates and that governments may one day require them.

Nor do governments always need new technology to impose their regulatory muscle. They can also rely on human intervention, just as Yahoo! now intends to do in order to ban auctions of Nazi and Ku Klux Klan items on its site. Although it is coy about details, the company says it will use software to filter out objectionable material and human reviewers to decide borderline cases.

Indirect regulation can also do the job. In Myanmar, formerly Burma, access to the web is banned. To enforce this, the country's military regime imposes jail terms of up to 15 years for unauthorized use of a modem. China recently published sweeping new rules that require Internet companies to apply for a licence and hold them responsible for illegal content carried on their websites. And democratic governments are learning that illegal commercial activity, such as online gambling, can be regulated by controlling credit-card companies and other financial intermediaries.

Perhaps the most promising approach, from the governments' point of view, is co-ordinated action to gain some control over the online world. Faster than might be expected, countries have banded together to fight the threat of jurisdictional arbitrage and to solve conflicts of law. The most straightforward way for governments to do that is to devise a uniform international standard. One early example is the World Intellectual Property Organisation's copyright treaty of 1996, which strengthened international copyright rules.

The Council of Europe—a group of 41 countries which includes all 15 members of the European Union—is putting the finishing touches to the world's first international treaty on cybercrime. The United States, which has also been involved in the negotiations, supports the treaty's main points. Signatories to the agreement, which will probably be presented for ratification this summer, must have laws on their books that allow, for instance, quick seizure of incriminating computer data and its distribution to authorities in other countries.

Such harmonisation is not likely in areas of interest to big multinational corporations (copyright) or where the interests of countries are closely aligned (crime and taxation). On January 9th, the OECD countries announced that they had agreed on a series of rules determining what kind of e-commerce activities made a company liable to taxation: doing business through a website, they concluded, would not leave a company liable to tax in the country from which the website had been accessed. But even most democratic countries are unlikely to agree on standards for more controversial issues, above all freedom of speech. As a result, in many areas, governments are trying "softer" approaches.

In the case of privacy, for instance, the United States and the EU have agreed to disagree. America so far favours self-regulation and sectoral laws, for example for the health-care industry, in order to protect the personal data of its citizens. In contrast, the EU relies on comprehensive privacy legislation enforced by data-protection agencies. The EU privacy directive also authorizes member states to cut off the data flow to other countries, including the United States, which do not have (by its lights) adequate privacy laws.

To avoid a trade war over personal data, both sides devised a "safe-harbour" agreement that went into effect on November 1st. This protects companies from having their data flow severed, as long as their privacy policies comply with certain principles (such as letting consumers choose how data are used, and allowing access to that data). So far, however, only a dozen companies and organisations have registered with America's Department of Commerce, not least because many firms first want to see whether and how the agreement will be enforced.

The provisions of the Hague Convention could prove more popular. This treaty, which is due to be adopted at a diplomatic conference in June, was first proposed by the American government in the early 1990s to formalize worldwide what American courts already often do: enforce foreign judgments in matters such as intellectual-property claims, contractual disputes and libel. American citizens would thus also be able to collect awards abroad.

Under the treaty, an online store could be liable under laws in any of the 48 member-countries of the Hague conference. That is why the American government is opposing, among other things, a clause that would ensure that consumers could sue businesses in the courts of the country where the consumer lives.

Instead, the Department of Commerce and e-commerce firms are pushing for a different solution: in effect, a new system of private laws, which would avoid the requirement to abide by the laws of the countries where their customers live. As in the Safe Harbour agreement, web firms could seek a certification that they follow certain minimum rules of consumer protection and privacy. Conflicts would be resolved by so-called "alternative dispute resolution." Lessons from Yahoo!

Will these trends turn cyberspace into a place stuffed with even more rules than the real world, as online companies worry? Or, as free-speech advocates predict, will litigants and governments pursue service providers they don't like, leading to an ever-tighter standard for protected speech?

For now, these fears seem exaggerated. But much depends on how the legal and political battles of the next few years are settled, and how technology evolves. There have been some attempts to steer a middle course. The Brussels Convention, for instance, lets consumers sue a foreign website in their home country only if the site can be proved to have aimed at that country's market.

Many courts are likely to refuse to enforce foreign judgments on matters of widely differing practice, especially where free speech is concerned. For example, Yahoo! will probably successfully defend itself in the American courts, on first amendment grounds, against the French judgment. And yet this may not be enough. The company plans to go on fighting the legal case. On December 22nd it asked a federal court for a ruling stating that a French court cannot hold an American-based company accountable for breaking French law. Nevertheless, the company has already, in effect, caved in by banning Nazi memorabilia from its auction sites. So whatever the American courts decide, the outcome will be new restrictions on Yahoo!'s American operations.

The firms that will be easiest to regulate and restrict, and which will be subject to multiple jurisdictions, will be those with assets in several countries: big websites such as Yahoo!, Amazon and eBay. But this is nothing new, Mr. Goldsmith argues: multinational companies have always faced multiple regulatory burdens. In addition, new technology will make it much easier to comply. Several start-ups such as Mercury2, MyCustoms.com and tariffic.com already offer services that automate the process of making sure that cross-border trade complies with all the various rules.

For Michael Froomkin, a law professor at the University of Miami, all this represents a great irony about the Internet. What was supposed to be an anarchistic and liberating technology may in fact make the world less democratic, by forcing a huge increase in legal harmonisation. This will mostly be pursued by governments and vested interests banding together to enact multilateral treaties, which are difficult for national parliaments to scrutinize or change.

The Hague convention and the cybercrime treaty are cases in point. If the online industry creates its own way of resolving disputes, this could take away jurisdiction from courts worldwide and eliminate existing legal rights. And the fact that the American government let a relatively unknown European organisation develop such an important agreement as the cybercrime treaty is a sign that Washington did not want it widely discussed. Although negotiations began three years ago, the treaty was made public only last April, in its 22nd draft. Only recently, therefore, were Internet advocacy groups able to get involved. To them, the treaty is a document that "threatens the rights of the individual while extending the power of police authorities."

The treaty also exemplifies the risk that governments, especially democratic ones, run when they try to assert their authority in the online world. The legal tools and technologies they develop, though useful in that context, may well be abused not only by them but also by authoritarian governments. The means used by France to fight anti-Semitism on the web could also be used to prevent people living in less democratic countries from getting the information they need to strive for basic freedoms.

Those aiming to preserve the Internet's freedom-loving character also have new technologies to deploy in their battle with government regulators. So-called peer-to-peer networks could make it more difficult to control content on the Internet. FreeNet, for instance, automatically spreads copies of documents all over the web, so that they no longer belong to one place. And SafeWeb will soon launch a service called "Triangle Boy" that allows citizens in democratic countries to turn their PCs into so-called proxy servers. These can then be used by surfers in China, Saudi Arabia or Vietnam to pierce through their countries' firewalls.

On the Internet, the struggle between freedom and state control will rage for some time. But if recent trends in online regulation prove anything, it is that technology is being used by both sides in this battle and that freedom is by no means certain to win. The Internet could indeed become the most liberating technology since the printing press—but only if governments let it.

Photo Credits

Part 1	Giraudon/Art Resource, NY
Part 2	Giraudon/Art Resource, NY
Part 3	Detail. Claude Monet, *The Gare Saint-Lazare,* 1877. Oil on canvas, 80.33 cm x 98.11 cm. Courtesy of the Fogg Art Museum, Harvard University Art Museums, Bequest from the Collection of Maurice Wertheim, Class of 1906. Photo: David Mathews. © President and Fellows of Harvard College, Harvard University.
Part 4	National Gallery, London
Part 5	AKG London
Part 6	© Hulton/Archive/Getty
Part 7	© Bettmann/CORBIS
Part 8	Brown Brothers
Part 9	Die Proklamierung des Deutschen Kaiserreiches am 18. Januar 1871 im Spiegelsaal von Versailles (Friedrichsruher Fassung). Gemalde von Anton von Werner, 1885. Oil on canvas, 167 x 202 cm. Friedrichsruh, Bismarck-Museum, bildarchiv preussischer kulturbesitz, Berlin
Part 10	Corbis/Bettmann
Part 11	Corbis/Underwood
Part 12	The Bathers (Les Greande Baigneuses), by Paul Cezanne. Philadelphia Museum of Art: Purchased with the W.P. Wilstach Fund
Part 13	Popperfoto
Part 14	Franklin D. Roosevelt Library
Part 15	Corbis/Bettmann
Part 16	MARGARET BOURKE-WHITE/TimePix
Part 17	Corbis/AFP
Part 18	Corbis/Bettmann